Microsoft Certification Exam Objectives
Exam #70-297: Designing a Microsoft Windows Server 2003 Active Directory and Network Infrastructure

Creating the Conceptual Design by Gathering and Analyzing Business and Technical Requirements

Objective	Chapter
Analyze the impact of Active Directory on the existing technical environment.	1
Analyze DNS for Active Directory directory service implementation.	1
Analyze existing network operating system implementation.	1
Analyze security requirements for the Active Directory directory service.	1
Design the Active Directory infrastructure to meet business and technical requirements.	2
Design the network services infrastructure to meet business and technical requirements.	3
Identify network topology and performance levels.	1
Analyze the impact of the infrastructure design on the existing technical environment.	1

Creating the Logical Design for an Active Directory Infrastructure

Objective	Chapter
Design an OU structure.	4
Design a security group strategy.	4
Design a user and computer authentication strategy.	4
Design a user and computer account strategy.	4
Design an Active Directory naming strategy.	4
Design migration paths to Active Directory.	4
Design a strategy for Group Policy implementation.	4
Design an Active Directory directory service site topology.	4

Creating the Logical Design for a Network Services Infrastructure

Objective	Chapter
Design a DNS name resolution strategy.	5
Design a NetBIOS name resolution strategy.	5
Design security for remote access users.	6
Design a DNS service implementation.	5
Design a remote access strategy.	6
Design an IP address assignment strategy.	6

Creating the Physical Design for an Active Directory and Network Infrastructure

Objective	Chapter
Design DNS service placement.	7
Design an Active Directory implementation plan.	7
Specify the server specifications to meet system requirements.	7
Design Internet connectivity for a company.	8
Design a network and routing topology for a company.	8
Design the remote access infrastructure.	8

D1551970

MCSE Guide to
Designing a Microsoft® Windows® Server 2003 Active Directory and Network Infrastructure

Brian Barber

Michael Cross

Melissa Craft

Hal Kurz

Jeffrey Martin

Brian Mohr

Paul Summitt

Jay Adamson

COURSE TECHNOLOGY
CENGAGE Learning™

Australia • Brazil • Japan • Korea • Mexico • Singapore • Spain • United Kingdom • United States

COURSE TECHNOLOGY
CENGAGE Learning™

**MCSE Guide to Designing a Microsoft®
Windows® Server 2003 Active Directory
and Network Infrastructure**
Brian Barber, Michael Cross, Melissa Craft,
Hal Kurz, Jeffrey Martin, Brian Mohr,
Paul Summitt, and Jay Adamson

Managing Editor: William Pitkin III

Product Manager: Manya Chylinski

Development Editor: Jill Batistick

Senior Production Editor: Elena Montillo

Senior Manufacturing Coordinator: Trevor
Kallop

Quality Assurance/Technical Edit: Marianne
Snow Christian Kunciw Chris Scriver

Senior Marketing Manager: Karen Seitz

Associate Product Manager: Sarah Santoro

Editorial Assistant: Amanda Piantedosi

Cover Design: Steve Deschene

Text Designer: GEX Publishing Services

Compositor: GEX Publishing Services

For product information and technology assistance, contact us at
Cengage Learning Customer & Sales Support, 1-800-354-9706

For permission to use material from this text or product,
submit all requests online at **www.cengage.com/permissions**
Further permissions questions can be emailed to
permissionrequest@cengage.com

ISBN-13: 978-1-4239-0294-2

ISBN-10: 1-4239-0294-7

Course Technology
20 Channel Center Street
Boston, MA 02210
USA

Cengage Learning is a leading provider of customized learning solutions with
office locations around the globe, including Singapore, the United Kingdom,
Australia, Mexico, Brazil, and Japan. Locate your local office at
international.cengage.com/region

Cengage Learning products are represented in Canada by
Nelson Education, Ltd.

To learn more about Course Technology, visit
www.cengage.com/coursetechnology

Purchase any of our products at your local college store or at our preferred
online store **www.ichapters.com**

Printed in the United States of America
3 4 5 6 7 11 10 09

Brief Contents

Contents

Introduction

Welcome to *MCSE Guide to Designing a Microsoft® Windows® Server 2003 Active Directory and Network Infrastructure*. This book offers you real-world examples, interactive pedagogy, and hands-on activities that reinforce key concepts and help you prepare for a career in Microsoft network management and pass the Microsoft 70-297 exam. This book provides in-depth study of configuring, administering, and troubleshooting the services available within a Microsoft Windows Server 2003 network infrastructure. In the accompanying CD, we provide pointed review questions to reinforce the concepts introduced in each chapter. In addition to the review questions, we provide detailed hands-on activities that let you experience firsthand the processes involved in Windows Server 2003 Active Directory network configuration and management. Finally, to put a real-world slant on the concepts introduced in each chapter, we provide case projects to prepare you for situations that must be managed in a live networking environment.

Intended Audience

MCSE Guide to Designing a Microsoft® Windows® Server 2003 Active Directory and Network Infrastructure is intended for people who have at least one year of experience administering and supporting a network for a medium or large company; and at least one year of experience designing a network infrastructure and administering a desktop operating system. To best understand the material in this book, you should have a background in Windows Server 2003 and general networking concepts. Ideally you have worked with the material presented in Course Technology's *MCSE Guide to Managing a Microsoft Windows Server 2003 Network* and *MCSE Guide to Managing a Microsoft Windows Server 2003 Environment*.

Chapter Descriptions

Chapter 1, "The Assessment Stage," provides an introduction to assessing the technical environment of Active Directory. It includes a discussion of DNS and existing namespaces, physical networks, and the impact of proposed network designs on existing infrastructure.

Chapter 2, "Developing the Active Directory Infrastructure Design," outlines how to analyze and design an administrative model, to assess and define forest design, to create a domain design, and to develop an OU model and replication design.

Chapter 3, "Developing the Network Services Design," explains network services infrastructure designs, including a detailed analysis of the design principles and features of DNS, WINS, and DCHP.

Chapter 4, "Designing the Logical Components," describes the various methods of defining standards and the role of standardization, establishing forest structure, hierarchy, and naming strategies, working with authentication mechanisms, and defining group policy objects and strategies for account policies.

Chapter 5, "Name Resolution," describes in detail the namespace in DNS design, DNS zones and servers, and WINS designs and strategies, with a focus on interoperability.

Chapter 6, "Remote Access and Address Management," discusses the requirements for and implementation of remote access service servers and its Active Directory implications, as well as IP address management and DCHP.

Chapter 7, "Service Sizing and Placement," explains in detail the planning and implementation phases and creating a project plan. It also discusses sizing and availability in Active Directory, with a section on specification requirements.

Chapter 8, "The Physical Design," outlines networking and routing, including a detailed discussion of topologies. This chapter also describes requirements for remote access infrastructures, as well as how to determine sizing and availability of remote access components.

Features and Approach

MCSE Guide to Designing a Microsoft® Windows® Server 2003 Active Directory and Network Infrastructure differs from other networking books in its unique hands-on approach and its orientation to real-world situations and problem solving. To help you comprehend how Microsoft Windows Server 2003 Active Directory and network management concepts and techniques are applied in real-world organizations, this book incorporates the following features:

- **Chapter Objectives**—Each chapter begins with a detailed list of the concepts to be mastered. This list gives you a quick reference to the chapter's contents and is a useful study aid.

- **Summary**—Each chapter's text is followed by a summary of the concepts introduced in that chapter. These sections include a formal summary, a summary by objective, and a section with frequently asked questions.

- **Self Test**—This section gives you questions and answers that you can use to test your mastery of the content of the chapter.

The CD that accompanies this text contains additional elements to reinforce the concepts introduced in the main text:

- **Summary**—The content begins with a summary to refresh your memory before you begin working on the end-of-chapter material.

- **Review Questions**—The end-of-chapter assessment begins with a set of review questions that reinforce the ideas introduced in each chapter. Answering these questions will ensure that you have mastered the important concepts.

- **Activities**—Hands-on Activities are incorporated throughout the text, giving you practice in setting up, managing, and troubleshooting a network system. The activities give you a strong foundation for carrying out network administration tasks in the real world. Because of the book's progressive nature, completing the hands-on activities in each chapter is essential before moving on to the end-of-chapter projects and subsequent chapters.

- **Case Projects**—Finally, each chapter closes with a section that proposes certain situations. You are asked to evaluate the situations and decide upon the course of action to be taken to remedy the problems described. This valuable tool will help you sharpen your decision-making and troubleshooting skills, which are important aspects of network administration.

- **Test Preparation**—The CD-ROM includes CoursePrep® test preparation software, which provides over 100 sample MCSE exam questions mirroring the look and feel of the MCSE exams.

Text and Graphic Conventions

Additional information and exercises have been added to this book to help you better understand what's being discussed in the chapter. Icons throughout the text alert you to these additional materials. The icons and features used in this book and its CD are described below:

Tips offer extra information on resources, how to attack problems, and time-saving shortcuts.

Notes present additional helpful material related to the subject being discussed.

Exam Warning—These focus on specific elements to focus on in order to pass the exam.

Test Day Tip—Short tips to help you organize and remember information you will need for the exam.

Designing & Planning—These sidebars explain how certain exam objectives are implemented or used in professional environments

Configuring & Implementing—Sidebars that point out the differences and details needed to properly configure your network environment in Windows 2003 Server.

Head of the Class—Discussions of concepts and facts as they might be presented in the classroom, regarding issues and questions that most commonly are raised by students when studying a particular topic.

 The Caution icon identifies important information about potential mistakes or hazards.

 Each Hands-on Activity is preceded by the Activity icon.

 Case Project icons mark the end-of-chapter case projects, which are scenario-based assignments that ask you to independently apply what you have learned in the chapter.

Instructor's Resources

The following supplemental materials are available when this book is used in a classroom setting. All of the supplements available with this book are provided to the instructor on a single CD-ROM.

Electronic Instructor's Manual. The Instructor's Manual that accompanies this textbook includes Additional instructional material to assist in class preparation, including suggestions for classroom activities, discussion topics, and additional projects.

Solutions are provided for the end-of-chapter material, including Review Questions, and where applicable, Activities and Case Projects. Solutions to the Practice Exams are also included.

ExamView®. This textbook is accompanied by ExamView, a powerful testing software package that allows instructors to create and administer printed, computer (LAN-based), and Internet exams. ExamView includes hundreds of questions that correspond to the topics covered in this text, enabling students to generate detailed study guides that include page references for further review. The computer-based and Internet testing components allow students to take exams at their computers and also save the instructor time by grading each exam automatically.

PowerPoint presentations. This book comes with Microsoft PowerPoint slides for each chapter. These are included as a teaching aid for classroom presentation, to make available to students on the network for chapter review, or to be printed for classroom distribution. Instructors, please feel at liberty to add your own slides for additional topics you introduce to the class.

Figure files. All of the figures and tables in the book are reproduced on the Instructor's Resource CD, in bitmap format. Similar to the PowerPoint presentations, these are included as a teaching aid for classroom presentation, to make available to students for review, or to be printed for classroom distribution.

Minimum Lab Requirements

- **Hardware:**

Hardware	Requirement Component
CPU	Pentium III 533 or higher
Memory	256 MB RAM
Disk Space	Minimum 2GB (3GB if storing the installation files on local hard drive)
Drives	CD-ROM Floppy Disk
Networking	All labs assume a single instructor server acting as a domain controller. Two network cards are recommended to allow isolation from other networks.
	All student servers will require one network card to complete all of the exercises. The first network card is connected to the classroom network with the instructor server.
	Make sure to have Windows Server 2003-compatible network adapters.
	A connection to the Internet via some sort of NAT or Proxy server is required.

- **Software:**

Windows Server 2003 Enterprise Edition for each computer

The latest Windows Server 2003 Service Pack (if available)
Active Directory Sizer Tool
Group Policy Common Scenarios

■ **Set Up Instructions:**

To successfully complete the lab exercises, set up classroom computers as listed below:

1. The instructor computer should initially be installed with default configuration options. The name of the server should be *Instructor*. The initial password should be *Password*.

2. After installation, rename one of the network connections as *Classroom* with an IP address of 192.168.1.10, a subnet mask of 255.255.255.0, and 192.168.1.10 as the DNS server. Rename the other connection as External and configure it with the appropriate IP address, subnet mask, and default gateway to allow access to the Internet. Configure routing and remote access and network address translation (if necessary) to allow access to the Internet. If network address translation is configured on this server then Classroom will be the internal interface, and External will be the external interface.

3. Configure the Instructor computer as a domain controller for the domain *Arctic.local*. When asked to create an Administrator password for the domain, use *Password!*. Allow the Active Directory installation wizard to automatically install DNS and create the domain. If the server does not detect Internet connectivity during the installation of Active Directory it will create a root DNS domain on the instructor server. This prevents the server from performing Internet DNS lookups. Delete the root DNS domain if it is created.

4. Student servers are to be set up by the instructor prior to the beginning of class. Each student server should be installed with Windows Server 2003 Enterprise Edition and should not have any specific roles installed.

5. To make identification easier for students consider placing a paper label on the monitor of each server indicating the name of the server.

6. It is important to remember that when performing the activities included in this book that the student logs in as the Administrator for the Arctic.local domain. The local Administrator accounts on the student member servers do not have enough privileges to complete some of the activities.

7. The Active Directory Sizer Tool and the Group Policy Common Scenarios applications should be placed on the instructor's server in a share that all students can access.

8. Student servers should be reset back to their original configurations prior to participating in the end-of-chapter activities.

Acknowledgments

Thank you to the wonderful staff at Course Technology for the opportunity to work on this book. In particular I would like to thank Jill Batistick, Developmental Editor, for keeping me on track and Manya Chylinski, Product Manager, for guiding the book through the process. Thanks also go to Elena Montillo, Senior Production Editor, for her fine work on this book. The quality assurance team of Christian Kunciw, Marianne Snow, and Chris Scriver are key members of the project team, helping to ensure the accuracy of the text, review questions, and activities.

Chapter 1

MCSE 70-297

The Assessment Stage

Exam Objectives in This Chapter:

1.4	Analyze security requirements for the Active Directory directory service.
1.4.2	Identify the impact of Active Directory on the current security infrastructure.
1.1	Analyze the impact of Active Directory on the existing technical environment.
1.1.4	Analyze current network administration model.
1.4.1	Analyze current security policies, standards, and procedures.
1.1.3	Analyze current level of service within an existing technical environment.
1.1.1	Analyze hardware and software requirements.
1.3.3	Identify the configuration details of all servers on the network. Server types might include primary domain controllers, backup domain controllers, file servers, print servers, and Web servers.
1.1.2	Analyze interoperability requirements.
1.3.1	Identify the existing domain model.
1.4.3	Identify the existing trust relationships.
1.3.2	Identify the number and location of domain controllers on the network.
1.2.2	Analyze the current namespace.
1.2.1	Analyze the current DNS infrastructure.
1.7	Identify network topology and performance levels.
1.7.1	Identify constraints in the current network infrastructure.
1.7.2	Interpret current baseline performance requirements for each major subsystem.
1.8	Analyze the impact of the infrastructure design on the existing technical environment.
1.8.1	Analyze hardware and software requirements.
1.8.3	Analyze current level of service within the existing technical environment.
1.8.2	Analyze interoperability requirements.
1.8.4	Analyze network requirements.

Introduction

Before the design of any system implementation may commence, first one must assess the environment into which that system is to be deployed. This argument holds true especially for Active Directory (AD). Active Directory has the potential to affect every facet of your IT infrastructure and every team involved with IT, even in the largest of enterprises. Active Directory deployments can impact areas including the physical network topology, network bandwidth and resilience, IP addressing, name resolution hierarchies, administrative procedures, administrative models, and security policies, to name but a few.

This first chapter helps you to better understand which aspects of your environment are affected by Active Directory, and how to assess whether your IT environment is ready for the deployment of Active Directory.

We start with the assessment of the technical environment. This includes an analysis of the current administrative model, service levels, existing hardware and software deployments, and any interoperability issues that need to be considered.

Next we move onto the server environment and analyze the current domain model, domain controller (DC) and other infrastructure (including WINS and DHCP) placement and numbers, as well as create a detailed inventory of all servers installed, including file, print, and Web servers.

The assessment phase then moves onto the area of DNS. Here we analyze the existing DNS implementation and its hierarchy, and assess whether it is ready to support Active Directory.

Finally, the physical network must be scrutinized. Versions of Windows operating systems prior to Windows 2000 did not rely upon an understanding of the underlying network topology to function correctly. This is not the case with Active Directory—information can be replicated between domain controllers in an efficient and timely fashion only if both the network topology is understood and Active Directory is configured to use that same topology.

Assessing the Technical Environment

Preparation is the key to designing the structure of Active Directory and the network infrastructure used by Windows Server 2003. Long before you even unwrap the installation CD from its packaging, you should have a thorough understanding of the current network and the organization in which it's used. The hardware, software, and operating systems used on a network can impact your design and determine whether changes need to be made before Windows Server 2003 is deployed. By analyzing the technical environment and the company's structure, you can craft a network that will meet the needs of your organization.

In the sections that follow, we'll review the components that make up Active Directory (AD) and see how they are used to mirror the structure of your organization. We'll discuss how the administrative model and geographic layout of a company can affect your design of AD and examine issues that need to be addressed before installing Windows Server 2003 on the network. By performing this assessment of the existing environment, you will be well on your way to devising an effective deployment plan.

Administrative Models

Even in the smallest of businesses, there are those who make the decisions and those who follow them (even if they make no sense). This command structure becomes more complex as the business gets larger. Staff will be assigned to different departments, which fall under the jurisdiction of people in other departments, who answer to divisions of management, who ultimately answer to senior management. In some cases, the company may be further broken into branch offices or divisions that reside in different geographic locations, or are separated for business, political, or security reasons. Because the structure and chain of command of a business will vary from others, it is important to understand the administrative model being used before designing Active Directory.

An administrative model describes the organization of a company and shows how it is managed. As is seen in a company's organizational chart, an administrative model is a logical structure. In other words, it doesn't tell you where the vice president's office is located, only that he or she answers to the president of the company. Because the components making up Active Directory can be broken down into logical and physical elements, the logical components in Active Directory allow you to organize resources, so their layout in the directory reflects the logical structure of your company. By separating the logical and physical components of a network, users are better able to find resources, and administrators can more effectively manage them.

Components Used in the Logical Design of Active Directory

If you're new to Active Directory, you may be unfamiliar with the logical components that make up the directory's structure. These components are an important part of transferring a company's administrative model to a Windows 2003 network and must be understood before attempting to redesign an existing network or design a new one. The logical components in AD are:

- Domains
- Domain trees
- Forests
- Organizational Units (OUs)

Domains

Since the days of Windows NT, domains have been a cornerstone of a Microsoft network. A domain is a logical grouping of network elements, consisting of computers, users, printers, and other components that make up the network and allow people to perform their jobs. Because domains group these objects in a single unit, the domain acts as an administrative boundary within which you can control security on users and computers. In Windows Server 2003, a domain also shares a common directory database, security policies, and, if other domains exist in the network, relationships with other domains. They are important logical components of a network, because everything is built upon or resides within the domain structure.

In serving as an administrative boundary, each domain uses its own security policies. Group Policies can be applied at a domain level, so that any users and computers within that domain are affected by it. This allows you to control access to resources, password policies, and other configurations to everyone within the domain. These security settings and policies affect only the domain and won't be applied to other domains in the network. If large groups of users need different policies, you can either create multiple domains or apply settings in other ways (such as by using organizational units, which we'll discuss later).

When a domain is created, a DNS domain name is assigned to identify it. DNS is the *Domain Name System*, which is used on the Internet and other TCP/IP networks for resolving IP addresses to user-friendly names. As we'll discuss later in this chapter, because an Active Directory domain is integrated with DNS, this allows users, computers, applications, and other elements of the network to easily find domain controllers and other resources on the network.

As you can imagine, a significant number of objects can potentially exist within a domain. To allow for significant growth in a network, Microsoft designed Active Directory to support up to 10 million objects per domain. While Microsoft concedes this to be a theoretical estimate, the company provides a more practical estimate that each domain can support at least one million objects. In either case, chances are your domain will never reach either of these limits. If it does, you'll need to create additional domains, and split users, computers, groups, and other objects among them.

As we'll discuss later in this chapter, Active Directory resides on domain controllers, which are used to manage AD and control access to network resources. To ensure that each domain controller has an identical copy of the directory database, Active Directory information is replicated to every DC within a domain. Each domain uses its own directory database. Because the information isn't replicated to other domains, this makes the domain a boundary for replication as well as for administration and security.

Domain Trees

Although domains serve as administrative boundaries, this does not mean that you should use only one domain until you reach the limit of the number of objects supported per domain. You might want to use multiple domains for any of the following reasons:

- To decentralize administration
- To improve performance
- To control replication
- To use different security settings and policies for each domain
- If you have an enormous number of objects in the directory

For example, your company might have branch offices in several countries. If there is only one domain, directory information will have to be replicated among domain controllers in each country, or (if no DCs reside in those locations) users will need to log onto a DC in another country. Rather than replicating directory information across a WAN, and having to manage disparate parts of the network, you could break the network into several domains. For example, you might create one domain for each country.

Creating separate domains does not mean there will be no relationship between these different parts of your network. Active Directory allows multiple domains to be connected together in a hierarchy. As seen in Figure 1.1, a domain can be created beneath an existing one in the hierarchy. The pre-existing domain is referred to as a "parent domain," and the new domain created under it is referred to as a "child domain."

As seen in Figure 1.1, domains created in this parent-child structure share a common namespace and belong to a *domain tree*. Trees follow a DNS naming scheme, so that the relationship between the parent and child domains is obvious and easy to follow. To conform to this naming scheme, a child domain appends its name to the parent's name. For example, if a parent domain used the domain name course.com, a child domain located in the United Kingdom might have the name uk.course.com. Names can also indicate the function of a domain, rather than its geographical location. For example, the child domain used by developers might use the name dev.course.com. Because domain trees use a contiguous namespace, it is easy to see which domains are child domains of a particular parent domain.

Figure 1.1 A Domain Tree Consists of Parent and Child Domains in a Contiguous Namespace

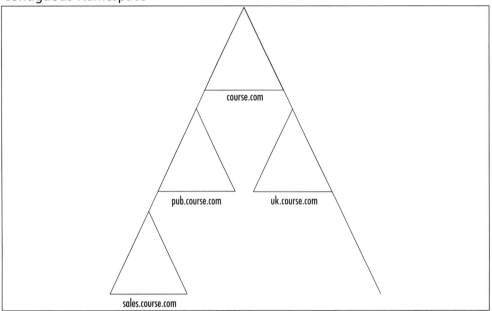

When a child domain is created, a two-way transitive trust relationship between the parent and child domains is automatically created. A trust relationship allows pass-through authentication, so users who are authenticated in a trusted domain can use resources in a trusting domain. Because the trust between a parent and child domain is bidirectional, this means that both domains trust each other, so users in either domain can access resources in the other (assuming, of course, that the users have the proper permissions for those resources).

The other feature of the trust relationship between parent and child domains is that they are transitive. A transitive relationship means that pass-through authentication is transferred across all domains that trust one another. For example, in Figure 1.2, Domain A has a two-way transitive trust with Domain B, so both trust each other. Domain B has a two-way transitive trust with Domain C, so they also trust each other, but there is no trust relationship between Domain A and Domain C. With the two-way transitive trust, Domain C will trust Domain A (and vice versa) because both trust Domain B. This will allow users in each of the domains to access resources from the other domains. Trusts can also be manually set up between domains so that they are one-way and non-transitive, but by default, transitive bidirectional trusts are used in domain trees and forests. These trusts are also *implicit,* meaning that they exist by default when you create the domains, unlike *explicit* trusts that must be created manually.

Figure 1.2 Adjoining Domains in a Domain Tree Use Two-Way Transitive Trusts

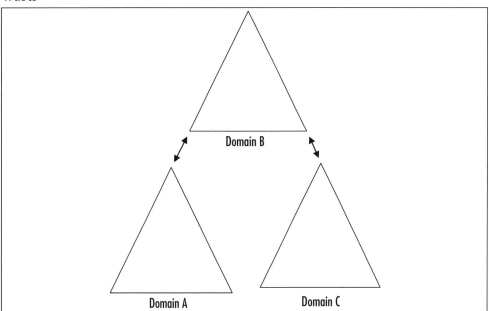

Forests

Just as domains can be interconnected into trees, trees can be interconnected into forests. As is the case with domain trees, domains in the same forests use two-way transitive trusts between the roots of all domain trees in the forest (that is, the top level domain in each tree) to allow pass-through authentication, so users can access resources in domains throughout the forest. As shown in Figure 1.3, although trees require a contiguous namespace, a forest can be made up of multiple trees that use different naming schemes. This allows your domains to share resources across the network, even though they don't share a contiguous namespace.

Figure 1.3 A Forest with Multiple Domain Trees

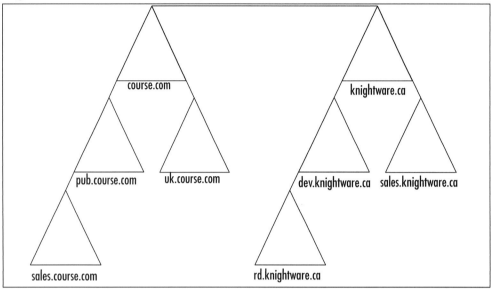

Every Active Directory structure has a forest, even if it consists only of a single domain. When the first Windows 2003 domain controller is installed on a network, you create the first domain that's also called the forest root domain. Additional domains can then be created that are part of this forest, or multiple forests can be created. This allows you to control which trees are connected and can share resources with one another (within the same forest), and which are separated so that users can't search other domains.

Organizational Units (OUs)

When looking at domain trees, you might think that the only way to create a directory structure that mirrors the organization of your company is to create multiple domains. However, in many companies, a single domain is all that's needed. To organize Active Directory objects within this single domain, organizational units can be used.

Organizational units (OUs) are containers that allow you to store users, computers, groups, and other OUs. By placing objects in different organizational units, you can design the layout of Active Directory to take the same shape as your company's logical structure, without creating separate domains. As shown in Figure 1.4, you can create OUs for different areas of your business, such as departments, functions, or locations. The users, computers, and groups relating to each area can then be stored inside the OU, so that you can find and manage them as a single unit.

Figure 1.4 Organizational Units Can Contain Other Active Directory Objects

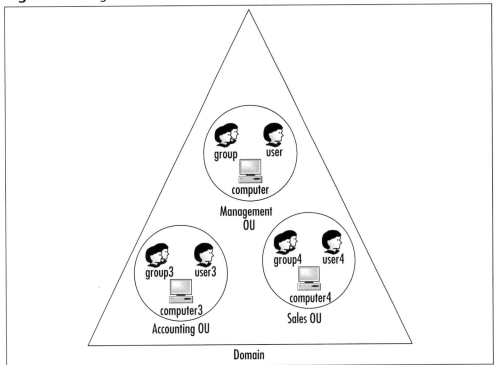

Organizational units are the smallest Active Directory unit to which you can delegate administrative authority. When you delegate authority, you give specific users or groups the ability to manage the users and resources in an OU. For example, you can give the manager of a department the ability to administer users within that department, thereby alleviating the need for you (the network administrator) to do it.

The Current Model

In looking at the components making up the logical structure of Active Directory, it is easy to see the need to understand the administrative model used by a business. By understanding how the business is organized, you can then apply that knowledge to the design of Active Directory. You'll be able to see which departments need their own organizational units, whether certain OUs need to be nested in others, and if a single domain is suitable for an entire corporation.

There are a number of ways in which you can identify the current model used by a company. These include:

- Use of organizational charts, which provide a graphical depiction of the business's logical structure

- Analyzing company processes and information flow
- Identifying geographical locations of business facilities
- Use of documentation dealing with previous network designs and administrative models
- Interviews with decision makers, departmental management, human-resources personnel, IT staff, and other knowledgeable sources

As we've mentioned throughout this chapter, organizational charts serve as a map of the company's administrative structure. Organizational charts flow from top to bottom, with the highest point of decision making at the top of the chart. As seen in Figure 1.5, the vice president of the company answers to the CEO, with numerous departments below them. These departments may have departments or divisions that are under their management, as in the case where the Payroll Department falls under the Finance Department. In looking at the components of the flowchart, you can see that each of these could become individual OUs within Active Directory, with some being nested within others. By following this model, you could easily create a design that works with the existing model used by the company.

Figure 1.5 Organizational Charts Depict the Administrative Model

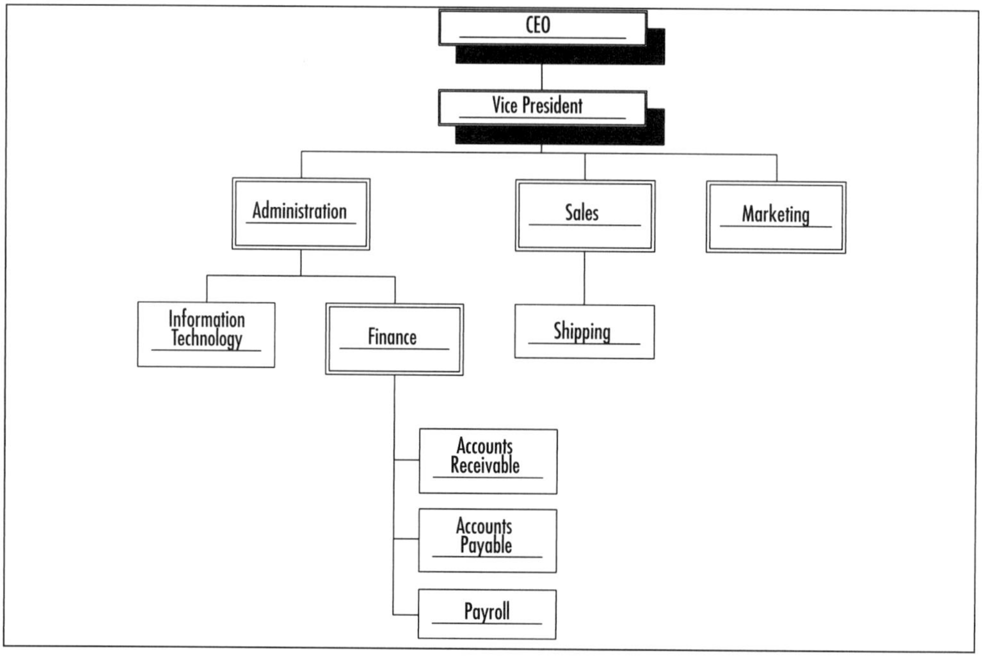

In looking at the organizational chart, you can get an idea of how communication and information flows through the company. A member of the Payroll Department would make a request to the manager of Finance, who would then take it to his supervisor in Administration, who would then forward it to her superiors at the executive level. When a decision is made at the top levels, it may also pass down through this same chain of command to the bottom levels. However, being that we live in the Information Age, you will need to determine if this is actually the case. For example, internal e-mail, instant messaging, or streaming video would allow any member of the organization to distribute information and communicate without going through a specific chain of command. Corporate policies that limit the material that can be distributed or firewall rules that keep certain information from being sent over the Internet should be identified early in the design stages.

TEST DAY TIP

Certification exams are naturally geared toward technology, but it is critical in design exams that business requirements drive the use of technology; therefore, the goals and structure of the organization are very important. It is important to pay attention to the flow of information, especially in relation to the purpose of the organization. For example, if the organization is a chain of retail stores, the critical flow of information may be the real-time transfer of inventory data between individual stores and a central warehousing operation.

The flow of information will also impact the file structure. Many companies will group employees into departments that need to work together, allowing you to create folders on the hard disk that the OU representing this group will have access to. However, because certain departments will need to collaborate on specific issues or projects, you will also need to allow them access to folders that are shared among them. All these processes must be realized and documented for your design. To accommodate information sharing and keep other information confidential, you must give all users access to hard disk space for private, departmental, collaborative, and companywide purposes.

Because you will need to identify the companywide needs of a business, you will need to identify its geographic scope. There are three types of models that may be used by a company in this regard:

- Regional model, in which facilities are located within a city or nearby surrounding areas

- National model, in which facilities are located in different areas of one country

- International model, in which facilities are located throughout the world

While many smaller companies do business on an international level, this does not mean that an international model applies to them. For example, if a business sold widgets on the Internet, they might consider themselves a global presence in the business world, even though they use a regional model in which all of the computers are centralized in a single office. In determining the actual size of the company (as it applies to location of equipment, users, and other resources), you will be better able to identify how Active Directory and the network infrastructure will need to be designed to accommodate their needs.

 EXAM WARNING

> Pay careful attention to the comments by the CEO and CIO in the business cases on your exam. The comments by the network manager will be at an operational level and will supply details on the choice of technology, but comments from the executive ranks will provide strategic direction that will dictate the current and future technology requirements in support of short- and long-term business goals.

With all the possible documentation that could be used as part of the design process, it is important that you don't forget the people for whom you're creating this system. It is imperative to interview many different people in the design process. Discussions with decision makers, department heads, and other managerial staff are an excellent source of information. Management can provide a broad picture of processes, organization, and provide insight into changes that may occur in the company. In addition to this, discussions with members of the Human Resources Department can provide information on different positions and departments within the company, and which ones supervise and oversee others. Finally, and perhaps most importantly, you should interview members of the IT staff. Those who work in information technology will have first-hand experience with issues that could affect your design of Active Directory and any changes you make to the network infrastructure. In addition, they may be able to provide documentation that may be useful later, such as hardware inventories (which we will discuss shortly).

Identifying Limitations

In assessing information about the administrative model of the company and how it relates to AD and the network infrastructure, it is common to find limitations. Such discoveries aren't necessarily a bad thing. A company might have business processes that have become outdated or can be improved upon. Through the process of designing Active Directory and the network infrastructure, these limitations can be remedied and the company's administrative model improved.

In assessing the various aspects of a company, it is common to find documentation that is sorely outdated and/or has never been used. Sometimes, documentation that would be important has never been created. The business you're dealing with might have never considered creating an organizational chart, or they could have kept inaccurate records of such things as computer equipment and their configurations. In other cases, they may have squirreled away every piece of documentation that ever has been created, so that no one can determine what's still needed.

In using organizational charts and other documentation generated by the company, it is important to determine the time it was last updated. In some cases, it may have been years since anyone thought to update the organizational chart, so now it barely resembles the current model. Because its archaic structure might not reflect the current administration, employees might be forced to go outside of the existing chain of command to get their jobs done. In such cases, the work you do in designing Active Directory can be used to provide up-to-date information for the company.

In other instances, the limitations you identify could be there for specific reasons. Laws may restrict how data is accessed, or certain departments may require an autonomy that isn't there for obvious reasons. These may exist due to reasons that are unique to the organization and need to be discovered before changes are made to AD or the network infrastructure.

Head of the Class...

Limitations Might Be a Result of Politics

Limitations within the administrative model used by a company mig13ht be there for a specific reason that goes beyond any functional purpose. In one organization, I found that there were two domains set up when only one was needed. I quickly found that one of the senior members in the organization had created his own empire, with his son (who "knew all about computers") running the domain. Because of the office politics involved, this domain existed for another two years until the problems they'd caused finally resulted in its demise. Although it may seem prudent to redesign obvious faults in the administrative model or network design, such politics might prevent you from doing so.

When dealing with changes that will affect the administrative model of a company, it is important that someone high in the chain of command signs off on those changes. The limitations in a model might be there for a specific purpose, or they may be the result of something that makes little sense to someone thinking solely of making logical changes.

Limitations might also exist with the international scope of a company. As we mentioned in the previous section, a company can have a regional, national, or international scope. Depending on the size of the company, this will have an effect on how the company addresses supporting users, equipment, and security issues, and might also affect how the network is designed.

A company with a regional geographic scope has its facilities within a city, or areas surrounding that city. This is the smallest of the three models, and generally allows all facilities to be connected to the network at high speed. Being the smallest, it is also the easiest to manage. All of the computers might be located in the same building, nearby buildings, or in facilities that are within driving distance of one another. This means that you can provide support using a single IT Department and Help Desk that can deal with problems and access equipment quickly and efficiently.

A national model has facilities scattered across a much larger area, with offices located in different states or provinces. Unless the company is located in a small nation (such as many of those in Europe), an IT Department located in a single city would most probably not be able to send an employee to visit remote sites to maintain, repair, or replace equipment. Although it might be a nice thought, no company would approve network administrators flying from Detroit to San Diego every time a backup tape needed to be replaced. As such, IT staff might need to be set up at different locations, or outsourcing might need to be considered.

Many national companies eventually expand to an international level, with branch offices and divisions located in foreign countries. This creates a number of challenges for a business. Different countries might have laws that conflict with the laws of your nation, and these laws could create issues dealing with how information is distributed. For example, some types of data sent across international boundaries might be prohibited. For example, if a company had government contracts, transmitting information dealing with those contracts to other countries might be considered espionage. In another instance, if an advertisement created in the Netherlands contained a semi-nude image of a teenager, this might be considered child pornography in other countries. It is important that laws affecting the company are identified before instituting changes.

The international model also might cause issues with technology. If the network used encryption on data that's sent to branch offices, this encryption might not be allowed in other countries. Even if they are allowed, you might have trouble transmitting this data, as T1 lines or other methods of sending data at high speed would be impossible to implement in certain nations or areas of those countries. If these problems aren't enough, the infrastructure of the country may cause further issues, such as electricity being unreliable or unavailable. The availability of certain technologies, and the legality and feasibility of implementing them, might be prohibitive. These issues need to be identified before you attempt to deploy them.

Formulating New Candidate Models

In designing Active Directory, you will be transferring the knowledge of the company's logical structure to AD's logical structure. In doing so, you might find that certain arrangements of organizational units and other components work better than others. The work you do designing Active Directory and the network infrastructure can reveal areas for change in the existing administrative model. These discoveries can then be transferred to the actual organization of the company to improve other business practices.

In some cases, you might find that certain departments would work better if some minor restructuring took place within the company. For example, a company might have the Shipping Department answering directly to an executive level. Because of the need for information to flow between Sales and Shipping, you might find that it would be better for Shipping to fall under the direction of the Sales Department. In doing so, improved communication between these departments might improve how sold products are sent to the customer. In other cases, you might find that certain departments would be better off merged together, so they could share resources they need and exchange information more readily.

Although Active Directory allows you to map the logical structure of an organization to AD's design, this doesn't mean that the infrastructure must exactly match the organization of the company. In some cases, it might be wiser to change the Active Directory and file structures so that they don't exactly match the company's organizational chart. For example, Police Departments have Internal Affairs units that monitor the actions of officers and investigate complaints made about them. Because such investigations could involve members at any level in the Police Department, it is important that others can't access files dealing with their investigations. Although their unit might fall under the jurisdiction of an executive branch dealing with detectives, they would be separated from other groups to accommodate specific needs.

Even if all documentation is current, and it seems that the design of Active Directory and the network infrastructure will be straightforward, it is important to realize that change is a common occurrence in business. The directory services architecture must not only reflect the current structure but also be aware of the potential for all kinds of corporate change.

It is important that you understand the growth strategy and any planned acquisitions made by the company. If the company planned to expand into other geographic locations, or expand into new core businesses, it might impact the number of domains needed by the company. If they planned to acquire new companies or merge with established businesses, this might mean connecting the current network to another disparate network. For example, you might need to connect your Windows Server 2003 network to a Novell network and have them exchange information and work together to control security. In other instances, downsizing might come into play, when some of the OUs currently in use will no longer be needed.

Such changes can create a number of challenges that weren't present when the current business model was established.

Information on planned changes in the organization is often acquired through interviews with decision makers and may be difficult to obtain. They might not want certain information on mergers, expansions, or downsizing to be known beyond a group of key personnel involved in these activities. As such, it is important that you ensure management that such information will be kept confidential and is essential to effectively designing the network.

The introduction of any new model might necessitate a change in the level of expectations on the part of users who connect to the network. These changes in expectations could be positive or negative depending on the amount of change the users can bear. To assist in managing these expectations, service levels should be negotiated or renegotiated. Service levels are discussed in detail in the following section.

Service Levels

A *Service Level Agreement (SLA)* is an agreement between those who will use a particular service and those who will provide it. It serves as a contract between clients and service providers, and spells out what services will be supplied, what is expected from the service, and who will fix the service if it doesn't meet an expected level of performance. Through an SLA, the expectations and needs are clearly specified, so that no misunderstandings about the system should occur at a later time.

An SLA is often used when an organization uses an outside party to implement a new system. For example, if the company wanted Internet access for all its employees, the company might order a WAN link from an Internet Service Provider (ISP). An SLA would be created to specify expected amounts of uptime, bandwidth, and performance. The SLA could also specify who will fix certain problems (such as the T1 line going down), who will maintain the routers connecting the company to the Internet, and other issues related to the project. To enforce the SLA, penalties or financial incentives might be specified to deal with failing or exceeding the expectations of a service.

SLAs can also be used internally, specifying what users of the network can expect from IT staff and procedures related to the network. When designing AD, you might outline the level of access needed by users to specific resources. When addressing the requirements of servers, you might outline the level of performance that's acceptable and what areas of the business need access to specific servers at all times.

An SLA often includes information on the amount of downtime (when customers will be unable to use a particular server, service, software, or equipment) that can be expected from systems. This information will usually include the expected availability of the system in a percentage format, which is commonly called the "Number of Nines." As Table 1.1 demonstrates, the Number of Nines can be translated into the amount of time a system might be down during a 12-month period. If the estimated downtime is longer than that specified in the SLA, then additional losses might be experienced by a company because employees are unable to perform their jobs or customers are unable to use services or purchase items provided by the company.

Table 1.1 Availability Expectations ("Number of Nines")

Percentage Availability (%)	Allowed Downtime per Year
99.9999	32 seconds
99.999	5.3 minutes
99.99	53 minutes
99.9	8.7 hours
99.0	87 hours

Before any discussion can take place around the amount of permissible downtime, the term *downtime* must be defined. In the broadest sense of the term, downtime equates to any period of time when a service is not available. There is accepted scheduled downtime, such as unavailability due to routine preventive maintenance and hardware upgrades, and unscheduled downtime, such as time lost due to hardware failure or an unresponsive application. You might want to add additional hardware to ensure that a critical application is always available even when one of the servers that hosts the application is down for maintenance. In addition, you'll want to guarantee access to the application during periods of high utilization. For example, the hardware could still be functioning even while being bombarded by connections that render the application unresponsive. The exact definition of *availability* (the converse of downtime) must be identified and explained in any Service Level Agreement in a way that each party that enters into it has reasonable levels of expectation.

Identifying Existing Service Levels

Many companies have a number of SLAs already in place. As mentioned previously, these may be included in contracts with external businesses that provide a particular service to the company. By reviewing documentation generated by the IT staff, you might also find service levels that were set during previous upgrades, or when new equipment or technologies were implemented. These can be reviewed during the planning stage to determine levels that were previously set.

Because the service levels will outline specific services, software, or equipment, the agreements can provide additional information on the company's physical structure. For example, if a service level specified that two divisions of the company were connected by an ISDN line, and a secondary one that's required if the first fails, you would not only identify the service level required by the company but the bandwidth between the different divisions. As you can see from this, this is useful in other areas of planning, which we'll discuss later in this chapter.

Network Speed and Availability

Connectivity and bandwidth are common issues for creating service level agreements. If the media and equipment transferring data are too slow, this can result in delays in logging onto the network, opening and closing files, and performing other tasks necessary to a person's job. Similarly, if a connection goes down, then that section of the network will be cut off and employees will be unable to do work. In addition to this, if the speed of a network is an issue, it can prevent new technologies such as video-conferencing from being used. Because of the impact your network's bandwidth and availability can have on its users, it is important that you review the existing service needs related to these areas.

As seen in Table 1.2, there are a number of different speeds that can be used for your network infrastructure, or in providing Internet access to users. As you can imagine, the slower the speed, the less expensive it is. This means that a compromise has been made between performance and cost. As we'll see in the next section, this might need to be reviewed and additional tradeoffs made between these two issues.

Table 1.2 Speeds of Different Network Media

Type of Media	Speed
Dial-up	56 Kbps (typically)
ISDN	64 Kbps or 128 Kbps
Frame Relay	Variable rate between 56 Kbps to 1.5 Mbps
T1	1.5 Mbps
T3	45 Mbps
10BaseT	10 Mbps
ATM	Variable rate between 155 Mbps and 622 Mbps
100BaseT	100 Mbps
Gigabyte Ethernet	1 Gbps

If it is imperative for connectivity between areas to always be available, then secondary connections might also be in place. These secondary connections might be used only if the primary one fails. Because they are used only in emergencies, slower and less expensive connections may be used. For example, if a company had a T1 connection connecting facilities, the secondary connection might be through an ISDN line. Although slower, this still allows the facilities to exchange information and access resources. It provides an emergency alternative until the primary connection is re-established and is considerably slower than implementing a second T1 connection that is rarely (if ever) used.

Domain Controllers

As mentioned earlier, Active Directory also includes a number of components that represent physical elements of your network. One of the most important parts of a Windows 2003 network is the domain controller (DC). Domain controllers are used to manage domains and are used to modify the directory, allowing network administrators to make changes to user and computer accounts, domain structure, site topology, and control access. When changes are made to these components of the directory, they are then copied to other domain controllers on the network.

Domain controllers are servers that store a writable copy of Active Directory. However, not every computer on your network can act as a DC. Windows Server 2003 Active Directory can be installed only on Microsoft Windows Server 2003, Standard Edition; Windows Server 2003, Enterprise Edition; and Windows Server 2003, Datacenter Edition. Servers running the Web Edition of Windows 2003 Server cannot be domain controllers, although they can be member servers that provide resources and services to the network.

When a domain controller is installed on the network, the first domain, forest, and site are created automatically. Additional domains, forests, and sites can be created as needed, just as additional domain controllers can be added. This allows you to design your network in a way that reflects the structure and needs of your organization.

While only one domain controller is required to create a domain, multiple DCs can (and usually should) be implemented for fault tolerance and high availability. If more than one domain controller is used and one of these fails, users will be able to log onto another DC that is available. This will allow users to continue working while the DC is down. In larger companies, a number of domain controllers can be added to accommodate significant numbers of users who might log on and off at the same times of day or users who need to access resources from these servers.

Determining the number of domain controllers needed on a network is important to performance and availability. Service levels should include information on the number of existing domain controllers and the number of users who will be using them. Table 1.3 shows the number of domain controllers needed for a specific number of users and the CPU speed necessary to support them. Based on this information, you could analyze the existing service levels and determine if additional domain controllers need to be added to the network. However, for fault tolerance, a minimum of two domain controllers in each domain would be needed.

Table 1.3 Number of Domain Controllers Needed Based on Number of Users

Number of Users in a Domain	Number of Domain Controllers Required in Each Domain	Minimum CPU Speed
1–499	1	850MHz Uniprocessor
500–999	1	850MHz Dual Processor
1,000–2,999	2	850MHz Dual Processor
3,000–10,000	2	850MHz Quad Processor
Over 10,000	1 per 5,000 Users	850MHz Quad Processor

Identifying Service Levels Requiring Change

As mentioned, even if SLAs exist, changes might be required before deploying Windows Server 2003 and making adjustments to the current network design. Additional domain controllers might need to be installed, redundant connectivity might need to be added, or any number of other changes might be required. Determining whether changes are necessary requires comparing the existing service levels to the current and future needs of the business.

One of the obvious changes to the agreements will be the inclusion of Windows Server 2003. In addition to changes in software and operating systems used on the network, you will also be adjusting expectations to reflect these systems. If an existing SLA was for Windows NT 4.0 servers on the network, then the performance levels would increase based both on Windows Server 2003's capacity to do more and the need for better servers to support this newer operating system.

This also leads to the need to identify service levels dealing with outdated or retired equipment, technologies, and services. For example, if the company previously used dial-up services to access the Internet, these might have been replaced by a T1 connection or another high-speed solution. In such a case, the ISP providing this service might also have changed, requiring updates to documentation on who provides the service. Also, as we'll discuss later in this chapter, after upgrading to Windows Server 2003 certain software might not work, requiring the software to be upgraded to newer versions or replaced with comparable software. Finally, in performing any of these upgrades, the opportunity is presented to replace other equipment, such as old routers, hubs, cabling, and so forth. All of these changes must be identified so the SLAs can be adjusted appropriately.

As changes occur, the expectations of the company will also be altered. Improvements to network speed, servers with greater processing power and hard disk space, or other changes will cause the company to have increased expectations. This is reasonable to assume, because the reason they paid for these changes was to expect more from their network. Discussions with decision makers will need to be conducted to achieve an agreement on what is considered to be acceptable performance from these changes.

It isn't inconceivable that the management and other people involved in these discussions may have unattainable expectations, or that these unattainable hopes were part of a previous SLA. In some cases, this might stem from the client receiving bad information from the media or entertainment industry (such as when a movie shows computers performing the impossible), or the knowledge of other companies having a performance level that their company isn't willing or able to pay for. For example, the company might want servers running 24 hours a day, 7 days a week, with no downtime. This is an unachievable goal because servers will eventually need to be rebooted or shut down because of upgrades and routine maintenance. Unless the company is willing to pay for additional servers providing duplicate services and storing identical data, this isn't a realistic expectation. As part of the planning process, you will need to identify such problems and adjust service levels to mesh with reality.

Hardware and Software Deployments

Before you're ready to deploy Windows Server 2003, you'll need to determine which servers are capable of supporting this operating system and what software on the machines will be able to run. This involves creating an inventory of hardware and software installed on servers that will be upgraded, as well as documenting the software and hardware on new servers that will run Windows Server 2003. You should also identify other hardware and software making up the infrastructure, including that on workstations and other network components. By creating such an inventory, you'll have a firm understanding of the network's components and be in a better position to determine what additional steps are needed before upgrading existing servers and installing Windows Server 2003 on new ones.

Performing a Hardware Inventory

Hardware inventories are simply lists of individual components making up a larger structure. When conducting an inventory of the hardware on a network, you would make a listing of the makes, models, serial numbers, and other pertinent data for each switch, hub, printer, and other piece of equipment. This lets you know what network assets the company owns and can be useful when problems arise and you need to contact the manufacturer to repair or replace the equipment.

When hardware inventories are performed on computers, the information becomes more granular. Rather than simply documenting information on the computer case itself, you would document the individual components that make up the computer. In addition to documenting the computer's name, IP address, and other identifiers, taking an inventory of a computer includes gathering the following specifications:

- CPU

- RAM

- Hard disk size

- CD-ROM, DVD-ROM, or CD/DVD burners

- Floppy disk

- BIOS

- Video card

- Sound card

- Network interface card (NIC)

In addition to providing information necessary to upgrading or installing Windows Server 2003, hardware inventories also provide numerous other benefits. They are useful in identifying hardware that needs replacement. In terms of computers, there is generally a three-year life cycle, meaning that after three years, the computer is scheduled for upgrade or replacement. Keeping a computer indefinitely makes little sense, considering that it would diminish performance and eventually become unusable. Just imagine keeping a "286" computer as a server after all these years, when even Pentium computers are considered outdated.

Another benefit of a hardware inventory is identification. By cataloging information about the equipment, it is easy to know which ones can potentially be used to violate corporate policy or become security issues. If IT staff found that users were installing games or watching movies on their systems, they might decide to enact a policy forbidding it. The hardware inventory could tell them which machines had CD/DVD-ROMs and thereby had the capability to have software installed. In the same way, they might decide to stop users from copying data from the server and leaving the building with it. The inventory would reveal which computers had the capability of having data copied to removable disks, allowing the IT staff to lock down or remove the devices from these systems.

Analyzing Hardware Requirements

By analyzing the data collected in a hardware inventory, you can identify which servers meet or exceed the minimum hardware requirements for installing Windows 2003 Server. In looking at the comparison of requirements between different versions of Windows servers, you can see that there are great differences in the hardware requirements of Windows NT 4.0 Server, Windows 2000 Server, and the four incarnations of Windows 2003 Server. If the hardware on your computer doesn't match or exceed these requirements, you will need to decide whether the server will be upgraded or replaced with a newer one. Table 1.4 displays a comparison of the minimum hardware requirements for the Windows family of server products.

Table 1.4 Comparison of Minimum Hardware Requirements

Requirement	Windows NT 4.0 Server	Windows 2000 Server	Windows 2003 Server, Standard Edition	Windows 2003 Server, Enterprise Edition	Windows 2003 Server, Datacenter Edition	Windows 2003 Server, Web Edition
CPU	486/33 MHz or Pentium or Pentium Pro	133 MHz Pentium	133 MHz (550MHz Recommended)	133 MHz (733 MHz Recommended and required for Itanium processors)	400 MHz (733 MHz Recommended and required for Itanium processors)	133 MHz (550 MHz Recommended)
RAM	16 MB (32 MB Recommended)	128 MB (256 MB Recommended and 4 GB Maximum)	128 MB (256 MB Recommended and 4 GB Maximum)	128 MB (256 MB Recommended and 32GB Maximum. 64 GB Maximum on Itanium-based computers)	512 MB (1GB Recommended and 64 GB Maximum. 512 GB Maximum on Itanium-based computers)	128 MB (256 MB Recommended and 2 GB Maximum)
Hard disk space	125 MB	2 GB with at least 1 GB of free space	1.5 GB	1.5 GB (2 GB for Itanium-based computers	1.5 GB (2 GB for Itanium-based computers	1.5 GB
Multiprocessor support	Up to 4	Up to 4	Up to 4	Up to 8	Minimum 8-way capable required. Up to 64	Up to 2

In looking at these requirements, there are a few additional hardware requirements to consider. You will need a keyboard and mouse so you can navigate and
enter data during the installation process, and an optical disk drive (CD or DVD) so
that you can use the installation CD. Once you have confirmed that the minimum
requirements of the operating system have been met, you can then deal with any
software needed on the machine.

While the requirements discussed here focus on Windows Server 2003, it is also
important to remember that other operating systems and software installed on network computers will have minimum requirements. These requirements should appear
on the software's packaging, in its documentation, or on the manufacturer's Web site.
It is important that when considering minimum hardware requirements that you also
consider the additional load of software installed on these machines. Such software
will also need a certain amount of hard disk space as part of its installation and will
use a certain amount of memory. If the computer isn't able to support this software,
then you will need to either upgrade the computer or install the programs on
another machine.

As far as creating the initial inventory and keeping it updated is concerned, there
is an easy way and a hard way. The hard way involves physically inspecting servers and
workstations and manually compiling a list of hardware and how it has been configured. Alternatively, there are a number of tools, such as Microsoft Systems
Management Server (SMS) that can discover and collect information about the hardware devices in your network and the software that is installed. In either case you will
need to audit the information on a periodic basis to ensure that it is still accurate and
make corrections as required. This information will tell you if your current hardware
will support Windows Server 2003 and any of its services you intend to deploy. In
cases in which the hardware will not support the new product, you might need to
procure new hardware or look at consolidating services from older hardware onto
newer hardware with greater capacity.

Performing a Software Inventory

A software inventory lists each program purchased by a company and how many
copies are available to install on machines. Separate inventory sheets are also created
that identify all the programs that are installed on each machine and all the machines
on which each program is installed.

Software inventories are important for new deployments, because a new or
upgraded server or workstation would need the same or comparable software
installed on it. By installing identical or similar software on servers and other
machines, users can continue benefiting from their functionality and services. In
many cases, failing to install this software on new deployments could prevent certain users from performing their jobs. Imagine a programmer not having Visual
Basic installed or a SQL Server no longer providing database services.

Inventories are also useful in keeping the company honest, so that illegal copies of software aren't installed. When a company purchases software to install on hundreds or even thousands of computers, they do not have huge trucks roll into the parking lot filled with copies of Windows. They get one or several copies and purchase licenses for each computer the program is installed on. Because it would be illegal to install the software on more computers than they have licenses for, it is important that each installation is carefully monitored. To that end, a software inventory allows companies to keep track of this.

Inventorying the software on each computer is important to identify conflicts that may occur after installation. If a new program was installed on a server or workstation and a problem occurred shortly thereafter, it would be easy to check the inventory and see that the problem arose just after new software was installed.

Software inventories must be updated just as hardware inventories need to be. Even though a computer initially had certain software installed on it when it was deployed, additional software might be added afterward. When new software is installed, the inventory sheet for that computer must be updated.

As described in the previous section, you will need to manually compile a list of running software or use the same tools that were used for collecting information about hardware assets. In addition, this list will need to be revisited on a periodic basis and updated if any changes occur without being reported to the keeper of the list. The compiled list of software will indicate to you if you are adequately licensed, and it will alert you of any interoperability issues.

Analyzing Software Requirements

Just as software has specific hardware specifications, it might also have software requirements. Programs are designed to run on certain operating systems and might not run on others. For example, those written for Apple computers will never run on Windows, while those for Windows NT might or might not run on Windows Server 2003. Before attempting to install these programs, you will need to identify what platforms the software will run on.

Numerous programs are also written to work with other software. Programs might be designed to access data from a SQL Server or access e-mail from an Exchange Server on your network. If this software no longer exists on the network after a server upgrade, then users of the network will no longer be able to use the client software on their machines. By identifying the software required by other programs, you will be able to prevent these failures in service.

When analyzing the software installed on the network, you should also determine which computers have software that is no longer needed or supported. For example, your company might have switched from one word processing program to Microsoft Word. When upgrading computers to this software, it is possible that the old software wasn't uninstalled. Similarly, servers and computers might have software that was used at one point but became unnecessary over time. Database servers providing information on products that are no longer available would rarely if ever be used and could simply be backed up and removed from the servers. By identifying these unneeded programs, you can free up valuable hard disk space and other resources on the machine.

When analyzing the software requirements of users, you should also identify whether software that wasn't previously available is needed. As technology and business change, new programs may be effective in increasing productivity and have benefits that would far outweigh the initial purchase costs. By discussing these matters with department heads and other management, you will be able to identify and meet these new needs. Once you have gathered all of the required information on the hardware and software that is connected to your network, you can delve a little deeper and assess the requirements for how disparate hardware platforms and applications interact with each other.

Interoperability Issues

Just because Windows supports Plug and Play doesn't mean that hardware and software will play nicely together. Installing new hardware and software on a network can cause issues such as the devices and/or program not functioning as expected, if at all. The software must interact with other programming code on the computer, and the operating system must be able to recognize and work with any hardware installed. These interoperability issues must be resolved for users to be able to utilize the programs and components and for the business to get what's expected from their purchase.

Microsoft provides information on which hardware and software products have been tested on Windows Server 2003 and provides tools to assess whether they will run on a computer being upgraded to this operating system. Using these tools and information, you can effectively assess how to approach problems with hardware and software needed by your organization.

In addition to discussing this in the paragraphs that follow, we will also look at interoperability requirements for Active Directory itself. Because Active Directory might not be the only directory service that exists on the network, we will discuss its capability of working with other directory services and their capability of exchanging information between them.

Identifying Current Interoperability Instances

Identifying issues that occur before or just after installing Windows Server 2003 is vital to the functionality of the server. Many times, when software is installed on workstations or servers running other operating systems, and that software doesn't work correctly or at all, you are stuck experimenting with different settings or trying to figure out which programs are interfering with others. With Windows Server 2003, this is a significantly different process.

Software Compatibility

Windows Server 2003 includes tools for analysis and adjustments to software settings, and tools for determining if a particular piece of software should be installed on the server. As part of the Help and Support Center, the Program Compatibility Wizard is used when problems occur with programs that ran fine under earlier versions of Windows. This tool allows you to test compatibility settings, which may resolve any issues and allow them to run on Windows Server 2003. By modifying settings, a program that couldn't start, denied you access, or had other issues that made it difficult or impossible to run might be fixed. This is something we'll see first-hand when we do Exercise 1.01:

EXERCISE 1.01

TESTING PROGRAM COMPATIBILITY

1. From the Windows Start menu, point to **All Programs**, point to **Accessories**, and then click **Program Compatibility Wizard**.

2. When the Program Compatibility Wizard appears, click **Next** to continue.

3. When the screen that's shown in Figure 1.6 appears, select the **I want to use the program in the CD-ROM drive** option.

Figure 1.6 Selecting the Program to Test with the Program Compatibility Wizard

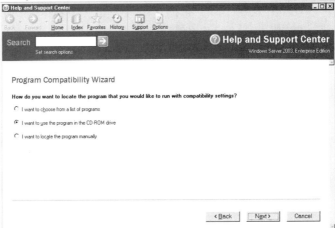

4. Insert an installation CD for another program into the CD-ROM. Click **Next** to continue.

5. When the next screen appears, choose the operating system that supported the program. As seen in Figure 1.7, this screen offers a wide variety of previous Windows versions to choose from. After selecting the operating system this program was compatible with, click **Next** to continue.

Figure 1.7 Selecting a Compatibility Mode with the Program Compatibility Wizard

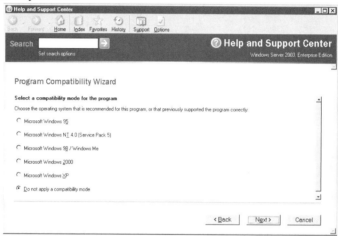

6. Select the check boxes to set whether you want the program to run in 256 colors and/or have 640 x 480 resolution. Click **Next** to continue. See Figure 1.8.

Figure 1.8 Display Settings Controlled Through the Program Compatibility Wizard

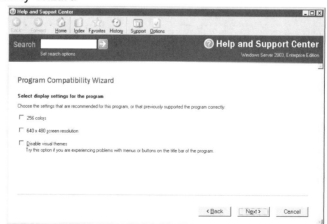

7. Select the check box on the next screen if you have experienced user account issues, which may result in receiving error messages stating you can't access the program, or if the program won't start. Click **Next** to continue. See Figure 1.9.

Figure 1.9 User Privileges Screen of Program Compatibility Wizard

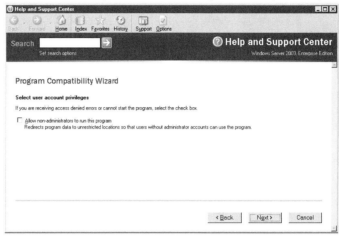

8. On the next screen you will be informed that Windows Server 2003 will attempt to test the program with the new settings. Click **Next** to continue.

9. Windows Server 2003 will then launch the installation of the CD you entered. Follow the setup program's prompts to install the program.

10. Upon finishing installation, try the program to see if it works, and then return to the **Program Compatibility Wizard**. As shown in Figure 1.10, answer whether the changes to compatibility settings worked and should be set, if you'd like to try others, or if you're finished trying compatibility settings. Click **Next** to continue.

Figure 1.10 Specifying Results of Running the Program
Compatibility Wizard

11. If you choose to set the settings, Windows Server 2003 will
    gather information about the program and apply them to the
    system. Upon completing this task, you can then click **Finish** to
    exit the wizard.

If you are comfortable with configuring a program without the use of a wizard,
you can modify settings for an installed program through the properties for that program. You can display the properties by right-clicking the desktop icon or Start menu
shortcut of an installed program, and then clicking Properties from the menu that
appears. As shown in Figure 1.11, the Compatibility tab allows you to view and
modify different compatibility settings for that program. Note that this tab has the
same settings as the wizard.

Figure 1.11 Compatibility Tab of a Program's Properties

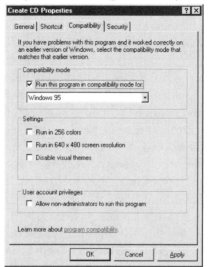

The Compatibility mode section of the Compatibility tab allows you to select a previous version of Windows on which the program ran without issue. By selecting the Run this program in compatibility mode for check box, a dropdown list with the following options becomes enabled:

- Windows 95

- Windows 98 / Windows Me

- Windows NT 4.0 (Service Pack 5)

- Windows 2000

- Windows XP

Selecting one of these options will alter settings that might enable the program to run under Windows Server 2003 as it did in the previous version. You can then set display settings for this program as well as check the Allow non-administrators to run this program check box to solve issues related to security problems. If the initial settings still don't allow the program to run, you can return to these settings and try different variations to fix any problems.

Hardware Compatibility

Microsoft also provides information and tools for determining the compatibility of hardware installed on a server. Using this documentation and software, you can determine which hardware components have been tested with Windows Server 2003 and found to work without issue. These should always be used prior to actually installing Windows Server 2003 on any server.

Microsoft's Web site provides a catalog of hardware products that have been designed for use with Windows Server 2003. The Windows Server Catalog for Windows Server 2003 can be viewed at www.microsoft.com/windows/ catalog/server, where you can browse various products tested with this operating system.

You can check hardware and software compatibility before installation by using the Microsoft Windows Upgrade Advisor. This tool will analyze your system to determine if the software and hardware running on it will allow you to upgrade to Windows Server 2003. To run this program, you would insert your installation CD into the computer you want to upgrade, click the Start menu's Run command, and then type the following command (where <drive letter> is the letter of the CD-ROM): <drive letter>\i386\winnt32.exe/checkupgradeonly.

After running this program, the Microsoft Windows Upgrade Advisor will start and begin analyzing your system. Once it has completed, a screen similar to that shown in Figure 1.12 will be displayed. As shown in this figure, a list of incompatible hardware and software is displayed. By selecting one of these entries and clicking the Details button, a report on that particular piece of hardware of software can be viewed.

Figure 1.12 Report System Compatibility Screen of Microsoft Windows Upgrade Advisor

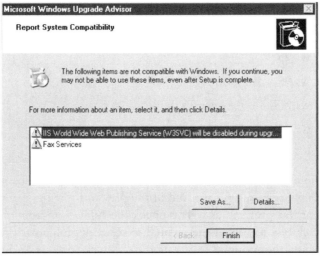

In viewing the entries in the Microsoft Windows Upgrade Advisor, it is important to note that not all items included are incompatible. For example, some programs (such as Internet Information Server) might be disabled during an upgrade. For those that are actually incompatible pieces of hardware or software, you will need to determine whether they are needed for your purposes and if so, if they can be upgraded to compatible versions.

Assessing Additional Active Directory Interoperability Requirements

In addition to being able to install Windows Server 2003 on a server, those acting as domain controllers will also have Active Directory installed. Because Active Directory stores data pertaining to the physical and logical aspects of a network, and is necessary for authenticating users, it is important for AD to be able to perform as effectively as possible. Depending on the network, however, this may require AD to interoperate with any number of other services.

Active Directory uses the Lightweight Directory Access Protocol (LDAP) for communications between clients and directory servers. This enables clients to access directory information and perform various operations in AD. It gets its name because it is a version of the X.500 Directory Access Protocol (DAP) and is considered lightweight because it uses less code than DAP.

X.500 is an established standard that defines directory services. It was developed by the International Telecommunication Union and published by the International Organization for Standardization. One of the protocols defined by X.500 is the Directory Access Protocol. Because it contains too many features to be efficient with personal computers, thin clients, and communication over the Internet, a more lightweight version was developed that contained fewer features. As mentioned, this light version of DAP is LDAP.

The Internet Engineering Task Force established industry standards for LDAP, enabling LDAP to be used over local networks and the Internet by a variety of directory services. Many network operating systems that use directory services (including Novell NetWare, Windows 2000, and Windows Server 2003) implement LDAP for accessing the directory, while other products (such as Internet browsers) support it as a method for finding resources or managing the directory. Since its inception in 1994, there have been several versions of LDAP, with features being added to accommodate changing needs. Active Directory supports versions 2 and 3.

Active Directory has enhanced security for LDAP communications in Windows Server 2003. By default, the administrative tools for Active Directory encrypt LDAP traffic using signing to ensure that packets haven't been tampered with. This makes Active Directory in Windows Server 2003 a more secure directory service that is better protected from hacking attempts.

In addition to its interoperability with other directory services, Active Directory also has interoperability with DNS (which we'll discuss later in this chapter) and Group Policies. Group Policies allow you to force specific settings on user accounts, including:

- Password policies, including minimum password length and how long a password is valid

- Assignment of scripts to computer or user accounts that are run at logon, logoff, startup, or shutdown

- Automatic installation of software on specific computers

- Display, backgrounds, and other settings used on computers

When policies are created, they are stored as Group Policy Objects (GPOs) in Active Directory. The settings in a GPO can be applied to a site (discussed later in this chapter), domain, or organizational unit. Because GPOs can be applied at different levels, you can set different policies for different areas of your company. For example, you could create a Group Policy for users in the Finance Department and another for the Sales Department (by placing Finance users in one OU and Sales users in another). If you had different domains for different branch offices, you could have different settings for the Sales divisions in each of these domains. Using GPOs in this manner, you can control the configuration of specific groups of users and computers.

Assessing the Current Server Infrastructure

If you aren't creating a Windows network from scratch, then a network infrastructure already exists. The Microsoft network would then come complete with domains, domain controllers, and other elements that are common to this network design. You might think that this would make your job easier, but this might not always be the case. You will need to examine the existing domains to see how they are modeled, where servers are located, and what steps are necessary to changing the infrastructure so it is suitable for use with Windows Server 2003 Active Directory.

The Current Domain Model

The domain models used on an existing Microsoft network will come in one of two forms: a Windows 2000 design that matches that of Windows Server 2003 or a Windows NT design that will need to be redesigned. Because Windows 2000 domains are the same as those used for Windows Server 2003, no changes will be needed as long as the network architecture was done properly the first time. However, before you can make this assumption, you will need to perform the same tasks that would be required if an NT domain were in place. In other words, you need to look at the number of domains in the network, determine why they exist, and then analyze whether additional or fewer domains are needed.

Identifying Existing Windows Domain Installations

In Windows Server 2003, most organizations need only a single domain to accommodate all of their users and resources. This is also true of Windows 2000 networks.

There will be times, however, when a company will want to add additional domains through the creation of child domains, thereby creating a domain tree. Some possible reasons to do this include:

- The addition of distant locations
- A move toward decentralized administration
- Namespace changes
- Group Policy requirements

If the company uses a national or international administrative model, divisions or branch offices of a company might be located in different parts of the country or world. If these branches of the company are connected with slow or unreliable links, this would make it difficult for Windows Server 2003 domain controllers to replicate Active Directory information between each another. Although this could also be dealt with by implementing sites (which we'll discuss later in this chapter), it is a mitigating factor to having multiple domains.

Decentralized administration is another benefit of multiple domains. Geographic distances between offices might mean that these offices are in different time zones, or in areas that use a different language, making it difficult for a network administrator to communicate with or work on the same schedules as users in those remote areas. The different branches might also be set up to manage their own domains, and there might be no immediate plans to centralize administration. Because domains are administrative boundaries, administration cannot be performed from outside of the domain. If decentralized management is unavoidable, then these additional domains might need to be left intact.

As we saw earlier, and will discuss in greater detail later in this chapter, domain trees use a contiguous namespace in which the child domain's name is added to the beginning of the parent domain's name. For example, course.com would be a parent domain name, with uk.course.com or dev.course.com being child domains within that namespace. If a company merged with another or had different divisions that wanted to continue using their own domain name, then you would need to create different domains to accommodate these needs. For example, if course.com purchased another company with a different registered domain name, then they might want to keep the two entities separate.

Another reason additional domains might be required is to allow administration of Group Policies. Group Policies can be applied at the domain level, so that any object in that domain is subject to its settings. For example, password policies are set at the domain level. If you wanted different areas of the company to have varying password policies, then this could be a factor in deciding to have more than one domain.

Windows NT 4.0 networks may also have multiple domains because of geographic limitations or the need for decentralized administration. In extreme situations, they might also have exceeded the maximum number of users that NT could support. The theoretical limit for how many user accounts and other objects NT 4.0 domains could support is 40,000, but the practical limit is 15,000 objects. In such cases, previous administrators might have moved from using a single domain to multiple domains. Please refer to the section entitled Assessing and Creating a Domain Design in Chapter 2, "Developing the Active Directory Infrastructure Design," where these design considerations are discussed in greater detail.

Identifying the Current Domain Models

If you're upgrading from Windows NT, there might be any number of different models in place. Before documenting them and incorporating Windows Server 2003 domains, you need to have an understanding of legacy Windows NT domain models on which this environment is based. In discussing these domain models, it is important to realize that in many cases, NT environments use a hybrid of different models. Generally, there is a reason for breaking away from a particular model, and you will need to identify why the hybridization occurred.

In Windows NT, there are four domain models:

- Single domain model

- Master domain model

- Multiple master domain model

- Complete trust domain model

As we look at these different domain models in greater detail, you will notice that a major facet of these models is their use of trust relationships. Trust relationships in legacy NT domains are one-way, meaning that just because one domain trusts another, the reverse might not be true. As seen in Figure 1.13, NT trust relationships consist of a trusting domain and a trusted domain. The trusting domain allows users from another domain to use its resources, while the trusted domain contains the user accounts that need to access these resources.

Figure 1.13 Legacy NT Trust Relationships

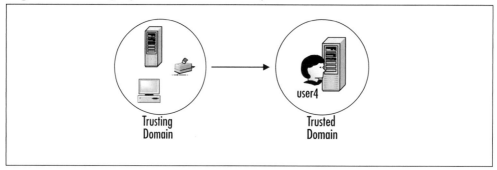

Another aspect of the legacy NT relationships is that they are non-transitive, meaning that they don't extend to other domains. As seen in Figure 1.14, the NT domains are depicted as circles, and trust relationships have been set up between Domain A and Domain B, and also between Domain B and Domain C. However, trust relationships are between two and only two domains. Although Domain C can access resources in Domain B, the trust relationship doesn't extend to allow them to access resources in Domain A. The logic behind this limitation is that the non-transitive trust would keep resources safe from being used by a domain that doesn't have an explicit trust set up with the trusting domain.

Figure 1.14 Comparison of Trust Relationships

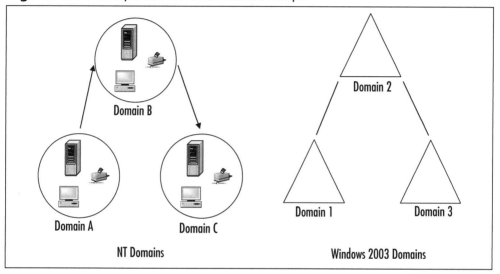

Domain B

Domain A

Domain C

NT Domains

Domain 2

Domain 1

Domain 3

Windows 2003 Domains

This is considerably different from the way trust relationships work in Windows 2000 and Windows Server 2003, in which trust relationships are two-way and transitive. Because it is two-way, if a relationship is set up between two domains, each can access relationships in the other's domain. Because it is transitive, this relationship also extends to other domains with trust relationships. In looking at Figure 1.14, you can see that a trust relationship is established between Domain 1 and Domain 2, and another relationship exists between Domain 2 and Domain 3. If a user in Domain 1 needs to access resources in Domain 3, the trust relationships connecting them would allow the request to be passed through. Even though no relationship exists between Domain 1 and Domain 3, the two-way transitive relationship allows them to use one another's resources. Bear in mind that Windows Server 2003 trusts are indeed two-way and transitive, but only between domains in the same forest; they are not transitive between or among multiple forests.

Single Domain Model

The single domain model is the simplest of the different legacy NT models. As seen in Figure 1.15, this model doesn't use any relationships because it consists of a single domain. All users, groups, and computers reside in this domain, thereby removing the need to manage trusts.

Figure 1.15 Single Domain Model

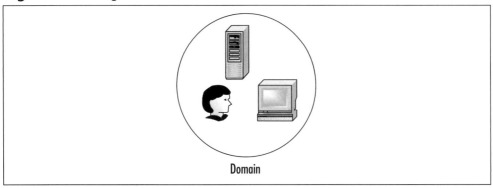

Master Domain Model

The master domain model is more complex than the single domain model. As seen in Figure 1.16, it consists of one domain that contains user accounts, and one or more other domains containing resources. The single domain containing user accounts is referred to as the "master domain" or "account domain," while those containing resources are called "resource domains."

Figure 1.16 Master Domain Model

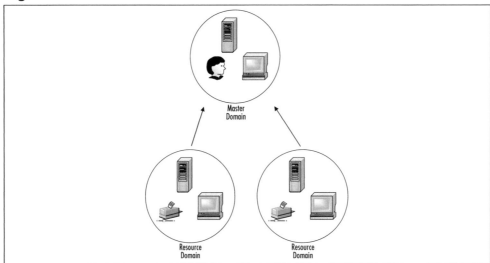

In a master domain model, the resource domains are trusting while the master domain is trusted. This means that accounts in the master domain have access to the resource domains, allowing the master domain to act as an administrative unit for accounts. Because all other domains trust the master domain, they recognize all of the users and groups in this domain. This allows users to log onto the master domain, and then access resources in the resource domains.

Multiple Master Domain Model

In the previous models, all user accounts were stored in a single domain, meaning that the theoretical limit of 40,000 objects on the number of users and related objects applied to the network. In larger companies, additional master domains might be required to support a larger number of objects. This is something that wasn't available using the previous models.

With the multiple master domain model, more than one master domain is used, thereby increasing the number of objects supported by the network. It is similar to the previous model in that user accounts are stored in a domain that's separate from those used solely for resources. What makes it different is that more than one master domain is used to store accounts, and considerably more trusts are used to make it usable. As seen in Figure 1.17, two one-way trusts are created between the two account domains, while each resource domain has a one-way trust with each of the account domains. In doing so, users in either of the two master domains can use resources in any of the resource domains.

Figure 1.17 Multiple Master Domain Model

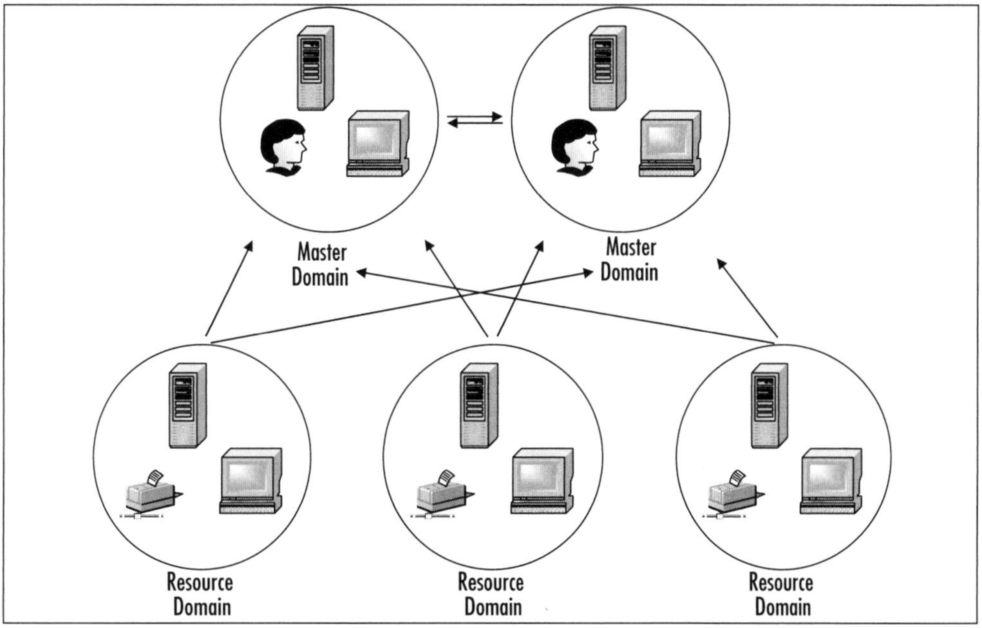

The number of trust relationships between domains in this model increases with the number of master domains and resource domains used. Determining the number of trusts required by these legacy models is done through the following formula: (M x (M − 1)) + (R x M)

In this formula, *M* is the number of master domains, while *R* is the number of resource domains. To explain this further, let's look at the multiple master domain depicted in the previous figure. In this figure, there are two master domains, and three resource domains. This would make the following equation: (2 x (2 − 1)) + (3 x 2)

This would equal (2 x 1)+6, which equals 8. When comparing this to the number of trust relationships shown in Figure 1.17, you can see that this accurately shows the same number of trusts. As we'll see later in this chapter, while this formula was designed to show the minimum number of trusts required when creating these domains, it is also useful in determining the minimum number of trusts in place for a multiple master domain model that's being migrated to Windows Server 2003.

Complete Trust Domain Model

As was the case with the multiple master domain model, the complete trust domain model also allows a scalable number of users. Unlike this previous model, the complete trust domain model has user accounts and resources within the same domains. As seen in Figure 1.18, each domain has two one-way trust relationships between itself and every other domain, thereby creating two-way trusts between each domain. This allows users in each domain to use resources in other domains. In this way, it is more like a multiple number of single domains with trusts created between them.

Figure 1.18 Complete Trust Domain Model

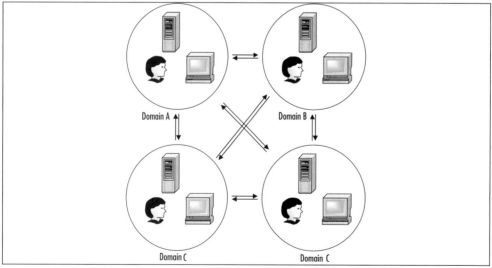

Domain A

Domain B

Domain C

Domain C

As was the case with the multiple master domain model, a significant number of trust relationships might be needed for this model. To determine the number of trusts required in such a model, the following formula can be used:

n x (n − 1)

In this formula, *n* is the number of domains. If we were to use this formula with the number of domains shown in Figure 1.18, we would see that this formula would become 4 x (4 − 1) or 4 x 3. This would mean that a network with four domains using the complete trust domain model would require 12 trust relationships.

TEST DAY TIP

Watch out for vocabulary and terms that are associated with other versions of Windows server products. You would be wise to make a list of similar or identical terms that are used in Windows NT 4.0 and Windows Server 2003 and indicate how each term is used differently in each version. For example, trust relationships and domain controllers are different in Windows NT 4.0 than in Windows Server 2003. The exam might use wording to cause confusion between the two versions. Your ability to distinguish between the two might be the difference between correct and incorrect answers on more than a few questions.

Comparing Models with Your Envisaged Design

In looking at the various models used in an NT environment, it might seem difficult moving the existing models to the envisaged design of your network. The process to migrate these domains to one or more Windows Server 2003 domains might take a few additional steps, but in most cases the number of existing domains can be diminished to a single or, at the very least, considerably fewer domains.

Migrating the Windows NT Single Domain Model

Because the Windows NT single domain model consists of just one domain, this is the easiest model to migrate to Windows Server 2003. The single domain will contain a server acting in the role of primary domain controller (PDC) that contains information on user accounts and passwords, and possibly one or more backup domain controllers (BDCs), which contains a backup of information from the PDC and is used for authenticating users.

The PDC must be the first domain controller upgraded to a Windows Server 2003 domain controller. Once you've run the Windows Server 2003 installation disk and upgraded this NT server, the Active Directory Installation Wizard (DCPROMO.exe) will automatically run so that the information in Windows NT's Security Account Manager (SAM) can be upgraded to Active Directory. Once DCPROMO has finished running, a single Windows Server 2003 domain will exist.

Migrating the Windows NT Master Domain Model

Migrating NT's master domain model to Windows Server 2003 begins by upgrading the master domain. This follows the same process used in the single domain model: the PDC is upgraded and Active Directory is installed. Where the differences appear in the migration scheme is when resource domains are migrated. The migration can use either a centralized or decentralized approach.

With a centralized approach, the resource domains are migrated into organizational units within the already migrated master domain. In resource domains, resources are managed on the basis of department or geographical location. Therefore, it makes perfect sense to remove them as domains and create organizational units in Active Directory containing exactly the same resources. After doing this, only one domain remains, with a series of OUs replacing the resource domains.

With a decentralized approach, the original domain structure of the master domain model is retained, but a domain tree is created. The master domain becomes the parent domain, while each of the resource domains become child domains using the same contiguous namespace. Because each domain is now a separate Windows Server 2003 domain, the user accounts and resources are decentralized into their appropriate domains. However, this approach should be used only if separate domains are required for specific reasons (which we discussed earlier).

Migrating the Windows NT Multiple Master Domain Model

When multiple domain models are created, the master domains are often created as organizational or geographic boundaries, or due to a high volume of objects. For the former reason, there would not be a need to collapse the domains into a single domain, because the needs of the business might still require multiple Windows Server 2003 domains. However, through the use of organizational units and sites in Active Directory, collapsing multiple domains into a single Active Directory domain in Windows Server 2003 might prove to be both feasible and prudent. Because it provides the ability to delegate administrative responsibilities at a granular level, having separate OUs could be more desirable than creating and managing separate domains.

Because more than one master domain is used in the multiple master domain model, the master domains are migrated so that they each become root domains of a domain tree, with both trees existing in the same forest. As was seen with the previous model, the resource domains then become child domains under the most appropriate domain tree root.

Migrating the Windows NT Complete Trust Domain Model

There are different ways in which an NT network using a complete trust domain model can be migrated to Windows Server 2003. Because there are numerous domains containing user accounts, these can individually be converted into separate Windows Server 2003 domains. One of the domains can be a parent domain, with other domains becoming child domains beneath the domain tree root. These domains can also be collapsed so that they become organizational units within the root domain.

An alternative to creating a single domain tree is to create multiple ones. If there is a need for more than one Windows Server 2003 domain tree within the network's structure, then two or more of the domains can be migrated to parent domains, and others can be migrated to become child domains beneath the appropriate tree root. You will explore designing Windows 2003 domains in Exercise 1.02.

EXERCISE 1.02

DESIGNING WINDOWS 2003 DOMAINS

You have decided to upgrade your network from Windows NT 4.0 to Windows Server 2003 and are preparing to change the existing domains into ones that will be more effective with Active Directory. After conducting interviews with decision makers and IT staff, you have compiled information and a series of requirements for the new domain. Based on this information, how will you redesign this network? Here is the information:

- The current domain model is shown in Figure 1.19.

- Company policy requires passwords to be a minimum of six characters and changed every 90 days.

- The Sales Department wants to be able to administer access to their resources.

- The Development Department is administered by programmers in the IT Department. Because it is used by the programming staff to develop new software that's sold by the company, they do not want anyone else having administrative privileges over their resources.

- The Development Department has more stringent policies and needs passwords that are at least eight characters long and changed every 30 days.

Figure 1.19 Current Windows NT 4.0 Domain Model

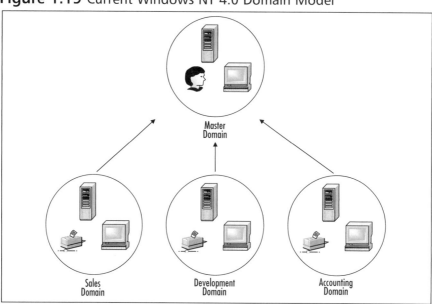

Solution: Because the Development domain requires that no one out-side of that department has administrative privileges over their resources, and two distinct password policies are required, two domains will need to be used in the new design. A domain tree could be created with all other domains migrated into the parent domain and the Development domain existing as a child domain. Group Policies with the different pass-word policies could then be applied to each domain. The Sales and Accounting Departments would have their own OUs inside the parent domain, with resources assigned to the respective OUs. In creating this design, the new domains would appear as shown in Figure 1.20.

Figure 1.20 New Design of Domains

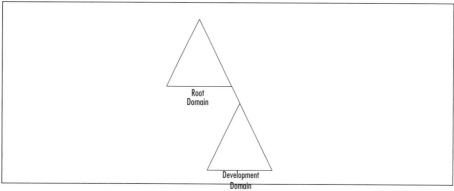

Infrastructure Placement

The placement of domain controllers and servers on the network is an important part of deploying Windows Server 2003 and Active Directory. In Windows Server 2003, domain controllers might play any number of different roles on a network and must be included in certain parts of the domain structure. Without these servers being placed on the network, Active Directory would be unable to function. As you proceed through the next few sections, feel free to refer to Chapter 7, "Service Placement," where the roles for and the placement of servers is discussed in greater detail.

Domain Controllers in Master Roles

Domain controllers might act in special roles on a Windows Server 2003 network, with certain changes to Active Directory being replicated only to them. Operations masters are domain controllers that provide special services to the network by keeping a master copy of certain data in Active Directory and copying data to other domain controllers for backup purposes. Because only one machine in a domain or forest can contain the master copy of this data, they are also referred to as Flexible Single Master Operations (FSMO) roles.

EXAM WARNING

There will be questions on where domain controllers should be situated in your network. For these questions, a map of the physical network will be your friend. The proximity of locations and the amount of available bandwidth will be the critical factors in determining where domain controllers will be located and what services each server will be hosting. The goal is the optimal performance of fundamental network activities, such as authentication and DNS queries, that is unhampered by excessive Active Directory replication.

There are five different types of master roles that are used in an Active Directory forest, with each providing a specific purpose. Two of these master roles are applied to a single domain controller in a forest (forestwide roles), while three others must be applied to a DC in each domain (domainwide roles). Only one domain controller in a forest can have a forestwide master role. This role consists of the following:

- Schema master
- Domain naming master

The *schema master* is a domain controller that is in charge of all changes to the Active Directory schema. The schema defines what object classes and attributes are used by AD within the forest. The schema master is used to write to the directory's schema, which is then replicated to other domain controllers in the forest. Updates to the schema can be performed only on the domain controller acting in this role.

The *domain naming master* is a domain controller that is in charge of adding new domains and removing unneeded ones from the forest. It is responsible for any changes to the domain namespace. The fact that such changes can be performed only on the domain naming master prevents conflicts that could occur if changes were performed on multiple machines.

In addition to forestwide master roles, there are also domainwide master roles. There are three master roles of this type, as follows:

- Relative ID (RID) master
- Primary Domain Controller (PDC) Emulator
- Infrastructure master

The *Relative ID master* is responsible for creating a unique identifying number for every object in a domain. These numbers are issued to other domain controllers in the domain. When an object is created, a sequence of numbers that uniquely identifies the object is applied to it. This number consists of two parts: a domain security ID and a relative ID (RID). The domain security ID is the same for all objects in that domain, while the relative ID is unique to each object. Instead of using the name of a user, computer, or group, this security ID (SID) is used by Windows to identify and reference the objects. To avoid potential conflicts of domain controllers issuing the same number to more than one object, only one RID master exists in a domain. The RID master controls the allocation of ID numbers to each DC, which the DC can then hand out to objects when they are created.

The *Primary Domain Controller (PDC) Emulator* is designed to act as a Windows NT primary domain controller. This is needed if there are computers running pre-Windows 2000 and XP operating systems, or if Windows NT backup domain controllers (BDCs) still exist on the network. The PDC Emulator is responsible for processing password changes, and replicating these changes to BDCs on the network. It also synchronizes the time on all domain controllers in a domain, so that servers don't have time discrepancies between them. Because there could be only one Windows NT primary domain controller in a domain, there can be only one PDC Emulator.

Even if there aren't any servers running as BDCs on the network, the PDC Emulator still has a purpose in each domain. The PDC Emulator receives preferred replication of all password changes performed by other domain controllers within the domain. When a password is changed on a domain controller, it is sent to the PDC Emulator. The reason the PDC Emulator is responsible for this is because it can take time to replicate password changes to all domain controllers in a domain. If a user changed his or her password on one domain controller and then attempted to log onto another, the second domain controller he or she is logging onto might still have old password information. Because this domain controller would consider it a bad password, it forwards the authentication request to the PDC Emulator to determine whether the password is actually valid. Whenever a logon authentication fails, a DC will always forward it to the PDC Emulator before rejecting it.

The *infrastructure master* is in charge of updating changes that are made to group memberships. When a user moves to a different domain and his or her group membership changes, it might take time for these changes to be reflected in the group. To remedy this, the Infrastructure Manager is used to update such changes in its domain. The domain controller in the infrastructure master role compares its data to the Global Catalog, which is a subset of directory information for all domains in the forest. When changes occur to group membership, it updates its group-to-user references and replicates these changes to other DCs in the domain.

Global Catalog Servers

The *Global Catalog* (GC) is a partial set of attributes of every object in an Active Directory forest. The attributes included in the Global Catalog are used in searches to locate objects in the directory. By default, there is only one GC in a forest. Subsequent GCs must be added manually. It is maintained on domain controllers that are designated as Global Catalog servers, which store a complete replica of the domain in which the DC is located, and a partial replica of every other domain in the forest that facilitates forestwide searches. By default, there is one Global Catalog Server in each site on the network.

Documenting Existing Infrastructure Locations

Domain controllers might provide various services or resources needed by various users or applications on the network. For example, one server might run SQL Server and provide data that's necessary to the Finance Department's ability to function. Just imagine the problems that would occur if the Payroll Department wasn't able to issue checks that week because of "improvements" you've been making. Before upgrading the network to Windows Server 2003, you will need to identify the location of these servers and identify whether they will be accessible after the existing network has been redesigned.

The location of each server on the current network must be documented and, as we discussed earlier, an inventory of hardware and software on that server taken. You will need to identify the roles a server plays on the network, data stored on it, and ascertain whether it is connected to the rest of the network using slow or unreliable media. By understanding these issues, you'll be better able to decide on whether the server must be moved, stay in its current location, or be removed from the network.

In addition to domain controllers, you should document the locations of any other equipment that is necessary to the network's normal operation. This includes routers, hubs, switches, Internet connectivity devices, and other hardware that's used. As we'll see later in this chapter, this information can then be used for creating a map of where various components of the network can be found and for identifying whether they need replacement or upgrading.

Identifying Bottlenecks

Bottlenecks are areas of a network that can slow performance or even stop a process from being performed. These can appear almost anywhere in the network infrastructure for a variety of reasons. It is important to determine where these bottlenecks are prior to upgrading to allow the upgrade to go more smoothly and also to avoid misdiagnosing performance issues as something relating to this change.

WAN links are a common area where bottlenecks occur. A slow or unreliable link can cause network traffic to bog down at that point, preventing data from being exchanged between the two sides. This can be particularly problematic if the link connects a branch office to a domain controller that's used to log onto the network. During times when the connection is down, users would be unable to log on or do their work. In some cases, this can be the result of outdated, damaged, or incorrectly configured equipment connecting the sites together. For example, if a branch office dialed into the network using a 56 Kbps connection, but had only a 28.8 modem, then the modem on their end would present a bottleneck, as they are not able to connect at the proper speed. In other situations, it can be a problem with the domain controller they're connecting to. You will need to identify where the bottleneck resides, and then take the appropriate steps to correct the problem.

Bottlenecks on a domain controller or another server might be identified using a program called Performance Monitor. This tool is available on Windows NT 4.0 Servers and can be accessed through the Administrative Tools menu on the Start menu. Using Performance Monitor, you can monitor memory usage, hard disk space, disk writes and reads, network performance, processor performance, and a variety of other aspects of a server. By analyzing this information, you can determine whether any parts of the server are acting abnormally or creating a bottleneck that might affect the network. A version of this tool is also available on Windows 2000 and Windows Server 2003, which we'll discuss later in this chapter.

Assessing DNS

The Domain Name System (DNS) is used to resolve domain names to IP addresses. It is a distributed database that maps host names to IP addresses (and vice versa). You're probably familiar with this method from using the Internet. It would be difficult or impossible to remember the IP address for every Web site or server that you want to access. DNS is a hierarchical, distributed database that allows users to find a particular resource by entering a user-friendly domain name such as www.cengage.com/coursetechnology, and then it looks up the IP address for that domain. Chapter 3, "Developing the Network Services Design," and Chapter 5, "Name Resolution," deal with DNS in greater detail.

DNS is highly integrated into Windows Server 2003. In Active Directory, domains are usually given names that are DNS names (such as www.cengage.com/coursetechnology.). Because Windows domains didn't use this naming scheme prior to Windows 2000, each domain is also given a name that's compatible with those used in Windows NT networks. These pre-Windows 2000 names are *NetBIOS* names and are single word names that users of older operating systems can use to log onto Active Directory. This allows clients to log onto domains by entering the domain name and username using the format: *domain name\username.*

Every computer account that is created in Active Directory also has multiple names, so that the account can be identified and accessed in a variety of ways. When a computer account is created in Active Directory, you need to enter a name for the computer, which will uniquely identify it in the domain. This is the host name for the machine, which can be used by DNS to indicate its place in the domain and can be used to help find the computer when clients search for it and its resources on the network.

In DNS, the host name is combined with the domain name separated by a dot to create the computer's fully qualified domain name (FQDN). For example, if you have a computer named COMP100 in the domain called knightware.ca, the FQDN for this computer would be comp100.knightware.ca. No two computers in a domain can have the same name, as this would create conflicts.

Head of the Class…

Universal Principal Names

Logons in Windows 2000 and Windows Server 2003 are different from previous versions and use Universal Principal Names (UPNs). *Universal Principal Names* are based on the Internet Engineering Task Force's RFC 822. Each user account in Active Directory has a logon name and UPN suffix. The logon name is the account name, while the UPN suffix is the domain that the user will log onto. The two are connected by the @ symbol, making the logon appear like an Internet e-mail address (*username@domain).* After entering a username, the user will generally be required to enter a password to prove he or she is authorized to use this account.

When the UPN is created for a user account, it also suggests a pre-Windows 2000 logon name that is used by the Security Account Manager (SAM) to log onto a server. The SAM is a service that stores information about user accounts and groups to which they belong. Local computer accounts use the SAM to store accounts that are used to access the local computer, and Windows NT servers use it for allowing network users access to resources on the server. Although you can create your own logon name, Active Directory will suggest a pre-Windows 2000 user logon name that's based on the first 20 bytes of the Active Directory logon name.

Continued

(Continued)

> When the computer account is created, it will also require the computer be given a pre-Windows 2000 name, so older clients and servers can identify and access it. As with user accounts, Windows Server 2003 will suggest a name for the computer that is based on the first 15 bytes of the name used to create the account. If you don't want to use this default name, you can enter a new one at any time.

Analyzing the Existing Namespaces

A DNS namespace is a naming scheme used by servers in a network; it shows the relationship of servers to one another in a domain tree and forest. As a hierarchy, it takes the shape of an upside-down tree. At the top of the DNS tree, the "root" is commonly shown as a single dot (.). Beneath the root domain are top level domains that use a two- or three-letter abbreviation. You are probably familiar with the domain abbreviations in Table 1.5 from the Internet.

Table 1.5 Domain Name Suffixes

Domain Suffix	Description	Original Purpose
.arpa	Advanced Research Project Agency	For reverse mapping of IP version 4 addresses on the Internet (in-addr.arpa)
.com	Commercial	Commercial/business use
.edu	Education	Schools, colleges, and universities
.gov	Government	For use by local, state, and federal government (aside from the military) in the United States
.int	International	For reverse mapping of IP version 6 addresses on the Internet
.mil	Military	United States military
.net	Network resources	For large scale Internet and telephone service providers that are the backbone of the Internet
.org	Organizations	Non-profit and non-commercial organizations, such as charities and religious organizations

These top-level domains branch off even further into second level domains, which use the abbreviations as a suffix to their domain names. For example, course.com and microsoft.com are both domain names that fall under the .com top-level domain. Because domain names need to be unique under a particular branch of the namespace, this allows for different names to be used under various top-level domains such as microsoft.com, microsoft.net, and so forth.

Originally, the domain suffixes in Table 1.5 were meant to represent American domains, but this philosophy has gone by the wayside over the years, with various organizations and individuals throughout the world registering them for their own use. To convolute things even more, many organizations registered .com domains, regardless of whether the sites were for business use. The reason behind this is because they are more familiar to most people on the Internet. In addition to these suffixes, there are also those representing countries. For example, .ca is for Canadian domains, .de is for German domains, and .uk is used to represent British domains. These too have somewhat lost their meaning, as many television programs are registering their sites under Tuvalu (a small nation in the Pacific), which has the suffix .tv.

It is at this point (where the domains take on a name combined with a domain suffix) that the DNS naming scheme should become familiar from our previous discussions of domains, domain trees, and forests. The DNS domain name selected for your network will be the namespace used by Active Directory and DNS servers in your organization. As we saw earlier in this chapter, the namespace can even be further broken down into child domains, such as dev.course.com or pub.course.com.

Documenting All Namespaces

Before installing Active Directory and DNS on your network, you should document all namespaces that are currently used on the network. Domain names will need to be unique within the network. In other words, you couldn't have two domains within the forest named course.com, or two child domains named dev.course.com. If you did, DNS would be confused as to which domain users were attempting to log onto or access resources from.

While domain names must be unique on the network, to a degree they should also be unique throughout all networks. If you're creating a new domain, you could name it almost anything you wanted. This means that if you really wanted to, you could name your domain microsoft.com or anything else you liked, but this could cause major issues if you needed to connect to this domain. For example, if you needed to obtain service packs or upgrades from windowsupdate.microsoft.com, DNS would assume that you're attempting to connect to a host computer or child domain on the local network.

Because many companies also have a Web site on the Internet, they also have a registered DNS domain. This can be used as the name of their Windows Server 2003 parent domain and avoids conflicts with other registered domains on the Internet. To keep their public presence separate from their internal network, the company could also register a second domain name, which is then used exclusively for the internal network. This is the method Microsoft recommends. However, being that many feel that all the good domain names are taken (hence the reason some are registering in Tuvalu), you might need to be creative in finding one that management will approve of.

In documenting the existing namespace or creating new ones, you should analyze the existing structure to identify any problems with the naming scheme. If a large number of domains are present, this might create a cumbersome structure that's hard to navigate. If enough domains branched off from one another, you might accidentally create a child domain that isn't globally unique. It is for this reason that the number of domains used in an organization is best kept to a minimum.

Identifying and Providing Remediation for Potential Issues

As you can see, there is a lot to consider when planning a namespace for your Windows Server 2003 network. Although we've discussed some of the issues that you might notice when documenting an existing or new namespace, these aren't the only ones that might arise. Not the least of these issues is actually choosing a name that fits normal conventions.

DNS domain naming in Windows Server 2003 allows some flexibility in the names you choose, but it is recommended by Microsoft that you follow the Internet naming conventions outlined in RFC 1123. This document states that DNS domain names should use only the following:

- Lowercase letters (a–z)

- Uppercase letters (A–Z)

- Numbers (0–9)

- Hyphen (-)

Other characters should not be included in your domain name. Because computers that used NetBIOS names might include other characters, Microsoft allows support for extended characters on networks running Windows 2000 Server and Windows Server 2003. However, because this support is provided for backward compatibility to older naming schemes, you should rename any computers and domains that don't meet RFC 1123.

Other naming issues might result from a company growing and the number of domain names becoming difficult to follow. Your goal should be to achieve the fewest possible domains your organization needs. As we discussed earlier, many times, domains that date back to NT environments could be migrated into other domains, with resources and users organized into OUs.

When documenting the namespaces used by your organization, you might find that they are based solely on purpose. This was seen in previous examples, such as when we specified developmental departments of companies as dev.*domainname*.com. In some situations in which there is a wide variety of such domains, you might find that the number of domains could be better managed by using a geographical approach. A corporation using a national or international model might be better suited to having users and resources grouped in child domains that reflect their location. In such a case, divisions in different countries of the course.com domain would become uk.course.com or us.course.com. Such a plan would also be less expensive then registering domains in each country (as we saw earlier when we discussed country domain suffixes).

In the previous section, we also mentioned some of the problems that could occur if your network used a domain name that was registered on the Internet. Although this generally isn't an issue if you're not going to use a particular Internet domain, it does become a problem if you plan to set up DNS on the Internet. If your network already uses a domain name that's registered to someone else, then this would present a conflict once your DNS servers and domain joins other DNS servers on the Internet. In such a case, you would need to either acquire the domain name from whomever it's currently registered to or change the domain name used on your network.

Developing & Deploying…

Renaming Domains

The ability to rename domains was non-existent in Windows NT Server. With Windows 2000 Server, you could rename a domain if it wasn't the forest root domain. You'll remember from earlier in this chapter that when the first domain controller is installed on a network, it creates the first domain. This domain is the forest root domain, and additional domains are created below it in the hierarchy. In Windows Server 2003, you are able to rename any domain including the forest root if the following conditions are met:

- All of the domain controllers in the forest are running Windows Server 2003.

- The forest functionality level is raised to that of Windows Server 2003.

This requires all domain controllers to be running Windows Server 2003, and the forest functionality level to be raised so that no previous versions of the Windows server operating system are running on any domain controllers. This also prevents older versions of Windows Server from being added later. As such, you should be extremely careful when selecting the domain name that will be used for your organization.

Assessing the DNS Infrastructure

A DNS infrastructure is the placement of DNS servers on a network. Because DNS servers are necessary to Active Directory's functioning, it should come as no surprise that their placement and configuration can have a major impact on your network. By failing to assess the DNS infrastructure, Active Directory might not function properly or users might have problems locating resources on the network.

Document DNS Server Locations

The location of DNS servers on the network is vital to document. It is important that all users are able to access any DNS servers used in the new infrastructure so they can thereby access domain controllers, Active Directory, and any services or resources they might need to do their work. It is also important for domain controllers to be capable of connecting to the other DNS servers on the network, so that they can replicate information from the DNS database to the other servers for the purpose of making sure each DNS server has identical information.

When documenting locations, you will also be determining the number of DNS servers on the network. This is important, because a change in the number of DNS servers on your network can improve or diminish performance. If there are too few DNS servers, then servers will be burdened by requests from users and computers to locate hosts and DCs on the network. If there are too many, then replication traffic can bog down the network.

Any DNS servers used on your network should be centrally located so that they are accessible throughout a domain or subnet. It is often wise to include a DNS server on each subnet. By doing so, requests won't need to be transferred across the entire network and possibly across slow links between sites.

EXAM WARNING

> There will be questions on the exam concerning the placement of DNS servers. The key considerations for DNS server placement are proximity to zone boundaries, available bandwidth, and DNS server type. For example, does the particular zone require a primary server and several secondary servers in remote offices, or will a primary server and several caching-only servers suffice? The answer will be based on the speed of the WAN links that interconnect the offices and the replication paths in the DNS infrastructure.

As is the case with other types of servers, if you have a small network, you should have more than one DNS server supporting the entire network. To achieve fault tolerance, you should have a minimum of two DNS servers. If one fails, users and computers will still be able to access the other DNS server, and thereby log onto domain controllers and use resources.

Analyzing Zone Configuration and Transfers

Each "level" of the DNS hierarchy represents a particular zone within DNS and contains resource records for all of the names within that zone. For the actual DNS database, a *zone* is a contiguous portion of the domain tree that is administered as a single separate entity by a DNS server. *Zone transfer* is the process of copying the contents of the zone file located on a primary DNS server to a secondary DNS server. In Windows Server 2003 DNS, the following types of zones are available:

- Primary
- Secondary
- Active Directory integrated
- Reverse lookup
- Stub

Primary and secondary zones are standard (that is, non-Active Directory-integrated) forward lookup zones. The principal difference between the two is the ability to add records. A standard primary zone is hosted on the master servers in a zone replication scheme. Primary zones are the only zones that can be edited, whereas secondary zones are read-only and are updated only through zone transfer. DNS master servers replicate a copy of their zones to one or more servers that host secondary zones.

An Active Directory-integrated zone is an authoritative primary (forward lookup) zone in which all of the zone data is stored in Active Directory. Active Directory-integrated is the only type of zone that can use multi-master replication and Active Directory security features. Standard and Active Directory-integrated zones will be compared and contrasted in Chapter 5, "Name Resolution."

A reverse lookup zone is an authoritative DNS zone that is used primarily to resolve IP addresses to network resource names. This zone type can be primary, secondary, or Active Directory-integrated. Reverse lookups traverse the DNS hierarchy in exactly the same way as the more common forward lookups.

Stub zones are a new feature introduced in Windows Server 2003. They contain a partial copy of a zone that can be hosted by a DNS server and used to resolve recursive or iterative queries. Stub zones contain the Start of Authority (SOA) resource records of the zone, the DNS resource records that list the zone's authoritative servers, and the glue address (A) resource records that are required for contacting the zone's authoritative servers. Stub zones are useful for reducing the number of DNS queries on a network and consequently the resource consumption on the primary DNS servers for that particular namespace.

Using zone transfer provides fault tolerance by synchronizing the zone file in a primary DNS server with the zone file in a secondary DNS server. The secondary DNS server can continue performing name resolution if the primary DNS server fails. Furthermore, secondary DNS servers can transfer to other secondary DNS servers in the same hierarchical fashion, which renders the higher level secondary DNS server as a master to other secondary servers. Three transfer modes are used in a Windows Server 2003 DNS configuration:

- **Full Transfer** When you bring a new DNS server online and configure it to be a secondary server for an existing zone in your environment, it will perform a full transfer of all the zone information in order to replicate all the existing resource records for that zone.

- **Incremental Transfer** When using incremental zone transfers, the secondary server retrieves only resource records that have changed within a zone so that it remains synchronized with the primary DNS server.

- **DNS Notify** The third method for transferring DNS zone records is not actually a transfer method at all. DNS Notify allows a primary DNS server to utilize a "push" mechanism for notifying secondary servers that it has been updated with records that need to be replicated. Servers that are notified can then initiate a zone transfer (either full or incremental) to "pull" zone changes from their primary servers as they normally would.

DNS zones and zone transfer are covered in greater detail in Chapter 5.

The primary concerns for zone and server placement in DNS are to provide the fastest resolution time for DNS queries and to conserve the amount of bandwidth consumed by queries and by zone transfers. The most significant metric to assess is the number of users and how they are grouped. For example, if you have offices of 400 users in New York and 500 in Chicago, the latter of which has the company's only connection to the Internet, and there is a 128 Kbps ISDN connection between them, it would be a particularly bad idea to have a single primary DNS server in Chicago and force users in New York to resolve queries across this slow WAN connection. It would be a better idea to place a primary server in Chicago and a secondary server in New York, and configure the replication for incremental zone transfer. It would be better still to create an Active Directory-integrated zone that encompasses both locations and schedule replication outside of business hours. The number of users and the amount of bandwidth will be the key pieces of information to gather when conducting your assessment.

Identifying Supportability for Active Directory

As we mentioned earlier, Active Directory requires DNS as a locator service to find clients and servers on the network. This locator service requires that DNS servers use a number of features that weren't supported in older versions of DNS, such as Windows NT 4.0 DNS. As such, for Active Directory to work with any existing DNS servers on the network, you'll need to determine what is supported by the current servers and whether you'll need to install a new DNS server (such as that included with Windows

Server 2003). The sections entitled Developing DNS Designs in Chapter 3 and Understanding DNS Design in Chapter 5 discuss DNS design in detail.

Assessing BIND Implementations

BIND is an acronym for Berkeley Internet Name Domain, which is an implementation of DNS that has run in many variations on UNIX servers. Windows Server 2003 DNS is interoperable with different versions of BIND and has been tested with the following versions:

- BIND 4.9.7
- BIND 8.1.2
- BIND 8.2
- BIND 9.1.0

If other servers on your network are running different versions of BIND, then Windows Server 2003 might not be interoperable with them, and you will need to either retire those servers or upgrade them to BIND 8.1.2 or later.

 TEST DAY TIP

There might be only a few questions on the exam that involve a homogeneous Windows Server 2003 DNS infrastructure. Many of the questions will relate to interoperability with DNS in older versions of Windows such as Windows NT 4.0 and with DNS that uses BIND. Identifying the features of Windows Server 2003 DNS that are supported by Windows NT 4.0 DNS and particular versions of BIND is critical for providing a correct response. There is a detailed table in Chapter 5.

Identifying Non-Supported Aspects

Older versions of BIND do not include elements that Active Directory needs to function. These include support for:

- Service Location Resource Records (SRV RRs)
- Incremental Zone Transfers (IXFRs)
- Dynamic updates

Service Location Resource Records are used to map the name of a service to the server on which it is located. When a user or application requests a particular service, the SRV RR is referred to, and they can then be redirected to the proper server. Active Directory and Windows Server 2003 require Service Location Resource

Records because clients and domain controllers use them to find other domain controllers on the network. Without this support, AD is unable to function because other domain controllers won't be found.

As we discussed earlier, incremental zone transfers are used to replicate changes to other DNS servers on the network. If IXFRs aren't supported, then the DNS servers would be able only to replicate the entire DNS database to other DNS servers. Because this would increase network traffic, this could cause performance issues for your network.

Dynamic updates allow changes made to hosts and domain names to be automatically updated on the DNS server. If a host computer or domain's name were modified in Active Directory, these changes would be sent to the DNS server, which would then update any mappings to the machine's name and IP address. Although support for this isn't essential in other DNS servers on the network, as changes could be made manually on them, it is an important part of Windows Server 2003 DNS that makes an administrator's job easier.

Assessing the Physical Network

Finally, we must undertake an assessment of the underlying network. Active Directory is replicated throughout the network, and as such, any replication scheme must be based upon the network topology. Therefore, it is imperative that the network be understood and fully documented. We must collate subnets, locations, sites, link speeds, and so on, and build up a map that can then be "fed" into Active Directory to create a replication topology. We must also closely analyze the network for performance and bottlenecks, because Active Directory can place far heavier demands upon the network than earlier versions of Windows ever did.

At a high level, assessing the physical network consists of the following activities:

- Analyzing the topology
- Creating a network map
- Analyzing network performance

Once the topology has been analyzed and all of its elements have been identified, you will be able to create a map of the network. The order is essential because analyzing the performance of the network will proceed more smoothly once you are armed with the knowledge and documentation on its layout and pathways.

Analyzing the Topology

Network topology is defined as the pattern of interconnection between nodes. As a topographical map identifies the surface features including relative positions and elevations of a tract of land, a network topology is the layout of a network that identifies

the relationships and connections among nodes that are connected to it. As a cartographer will use all kinds of tools and methods to gather information on a region to
create an accurate map, you as the "network cartographer" will need to complete the
following activities to gather accurate information on your network:

- Developing tools and methods to interrogate the network

- Collating routes, links, and bandwidths

- Collating subnet data

Chapter 2 discusses design considerations relative to the impact of replication on
network topologies.

Developing Tools and
Methods to Interrogate the Network

Just as the early explorers had compasses, sextants, and the stars to guide them and
assist in mapping new worlds, network designers need to collect tools and develop
methods for creating their own maps. The explorer's advantage is that the terrain of
these new worlds does not change, while network maps are often obsolete within
hours of being created. Because of the rapid pace of change in networking, updating
network diagrams could very well be a frequent activity. Therefore, honing your tools
and methods will make your job easier and save you valuable time.

Auto-discovery tools actively gather information on new and existing network
nodes and the health of the network, and can produce diagrams and reports on the fly.
These enterprise systems management tools are expensive, but on a large network their
utility can quickly justify the costs, especially if they can reduce the number of people
needed to manage the network or can be used to quickly diagnose and resolve costly
outages. Diagramming software is also bundled in network-discovery tools to quickly
generate diagrams.

Sniffers and protocol analyzers discover the protocols in use and the hosts that are
using them. They can also isolate individual links and measure the bandwidth being used
for individual services, such as DNS, HTTP, FTP, RTSP, and Quake2. Bandwidth consumption is especially important in a distributed network in which slow WAN links can
become bottlenecks for replication.

You can also employ less scientific methods for gathering information. For information on the technical details of your WAN links, the first place you should check
is with your telecommunications carrier(s). They should quickly be able to supply
information on the links they are providing to you. Second, if you are one of those
types who have to see it to believe it, then site inspections might be in order. Taking
copious notes, capturing screenshots, and even taking pictures with a digital camera
can ensure that information you received from others or through network discovery
tools are complete and accurate. Finally, you can produce some rudimentary network

performance statistics by capturing response times and other metrics through basic TCP/IP utilities such as tracert and ping. Enterprise systems management tools, if available, can be used to produce more sophisticated measurements.

Collating Routes, Links, and Bandwidths

Once you have developed the ways and means to collect data about your network, you will need not only to gather the information, but to produce something meaningful with it. As you work through your notes and reports, you should begin distilling the data you captured into layers that will later be depicted in a network diagram or series of diagrams. Beginning with basic geographic locations, you can identify what offices, campuses, countries, or even continents are connected to each other. Once this base layer is complete, you can begin attributing bandwidth capacities to these links.

 EXAM WARNING

Pay extra attention to the size (speed) of WAN links that interconnect the organization's physical locations for each business case. Your ability to make decisions on all aspects of Active Directory and network design will be based on the available WAN links.

With all of the pathways identified and quantified, you will need to analyze the paths to determine the most efficient routing scheme. For example, heavy replication should not be routed over a slow link or over a multitude of links. To accomplish this path analysis you will need to identify the services and types of traffic that are running over the network and estimate the amount of bandwidth consumed by each service. Once the services and bandwidth usage have been enumerated, you can begin prioritizing the services so that you can configure the routing of high priority traffic over the most appropriate routes and lower priority traffic over other links, or even reschedule certain types of traffic in off-peak hours.

Collating Subnet Data

Based on the IP address type and subnet mask in use on your network, you should be able to make a fairly well-educated guess as to what subnets are being used. You should be able to gather this information over the phone with enlightened colleagues and validate this information using Windows-based TCP/IP utilities such as tracert and ping.

In the event that you are left to your own devices to collect data on what subnets are in use on your network, one of the better methods is to examine the configuration of your DHCP servers. You should be able to open DHCP Manager in Windows or the configuration file in a text editor (such as Dhcpd.conf in UNIX or Linux) from the DHCP servers in locations around your network and document all of the configured subnets. It is critical that the subnet data be associated with sites on your network, especially if any reconfiguration is required during your Windows Server 2003 migration planning. The last thing you would want is to omit a location.

Creating a Network Map

"A picture is worth a thousand words." This adage is true of many things, but it is especially true with respect to network documentation. There is no more fundamental a tool for planning or troubleshooting than a graphic representation of your organization's network. That being said, there is also a maxim in IT that declares that a network diagram is obsolete as soon as you finish creating it. For this reason, creating and maintaining a map of your network is a critical task that must be performed on a frequent basis. Creating a new network map or even validating an existing map requires the execution of the following activities:

- Documenting site and subnet boundaries
- Drawing a routes, links, and bandwidths map

Documenting Site and Subnet Boundaries

The best place to start creating the network map is with the physical geography. Identify all of the continents, countries, cities, and buildings where your organization has facilities. Once these physical locations have been identified, you can move onto documenting virtual or logical sites. According to Microsoft, a site is "a combination of subnets, which consist of computers using the same grouping of IP addresses." If your organization has already rolled out Active Directory with Windows 2000 you should have some sites set up to manage areas of low bandwidth on your WAN. If this is the case, documenting the sites and their subnets will be as simple as opening Active Directory Sites and Services, as seen in Figure 1.21. The listing shows all of the configured sites and connectors that constitute the network topology and replication paths.

Figure 1.21 Gathering Data from Active Directory Sites and Services

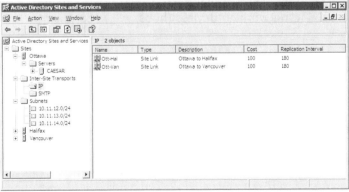

If Active Directory has not yet been deployed or you have not set up any sites, you will need to construct your own virtual boundaries. This might require visits to the various locations, or at least collaboration with people in those locations who can provide you with reliable, accurate data. It is critical that the subnets used in a campus, building, or area within a building are gathered and associated with a physical location. If you are running Windows NT 4.0 and using more than one domain, you might be able to construct these sites and subnets using domain boundaries.

TEST DAY TIP

The Knowledge Consistency Checker (KCC) is a key piece of the Active Directory replication topology. It is a process that runs on every domain controller every 15 minutes and automatically creates a replication topology, selecting which domain controllers to replicate with and when. The choice is based on the settings you choose when you create sites, links, and schedules within the Active Directory Sites and Services console.

Drawing a Routes, Links, and Bandwidths Map

Once you have documented the geographic layout of your network and identified the boundaries of your organization's physical and logical sites, you would be wise to follow the bottom four layers of the OSI model for networks as you build the remaining layers of your network map. Table 1.6 can be used as a guideline for drawing the required layers. Please note that the layers in this table are presented in the order that the information should be collected.

Table 1.6 Using the OSI Network Model Layers to Categorize Physical Network Information

OSI Model Layer	Infrastructure Components	Key Information
Physical	Cabling (copper, fiber), simple networking devices (hubs, repeaters)	Topologies, available bandwidth
Data Link	Switches, MAC (device) addressing	LAN hardware, MAC addressing
Network	Routers, protocols	WAN hardware, network routes
Transport	Protocols	TCP/IP addressing

You will notice that the layers in this table are presented in the reverse order (that is, from the bottom up). By beginning with the physical layer, you can first map out where and how the copper and fiber (and radio waves) connect the physical locations. Once the connection paths have been documented, you can then identify the networking equipment that has been deployed to joins the paths together. Once this "plumbing" has been captured, you can start building routes, compiling a list of network protocols, and noting the addressing schemes for each of these protocols.

The significance of documenting the available bandwidth, network paths, and configured routes will come into play when devising replication schemes for the various services that support Active Directory. Active Directory will need to be replicated to all domain controllers regardless of location, and the same is true for Global Catalogs and DNS and file system replication, among others. The creation of Active Directory sites and site replication will help in making the best use of available network paths and bandwidth.

Analyzing Network Performance

Network performance, like beauty, is in the eye of the beholder. If you were to survey employees in your organization about how the network is performing, you would receive a range of answers ranging from "It's as slow as molasses" to "It seems like it is working fine to me." Normally these answers are based on a comparison of some sort, either to the performance of other activities on the network or on the performance of a particular activity over a period of time. In order to make the measurement of network performance as objective as possible, you should perform the following activities:

- Collect current network performance measurements to generate statistics and create a performance baseline.

- Identify issues and constraints that will have an impact on network performance.

Once the baselines have been established, you will have objective, quantifiable data and a method for capturing that data to measure against when reports of "The network is slow" find their way to your phone or e-mail address.

Documenting Current Baselines

When it comes to measuring performance, you will not be able to measure "where you are" if you do not know "where you have been." Without establishing baseline metrics, you will not be able to measure the impact of introducing new services on your network and on existing services. A *baseline* is defined as a snapshot or a position that is recorded and remains unchanged and available as a reference of the original state and as a comparison against the current position. The process of constructing a baseline is commonly referred to as benchmarking. The data collected from the monitoring should be analyzed to identify trends from which the normal utilization and service level, or baseline, can be established. By regular monitoring and comparison with your established baseline, any conditions in the utilization of individual components or service thresholds that deviate from the baseline can be documented, and breaches or near misses in the SLAs can be used for reporting. In addition, the data collected from monitoring can be used to predict future resource usage or to monitor actual growth against predicted growth.

A protocol analyzer, or network sniffer, is a very valuable tool for capturing network resource usage. It can capture protocol usage information, traffic patterns over periods of time, and can quantify in logs the amount of bandwidth consumed by various services and individuals. The logs can be used to chart this data. Identifying patterns over time is especially critical. *Microsoft Operations Manager (MOM)* and *perfmon*, the integrated network monitoring utility in Windows Server 2003, can be used to accomplish these tasks as well. As an example, there will probably be less available bandwidth between 8:00a.m. and 9:00a.m. because people are authenticating, receiving TCP/IP addresses through DHCP, refreshing local DNS caches, and downloading e-mail and anti-virus updates. It would be a very bad time to schedule across-the-network backups.

Identifying Issues and Constraints

One of the best ways to start identifying future potential problem areas is to identify where your organization has encountered problems in the past. Using your organization's Help Desk records to plumb the depths of known network errors and problems could prove to be a very worthwhile exercise. For example, you might discover that the consolidation of financial records from all locations for biweekly payroll processing congests the network and slows down e-mail delivery and forms processing on your intranet site. You might decide to force the replication of all but the most critical Active Directory information to occur at off-peak hours so that it does not add to the congestion when the regions send in their financial records.

You can also look at service records on the networking equipment. The fact that a particular core router has had its memory upgraded three times in the past year might indicate that it is already working to capacity, and choosing an alternate route for replicating Active Directory data that avoids this router would be a better option. Alternatively, you could analyze the traffic being handled by this router to see if particular traffic streams could be configured to use different routes or be eliminated altogether.

Regardless of what is found, everything that even remotely resembles an issue or constraint should be captured. Some issues and constraints might appear to be minor in isolation, but considered together with others, they might prove to be more significant than originally observed.

Assessing the Impact of Proposed Designs

Once all of the assessments are complete, the next step in planning is to mock up the potential designs as a proof of concept to verify which designs are the most suitable for implementation into the production environment. Assessing the impact of proposed designs consists of undertaking the following tasks:

- Examining the existing infrastructure
- Determining interoperability
- Examining the physical network

Examining the Existing Infrastructure

Now that we have looked at the factors that affect our choice of possible designs, we need to look at how these factors and the required products, notably Active Directory, could impact the production environment. This consists of examining the physical infrastructure—the servers, how they are managed, and the applications they are running. For each of these components, we will need to assess if remedial work will be required to bring it up to specification, and if it is required, how much effort would be involved.

EXAM WARNING

Take a holistic, cautious approach for proposing a new design. In this situation, *holistic* should be taken to mean considering all factors together, such as business requirements, existing technology, available technology options, geographic limitations, and the primary function of the organization. Create a design (or designs) that addresses all requirements but is not overly complicated and does not contain elements that are not required.

Server Infrastructure

With a new set of system requirements, Windows Server 2003 might require you to upgrade the hardware that will host it. Processor speed, the amount of memory, and required disk space will need to be measured not only to enable Windows Server 2003 to run efficiently, but to enable all of the services that Windows Server 2003 will host to run efficiently for all of the users who connect.

Service Levels

The key consideration with respect to service levels is whether or not they are expected to change in the short- or long-term future of the organization. For example, is it expected that the status of particular applications will be elevated to mission critical in the short term after the organization is restructured? Perhaps more robust hardware or high-availability solutions will be required to meet elevated expectations of service. It is during this phase that the technical and organizational requirements for and the costs of maintaining current service levels should be identified. It might end up that new technology is introduced or that current service levels are renegotiated in light of these new developments.

Applications

We discussed compatibility earlier in the chapter; however, at this point in the planning process, the actual compatibility and performance of corporate applications will be assessed in coexistence with each other. Windows Server 2003 has demands of its own and applications might or might not function or perform better on this new platform. This is the phase in which any unexpected aspects of application compatibility and performance are identified, assessed, and if possible, quantified. Any deviation from current expectations should be communicated to the user community.

Determining Interoperability

Not all environments are homogeneous. Life would be easier if they were. There might be a number of reasons and requirements for maintaining a variety of platforms, and fortunately there are many new means of fostering interoperability among disparate operating systems. Interoperability consists of taking the following realities into consideration:

- There might be other network operating systems on your network.
- There might be other directory services that need to connect with Active Directory.

Other Network Operating Systems

As stated earlier, there might be a number of technical reasons and business requirements for maintaining platforms that run a variety of network operating systems. For example, your corporate standard for Web servers or database servers might be a particular flavor of UNIX, or your corporate financial management application might run only on a particular platform. These requirements must be taken into consideration when planning the deployment of Windows Server 2003 so that users in your organization can use services on all platforms with a minimal amount of inconvenience.

UNIX and Linux share a network protocol with Windows Server 2003, but each system has fundamentally incompatible file systems and authentication mechanisms. Microsoft has included many TCP/IP utilities with Windows Server 2003 and earlier versions. For example, Windows Server 2003 users can connect with UNIX and Linux systems using telnet. If more sophisticated functionality is required such as a UNIX shell or the ability to mount directories with NFS, a separate set of utilities, such as Microsoft Services for UNIX or MKS UNIX ToolKit, is required.

With Novell NetWare, the degree of interoperability depends on the version of NetWare. Older versions use IPX/SPX, a compatible version of which is included in all versions of Windows, but client software from Novell might be required for full functionality. Additional products from either Novell or Microsoft are required for parallel operation, such as Novell Account Manager or DirXML, or Microsoft Services for NetWare. Newer versions of NetWare use TCP/IP, which is a compatible protocol, but does not provide for native seamless interoperability because of incompatible file systems and authentication mechanisms.

Other Directories

Although Active Directory will be consuming your thoughts as you conduct your assessment, there are other directory services, notable enterprise directory services, and application directories to which you should devote some thought. *Enterprise directory services* are directories of names, profile information. and machine addresses for users and resources to manage user accounts and network permissions on a network. Active Directory is one example of an enterprise directory service. However, you might need to integrate with others, such as X.500 directory service products from Isode or HP, slapd (an Open Source stand-alone LDAP daemon), and Novell eDirectory, formerly known as Novell Directory Services (NDS). Application directory services are used to provide a central directory of searchable information within a specific application. For example, both PeopleSoft and Oracle have central directories in their Enterprise Resource Planning (ERP) products.

Although you might question the value of taking application directories into consideration in the context of Active Directory, there might prove to be an advantage to using the existing data stored in your central applications. This advantage can be realized through replicating the data into Active Directory or from Active Directory to another directory or directories. For example, you can use a metadirectory service to designate your organization's ERP (Enterprise Resource Planning) application directory service as the primary authority for employee contact information. The metadirectory service would be configured to push the contact information to equivalent fields in Active Directory and any other available directories that store contact information. The use of a metadirectory service, such as Microsoft Metadirectory Services, should be a factor in your assessment to avoid the redundant maintenance of duplicated data around your network.

The simplest description of a *metadirectory* is that it is a directory of directories. It is a mechanism for synchronizing and storing the information of multiple directories so that the same information does not need to be maintained in multiple locations. Although it does not actually contain the data, the metadirectory can declare a particular directory as the master—the authoritative source for a particular type of information. For example, a metadirectory service that incorporates Active Directory and other directories can be configured to declare the directory at the core of your organization's human resources system as the authoritative source for employee contact information and will govern the synchronization of this information to equivalent attributes of user objects in Active Directory.

Examining the Physical Network

The final area to assess is how the physical network will be impacted. With the knowledge of existing requirements and demands on the technical environment, we now need to focus on additional demands that might be required in the future. Furthermore, we need to identify potential bottlenecks that could be introduced with a migration to Windows Server 2003 and remediate them before Active Directory is deployed.

> ## TEST DAY TIP
>
> Because you will not have a lab in the test center, you will need to use the paper that is supplied to you when you register to draw your designs. The exhibits in each business case are valuable, but you might save time by combining the exhibits in a single diagram and creating possible designs that are based on the diagram. If you have the diagram and your designs in front of you, you will not waste valuable time switching back and forth between the exhibits and the questions.

Additional Demands

There will be traffic that is common to all networks and cannot be avoided. People need to authenticate, map network drives, and read their e-mail. There will be traffic that can be scheduled more appropriate times, such as across-the-network backups happening at 2:00 a.m. The difficulty will lie in anticipating future demands.

This would be a good time to investigate the IT strategy for your organization. Ask questions about the potential future implementations of Voice Over IP, streaming multimedia, and videoconferencing. Will services that are currently running on servers in branch offices be consolidated in the corporate headquarters where all employees will access these newly consolidated services over existing WAN links? Anything that will consume bandwidth and affect network performance must be taken into consideration, especially if it has an effect on particular fundamental ser-vices required for Active Directory, such as domain controller replication and DNS zone transfer.

Identify Bottlenecks

When speaking of bottlenecks in an enterprise, one's mind immediately jumps to areas of the network where network traffic is constricted by an older piece of net-working hardware or a slow WAN link. Most of the time situations like this would be the cause; however, the network is not the only source of bottlenecks. An under-powered (and overwhelmed) domain controller, an ill-configured DHCP server, or a DNS server with a database overflowing with stale records can cause slow response times. Good design would suggest that all possible bottlenecks be identified during the planning phase and tested during a pilot deployment. The majority of bottlenecks can be caught that way. However, the best method of identifying bottlenecks is to analyze the historical performance of the network to identify the cause of past bottle-necks, whether it was the network or the server infrastructure or particular services running on the wrong choice of platform. You will be able to avoid or at least plan around potential bottlenecks with the knowledge of where your network has been.

Summary of Exam Objectives

Regardless of whether an application or operating system platform is new or old, it cannot be introduced into an environment with the complete confidence that it will work to expectations without making sure that it can peacefully coexist with existing technology and practices. You could be upgrading from Windows 2000 to Windows Server 2003 or building a network and directory services infrastructure based on Windows Server 2003 from scratch. The implementation of new software and hardware requires very careful and thorough assessment before anything is even purchased. The following paragraphs summarize the various analyses and evaluations that should take place as part of the due diligence for any implementation project, and specifically for the implementation of Windows Server 2003 and Active Directory.

First, the impact of introducing Active Directory on the existing technical environment should be investigated. This requires the analysis of hardware and software requirements, any interoperability requirements for software and hardware that will continue to be in operation, and network requirements. In addition, once the analysis of the infrastructure components is complete, you will need to review current levels of service within your technical environment and the current network administration model. These two items might require changes depending on how the new platform and directory service will be implemented and managed.

Second, you will need to examine the existing implementation of the various network operating systems that are running on your organization's network. You should identify the existing domain model, discover the number and location of domain controllers on the network, and gather the configuration details of all servers on the network. Server types might include primary domain controllers, backup domain controllers, file servers, print servers, and Web servers. The output of this phase of the overall assessment is a logical map of the network that displays how resources are organized and a detailed inventory of the purpose and location of all servers.

Third, you will need to analyze the state of your existing DNS to determine what changes need to be made (if any) so that Active Directory is adequately supported. DNS is so deeply intertwined with Active Directory that it must be functioning properly or else your life as a network administrator will take on a whole new meaning. Preparing for Windows Server 2003 DNS includes a thorough analysis of the current DNS infrastructure and the current namespace.

Fourth, the network topology needs to be identified and network performance levels need to be measured. This includes investigating performance constraints in the existing network infrastructure and establishing baseline performance requirements for each major subsystem before any changes are introduced. Without the knowledge of how well (or poorly) your network is currently performing, you will not be able to establish whether the introduction of Windows Server 2003's new services is having a beneficial or detrimental effect on performance. The network performance evaluation will also enable you and your team to justify the design and procurement decisions you will need to make.

Finally, you will need to analyze the impact of your new infrastructure designs on the existing technical environment. To accurately gauge the impact, you should analyze requirements for hardware, software, and for interoperability between new and legacy systems and among services that will be running on different platforms. Again, you will need to review current levels of service within the existing technical environment and requirements for network performance against expectations that might be developing with the introduction of Windows Server 2003. To accomplish this, a lab environment and potentially a pilot deployment might prove to be especially helpful.

All of this investigation, analysis, and documenting might sound like a tall order, and frankly, it can be. By persevering and conducting a thorough, detailed assessment, however, you will avoid all kinds of headaches (and maybe even unemployment). The fruit of your labor will be that you have all of the information you need to make informed and accurate design decisions at every juncture during the project. Costly risks can be minimized, and time-consuming wrong turns can be eliminated by arming yourself and your design team with all of the information required to produce sound technical architecture.

Exam Objectives Fast Track

Assessing the Technical Environment

- ☑ Create your assessment based on communication and information flows. Communication is both technical (such as network traffic) and organizational (such as reporting hierarchy between levels of management).

- ☑ Assess the capabilities of hardware, software, and the network, and ensure that there are appropriate levels of support and management staffing.

- ☑ Service levels are key considerations. There is a vast difference in cost and management effort between 99.9% and 99.999% reliability.

Assessing the Current Server Infrastructure

- ☑ Ensure that the physical deployment of server hardware and server roles is captured. It is important that the geography and distribution of people is also documented.

- ☑ Identify the logical arrangement of servers. You can use the existing domain structure or even organization workgroups to identify where servers are and how they are used.

☑ Measure the capacity of servers against the services they need to provide and the service levels they need to achieve. It might be necessary to redeploy servers to ensure that appropriately sized hardware is provided so that service levels are met or exceeded.

Assessing DNS

☑ Identify any aspects of the current DNS infrastructure that might need to change prior to migrating to Windows Server 2003 DNS. Any potential incompatibilities might inhibit or prevent a smooth transition to the new product.

☑ The namespace should be reflective of the physical and logical organization. Zones within the DNS namespace should be created around physical locations so that the bandwidth consumed by zone transfers can be managed. The namespace should also be subdivided into zones to enhance the manageability of the DNS infrastructure.

☑ Establishing the appropriate replication scheme is critical. Place servers close to the users who need them and choose the appropriate server type for the amount of bandwidth that is available (such as a caching-only server in a small branch office that is connected to headquarters with a dial-up connection).

Assessing the Physical Network

☑ Identify the physical locations that constitute your organization and the links that interconnect them against the types and criticality of the services that need to be provided. Identifying bottlenecks is easier when you are equipped with the knowledge of which servers are providing particular services across the various capacities of network links.

☑ Establish a baseline for network performance. Again, this makes trouble-shooting easier because you should be able to identify when a newly introduced service has an adverse effect on the network by the amount it deviates from the baseline.

☑ Identify existing and potential Active Directory sites to better manage the amount of bandwidth consumed during replication and the time when replication occurs.

Exam Objectives
Frequently Asked Questions

The following Frequently Asked Questions, answered by the authors of this book, are designed to both measure your understanding of the Exam Objectives presented in this chapter and to assist you with real-life implementation of these concepts. You will also gain access to thousands of other FAQs at *www.ITFAQnet.com*.

Q: We are running Windows 2000 and are merely upgrading to Windows Server 2003. Why is an assessment so important to us in our situation?

A: Forewarned is forearmed. Depending on the complexity of your environment, there might be unseen factors that can hinder the progress of even the most straightforward-seeming upgrades. Although the jump from Windows 2000 to Windows Server 2003 might not be as big as a migration from other platforms; there are still risks that can be mitigated by ensuring that you are adequately informed prior to starting the actual implementation.

Q: We have decided not to preserve any aspect of our existing network and will be building our new environment from scratch. Do we still need to do an assessment?

A: Yes. Even though you will not be building on any existing technology, you will still need to identify all of the business requirements, organizational factors, and resource costs (people, time, and finances) that come to bear on your design. An assessment of these "soft" elements will determine what "hard" (technology) components are required, how they should be used, and where they should be deployed.

Q: This seems like a lot of work for creating the design. Is all this effort really required?

A: The quantity and quality of data you gather will determine the quality of your design and the success of your project. A thorough, detailed assessment will produce three benefits. First, you will be able to make the most informed decisions when creating your design and justifying your recommendations to management. Second, you will be able to accurately measure the success of the implementation project because you will have established expectations for the outcome before you start the deployment. Third, you will have the foundation for developing sound network documentation that will be required for managing and supporting the new network environment after the project has concluded.

Q: Everything is running fine now. What is wrong with starting to upgrade our servers and fixing things that go wrong as we proceed?

A: Even if the risks are assumed to be low, proceeding with a deployment without first conducting an assessment and actually identifying and potentially quantifying areas of your technology environment that require particular attention can introduce problems that could have been avoided. In addition, there might come a point in the deployment at which you cannot roll back to a previously harmonious state. You would not want to introduce instability where it could have potentially been avoided through planning.

Self Test

A Quick Answer Key follows the Self Test questions. For complete questions, answers, and explanations to the Self Test questions in this chapter as well as the other chapters in this book, see the Self Test Appendix.

1. You are part of a team of consultants that will be designing the network infrastructure and Active Directory for a multinational company. Your team is approached by the head of one of the organization's business units, who is proposing his own design for Active Directory that has been modeled after the organization chart, with each business unit having an OU that is named after its director. How would you rate this design?

    A. It is a good design because it follows the organization chart.

    B. It is a good design because it follows the flow of information from management to employees.

    C. It is a bad design because it does not account for changes in the organization.

    D. It is a bad design because it does not account for available bandwidth.

2. You have been asked to assess your current domain structure as part of the planning to migrate to the version of Active Directory on Windows Server 2003. You have been asked to keep the company's business objectives at the front of your mind when conducting your assessment. What documents will be especially useful to you?

    A. Organization charts

    B. Documented business processes

    C. The annual report to shareholders

    D. Financial statements

    E. The geographic locations of offices

3. Your design team is handed documents that describe the company's organization and is assured that they are current, although no one can tell you when the documents were last updated. How should you proceed with this new-found information?

    A. Trust the documents and proceed.

    B. Verify when they were last updated and make changes if necessary.

    C. Ignore the documents and create new ones by conducting your own investigation.

    D. Create a design based on industry best practices and recommend making organizational changes to accommodate the design.

4. When they find out about the impending upgrade of the network infrastructure, representatives from your company's business units approach you demanding assurances that existing service levels will apply after the migration is complete. How should you respond?

    A. Inform them that you cannot make any promises at this point in the migration.

    B. Inform them that you will assess past performance against the existing service levels to see if the existing service levels are still valid.

    C. Inform them that Windows Server 2003 is definitely more reliable than what is currently running and they should expect an improvement in service.

    D. Inform them that the new network infrastructure design is being constructed with the existing service levels as a primary consideration and they will be kept informed as the design evolves.

5. You have been asked to conduct a hardware inventory of all of the servers running in your company to determine their state of readiness for the impending upgrade to Windows Server 2003. What hardware information should you capture? (Select all that apply.)

    A. Hard disk size

    B. Serial number

    C. Date of manufacture

    D. CPU

E. Amount of RAM

F. Warranty status

6. You are migrating your company's Web servers from Windows NT 4.0 to Windows Server 2003, Standard Edition. What are the most important components to examine to see if your existing hardware can support the new version? (Select all that apply.)

A. SSL accelerator

B. Amount of RAM

C. NIC type and speed

D. Hard disk capacity

E. Number of processors

7. You have been asked to conduct an inventory of all software that is running on your company's servers. What are the primary benefits for creating a design that can be derived from the data collected during a software inventory? (Select all that apply.)

A. Determining if your company has an adequate number of licenses for the number of users

B. The portability of applications from Windows to UNIX

C. The degree of compatibility of the software that will be installed with existing software that will not be upgraded

D. Finding software that is no longer in use

8. You are assessing your current version of the DNS design for your company, specifically the placement of DNS zones. The company is based in North America and has many branch offices throughout the continent. What are the key issues you need to consider when making your assessment? (Select all that apply.)

A. Use of caching-only servers

B. The version of Windows DNS that is being used in the branch offices

C. Link speed

D. Traffic patterns

E. Use of conditional forwarders

F. Client configuration

Self Test Quick Answer Key

For complete questions, answers, and explanations to the Self Test questions in this chapter as well as the other chapters in this book, see the Self Test Appendix.

1. **C**
2. **A, B, E**
3. **B**
4. **D**

5. **A, D, E**
6. **B, D**
7. **A, C**
8. **A, C, D**

MCSE 70-297

Developing the Active Directory Infrastructure Design

Exam Objectives in This Chapter:

1.5   Design the Active Directory infrastructure to meet business and technical requirements.

1.5.1   Design the envisioned administration model.

1.5.2   Create the conceptual design of the Active Directory forest structure.

1.5.3   Create the conceptual design of the Active Directory domain structure.

1.5.5   Create the conceptual design of the organizational unit (OU) structure.

1.5.4   Design the Active Directory replication strategy.

Introduction

Once the environment has been assessed and fully documented, the actual Active Directory designs can now be developed. You should by now have sufficient data relating to your organization to start putting together designs that are appropriate for the organization and meet any requirements to which you must adhere.

During the initial stages of an Active Directory services infrastructure design phase, one should identify the administrative model that will be implemented. This can be done only when the current model has been assessed, the service and data administrators have been identified, and those sections of the organization requiring isolation and/or autonomy have been identified. These factors, together, will determine the forest and domain design(s).

This chapter will help you to understand those factors, what they are, and how they affect the designs. You will appreciate how isolation and autonomy issues (due to political and/or legal reasons) will affect the number of as well as the hierarchy within each forest. The chapter discusses the different approaches that can be taken to "carve up" the forest, based on geography, function, politics, and law. The structure and naming of the namespace(s) will be discussed as will the idea of a "dedicated" root domain, within the forest(s).

After examining the forest design, we move on to domain and OU design. For each aspect of the design, we look at the pertinent factors that affect the designs and then typical models that are used by many organizations today.

The final design aspect considered is that of replication. In this chapter, we explore some of the basic concepts and models available. A more thorough discussion of the more advanced techniques available can be found in Chapter 4, "Designing the Logical Components."

The subjects of ownership and responsibilities will also be covered. These are areas often overlooked when designing a system that encompasses multiple entities within a single organization. It is important that controlling groups are created that then own and manage the environment as a whole, while each entity within the organization still retains the option of autonomy. The topic of ownership is covered for each phase of the design, such as forest, domain, OU, and replication.

Assessing and Designing the Administrative Model

When originally released, the domain was documented and designed to be the security boundary within an Active Directory. This implied that resources within any one domain within the forest would be isolated and autonomous from all other resources outside the domain. In other words, multiple domains could coexist within the same forest, in the knowledge that administrators from one domain could not access resources in any other domain, unless granted specific rights to do so.

However, several loopholes have since been found that allow an administrator in any one domain in the forest to elevate his rights in other domains. Ultimately, the administrator can elevate his privileges so he has domain admin rights in all domains in the forest. This has led Microsoft to rethink security boundaries and whether the domains actually represent a boundary, or whether, in fact, the forest should be viewed as the new security boundary. These issues must be carefully considered when designing the Active Directory infrastructure, as to whether they will actually change the designs implemented or whether the organization is happy to accept that these loopholes exist and to simply mitigate against them, as best it can.

To assess whether an organization (that would traditionally have considered a single forest design appropriate) requires multiple forests, several new terms and concepts need to be defined. This includes the notions of a *service administrator*, *data administrator*, *isolation*, and *autonomy*. These terms are described and explained in the sections that follow, all of which when applied to your organization will help to identify the appropriate forest design.

Service Administrators and Data Administrators

Service administrators are responsible for maintaining the Active Directory infrastructure and for ensuring that this infrastructure provides the necessary functions and services to end users, so that any service levels established are met. It is important that this type of administrator is not confused with the data administrator, who is responsible for the maintenance and management of the objects stored within Active Directory, including users, groups, and machine objects.

More often than not, especially in larger organizations, the service administrators are not the same people performing the data administrator role; therefore, this demarcation must be understood and allowed for in the design of Active Directory. The owners of the service and data administrators' roles should all be closely involved with any designs, because their needs must be incorporated into any design implemented. If either group requires autonomy or isolation, then that requirement might alter the design principles adopted.

EXAM WARNING

While some larger organizations have traditionally used the approach where service and data administrators are viewed as separate groups, the concept is new to Microsoft material. It is therefore likely that these terms appear in the associated exam, and those wanting to take Exam 70-297 should be conversant with these new concepts and ideas.

The Role of the Service Administrator

The service administrator will typically be responsible for the following aspects of Active Directory:

- Management and maintenance of domain controllers (DCs)

- Management and maintenance of a Domain Name System (DNS)

- Management and maintenance of forestwide components

- Management and maintenance of Active Directory replication within the forest

- Deployment of Active Directory infrastructure throughout the organization

- Management and maintenance of trusts within the forest

- Management and maintenance of trusts with external domains, forests, and Kerberos realms

It can clearly be seen from this list that the service administrator holds a very powerful position within the enterprise. It is therefore of utmost importance that the role of service administrator is handed only to trusted employees if they can demonstrate a deep understanding of various technical, security-related, and political aspects of the organization. The number of users holding such a role should be minimized due to the nature of the rights held by these users. The fewer the number of service administrators, the better, because the management of the infrastructure can be more tightly controlled if a small team of highly specialized admins have control of the environment, versus a larger number of less knowledgeable users holding the same role.

As already stated, administrators in any one domain can elevate their privileges in any other domain. As a result, the service administrators must be trusted by all entities within the organization, because all service administrators will have access to all files, resources, and objects across the entire forest, whether they are granted the necessary rights (via membership of the Enterprise Admins groups) or simply are granted Domain Admins rights in one or more domains in the forest.

To summarize, the service administrator role should be viewed as a separate role to that held by the data administrator, but must also be viewed as a forestwide role, because the forest (and not the domain) must now be seen as where the security boundary exists.

The Role of the Data Administrator

The data administrator will typically be responsible for the following aspects of Active Directory:

- Management of user objects

- Management of group objects

- Management of machine objects

- Management of printer objects

- Management of NTFS file and share access control lists (ACLs)

- Management of member servers and workstations

Data administrators, unlike service administrators, are responsible only for a subset of objects within Active Directory. For example, a group of data administrators might be delegated administration of user objects in one particular OU, within one specific domain.

Unlike service administrators, the rights granted to data administrators can be delegated to a subset of objects, rather than at the domain or forest level. Data administrators do not have any access to the Active Directory infrastructure; instead, they simply manage the objects, or a subset thereof, within an Active Directory domain.

Another difference between service and data admins is that service administrator roles exist within Active Directory by default—including Enterprise Admins, DNS Admins, Domain Admins, and so on. Data administrator roles, however, need to be created manually to suit the needs of the organization. For example, the role "London Users Administrators" can be created and granted the right Full Control on all user objects in an OU named "London." This example also demonstrates how the rights of data admins can be granted in a granular fashion, because the group "London Users Administrators" has rights on user objects in the "London" OU but has no rights elsewhere in the domain or in any other domain.

Because the data administrator role can be managed in this granular fashion, it is likely that many such roles are created so that management of objects can be delegated to the appropriate support groups within your organization. This leads to a much lower cost of ownership (when compared to that found in a Windows NT environment), because only a small number of service admins are created, and the remaining roles are data admins with very restricted and specific rights. This allows service admins to concentrate on ensuring that the Active Directory functions correctly, while data admins manage the objects within Active Directory. This should be a far more efficient and less expensive way to manage an environment when compared to the approach used in Windows NT, where all administrators were in essence service administrators.

To summarize, the data administrator is responsible for a subset of objects in Active Directory and has no rights to any objects elsewhere in the forest. This role allows the organization to distribute the delegation of object management to a very granular level, thus allowing the service admins to concentrate on service delivery.

Understanding Isolation and Autonomy

To better understand which Active Directory model is most appropriate, the terms *autonomy* and *isolation* must be understood and factored into any design. Political, technical, and security-related aspects of the enterprise require that autonomy and/or isolation might be needed by various factions within the organization.

These terms and how they relate to design principles are discussed further in subsequent sections. Isolation and autonomy and how these terms relate back to service and data admins are also explained.

EXAM WARNING

The terms *autonomy* and *isolation* are new to Microsoft literature. Microsoft has stressed the importance of these terms and their relation to forest design recently, and it is therefore essential that these terms are understood and that the readers appreciate fully how these terms relate to their organization and the resultant designs.

The reader should carefully consult with all interested parties and decide early in the design phase whether and where isolation and/or autonomy are required. These requirements have a fundamental effect on the design and must be established early in the project.

Autonomy

If an entity requires autonomy, then a degree of independence is required, but without precluding other entities from accessing resources inside that boundary autonomy.

Autonomy can be achieved at the service admin level, implying that domain service admins have independence from service admins in other domains, but that these service admins accept that there are admins elsewhere in the forest with greater rights. These latter admins have the ability to remove rights from domain service admins and to make changes to the Active Directory infrastructure within any domain in the forest. For example, domain service admins in emea.company.net have service autonomy from all other service admins in all other domains in the same forest, but must accept that forest service admins in company.net have domain service admin rights in all domains in the forest, including emea.company.net.

Autonomy can also be achieved at the data administrator level. The data administrators have a similar situation to the service administrators. Although they have complete control over the objects within their jurisdiction, they must accept that there are admins elsewhere with greater rights who can remove the rights granted to the data administrators and who have the ability to manage those same objects for which the data admins are responsible. Indeed, the administrators with greater powers could in theory remove rights from the data admins, so they can no longer manage their objects.

In the autonomy model, administrators of all types must accept that there exist other administrators with greater rights and therefore greater control over the Active

Directory and its objects. If this level of independence is deemed insufficient, then isolation might be required rather than simple autonomy.

Isolation

The concept of isolation takes autonomy to the next logical level. With isolation, one has both independence and exclusive access and control of one's resource, be it a forest, domain, or OU.

In contrast to autonomy, where independence was assured but exclusive access was not, isolation implies that only the administrators of the resource have access and that there are no other administrators elsewhere with sufficient rights to access or manage those same resources.

The reason for stressing the importance between autonomy and isolation is that if isolation is required, the forest should be viewed as the security boundary and not the domain. This implies that if service isolation is required, then a separate forest must be established, because any other solution can only guarantee autonomy, not isolation. Similarly, if data isolation is required for any data within the enterprise, then a separate forest must be deployed to house that data, because again, any other solution cannot guarantee isolation, only autonomy.

Figure 2.1 is a flow diagram illustrating the design options available, depending on whether isolation, autonomy, or both are required.

Figure 2.1 Autonomy and Isolation Flow Chart

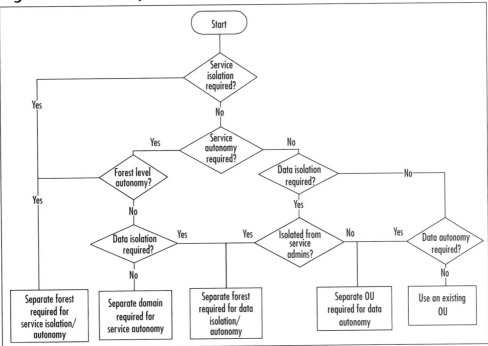

The degree of isolation and/or autonomy required within your organization must be carefully assessed and evaluated before designs are constructed. This starts with the assessment of the current administrative models and domain models. These subjects were covered in detail in Chapter 1, "The Assessment Stage."

Only once these models have been assessed can design objectives be created, which include isolation and autonomy requirements. Naturally, the more complex the design, the more complex the environment and the more costly it is to manage and administer. The business benefits of a more complex environment must therefore be weighed against the increase in administrative overhead. Table 2.1, on pages 96–97, lists pros and cons of multiple- versus single-forest designs.

More details regarding these terms and how they relate to Active Directory design principles can be found in subsequent sections, *Assessing and Defining the Forest Design*, *Assessing and Creating the Domain Design*, and *Developing the OU Model*, where different design alternatives are discussed along with the factors that make certain designs more appropriate than others.

Assessing and Defining the Forest Design

The previous section covered the administrative models and how they can influence design-related decisions. It also explained how some design criteria and principles that have changed since Windows 2000 should be incorporated into any new designs (and factored into existing designs where possible).

In this section, we start to examine the different forest designs, which scenarios they are particularly relevant to, and how to decide which design best suits your organization. The section starts by looking at factors that can influence forest designs and how one should choose forest namespaces carefully (a namespace being a contiguous DNS hierarchy), so that the new environment can be easily incorporated into any existing naming systems (such as DNS).

When deploying Active Directory within any organization, either one or more than one forest will be designed and implemented. The pros and cons of both options along with the different subtypes of both options are discussed. Finally, subjects often omitted in the design phase include ownership, accountability, and change management. Designing and deploying an environment is all well and good, but without proper management and control, the environment can easily fall into chaos, and in time, fail to meet its objectives and service levels.

Forest Design Factors

Before embarking on a discussion of the various forest design options, we need to examine the factors that will influence the design. We have already looked at service and data administrators as well as the concepts of isolation and autonomy, but what other factors are likely to dictate which of these concepts are most applicable? The following is a list of topics that will play into decisions made regarding forest design and are discussed in further detail:

- Organizational
- Operational
- Legal
- Naming considerations
- Timescales
- Management overhead
- Test environments
- External facing environments

Organizational

Many large companies are comprised of many smaller organizations or businesses. This is often the result of mergers and acquisitions, where several previously independent companies have "joined together" to form a new, much larger company. It can also be because of the existence of different business streams within the organization, such as Manufacturing, Sales, and Marketing.

Although the businesses within the company are all part of the same group of businesses, and share many aspects of the IT infrastructure, there is often a need for independence within each business, for various reasons. These reasons are described in the subsequent sections.

This independence, as previously described, can be achieved in one of two ways—the business might deem that autonomy is sufficient and therefore co-exist in the same forest as other businesses. However, if isolation is required, then the business must deploy its own forest to achieve that requirement.

Operational

Again, focusing on larger companies made up of several businesses, the need might arise where one business needs to store different data in the shared components of Active Directory, compared to the other businesses.

For example, one business might need to make schema changes that are not required by the other businesses. If a compromise cannot be reached, where a common schema is designed to meet the needs of all businesses, then a separate forest must be deployed by the business requiring its own unique schema changes.

Alternatively, the organization might require that multiple forests be deployed so that each business entity has complete isolation from a security point of view. For example, in a hosting environment, the ISP might need to deploy one forest per hosted environment, so that each environment is isolated from each other environment.

Legal

Although operational factors are largely technical in nature, legal factors are normally more political in nature. Often, businesses would gain advantage financially from sharing infrastructure costs, but the legal requirements of the country or the nature of the business conducted means that isolation must be established between different parts of the organization.

This is frequently the case within financial institutions, where various parts of the organization must be isolated, so as to meet the requirements of the regulatory body that has control in that country. A specific example is private banking and private bank account details. The details held within each private bank branch cannot be accessed outside of that jurisdiction (normally a country boundary). This implies data isolation, and therefore a separate forest per private banking jurisdiction, such that branches within the same jurisdiction can share data with each other, but cannot share data with branches in other jurisdictions. This applies even to branches that are part of the same business.

Naming Considerations

Within each forest, there will exist at least one DNS namespace, and one additional namespace per additional tree created. If multiple forests with multiple trees are to be created, the management and control over namespaces needs to be carefully considered and maintained. For additional details on DNS, refer to Chapter 5, "Name Resolution."

Each DNS namespace within the organization must be unique (unless housed on a segmented network), and the corresponding NetBIOS names of all domains within the forests must be unique across the whole enterprise.

For example, if splitting the forests by business, then the namespaces might be called business1.com, business2.com, business3.com, and so on. Each business then has complete control over its namespace and the hierarchy and DNS names contained therein. However, a degree of collaboration is required when NetBIOS names are chosen for each domain within each forest. Because each domain NetBIOS name must be unique across the whole enterprise, the various administrators and owners (defined later) must all agree on naming standards such that the uniqueness of NetBIOS domain names exists.

All of the preceding considerations and factors can influence the forest designs—more domain trees might be required to satisfy naming requirements, for example.

Timescales

The design phase of Active Directory can be a lengthy process, and if multiple businesses are involved with that design phase, a common, mutually agreed-upon design might not be reached within the agreed timescales.

Often, one particular business will have different planning and testing requirements than the other businesses, or one business might need to deploy Active Directory in a tighter timescale. One particular application might act as a driver for the deployment of Active Directory, such as Exchange 2000 or Exchange 2003, yet this might not be a driver across all businesses within the organization.

This demonstrates how timescales and business drivers can influence the design in an indirect way. Although all parties might agree in principle that one particular design is appropriate, if some businesses are not ready to participate in a shared infrastructure, they might choose to deploy their own forest once their own planning phase has been completed, within their timescales, based on their business drivers.

Although the timescales dictated by one business might not suit other businesses, it is highly recommended that the designs be created so that other businesses, not currently ready to deploy Active Directory, can join the Active Directory implementation with little or no disruption. A separate forest should be deployed only "as a last resort" if timescales cannot be agreed to.

Management Overhead

The final factor is the subject of management overhead. Although a shared infrastructure is obviously the most cost-effective solution from an administrative point of view, that model might not suit the needs of all businesses involved. Conversely, a multiforest deployment requires additional hardware and incurs additional admin management overhead, because more administrators are required to manage the infrastructure, including additional DNS namespaces, DCs, and so forth.

However, if isolation is not required, then it should be possible to give each business autonomy from each other business, within the same shared forest. The final solution might need to be a combination of centralized admin (at the forest service admin level) and decentralized admin (within each business).

In essence, the model needs to weigh cost effectiveness versus benefit. Cost-effective solutions require the minimum amount of infrastructure and administrators, while business benefit might require that each business have a degree of autonomy or even isolation from the rest of the organization. This dilemma needs to be discussed and addressed by the owners of the design. (Ownership is discussed later in the chapter.)

Test Environments

The final factor relates to testing, research, and development, which we'll collectively term *test environments*. When testing, researching, or developing a new technology, often there is a need to do so in an isolated environment. This can be accomplished through the use of a separate Active Directory implementation and/or segregated networks.

Testing new technology often calls for an environment that can quickly and easily be re-established on short notice, with minimal disruption to other users. By definition, this cannot be achieved within the main production environment, and so a test, research, and development environment is required to meet this objective.

Test environments should, ideally, mirror the production environment. For example, similar (or matching) domain names should be employed, along with matching OU and DNS implementations. If detailed stress testing is to be performed in the test environment, then it should also be populated with a similar number of user, group, and computer objects as found in the production environment.

Externally Facing Environments

Many organizations have externally facing networks and applications that are accessible by external clients. Often, these clients need to authenticate themselves before being granted access to resources in the external-facing environment. Rather than deploy a new authentication mechanism in the external environment, it might be prudent to deploy an Active Directory implementation within the external environment.

For reasons of security and isolation, the externally facing Active Directory implementation must be totally isolated from the internal production implementation, and so a separate forest must be deployed to meet this requirement. This split model also provides the organization with a mechanism for segregating external client users and data from its own internal users and data.

Forest Models

We looked at the myriad factors that can influence the design and just how they can dictate what options are most appropriate or feasible. We now examine the different multiple forest scenarios and which is appropriate based on the factors explained previously, including:

- The Service Provider model

- The Restricted Access model

- The Resource model

- The Organizational model

- The Single-Forest model

It should be pointed out at this stage in the design phase that the ideal scenario is that of a single forest. This model will always offer the lowest administrative overhead and total cost of ownership. Always attempt to design Active Directory as a single forest wherever possible. Only resort to the multiple forest designs if there is a real and evident requirement to do so.

The Service Provider Model

The first model considered includes multiple forests, each being completely isolated from the others. We call this the Service Provider model because this is applicable to ISPs hosting environments for multiple organizations. Refer to Figure 2.2 for an example.

Figure 2.2 The Service Provider Forest Model

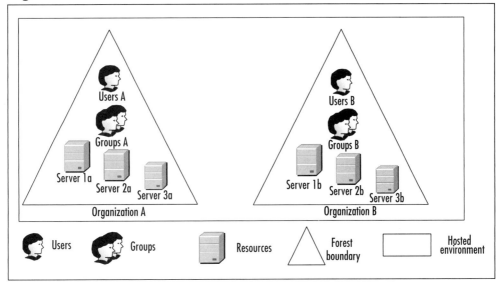

The ISP is responsible for both hosting environments on behalf of various companies and ensuring that data stored within each environment is isolated from every other hosted environment. This can be achieved only by deploying a separate forest for each organization. The ISP must establish a separate forest for each hosted environment and ensure that no trusts exist between any of these forests, so that isolation is guaranteed.

Although this obviously represents the least cost-efficient approach for the ISP, it does, however, meet the requirements of the hosted environments. In this scenario, the need for a secure, isolated environment clearly outweighs the fact that the multiple environments incur a larger maintenance overhead. Indeed, the ISP will no doubt charge a premium rate for such a service, but the hosted companies should be prepared to pay that little extra so as to guarantee isolation, which in turn ensures integrity of what might be highly sensitive business data.

The Restricted Access Model

A closely related scenario to the previously described model is the Restricted Access model. In this scenario, there is a need to isolate sensitive data within the same organization, such that users can only access that data if granted explicit rights to do so. Figure 2.3 illustrates such a model.

Figure 2.3 The Restricted Access Forest Model

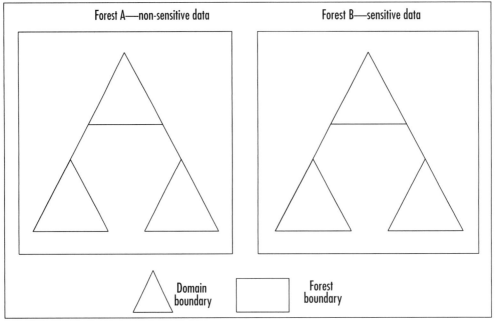

At first glance, this requirement appears to be met by the Single Forest model, because NTFS permissions can be used to grant and deny access to resources. However, remember that domain admins in any domain can in theory raise their privileges within the forest and thus gain access to any resource anywhere in the forest. Therefore, if data (or service) isolation is required, a separate forest must be deployed to house this sensitive (isolated) data.

This requirement, then, is met by the deployment of a separate forest. In fact, not only is a separate forest required, but complete isolation of that forest from any others is required. This can be achieved by ensuring that no trusts exist between the isolated forest (or any domain within the forest) and any other forest or domain elsewhere in the organization.

Each user within the organization will, therefore, have two user accounts. One account will be used to log in and access resources in the forest where sensitive data does not reside, and the other account will be used to access sensitive data in the isolated forest. Service administrators in one forest cannot access or gain access to resources in the other forest, because the two forests are isolated from each other.

This model can be taken a step further—the two environments can be placed on separate, isolated networks. This implies that if access to the sensitive data is required, then the user requires both a user account in the isolated forest and access to a machine located on the isolated network. This further restricts access to the sensitive data and is likely to be popular in government and military organizations.

EXAM WARNING

Many of the questions and answers in Exam 70-297 will revolve around the security boundary. Windows 2000 exams were based on the concept of the domain security boundary, but the newer Windows Server 2003 exams will expect the forest to be considered the new boundary.

If readers have previously taken Windows 2000 design exams, they should be conversant with the new ideas examined in this book, which covers topics such as isolation, autonomy, and security boundaries. Although the readers' design principles might have evolved over the years to match those held by Microsoft, they should ensure that they are aware of all the new design principles before embarking on the new Windows Server 2003 exams.

The Resource Model

The next model is the Resource model. In this model, a separate forest is deployed that houses resources that relate to a specific project or business. Refer to Figure 2.4 for an example of such an implementation.

Figure 2.4 The Resource Forest Model

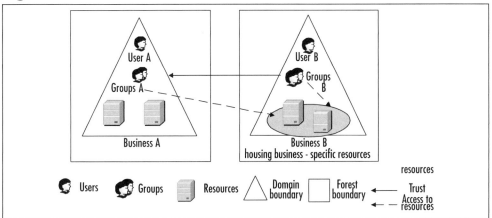

Although user accounts are all stored centrally in one "accounts forest," all resources relating to a project or business are stored in a separate forest, along with "backup" user accounts that can also be used to gain access to the resources in the resource forest. Users in the accounts forest can access resources in the resource forest via a one-way trust (there is no need to grant access to the users forest from the resource forest).

The purpose of this scenario might not appear obvious at first glance. The model becomes more relevant when one asks the question, "What happens if the users forest becomes unavailable?" Assuming that the data stored in the resource forest is highly important (although not necessarily sensitive), then we must ensure that access to that data is available 24x7. This can be achieved via the backup accounts mentioned earlier—if the users forest is unavailable, then users simply resort to using their backup accounts instead, which are located in the resource forest and have access to appropriate resources.

Such a model might prove relevant to organizations that have one particular aspect of their business that must be available 24x7. For example, an automobile company might have manufacturing and sales business components, and the former has the requirement that its resources be available 24x7. The Resource model could be used in this scenario, because it offers both centralized management of user accounts (within a users forest) and the fallback option that manufacturing resources are still available if the users forest is unavailable, via backup accounts that exist in the resource forest. Again, cost efficiency versus benefit must be carefully weighed before such a model is designed and deployed, because it clearly increases the total cost of ownership (TCO) of the whole environment.

The Organizational Model

The final multiple-forest model considered is the Organizational model. This is probably the most widely used multiple forest model, especially in larger companies where multiple, independent business units exist. Figure 2.5 depicts such a scenario.

Figure 2.5 The Organizational Forest Model

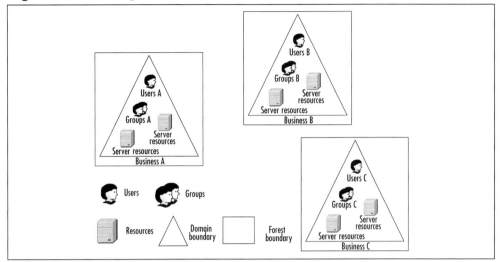

As previously mentioned, within a larger organization, the smaller businesses might have different requirements and/or timescales for deploying Active Directory; therefore, a single forest design might not meet the needs of all involved parties.

This leads the various businesses within the organization to create their own forests, each of which meets the needs of the business unit using that forest. This model also has the added advantage that each business unit has both autonomy and isolation from all other forests, but has the option to establish trusts with other forests and domains as necessary.

Reasons for establishing separate organization forests include the need to make schema modifications or changes to the configuration partition that are not required or contradict those required by other businesses. Alternatively, each business might need service and/or data isolation from all other businesses, and as already mentioned, this can be achieved only with separate (organization) forests.

In this model, each forest would contain all objects relating to the business the forest represents. All users, groups, printers, machines, and so forth would be contained in the one forest; the same scenario would also exist for each additional organization forest. It is likely that resource sharing would be required in such a model, which can be achieved with domain and/or forest trusts.

Again, the subject of cost versus benefit needs to be carefully considered. This model involves a lot of duplication of effort—sites and subnets need to be defined multiple times, and much more infrastructure needs to be deployed to support this model. However, if service and/or data isolation is of paramount importance (and indeed of a legal requirement perhaps), then isolation through the deployment of multiple forests is the only viable solution.

The Single Forest Model

So far, we have discussed scenarios where multiple forests are required such that the various technical and political requirements can be met. However, none of these requirements might exist and the single forest scenario might be the most appropriate.

It should be clear by now that the single forest model is the simplest to design, engineer, and deploy. It should also be clear by now that it is the cheapest option to deploy and the cheapest to own (with the lowest TCO). If none of the factors that require multiple forests to be deployed exists, your organization should strongly consider the deployment of a single forest.

If autonomy is a factor but isolation is not, then a single forest with multiple domains and/or trees should meet such requirements. Again, it should be clear by now that isolation requires a separate forest to be established, because this represents the security boundary, while autonomy merely needs a separate domain (or OU) because it needs independence without exclusive control and access.

The various factors and scenarios available within a single forest are discussed further in the next section, *Assessing and Creating the Domain Design*.

Summary of Forest Models

Table 2.1 contains a summary of the pros and cons of multiple versus a single forest design.

Table 2.1 Forest Advantages and Disadvantages

Multiple Forests	
Advantages	**Disadvantages**
Separate schemas, allowing for forest autonomy at the schema level.	No simple sharing of network resources; collaboration between forests needed.
Separate configuration partitions, allowing for forest autonomy at the configuration level.	Requires an external trust(s) to domain(s) in other forest(s) in order to share resources.
No requirements for interbusiness trusts; each forest is isolated from every other forest.	Global catalog (GC) queries can access objects only in the local forest.
Separate forest service admins, allowing for business autonomy and isolation.	A number of disparate schemas might exist—consolidation of forests at a later date might prove difficult.
Mitigates against known Active Directory vulnerabilities (because each business is isolated from every other).	Requires some Meta-Directory to manage inter-forest synchronization and generation of a common global address book (if a common, global address book is required).

Continued

Table 2.1 Forest Advantages and Disadvantages (Continued)

Multiple Forests	
Advantages	**Disadvantages**
No dependency on any other business; each business has complete independence in its own forest.	Higher design and implementation costs.
Can completely and easily separate DNS hierarchies—each business can choose its own namespace and no interoperability is necessarily required between these namespaces.	
Allows for the segregation of externally facing Active Directory environments.	
Allows for the segregation of test Active Directory environments.	

Single Forest	
Advantages	**Disadvantages**
Single forest—allows for simple sharing of objects across domains.	Controlled change management plan required for forestwide operations, because of potential impact to all domains.
A single exchange organization can be deployed, using the same directory as Active Directory.	Control over Enterprise components required, which are shared across multiple domains.
Single replicated GC and therefore, a common Global Address Book view in Exchange.	Thought, collaboration, and planning required to meet each domain's security needs.
Single set of object entities to manage, such as schema and configuration.	Thought and planning required to deliver horizontal Exchange system management vs. vertical divisional Active Directory management.
Lower design and implementation costs.	Does not cater to test environments. Does not cater to externally facing environments.

Ownership, Accountability, and Change Management

The final topic that needs further discussion with regard to forest design is the subject of ownership. All too often, this subject is overlooked during the design phase, and procedures are hurriedly implemented in order to properly maintain and control the environment(s).

This section discusses the importance of subjects such as ownership, accountability, and change management, because without these aspects the environment can quickly fall into chaos.

TEST DAY TIP

The concepts of *ownership* and *sponsorship* have traditionally not been covered in enough depth in Microsoft literature. Fortunately, this is changing, and more documents now have these subjects included. Rest assured that when the reader takes Exam 70-297, these subjects will now be included and are therefore covered in this book in some detail.

Sponsors

This chapter demonstrates how the need for collaboration between disparate business units within an organization is an important aspect of the design phase. Without this collaboration, each business unit will be forced to implement its own separate Active Directory infrastructure, thus increasing TCO to the organization.

In order that the business units are brought together and forced to collaborate, a sponsor from each business unit should be nominated who are responsible for ensuring that each business's requirements are voiced during the design phase and for ensuring that designs are appropriate and relevant to each participating business. These sponsors should also ensure that the necessary time and effort are assigned to the design phase, such that no one business is responsible for failing to meet deadlines throughout the project.

In addition, an executive sponsor should be assigned to the project. This person, although not aligned to any one business, will be in a position to resolve conflicts between businesses as they arise. He or she will also have the backing of the executive board within the organization, which ensures the project is exposed and supported at the highest level within the organization.

Owners

In addition to sponsors, each forest deployed will also need an owner, or a committee of owners. Again, this is because a degree of collaboration might be required within each forest, and it helps to identify the person or group that is ultimately accountable for the delivery of service within the forest environment.

The forest owner, although responsible for the operation of the forest, does not necessarily make operational changes to the environment; instead, he or she is responsible for assigning the appropriate people to the appropriate roles. These roles include service administration and data administration.

For example, the forest owner will be responsible for:

- Assigning owners to each OU, who will act as data administrators within the appropriate OU

- Assigning service admins within each domain

- Assigning forest service admins

- The forest root domain

- Sites and subnets

- The schema

- Replication

- Domain-level security group policies, such as password, account lockout, and Kerberos policies

- DC group policies

- Site group policies

Within a forest that houses multiple businesses, it is suggested that the forest owner be a committee comprised of members from each participating business. This means that all decisions that the forest owner is responsible for can be made by a collective unit and not just one person. This ensures that all decisions are agreed on and relevant to all businesses within the forest and should make for much closer collaboration and agreement between the disparate businesses.

Change Management

Although ownership covers the issue of accountability, the topic of change management remains outstanding. Changes made within a forest, especially within a forest shared by multiple businesses, must be carefully tested, discussed, and implemented.

It is highly recommended in the experience of the author that the same committee described previously be used to discuss and agree any on changes to the forest. Again, this ensures that all businesses are aware of the change and can assess the impact of that change on their business and end users.

It is also recommended that this committee document what components within a forest fall under its control and what can be controlled in an autonomous fashion within each business domain. This ensures that all changes have a clear route from inception, through testing to deployment, with the relevant approvers being involved, depending on the nature of the change.

For example, the following changes should be deemed forestwide and thus owned by the committee:

- Addition and removal of DCs in any domain

- Addition and removal of GC servers in any domain

- Amendments to the schema

- Amendments to sites

- Amendments to subnets

- Installation to, change, or removal of an enterprise PKI instance

- Changes to group membership of any service administrator group (domain admins, enterprise admins, DNS admins, backup operators, account operators, print operators)

- Changes to domain security group policy

- Changes to DC group policy, in any domain within the forest

Please note that the preceding list is not exhaustive and that the list of changes should be created as appropriate to your environment. The list is merely a sample of those changes that should be included and thus under the control of the forest owner(s).

Conversely, the following changes should be deemed domainwide and thus controlled by the domain owner(s):

- Addition and removal of member servers

- Addition and removal of workstations

- Amendments to the nonservice admin groups

- Amendments to NTFS permissions on member servers

- Amendments to group policy on OUs

Please note again that the preceding list is not exhaustive and that the list of changes should be created as appropriate to your environment. The list is merely a sample of those changes that should be included and thus under the control of the domain owner(s). The subject of domain ownership is covered fully in the section *Assessing and Creating the Domain Design*.

Assessing and Creating the Domain Design

We have now finished discussing the various forest design options and which factors affect the design principles. Hopefully, it is now clear which forest design is most appropriate for your requirements and organization and we can now focus our attention at the domain level, within the forest.

This section is structured in a similar way to the previous one, in that we start by examining the factors that affect the domain design within a forest. We then move on to namespace considerations and how the topic of DNS starts to become more relevant when designing Active Directory forests and domains.

We then examine the different ways of implementing a domain structure within a forest, starting with the idea of a "dedicated" forest root domain. This then leads to the different designs available when choosing a multiple domain design within a forest—regional versus functional. In addition to the multiple domain approach, obviously a forest can contain one domain, and this is considered next. This section concludes with the subjects of ownership and responsibility, in a similar fashion to the previous section, but here relating to domains.

Domain Design Factors

We previously saw that various factors can influence the forest design, and similarly, several factors can influence the domain design within those forests. These factors will be relevant within each forest deployed within your organization and will need to be incorporated within each forest design.

All forests contain at least one domain, but the decision to deploy additional domains is influenced by geographic, network, and service autonomy factors. Details on these factors are discussed throughout the remainder of the chapter.

Geographic Separation

Many organizations have users and resources spread throughout the globe, in tens, hundreds, or even thousands of distinct locations. When deploying a Windows NT network infrastructure, geographic factors were often the largest influence on the designs considered, because domains were limited to a comparatively small number of objects and replication could not be managed in the way Active Directory permits.

Active Directory, however, offers a much more granular replication model, which can be designed and tailored to meet the needs of most organizations. That said, some organizations still feel the need to "segment" network traffic such that traffic is restricted to one geographic region, where possible, so the wide area network (WAN) links are not flooded and because these regional boundaries are seen as an appropriate way to segment the organization from an administrative point of view. Whereas this model might appear inappropriate in an Active Directory design, it can be the simplest approach, especially if an in-place upgrade is seen as the way forward and the existing Windows NT domain model is based on geography.

Given that Active Directory data is replicated per partition, a geographic domain design can also be used to better control and manage replication across disparate regions. For example, if Europe were assigned one domain, the Americas another, and Asia Pacific another, then DCs in each region would replicate only local domain data with other DCs in the same region. Furthermore, GCs in any one region would replicate only local domain data with DCs/GCs in the same region and would replicate only partial (around 50 percent) data from other regional domains. Such a regional design split can therefore be used to better control replication between the different regions within an enterprise.

As always, however, one must weigh the benefits versus cost, and in this particular scenario, the organization would incur greater costs than if it had deployed a single domain, but then it gains the advantage that it has better control over replication within the enterprise. The cost versus benefit issue must be carefully considered before any designs are advanced to the deployment phase of any project.

Network Limitations

In certain parts of the world, WAN links between small offices and the nearest hub site can prove costly to implement, costly to maintain, and are often unreliable. If this is the case within your organization, then the domain design might be influenced by these links.

Microsoft has recently published in the *Windows Server 2003 Deployment Guide* a recommendation for the maximum number of users that can be supported by WAN links of varying sizes, depending on the amount of bandwidth that can be dedicated to Active Directory. This is depicted in Table 2.2.

Table 2.2 Maximum Number of Users Supported in a Single Domain

Slowest Link to DC (KBps)	Maximum Number of Users if 1% Bandwidth Available	Maximum Number of Users if 5% Bandwidth Available	Maximum Number of Users if 10% Bandwidth Available
28.8	10,000	25,000	40,000
32	10,000	25,000	50,000
56	10,000	50,000	100,000
64	10,000	50,000	100,000
128	25,000	100,000	100,000
256	50,000	100,000	100,000
512	80,000	100,000	100,000
1500	100,000	100,000	100,000

NOTE

The *Windows Server 2003 Deployment Guide* can be found at www.microsoft.com/windowsserver2003/techinfo/reskit/deploykit.mspx. Table 2.2 can be found in Chapter 2 of the guide, *Designing and Deploying Directory and Security Services*.

The reader should use Table 2.2 as follows: determine the slowest WAN speed that a DC will replicate data across, and then decide on the maximum bandwidth that can be allocated to Active Directory. Table 2.2 will then give an approximate value for the maximum number of users that the forest can support if a single domain is deployed.

For example, if the smallest link size where Active Directory data is replicated to is found to be 64Kbps and the maximum bandwidth that Active Directory can be allocated is 5 percent, then the maximum number of users that a single domain forest can support is 50,000. If the organization in question has more than 50,000 users, then naturally Table 2.2 suggests that multiple domains be deployed. These domains can be assigned by region or function as appropriate (see later); either way, each domain can support at most 50,000 users.

It should be noted that even if Table 2.2 suggests that your organization can cope with a single domain forest, future growth and changes in replication behavior should be factored into the model. Alternatively, if Table 2.2 suggests multiple domains, then consider either upgrading WAN links or allocating more bandwidth to Active Directory. If either or both of these aspects are changed, then a single domain forest might prove feasible.

Service Autonomy

The third and probably most relevant factor when deciding on the domain design is the issue of service autonomy. If an organization is made up of independent businesses, these different entities, although keen to share a common infrastructure and realize the lower associated TCO, might require a degree of autonomy within their own domain.

This autonomy might simply be born out of the need to have their own service administrators, or it might be a result of requiring different domain security group policies than other businesses within the organization. In either case, the best solution available is that the business deploys a separate domain within the forest. It should be noted that the key word here is *autonomy*, which implies a need for independence without exclusive access, as opposed to *isolation*, which implies exclusive access and control. The business has agreed to share a forest with other businesses and is happy that there are more powerful administrators elsewhere in the forest. This must mean they are happy that they do not require isolation.

Examples of such a scenario can occur in a large financial institution, where businesses exist that manage asset management and investment banking. While the two business units might be happy to share a common forest, each business might want to implement different security policies at the domain level. This implies that separate domains must be deployed, one for each business.

As ever, the cost versus benefit argument must be carefully considered. However, more often than not, the service autonomy factor has a political or even legal element to it, and so the cost argument cannot be weighed against the (huge) benefit argument.

Names and Hierarchies

We have reached the stage now where, hopefully, both the forest model and the domain model applicable to your organization are becoming apparent. Before embarking on a more thorough examination of the domain models, we must first decide on naming strategies within each forest.

Within each forest there are general best practices and rules that should be adhered to as well as special considerations for the dedicated root or root domain (the first domain in any forest). Finally, each subsequent domain in the forest should adhere to various naming practices. All these aspects of forest naming strategies are discussed in the following sections.

General Considerations

When designing Active Directory forests and domains, one must remember that each domain has two names: a NetBIOS name and a DNS name. Both must be unique within the enterprise. Active Directory domains, therefore, have an additional aspect to be mindful of, because Windows NT domains only had a single NetBIOS name.

Aside from ensuring uniqueness, several other factors can influence the names chosen within each forest. First, if domains are being upgraded from Windows NT, then the existing NetBIOS names should be maintained so that clients can continue to log on to the domain without reconfiguration. If this is the case, then the existing NT domain names must adhere to the naming rules permitted within Active Directory.

Unfortunately, the NetBIOS rules changed slightly between Windows NT and Active Directory. For example, if Windows NT domains contain a "." (dot), then those domains cannot be upgraded and retain the same NetBIOS domain name. The NetBIOS rules for Active Directory domains are as follows:

- Choose names that are not likely to requiring change.

- Choose Internet standard characters (A–Z, a–z, 0–9, and "-" (not all numeric characters)).

- Include 15 characters or less.

For example, the NetBIOS name mycompany1A is permitted because it contains the characters allowed, is generic enough that it is unlikely to need to be changed, and has 11 characters. The NetBIOS name my.company.europe is not permitted because it contains the character "." (dot) and contains more than 15 characters.

The next consideration is the DNS domain name. DNS domain names consist of a prefix and a suffix. For example, mycompany.com has the prefix of mycompany and suffix of com. Where possible, the prefix should match the NetBIOS name assigned to the domain and should be indicative of the nature of the domain (a geographic name or a functional name, etc.).

Head of the Class…

Unique NetBIOS Domain Names

It is easy to forget that all Active Directory domains require a unique NetBIOS name and a unique DNS name. Because most organizations will have existing Windows NT domains, each with a unique NetBIOS name, it is important to ensure that new Active Directory domains are planned such that they have NetBIOS names that do not clash with existing Windows NT domain names.

For example, if a company already has a Windows NT domain called SALES (which is by definition its NetBIOS name), then a new Active Directory domain named sales.company.net will not be able to use the default NetBIOS name of SALES, because that name is already in use. In fact, dcpromo will detect the naming conflict and will suggest an alternative NetBIOS name for the new Active Directory domain. Without upfront planning, however, this conflict will not be expected and could result in a redesign, especially if it was assumed that the new domain would use the NetBIOS name of SALES.

Dedicated Root Domain

Following on from the previous section, we now discuss the DNS suffix. When deploying the first domain in a forest, the DNS name chosen is used as the suffix for all other domains in the same tree of the forest. (Trees are discussed further in the section *Single versus Multiple Trees*.)

For example, if the first domain in a forest is assigned the DNS domain name mycompany.com, then all domains created as children of that root domain must have the DNS domain name suffix mycompany.com. Furthermore, the NetBIOS name assigned to that domain should be mycompany, as per the rules described previously.

When selecting a suffix for the root domain, it should be unique within the organization and it is further recommended that this suffix be created and assigned for use exclusively within the Active Directory forest. This ensures that a new DNS name-space is used by the forest and thus no dependencies are established between the existing DNS systems and the new forest. Finally, it is strongly recommended that all DNS suffixes created for use within Active Directory forests should be registered with an Internet authority. This ensures uniqueness across the globe, within all organizations. (This applies to suffixes used in both internal and external networks.) This is recommended because one organization could merge with another, and the latter might have registered the same suffix that the former is using, with no registration. This implies that the two companies cannot be merged without some (very intrusive) reconfiguration.

Additional Domains

As previously mentioned, all domains across the enterprise must be assigned both a unique NetBIOS name and a unique DNS name (specifically, a unique fully qualified domain name (FQDN)). It is also true that each additional new domain must follow the DNS suffix used by the first domain created in the parent tree.

For example, if the root domain is named mycompany.com, then regional child domains within that same suffix (and hence the Active Directory tree) would be named emea.mycompany.com, americas.mycompany.com, and apac.mycompany.com. Using arguments given previously, the NetBIOS names for these domains would be EMEA, AMERICAS, and APAC, respectively.

The Dedicated Root Domain

The first domain deployed into any forest is known as the root domain. While in many respects it can be viewed as just another domain, because it must adhere to naming rules and so forth, it has unique properties that no other domain in the forest has.

The root domain is where special forestwide groups live—Schema Admins and Enterprise Admins. These two groups are used to manage forestwide operations, such as the addition of domains and modifications to the schema.

It is necessary, therefore, to decide whether the root domain should be one of the domains designed within the forest or whether it should be a dedicated domain. These options are examined more closely in the following section.

The root domain is also by default the location of the two forestwide Flexible Single Operations Master (FSMO) roles: the Schema Master and Domain Naming Master. The Schema Master role holder is the only DC on which schema modifications are permitted, while the Domain Naming Master must be contacted in order that domains can be created, renamed, or removed.

Using a Dedicated Root Domain

A dedicated root (or dedicated) forest root domain is deployed simply to exist as the root domain. Figure 2.6 shows an example scenario. It does not house users or groups beyond the default service administrator accounts, which are created automatically. The creation of this additional domain does not, therefore, incur any significant overhead regarding replication. The domain houses only DC computer accounts and default user and group objects. The impact of this on the database size and replication traffic will be negligible.

Figure 2.6 The Dedicated Root Domain Model

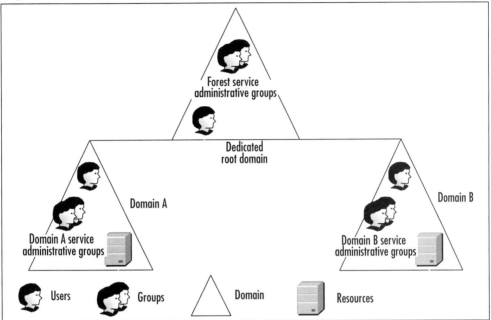

Subsequent domains can be created as child domains of the dedicated root, using the same DNS namespace as that used by the dedicated root domain. They can also be used to establish new trees with a new DNS namespace or as a child domain within another existing tree in the forest.

Furthermore, it is not explicitly associated with any region or business within the organization. Control of the dedicated root domain can be passed from one organization entity to another, without deploying or renaming any domains. The dedicated root domain is in fact politically and geographically neutral, and it is this neutrality that offers these benefits:

- **Forest service admins are separated from domain service admins** The dedicated root domain approach has the advantage that domain admins outside of the dedicated root domain cannot elevate their rights so they have EA or SA rights, which they would be able to do in a single domain model, for example. This ensures that forest service admin roles can be clearly separated from domain service admin roles.

- **Simpler to reconfigure the forest** If a dedicated root domain were not used, then any changes required to the name of the first domain created would result in a complete rebuild of the forest and all the domains therein. If a dedicated root domain is used, with a generic name that is not likely to require change, then all other domains in the forest can be renamed or restructured without resulting in a forest rebuild.

- **Politically neutral** If a dedicated root domain did not exist, then the first domain created in a forest would house and therefore own the forest service admin roles, such as Enterprise Admins and Schema Admins. In an environment where the forest is to be shared by multiple businesses, this might not be politically acceptable to the other businesses.

However, there is the disadvantage that additional service administrator roles need to be managed, along with an additional DNS zone and additional DCs. It is widely accepted, though, that this disadvantage is outweighed by the numerous advantages previously described.

Head of the Class…

Malicious Administrators

Even though we have discussed how a dedicated root domain stops domain admins in other domains from elevating their rights so they have EA or SA rights, it is still possible for malicious administrators to grant themselves forest service admin rights or indeed DA rights in any other domain, using specialized tools and procedures.

It is, therefore, of paramount importance that all service administrators are vetted, trained, and above all trusted to perform the role expected of them. It is the responsibility of the forest owner to select appropriate service administrators and to ensure that they meet the previously listed requirements and any additional requirements that your organization demands.

Nondedicated Domain

If a dedicated root domain is not used, then the first domain created will assume the role of the root domain. The decision now becomes one of "which regional or functional domain should be deployed first and therefore assume the role of root domain?" Refer to Figure 2.7, which illustrates this concept.

This decision must be made because the first domain deployed will house the forest service admin roles as well as domain-specific service admin roles. Administrators within this first domain will therefore have control over both the local domain and the forest, and even if users are removed from the forest service admins groups, they can simply add themselves back in by virtue of their membership to the domain admin group. Refer to Figure 2.7 for an example deployment.

Figure 2.7 The Nondedicated Root Domain Model

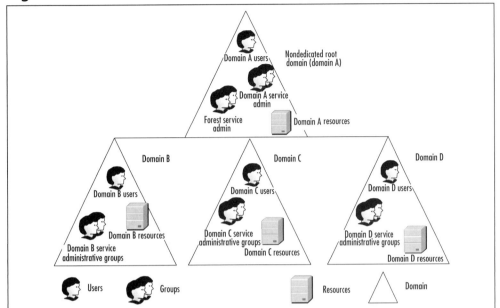

Although Figure 2.7 depicts a disadvantageous situation (especially in a politically sensitive organization), this approach does carry the advantage that an additional domain, DNS zone, and group of service admins do not need to be managed, thus lowering the admin overhead and overall TCO.

To mitigate the risk associated with the previously discussed disadvantages, the first domain built should be associated either with the main headquarters location of the organization (if using a regional model) or the main function group (most likely the IT group responsible for the management of infrastructure) if using a functional approach. This ensures that the issue of forest versus domain service admins is minimized, because the controller faction within your organization owns both roles in the first domain and has overall ownership or control of the forest in any case.

If this approach is not feasible in your organization and no one region or function can easily be identified as owning the forest service admin roles, then a dedicated root domain should be implemented.

Root Domain Availability

The availability of the root domain and specifically the _msdcs DNS domain under Windows 2000 was of paramount importance. The _msdcs zone houses forestwide DNS records, such as GC service records and the unique GUID records for each domain and DC. Administrators generally ensured that secondary copies of the root domain DNS zone were transferred to several DC/DNS servers outside the root domain to ensure 24x7 availability.

However, Windows Server 2003 introduces Application Directory Partitions, and by default stores the _msdcs DNS zone in a forestwide application partition (if the zone is stored in Active Directory) that is replicated to every DC in the forest. Such concerns regarding availability are therefore largely mitigated by this change in approach and should be kept in mind when designing the root domain and associated DNS zones.

Regional Domains

We previously discussed domain design factors, one of which is geographic dispersion. The domain design that follows naturally if these factors are a major influence on designs is the regional domain model.

The regional model simply implies that a separate domain is created for each distinct region within the organization. As already discussed, this has the advantage that replication can be better restricted to the local region, and segregation of objects can be achieved by setting domain boundaries at corresponding regional boundaries that already exist within the organization. An example of a regional model is illustrated in Figure 2.8.

Figure 2.8 The Regional Domain Model

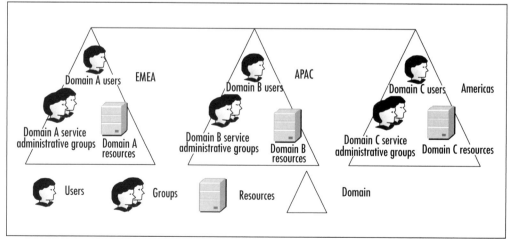

Naturally, the simplest and most cost-efficient design is the single domain forest, but this does not meet the requirements of most organizations. However, there are several disadvantages associated with introducing additional regional domains:

- **Multiple service admin groups** With the addition of each new domain, the environment acquires a set of new service admins who need to be controlled, regulated, and managed. This adds to the admin overhead associated with the forest and increases the TCO accordingly.

- **Additional overhead in duplicating settings** Usually, even if multiple domains are deployed, there is a need for consistency of certain settings across all domains. For example, the organization might mandate that all domains have the same domain security group policy settings relating to passwords and account lockout. These settings will need to be established and maintained across multiple domains, and any changes to the mandate will result in multiple, managed changes being made across all domains in the forest. Other settings that might need to be managed across multiple domains include DC policy settings, auditing settings, DNS server and DNS zone settings, and access control lists (ACLs) to objects such as group policy. Again, this increases admin overhead within the forest, when compared to the single domain model.

- **Interdomain object moves** The regional domain model places objects into a domain that is representative of their location within the organization. From time to time, these objects will move, such as users and computers, from one region to another. In a single domain model, this is a relatively trivial operation, because the objects(s) in essence are "dragged and dropped" from the old location to the new one. Within a multiple domain model, however, this "drag and drop" approach is not available, so the objects must instead be migrated using special tools. Refer to the sidebar *Group Policy Modeling* for further suggestions on how to best handle object moves.

If any or all of the previously described issues exist within your organization and are seen as major hurdles to overcome if multiple domains were deployed, you should consider deploying a single domain and segmenting objects into separate OUs instead. (This topic is covered in more depth in the section *Developing the OU Model*).

Configuring & Implementing...

Group Policy Modeling

It was previously mentioned that an object move within a domain was a trivial task and that the object can simply be "dragged and dropped" from old to new locations. While this is in essence true, there are tests and checks that one should carry out before performing such an object move.

It is suggested that group policy modeling be performed before an object is moved either intra- or inter-domain, so that effective policy settings can be generated in a "what if" scenario, so that the administrator can predict which new settings will be applied to the user and/or computer as a result of the move. Modeling can be performed using the new Group Policy Management Console, for example (as long as at least one Windows Server 2003 DC exists in the forest). A model can be created for any machine and user combination, regardless of the machine type used by that user. This should take much of the guesswork out of moving objects around, because the behavior can be predicted using the modeling tools before the move is carried out.

Functional Domains

While geographic issues can influence the domain design toward a regional domain model, factors such as autonomy might require that you adopt another, similar model—the functional domain model. An example can be found in Figure 2.9.

Figure 2.9 The Functional Domain Model

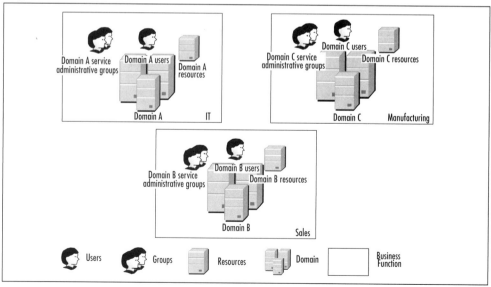

Functional domains rather than being created per region are established per functional group or business group within the organization. This is often a requirement where different business units within the organization have different requirements from Active Directory or require service autonomy. For example, if an organization is made up of manufacturing, sales, and IT functions, and each of these functions requires a degree of autonomy, then separate functional domains should be deployed within the same forest.

The functional domain model has the same issues associated with it as does the regional domain model described previously, but has the additional requirement of general collaboration between domains.

Within a regional domain mode, it is likely that one business exists within the forest and that collaboration between domains is therefore implicit. However, in the functional domain model, the forest might be home to multiple, disparate, autonomous businesses that would not normally need to collaborate with each other at either a technical or political level. In order for multiple businesses to exist in the same forest, however, a degree of collaboration is required so that security within any one domain is not compromised. For example, the businesses should discuss and agree on the minimum security policies that are deployed within each domain and the service admin personnel within each domain. Refer to the sidebar *The Weakest Link in the Chain* for insight into the importance of this point.

If any or all of the issues mentioned in the regional domain or the functional domain model sections exist within your organization and are seen as major hurdles to overcome if multiple domains were deployed, then you should consider deploying a single domain and segmenting objects into separate OUs instead. (This topic is covered in more depth in the section *Developing the OU Model*.)

Head of the Class…

The Weakest Link in the Chain

It is worthwhile at this point to revisit the forest versus domain security boundary issue. While this might appear as a subtle change, it does in fact represent a complete rethink and redesign for many larger organizations that deploy domains for purposes of service isolation.

Previously, it was assumed that in a multiple domain forest with multiple disparate businesses that each business could grant service admin rights to as many persons as they saw fit, without impacting the forest and all other domains therein. This was because in Windows 2000 Active Directory the domain was deemed a security boundary within which the business had implicit isolation from all other domains and their service admins. This is clearly not the case now that it is accepted that the boundary has "moved" to the forest, and each business should be aware that any service admins any-

Continued

where in the forest can elevate their rights and gain access to any domain in the forest. This is why it is important that all service admins in each domain be vetted and agreed upon by all businesses in the forest and not just the individual business. Clearly, one single rogue or malicious administrator in one domain can compromise security in the whole forest, and that administrator represents the "weakest link in the chain."

Comparing Trees with Domains

We have now covered the forest design and the domain design aspects of Active Directory design. When deploying multiple domains, however, they can be created to form one or more trees within the forest. Each tree within the forest has its own DNS namespace, and all domains within that tree use that same namespace. The root domain in a forest therefore establishes the first tree and first DNS namespace in the forest.

So, should new domains be created as the root of a new tree, within an existing tree, or within the root tree? The answers to these questions depend on the reasons used to deploy new domains and the nature of the organization. Various different scenarios are considered in the following sections—the first examines the forest with a single tree and DNS namespace, and the second discusses forests with multiple trees.

Single Tree

The simplest approach is to just deploy the first (root) domain and then add additional domains within that same tree, thus using the same DNS namespace, as shown in Figure 2.10. Figure 2.10 shows an example where the domains are split by function (marketing, sales, and IT) within mycompany and the DNS namespace chosen is mycompany.net.

Figure 2.10 A Single Tree

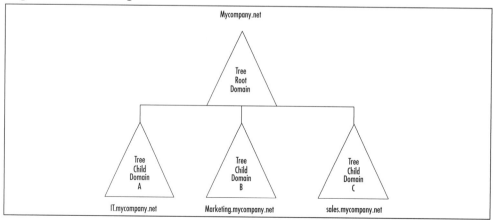

This approach has the following advantages:

- **Only one namespace needs to be created and managed** If a new DNS namespace is created for the Active Directory forest, and all domains are created within the same tree, then there is only the need for that one namespace to be created, which helps to minimize admin overhead.

- **No interoperability issues exist between disparate namespaces** Because only one namespace exists, there are no issues regarding interoperability and name resolution across disparate namespaces. If delegation is implemented correctly within the namespace, name resolution should function correctly, with little administrative effort. If multiple trees (and therefore DNS namespaces) exist, however, then interoperability at the DNS level must be carefully incorporated into any designs.

Conversely, the single tree approach has several disadvantages:

- **Disparate, autonomous businesses are constrained to using the first namespace** Although the management of a single namespace might prove advantageous from an administrative point of view, it does imply that all domains deployed must exist within that same tree and namespace. This removes flexibility and choice from disparate businesses.

- **Businesses do not have autonomy within their own namespace** Following closely from the aforementioned consideration, the deployment of a single tree and namespace also implies that each disparate, autonomous business within the organization has no freedom to choose a namespace hierarchy as they see fit. Instead of using their own namespace, of which they have complete control, they are forced to use the namespace established by the first tree and to follow the rules contained therein.

If either of the scenarios exists within your organization and these cannot be overcome through compromise or collaboration, then multiple trees and namespaces should be considered. However, the single tree approach should be favored and designed where possible, because it is the simplest and most cost-efficient option.

Multiple Trees

If a degree of autonomy is required with respect to the namespace design by one business within the organization, then a separate tree should be created for that business. This will give them the freedom to both the name of the namespace and to create a hierarchy within that namespace as they require. An example can be found in Figure 2.11, which shows how the forest is split into separate trees for each function (banking and sales), and each function is then split by region, with one domain for each region per function.

Figure 2.11 A Forest with Multiple Trees

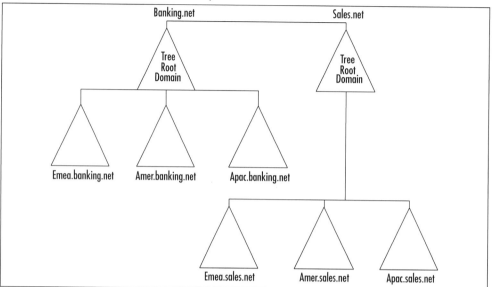

If, for example, the IT department creates a new forest with domain name IT.net as the root domain and therefore namespace name, then other businesses such as manufacturing or sales might not want to participate in that same namespace. Instead, they might want to use manufacturing.net and sales.net, respectively. Both non-IT departments can then choose a namespace hierarchy as they see fit, with no dependence on the IT department to create additional domains or zones on their behalf.

This approach has the following advantages:

- **Disparate businesses can use their own different namespaces** As previously discussed, having multiple trees enables each business to establish its own namespace with a DNS name that it selects and that is not therefore chosen by the first entity to create a domain in the forest. This is often preferred by businesses that want to have their own "identity" within the forest and not be seen as departments within another business.

- **Autonomy within the business namespace** Not only can the business choose its own "identity" when creating a new tree and namespace, but it also has complete control over that namespace. This means that it can choose its own domain hierarchy within the tree and not use the same design as that used within other trees.

This approach, however, has the following disadvantages:

- **Multiple DNS names** Each tree is assigned its own unique DNS namespace, and each of these namespaces should be registered with the local

Internet authority. This will potentially add the time taken to deploy the new trees, if not already registered, and also implies that more DNS names need to have their registration managed by the internal department for DNS within the organization. This all leads to increased admin overhead, which needs to be weighed against the benefit of deploying multiple trees and namespaces.

- **Increased DNS maintenance** With the addition of each new namespace in the organization comes additional complexity within the DNS environment. This is because of the additional effort required to ensure that all namespaces can resolve and communicate with each other, so that name resolution continues to work across these multiple, disparate namespaces. As before, this increases the admin overhead associated with DNS within the organization.

If namespace autonomy is important in your organization, then separate trees should be deployed, but weigh this carefully against the increased overhead incurred by the DNS management staff who have to manage and maintain multiple associated DNS namespaces. An example of a forest with multiple trees can be found in Figure 2.11.

Single Domain Forest

Naturally, the simplest design within any one forest is to deploy one single domain. This domain will house all objects, including:

- Forest service admins

- Domain service admins

- Users

- Groups

- Computers

- DCs

If none of these requirements or factors regarding multiple domains and/or multiple trees applies to your organization, and all departments and businesses within the organization believe they can co-exist in the same domain, then this is the ideal option. A recap of advantages and disadvantages associated with the single domain model are provided in Table 2.3 to further help you decide if this approach is applicable to your requirements.

Table 2.3 Advantages and Disadvantages of a Single Domain Forest

Advantages	Disadvantages
Reduced administrative overhead.	The domain can never be renamed (without being rebuilt).
Reduced hardware.	Forest service admins cannot be separated from domain service admins.
Reduced design effort. All DCs can also be GCs, thus removing the need to design GC placement.	This domain will always own the forest service admins roles. This might not be appropriate politically if further domains join the forest.
	All objects are replicated to every DC in every region, which can result in unacceptable levels of replication traffic.

Based on these points, it is clear that if a single domain is deployed, then this design cannot easily be changed later. For example, if forest service admins and domain service admins need to be segregated, then a migration will need to be effected, at some considerable cost. Furthermore, if the domain ever needs to be renamed—due to a merger, acquisition, or rebranding exercise—then the forest must be rebuilt and restored, at a huge cost and risk to the business.

It is therefore highly recommended that the single domain model be deployed only if the organization can guarantee that none of the mentioned requirements will ever exist. If there is any doubt, then additional domains should be deployed, depending on the nature of your requirements.

Ownership and Responsibilities

We previously examined the importance of ownership within each forest. This concept is relevant in each domain too, however, because without overall ownership the domain will cease to be properly managed, maintained, and controlled. The forest needs ownership and sponsorship, and each domain within the forest requires an owner. The domain owner should perform two basic tasks:

- **Act as a representative within the forest** In a multidomain and multibusiness forest, each domain and business should be represented at the forest level. This will help to ensure that decisions that have a forestwide impact will be open to discussion by all participants of the forest. The domain owner should be such a person to represent the domain.

- **Assist in choosing service admins and security policy** Within each domain, service admins need to be chosen who can be trusted across the entire forest or organization. The domain owner should be responsible for selecting these people and proposing them to the forest committee or owner. The domain owner should also be responsible for selecting domain security policies and DC security policies.

Configuring & Implementing…

Collaboration in the Forest

The relationship between the domain and forest owners should not be underestimated, especially in a forest where disparate businesses co-exist. Where previously the domains in a forest could consider themselves isolated and unaffected by the actions of other domains in the forest, this is now known to not be the case.

As a result, the domains in a forest must collaborate with each other on topics that might affect the security or availability of the other domains in the forest. It is for these reasons that a committee was suggested earlier, which is represented by all member domains and businesses. This committee is then responsible for maintaining security of the forest and for ensuring that all domains adhere to any forestwide policies implemented.

EXAM
70-297
OBJECTIVE
1.5.5

Developing the OU Model

We have so far covered forest and domain design principles and concepts. Working from the top to the bottom in the forest hierarchy, we arrive at the OU level. The OU represents the most granular piece of the forest and domain at the end of the hierarchy in which the actual objects exist.

OUs are generally created for one of two reasons—delegation of rights or group policy. One of the big advantages of Active Directory over Windows NT domains is the ability to delegate rights at a very granular level. The vehicle used to achieve this level of granularity is the OU. In addition, Active Directory allows the administrator to set policies across discrete groups of objects, where again this discrete group boundary is the OU. The section *OU Design Factors* examines delegation and group policy and how they might affect the OU design chosen.

Having looked at the factors that can influence the OU design, we then examine the different designs. While the OU structure can be designed in many different ways, most structures adhere (in a general sense) to one of three models. These models are discussed in the section *OU Design Models*.

OU Design Factors

We saw previously how different technical and political factors can influence Active Directory designs. Now we have arrived at the OU design phase, and that fact remains unchanged. The OU design is generally dictated by three factors—the way in which the business is administered, the way in which group policy needs to be deployed, and the need to hide sensitive objects from users.

The OU structure within each domain can be designed in one of many different ways. It is therefore important to examine those factors that affect the design closely, so that the design options available can be narrowed down to a small subset of all available options. The sections *Delegation and Admin Models* and *Group Policy* examine how the design is influenced, while the *OU Design Models* section discusses different, popular models.

Delegation and Admin Models

The way in which rights are delegated within Active Directory need not reflect the structure of the business itself. For example, if one group manages user objects across the business, regardless of which aspect of the business the user works within, then there might not be any advantage to segmenting the user objects into multiple OUs.

Many organizations fall into the trap of designing their OU structure to match precisely their underlying business model. Although this implies that the OU model is simple to understand, because it matches the business model, it suffers in two ways:

- **Business models change frequently** Large organizations (and even smaller ones) are likely to change their political business structure on a regular basis to reflect the state of the market in which they operate. As a result, the OU model deployed today might not be appropriate in one or two years. It is therefore recommended that the OU structure not be too granular and not necessarily be reflective of the business model. Instead, OUs should be created where delegation needs to be granted. Refer to Figure 2.12 for a basic example.

- **Delegation becomes complex** If the OU hierarchy is created to match the business model, then delegation might become a complex task, because one group might need rights to manage objects across many disparate OUs. This group will need to be granted those rights separately, in each OU where rights are required.

The recommended approach is to create an OU so that all objects inside that OU are managed by the same group, and that group can therefore be granted the same rights on the OU and all objects contained therein.

As already discussed, if autonomy at the forest or domain level is not required, then the next level of segregation is the OU. Therefore, if a group needs autonomy over its objects, then those objects should be placed inside an OU, and the group in question should be granted appropriate rights over the OU, while no other group has access (other than service administrators).

Focusing on Figure 2.12, we can see that the following has been implemented:

- Sales and Marketing departments require autonomy from each other.

- A separate OU has been created for each department.

- All Sales objects are located in the Sales OU, and the same applies to the Marketing OU.

- A group has been created that has full control over all Sales user objects.

- A group has been created that has full control over all Sales group objects.

- A group has been created that has full control over all Marketing user objects.

- A group has been created that has full control over all Marketing group objects.

While Sales and Marketing departments might have further subdepartments, if users and groups are managed at the parent department level, then there is no need to further segment the Sales and Marketing OUs unless delegation at a more granular level is needed.

One further point to note regarding Figure 2.12 is that each group has full control over only user or group objects—no one group has control over both object types. For further visibility, the user and group objects can be split into separate OUs, but if this is not required, a separate OU will suffice, with access granted to specific object types only. A more thorough examination of these factors is given in Chapter 4.

Figure 2.12 Using OUs to Delegate Rights

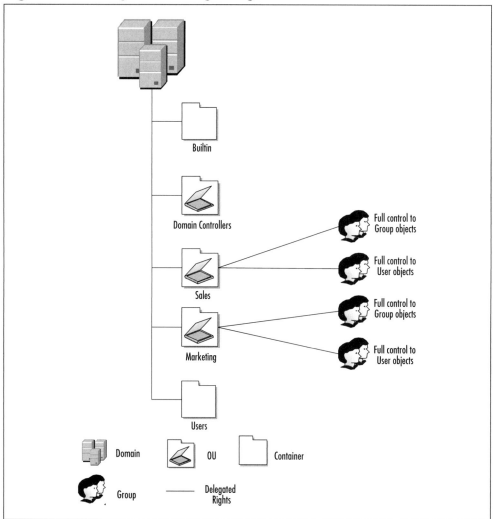

Group Policy

In addition to being used to segment objects that require the same delegation, OUs are also useful when applying group policy. Group Policy Objects (GPOs) are linked to OUs (and can be linked to domains and sites too), and so the OU is a convenient way to group objects together, such as those that need the same security policies. Group policy is described in further detail in Chapter 4.

As an example, let's assume that a business wants to apply a core set of policies to all servers, but then also apply role-based policy settings, depending on the role the server plays in the environment. An OU structure as shown in Figure 2.13 can then be used.

The net effect of the scenario depicted in Figure 2.13 is the following:

- All servers, regardless of role, receive settings applied at the Servers OU.
- Only file servers receive settings applied at the File Servers OU.
- Only application servers receive settings applied at the Application Servers OU.

Figure 2.13 Using OUs to Apply Group Policy

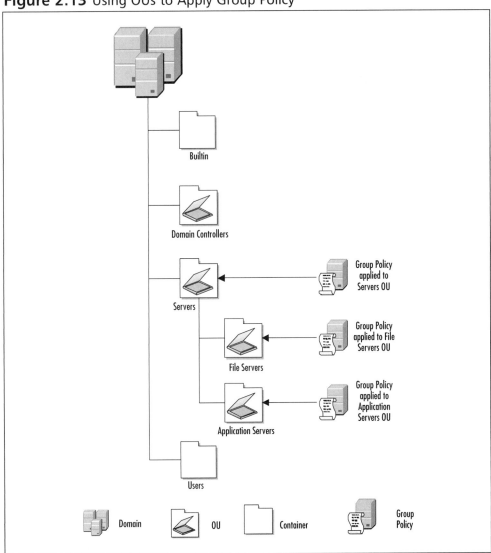

TEST DAY TIP

There is no technical limitation to the depth an OU structure can be given. However, it is recommended that the depth not be greater than 10 levels of OU. This is because objects at the 10th level must process group policy settings from (potentially) 10 levels of OU, which can increase the time to start up and log on significantly. Furthermore, certain applications might not install correctly if the LDAP path to the object being installed to is too long.

Further information regarding the use of OUs to better aid the deployment of group policy, and group policies themselves, can be found in Chapter 4.

Hiding Sensitive Objects

The third and final way in which OUs are generally used to manage and organize a domain's objects is to hide those objects of a more sensitive nature. We have already seen how the service admins within forests and domains are very powerful roles, and the groups that grant them these rights should therefore be protected and closely managed.

It is therefore highly recommended that all service admin objects be segregated from the rest of the domain objects so that their attributes are not viewable by all users in the domain. This has the advantage that users cannot view the memberships of the sensitive service admins groups, such as domain admins, and conversely implies that the membership that service admins users have cannot be viewed, except by other service admins. An example is shown in Figure 2.14, where service admin objects are segregated and further split into their separate OUs by object type. This has the further advantage that group policy can be applied to the OUs so that only service admin users have access to service admin machines and DCs, for example.

Figure 2.14 Using OUs to Segregate Service Admins

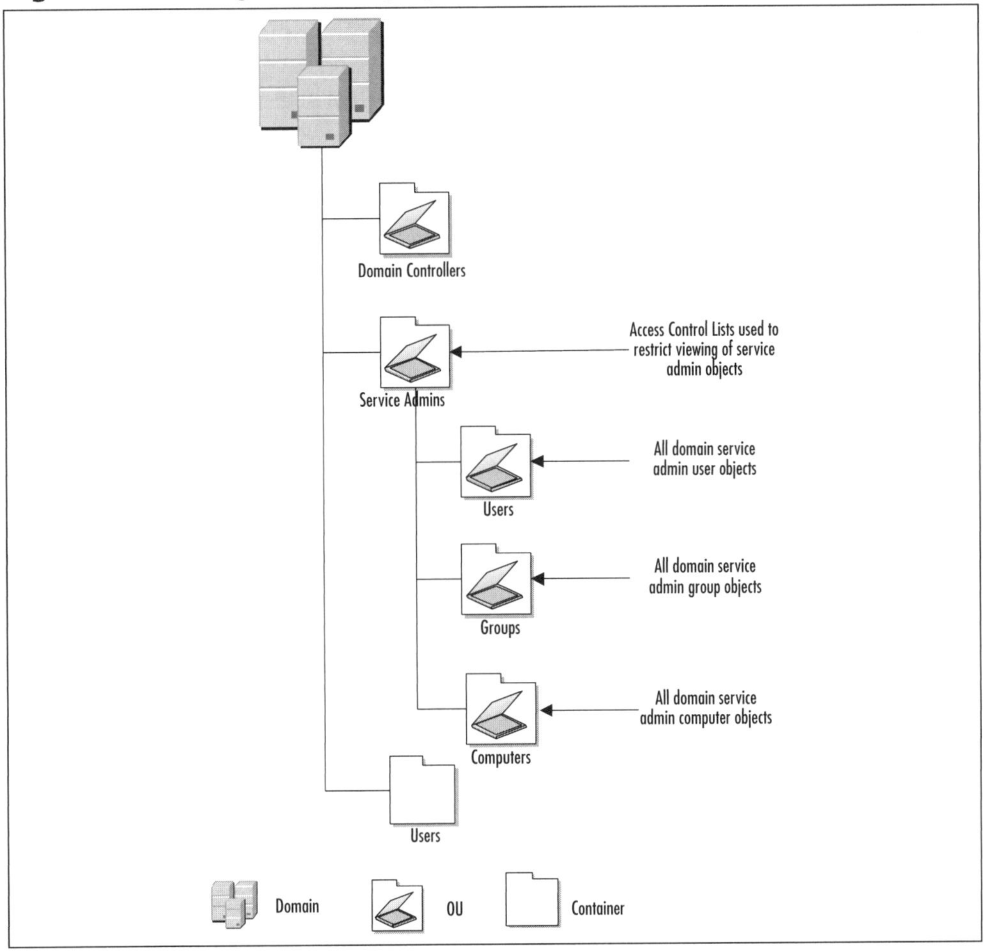

Restricting Access to Service Admin Functions

Access to the DCs in the forest, both physically and to the operating system (OS), must be carefully controlled and managed. Although access to the OS can be controlled through ACLs and group membership, often DCs have remote management boards installed so they can be managed remotely, even when the OS is not running. These boards give the malicious user another way in to the DC, so access to the boards must also be managed. One such method is to restrict access to these boards so they can be accessed only from specific IP addresses and/or specific machine names.

Another more generic method is to insist that all terminal services (using the RDP protocol) traffic to and from a DC must be protected using IPSec. A

Continued

(Continued)

> group policy can then be applied to service admin computers (because they all exist in a common OU) that insists they use IPSec for RDP traffic to DCs. Another policy must also be applied at the DC OU, which insists that all RDP traffic be similarly protected. All RDP traffic to a DC from outside this group of machines will be discarded, because all other clients will not try to establish an IPSec session over RDP.

OU Design Models

The following section outlines the three basic, most popularly used OU models. Although it is possible to design an OU structure in thousands of different ways and to change the structure on a regular basis to meet business requirements, it is suggested that one of the following basic models be chosen as a starting point and tailored to your environment as appropriate.

A basic introduction to the models is given here, while more detailed examinations of the models and their applicability to the environment are given in Chapter 4.

Geographic Models

If the administrative model and therefore delegation model needs to be performed on a geographic basis, then the geographic OU model might be the starting point for your organization. This model simply starts by creating geography-based OUs at the root of the domain and then further segregating objects below that, as appropriate. An example can be found in Figure 2.15.

Figure 2.15 shows how the three main regions within the organization are depicted by OUs at the root of the domain, and separate OUs are then created within each region to further segregate the environment. This split within the region can be based on object type, function, or whatever the administrative model, delegation model, and group policy dictate.

Figure 2.15 The Geographic OU Model

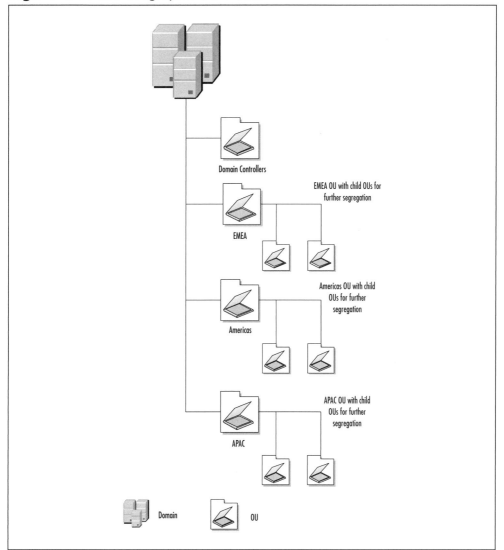

Functional Models

If, however, the administrative model and therefore delegation model needs to be performed on a functional basis, then the functional OU model might be the starting point for your organization. This model simply starts by creating functional-based OUs at the root of the domain, and then further segregating objects below that as appropriate. An example can be found in Figure 2.16.

Figure 2.16 shows how the three main functions within the organization are depicted by OUs at the root of the domain, and separate OUs are then created within each function to further segregate the environment. This split can be based on object type, region, or whatever the administrative model, delegation model, and group policy dictate.

Figure 2.16 The Functional OU Model

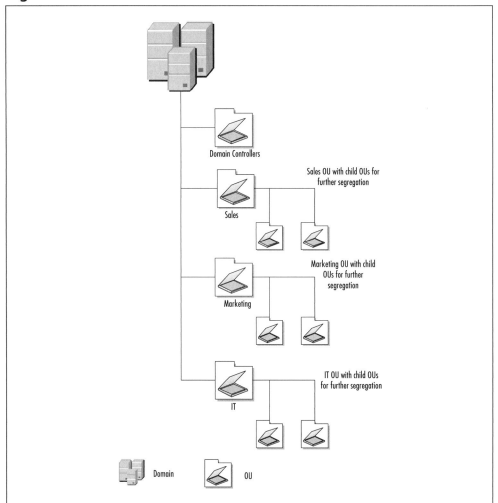

Object Type Models

The final model considered is the object type model. If the administrative model and therefore delegation model needs to be performed on an object type basis, then the object type OU model might be the starting point for your organization. This model simply starts by creating object type-based OUs at the root of the domain, and then further segregating objects below that as appropriate. An example can be found in Figure 2.17.

Figure 2.17 shows how the three main object types within the organization are depicted by OUs at the root of the domain, and separate OUs are then created within each object type OU to further segregate the environment. This split can be based on geography, function, or whatever the administrative model, delegation model, and group policy dictate.

Figure 2.17 The Object Type OU Model

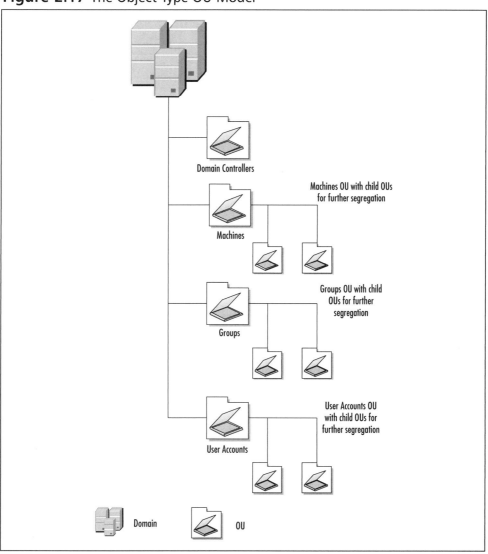

Ownership

We already discussed forest and domain ownership, and the subject of OU ownership is also an aspect of the overall design that should be carefully considered. An OU is a useful tool for granting autonomy to a group over objects that the group manages. However, the rights for a group must be clearly defined, so that the group is accountable for the data contained within its OU. It is suggested that each OU be assigned an owner, and that the OU owner be responsible for the following in his or her own OUs:

- Delegation of rights over objects
- Group policy assignments
- Creation and deletion of child OUs

TEST DAY TIP

The ownership of an OU is a good example of how autonomy differs from isolation. Whereas isolation guarantees exclusive access to objects, *autonomy* simply means that objects can be managed only by those with explicit rights plus the service admins within the domain and forest. Objects within an OU will therefore always be accessible by forest and domain admins, and the OU owner must accept that this is the case. Indeed, this is a highly recommended relationship, because errors made by OU owners that block access to the OU administrators can be undone by service administrators.

EXAM
70-297
OBJECTIVE
1.5.4

Developing the Replication Design

The one remaining Active Directory infrastructure-related piece of the puzzle is that of replication design. Without a replication design and topology, all the designs arrived at previously relating to forests and domains and OUs are moot.

Active Directory is a distributed, multimaster replicated database that should be located as "'near" to user populations as is feasible. (More about service placement in Chapter 7, "Service Placement.") As a result, it is imperative that a scalable, available, and robust replication design is implemented.

Although the more advanced concepts are discussed in Chapter 4, now is a good opportunity to cover the basic principles and concepts surrounding replication within Active Directory. In this section, we look at concepts, typical replication options, and ownership.

Active Directory replication involves various terms, concepts, and objects that are used to create a replication topology, including:

- Sites

- Subnets

- Site links

- Site link bridges

- Connection objects

- Multimaster replication

- Knowledge Consistency Checker (KCC)

- Inter Site Topology Generator and bridgehead servers

- SYSVOL

- File Replication System (FRS)

- Topology options

- Ownership

Each of these considerations is described in additional detail in the sections that follow.

Sites

A site is a collection of well-connected IP subnets. The definition of *well-connected* is open to interpretation and will vary from one organization to another. As a result, a site might be classified as a building, a collection of buildings connected by a high-speed local area network (LAN) or metropolitan area network (MAN), or all buildings within a region, such as a city. Sites might house DCs from multiple domains and domains might have DCs in multiple sites. The purpose of a site is twofold:

- A site is used as a resource locator boundary, such that clients are only offered the services available in or assigned to their site.

- A site is used as a replication boundary, such that replication can be better managed and configured.

Resource Location

When searching for local resources, such as a DC, a Windows client will query DNS for a list of DCs in its local site. Therefore, instead of providing the client with a list of all DCs in the client's domain, DNS will provide the client with only a subset of DCs, those that exist in the same site as the client. This mechanism implies that a client will always use resources located within its local site (if available) and not traverse an expensive WAN link to locate a resource.

Replication Boundary

Changes made to Active Directory on one DC will be replicated (eventually) to all other DCs (hosting a copy of the partition where the change occurred) as per the replication topology designed and implemented. As a result, sites could also be designed to better manage replication of Active Directory data, because replication occurs between predefined DCs in predefined sites.

Head of the Class…

Windows Server 2003 Replication versus Windows NT Replication

For those of you making the leap from Windows NT to Windows Server 2003 and Active Directory, this is one area where a huge benefit can be gained. In the Windows NT replication model, all changes occur on the primary domain controller (PDC), which then sends the change to each backup domain controller (BDC) simultaneously. If the change represents 100Kb of network traffic and the domain has 100 BDCs, then this change results in 100*100Kb or 10Mb of total network traffic. This 10Mb of traffic cannot be managed or throttled by the administrator.

However, sites and site links, as we'll see later, can help the administrator to manage, control, and throttle the replication traffic to meet the requirements of the organization.

Subnets

A subnet is a logical collection of contiguous IP addresses, all within the same LAN segment or virtual segment. For example, all addresses within network 192.168.1.0 with a 24-bit mask of 255.255.255.0 represent a subnet. Each subnet within the organization should be defined within the Active Directory configuration and assigned to a specific site. Subnets must be defined with both a network ID and a subnet mask to uniquely identify them.

Site Links

Once the appropriate sites and subnets are defined, links between sites must be established to determine the direction and nature of flow of Active Directory data replication between sites. The links should be established to create a topology that matches the actual physical topology of the underlying network.

For example, if the network has a hub and spoke design, with many small satellite sites connecting to a small number of hub sites, then the sites and site links should be configured in a similar fashion. Site links are manually assigned a cost, a replication interval, and a replication schedule. These are discussed next.

Cost

A cost indicates the cost of the physical link between two sites. Therefore, a 64Kb WAN link will have a higher cost associated with it than will a 1Mb link. Costs are used to construct optimal paths between one site and another, so that low-cost routes are used with preference above higher cost routes.

For example (illustrated in Figure 2.18):

- Site A is linked to site B with a cost of 1000

- Site A is linked to site C with a cost of 500

- Site C is linked to site B with a cost of 400

Figure 2.18 Sites and Costs

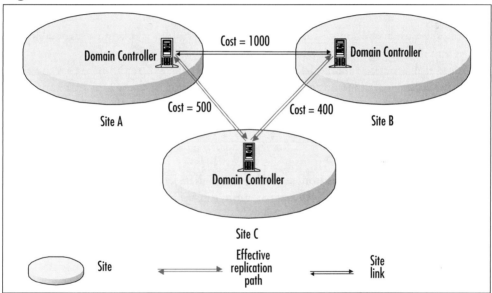

The optimal replication path from site A to site B is A − C − B at a cost of 900, and not A − B at a cost of 1000.

Interval

Data is replicated across site links at regular, predefined time intervals. So as not to saturate slow WAN links, intersite traffic is replicated in "batches," with all changes stored since the last replication event occurred.

The interval should be set to a suitable value that is neither too low such that data is replicated too frequently, thus saturating the link, nor too high such that changes take a long time to propagate throughout the enterprise.

It is recommended that the interval be set lower (for example, 15 minutes) across low cost links and higher (up to 180 minutes) across higher cost links. A sample cost versus interval matrix can be seen in Table 2.4.

Table 2.4 Sample Cost versus Interval Matrix for Data Replication

Cost	Interval
0–100	15
101–200	30
201–300	60
301+	90

Schedule

Schedules are used in conjunction with intervals to create a "replication timetable." For example, if the replication schedule across a site link is "Mon to Fri, 9 a.m. to 5 p.m." and the associated interval is 60 minutes, then data will replicate across the site link at the following times on Monday through Friday inclusive: 9 a.m., 10 a.m., 11 a.m., 12 p.m., 1 p.m., 2 p.m., 3 p.m., 4 p.m., and 5 p.m. This implies that data will be replicated across the site link nine times per day, five days per week.

Site Link Bridges

Sites that do not share a common site link but do share common Active Directory data, such as an Application Directory partition, can be bridged using site link bridges.

This enables DCs that are not directly connected via connection objects to replicate with each other using a site link bridge. For example, if site A has a DC hosting application partition abc.net, but its site partner does not host this same partition, then site A can be connected to another site (site C) that does host that partition via a site link bridge (refer to Figure 2.19).

It should be noted that by default, all sites are linked through transitive bridges, so the need for manual site link bridges is not required unless this feature is disabled. If bridging is disabled, then each site is completely isolated from every other site unless explicitly joined via a site link or a site link bridge.

Figure 2.19 Site Link Bridging

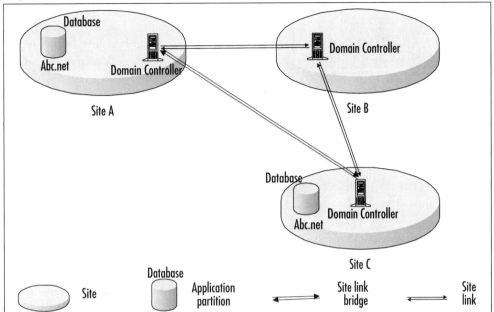

Connection Objects

In order that Active Directory data can be replicated both within and between sites, connection objects are established between DCs. It is along these connection object "paths" that Active Directory data is replicated. Connection objects can either be manually created (configured and managed by the administrator) or automatically created by a process that runs on all DCs, known as the Knowledge Consistency Checker (KCC). The KCC is described later in this section.

Automatic Connection Objects

By default, the KCC will evaluate the site topology created by the administrator using sites and site links, and from this model, it will construct inter-site connection objects along which replication of Active Directory data will flow based on the site and site link data stored within Active Directory. The KCC will also attempt to construct a resilient topology ring within a site, using connection objects between DCs in the same site.

Because the KCC evaluates the topology on a regular basis, it is able to make changes to connection objects based on the availability of the DCs in the forest. If, for example, Active Directory data is replicated between site A and site B using connection objects between DC 1 and DC 2 and DC 1 is unavailable, upon the next execution of the KCC on DC 2, new connection objects will be established between

DC 2 and another DC in the same site as DC 1. The connection objects between DC 1 and DC 2 will be removed.

The KCC is responsible for ensuring that data within each partition is replicated to and from each site. This can result in the KCC establishing multiple connection objects between a DC in one site and the DCs of another site. DC 1 in site A might replicate partitions x, y, and z to DC 2 in site B, but partition u and v to DC 3 in site B.

Manual Connection Objects

A manual connection object can be established between any two DCs in the forest. So that data can flow in both directions, two connection objects should be created— one from DC a to DC b, the other from DC b to DC a.

Manual connection objects can be created between DCs in the same or different sites, and replication schedule and frequency can be configured on a per-connection basis.

The generation of automatic connection objects (by the KCC) can be disabled at a per-site or forestwide basis, thus resulting in the need for manual connection objects to be established instead. However, if a DC fails, the administrator must then establish new connection objects or must have established multiple connection object paths to be used in the event of such a failure. It is self-evident that this manual approach involves a higher level of admin overhead than does the automatic (KCC) approach.

Multimaster Replication

Changes to a Windows NT-based object were always performed on the PDC for the domain and then replicated out to all BDCs in the domain, from that PDC. Naturally, this places a huge responsibility on the PDC in a Windows NT domain, because it is responsible for all changes, and if it were to fail, changes would not be possible (until the PDC role is moved to another BDC).

Active Directory, however, allows changes to be made on any DC that holds a read/write copy of the appropriate partition. Partitions are distributed according to Table 2.5.

Table 2.5 Active Directory Partition Distribution

Server Role versus Data Hosted	Local Domain Partition	Other Domain Partitions	Schema Partition	Config- uration Partition	Application Directory Partition
Domain controller	Read/write	N/A	Read only	Read/write	N/A
Global catalog	Read/write	Partial and read only	Read only	Read/write	N/A

Continued

Table 2.5 Active Directory Partition Distribution (Continued)

Server Role versus Data Hosted	Local Domain Partition	Other Domain Partitions	Schema Partition	Config-uration Partition	Application Directory Partition
Domain controller hosting application directory partition replica	Read/write	N/A	Read only	Read/write	Read/write
Global catalog hosting application directory partition replica	Read/write	Partial and read only	Read only	Read/write	Read/write

 NOTE

The DC or GC that hosts the Schema Master role has the only read/write copy of the Schema partition.

Application directory partitions are available only if the Domain Naming Master role is hosted by a Windows Server 2003 DC or above. Because changes can be made on any one of the DCs holding a read/write copy of the appropriate partition, replication is described as "multimaster," because no one server has the only changeable copy of any partition. Once a change is made, that change is replicated around the forest as per the replication topology designed and configured by the administrator. As a result, changes made on one DC might take some time to replicate to another DC if the receiving DC is several site links or "hops" away from the sending DC.

Knowledge Consistency Checker (KCC)

Running on every DC in the forest is a process known as the Knowledge Consistency Checker, or KCC. The KCC at regular intervals evaluates the site topology and available DCs and then generates intra-site connection objects for the local DC with other DCs in the same site to ensure efficient replication of Active Directory data. The parameters used by the KCC, which are stored in the registry, are described in Microsoft KB article 271988, which can be found at http://support. microsoft.com/default.aspx?scid=kb%3ben-us%3b271988.

The KCC will attempt to construct a ring topology within each site between the DCs in that site. Intersite connection objects are established by the Inter Site Topology Generator role, which is explained later in this same section.

NOTE

The KCC can be triggered manually to execute on a DC as follows:

- Execute repadmin /kcc.
- Execute "Check replication topology" against the NTDS Settings object, within the DC object, in the appropriate Site container, using the Sites and Services snap-in.

One enhancement made to the KCC in Windows Server 2003 that negates the need to disable the KCC (as discussed in the section *Manual Connection Objects*) is described in the sidebar *Disabling the KCC*.

TEST DAY TIP

The KCC algorithms and underlying code used were found to have serious limitations when used with Windows 2000 Active Directory. Organizations with more than around 200 sites (and multiple domains) found that the KCC would execute but never finish constructing the in-memory network map it uses to manage connection objects.

However, the KCC and related ISTG (described in the next section) algorithms have been greatly improved in Windows Server 2003. Microsoft has successfully tested an implementation with thousands of sites without experiencing any issues with the KCC. More information relating to the KCC and advanced aspects of replication design can be found in Chapter 4, along with a description of the new replication-related features and how they might be realized.

Inter Site Topology Generator and Bridgehead Servers

Although the KCC is responsible for intra-site connection objects, all inter-site connection objects are established by the Inter Site Topology Generator (ISTG). The first DC in each site (regardless of domain membership) will assume the role of the ISTG. This role cannot be viewed or changed using standard Microsoft tools, and precisely one ISTG role per site exists for sites that house one or more DCs.

The ISTG is responsible for assessing the replication needs of the site in which it resides in relation to other sites and the site links established by the administrator. The ISTG will ensure that DCs in the site receive a copy of the Schema, Configuration, and Local Domain partitions, while GCs receive the same and also partial copies of all other domain partitions.

This is done by assigning the role of bridgehead server (BS) to one or more DCs in the site. These BSs are then responsible for replicating changes with other BSs in other sites. Multiple BSs per site might be required to ensure that all partitions required are replicated across site links. Only BSs replicate with DCs in other domains. Therefore, when a change is made to an object on a DC, it first replicates (intra-site) with its partners (established by the KCC), and ultimately, the change arrives at the BS for that partition in the site. That BS then replicates (inter-site) with each of its BS partners.

The ISTG and BS roles might or might not exist on the same DC. Either way, the ISTG calculates which inter-site connection objects are required, and the BS "hosts" these connections and performs the actual replication of data across site links. This relationship is illustrated in Figure 2.20.

Figure 2.20 The Bridgehead and ISTG Roles

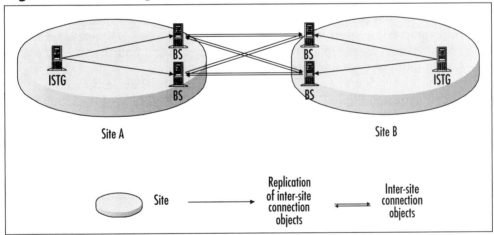

The ISTG writes to the *interSiteTopologyGenerator* attribute on the NTDS Settings object within its DC object, in the config NC every 30 minutes, by default, so as to inform other DCs in the site that it is still actively performing the ISTG role.

The NTDS Settings can be found as follows:

1. Open the ADSIedit snap-in.

2. Add the Configuration partition to the view, if not already visible.

3.   Expand the Sites container.

4.   Expand the site container in question.

5.   Expand the Servers container.

6.   Expand the DC container in question.

7.   Right-click the NTDS Settings object and choose Properties.

8.   Inspect the *interSiteTopologyGenerator* attribute.

In the event that the ISTG role holder is unavailable, and the role holder fails to update the attribute, then all DCs in the site order the GUIDs of each DC in that site and elect the DC at the top of the list as the new ISTG role holder. That DC then writes to the *interSiteTopologyGenerator* attribute on the NTDS Settings object, within the DC object, in the Configuration partition. The role holder can be viewed by following the preceding steps.

For more detailed information regarding advanced replication techniques, refer to Chapter 4.

TEST DAY TIP

Previously, using Windows 2000 DCs, within each site each partition that needed to be replicated to that site was "hosted" by only one BS in the site. For example, if a forest had three domains, then in siteA we might find that domains1 and 2 are replicated by DCn, while domain3 and the Schema and Config partitions are replicated by DCm.

Using Windows Server 2003 DCs, however, the BS role is load balanced across multiple DCs in the site, such that the task of replicating data is spread across those same DCs. This offers the advantage that the replication overhead is spread over multiple servers, thus not burdening any one DC, while also offering increased availability of Active Directory, because if one BS fails, the other(s) will continue to replicate changes, regardless.

SYSVOL

In addition to replicating Active Directory changes, the same underlying topology is used to replicate changes to the SYSVOL (domain system volume) area. SYSVOL is typically used to house scripts and group policies, which are stored on each DC on an NT File System (NTFS) partition and replicated to all DCs in the same domain using the FRS replication mechanism. A thorough description of the SYSVOL share, in conjunction with Group Policy, can be found in Chapter 4.

File Replication System (FRS)

FRS is used to replicate SYSVOL data between DCs in the same domain. Where Active Directory replication occurs at the object and attribute level, FRS replicates at the file and directory level.

Active Directory changes are replicated at the attribute level, so that only the change made to an object is actually replicated. However, FRS replicates at the file level, so if a SYSVOL housed file is changed, then the entire file is replicated, not just the changes. The FRS replication mechanism is described in further detail in Chapter 4.

Topology Options

Having explained the basic concepts and terms related to replication designs, we now explore the typical topologies used when designing replication for Active Directory. The topologies most often used are the ring, full mesh, hub and spoke, and a hybrid (which can include some or all of the aforementioned).

Intra-Site Replication

Intra-site replication differs from inter-site replication in several ways:

- **Structure** Replication topology within a site is constructed as a ring. This means that every DC in a site will have at least two in-bound and out-bound replication partners (assuming the site has sufficient DCs to accommodate this). The ring is constructed by the KCC process and is maintained until there are seven DCs in a site. The KCC will construct a hybrid mesh/ring topology if a site has more than seven DCs.

- **Compression** Intra-site replication is not compressed, whereas inter-site replication traffic is compressed. This is due to the fact that it is assumed within a site that connectivity is sound and sufficient bandwidth is available for intra-site replication.

- **Notification** The final difference is that intra-site replication uses a notification process to inform partners of changes and does not use costs or schedules. This implies that when a change is received at the site BS server, it notifies each of its partners, who then request that the changes be sent. They in turn inform their partners in a similar fashion, who pull the changes. This process repeats until all DCs in the site have received the changes.

Inter-Site Replication

Inter-site replication mechanisms differ from those used intra-site, because inter-site connections are normally able to accommodate less traffic than intra-site connections.

- **Structure** Rather than construct a ring, the KCC builds two one-way connection objects between BSs in sites that participate in a site link. For example, if a site link is created that links site A with site B, and site A has BS DC 1 and site B has BS DC 2, then the KCC will construct two one-way connection objects between DC 1 and DC 2. This process is repeated for each site link of which a site is a member.

- **Compression** Because inter-site replication frequently traverses expensive WAN links, all replication traffic across an inter-site link is compressed. The compression is performed by the bridgehead DC(s) before sending the data across the network. This represents an additional overhead for the BS, and BSs should be designed with this fact in mind. Typically, data is compressed to around 10 percent of its original size.

- **Store and forward** Intra-site replication is sent via a notification mechanism, as described earlier; however, inter-site replication uses a store and forward mechanism. This implies that all changes are stored on the sending DC until the next replication event time is reached, as per the interval and schedule defined for the site link (refer to the previous descriptions of *interval* and *schedule*).

Ring

A ring topology involves constructing a loop with each site connected to two neighbor sites as per Figure 2.21. Such a design is redundant but not scalable, and therefore not suitable in large organizations.

If an organization has a small number of sites and does not need the high redundancy offered by the full mesh design, then the ring design might prove suitable.

A ring topology requires $2n$ unidirectional (or n bidirectional) site links, where n is the number of sites in the ring. A ring of four sites requires eight unidirectional or four bidirectional links.

Figure 2.21 The Ring Topology

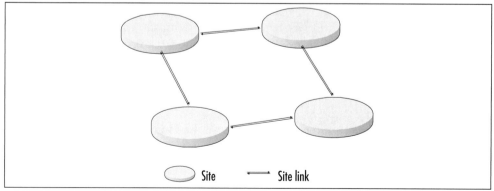

Fully Meshed

The full mesh design connects each site to all other sites, as per Figure 2.22. Such a design is highly redundant, very expensive to implement and manage, and not scalable. It is therefore not practical in a large organization with many sites.

A full mesh design might be suitable for a small organization with a small number of sites and where redundancy is important. Otherwise, a hub and spoke design is probably more suitable.

A mesh topology requires $n(n-1)$ unidirectional (or ? $n(n-1)$ bidirectional site links, where n is the number of sites in the mesh. A mesh of four sites requires twelve unidirectional or six bidirectional links.

Figure 2.22 The Fully Meshed Topology

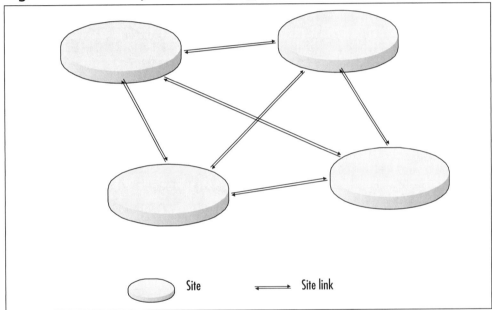

Site   ⟷ Site link

Hub and Spoke

The most popular design is the hub and spoke, as seen in Figure 2.23. This design offers less redundancy than previous designs, but is far more scalable and therefore more suited to large organizations.

The hub and spoke design relies on one or more hub sites that have slower WAN connections to multiple spoke or satellite sites. The hub sites are also generally connected to each other in a full mesh style, with very high-speed WAN connections.

Hub and spoke designs offer the ability to segment data within a specific geographic area. This has an obvious advantage in a large organization with sites spread all over the globe. Each regional hub manages replication to and from its connected satellite sites, and the replication between itself and other hub sites.

This design introduces larger latency times than do ring or full mesh designs, but in a large network this is offset by the increased management of replication traffic, which is a result of the segmentation.

A hub and spoke topology requires 2n unidirectional (or n bidirectional) site links, where n is the number of spoke sites. A topology of one hub and four spoke sites requires eight unidirectional or four bidirectional links.

Figure 2.23 The Hub and Spoke Topology

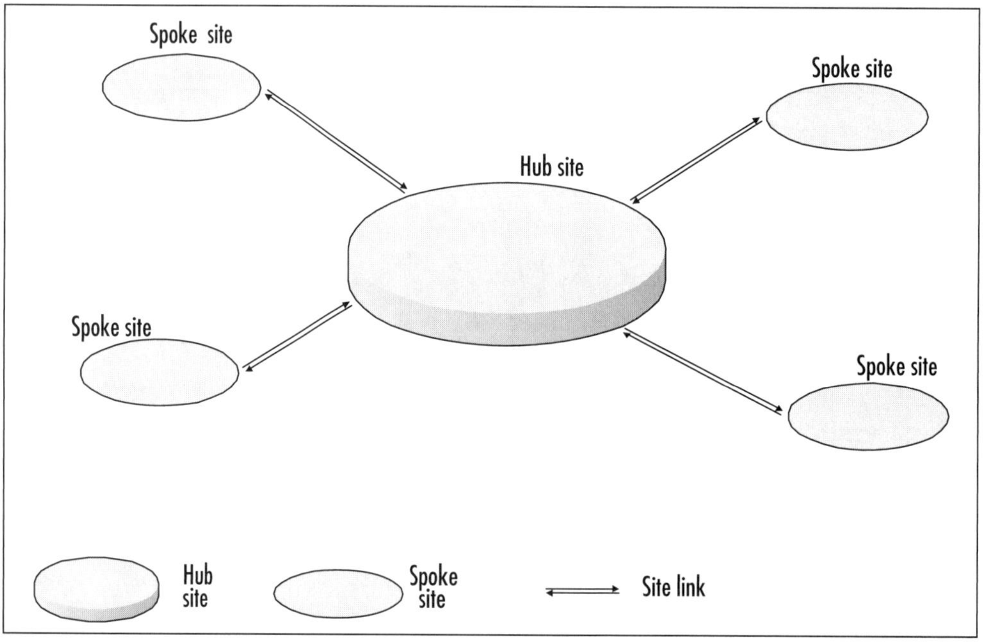

Hybrid

The hybrid model uses a combination of any or all of the models discussed previously. For example, an organization can have multiple hub sites and multiple spoke sites connected to each. The hub sites can be joined in a mesh topology, while the satellites are joined to hubs in a hub and spoke fashion. An example can be found in Figure 2.24. This model is often found in larger organizations with complex underlying network structures that have regional hub sites, each with multiple satellite or spoke sites.

A topology requires 2n unidirectional (or n bidirectional) site links per hub site, where n is the number of spoke sites connected and 2m unidirectional (or m bidirectional) site links per hub site, where m is the number of hub sites. A topology of three hub and eight spoke sites (as seen in Figure 2.24) requires (2 × 3) + (2 × 3) + (2 × 2) = 16 unidirectional or 8 bidirectional links for the spokes, and 6 unidirectional or 3 bidirectional links for the hubs, for a grand total of 22 unidirectional or 11 bidirectional links.

Figure 2.24 The Hybrid Topology

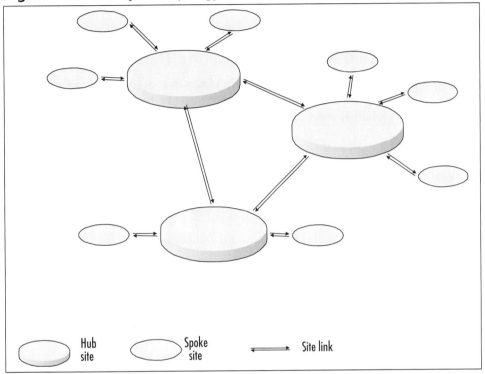

>
> **NOTE**
>
> Although the hub and spoke model might be the most popular model, it is rarely deployed in the simplistic sense described previously. In very large networks with perhaps hundreds of locations (and thus sites), a secondary layer of "sub-hub" sites are frequently used. These sub-hubs are used to further segment traffic within the local region.

Ownership

The final subject covered under the heading of replication is that of ownership. Again, as with forests and domains (and indeed with OUs as we'll see later), the subject of ownership plays an important part in the well-being of any Active Directory implementation.

It is therefore suggested that a topology owner be assigned who has sole control and access to the replication topology within Active Directory. This person (or indeed team) will assume the following responsibilities:

- Liaise with personnel responsible for managing the physical network and documenting the network, subnets, bandwidth, WAN link speeds, and so forth on a perpetual basis.

- Document the Active Directory replication topology, including sites, sub-nets, links, and bridges.

- Manage and perform changes to the replication topology within Active Directory based on the documentation created and changes made to the underlying network.

Summary of Exam Objectives

The main objective of this chapter was to "design the Active Directory infrastructure to meet business and technical requirements." This objective is further split into five subobjectives, each of which were covered in this chapter and are summarized here.

We started with the objective "design the envisioned administrative model," which was discussed in the section *Assessing and Designing the Administrative Model*. This section focused on examining the current administrative model in use within the organization, the role of service administrators and data administrators, and isolation and autonomy. We then discussed how a suitable admin model might be arrived at by carefully considering these factors and how they relate to and affect the Active Directory design project as a whole.

The first phase of the project and the aspect most affected by the administrative model is discussed in the section *Assessing and Defining the Forest Design*, which maps to the objective "Create the conceptual design of the Active Directory forest structure." We applied the principles discussed in the previous section to this section and compared various multiple forest models with the single forest model.

We then moved onto the domain design phase, which maps to the objective "Create the conceptual design of the Active Directory domain structure." Again, we examined the pertinent factors and popular models, which are each a result of one or more of those factors.

Next, we looked at OU design, which maps to the objective "Create the conceptual design of the organizational unit (OU) structure". Again, we considered the various factors that influence this phase of the project and the different resultant approaches to structuring the OU design.

Finally, we examined replication design, which maps to the objective "Design the Active Directory replication strategy." Here we discussed the concepts that surround Active Directory replication and topology considerations. Several popular models were considered that correspond to the most widely found network topologies.

Throughout the chapter, we discussed the subjects of ownership, sponsorship, responsibilities, and change management. Each of these aspects has its own place and relevance within each of the design phases, and each was therefore discussed in some detail.

Exam Objectives Fast Track

Assessing and Designing the Administrative Model

- ☑ Service administrators manage the Active Directory infrastructure.
- ☑ Data administrators manage the data contained within Active Directory and member computers.

☑ Isolation implies exclusive access to a resource.

☑ Autonomy implies independence from all other users, with the exception of the service administrators.

Assessing and Designing the Forest Design

☑ If service or data isolation is required, create a separate forest.

☑ If disparate schemas or Configuration partition data is required, create a separate forest.

☑ Carefully consider legal, political, technical, organizational, and operational factors.

☑ A single forest model is the simplest to administer, with the lowest TCO.

☑ Ensure each forest has an owner and each design project has a sponsor.

Assessing and Creating the Domain Design

☑ Consider geographic domains to better manage replication.

☑ Consider functional domains for service autonomy.

☑ Consider the use of a dedicated root domain and associated pros and cons.

☑ Carefully select the domain names, especially the root domain name.

☑ Separate trees can be deployed to allow autonomy within a DNS namespace.

☑ The single domain model is simplest to administer, with the lowest TCO.

Developing the OU Model

☑ Administrative models, group policy, and the protection of sensitive objects are the biggest OU design influences.

☑ Create geographic, functional, or object-type OUs at the root of the domain—use these models as starting points.

☑ OU structures should not be too deep (>10 levels) due to startup and logon times and application deployment issues.

Developing the Replication Design

☑ Be conversant with replication concepts.

☑ Be aware of the improvements and new features found in Windows Server 2003.

☑ The replication topology should match the underlying network structure as closely as possible.

Exam Objectives Frequently Asked Questions

The following Frequently Asked Questions, answered by the authors of this book, are designed to both measure your understanding of the Exam Objectives presented in this chapter and to assist you with real-life implementation of these concepts. You will also gain access to thousands of other FAQs at *www.ITFAQnet.com*.

Q: What is the security boundary when designing Active Directory, assuming that service or data isolation is required?

A: The forest is the security boundary.

Q: I need data isolation but not service isolation. Do I need a separate forest?

A: Yes. Data isolation can be achieved only with a separate forest.

Q: Will schema changes affect all domains in the forest?

A: Yes. Schema data is replicated to all DCs in the forest.

Q: Can multiple password policies be set in the same domain?

A: No. A separate domain is required for each password policy required.

Q: Why would I deploy a separate tree?

A: A separate tree gives a business the opportunity to deploy a different, business-specific DNS namespace.

Q: How can I mitigate the risk of a redesign in the event of a merger?

A: Deploy a dedicated root, root domain in the forest. This segregates the forest service admin roles from the other domains and allows for other domains to be redeployed with new names without destroying the forest.

Q: Why should I create multiple sites?

A: Create a site topology to closely match the underlying network. This ensures that data is replicated according to the underlying topology.

Q: All branch offices are connected via WAN links to a main office. How should I design the replication topology?

A: Use a hub and spoke design.

Q: Users in different regions need to have different group policy applied. How do I achieve that?

A: Deploy separate user OUs within a parent "User" OU and deploy GPOs at each regional OU.

Q: How do I grant autonomy to objects without isolation?

A: Deploy an OU and place the objects in the OU. Delegate rights over the OU and its objects to the group owning those objects.

Self Test

A Quick Answer Key follows the Self Test questions. For complete questions, answers, and explanations to the Self Test questions in this chapter as well as the other chapters in this book, see the Self Test Appendix.

1. Your organization is comprised of six different business units. Each requires a certain level of independence from each of the other businesses within the Active Directory environment. Which of the following terms are relevant when considering the level of independence required? (Choose all that apply.)

   A. Isolation

   B. Autonomy

   C. Independence

   D. Restriction

2. You are the project manager for a large Active Directory design and deployment project within an organization. Several disparate businesses want to coexist in the same Active Directory environment. Which administrative roles need to be defined within each business, such that the level of isolation and autonomy can be designed appropriately to meet the needs of these administrative groups? (Choose all that apply.)

   A. Service administrators

   B. Domain administrators

   C. Server administrators

   D. Data administrators

3. During the assessment of administrative requirements, one group expresses the need to have complete, exclusive access to and control over the schema within Active Directory. Which of the following terms describes their requirement in terms of independence?

   A. Autonomy

   B. Isolation

   C. Exclusive access

   D. Restricted access

4. An organization has several disparate businesses, which for legal reasons cannot share data with any other part of the organization. These businesses must ensure that their data cannot be accessed from any other business. Which of the following models meets these requirements?

   A. Separate OU per business

   B. Separate domain per business

   C. Separate forest per business

   D. Separate, segmented network per business

5. An application requires that extensions to the schema be made. However, the existing Active Directory design houses several disparate businesses, some of which do not require these schema changes. How might the application be deployed while leaving the schema in the "'shared" forest unchanged so that users can access the application with existing credentials?

   A. Deploy a separate domain within the existing forest. Deploy the application in the new domain.

   B. Deploy a separate forest. Deploy the application in the new forest with no trust to the other forest.

C. Deploy a separate forest. Deploy the application in the new forest and establish a trust to the other forest.

D. Deploy the application in the existing forest.

6. Two Active Directory sites each have a DC that hosts a replica of an application partition. No site link exists between these two sites. What can be done to initiate replication of the application partition data between these two sites?

A. Create manual connection objects.

B. Create a site link bridge.

C. Create a site link.

D. Merge the sites into one new site encompassing both DCs.

7. You are designing Active Directory for an organization comprised of several functional groups. Each group needs autonomous control over its objects but not isolation at the service or data level. How should each group be segregated from other groups to meet these requirements in the simplest way possible?

A. Create a separate domain.

B. Create a separate forest.

C. Create a separate OU.

D. Create a separate site.

8. Your organization has three regional Windows NT 4 user domains. This split was designed due to the limitations of the Windows NT Secure Accounts Manager (SAM) database. Each user domain is managed autonomously by its own region. When designing Active Directory for the organization, how should these regions be segregated so that no change to the administrative model is required?

A. In separate domains

B. In separate forests

C. In separate sites

D. In separate OUs

9. When designing a group policy strategy for your Active Directory implementation, the following requirements are identified: all member servers must receive a core set of policies; all servers must receive a role-specific set of policies; all servers must receive a regional-specific set of policies. How can this be achieved?

A. Create an OU structure that splits servers by role, and then by region.

B. Create an OU structure that splits servers by region, and then by role.

C. Create an OU structure that splits servers by role. Apply local policies on each server as appropriate.

D. Create an OU structure that splits servers by region. Apply local policies on each server as appropriate.

Self Test Quick Answer Key

For complete questions, answers, and explanations to the Self Test questions in this chapter as well as the other chapters in this book, see the Self Test Appendix.

1.	**A, B**		6.	**A, B, C, D**
2.	**A, D**		7.	**C**
3.	**B**		8.	**D**
4.	**C**		9.	**B**
5.	**C**			

Chapter 3

MCSE 70-297

Developing the Network Services Design

Exam Objectives in This Chapter:

1.6 Design the network services infrastructure to meet business and technical requirements.

1.6.1 Create the conceptual design of the DNS infrastructure.

1.6.2 Create the conceptual design of the WINS infrastructure.

1.6.3 Create the conceptual design of the DHCP infrastructure.

1.6.4 Create the conceptual design of the remote access infrastructure.

Introduction

In this chapter, we discuss how to develop a network services infrastructure design, and approach that design from the standpoint of a Windows Server 2003 rollout with Active Directory. Networks are often already running one or more network services such as Domain Name System (DNS), Windows Internet Naming Service (WINS), Dynamic Host Configuration Protocol (DHCP), and Remote Access Services. These are common services used on Transmission Control Protocol/Internet Protocol (TCP/IP) networks.

One challenge of designing a service on an internetwork that already provides that service is that it might seem you are reinventing the wheel. A good design process should start with a blank slate and be led by the organization's business objectives. If you work within the limits of the existing services, you might not be able to achieve the business objectives. Keeping an existing service can also result in inheriting its existing problems. Once the ideal system is designed, then existing systems can be worked into the design or discarded.

This chapter takes you through the design process for TCP/IP-based services on a Windows Server 2003 network. We will look at the incorporation of redundancy and reliability into the design. Finally, we will review how these services work within the overall Windows Server 2003 network.

Developing the Network Services Infrastructure Designs

Of the services we will discuss in this chapter—DNS, DHCP, WINS, and Remote Access—the one that must be completely designed before implementation of an Active Directory network is DNS. DNS is the basis of the naming structure for Active Directory domains and provides the lookup service for communications between all Active Directory member computers and domain controllers (DCs). With the Active Directory's reliance on DNS, you must take a great deal of care in ensuring that your initial designs will meet your organization's business requirements, and that the design can grow and expand with the network.

DHCP, WINS, and Remote Access services need never be implemented in order for an Active Directory DC to be installed or for it to function. However, these three services provide functionality that reduces administrative overhead, enables integration with older Windows systems, and allows users to connect to the network from remote locations. Although not a requirement, they are of extreme value to a network administrator. For optimum performance, they should be designed with as much care and consideration as the DNS design.

Developing DNS Designs

Windows Server 2003, like its predecessor Windows Server 2000, uses the Domain Naming System (DNS) for name resolution. Windows pulls upon DNS' hierarchical, distributed, and scalable database. In fact, DNS is integrated within the Active Directory domain structure itself to the degree that a DC for an Active Directory domain cannot be installed without DNS being installed somewhere on the network and configured on the DC as well. DNS is used to name the domain, to name the DC, and then to help clients and servers locate the Active Directory services available on the network. For example, an Active Directory domain might be named course.com or, perhaps, example.course.com. Each is a DNS name. A DC in the course.com domain could be called dc.course.com, also a DNS name. Past versions of Windows NT did not require DNS (nor they did not require the TCP/IP protocol stack). Because Windows NT used NetBIOS naming, they relied on the Windows Internet Naming Service (WINS) for name resolution when TCP/IP was configured. WINS is discussed later in this chapter.

Computers use DNS as a name resolution service to communicate on a TCP/IP network and for directly locating Active Directory services. For example, client computers use DNS to locate DCs at logon, and DCs use DNS to locate their peer DCs when performing updates to the Active Directory. The DNS service incorporated into the Windows Server 2003 operating system is compatible with Internet name resolution standards.

When you plan an Active Directory network, you must be aware of how DNS is currently used on the network. This will include the existing TCP/IP configuration and names that exist on the network. You should look at both the company's Internet presence and corporate structure. Behind the scenes, you need to check the version of DNS that is currently being used and whether that version can interoperate with the Active Directory. All of these factors will affect how you design the resulting DNS structure.

Head of the Class…

History Course on DNS

Most systems administrators and engineers encounter DNS in their daily activities. Even so, it doesn't hurt to refresh your memory about how DNS originated.

DNS grew out of the need for users to be able to translate human names into IP addresses, and vice versa. On a TCP/IP network, each host is identified by the 32-bit IP address. Even though the dotted decimal IP addresses (those that are in the format of 129.88.3.254) are easier to remember than 32 ones and zeroes, a friendly name such as joe.course.com is far easier for a human to remember. Before DNS, each host had a file called "hosts" that listed the computers on the network and their associated IP addresses. This system was tedious to manage. At the addition of each new host or the removal of one,

Continued

(Continued)

an administrator needed to update the host's file on each computer. It was from these humble beginnings that the centralized, hierarchical, and distributed DNS system was devised in order to allow a small set of computers to provide the name and address records to other computers on the network.

Although each DNS server provided a central location for DNS data, these servers were further connected into a hierarchy so that name resolution could easily be passed to the correct computer that held the data for that portion of the network. The DNS database is distributed in the form of *zones*. Each zone holds the records that match IP addresses to names, but the zones list only a subset of the DNS database. For example, the zone for course.com will hold the records for course.com. This zone might also contain a subdomain corp.course.com, or the administrator can create an additional zone for corp.course.com. The DNS servers are configured to pass along requests for unknown names or IP addresses to their parent servers. When a request is sent to the top, it is then sent down the hierarchy to the DNS server that holds the record.

The system of DNS is so efficient that it can serve the hosts of the entire Internet, regardless of how many millions, or even billions, of IP addresses and names need to be resolved.

The process that is generally used in developing a DNS design is shown in Figure 3.1.

Figure 3.1 The General Process in Developing the DNS Design

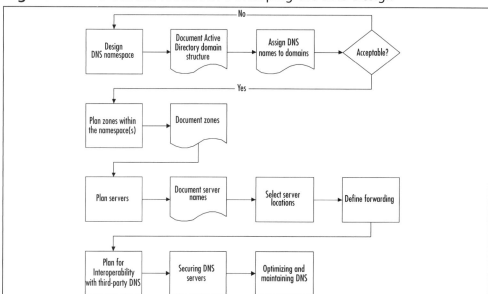

DNS Design Principles

The first major task in the DNS design process is to develop the DNS namespace. This step might normally be a simple selection of one or two DNS namespaces. However, because each Active Directory domain requires its own DNS domain name, both the structural design and the naming of Active Directory domains must be included in the process. You must document each DNS name that you intend to use in the internetwork before you plan for DNS zones, servers, and interoperating with third-party DNS systems.

EXAM WARNING

Check for conflicts when asked questions regarding DNS namespace designs. For example, if the scenario states that a particular namespace is already being used for another purpose, it is likely not going to be the first choice for an Active Directory root domain namespace.

Zone Design

You have several options for planning your zones; however, there are a few rules:

- Each DNS name that ends with a different domain suffix will require a separate zone. For example, course.com and course.local would each require a separate zone.

- Parent and child namespaces can either be included in a single zone or separated into multiple zones. For example, if you have course.com and corp.course.com, you can create a single zone that is authoritative for the records in both course.com and corp.course.com, or you can create two separate zones.

- Sibling namespaces that do not include their parent namespace cannot share a single zone. For example, corp.course.com and pub.course.com cannot be in the same zone unless that zone also includes course.com.

Figure 3.2 shows a correct set of DNS zones.

Figure 3.2 Zones Can Include One or More DNS Names, as Long as They Follow the Parent and Child Rules

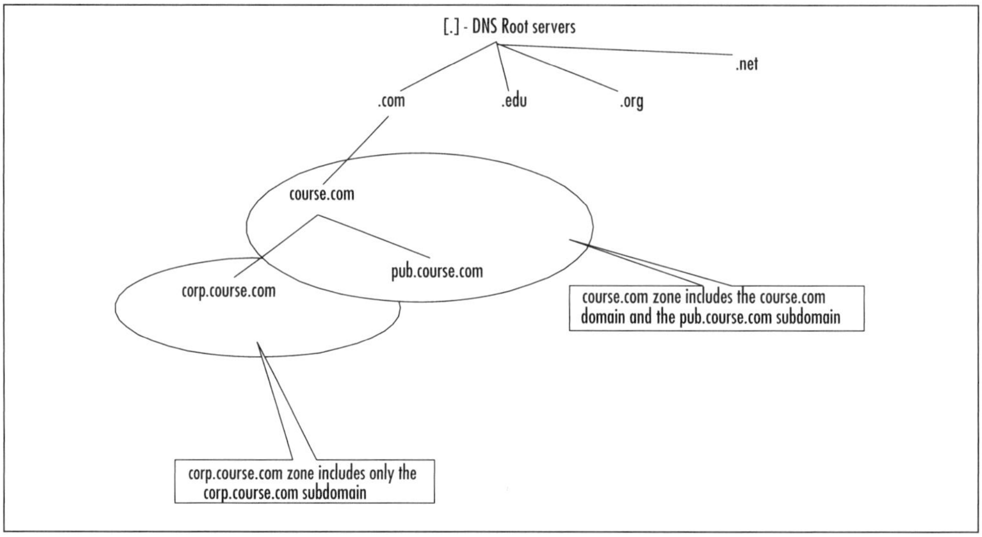

Each zone is maintained by a primary name server. The primary name server is considered authoritative for the zone. For redundancy and distribution purposes, additional name servers can hold the same zone as the primary name servers. These are called secondary name servers. A secondary name server holds a copy of the zone that clients can use to resolve names, but this is for read-only purposes. The primary server is the only place where new records, deletions, and updates can take place.

Active Directory Integrated zones are a special case, when you consider how zone information is updated across DNS servers. Because the Active Directory Integrated zone information is incorporated directly into the Active Directory database, the data is replicated in the multimaster fashion used by the Active Directory. Any DNS record that is updated in the Active Directory Integrated zone is replicated to the other DNS servers with the zone, instead of the entire zone being replicated.

TEST DAY TIP

Review DNS zone types and zone replication processes. You will need to know these for the exam.

Name Resolution

You need to know how the clients resolve DNS requests, as well as the setup of the internetwork in order to determine where to place primary name servers and secondary name servers. Each DNS client uses a resolver to query the name server that they have been configured to use. On each DNS name server, a responding application (also called a resolver) receives the requests and extracts the data from the local DNS database to send back to the DNS client. When the data is not available on the DNS server because that server is not authoritative for the requested IP address or name, the resolver will query the DNS database through a recursive process of referrals to other name servers. This process is shown in Figure 3.3.

Figure 3.3 Resolvers Refer to Other Name Servers to Resolve a Nonlocal Query

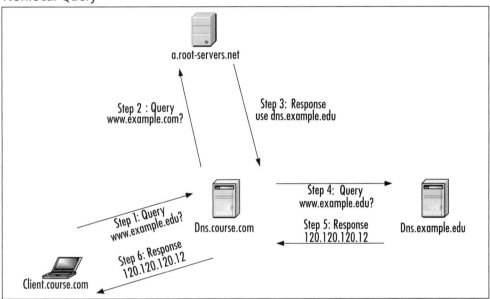

Figure 3.3 shows the following recursive process:

1. The computer named client.course.com is attempting to reach the Uniform Resource Locator (URL) www.example.edu.

2. The DNS client resolver determines that the local computer does not have the IP address for this URL and queries the name server dns.course.com.

3. The name server dns.course.com determines that it is not authoritative for the example.edu zone and does not have the IP address available in its local cache.

4. dns.course.com's resolver application refers the query to the root servers. (Note that the dns.course.com root server must be configured with the root server's forwarding information for this to function properly.)

5. A root server replies that dns.course.com should pass the query on to dns.example.edu and includes the IP address of dns.example.edu in the response.

6. dns.course.com then refers the query to dns.example.edu. Because dns.example.edu is authoritative for that name, it responds with the IP address www.example.edu.

7. dns.course.com then returns the IP address 120.120.120.12 to client.course.com, which then contacts the www.example.edu host directly to continue its process.

8. If the client had attempted to access an IP address for www.sub.example.edu, the root servers would have still referred the query to dns.example.edu. However, if dns.example.edu were not authoritative for that zone, it would have referred the query to dns.sub.example.edu, where it could then be resolved.

Forwarding and root hints are two different methods of moving name resolution queries around the network with similar results. When you use root hints, your server is configured to contact the root of the DNS tree directly for all external requests. When you use forwarding, your server is configured to contact a local DNS server for all external requests, and (presumably) that server is configured to contact the root servers. The use of forwarders helps in a few ways:

- Forwarders can direct DNS traffic in a preset pattern through your network.

- Forwarders can be designed to ensure that only certain DNS servers communicate with the public Internet.

- Forwarders can be used to establish Split Brain DNS, which is discussed later in this chapter.

Record Management

The DNS system, once configured correctly, is transparent to the user. However, it is not transparent to administrators. They must still manually add each host name and IP address record (known as host address (A) records and pointer (PTR) records) for clients. Host (A) records are in the forward lookup zones, providing host name to IP address resolution. PTR records are in the reverse lookup zones, providing IP address to host name resolution for those instances when an IP address is known but the host name is not. If a client's IP address changes, then the existing records must be updated with the new IP address. In a server-centric network, where client computers are not accessed by others, the need to update DNS with every client IP address is reduced. However, in a peer-to-peer network where clients are providing services and resources to other clients, the administrative overhead can grow quite large. Even in the server-centric network, there can be so many servers with a variety of changes that the system can become quite cumbersome.

These problems have been resolved by a DNS feature called Dynamic DNS updates (DDNS). When DDNS is incorporated into the DNS server, DDNS clients can dynamically register their IP addresses and associated host names with the DNS server. This is especially helpful in an environment where DHCP is used, and we will review DHCP, as well as its use with DDNS, in the section *Developing DHCP Approach* later in this chapter.

EXAM WARNING

Be aware that both Windows 2000 and Windows Server 2003 DNS services will support DDNS. In addition, some (but not all) third-party DNS services do support DDNS.

Windows 2000 Professional, Windows 2000 Server, Windows XP, and Windows Server 2003 DNS clients all have the ability to use DDNS. Figure 3.4 shows the Advanced TCP/IP Settings dialog box in which you can check the box for "Register this connection's address in DNS." By default, these DNS clients will have this box already checked, so that if DDNS is running on the network, these clients will already be configured to work with it. The DNS server service must be configured to specifically allow or disallow DDNS.

Figure 3.4 DDNS Is Enabled in the Advanced TCP/IP Settings Dialog Box of Any Network Connection

Ownership of the Namespace

As discussed previously, the DNS system is organized into a hierarchical structure to resolve names to IP addresses, and vice versa. The DNS namespace is used to organize DNS into the hierarchy. It is similar to the way in which a directory structure is organized on a hard drive. For example, if you opened Windows Explorer, you would see the C:\ drive at the top of the directory tree. Below that, you would see a set of folders, such as Program Files and Windows. Within either of these folders, you will find more folders. Some of the folders contain files. You could find a readme.txt file in the Windows folder, and a file named readme.txt within the Program Files folder. These are not the same files and can easily coexist on the same hard drive because they are contained in different folders. Likewise, you can have two computers named NED. They can both coexist on the same network as long as they are not in the same namespace. One could be NED.course.com and the other could be NED.example.com. In addition, like folders that can contain both other files and other folders, domain namespaces can contain other domain namespaces as well as host names. For example, the domain course.com can contain the host name ned.course.com and the domain name domain.course.com.

The summit of the DNS namespace hierarchy is the root, which has several servers managed by the Internet Name Registration Authority (INRA). Immediately below the root are the COM, NET, EDU, and other top-level domains listed in Table 3.1. Each of these domains is further divided into namespaces that are managed by the organizations that register them. For example, course.com is managed by a different organization than umich.edu is.

Table 3.1 Domain Suffixes Used on the Internet

Domain Suffix	Typical Usage
.mil	United States military
.edu	Educational facilities
.com	Commercial organizations
.net	Networks
.org	Nonprofit organizations
.gov	United States government—nonmilitary
.us	United States
.uk	United Kingdom
.au	Australia
.de	Germany
Other two-letter abbreviations (.xx)	Other countries

In addition to the domain suffixes shown in Table 3.1, you will also find the occasional privately used domain suffix .local. The .local suffix is not managed by a DNS root server, so the namespace cannot be published on the Internet. When you design the namespace for an Active Directory network, you can choose to use the .local suffix for domains that will not have any hosts on the Internet. Keep in mind that using the .local namespace internally will not prevent an organization from using Internet resources, such as browsing the Web. The DNS hierarchy is typically shown as a tree structure with the root shown at the top, as depicted in Figure 3.5. Usually you will see the root domain represented by a dot. Following the root, you will see the top-level domain suffixes. Below those are the second-level domain names with which users are most familiar. These second-level domains can be further subdivided, or not, as the organization desires.

Organizations often split the ownership of their DNS namespace. One team might be responsible for everything inside the firewall, while another team is responsible for the namespace that faces the public. Because Active Directory often replaces Windows NT as an upgrade, the team responsible for Windows NT will often take over the DNS namespace management for Active Directory domains. Because Active Directory DNS design and implementation does differ somewhat from the standard DNS' design and implementation, you can often find the two types of tasks split between two different groups in the same organization.

Figure 3.5 The DNS Hierarchy Is Displayed in a Tree Structure with the Root at the Top

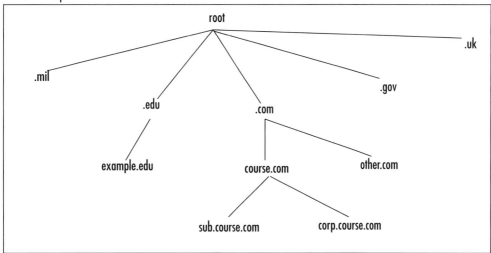

When designing a DNS network, you need to consider whether searches need to be fast, or if slower DNS queries that are experienced as a slow network response will be acceptable. This issue should affect only large networks. Let's consider that you

might have a network that has 100,000 client computers. These computers share resources in addition to consuming them. As such, every network host—client or server—must be listed in DNS. If you have a single DNS domain that houses all of these address records in addition to other types of DNS records, the time it takes for a DNS server to respond to a query for a resource could become excessively long. To speed up the response, you could use subdomains. If you had five subdomains with 20,000 hosts each, your response would be nearly five times faster whenever you performed a DNS query. Although performance would not necessarily improve linearly, think about how the DNS server using subdomains would function. Instead of searching every record in a 100,000 set of records, the server would point to a subdomain and search through only 20,000 records, thus greatly improving the speed of the server. This is something to keep in mind when designing your Active Directory namespace, especially if you have a very large internetwork.

Developing the DNS Design for Your Network

There are few limitations to developing DNS designs and deploying the service thereafter. You should consider the following points during your design process:

- Each domain contains a set of resource records. Resource records map names to IP addresses or vice versa depending on which type of record it is. There are special resource records to identify types of servers on the networks. For example, an MX resource record identifies a mail server.

- If the organization has a large number of hosts, use subdomains to speed up the DNS response.

- The only limitation to using subdomains on a single DNS server is the server's own memory and disk capacity.

- A zone contains one or more domains and their resource records. Zones can contain multiple domains if they have a parent and child relationship.

- A DNS server with a primary zone is authoritative for the zone, and updates can be made on that server. There can be only one primary zone for each zone defined.

- A DNS server with a secondary zone contains a read-only copy of the zone. Secondary zones provide redundancy and speed up query responses by being placed near the computers that place DNS queries.

- DNS servers can use primary and secondary zones whether they are running Windows Server 2003 or are a third-party DNS server.

Developing & Deploying...

Continued

(Continued)

- Windows Server 2003 and Windows 2000 Server both support Active Directory integrated zones, but these are not supported by third-party DNS servers.

Design Features

Networks typically connect to the Internet, and you must consider how to handle name resolution within your network and on the Internet. Depending on your requirements, you might decide to use root hints or a combination of forwarding and root hints. To increase DNS performance, you might decide on a Round Robin system. Security will also come into play within your DNS design. We will now drill down into features that drive DNS designs, including:

- Security options within DNS

- Use of forwarding and root hints

- Performance enhancement with Round Robin DNS

- Designing DNS for Active Directory

As discussed earlier, a DNS network allows multiple hosts to have the same common name on the network. This is because the entire name, called a fully qualified domain name (FQDN), of the host is actually the common name concatenated with the domain name. The host named joe in the course.com domain has the FQDN of joe.course.com, while the host named joe in umich.edu has the FQDN of joe.umich.edu. Because joe.course.com is a different name from joe.umich.edu, the two hosts can have the same first name of joe and be able to coexist on the Internet. The only limits that you have to the names, then, is that two different hosts cannot have the same FQDN, and that a subdomain cannot have the same name as a host's FQDN. For example, you cannot have a subdomain named jack.course.com and a host named jack.course.com. Within each domain, all names must be unique.

Security Options Within DNS

Security is something you do need to consider when designing DNS. Although you might think of security as a feature, it has an impact on the performance of the network. When there are too many security gatekeepers in a network (regardless of what aspect of security is being applied), performance suffers. Conversely, when you do not implement any security, then the network could have the ultimate performance problem because a major security breach could cause the network to stop performing.

Balancing security with performance is the key to a solidly performing network. There are some simple things that you must consider:

- When you implement security at the protocol level, such as using the DNSSEC protocol that is discussed later in this chapter, every packet will take longer to transmit because both the sender and receiver will need to code or decode the security protocol.

- When you implement security at the protocol level, packets generally are larger. This will consume more bandwidth and affect other data transmissions.

- When you implement security by placing a firewall or other type of gateway system, you will have a single bottleneck that will affect only the data that is transmitted through that bottleneck.

- When you implement a design to enhance security, especially in the case of Split Brain DNS, you will often have a higher level of administrative overhead, and performance might or might not be affected depending on the other features of the design.

Security should always be the first consideration on the network. You should be able to discern when additional security is required. For example, if you have a single site with a single domain that uses a DNS namespace that is not shared on the Internet, and the network is protected from the Internet by a firewall and Network Address Translation (NAT), the need for protocol-level security will be limited to verifying whether the security policies of the organization require it.

Forwarding and Root Hints

Root hints are used by DNS servers to communicate directly with the root name servers on the Internet. They are used in simple recursive queries for name resolution to any host on the Internet. In a recursive query, the client is asking for an authoritative resolution of the name. Clients always forward recursive queries to their configured DNS servers. If their own DNS server is not authoritative for the name and does not have that name in its local cache, it will use an iterative query to the root DNS server that is configured in the server's root hints. The root server will respond with an appropriate DNS server name to request the information from. If that DNS server delegates the zone rather than is authoritative for it, it will provide the local DNS server with its child DNS server to request the information from. When the DNS server that is authoritative for the queried zone is reached, it responds with the correct information and that information is sent back to the client.

Large internetworks with many DNS servers will likely cause excess bandwidth consumption if all the DNS servers are configured to use root hints. For example, imagine a network with a site in San Diego that is connected to Los Angeles, which is connected to New York, which is then connected to the Internet. If the DNS server in San Diego is configured with root hints, it will bypass all the other DNS servers on the network and connect all the way to the Internet to try to resolve a query. Because organizations tend to have searches to the same sites on the Internet, the query's results might be in cache in a Los Angeles DNS server or in a New York DNS server.

One design method that you can use is forwarding. When you enable forwarding in the network, you can route all DNS queries to a specific DNS server on the network before transmitting them across the Internet. This can reduce the bandwidth consumption throughout the network, leaving it available for more important traffic. The query process when using forwarding is as follows:

1. A client queries its local DNS server.

2. The local DNS server is not authoritative for the queried zone, nor does it have the query result in its local cache, so it forwards the query to a DNS server known as a forwarder.

3. The forwarder DNS server is not authoritative for the queried zone, nor does it have the query result in its local cache, so it uses root hints to forward the query to a root name server.

4. The forwarder then conducts all iterative queries until it resolves the name. The forwarder returns its result to the local DNS server.

5. The local DNS server returns the result to the client.

Another design option within forwarding is the ability in Windows Server 2003 to have conditional forwarding. Rather than a DNS server using a single forwarder for all queries it cannot resolve, in conditional forwarding, you can forward queries to different DNS servers based on the specific domain name included in the query. This improves the DNS performance in a large internetwork that contains several zones because it provides a shortcut through the tree to the correct branch for name resolution.

When using conditional forwarding, the client will send a query to its local DNS server. The local DNS server will look to see if it can resolve the query from its own zone or from its local cache. If not, the local DNS server then checks a list of forwarders. If there is a match between the domain name stated in the query and a DNS forwarder, the query is sent directly to that DNS forwarder. If there is no match in the conditional forwarding list, the DNS server follows the standard recursive query process to resolve the name.

Another design option for performance enhancement, which is available in Windows Server 2003 DNS, is the stub zone. This stub zone contains a read-only copy of a zone with a set of specific resource records. These records are the original zone's start of authority (SOA) record and the name server (NS) records. The NS records identify the DNS servers that are authoritative for the zone and are accompanied by the appropriate address (A) records and pointer (PTR) records. Because a stub zone is read only, the administrator of a stub zone server cannot modify its resource records. Instead, the records must be modified in the original primary zone.

The use of a stub zone is simply to bypass the tree, much like conditional forwarding. When a client contacts a DNS server with a query that is directed to a stub zone on that DNS server, the DNS server automatically sends the query to the DNS servers that are authoritative for the zone.

When a DNS server loads a stub zone, it will query the zone's primary server for the SOA, NS, and A records. All updates also are pulled from the primary zone server. A stub zone can be Active Directory Integrated, but it is not necessary for it to be.

DNS and the Internet

One of the issues that you might run into with an Active Directory network is whether you should select a domain name that is already used on the Internet for an Active Directory domain. For example, a company that uses company.com as its domain name for Internet services might also want to use company.com for the root domain of its Active Directory forest. Using that same domain name can cause a serious security breach, because Internet users could potentially access and infiltrate the root domain of the forest. There are a few ways to handle security with the name issue.

- Select a different domain name for the Active Directory domains, for example, Company.local.

- Select a subdomain name for the Active Directory; for example, sub.company.com.

- Use Split Brain DNS.

In the first option, you can secure the Active Directory network by simply not using names that are accessible from the Internet. You do not even need to have these names registered on the Internet if you intend to use .local as the domain extension. When a query initiates from the public Internet, it will not return any names of servers on the private network. Because the Active Directory database can contain private information about organization members or employees, it is often preferable not to allow any Active Directory members—whether servers, client computers, or DCs—to be accessible from the Internet. Keep in mind that using this method will not prevent you from enabling virtual private network (VPN) access to your internal network, so accessibility is not completely cut off from network users.

In the second option, using a subdomain name of a registered domain name also allows you to have some privacy for the Active Directory network. You can configure DNS so queries are not resolved for the subdomain from the public DNS servers.

It is considered good policy not to use the same name used on the Internet for your Active Directory domain name for security reasons. The use of a private domain name is much easier to keep secure. The use of a subdomain name is also fairly easy to maintain security. You can, however, use the same name on the Internet as you do for the Active Directory and still secure the network from public DNS queries. This is done using the third option—Split Brain DNS.

Split Brain DNS is a system that uses separate internal and external DNS, as shown in Figure 3.6. This method requires that there are two separate DNS servers with different DNS records. These servers are updated independently of each other. Security comes from the fact that no DNS server on the public network stores the IP address records of private IP hosts. An Active Directory DC cannot be located, much less infiltrated, by an external IP host, because the external DNS server does not have any resource records for the internal IP DCs or any other internal computers.

The advantages to Split Brain DNS are simple. You can use a registered DNS name without having to register another DNS name. Users who are familiar with the Web DNS name can use that name for all Active Directory queries. You don't need to add another user principal name (UPN) to the forest to allow users to use the domain name with which they are familiar. Moreover, the network is secure from public queries.

Figure 3.6 Split Brain DNS

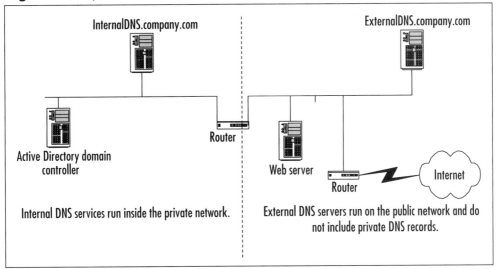

There is one disadvantage to using Split Brain DNS. By having two separately administered DNS zones, the administrative overhead doubles. To configure Split Brain DNS, the internal DNS servers must be configured to forward the queries that they cannot resolve to external DNS servers. External DNS servers must be configured to contain only the records for the external Web, mail, and File Transfer Protocol (FTP) servers, in addition to any hosts that are also to be made public. Internal DNS servers include the DNS records for all the private hosts.

When an internal DNS client tries to resolve a host name to an IP address, the internal DNS server responds to the query. If the internal DNS server is not authoritative for that record, the query will be passed to an external DNS server and then follows the typical recursive query system.

An internal client can still connect to the company's external Web site. This can be done by including the external servers' DNS records in the internal zone, even though they would be duplicates.

When an external DNS client tries to query for a host name that is private to the domain, the query is answered by the external DNS server. Because the external DNS server is not authoritative for that record, and because it is not configured to forward queries to the internal DNS server, the response is that the private host is not found. Figure 3.7 shows the forwarding system in Split Brain DNS.

Figure 3.7 Split Brain Internal DNS Servers Forward Queries Out, but Do Not Receive Queries from the Internet

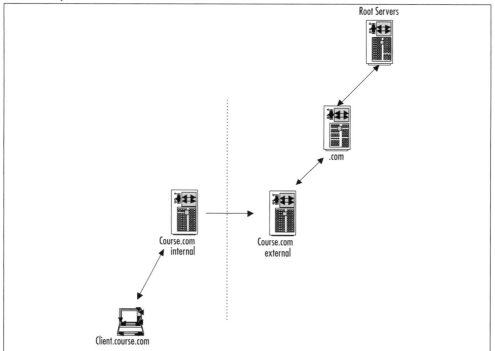

Exercise 3.01

Configuring Split Brain DNS

To complete this exercise, you must have two Windows Server 2003 DNS servers on separate network segments.

1. Log on to the server that is attached to an "external" network.

2. Click **Start**, select the **Administrative Tools menu**, and then select **DNS**. The DNS Management console will open.

3. Right-click the **Server** icon in the left pane, and then select **Configure a DNS Server** from the pop-up menu. The Configure a DNS Server Wizard will start, as shown in Figure 3.8.

Figure 3.8 The Configure a DNS Server Wizard Can Be Started from the DNS Management Console

4. Click **Next**. Select **Create a forward lookup zone**, and then click **Next**.

5. Select **This server maintains the zone** and click **Next**.

6. Provide a zone name (the DNS name of the domain) that will be the same as the DNS name that you will be using internally. This is shown in Figure 3.9.

Figure 3.9 A Zone Is Named the Same as Its DNS Domain Name

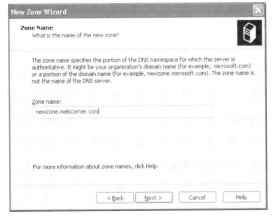

7. Click **Next**. Your screen should resemble Figure 3.10. Select whether you will allow secure, nonsecure, and/or dynamic updates for the zone. Note that you will be able to use only secure updates with Active Directory Integrated zones. For this exercise, select the option to **Allow both nonsecure and secure dynamic updates**.

Figure 3.10 Each Zone Is Configured with the Updates Allowed— Secure, Nonsecure, and Dynamic

8. Click **Next**. You are now given the ability to configure the forwarding of the DNS server queries. You should select the option for **No, it should not forward queries**. This option will still allow you to use root server hints to forward queries outside of the zone.

9. Click **Next**. When the server has completed looking for root hints, you will reach the summary dialog screen for the wizard.

10. Click **Finish**.

11. Log on to the DNS server that is connected to your "internal" network.

12. Open the DNS Management console and begin the Configure a DNS Server Wizard.

13. Select **Create a forward lookup zone**.

14. Select **This server maintains the zone** and click **Next**.

15. Provide the same zone name as you used for the external DNS server.

16. Select the option to **Allow both nonsecure and secure dynamic updates**.

17. The next screen is different from the "external" DNS server configuration. Instead of selecting **No** and allowing the server to look
for root hints, you will select **Yes** and configure the server to forward queries to the "external" DNS server's IP address. This is
shown in Figure 3.11.

Figure 3.11 The Internal DNS Server in Split Brain DNS Points to the
External DNS Server

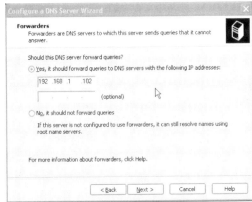

18. At the summary screen, click **Finish**.

Windows Server 2003 supports the DNS Security Extensions (DNSSEC) protocol. This protocol is defined in Request for Comments (RFC) 2535, "Domain
Name System Security Extensions," which you can find at www.ietf.org/rfc/
rfc2535.txt?number=2535. As a new feature to Windows Server 2003, this protocol
can be used with Windows Server 2003 DNS servers, or with compatible third-party
DNS servers to ensure that DNS data is secured in transit.

Round Robin DNS

Round Robin DNS provides a performance boost to DNS through its design. A small
organization would probably not need to have Round Robin DNS. Small organizations often have few servers that provide identical services to the network. However, in
an organization that has, for example, more than 50,000 clients, DNS performance
would likely benefit from a boost. In a large organization, usually one or more services
are provided in duplicate. Web servers are typically configured with Round Robin
DNS because there can be several of them providing the same services.

Round Robin DNS works in a similar fashion to a cluster in which multiple
servers act as a single system when viewed from a client's perspective. In this type of

system, multiple servers are each assigned the same IP address. When a client resolves the name of a server, it will forward the request to the DNS server, and it will respond with one of the IP addresses. The servers take turns in a "round robin" method; hence, the name.

Using a pool of DNS records increases performance because no single server becomes so overloaded with client requests that it slows down. Instead, another server takes over as each new client is redirected to a different server. Another benefit to Round Robin DNS is that, once configured, you can increase performance simply by adding additional DNS records for each additional server. You do not need to reconfigure any DNS clients.

Increasing Performance with Clusters

Windows Server 2003 offers two methods for increasing performance through clusters. Because the DNS service that runs on Windows Server 2003 supports clustering, you can use either method to ensure a highly available DNS server.

- Cluster services
- Network load balancing

Cluster services are intended for systems with shared disk storage. A cluster can be created with multiple servers, but they all share a storage system of some type. If you are using a storage area network (SAN), you should select cluster services for the cluster. Cluster services are automatically installed as part of Windows Server 2003. To configure a cluster, open Cluster Administrator.

Network load balancing is a cluster of servers that provide the same services. By using network load balancing, users contact the IP address of the cluster in order to use the services that are shared by the cluster.

When using either method, DNS will provide faster responses to queries because the cluster will have more resources available for DNS to use.

Configuring & Implementing...

Active Directory and DNS

One of the main requirements that Active Directory has of any DNS system is that it supports Service Locator Resource Records (SRV). The SRV record allows multiple servers to provide the same type of service, such as peer DCs, on the same network. Furthermore, a query of SRV records can return multiple results for that type of service. For example, a DNS client can query for any DC. Instead of receiving only one result, the response would be several DC IP addresses. This process enhances performance of the network because a DC that was down or too busy is simply one of the crowd rather than the first and only response received from the query.

Each DC registers multiple SRV resource records as well as an A record, so that it can function as a standard TCP/IP-based host on the network.

Active Directory has an additional feature for DNS that is not available in any third-party DNS service—Active Directory integrated zones. An Active Directory Integrated zone is stored in the Active Directory database. Because the database is replicated throughout the network, this means that the zone has redundancy and is updated in the same multimaster fashion as the rest of the Active Directory database. DNS records can be updated on any DNS server and then replicated to all other DCs that contain that copy of the zone. DNS integration into the Active Directory is optional. However, once an Active Directory Integrated zone is created, all the DCs within the domain receive the zone data, *unless you create an application directory partition*. Application directory partitions are new with Windows Server 2003. They allow you to subdivide the data that is included in applications that integrate with Active Directory and replicate that data only to specified DCs. Using an Application directory partition with DNS allows you to select only the DCs that should have DNS zone data. These servers will perform multimaster replication of the zone data *only among themselves*. This reduces the impact on the network when updates are made. When you have multimaster replication, there is always the opportunity for a conflict to occur. For example, when two administrators each enter a new A record for the same host name into an Active Directory Integrated zone on different DNS servers, there will be a conflict when those zone changes are replicated throughout the network. With Active Directory, the last A record entered will "win" the conflict and be written to the zone.

If not using Active Directory Integrated zones, you are left only with standard text-based file storage of the zone. The standard text-based method allows for one primary zone server and anywhere from zero to multiple secondary zone servers. Text files for DNS zones are stored with the .dns extension on a Windows Server 2003 DNS server in the %SystemRoot%\System32\DNS directory. The first part of the name of the file is also the name of the zone.

TEST DAY TIP

You should review the keys to naming and planning a DNS namespace design for Active Directory, and be prepared to answer design questions that include an existing DNS infrastructure at the time the DNS planning begins.

EXAM WARNING

Be on the lookout for exam questions that distinguish Active Directory Integrated zones. Remember that these zones are synonymous with secure updates. When a question calls for secure DDNS, then an Active Directory

Integrated zone is required. Active Directory Integrated zones require you to have DNS servers that are also DCs.

When you plan DNS, you should consider how you will maintain it. When you use DNS under Windows Server 2003, you will have some capabilities that will reduce administration. For example, Windows Server 2003 DNS provides a time-stamp method for clearing out old records from the zone. This is helpful administratively because it does not require an administrator to determine whether a record should be removed from the zone. It is best used with DDNS, so that hosts can reregister their IP addresses and host names after old records have been scavenged.

EXERCISE 3.02

CONFIGURING DNS FOR AGING AND SCAVENGING

1. On a DNS server, open the DNS Management console.

2. In the left pane, navigate to the Forward Lookup zone for which you will configure aging.

3. Right-click the zone and select **Properties** in the pop-up menu.

4. The General tab should already be selected. Click the **Aging** button as shown in Figure 3.12.

Figure 3.12 The Aging Button Is Found on the General Tab of the Zone's Properties Dialog

5. Note that the box for Scavenging stale resource records is by default unchecked. Click the box to check it.

6. The default Refresh and No Refresh time intervals are set to seven days, as shown in Figure 3.13.

Figure 3.13 You Can Change the Refresh and No Refresh Time Intervals to Suit Your Network's Aging and Scavenging Requirements

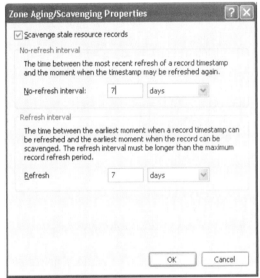

7. Click **OK** to close the Aging and Scavenging dialog box.

8. Click **OK** to close the zone Properties dialog box.

When you plan your Active Directory namespace, consider two aspects of your Active Directory design:

■ How many forests will you have?

■ How many domains will you have in each forest?

The answers to those two questions will tell you how many DNS namespaces you need to plan for. Each domain will require a separate DNS name. The domains are logical divisions of the forest. They are also considered an administrative division (remember that the forest is the final administrative division). Each domain can have a separate password and account lockout policy. However, organizational units (OUs) within the domain can be used to delegate administrative duties of portions of the network to a selected group or user.

A typical DNS plan for Active Directory will provide separate DNS zones for each domain. Furthermore, it will specify that there are at least two DNS servers for each zone. These can be the same two DNS servers carrying multiple zones, or different ones holding only one zone.

Planning the namespace should be done very carefully, although Windows Server 2003 offers more flexibility than in the past. It is difficult (although no longer impossible) to change an Active Directory domain's name. Merging domains must be handled with special programs such as a third-party migration tool, as must be splitting of domains. These processes will directly affect DNS host names and the A and PTR records associated with them.

Part of DNS design planning is analysis of the existing network topology. Wide area network (WAN) links can cause a problem if they are unstable or have a significant outage. For those organizations that have multiple locations with WAN links between them, you should consider placing at least one DNS server in each site that is separated from other sites by unstable WAN links. Each DNS client should be configured with two DNS servers' IP addresses. When you place your DNS servers on the network, you should also keep in mind where the DCs are located. DNS servers must be available to all Active Directory DCs and clients at all times. If a DNS server cannot be located, communication ceases. This is the purpose behind using at least two DNS servers for each zone.

Your evaluation of the network topology should include traffic considerations. DNS traffic is fast and small. When the data is returned to a query, it is not the same as querying a large database and receiving a query file of several megabytes in size. Even so, you should look at how replication of DNS zone data across the internetwork will affect traffic. A full zone transfer between a primary zone server and its secondary zone servers can become extensive. Active Directory Integrated zones do not use full zone transfers because they use multimaster replication. For large internetworks, even using Active Directory Integrated zones might cause too much replication traffic on the network because the zone data updates are replicated to all DCs under the default configuration. Under Windows Server 2003, a DNS Application directory partition can be configured to limit the scope of the DNS-driven replication traffic to the selected DCs with DNS.

Namespace planning should incorporate any anticipated (or unanticipated) growth of the network. With a sudden increase in DNS clients, you might need to plan for additional domain names or DNS servers to accommodate them. Of the names themselves, you should consider using names that are meaningful yet somewhat generic. For example, the name "corp.company.com" can be used to hold the users and network resources for a variety of purposes, while the name "color-printers.company.com" implies that the domain hosts only color printers. This can be confusing to users. Even if they are using a specific nickname for a domain today, that name might change or be discarded in the future.

Integrating DNS Designs with Existing Deployments

There are several things that you must be aware of when you integrate a third-party DNS system with Active Directory. You should also be aware of issues that occur when you integrate third-party DNS with Windows Server 2003 DNS. The main question of whether you can use a third party DNS server is answered by a resounding "Yes." You have several options:

- Use only the third-party DNS servers for the entire network, including the new Windows Server 2003 Active Directory.

- Use only Windows Server 2003 DNS for the entire network.

- Use Windows Server 2003 DNS as secondary name servers for existing zones, and third-party DNS servers as the primary name servers, or vice versa.

- Use the third-party DNS services for a selected zone or zones, and Windows Server 2003 DNS for the remaining zones.

- Migrate from a third-party DNS service to Windows Server 2003 DNS before implementing Active Directory.

- Migrate from a third-party DNS service to Windows Server 2003 DNS during or after implementing Active Directory.

- Migrate from an incompatible third-party DNS service to a compatible third-party DNS service before implementing Active Directory.

Your DNS design will drive certain configurations. For example, if you have an existing DNS service that is not compatible with Active Directory and you intend to use the same zone for an Active Directory domain, then you will be forced to migrate to a compatible third-party DNS service or to Windows Server 2003 DNS prior to implementing the first Active Directory domain. Before you decide which route to take, you must first determine the following:

- Is the third-party DNS service compatible with Active Directory?

- Does the third-party DNS service support DDNS (if you are planning to use DDNS)?

- Does the third-party DNS service support DNSSEC (if you are planning to use DNSSEC)?

- Will you be using Active Directory Integrated zones?

If you answer "No" to any of these questions, then you can work only with the third-party DNS service by configuring it as a server for a different zone outside of Active Directory that you forward queries to. You might even be able to use that service in Split Brain DNS for the external server. However, you will not be able to use that third-party DNS server as either a primary or secondary zone server on any zone that serves an Active Directory domain. Table 3.2 lists a variety of common DNS services that are compatible with Active Directory, along with their supported features. Keep in mind that the main feature that all DNS services must include in order to be compatible with Active Directory is Service Locator Resource Records (SRV RRs).

Table 3.2 Compatible DNS Services

Supported Feature	Unix BIND v 9.1.0	Unix BIND 4.9.7	Windows NT 4.0 DNS	Windows Server 2003 DNS
SRV RECORDS	Supported	Supported	Supported	Supported
Dynamic DNS (DDNS)	Supported	Not Available	Not Available	Supported
WINS integration	Not Available	Not Available	Supported	Supported
Active Directory Integrated zones	Not Available	Not Available	Not Available	Supported
Conditional forwarding	Supported	Not Available	Not Available	Supported
Stub zones	Supported	Not Available	Not Available	Supported

You should diagram the existing DNS infrastructure, whether you plan to upgrade, migrate, or integrate it with the Active Directory. The infrastructure diagram will assist you in making decisions on where to place new DNS servers.

Begin your design process by determining how many DNS servers are required for the new Active Directory. You should look at the minimum number of DNS servers to reduce administrative overhead; however, you should always have at least two DNS servers authoritative for any particular zone to provide redundancy and load balancing. You should add servers for the following reasons:

- Increase performance
- Provide additional redundancy
- Provide DNS services locally to a site that is connected via an unstable WAN link
- Reduce the amount of traffic across a WAN that is generated by DNS queries

Developing WINS Designs

Prior to the Active Directory, a Microsoft network used NetBIOS names with TCP/IP, rather than DNS names. To resolve NetBIOS names to IP addresses, the network used the Windows Internet Naming Service, or WINS. WINS was an absolute requirement for a Windows NT network. However, in an Active Directory network it is not required. WINS is required only for those networks that use NetBIOS names, and a network might require NetBIOS names if it has an application that uses NetBIOS naming. An example of such an application is Microsoft Exchange Server.

EXAM WARNING

The exam will expect you to know the behavior of NetBIOS name resolution when using multiple subnets connected by routers. When a client uses NetBIOS naming, that client will communicate by broadcasts to see what other computers are on the subnet. Broadcasts are not allowed across routers. In order to reach other subnets, the computers must use either LMHOSTS files or WINS servers for name resolution across a TCP/IP infrastructure.

NetBIOS depends on broadcasts for hosts on the network to resolve names; a limitation that will affect the design of a WINS network. Because broadcasts are limited to the local subnet, a computer on one subnet will not be aware of the computers on any other subnet. That is, unless you implement either LMHOSTS or WINS. LMHOSTS is the name of the text file that contains NetBIOS names mapped to IP addresses on the network. In its simplest terms, WINS could be considered the shared server version of LMHOSTS.

EXAM WARNING

Look out for questions asking about a client on a subnet that can no longer communicate with a server on a different subnet after the server is renamed. This often points to an incorrect static entry in the WINS database or LMHOSTS file.

It is important to remember that only Microsoft clients can use WINS for NetBIOS name resolution. In order for a computer to register its own name in the WINS database, it must be configured as a WINS client. WINS Proxy servers are used for non-WINS clients such as Unix. It does not matter which subnet the non-WINS clients are on, whether local or other subnet, they must use a WINS Proxy server.

TEST DAY TIP

Review the hub and spoke topology as a design method for WINS. You should also understand how push and pull replication work under WINS.

Design Principles

Your first task in developing a WINS design is to determine whether you need WINS at all. One thing that you need to test for is whether NetBIOS over TCP/IP is being used to communicate across the network. You can do this through the Performance Monitor. Exercise 3.03 shows how to view WINS counters on a local computer. You can use Performance Monitor to connect to remote computers and monitor them as well. Once you determine whether NetBIOS naming is currently needed, your next task is to determine whether the network can function without NetBIOS naming at all. This will require you to test applications and services on a test network in a lab without using NetBIOS, LMHOSTS, or WINS.

EXERCISE 3.03

DETERMINING TO WHAT EXTENT WINS IS USED ON THE NETWORK

1. Click **Start**, then **Administrative Tools**, and select **Performance**.

2. Delete the counters in the existing System Monitor by clicking the **X** above the monitor's moving chart.

3. Add the WINS counters by clicking the **Plus (+)** symbol above the monitor's moving chart, as shown in Figure 3.14.

Figure 3.14 Click the Plus (+) to Add Counters to a Chart

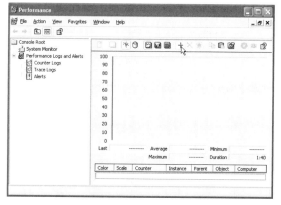

4. In the Add Counters dialog box, drop down the list for **Performance Object** and select **NBT Connection**.

5. Select counters from the list by clicking them and then clicking the **Add** button.

6. If the chart is flat, or nearly flat, such as the one shown in Figure 3.15, then you can surmise that WINS is rarely used on the network and can be discarded.

Figure 3.15 NBT Connection Will Show NetBIOS Usage Across TCP/IP

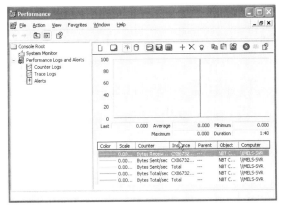

The design of a WINS topology should take into account how WINS servers replicate. Each WINS server pushes or pulls the database from its replication partners. If you configure the replication partners so that they replicate in a domino fashion, it will take several steps for any change to be updated across the network. The time for replication to fully synchronize across all WINS servers is called *convergence time*. The longer convergence takes, the higher the likelihood of errors. To reduce convergence time, you can create a hub and spoke topology in which all WINS servers replicate with a central WINS server. In this topology, you will have the result of a two-step replication process at any point in time when an update is made on any WINS server in the network.

Windows Server 2003 DNS is compatible with WINS. You can use both in a network environment that has WINS clients and DNS clients.

Keep in mind that WINS is a flat file database. All names are considered equal, and as such, must be unique. This means that you can have only one computer named Ned and one computer named Joe. When there are two computers configured with the same NetBIOS name, only the first will be able to access the network.

Older Microsoft networks not only used WINS, but also transmitted data across NetBEUI, a protocol that does not incorporate a network layer. Without a network layer, NetBEUI is not routable. However, NetBIOS can be routed over TCP/IP or even over IPX. In the Windows Server 2003 operating system, NetBIOS is only routed over TCP/IP, if it is used at all.

If you determine that you will install or upgrade an existing WINS network, you must first determine whether the hardware of your server will be sufficient for WINS. WINS servers use their hard disks quite heavily, so you should make certain that you have sufficient hard disk performance.

You should also determine how many WINS servers you should deploy. A single WINS server with sufficient hardware and network performance can provide services to 10,000 clients. You should always plan for at least two WINS servers for redundancy.

WINS has the ability to integrate with DNS so that DNS clients can use DNS to look up records in the WINS database. This helps in the case of a network that has client computers running non-Microsoft operating systems, such as Unix or Linux. To use the WINS Lookup Integration feature, you must add a special WINS resource record for the WINS servers on the network. This resource record is available only within a Windows Server 2003 or Windows 2000 Server DNS.

From the client perspective, you should be aware of how the node types will affect the communication preferences of the client computer. Node types affect the type of WINS traffic that traverses the network. For example, if you want to avoid all broadcast traffic, you would configure WINS clients to be p-nodes because they do not invoke broadcasts to resolve NetBIOS names. You can configure DHCP to tell a computer what type of WINS node it will be. The options you have are:

- **b-node** A b-node depends on broadcasts to register and resolve names. If there are no WINS servers configured, this is the default node type used.

- **h-node** An h-node will search the configured WINS server first, and then resort to broadcasts, followed by LMHOSTS, and then DNS to register and resolve names.

- **m-node** The m-node is the opposite of an h-node. It will broadcast first, and then search the configured WINS server.

- **p-node** A p-node uses only point-to-point connections with a configured WINS server.

Active Directory Requirements

Windows Server 2003 Active Directory does not require WINS. In fact, when you install a Windows Server 2003 member server and then promote it to a DC, you will never be prompted to install WINS, whether there is a WINS server on the network already or not. The WINS console will not be available until you actually install

WINS as an added feature. There are some circumstances in which you will need NetBIOS naming and WINS on the network:

- You are running legacy applications that use NetBIOS naming.

- You have an existing Windows NT 4.0 network.

- A domain in your Active Directory forest has an external trust relationship to a Windows NT 4.0 domain. (Realms and other Active Directory domains use DNS, not WINS.)

- Some clients on the network require NetBIOS naming in order to locate other network hosts.

Design Features

Even though WINS is not a requirement for Windows Server 2003 to function normally in a pure Active Directory environment, Windows Server 2003 brings new functionality to WINS. When you install WINS on the network, you can configure up to 12 WINS servers on a Windows XP or Windows 2000 WINS client to provide redundancy. You can have many more on the network if you need them for performance reasons. The new features that Windows Server 2003 WINS brings are record filtering and replication partner blocking.

Record Filtering

When your network uses an extensive WINS installation, you could have thousands of records in the WINS database. WINS can have both static and dynamic entries in the database. If there is a problem with connectivity for a particular network node, you might need to find that node's entry in the WINS database to see if there is an error with the entry or if there is some other problem that needs attention. Sifting through thousands of records can be extremely time consuming.

WINS under Windows Server 2003 has the new capability to filter records. By using record filtering with a search function, you can specify the records that you are looking for and quickly locate them. You have the ability to specify the record type, its owner, its name, or its IP address. You can further look for a group of records matching a name pattern or search for all the WINS records within an entire IP subnet. Figure 3.16 shows the filter options.

Figure 3.16 You Can Filter Records to Display Only Those that Apply to Your Criteria

Replication Partner Blocking

One of the difficulties in managing a WINS topology is that replication is not easy to manage and direct. Windows Server 2003 brings a feature to WINS that puts an end to this limitation—Replication Partner Blocking. When you implement Replication Partner Blocking, you can do any of the following:

- You can define the replication partner list to accept record updates only by specific WINS servers.
- You can define a list of WINS servers to block record updates.

Phasing Out WINS

WINS can be used in a combination WINS/DNS environment. Alternatively, you might consider phasing WINS out completely. To do so, you should leverage the DNS network and monitor the NetBIOS usage on the network. It might turn out that only one application requires a NetBIOS name while everything else on the network is solely DNS-aware. When this is the case, you can replace the application or retire it. Optionally, you might decide to implement LMHOSTS files for the clients that use the NetBIOS application, which should be considered if there are very few clients that use NetBIOS and only one or two applications on the network that require it.

Developing DHCP Approach

The Dynamic Host Configuration Protocol (DHCP) has saved thousands of hours of IP address management for administrators. Instead of manually configuring each computer with its own IP address, retiring computers and putting their IP addresses back into the available pool, and ensuring that there are no conflicts on the network, DHCP handles the entire task seamlessly and behind the scenes. Although the main function of DHCP is to deliver an IP address to a DHCP client, it also provides additional information such as the DNS server addresses, WINS server addresses, domain name suffix, and more.

> ### TEST DAY TIP
>
> Review the way in which DHCP traffic is affected by placement of DHCP servers. For example, when servers are placed locally, the traffic remains on the subnet. You should also understand how subnetting works when designing DHCP scopes.

DHCP Background

The way DHCP works is fairly simple. Using a client/server model, a DHCP server maintains a pool of IP addresses. DHCP clients request and obtain leases for IP addresses during the boot process. DHCP is derived from the Bootstrap Protocol (BOOTP), which was a protocol typically used to allow clients to boot from the network rather than from a hard drive. Through this boot process, BOOTP assigned an IP address dynamically to the client computer.

Some benefits of using a Windows Server 2003 DHCP server include:

- **DNS integration** Windows Server 2003 DHCP integrates directly with DDNS. When a computer obtains a lease for an IP address, the DHCP server can then register or update the computer's address (A) records and pointer (PTR) records in the DNS database via Dynamic DNS on behalf of the client computer. The result of the two—DHCP used with DDNS—is true dynamic IP address management. Any computer can start up on the network and receive an IP address that is further registered in the DNS name server.

- **Multicast address allocation** The Windows Server 2003 DHCP can assign IP addresses to multicast groups in addition to the standard individual hosts. Multicast addresses are used to communicate with groups such as server clusters using network load balancing.

- **Detection of unauthorized DHCP servers** By restricting DHCP servers to those that are authorized, you can prevent conflicts and problems on the network. An administrator must configure Active Directory to recognize the DHCP server before it begins functioning on the network. The Windows Server 2003 DHCP service contacts Active Directory to determine whether it is an authorized DHCP server. The Active Directory also enables you to configure which clients a DHCP Server can service.

- **Enhanced monitoring** With the Windows Server 2003 DHCP service, you have the ability to monitor the pool of IP addresses and receive notification when the address pool is utilized at a threshold level. For example, you might monitor for a threshold of 90 percent or above.

- **Vendor and user classes** Vendor and user classes enable you to distinguish the types of machines that are obtaining DHCP leases. For example, you can use a predefined class to determine which users are remote access clients.

- **Clustering** Windows Server 2003 DHCP services support clustering. Through a cluster, you can ensure a higher reliability and availability of DHCP services to clients.

Figure 3.17 illustrates the negotiation between a DHCP client and server when the client boots up on the network.

Figure 3.17 The DHCP Negotiation Process

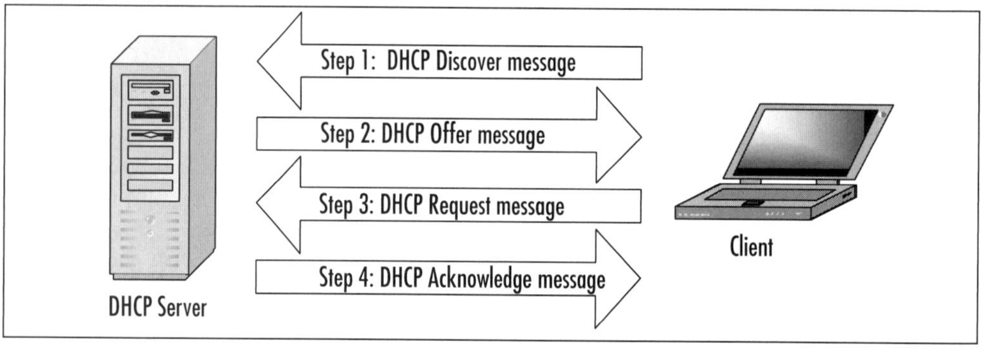

The negotiation process consists of only four messages, two from the client and two from the server. The first message is the DHCP Discover message from the client to the server. This message looks to a DHCP server and asks for an IP address lease. The second message is the DHCP Offer message responding from the server to the client. A DHCP Offer tells the client that the server has an IP address available. The third message is a DHCP Request message from the client to the server. In this message, the client accepts the offer and requests the IP address for lease. The fourth and final message is the DHCP Acknowledge message from the server to the client. With the DHCP Acknowledge message, the server officially assigns the IP address lease to the client.

 EXAM WARNING

You should be able to identify the DNS default order of name resolution. A computer will search its local cache first, its HOSTS file second, and then it will try DNS. It can further search WINS, broadcast, and the LMHOSTS file.

DHCP Design Principles

DHCP is heavily reliant on the network topology and is heavily relied on by the hosts within the network. For DHCP to function at an optimal level, client computers must be able to access at least one DHCP server at all times.

When you develop a DHCP approach for your network, you have some things to consider:

- How many clients will be using DHCP for IP addresses?

- Where are these clients located and what roles do they have?

- What does the network topology look like?

- Are there any unstable WAN links that might cause a network outage if DHCP clients cannot contact a DHCP server for an IP address lease?

- Are there any clients that cannot use DHCP?

- Are there any clients that will be using BOOTP?

- Which IP addresses are dedicated and must be held outside the IP address pool?

- Will you be using Dynamic DNS?

Each DHCP server requires a statically applied IP address for renewal of IP address leases. For example, let's say that a computer receives an IP address from the DHCP server while the DHCP server's IP address is 192.168.1.1. Then, the DHCP server's IP address changes to 192.168.1.2. The client cannot renew the lease because it tries to contact the 192.168.1.1 address. Therefore, the client registers a new address with the 192.168.1.2 address. When the server's IP address changes again, the same process occurs. To avoid this, you must have a static IP address assigned to the DHCP server. If you've configured BOOTP forwarding on your router, and then you change the IP address of the DHCP server, then BOOTP will no longer forward requests. Of course, you can see a "chicken and egg" problem evolving if you try to use a dynamic IP address on a DHCP server. If the server receives a dynamic address, where did it originate from? The DHCP server would have to deliver its own IP address to itself because it would have the active scope for that segment.

DHCP clients do not wait for the DHCP lease to be over before beginning renewal. Instead, they begin the renewal at the point when 50 percent of the lease is up. For example, when a client has a 10-day lease, then after 5 days, the client sends the DHCP Request message to the DHCP server. If the server agrees to renew the lease, it responds with a DHCP Acknowledge message. If the client does not receive the DHCP Acknowledge response, the client waits for 50 percent of the remaining time (at 7.5 days since the original lease was made) before sending another DHCP Request message. This is repeated at another 50 percent of remaining time, or at 8.75 days since the original IP address lease. If the client cannot renew the address, or if the DHCP server sends a DHCP Not Acknowledged response, then the client must begin a new lease process.

There are only a couple of design requirements with DHCP:

- You should have at least two DHCP servers to ensure redundancy. You can use clustering to ensure availability, but also keep in mind that two separate DHCP servers at different locations in the network can prevent DHCP problems resulting from a network link failure.

- You must either provide a DHCP server on each network segment or con-figure routers in between those segments to forward the DHCP messages.

When planning the DHCP servers, the network topology comes into play. It is critical that you place DHCP servers at the locations that are most available to the computers that need IP addresses.

Placing DHCP Servers

Configuring & Implementing...

I once consulted for a company whose IT Department decided that central-izing all servers to a single site would be best for everyone. This company had a large Novell NetWare implementation, as well as a significant Microsoft implementation, consisting of several hundred servers and at least 60,000 clients. One of the services that the IT Department decided to "bring in-house" and manage from a single location was DHCP. They installed DHCP servers at their site and defined them as the only authorized DHCP servers. They configured BOOTP and DHCP forwarding on all the routers. They brought all the former DHCP servers down. And the system worked. Yes, they had higher network traffic on the WAN, but all systems received their IP addresses.

There was still a flaw in the design, and they didn't see it coming. During the time that I worked on a project at one of the satellite offices,

Continued

(Continued)

which had about 4000 employees, the WAN link to the headquarters went down. The DHCP lease was short enough that not one system had an existing IP address leased, nor could it obtain an IP address. Four thousand people were unproductive while local administrators went from desk to desk assigning static IP addresses as a stopgap measure. When the WAN finally came back up, the statically assigned IP addresses conflicted with the newly DHCP-leased IP addresses. The local administrators had to undo each desktop's network configuration a second time.

These are the types of situations that a poor network design will cause. You should always assume that network links can be unstable, even if they've never been a problem in the past. You should take the time to think about what would happen if a network link went down. Distribute DHCP servers near large concentrations of DHCP client computers. Implement server-side conflict detection so that when an alternative address configuration is used, there won't be a problem when the server comes back online. Implement a failover method such as:

- **Standby server** The standby DHCP server must be manually transitioned and might not be as easy to actually use in failover as other methods. In a standby server configuration, you configure a DHCP server with an identical scope. This server will be brought online only in the event of a failure of the first server.

- **Split scopes** Two (or more) DHCP servers are configured with the same scope, except that each server is also configured to exclude part of the scope. If one of the servers fails, the other continues to provide DHCP services. You can use split scopes with servers that are placed on separate subnets to provide failover in the event of server failure or even subnet failure. When configuring the split scope, you do not need to split the scope in equal portions. You should place the larger amount of the scope on the server that is local to the subnet that is being served.

- **Clustered server** A clustered server will provide failover; however, it will do little to correct the problems with a failed network link.

When your client computers support it, you should consider using Automatic Private IP Addressing (APIPA) for a stopgap measure when DHCP fails or have an alternate IP configuration that can go into effect. APIPA is an

Continued

(Continued)

addressing technique that enables a client to assign itself an IP address in the range of 169.254.0.0 with a submask 255.255.0.0.

Figure 3.18 shows the TCP/IP Properties dialog for a network connection on a Windows XP Professional computer. As you can see, a client computer with an alternate IP configuration can continue to function on the network even if the DHCP server is not able to provide a lease.

Figure 3.18 Alternate IP Address Configuration Can Be Used Instead of APIPA

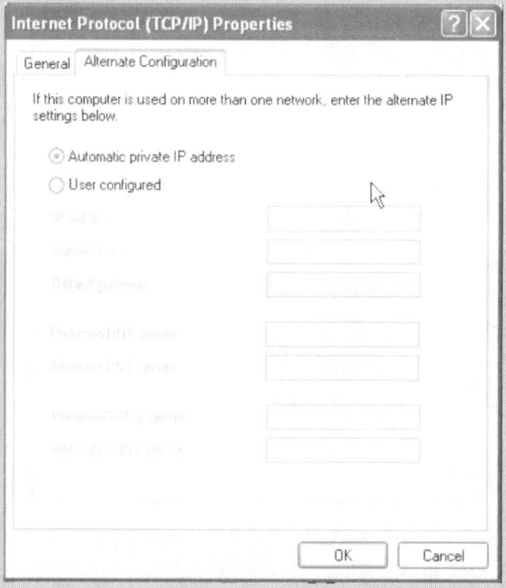

DHCP Servers and Placement

The number of DHCP servers you need on a network is driven by the number of clients, availability requirements for the DHCP server, and the network topology. The number of clients that a DHCP server can serve varies based on the hardware of the server and whether it provides multiple roles or is strictly a DHCP server. Most can provide IP addresses to thousands of hosts. Server hardware that will have the greatest impact on DHCP performance includes the network interface and hard disk. The faster the network interface card (NIC) and disk access, the better. In addition, multiple NICs will greatly improve performance, because NIC speed in no way compares to the speed of the internal PC hardware, and adding NICs literally relieves a bottleneck.

The availability of the DHCP services to the network drives multiple DHCP servers. You must have at least two DHCP servers. You might want to cluster the server if you have a large scope of addresses that are provided to a network segment.

The network topology will drive additional servers as well. This is something that must be reviewed and then planned. Ideally, a network should have a DHCP server on each segment, although this becomes impractical. Because you can configure routers to forward DHCP requests using a DHCP Relay Agent, you can place DHCP servers at any location on the network. Therefore, you should probably look at the unstable WAN links as the deciding factors for additional DHCP servers. A network that has a highly unstable satellite link to a location that has thousands of clients will require its own DHCP server. However, a network with a highly unstable satellite link to a location that has only a few clients will probably be better served by a statically applied IP address or alternate IP configuration used with DHCP from across the link.

DHCP Design Features

When you plan the design around a network service, you must take into account its features. One of the features of DHCP is also a limitation—DHCP Relay Agents. DHCP Relay Agents are used in networks that use routing between subnets and do not have DHCP servers on those subnets. They provide a way to move DHCP data through the network.

Another feature of DHCP is its ability to integrate with DNS. These two services running congruently can automate IP addressing management to a great degree. Let's take a closer look.

DHCP Relays

The DHCP Discover message is a broadcast message. Broadcasts are kept within the same segment unless they are specifically routed. Because of this issue, you must configure a DHCP Relay Agent on a router in order to ensure that messages can be forwarded to the DHCP server, or you can configure the router to forward BOOTP and DHCP messages. Without a DHCP Relay Agent or forwarding configuration, a router will by default reject DHCP broadcast messages. With the Relay Agent, a router can accept broadcast messages from DHCP clients on the local subnet, and then forward them to the DHCP server. The server replies to the DHCP Relay Agent, and the server's IP address is broadcast back to the client. From that point forward, the client communicates directly with the DHCP server. In Figure 3.19, you will see a network topology showing which routers would require DHCP Relay Agents. As you can see, the subnets containing client computers are indicated by ellipses. The DHCP Relay Agent is required only on routers leading to subnets without clients. In the example, one DHCP server provides DHCP services to two subnets, and the other DHCP server provides DHCP services to its own subnet.

Figure 3.19 Routers Require DHCP Relay Agents in Order to Forward Broadcasts Between DHCP Servers and Clients

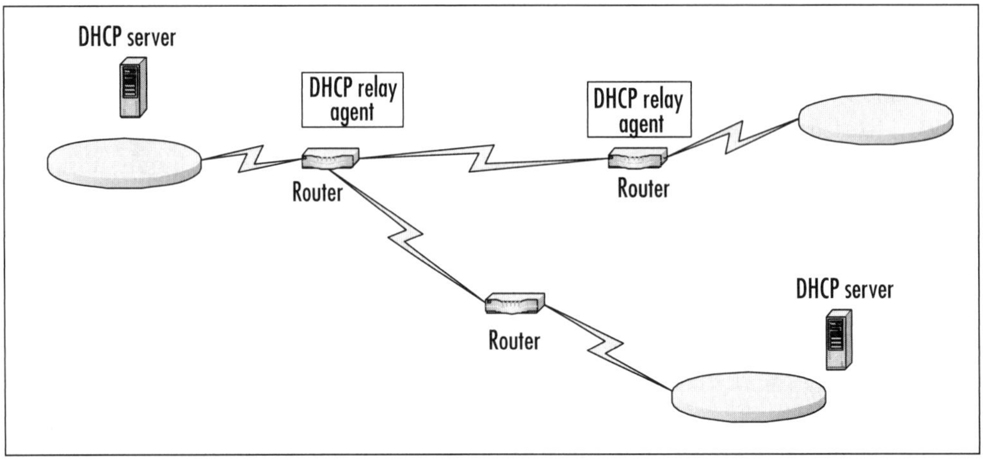

DHCP servers can be configured with multiple network interfaces so that they can directly communicate on multiple network segments. Multihoming a DHCP server works only in cases where the subnets are located in the same geographic location. For a local area network (LAN) with many subnets, a multihomed DHCP server is limited to serving only as many networks as NICs it can contain.

EXERCISE 3.04

CONFIGURING A DHCP SCOPE

This exercise walks you through the configuration of a DHCP scope. Before you configure a scope, you must install the DHCP service.

1. To install the DHCP service, click **Start** and then **Control Panel**.

2. Select **Add or Remove Programs**.

3. Click **Add or Remove Windows Components**.

4. Select **Networking Services** and click the **Details** button.

5. Check the box for **Dynamic Host Configuration Protocol (DHCP)** and click **OK**.

6. You will be returned to the Add or Remove Windows Components dialog screen. Click **Next**.

7. The DHCP Service will require a statically applied IP address and prompt you to change to a static IP address if the server currently uses a DHCP address.

8. Click **Start**, then **Administrative Tools**, and select **DHCP**.

9. Right-click the server and select **New Scope**, as shown in Figure 3.20.

Figure 3.20 Creating a New Scope Is an Option in the Pop-Up Menu that Appears when You Right-Click a Server in the DHCP Console

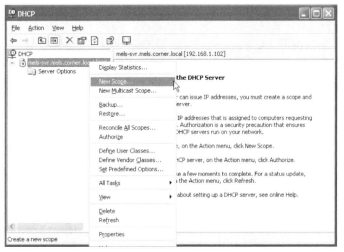

10. The New Scope wizard will start. Click **Next**.

11. In the Scope Name screen, provide a name and description for the scope. Click **Next**.

12. In the screen shown in Figure 3.21, type the address range that will be delivered by the scope. Click **Next**.

Figure 3.21 The Address Pool Is the Range of IP Addresses that Are Delivered by the Scope

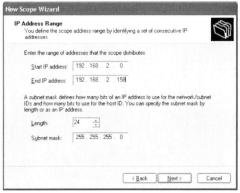

13. The following dialog allows you to eliminate certain IP addresses from being part of the IP address pool. These addresses can be reserved for use in static IP address assignments. The Exclusions screen is shown in Figure 3.22. Click **Next**. You can use the exclusion to create a split scope. You should configure the exclusion on two or more servers such that each of the servers has a separate portion of the scope without any duplication of IP addresses.

Figure 3.22 You Can Exclude IP Addresses that Should Not Be Delivered by a Scope, Even if They Are Included in the Address Range

14. You are next shown a screen where you can configure the lease duration. The default time period is eight days. You should select a longer period of time if you have little change on the network. You should configure a shorter period of time if you have an active network with many installs, moves, adds, changes, and retirements. Click **Next**.

15. You are next asked whether you want to configure DHCP options. Select the option for **Yes** and click **Next**.

16. The first DHCP option you can configure is the gateway address for the scope. This is important. When a client leases an IP address from the DHCP server, this will be the address of the router that it should forward IP messages to when the client is not on the current network. This screen is shown in Figure 3.23. Click **Next**.

Figure 3.23 The Gateway Address Is One of the DHCP Options You Can Configure for a Scope

17. The next DHCP option to configure is the DNS name and DNS server IP addresses. Add the correct information and click **Next**.

18. The following screen allows you to input the WINS server IP addresses. Configure these and click **Next**.

19. Before the scope can be used, you must activate it. You can do so in the next dialog screen, or wait until later. Select **Yes**, and then click **Next**.

20. On the final screen of the wizard, click **Finish**.

DHCP and DNS Integration

Dynamic DNS allows a client computer to register its own IP address and host name with a DNS server. Dynamic DNS works well for statically configured IP addresses. However, when a client receives an IP address from a DHCP server, it will not contact a DNS server and register the IP address for DDNS. Instead, the DHCP server must be able to register the IP addresses on behalf of clients.

Windows Server 2003 DHCP offers three options for registering IP addresses in DNS. These options can be configured for an entire server or on a per-scope basis.

■ The default option is that the DHCP server will register the IP address with the authoritative DNS server according to the client request.

■ One option is to configure the DHCP server to always register the IP address of each client.

■   You can also configure the DHCP server to never register the IP address of clients.

To configure either the server or the scope, right-click that object in the left pane of the DHCP console. Select **Properties** from the pop-up menu. Click the **DNS** tab and you will see the options shown in Figure 3.24.

Figure 3.24 A DHCP Scope Can Be Configured to Work with DDNS in Different Ways

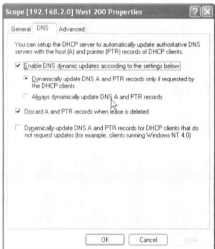

When a Windows XP client boots up and obtains a DHCP lease of an IP address, DHCP sends a Start of Authority (SOA) message to locate the primary DNS server. When the primary DNS server responds, DHCP sends an update request to the DNS server. The server processes the update request and adds the records for the DHCP client.

Integration with Existing Deployments

DHCP is a standard protocol. Being standardized, client computers can integrate with any manufacturer's DHCP service. Problems rarely arise from DHCP not functioning because the manufacturer's implementation is not compatible. Instead of it not working, you are more likely to find that you miss the extra features that Windows Server 2003 DHCP offers.

Developing Remote Access Strategy

Routing and remote access (RRAS) is the software within Windows Server 2003 that allows a server to act as either a router, a remote access server, or both. The functions of a router and a remote access server are nearly identical. A router receives data from one network subnet and forwards it to another network subnet. Likewise, a remote access server receives data from a dial-up line or the Internet, and then forwards that data to the private network. RRAS can be configured to do the following:

- Provide a route between two private networks
- Allow remote networks to establish a dial-up connection to the current private network
- Allow remote users to dial up into the private network
- Act as a VPN gateway
- Perform Network Address Translation (NAT)
- Act as a firewall

EXAM WARNING

The exam will expect you to know the new features of RRAS for design purposes. For example, if a proposed design includes a NAT router, you should know that a VPN design using L2TP will require IPSec NAT transversal.

Design Principles

Designing an RRAS system is a matter of first selecting which functions you need to implement on the network. For example, if you want to implement a VPN gateway, you will select vastly different RRAS options from those needed to provide a firewall. Although organizations are usually very aware of their needs as far as routing data is concerned, the choice between implementing a dial-up RRAS solution versus a VPN RRAS solution is usually a big planning decision. The fact is that VPN and dial-up RRAS provide the same result to the network; the data simply takes a different path. VPNs provide a remote user access to the network. Dial-up solutions provide a remote user access to the network. The difference is that VPNs bring a remote user's data through the Internet connection to the network, while a dial-up solution brings that data in through the telephone network. Often, a VPN solution is much cheaper. It has fewer costs associated because you have to maintain only a single Internet connection instead of tens or even hundreds of telephone lines. Therefore, your design of a remote access solution should include a thorough review of the costs and how they impact the budget for the project and ongoing.

The next design impact is defining the usage of the server. In the case of a route between two private networks, whether through a server using two NICs or a server that routed data between a modem and a NIC, you would look at the traffic patterns on each network and how much traffic you need to estimate and then anticipate growth between those networks. This will tell you what hardware you should select for the server to meet your performance requirements. Keep in mind that the RRAS server's CPU and memory will be the main factors that you will select to meet performance. It is unlikely that hard drive size will have much of an impact.

The other type of usage that you should consider for the RRAS server is whether it will also perform other functions, such as file sharing, printer sharing, or other services. When you combine functions of servers, you lose performance on both sides. When a client needs streaming data through an RRAS router, you don't want that data stream to be interrupted by another user's file download or print job.

The next decision you need to consider is where to place the RRAS server. With routing, you are usually left with few options—place the server between the two subnets. With a dial-up server, you should place the RRAS server close to the location of incoming dial lines. If these can be placed anywhere, then you would want to place the RRAS server close to the resources that users would access. When you have a server that acts as a VPN gateway, you should place the server on the edge of the Internet.

NAT and firewall services performed by an RRAS server are both similar in that they translate data between a public and private network. The firewall forwards data based on an access control list (ACL). NAT takes incoming data from the public network and strips out the public IP address to be replaced by the destination's private IP address. It performs the reverse operation when sending data back out through the public network. Both RRAS configurations must have a NIC connected to the private network and another interface (NIC or modem) connected to the public network.

A key decision when designing a VPN with a firewall is whether to place the VPN server on the Internet or to place it behind the firewall on the private network. If you place the VPN server on the Internet, it will decrypt data before transmitting the data to the firewall and into the network. If you place the VPN server behind the firewall, the data received will already be filtered, and decryption while still on the private network poses a much lower security consideration.

Finally, you should consider the availability and redundancy needs for the network. If the server should be available at all times, then you can configure a cluster. If you need to provide the same services but in two very different locations on the network, you can simply configure two separate RRAS servers in different locations.

TEST DAY TIP

Make sure you know the protocols that you can use under RRAS and when to use these protocols—RIP I, RIP II, OSPF, L2TP, PPTP, IPSec, and EAP.

Requirements

Planning an RRAS implementation begins with a full understanding of the organization's business and technical requirements. Business requirements don't necessarily come packaged neatly so that a single solution is obvious. For example, you might be using DHCP on the internal network. It comes to your attention that there simply aren't enough IP addresses to serve the clients on the network. You can reduce the lease length of the DHCP address to clear out the unused IP addresses. You might register a new IP address to add more to the network. Alternatively, you might consider using NAT. If you select NAT as the best solution, you then need to determine the scope of the project. Where will you implement NAT? Who will be affected? What will you need for hardware, software, and tools? How much will it cost to implement? How will you handle problems such as lack of Internet access? The next step is to begin the planning and design—which manufacturer's solution do you use? Where will you implement it? And so on. Business requirements should always drive a final solution.

When you decide on using Windows Server 2003 RRAS, you will receive the ability to use Remote Access Policies under Group Policy. Group Policy offers the ability to control some of the user-specific RRAS configuration such as the times that users connect to the network, and the methods used to connect. Because these policies are included in Group Policy, you can apply different settings to each OU, domain, or site.

Integrating with Existing Deployments

RRAS can function seamlessly with a network that already has existing routers and remote access servers. Depending on the function that the RRAS server provides, it might be able to integrate with the existing servers. For example, an RRAS server that is configured as a router will simply integrate with the network and forward data to any other router on the network depending on how you configure it. An RRAS server that is configured as a remote access server can be fully integrated with a RADIUS implementation.

Remote Authentication Dial-In User Service

Remote Authentication Dial-In User Service, or RADIUS, is a special system in which remote access servers configured as RADIUS clients interact with a centralized RADIUS server to verify user credentials and audit and log a variety of events. Because RADIUS uses a protocol standard, you can have different manufacturers' remote access servers all sharing data with the RADIUS server. From a security standpoint, this can help an administrator track any security breach attempts.

The process of configuring an RRAS server to work with RADIUS is to configure RRAS as a remote access server, and then configure it to handle RADIUS authentication and RADIUS accounting. Figure 3.25 shows an RRAS server integrated with an existing RADIUS solution.

Figure 3.25 RRAS and Third-Party Remote Access Servers Can Work with a Central RADIUS Server

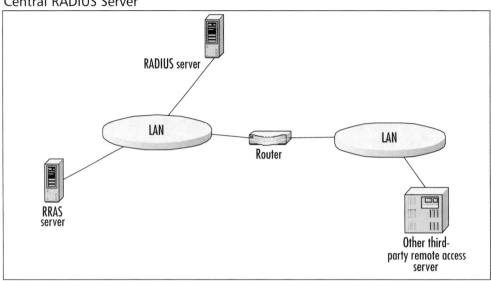

To integrate with RADIUS, the RRAS server must be configured as either a dial-up remote access server or a VPN gateway. These two types of servers authenticate clients from outside the network.

Windows Server 2003 includes a supporting technology for RRAS called the Internet Authentication Service (IAS). IAS can be configured to act as a RADIUS server. IAS can then perform client authentication on behalf of any RRAS server. The way in which RRAS and IAS interact follows a simple process:

1. A remote access client connects, either through dial-up or VPN, to an RRAS server.

2. RRAS needs approval in order to allow the connection, so it sends a request to the RADIUS server, which in this case is IAS.

3. IAS reviews the RADIUS Access-Request message and validates the user's credentials.

4. If the user's credentials are not valid, the connection is terminated.

5. If the user's credentials are valid, the user's Remote Access Policies are then checked.

6. IAS then tells RRAS how to handle the user's remote connection and the link is made.

To configure RRAS, click **Start**, then **Administrative Tools**, and select **Routing and Remote Access Service**. The RRAS console will appear. Right-click a server in the RRAS window and select **Configure and Enable Routing and Remote Access** from the pop-up menu, as shown in Figure 3.26.

Figure 3.26 You Can Configure RRAS in the Routing and Remote Access Service Console

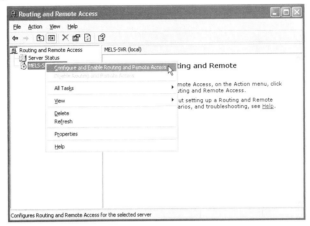

After selecting this option, the RRAS setup wizard allows you to select from predefined roles or a custom configuration, as shown in Figure 3.27.

Figure 3.27 The RRAS Configuration Wizard Has Several Options

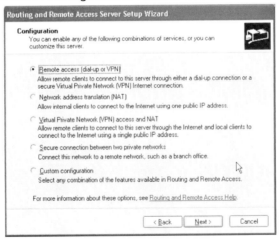

Once RRAS is configured on the server, you will see the tree structure in the RRAS structure that is shown in Figure 3.28.

Figure 3.28 RRAS Servers Are Displayed with Additional Folders in the RRAS Console

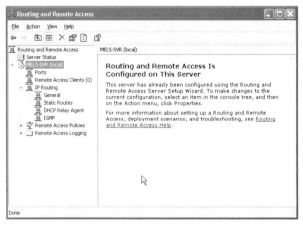

To configure the server for authentication via RADIUS, right-click the server and select **Properties**. Click the **Security** tab, then select **RADIUS authentication** from the drop-down box for Authentication provider, as depicted in Figure 3.29.

Figure 3.29 RADIUS Authentication Is Found on the Security Tab of the RRAS Server Properties Dialog

To configure the server for RADIUS accounting, click the drop-down box for **Accounting provider** on the same Security tab and select **RADIUS Accounting**. Once the RADIUS Authentication and RADIUS Accounting options are selected, the Configure button becomes active and you can add the RADIUS server.

Summary of Exam Objectives

The *Developing the Network Services Infrastructure Designs* exam objective consists of four subobjectives:

- Developing DNS Designs
- Developing WINS Designs
- Developing DHCP Approach
- Developing Remote Access Strategies

DNS is the service that resolves host names to IP addresses, and vice versa. You must develop a DNS design that is capable of interacting with the Windows Server 2003 Active Directory. The DNS design will consist of selecting a DNS namespace that must incorporate each Active Directory domain. The next design consideration is how to configure zones. Finally, you must decide where to place servers. A DNS design should take into account the organization's needs for availability and performance. It should also provide for integration with third-party DNS services.

WINS is the service that resolves NetBIOS names to IP addresses. NetBIOS names are being phased out on Microsoft networks and are not required for a pure Windows Server 2003 implementation. However, some applications require NetBIOS naming. In addition, a network that includes older Microsoft servers and clients will require NetBIOS naming. In these networks, you must develop a WINS design that will provide name resolution services to the network and meet the availability requirements of the organization.

DHCP is the service that leases IP addresses and IP-related information to clients. The DHCP design approach incorporates factors such as the network topology, use of multihomed DHCP servers, the need for DHCP Relay Agents or forwarding configuration on routers, the scopes of IP addresses that are delivered to the subnets, and the number of DHCP servers placed throughout the network. This approach should meet the business objectives for availability and performance.

RRAS is the remote access service incorporated in the Windows Server 2003 operating system. An RRAS server can be configured in a variety of roles, including dial-up remote access server, VPN gateway, router, firewall, and even as a NAT provider. In the RRAS strategy, you must consider whether to have multiple servers, use clustering for availability, or even whether to incorporate the remote access server with a RADIUS server and third-party remote access services.

Exam Objectives Fast Track

Developing the Network Services Infrastructure Designs

☑ Windows Server 2003 Active Directory requires DNS to function.

☑ DNS designs incorporate the namespace, server placement, availability, security, and integration with third-party DNS systems.

☑ Split Brain DNS requires an internal DNS server and an external DNS server, both of which manage the same zone namespace. However, the internal DNS server includes private host records, while the external DNS server provides only public host records.

☑ Round Robin DNS is one method of using multiple DNS records to increase the availability and performance of two or more servers providing identical services.

☑ The WINS service does not need to be designed and implemented unless an application or network clients require it.

☑ WINS is used for resolving NetBIOS names to IP addresses.

☑ DHCP uses broadcast messages for the initial communication between DHCP clients and DHCP servers. These broadcast messages must be forwarded if a DHCP server is not placed on the same network as the DHCP clients.

☑ Windows Server 2003 RRAS can be integrated with RADIUS for client authentication and accounting.

Exam Objectives
Frequently Asked Questions

The following Frequently Asked Questions, answered by the authors of this book, are designed to both measure your understanding of the Exam Objectives presented in this chapter and to assist you with real-life implementation of these concepts. You will also gain access to thousands of other FAQs at *www.ITFAQnet.com*.

Q: What benefit can be derived from splitting a large DNS namespace into multiple smaller subdomains?

A: When a large namespace is split into multiple smaller subdomains, the result is speedier DNS searches.

Q: What is Split Brain DNS?

A: Split Brain DNS refers to the use of two views into the same zone on the network. The public, or external, zone contains only public host records so that a query coming from the public network will return only public host record results. The internal zone contains private records, and queries coming from within the internal network will return private host records. Because the internal DNS server is configured to forward any unknown queries to the external DNS server, queries from the internal network can also return public network results.

Q: How many IP hosts can I have with the name joe on my network using DNS?

A: Because the DNS system is hierarchical and uses fully qualified domain names (FQDNs) that concatenate the common host name with the domain name, you can have one host named joe in each domain on your network. If you have two domains, then you would have joe.domainone.com and joe.domaintwo.com.

Q: Do I need to have WINS on my network if I am migrating from Windows NT 4.0 to Windows Server 2003?

A: The answer could be yes or no depending on your network's configuration. If you have older applications or network clients that require NetBIOS naming, then you will most likely need WINS present on the network.

Q: What are the four phases of the DHCP lease procedure?

A: The four phases of the DHCP lease procedure are as follows:

1. Discover (DHCPDISCOVER) from client to server
2. Offer (DHCPOFFER) from server to client
3. Request (DHCPREQUEST) from client to server
4. Acknowledgment (DHCPACK) from server to client *or* Not Acknowledged (DHCPNACK) from server to client

Q: If I have seven subnets and one DHCP server, will I be able to use DHCP on all the clients?

A: Yes. You will need to either multihome the DHCP server or configure the routers between the subnets to forward the DHCP broadcast messages.

Q: Can I use RRAS with RADIUS?

A: You can implement RADIUS Authentication and RADIUS Accounting on a Windows Server 2003 RRAS server. You can also use RRAS and RADIUS in conjunction with a third-party remote access service.

Self Test

A Quick Answer Key follows the Self Test questions. For complete questions, answers, and explanations to the Self Test questions in this chapter as well as the other chapters in this book, see the Self Test Appendix.

1. You have been hired to design the network services for BlueBell Corp. BlueBell is planning on implementing Windows Server 2003 network services with Active Directory, which will be migrated from their existing Novell NetWare and Unix systems. Which of the following services must you design before implementing these network services?

   A. DHCP
   B. DNS
   C. WINS
   D. RRAS

2. You are the network administrator for Jim's Garages. The Jim's Garages network is distributed throughout the United States and Canada. The main location has several hundred users, while there are 75 satellite locations directly connected to the main location with fewer than 10 users at each site. You want to deploy DHCP. You have configured all satellite offices to use APIPA in the event of a WAN link failure. How many DHCP servers will you require if you want to make certain the DHCP service has high availability to the network?

A. 1

B. 2

C. 75

D. 76

3. You have configured a DHCP server on segment A. Your client is connected to segment B. You cannot obtain an IP address lease. Which of the following can be configured to resolve the problem?

A. DHCP Relay Agent

B. DHCP Discover

C. DHCP Offer

D. DHCP Request

4. You have been monitoring the network traffic on a segment of your network. This segment is one where no client has been able to lease an IP address from the DHCP server that has been configured on a different segment. You find that there is a DHCP message type that is being transmitted on the network. Which of the following messages are you most likely seeing?

A. DHCPDISCOVER

B. DHCPOFFER

C. DHCPREQUEST

D. DHCPACK

5. You are upgrading a Windows NT network to Windows Server 2003. The current network has three domains, which you intend to keep. You want to make certain that each domain has its own DNS zone, and that the solution is redundant. Take into consideration that each zone consists of 5000 or fewer hosts. What is the minimum number of DNS servers that will you need to plan for?

A. 2

B. 3

C. 4

D. 6

6. You are the network administrator for Blue Bell Corp. Blue Bell uses the Web site *www.bluebell.com*. Users are comfortable with the bluebell.com name and are expecting to use that for the Active Directory you are implementing. You are concerned about the security of internal hosts if you use the same

domain name for the Web site as well as the Active Directory. Which of the following can you implement to provide security?

A. Dynamic DNS

B. Round Robin DNS

C. Clustered DNS servers

D. Split Brain DNS

7. You have been recently hired by Jim's Garages to design their DNS network. Jim's Garages has had a heavy load on their existing DNS server and performance has been slow. Which of the following methods can increase performance?

A. Dynamic DNS

B. DHCP

C. Cluster services

D. Split Brain DNS

8. You are the network administrator for Blue Bell Corp. You have 1200 servers that provide network services such as file sharing and printer sharing on the network. These servers are frequently installed, moved, added, changed, or retired from the network. You want to implement an automatic method for managing the DNS record registration for the servers. Which of the following should you implement?

A. Dynamic DNS

B. DHCP

C. Round Robin DNS

D. Split Brain DNS

9. You are the network designer for Jim's Garages. You have been asked by management to use the existing DNS servers for the migration to Windows Server 2003 with Active Directory. Which of the following should you do first?

A. Upgrade the servers to Windows NT 4.0.

B. Contact the manufacturer to find out if the existing DNS system is compatible.

C. Review the network topology to see if there will be sufficient availability.

D. Determine the number and size of each DNS server.

10. Your Unix network uses a version of BIND that is incompatible with Windows Server 2003 Active Directory. You want to maintain the existing BIND implementation for the namespace example.com. Your only Active Directory domain will be named example.local. Which of the following must you do to make this system function?

    A. Nothing, it should work fine using just the existing BIND implementation.

    B. Install another BIND server to manage example.local.

    C. Install a Windows Server 2003 DNS server to manage example.local.

    D. Create two primary zones for example.local.

11. You are the network administrator for Old School. Old School has a Windows NT 4.0 network with a couple of Windows NT 3.51 servers providing DNS and WINS services for name resolution. There is also a Windows NT 4.0 server providing RRAS and DHCP services. You have been given the go-ahead to install a new Windows Server 2003 DC. Your plans are to install the new server hardware with Windows NT 4.0 as a backup domain controller (BDC). Then, you intend to promote it to a primary domain controller (PDC), and finally you want to upgrade it to Windows Server 2003. Before you perform the upgrade to Windows Server 2003, which of the following must you install first to avoid any compatibility problems?

    A. DHCP

    B. WINS

    C. DNS

    D. RRAS

12. As the Webmaster for an intranet, you manage all servers and server design for any application that is shared on the intranet. Management has asked you to share a new application. You find out that the application requires NetBIOS names on the network. Which two of the following methods can you use to resolve NetBIOS names to IP addresses?

    A. WINS

    B. DNS

    C. HOSTS

    D. LMHOSTS

13. You are the network administrator for Fast Trax research department. Your business unit consists of 5000 users. The rest of the company is about 30,000 users. You install a DHCP server to provide IP addresses to your clients who dial in to

your own business unit's remote access server. You find that the server is not providing IP addresses. Which of the following could be the problem?

A.   You did not authorize the DHCP server in Active Directory.

B.   You did not activate the DHCP scope.

C.   You did not configure the routers to forward the DHCP broadcasts.

D.   Any or all of the above.

E.   None of the above.

14.   Your network has a RADIUS server that provides remote access client authentication and accounting services. The network also uses a third-party remote access solution. One of the company's business units wants to have a private remote access server with its own dial-up numbers. They already have a server running Windows Server 2003 that is not being used for any other purpose than DHCP services to 75 client computers. Which of the following is the most cost-effective method to comply with their request yet maintain RADIUS authentication?

A.   Install an additional third-party remote access server for the business unit.

B.   Add another third-party remote access server to the main pool.

C.   Enable and configure RRAS on the existing W2K3 server as a RADIUS client with RADIUS authentication back to the RADIUS server.

D.   Enable and configure DHCP on the existing W2K3 server.

15.   You have been tasked with designing a new Windows Server 2003 Active Directory forest. The network is currently a combination of Novell NetWare, Unix, and Windows NT 4.0. All client computers use HOSTS files and statically applied IP addresses. Your network is expecting to quadruple in the next year due to a merger that is being finalized. You want to reduce administration of IP addresses. Which of the following services must you implement before installing the first Active Directory DC?

A.   DHCP

B.   DNS

C.   WINS

D.   DDNS

16.   You are the network administrator for Black Jack Groceries. You have an existing Windows NT 4.0 domain infrastructure of three domains named HQ, Produce, and Wholesale. The network relies solely on WINS for name resolution. You are planning to install a new Active Directory domain named blackjack.com. You will

then restructure the HQ and Produce domains into blackjack.com. You do not plan to upgrade or restructure the Wholesale domain. All blackjack.com users will require access to the Wholesale domain, and all Wholesale users will require access to blackjack.com. Your company's written security policy prevents the use of LMHOSTS and HOSTS files. Which of the following is required?

A. DHCP must be configured on all servers in the Wholesale domain.

B. DNS must be configured on all servers in the Wholesale domain.

C. WINS must be configured on all DCs in the Wholesale and blackjack.com domains.

D. DNS must be configured on all DCs in the Wholesale and blackjack.com domains.

17. You have a network with two subnets. All the DCs for your Windows NT 4.0 domain named JHN are on Subnet A. WINS and DHCP run on a member server of the JHN domain. You have installed a new Active Directory domain named resources.ababab.com on Subnet B. DNS (which is configured to accept dynamic registrations from clients) runs on the DC dc1.resources.ababab.com. You have attempted to create a trust relationship between JHN and resources.ababab.com and it has failed. Which protocol is most likely at fault?

A. WINS

B. DNS

C. DHCP

D. DDNS

18. You have been hired to plan the WINS configuration for a large internetwork consisting of 50,000 client computers, 558 servers, and 40 DCs. These computers are distributed throughout 78 physical sites, 7 of which are considered "large" because each has over 4000 users. The majority of sites are connected directly to the headquarters site. Your goal is to reduce the WINS convergence time, yet maintain availability of WINS services. Which of the following can help meet that goal?

A. Add WINS to each of the 40 DCs. Have each DC contact its nearest neighbor for WINS replication.

B. Add WINS to a single server located at the headquarters site.

C. Install WINS servers at each large site. Configure all WINS servers to block all other replication partners except for the WINS server at the headquarters site.

D. Install WINS on servers at each large site. Configure all WINS servers to accept all other WINS servers as replication partners.

Self Test Quick Answer Key

For complete questions, answers, and explanations to the Self Test questions in this chapter as well as the other chapters in this book, see the Self Test Appendix.

1.	**B**	10.	**C**
2.	**B**	11.	**C**
3.	**A**	12.	**A, D**
4.	**A**	13.	**D**
5.	**A**	14.	**C**
6.	**D**	15.	**B**
7.	**C**	16.	**C**
8.	**A**	17.	**A**
9.	**B**	18.	**C**

Chapter 4

MCSE 70-297

Designing the Logical Components

Exam Objectives in This Chapter:

Introduction

Now that we have assessed the environment and considered the various design options available to us, it is time to choose the appropriate designs for each component.

We start with naming standards. Before we progress to design components, we must first decide which components are to have standardized naming strategies, whether those strategies extend across all forests, and what the naming conventions should be.

Next we move on to the top level—the forest or forests. We must first decide how many forests are required, their names, and whether they are to be located on a protected internal network or within a DMZ. Then we discuss the number, naming, and hierarchy of domains within each forest and the level of collaboration required between forests as well as between domains in the same forest. This includes the use of trusts to facilitate and optimize collaboration between domains and forests.

Different authentication protocols and standards are used by Windows 2000 and Active Directory from those used by Windows NT. We discuss the client require- ments and how to implement a design that allows for co-existence of multiple client types while providing a secure environment.

Next we discuss the organizational unit (OU) model design and how to select the appropriate model for your organization, based on the requirements of delegation and Group Policy.

This leads nicely to the subject of Group Policy itself—how first you should decide what GPOs can do for you, how they should be managed through delegation, where they need to be applied, and what the appropriate settings are for the default policies as well as for other available user and computer settings.

We then move on to groups and roles; these may be used effectively within an environment to best leverage the granular delegation model offered by Active Directory. We discuss how delegation should be split between data and administration and how roles should be defined, with a predefined subset of functions delegated to each role.

Finally, we discuss the replication design. The data stored within Active Directory must be available to all users in a timely fashion, and changes must be propagated to all locations within an acceptable time period. The replication design must identify site boundaries, subnets that are contained within those sites, how the sites are connected with links, and how this is all brought together to create an optimum replication model.

Defining Standards

Standards exist within every industry and are usually present within organizations and companies. Standards exist to provide consistency and predictability. Imagine the diffi- culty you would experience maintaining any type of machinery without standards—

every bolt would be different from the others, there would be no way to buy a wrench for bolts with any degree of certainty that it would work, and each piece of a machine would be handmade to match its counterpart. In this section, we look at the benefits to standardization in Active Directory design.

Why Standardize?

As mentioned, standardization provides consistency and predictability in a design. In the following sections, we will begin to look at the structure of Active Directory in an effort to see how standardization plays a key part in a successful Active Directory design and deployment. Let's first look at the benefits of a standardized design.

The Benefits

Standardizing a directory or database structure provides the benefit of consistency. In a given directory, you do not want duplicate names for different objects. Likewise, you do not want to list objects in an inconsistent fashion. Computer-based directories are searchable listings of items. Following a naming standard, for example, provides simplified searches. Imagine the phone book without standardized naming conventions. Some names might be listed by first name followed by last name. Others might be listed as last name first, while still others could use initials or address information. The lack of standardized naming in this case would make the directory nearly useless. This lack of standardization could spill over to other areas as well.

Standardization can also provide other benefits. For example, some data structures work more efficiently than others. Providing a standard for design may ensure a more efficient system. Another concern when designing a networked system is security and interaction of applications. Design standardization can ensure consistency in applications and configurations. This standardization can ensure a consistent user experience throughout the network environment. In the next section, we explore how standardization, or a lack thereof, affects administrative overhead.

Administrative Overhead

As administrators, we are expected to be responsible for an ever-growing list of duties. Most administrators consider a blessing any way that administrative overhead can be reduced. Standardization within your organization's Active Directory is certainly a way to reduce administrative overhead. Again, imagine a large organization that does not have a naming standard. You have to connect to a resource somewhere within the enterprise. Your Active Directory implementation will provide access to a resource by name. Inconsistent naming will prove to be an administrative nightmare when it comes to accessing network resources. Likewise, imagine having to create user accounts and then having to support user accounts without a standardized naming system. How many times have you helped a user log on to a PC after someone else has used it? Most users who regularly use a PC enter only their password to gain access to the machine;

the username is usually already entered for the user. Without a naming standard, you will have to manually search your directory for the user's account to provide her with the correct logon information. So, not only does this lack of standardization cause multiple headaches for the person administering this environment—it also adversely affects the users.

Standardization of applications and configuration settings also helps simplify administrative overhead and provide a consistent user experience. In the next section, we begin looking at the Active Directory logical structure and how standards play an integral part in a successful Active Directory design.

Understanding the Scope of the Standards

Because of the design of Active Directory's structure, standardization's scope differs within different parts of the Active Directory. In this section, we analyze various portions of Active Directory and discuss the effects of standardization within the various portions of the Active Directory logical structure. First, we will see how enterprisewide standardization will work within Active Directory. We will determine where standards will work best within the enterprise environment, and we will see what items should be standardized. Next, we will look at forestwide standardization. Again, we will determine where standards will work best within the Active Directory forest design. Finally, we will look at domainwide standardization and how standardization will work best within the Active Directory domains.

Before we can see how standards will aid in the design of our Active Directory infrastructure, we should review the logical structure of Active Directory itself. Active Directory is described as a globally distributed database. This database is organized in two ways: in a logical structure and in a physical structure. The physical structure comprises the servers that host Active Directory, the networks that they utilize for connectivity, and the various objects that are indexed within Active Directory. The physical structures represent actual, tangible entities within the database. The logical structure is broken into a series of containers. These containers are similar to the directories or folders that you see when navigating the file system of your PC using Windows Explorer, for example.

Each logical container serves to organize objects and other containers while providing other administrative capabilities. This logical organization is not mirrored in the physical representation of the dataset and is merely used as a way to logically group objects in some meaningful manner. The forest, for example, is the top level in the Active Directory container hierarchy. This container houses all other containers within the Active Directory logical structure. Before the advent of Microsoft's Active Directory, Windows administrative control rested at the domain level. Within Active Directory, the forest is the seat of administrative power. The forest hosts one or more domains, the directory schema, the global catalog, and a common directory configuration.

The next container within Active Directory's hierarchy is the domain. Domains in Active Directory are basically partitions of the forest. This partitioning helps control replication traffic while providing more granular administrative control.

Finally, the smallest container within the Active Directory logical structure is the organizational unit, or OU. OUs add even more granular administrative control to Active Directory, allowing delegation of control for administrative purposes as well as object grouping and OU nesting to provide a structure to organize Active Directory to mimic the business structure of the organization implementing Active Directory.

Now that we have a basic layout of Active Directory's logical structure, let's take a look at how standardization works with these container objects.

TEST DAY TIP

In designing an Active Directory environment, we focus on the scope of each item in the design. It pays to look at several Active Directory logical diagrams to see how the different containers interact with one another in Active Directory.

Enterprisewide

The term *enterprisewide* implies multiple Active Directory forests. In this situation, a trust relationship or multiple trust relationships exist between multiple forests. Before Windows 2000, security boundaries were defined and implemented by domains. Placing resources in different domains placed those resources in the hands of different administrators. Before Windows 2000, we could basically use domains only to delegate administration. When Microsoft introduced Active Directory with Windows 2000, domains took on a different role in the overall enterprise design. In Active Directory, forests define the security boundaries between administrative factions. *Enterprisewide standardization* refers to common elements between forests. This may refer to trust relationship configurations, remote access policies, VPN settings, or other items that provide a more consistent approach through standards. Enterprisewide standardization is not very common due to the fact that organizations do not typically need to host multiple forests.

The Importance of Name Selection

Let's look at a common enterprisewide standard. All resources in a Microsoft network are accessed via some form of naming system. The traditional naming system uses NetBIOS names. NetBIOS names, in contrast to the Domain Name System (DNS) and Fully Qualified Domain Names (FQDN), do not provide for a hierarchical design. This means that the 15-character name provides the only real name for a system.

If conflicting NetBIOS names exist somewhere within the organization, access will not be available to the conflicting resources. A functional NetBIOS name system design will provide unique names for all systems within an organization.

Forestwide

Because a forest provides the top-level container for Active Directory, the scope of forestwide standardization includes all aspects of a single Active Directory structure, including schema, directory configuration, global catalog, and domains. This standardization would typically be controlled within an organization, compared to enterprisewide standardization, which may affect multiple distinct organizations. Forestwide standardization and several examples are discussed in more detail later in this chapter.

Domainwide

Domainwide standardization works within a single partition of the Active Directory forest. This standardization will affect all objects and accounts housed within the domain, including users, computers, groups, and OUs. Domainwide standardization and examples are discussed in more detail later in this chapter.

What Should You Standardize?

Because certain objects and containers are common throughout a typical Active Directory infrastructure, they lend themselves to standardization. In the following sections, we look at several aspects of Active Directory and discuss typical standardization methods for various Active Directory objects. We also review the benefits we gain when we use standardization for each of these objects.

Any discussion about naming systems and standardization in Active Directory requires an overview of the various naming conventions used within Active Directory. Active Directory provides three different naming references for each object contained within the Active Directory. The naming references are as follows:

- **LDAP relative distinguished name** As the name implies, this provides a unique identity for the object within its parent container. The LDAP relative distinguished name of a user named *joeuser* is CN=joeuser.

- **LDAP distinguished names** These are globally unique. The distinguished name of a user named *joeuser* in the ManagementOrganizationalUnit organizational unit in the mycorp.local domain is CN=joeuser, OU=ManagmentOrganizationalUnit, DC=mycorp, DC=local.

- **Canonical names** These are similar to the distinguished name. The canonical name for our previous example would be Mycorp.local/ ManagementOrganizationalUnit/joeuser.

Let's take a look at usernames, how they can be standardized across the Active Directory, and limitations we need to be aware of when establishing a standard.

EXAM WARNING

Naming convention is very important in network design. We connect to nearly all resources by name. Be sure you understand the different naming conventions; each type has its significance in network design and operations.

Usernames

Because computer directories and networked systems are typically designed to provide information to human beings (users), one of the first concerns when standardizing objects in Active Directory is standardization of user accounts. Your design should reflect a standardized approach to user accounts, providing simplified administration and expandability. The idea here is to make sure that as your company grows, you will have a unique username for each user in your organization.

Although placement of user accounts in different domains or containers provides for global uniqueness in the distinguished name and canonical name, it is best to use a naming standard that provides global uniqueness for relative distinguished names in the event that accounts are moved from domain to domain or container to container. A system of first-name-only user accounts might work for an organization with fewer than 10 employees, but in an organization with hundreds or even thousands of employees, this will likely result in a conflict. Likewise, a first-initial/last-name system could result in the same problems. Many companies settle on a combination of first and last names or an alphanumeric combination of names and relevant numbers. Again, the concern here is the ability to provide unique usernames for each individual in your organization without hitting the 20-character maximum for user accounts. Also, a user account cannot consist entirely of *at* signs (@), spaces, or periods (.). Finally, leading periods or spaces are cropped from usernames. Table 4.1 lists valid usernames based on the previously described criteria for a user named John Quincy Public.

Table 4.1 Valid Usernames for the Hypothetical User John Quincy Public

John	Jpublic
JohnQPublic	JohnPublic
Jpublic0711	JQP0711

All the listings in Table 4.1 are valid user accounts. Again, plan for company expansion and ensure no future overlap problems with accounts; usernames that include the majority of a person's name or that include names with specific numbers tend to provide the greatest amount of expandability and potentially increased security when combining names with specific numbers. Table 4.2 illustrates invalid usernames based on previously described criteria, with a description elaborating why the account is not valid.

Table 4.2 Invalid Usernames for the Hypothetical User John Quincy Public

Invalid Username	Rule Preventing Username Usage
@@@	Username cannot contain all @ symbols
...	Username cannot contain all . symbols
John_Quincy_Public_0711	Username will be truncated beyond 11 characters
____	Username cannot contain all spaces

Now that our usernames are in order, let's take a look at machine names.

Machine Names

Again, the idea here is to implement a naming strategy that simplifies administration while providing unique names for existing systems and expandability for future additions. Different approaches are now in use for machine names. Some organizations use special number systems to identify machines. The number may give information about location, the service the machine provides, or the group responsible for administering the particular machine. Some organizations use a three- or four-character combination to identify the machine's location, followed by another three- or four-character combination to identify the services the machine offers, followed by a number to uniquely identify multiple machines that are providing the same services from the same location.

For example, a machine providing domain controller functionality in Miami might use the airport code for Miami followed by the machine service and a number, MIADC01. An Exchange server in Chicago may have a name like CHIEXC02.

Machine accounts, like user accounts, have a size limitation. Machine account names cannot exceed 15 characters; they cannot consist entirely of spaces, numbers, or periods; and leading spaces or periods are cropped from the name. It is possible to change security settings to allow machine names to contain more than 15 characters, but this practice is not recommended.

Now that we've looked at user and machine names, let's take a look at group names.

EXAM WARNING

Our modern networks have reached a point at which NetBIOS may be disabled on newer systems. Be aware, however, that NetBIOS has not completely disappeared from the network landscape; consequently, the NetBIOS questions will not simply disappear either.

Group Names

Like user accounts and machine accounts, there are several different approaches to group names. A group name standard should help simplify administration while providing uniqueness and expandability. Windows Server 2003 supports three different group scopes and two group types. The group types are:

- **Security groups** These work in conjunction with discretionary access control lists (DACLs) to provide a means for controlling users' access to network resources.

- **Distribution groups** These are used with e-mail applications to send e-mail to a particular group of users.

The group scopes are:

- **Domain local scope** Used to define and control access to resources within a single domain. The domain local scope is used within the DACL on a resource to control access. Users are added to global groups, which, in turn, are added to the domain local scope to control access to resources.

- **Global scope** Used in multiple domains to control directory access maintenance tasks. Global scope information is not replicated outside its home domain. If multiple domains will require the same type of global scope, the global group will have to be created in each domain.

- **Universal scope** Used to unite groups from multiple domains. Nesting other universal groups and global groups within universal groups provides forestwide access control while keeping replication traffic from group membership changes to a minimum.

Knowing how each group scope is used and understanding the breadth of coverage of a security group aids in the development of a standardized group-naming convention.

TEST DAY TIP

Note the differences between the groups and how they are used in real scenarios. Also, be acutely aware of the group nesting options and how domain functional level affects the group nesting capabilities.

Because domain local scope typically pertains only to resource access control within a domain, domain local groups usually follow a naming convention that reflects their limited coverage. Most domain local groups are named to reflect the access control that they provide or to reflect the group of individuals that the access control will affect.

As mentioned previously, global scope does not extend beyond its home domain. To simplify administration, it is common practice to use the same name for a global group in each domain that requires the group. For example, if the NAmerica domain and the SAmerica domain both have a group to control access to resources for their respective marketing departments, a group with global scope should be created in each domain. This group would likely be named GLMarketing in each domain to reflect the global scope for the marketing department. The GLMarketing group would be added to each domain local group where marketing department employees will need access to resources.

Universal scope is used to reduce replication traffic caused by changes in group membership. In our previous example, you should create a GLMarketing global group in both domains as well as a UMarketing group in one of the domains. To use universal scope, the domain functional level must be set to Windows 2000 or higher.

Like user and machine accounts, group accounts have their limitations. Group accounts can contain up to 63 characters. A group account cannot be made up entirely of spaces, periods, or numbers. Also, like the other accounts discussed so far, leading periods or spaces are removed. In the next section, we will look at standardization of other object types within Active Directory.

Other Object Types

Other account types used within Active Directory include the following:

- **Organizational units (OUs)** Used for storing users, computers, and other account objects to provide for administrative delegation or simplification.

- **Sites** Containers used to control authentication and replication traffic across links that are not well-connected (typically wide area network, or WAN).

- **Contact** These objects listed within Active Directory are e-mail contacts like those found in your Microsoft Outlook address book. The format for this type of object already lends itself to specific search criteria. In other words, when setting up a contact, you will be prompted for first name, last name, e-mail addresses, phone numbers, and the like.

- **InetOrgPerson** These objects are available in Active Directory for interoperability with other directory service systems. This account is almost the same as a standard user account and can follow the same type of standardization model.

- **MSMQ Queue Alias** These objects are used in connection with Microsoft Message Queues and will not be discussed here.

- **Printer** These objects provide directory access to shared printers within the forest. Standardization for printer naming provides simplified administration and ensures consistent naming, which in turn simplifies user searches for available printers. It is a recommended best practice to fill out the location information for printers to aid in directory searches as well.

- **Shared folder** These objects provide directory access to shared folders within the forest. Again, standardization simplifies administration while simplifying user searches for available shared folders.

In the previous section, we discussed standardization and its effect on Active Directory design. We looked at the various objects contained within the Active Directory infrastructure and some of their naming and operational limitations. In the following section, we will see how the design of Active Directory should model the organization that will implement Active Directory. We will look at various design decisions that will affect how Active Directory will model the implementing organization.

Defining the Forest Structure, Hierarchy, and Naming Strategy

We have looked at the various objects contained within the Active Directory infrastructure and have analyzed the scope of various containers within Active Directory. In this section, we analyze the structure and hierarchy of our Active Directory. We will see how the organizational requirements will affect the decisions regarding forest structure, hierarchy, and naming strategy. We will see how Active Directory name structures and the Domain Name Service (DNS) interact and how this affects naming strategy with single and multiple forests.

As we continue to detail our design requirements, we will see the role that domains play within the AD design. We will also see how domain hierarchy affects the AD namespace. This section also covers domain migration and upgrade designs as well as authentication and trust relationships. Let's begin by taking the highest-level look at Active Directory by analyzing the forest design.

Structure and Hierarchy

The forest is generally owned by a senior-level IT administrator. This individual is responsible for:

- The forest root domain deployment that is used to create the forest. (Forest design was covered in greater detail in Chapter 2 section 1.4.2.)

- The first domain controller deployment in each domain that is used to create each domain required for the forest. (Domain design was covered in greater detail in Chapter 2 section 1.4.3.)

- Selection and placement of service administrator group members in all domains of the forest.

- The design and creation of the OU structure for each domain in the forest. (OU design was covered in greater detail in Chapter 2 section 1.4.5.)

- Delegation of administrative authority to OU owners.

- Schema modification.

- Overall forestwide configuration settings and changes.

- Top-level Group Policies implementation, including:

  - Password complexity and account lockout policies for domain accounts

  - Domain controller policies

  - Any other Group Policies that are applied at the domain level

A few factors play a major part in the decision to use a single forest or multiple forests. While analyzing your organization's hierarchical structure, you need to determine how much autonomy is required within the various departments, divisions, and organizations in your organization. Does your organization require a completely centralized administrative structure, or is it necessary to grant complete autonomy to certain groups within your organization? Active Directory provides for significant granular control over containers within the AD. It is possible to delegate significant portions of administration to individuals or groups within an individual forest. Although it is possible to delegate a large degree of control within a single forest, different groups within an organization may require a certain level of autonomy or isolation. It is important to note that the forest or enterprise-level administrators will have control and access to all resources within the forest. This could pose a problem for some organizations. This degree of access that is afforded to forest-level administrators can be regulated by only creating multiple forests.

If an organization's design specifications dictate multiple forests, how do you design for collaboration between forests? The answer is trust relationships. Establishing trust relationships between forests provides for controlled access to resources for users external to a forest. Using trust relationships, forest administrators can grant access to resources for users in other forests without giving complete access and control to other administrators. We will look at trusts in more detail later in this chapter. For now, let's examine the factors that determine the number of forests required in an AD design.

 EXAM WARNING

The Active Directory namespace and its implied hierarchy are inseparable from the AD design. Specific designs warrant separate forests or separate domains. Be sure to review how separate forests or domains will be reflected in the hierarchical name.

Collaboration

In previous iterations of Microsoft Windows NT Server, the domain was considered the administrative or security boundary. With Windows Server 2003, Microsoft fully advocates the forest as the administrative or security boundary. This change brings about the need to connect forests in certain design scenarios. The mechanisms used for connecting forests in Windows Server 2003 are trusts and metadirectories.

Trust relationships allow users hosted by one forest to access resources located in a separate, external forest. This is a new feature for Windows Server 2003, extending the external trust capabilities that were introduced in Windows 2000 Server. Windows 2000 Server provided only nontransitive trusts between two domains in separate forests; the new forest trust capabilities for Windows Server 2003 provide transitive trusts between entire forests via the root domains of each forest. With the new forest trust capabilities, it is possible for implicit trusts to exist between forests. In other words, if Forest A trusts Forest B, and Forest B trusts Forest C, Forest A will trust Forest C through an implied trust, as shown in Figure 4.1.

Figure 4.1 Implied Trusts Between Forests

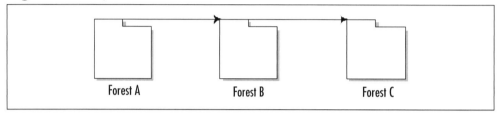

Windows Server 2003 forest trusts provide the following:

- A reduction in the number of necessary external trusts, providing simplified management of resources across Windows Server 2003 forests

- Two-way trust relationships with every domain in each forest

- User principal name (UPN) authentication across two forests

- Availability of Kerberos V5 and NTLM authentication protocols, providing improved interforest authorization data trustworthiness

- Flexibility of administration—administrative tasks can be unique to each forest

The world of information technology views security with a much greater awareness than it did in the not-so-distant past. To most administrators and engineers today, the thought of an external organization gaining access to internal company resources is a scary proposition. Fortunately, Microsoft introduces the authentication firewall with Windows Server 2003. The authentication firewall places a special security ID (SID) on incoming authentication requests that pass through the authentication firewall. This special SID, called the *other organization SID,* triggers a special allowed-to-authenticate check on authentication requests in an effort to control access to internal forest resources for external users. This added authentication check helps lock down the forest from unwanted external requests; it also helps prevent denial-of-service (DoS) attacks against your organization's domain controllers.

To create a forest trust between Windows Server 2003 forests, it is necessary to change the forest functional level to .NET native functionality. This eliminates the possibility of running any non–Windows Server 2003 domain controllers in either forest. Furthermore, to establish the trust between forests, the operators must be part of the Enterprise Administrators groups for each forest.

Products like Microsoft Identity Integration Server (formally known as Microsoft Metadirectory Services) provide metadirectory connectivity that facilitates simplified management of disparate systems. Metadirectory services provide synchronization for the following types of information:

- Public folders

- Directory objects

- Global Address Lists (GALs)

Microsoft provides for full or partial synchronization between the following directory products using Microsoft Identity Integration Server:

- Active Directory

- Active Directory Application Mode

- Attribute value-pair text files

- Delimited text files

- Directory Services Markup Language

- Fixed-width text files

- GALs (Exchange)

- LDAP Directory Interchange Format

- Lotus Notes/Domino 4.6 and 5.0

- Microsoft Windows NT 4 domains

- Microsoft Exchange 5.5 bridgeheads

- Microsoft Exchange 5.5, 2000, and 2003

- Microsoft SQL 7 and 2000 databases

- Novell eDirectory v8.6.2 and v8.7

- Oracle 8i and 9i databases

In the next section, we will see how forests relate to the Active Directory namespace, and we will determine the effects of Internet and extranet presence on the namespace.

Naming

Active Directory namespace correlates closely to DNS naming conventions. Delegation of authority as dictated through DNS naming follows the same basic delegation of authority for AD resources. If an organization requires an Internet or extranet presence, the AD namespace must correlate to registered public DNS namespace as provided through ICANN-authorized name service registration authorities. For example, a fictional company with an Internet presence of www.ourcorp.com might provide access to AD resources via this registered name. A VPN server may be accessed through the vpn001.ourcorp.com namespace. Other resources may be available through this publicly registered namespace.

This type of namespace design can provide for single sign-on access to resources by using an individual's e-mail address as a logon. This simplifies user account administration, but it could generate greater design complexity because of the potential to inadvertently expose resources to the public.

Let's take a closer look at forest design and see how external access requirements affect the AD namespace.

Internal Versus External Names

Internal namespace does not provide for access from external systems via the Internet or via extranet scenarios. Even though internal namespace designs may not require or may not desire connectivity from external systems, it is recommended to use a registered DNS namespace for the AD forest name. This ensures that as design requirements change or if other organizations merge with your organization in the future, the namespaces will be able to coexist.

Four options exist for organizations that require internal and external namespace:

- Use a child domain of an externally registered domain to accommodate internal namespace.

- Use *.local* or *.internal* top-level names for internal name resolution.

- Use *.com* for external namespace and *.net* for internal namespace.

- Use split-brain DNS between internally connected DNS servers and your ISP's DNS servers.

As mentioned, you may attach a new prefix to an existing, registered DNS namespace to accommodate a new AD design, such as internal.ourcorp.com, where *internal* is the prefix and *ourcorp.com* is the existing DNS suffix. The advantage to this type of design is that the namespace is consistent throughout. External connectivity and internal user connectivity are provided through the same namespace. This also presents a possible disadvantage due to the fact that internal, sensitive resources may be exposed to external requests if this design is not configured properly.

Microsoft currently recommends against using nonregistered, nonexistent names for internal use. This design was originally suggested with Windows 2000 Server's Active Directory; however, it presents problems as an organization expands and turns its connectivity needs to the Internet.

Using a *.com* registered domain name for your company's external DNS presence and a *.net* registered domain name for your company's internal requirements is another alternative. This presents a reasonably secure approach to DNS infrastructure design while still providing for network expansion and consolidation in the future. The disadvantage to this approach (and to basically all the solutions except split-brain DNS) is that the namespace is not consistent throughout. There may be confusion in this design between external and internal resources for some users.

Split-brain DNS utilizes two ISP-hosted external DNS servers and two internally hosted DNS servers. The internally hosted DNS servers provide name resolution for internal clients while the ISP-hosted DNS servers direct external, Internet-based requests to Internet servers. If a client's DNS request cannot be answered by the internal DNS servers, the request is forwarded to the ISP's DNS servers for resolution. This solution requires static configuration of DNS records on the internal DNS servers for any servers that reside on the Internet within the corporate namespace. Typically the ISP hosts Web and e-mail servers. In this case, the internal name servers must have manually added DNS records that point to the Web and e-mail servers. This design provides for consistent naming for internal and external clients and provides a relatively secure DNS infrastructure design. The disadvantage to this design is that internal DNS servers must be manually configured with records for external company resources such as Web servers and e-mail servers. If an ISP makes any changes to the external servers, the changes are not automatically updated on the internal servers. (Chapter 3 covers DNS design in greater detail.)

Now that we have determined the number of forests required and provided the namespace, it is time to determine how many domains will be required.

How Many Domains?

The domain model design selected in designing an Active Directory implementation is generally based on bandwidth and replication control. The simplest, least expensive domain model to implement and administer is the single-domain model. As more domains are added to a design, the design complexity and the overall total cost of ownership increase significantly. The number of users in your organization, as well as the amount of available bandwidth in each site, will influence the domain design requirements.

As mentioned, the simplest domain design model is the single-domain model. This is the preferred domain design model. In this model, all directory data in a forest is replicated to all domain controllers. If a design requires multiple domains, the preferred design approach is the regional domain model. The regional domain model breaks the forest into domains based on geographic location of users and resources. This is considered the preferred multiple-domain model because it generally provides a stable environment that does not fluctuate over time. If we use regional domains, boundaries are typically defined by continents or other stable geographic boundaries. This model also allows for a design that properly reflects varying political requirements from one socio-geographic area to another. (Section 1.4.3 of Chapter 2 provides greater detail on domain design.)

All AD designs begin with a single domain. Windows NT 4.0 domains exhibited an account limitation that required multiple domains based on the number of user and computer accounts in the enterprise. Since the advent of Active Directory, the operational account limitation has been removed from domain design, but due to logistics, replication traffic, and other factors, the number of user accounts still plays a part in domain design. Table 4.3 correlates the available bandwidth between domain controllers, the total number of user accounts within the forest, and the percentage of bandwidth that will be allotted to replication.

Table 4.3 Microsoft Recommended Maximum User Accounts in a Single Domain

Slowest Link Connecting a Domain Controller (KBps)	Maximum Number of Users at 1 Percent of Available Bandwidth	Maximum Number of Users at 5 Percent of Available Bandwidth	Maximum Number of Users at 10 Percent of Available Bandwidth
28.8	10,000	25,000	40,000
32	10,000	25,000	50,000
56	10,000	50,000	100,000
64	10,000	50,000	100,000
128	25,000	100,000	100,000
256	50,000	100,000	100,000
512	80,000	100,000	100,000
1500	100,000	100,000	100,000

To use this table, find the smallest amount of bandwidth available between domain controllers in your design, and determine the percentage of that bandwidth that will be made available to replication. If the number of user accounts in your forest design does not exceed the number listed in the bandwidth column, a single-domain model will suffice. If the number of user accounts in your forest exceeds the number listed below the bandwidth that will be made available, you should consider dividing your forest into multiple regional domains.

If the design requires a regional domain model, the number of user accounts and replication bandwidth available will affect the overall design. Because a certain portion of Active Directory will be replicated between domains, even in a regional domain model, bandwidth limitations may be affected by the overall number of user accounts in the forest. Table 4.4 illustrates the relationship between available allocated bandwidth and the number of user accounts in the forest.

Table 4.4 Microsoft Recommended Maximum User Accounts in a Forest

Slowest Link Connecting a Domain Controller (KBps)	Maximum Number of Users at 1 Percent of Available Bandwidth	Maximum Number of Users at 5 Percent of Available Bandwidth	Maximum Number of Users at 10 Percent of Available Bandwidth
28.8	10,000	50,000	75,000
32	10,000	50,000	75,000
56	10,000	75,000	100,000
64	25,000	75,000	100,000
128	50,000	100,000	100,000
256	75,000	100,000	100,000
512	100,000	100,000	100,000
1500	100,000	100,000	100,000

If the number of users in your forest design exceeds the number listed in the corresponding entry in Table 4.4, you should either allocate a greater percentage of bandwidth, increase the amount of minimum link speed, or deploy additional forests.

If the number of user accounts and available bandwidth in your design can be accommodated by a single-forest design, but a regional domain model is required, you should determine the number of accounts that each region can support. It is recommended that regional domain designs maintain a limitation of a maximum of 10 domains. Table 4.5 determines the maximum number of users that can be hosted in a region based on bandwidth.

Table 4.5 Microsoft Recommended Maximum User Accounts in a Region

Slowest Link Connecting a Domain Controller (KBps)	Maximum Number of Users at 1 Percent of Available Bandwidth	Maximum Number of Users at 5 Percent of Available Bandwidth	Maximum Number of Users at 10 Percent of Available Bandwidth
28.8	10,000	18,000	40,000
32	10,000	20,000	50,000
56	10,000	40,000	100,000
64	10,000	50,000	100,000
128	15,000	100,000	100,000
256	30,000	100,000	100,000
512	80,000	100,000	100,000
1500	100,000	100,000	100,000

If the number of user accounts in a region exceeds the number of accounts listed in the corresponding entry in Table 4.5, either allocate a greater percentage of bandwidth, increase the amount of minimum link speed, or deploy additional regional domains and recalculate. (For a less simplistic approach to domain design, follow the definitive information on this subject provided in Chapter 2 of this study guide.)

Beyond bandwidth availability and total accounts in an environment, political factors often influence domain designs. A design may include child domains or peer domains, depending on the situation. Typically, child domains are deployed as lower-level hierarchical units within an organization or in a scenario in which an organization prefers to create equality between grouped units.

Peer domains generally exist where some degree of autonomy or self-sufficiency is required within different portions of an organization. Peer domains stem from independent domain tree roots, each carrying its own namespace. Each domain tree has rights over its own domain hierarchy in this scenario, compared to the regional domain design discussed earlier in this chapter, in which control exists in a higher domain in the hierarchy.

EXERCISE 4.01

DOMAIN DESIGN

For this exercise, your existing network and its WAN infrastructure are documented in Figure 4.2. You have been instructed not to exceed 5 percent of the available bandwidth for site replication and determine the number of forests, domains, and sites for the network design.

Figure 4.2 Network Infrastructure Connectivity

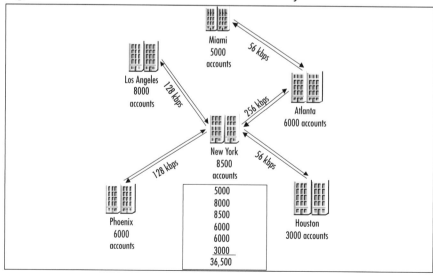

1. Begin by analyzing the connection speeds to find the slowest links. The Houston–New York link and the Miami–Atlanta link both constitute the slowest links for our infrastructure with a 56 kbps connection used for each link.

2. Comparing the 56 kbps link at 5 percent, we see that Table 4.3 claims support for up to 50,000 accounts. Our current design must accommodate 36,500 accounts, so a single domain will suffice.

3. Verifying the total number of accounts against Table 4.4 for a 56 kbps connection at 5 percent utilization determines that 75,000 accounts may be supported, so a single-forest design will suffice as well.

4. Finally, comparing the number of user accounts to Table 4.5, using 56 kbps and 5 percent utilization, we see that 40,000 accounts may be supported by any single region.

5. As our network grows, we already know that the 56 kbps connections will provide a bottleneck to the existing design, which will force an increase in bandwidth or a restructuring in the network infrastructure and Active Directory designs.

Now that we have discussed how to determine the number of domains required, let's see how domain designs correlate with the AD namespace.

Naming

Earlier in this chapter, we saw how our forest design would use a namespace similar to a DNS namespace as its root. This design utilized a registered DNS name like ourcorp.com or internal.ourcorp.com. As domains are added to a forest namespace, the domain becomes a prefix to the forest root. As noted earlier, the creation of the forest starts with the creation of a domain, so ourcorp.com or internal.ourcorp.com could represent the root domain in the forest.

Let's look at an example using ourcorp.com as the root of an AD forest. If multiple domains have to be created to accommodate design limitations, the regional domains created within the ourcorp.com domain will be added as prefixes. In the next section, we will look at the namespace and how this correlates to the domain hierarchy.

The Hierarchy

If our fictional company has offices in North and South America and the available bandwidth and number of user accounts dictates that a regional domain model should be used, the two separate regional domains could be namerica.ourcorp.com and samerica.ourcorp.com. In this example, the domains are peers in the ourcorp.com root. If the North America regional domain was divided into East and West sub-domains, the domains created would use names like east.namerica.ourcorp.com and west.namerica.ourcorp.com. In this example, the *east* and *west* domains are considered child domains to the namerica.ourcorp.com domain. Just as in our example, in any AD design, one of the first steps is determining the best hierarchical design for your organization. (For a more detailed reference to domain design, please refer to Chapter 2 in this study guide.)

Once the best hierarchy is designed, it is time to determine the best path to that design and which migration strategy will work best to achieve the desired design.

Assessing and Defining a Migration Path

If you are building a house, a car, a road system, or even a computer network, it is easier to start with a clean slate than it is to have to operate within previously defined limitations. Unfortunately for most engineers tasked with an Active Directory design, a clean slate is usually not an option. In this section we will analyze the various approaches available in upgrading an existing enterprise infrastructure to Windows Server 2003's Active Directory.

In-Place Upgrades

In designing an upgrade strategy for a migration to Active Directory, every domain in the new enterprise design will be either a new domain or a domain that has been upgraded in place. *In-place upgrades*, as the name implies, involve upgrading from a pre-Windows Server 2003 domain environment to Windows Server 2003's Active Directory using the same domain name and structure as that used in the original enterprise design. The advantage to an in-place upgrade is that user accounts do not have to be moved from one domain to another.

If an in-place upgrade is not executed, accounts from existing domains that will not be upgraded have to be moved into newly created domains in Active Directory. The obvious downside to this migration strategy is that user accounts have to be relocated from one domain to another. Relocating user accounts can adversely affect the end users involved in the migration. If you will be upgrading existing NT 4.0 *Master User Domains* (*MUDs*), the first step should include listing all the MUDs and comparing them against planned domains. After comparing your Windows NT 4.0 MUDs to your proposed domains, determine whether any of the MUDs will be migrated in place to new domains or whether new domains will be created for the proposed domains.

Two options exist within the in-place upgrade design. An in-place upgrade could mean upgrading to a regional domain in an existing forest or upgrading to a single-domain forest. Upgrading provides several simple advantages, including lower risk, shortest time, no need for new servers, and fewest resources needed.

Because a good plan always includes an exit strategy, your in-place upgrade design should have an exit strategy that includes an upgrade time frame in case things do not go well during the upgrade process. While upgrading an NT 4.0 domain to Windows Server 2003, it is considered best practice to take a domain controller offline to preserve the existing Windows NT 4.0 SAM as a fallback mechanism. This offline domain controller should be a backup domain controller (BDC) that has been synchronized with the existing primary domain controller (PDC) and removed from the network, either by shutting the system down or, preferably, by disconnecting it from the network. Once this fallback machine is taken offline, the PDC should be upgraded to Windows Server 2003.

If the upgrade does not go well and the upgrade time frame is exceeded, it is time to implement the rollback plan. The first step in a rollback plan should include removing Windows Server 2003 domain controllers, selecting a Windows NT 4.0 BDC to promote to PDC, and synchronizing all Windows NT 4.0 domain controllers. If testing proves that this process has failed, the final resort is to incorporate the offline domain controller back into the network. Promote the fallback BDC to PDC and perform synchronization between all NT 4.0 domain controllers. Once service is restored for end users, conduct a thorough inspection to determine the reason for the failed upgrade. This will help promote a successful future upgrade strategy.

Because Windows NT 4.0 domain controllers often perform more functions than just those of a domain controller, other functionality needs to be planned for during an in-place upgrade. One area that requires planning and proper design is the replication capabilities of Windows NT 4.0. Windows NT 4.0 uses export and import directories on domain controllers to handle replication of important files (typically logon scripts) between domain controllers. Windows 2000 Server and Windows Server 2003 do not support the LAN Manager Replication (LMRepl) capabilities supported by Windows NT 4.0. During an in-place upgrade from Windows NT 4.0 to Windows Server 2003, you should ensure that the export folder does not reside on the initial machine to be upgraded. If the preferred upgrade machine is hosting files in the export folder, you should prepare and test a different domain controller to handle the export functions for the domain during the upgrade process.

Windows 2000 Server and Windows Server 2003 use the File Replication Service (FRS) to handle replication. Generally, if your Windows NT 4.0 environment relies on LMRepl to replicate logon scripts, using FRS to replicate the contents of the sysvol folder on all Windows 2000 Server and Windows Server 2003 domain controllers should be a sufficient replacement solution. If your design has more elaborate needs than FRS can provide for, it may be necessary to configure the distributed file system (DFS) to handle the replication requirements for your organization's network design.

Our discussion to this point has revolved around domain upgrades from Windows NT 4.0 Server to Windows Server 2003. Although Windows 2000 Server supports Active Directory, it is important to note that an upgrade from Windows 2000 Server to Windows Server 2003 involves upgrading Active Directory because Windows Server 2003 supports an enhanced Active Directory compared to the Windows 2000 Server Active Directory. To upgrade Windows 2000 servers to support the enhancements to Active Directory provided by Windows Server 2003, it is necessary to use the Active Directory Preparation Tool (adprep.exe) located on the Windows Server 2003 operating system CD. Although Windows 2000 Server and Windows Server 2003 both support Active Directory, an upgrade is usually the best time to make modifications to an existing design, to improve functionality or to repair overlooked design criteria from the Windows 2000 Server network design. If you are upgrading from Windows 2000 Server, remember that the existing design is not set in stone and that this is a great opportunity to make adjustments to the existing design.

One of the advantages to Active Directory over Microsoft's original Windows NT 4.0 domain model is the change in domain replication. Windows NT 4.0 used a single-master replication model. This model uses only a single writeable version of the Security Accounts Manager (SAM) database. The PDC is the only machine hosting a writeable version of the SAM. Changes are made to the SAM on the PDC and are subsequently replicated to all the BDCs in the domain. Windows 2000 Server and Windows Server 2003 use a multiple-master replication model whereby each domain controller contains a writeable version of the Active Directory database. Changes made to items in the Active Directory database are replicated to all the other domain controllers within the domain.

Generally, smaller organizations benefit from an in-place upgrade because users, settings, groups, rights, and permissions are retained. Also, the in-place upgrade provides the benefit that you are usually not required to reinstall files and applications. Larger organizations, on the other hand, tend to benefit from a clean installation or a migration. If you are planning a server consolidation, for example, the preferred route is to begin with a clean installation. Furthermore, beginning with a newly formatted disk is often preferred because a notable increase in system performance may be gained compared to an upgraded installation. Reformatting also provides the designer with options to restructure the partition layout—modifying partition sizes or the number of partitions. If an effort to provide highly available servers is the ultimate goal of a design, a new installation would be preferred over an upgrade route. Lastly, upgrading the operating system on a server that has been previously upgraded from another operating system should be avoided whenever possible.

EXAM WARNING

This exam is a Windows Server 2003 exam, but the design strategies used in Windows NT 4.0 play a significant part. Understand the 40,000-account limitation for the NT 4.0 SAM and how it affects domain designs for Windows NT 4.0 domains. Also understand the Windows Server 2003 domain limitations discussed here.

Restructuring Domains

Restructuring domains involves moving accounts from a nonupgraded domain to a Windows Server 2003 Active Directory domain. Restructuring usually works best for organizations that cannot afford the downtime associated with a move to Windows Server 2003, whose existing organization structure does not meet design needs or who need an optimized domain structure.

The Microsoft recommended tool for migrating accounts is the aptly named Active Directory Migration Tool, or ADMT. The ADMT provides console, command-line, and script options for copying users, groups, and service accounts; moving computers; migrating trusts; and performing security translation. Using ADMT to migrate accounts from a Windows NT 4.0 domain to a Windows Server 2003 Active Directory domain provides a mechanism for copying accounts from an NT 4.0 source domain to a Windows Server 2003 destination domain. ADMT provides several benefits for organizations requiring a domain restructuring.

ADMT provides capabilities to analyze the effects of migration before and after the actual migration process is undertaken. Various migration scenarios may be tested with ADMT to determine best-case migration outcomes without actually performing the migration. Migration within a forest and between forests may both be accomplished with ADMT. Finally, ADMT contains several wizards to simplify many of the more common migration tasks. Because restructuring involves moving various accounts from one domain or forest to another, several factors require careful planning and coordination.

When accounts are created in a domain or forest, SIDs are created to correspond to the account. Each forest has its own pool of SIDs to associate to new accounts. Moving an account from one forest to another typically means associating new SIDs to the account. This could present a problem if a rollback strategy needs to be implemented. For this reason, a SID history is usually maintained to ensure that user accounts may be rolled back in the event of a failed domain restructuring. ADMT not only provides for user account and SID mapping capabilities—it also provides group account migration, computer account migration, security account translation, service account migration, trust migration, and group mapping and merging.

Group account migration provides a mechanism for copying groups from a source domain to the destination domain. Computer account migration provides migration capabilities for Windows NT 4.0, Windows 2000, and Windows XP machines from the source domain to the destination domain. Service account migration provides a transport for moving needed service accounts from the source domain to the destination domain. Trust migration, as the name implies, is used for migrating trust accounts from the source domain to the destination domain. Security account translation provides capabilities for migrating user profiles during a migration from a Windows NT 4.0 or Windows 2000 domain structure to a Windows Server 2003 Active Directory infrastructure.

Although the previous version of ADMT did not provide password migration capabilities, the current version of ADMT (version 2) does. As mentioned earlier, the three main reasons for restructuring are:

- The existing structure does not meet the organization's needs.

- Downtime for implementation is not acceptable.

- An optimum design structure is needed.

With all the discussion regarding ADMT and design, it should be noted that other third-party tools exist for simplifying the migration process. ADMT is a much improved, Microsoft-recommended utility for migration, but it is not the only migration tool, and others may provide greater flexibility and capabilities than ADMT.

Migrating to Pristine Environment

Not all migration paths provide for a direct upgrade from one operating environment to another. If the current domains in your environment are not running Windows NT 4.0 domain controllers, at a minimum, it is advisable to start with a pristine environment. Migrating to a pristine environment is less a migration and more a recreation process.

When migrating to a pristine environment, analyze your existing enterprise as though you were going to follow one of the previous migration strategies. Instead of "migrating," however, you'll create the accounts in new domains as if they were migrated from previous Windows versions. This approach is generally preferred if the previously described migration paths do not provide for a workable solution. Sometimes the existing environment requires more work to do a migration than it will to just build anew. It may be possible that none of the current environment or equipment is salvageable for an Active Directory upgrade project. Likewise, maybe your current operating system is not Windows NT 4.0 or Windows 2000. Novell networks and older Microsoft networks, for example, may work best as mere guidelines for a pristine Windows Server 2003 environment.

Defining Authentication Mechanisms

Authentication is the process of verifying an identity (ensuring a user really is who he purports to be) for the purpose of authorizing or granting certain permissions to that identity. Through the years, Microsoft has used various mechanisms for user authentication. In this section, we will analyze the mechanisms Microsoft has used to authenticate security principals (user and machine accounts) and for relaying authentication between servers. We also discuss the mechanisms supported by Microsoft client operating systems. Next, we analyze the authentication mechanisms supported by various Microsoft clients, seeing how they will determine the authentication mechanism used for our design. Finally, we explore trusts and the authentication mechanisms used both inside and between forests in a design.

Requirements

Different operating systems and service pack levels provide different authentication mechanisms for Microsoft clients. Windows Server 2003 provides full backward compatibility for previous Microsoft operating systems, but it is preferred to limit the use of or, whenever possible, to disable older authentication mechanisms. In the following sections, we analyze the effects of client operating systems and applications used within the enterprise on the Active Directory design. Next, we compare the LAN Manager authentication protocols to Microsoft's implementation of the Kerberos authentication system. Finally, we see how Microsoft's implementation of Kerberos may be used with other Kerberos-enabled operating systems for trusted authentication.

Let's start with an analysis of the clients that exist on today's networks and how Microsoft Windows Server 2003 provides an authentication mechanism for each.

The Client Community

Windows Server 2003 Active Directory provides authentication support for several Microsoft and non–Microsoft client operating systems. Older Microsoft clients are authenticated using the LAN Manager or newer NT LAN Manager (NTLM) protocol. More recent Microsoft clients use Microsoft's implementation of Kerberos version 5 authentication. We will analyze LAN Manager, NTLM, and Kerberos in the next section. Right now, let's take a look at the different client operating systems available from Microsoft that interoperate with Windows Server 2003 Active Directory.

Microsoft consumer operating systems such as Windows 95 and Windows 98 will work within a Windows Server 2003 Active Directory. These operating systems can take greater advantage of directory service features by installing the Active Directory Client Extensions for Windows 95/98 provided on the Windows Server 2003 installation CD. Installing the client extensions provides the following benefits for Windows 95/98 clients:

- **Site awareness** This is the ability to log on to the domain controller and access other resources that are closest to the client in the network. The client extensions also provide the ability to change passwords on any Windows Server 2003-based domain controller, not just the PDC.

- **Active Directory Service Interfaces (ADSIs)** These allow scripting to Active Directory, providing a common programming API for Active Directory programmers.

- **DFS fault-tolerance client** Provides access to Windows Server 2003 DFS fault-tolerant and failover file shares that are advertised in Active Directory.

- **Active Directory Windows Address Book (WAB) property pages** These allow users who have permission to change properties on user objects by means of the user object pages. This function is available by clicking **Start | Search | For People**.

- **NTLM version 2 authentication** Provides improved authentication features.

The previously listed features are also available to Windows NT 4.0 clients through the Active Directory Client Extensions for Windows NT 4.0, available as a downloadable file from the Microsoft Web site.

Windows 2000 and Windows XP clients have built-in capabilities to interoperate with Windows Server 2003 Active Directory. Full Active Directory functionality is available to these clients, including Group Policy and Intellimirror capabilities.

One of the major differences between the modern Microsoft client operating systems and the older Microsoft client operating systems is the available authentication mechanisms. In the next section, we compare and contrast the LAN Manager, NTLM, and Kerberos protocols.

 EXAM WARNING

Again, this exam is a Windows Server 2003 exam, but the existence of legacy client operating systems such as Windows 98 and Windows NT 4.0 plays an important part in the network design. Make sure you understand the benefits of installing the Active Directory Client Extensions for NT 4.0 and Windows 9x, as well as the limitations.

NTLM and Kerberos

Early Microsoft networking clients utilized LAN Manager authentication to provide user authentication for network access to resources. Windows NT 4.0 evolved from the LAN Manager network operating system. For backward compatibility, Windows NT 4.0 uses a version of LAN Manager authentication known as *LAN Manager challenge/response* as well as Windows NT challenge/response, known as *NTLM* for more recent systems. NTLM authentication is significantly stronger than LM authentication. Whether Windows NT is communicating with LM-only systems or systems capable of NTLM authentication, Windows NT will use both authentication methods. SP 4 for Windows NT 4.0 introduced a new version of Windows NT challenge/response authentication known as *NTLM v2*. Forcing NT 4.0 systems to use NTLM or NTLM v2 significantly increases the difficulty involved in brute-force or dictionary attacks against network password hashes. To take advantage of NTLM v2 authentication or to just disable LM authentication, your Windows NT 4.0 system requires SP 4 to be installed, and a registry modification is also needed.

Cryptographic methods that were once considered strong eventually succumb to Moore's Law. Moore's Law has plotted the pace of technology for more than 25 years. As the power of computing equipment has rapidly increased, so too has the potential to break cryptography that was once considered strong. With advances in hardware capabilities, coupled with the increased availability of cracking tools, LAN Manager authentication encryption is quickly becoming more vulnerable to attack than the newer forms of encryption. LAN Manager authentication should be restricted or eliminated whenever possible. Although Windows Server 2003 supports all versions of LAN Manager authentication in an effort to provide backward compatibility for clients that do not support newer authentication protocols, LAN Manager authentication is viewed as a security risk to any network.

If you are unable to eliminate LAN Manager authentication from your network, you can increase security by enabling support of NTLMv2 if possible. Password hash values can be removed from the network, resulting in increased network security by eliminating LM and NTLM v1 protocols from your enterprise. You can enable NTLMv2 support by doing the following:

- Upgrade Windows NT 4.0 clients to a minimum of Service Pack 4 (SP4). SP4 is available via download from the Microsoft Web site at *www.microsoft.com*.

- Install the directory services client on all client computers running Windows 95 or Windows 98. The directory services client is available from the Windows Server 2003 operating system CD.

- Tighten the LAN Manager authentication policies used on your network. It is preferred to set Domain Group Policy for LAN Manager Authentication Level to **Send NTLMv2 response only\refuse LM & NTLM**. This policy is configured through the Microsoft Group Policy Management Console under **Computer Configuration | Windows Settings | Security Settings | Local Policies | Security Options**.

NOTE

The LAN Manager authentication protocol is considered weak because of the method used to encrypt the password. If a password is fewer than seven characters long, breaking down the LAN Manager protocol to extract the clear-text password is simplified because the last half of the LM hash follows the same predictable pattern. Hackers know and exploit this weakness. Programs exist for extracting the LM hash and decrypting it. The best practice, if possible, is to not use LM authentication and to not store the LM hash.

NTLM v2 is the preferred authentication protocol for older Microsoft clients. The preferred authentication mechanism for modern Microsoft network designs revolves around the use of Kerberos. Kerberos authentication, originally designed and developed by the Massachusetts Institute of Technology (MIT) as a solution to the problems associated with authenticating clients over untrusted and insecure network infrastructure, uses a three-headed approach to authentication. Clients, servers, and an intermediary server known as a *Key Distribution Center (KDC)* form the authentication infrastructure, mimicking the three-headed Kerberos of Greek mythology. Client/server communication is verified for authenticity, and timestamp techniques are used to circumvent the possibility of replay attacks.

Microsoft's selection of the open-standard Kerberos provides for limited interoperability with other, non-Microsoft operating systems. The interoperability is limited because Microsoft's interpretation of the open standard and a decision to send authorization information embedded in the Kerberos traffic cause the use of non-Microsoft operating systems to provide limited functionality compared to an all-Microsoft environment. It is possible to authenticate Linux, UNIX, and Mac OS X clients against Active Directory through the Kerberos protocol, providing for simplified network management in just such a heterogeneous environment. Table 4.6 illustrates the available authentication mechanisms for various Microsoft client operating systems.

Table 4.6 Authentication Mechanisms for Various Microsoft Client Operating Systems

Operating System	LAN Manager	NTLM v1	NTLM v2	Kerberos
Windows 9x	Yes	Yes w/DS Client	Yes w/ DS Client	No
Windows NT 4.0	Yes	Yes	Yes - SP 4 or higher	No
Windows 2000	Yes	Yes	Yes	Yes
Windows XP/2003	Yes	Yes	Yes	Yes

A chain is only as strong as its weakest link, and a network is only as secure as its weakest cryptographic-sensitive network traffic. Consequently, if your environment contains clients that cannot authenticate via the preferred Kerberos system, your network security will be diminished through the use of weaker NTLM or LM authentication traffic. As mentioned previously, Windows 95, Windows 98, and Windows NT 4.0 clients will utilize the weaker LM or NTLM v1 authentication protocol unless specific measures are taken. Windows 95 and Windows 98 clients require the installation of the Active Directory Client Extensions as well as registry modification to force NTLM v2 authentication. Windows NT 4.0 clients require a minimum of SP 4 (SP 6a is preferred) as well as installation of the Active Directory Client Extensions and registry modifications to force NTLM v2 authentication. Again, Windows 2000, Windows Server 2003, and Windows XP clients rely on Kerberos authentication in an Active Directory environment by default.

EXERCISE 4.02

FORCING CLIENTS TO USE NTLM v2 AUTHENTICATION

Because Windows Server 2003 was designed to support legacy clients, the weakness of legacy client authentication protocols is a valid concern. In this exercise, we modify the registry to force NTLM v2 authentication, as opposed to the weaker LAN Manager or NTLM v1 authentication. This configuration should be applied to Windows 9x systems or Windows NT 4.0 systems with Service Pack 4 or newer applied. The Active Directory Client Extensions should also be installed.

1. Install the Microsoft Active Directory Client Extensions (available from the Windows 2000 Server CD-ROM).

2. From the Windows 98 client system, select **Start | Run |** and type **regedit**, then click **OK**.

EXAM WARNING

Incorrect use of the Registry Editor may cause serious problems that could require a reinstall of your operating system. Use the Registry Editor at your own risk.

3. Create an LSA registry key in the following registry key: **HKEY_LOCAL_MACHINE | System | CurrentControlSet | Control | LSA**, as shown in Figure 4.3.

Figure 4.3 Using the Registry Editor to Force NTLM v2
Authentication

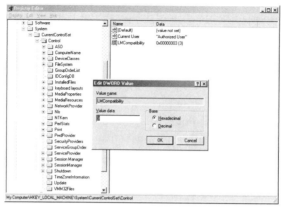

4. From the menu bar, select **Edit | New | DWORD value**, and then
   enter the following information:

   ■ Value Name: **LMCompatibility**

   ■ Data Type: **REG_DWORD**

   ■ Value: **3** (valid range is 0–3)

5. Adjusting the **lmcompatibilitylevel** registry key controls the type
   of challenge/response authentication that will be used. Table 4.7
   lists the possible settings for the lmcompatibilitylevel registry key.

Table 4.7 Possible Registry Settings for the LMCompatibilitylevel Registry Key

Registry Key Value	Effect of Registry Setting
Level 0	Send LM response and NTLM response; never use NTLM v2 session security
Level 1	Use NTLM v2 session security if negotiated
Level 2	Send NTLM authentication only
Level 3	Send NTLM v2 authentication only
Level 4	DC refuses LM authentication
Level 5	DC refuses LM and NTLM authentication (accepts only NTLM v2)

6. Adjusting the registry value to 3 will force the client to use only NTLM v2.

Because we now have a better understanding of client operating systems supported in Windows Server 2003 and the benefits and drawbacks of each, it's time to move our sights from individual machines and focus on the bigger picture. In the next section, we will see where trust relationships come into play in an Active Directory design. We will also see why we need trust relationships, how default trust relationships are established within an Active Directory forest, and how certain fine-tuning can be executed to improve the performance of the default trust relationships.

TEST DAY TIP

Make sure you know the difference between Windows Server 2003's various LAN authentication mechanisms. At the very least, know the order from LAN Manager (the weakest) to Kerberos (the strongest) and which operating systems support each protocol.

First, let's take a look at how authentication works within trusts and collaborative scenarios.

Trusts and Collaboration

Authentication is handled in different ways, depending on the design. In a workgroup or peer-to-peer design, systems handle authentication locally. In a domain environment, domain controllers handle the authentication duties. In a trust relationship, domain controllers from another domain or even another forest handle the authentication for clients. A client from a remote domain or forest may authenticate to a domain or forest that is not its native domain or forest in order to access resources in that domain.

Trust relationships are differentiated by the way the trust relationship is handled. Transitive trusts, for example, may be transferred between common forests or domains. One-way trusts, as the name implies, allow clients from one domain or forest to access resources in another domain or forest without providing a reciprocal trust relationship in return. Finally, a two-way trust relationship provides resource sharing and outside authentication in both directions.

Windows Server 2003 provides for different types of trust relationships within an Active Directory design. In this section, we analyze the trust relationships available and see how some trusts are set up by default. We will see how different Active Directory infrastructures may be joined through trust relationships between forests.

Next, we will see how different trust relationships may be established between domains. We will see the interplay of default trust relationships established in an Active Directory design, as well as specialized trust relationships that may be created to improve the Active Directory performance.

Between Forests

Earlier in this chapter, we explored how the design criteria for different groups within an organization affect the design and implementation of Active Directory forests. We analyzed the different Active Directory forest models and how data isolation, service isolation, data autonomy, service autonomy, and limited connectivity impact the forest model selection. Most of the forest models discussed involved some type of trust relationship between forests. This is a new and greatly improved feature for Windows Server 2003. Let's take a closer look at trust relationships used between forests and see why we need such trusts.

Active Directory forests provide a boundary for the Active Directory infrastructure. The forests in Active Directory are viewed the way domains were viewed in the days of Windows NT 4.0. Viewed this way, Active Directory forests provide a security or administrative boundary. Earlier in this chapter, we discussed scenarios whereby a single forest was not suitable for an AD design. In such a scenario, multiple forests are created. Often, user accounts are placed in a single forest while resources are placed in separate forests. In order for accounts to reach beyond the security boundary defined by a single forest, trust relationships must be established.

A trust relationship is a mechanism implemented by Enterprise Administrators of separate forests. The Enterprise Administrators are tasked with providing access to services or resources within their forest to users who are located in an external forest, or vice versa. Trusts in Windows Server 2003 may be created to trust other Windows domains or forests, or they may be created to establish trust with other Kerberos realms. A Kerberos realm is an administrative boundary for an environment utilizing Kerberos authentication. Table 4.8 illustrates the four different trust types for Windows Server 2003.

Table 4.8 Trust Types for Windows Server 2003

Trust Type	Transitivity	Direction	Description
External	Nontransitive	One-way or two-way	Generally used to connect to an NT 4.0 domain hosted within a separate forest
Realm	Transitive or Nontransitive	One-way or two-way	Used to connect to non-Windows Kerberos realms
Forest	Transitive	One-way or two-way	Used to share resources between forests

Continued

Table 4.8 Trust Types for Windows Server 2003 (**Continued**)

Trust Type	Transitivity	Direction	Description
Shortcut	Transitive	One-way or two-way	Used to shorten logon times between domains in a common Windows Server 2003 forest

Transitivity describes the capability for a trust relationship between two domains to be applied to a separate forest or domain through one of the common, shared trusted domains. In Figure 4.4, if Domain B trusts Domain A, and Domain C trusts Domain B, the transitive nature of the trusts says that Domain C will trust Domain A.

Figure 4.4 Trust Transitivity

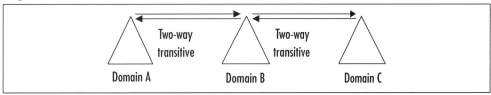

One-way trusts, as the name implies, provide a trust relationship in which users in one forest or domain (an organizational forest, for example) are granted access to resources in a separate external forest or domain (a resource forest) without providing the users in the resource forest access to resources in the organizational forest. This concept is illustrated in Figure 4.5.

Figure 4.5 One-Way Trust Relationship Between an Organizational Forest and a Resource Forest

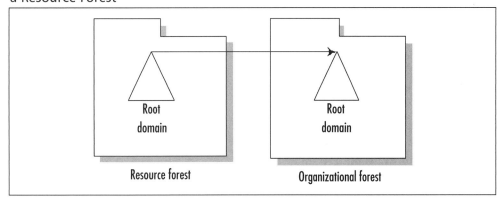

Figure 4.6 illustrates a trust relationship between a Windows NT 4.0 domain and a Windows Server 2003 Active Directory domain in which the users in the Active Directory forest will access resources in the Windows NT 4.0 domain but not vice versa.

Figure 4.6 Windows NT 4.0 Trust with Windows Server 2003

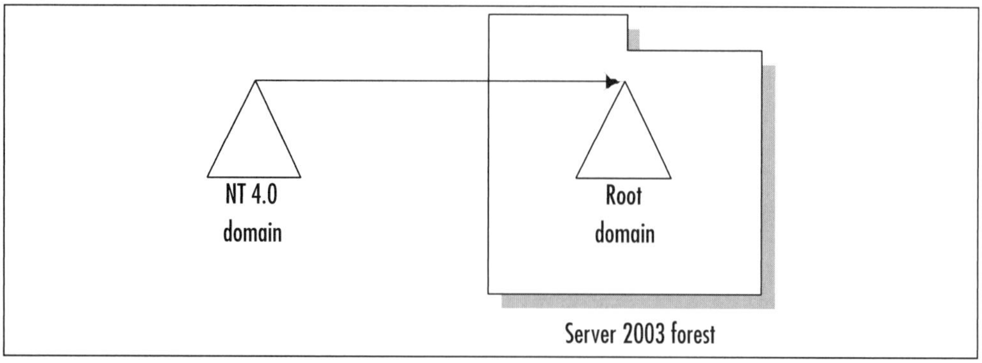

NT 4.0
domain

Root
domain

Server 2003 forest

EXAM WARNING

In this age of interoperability between different operating systems, trust relationships play a significant part. Understand each of the four types of trust relationships that exist in a Windows Server 2003 environment as well as how the domain and forest functional levels affect each.

A two-way trust is made up of two one-way trusts. In this scenario, access to resources is granted in both directions for users in each domain or forest. Typically, each forest is an organizational forest consisting of users and resources.

To understand trusts, you should view them as authentication paths. For users to gain access to specific resources, a path must exist to direct the authentication requests to the proper entity. This authentication path, or trust path, defines the direction that authentication requests will be sent. Within a single forest, the trust path ultimately leads back to the forest root. Now let's take a look at trust relationships between domains.

Windows Server 2003 introduces a new method for extending the Active Directory forest design to other forests—the cross-forest external trust relationship. Cross-forest trusts are created between forest roots to provide a one-way or two-way transitive trust relationship between all domains in each forest. This type of trust requires the forest functional level to be raised to Windows Server 2003 functional level—a process that cannot be reversed. Because cross-forest trusts provide access to resources for individuals outside your organization's forest (the administrative security boundary), Microsoft has provided mechanisms to restrict authentication traffic between forests. We discussed the authentication firewall earlier in this chapter. This new feature provides capabilities to lock down cross-forest trusts through the use of the "other organization" SID. This prevents unwanted access and reduces the likelihood of DoS attacks against your organization's domain controllers. In the next section, we look at other trusts that exist in a Windows Server 2003 Active Directory design.

Other Trusts

Two other trusts that are used within a Windows Server 2003 Active Directory design are realm trusts and shortcut trusts. *Shortcut trusts* shorten the authentication path within an Active Directory forest. They connect peer domains that would otherwise have an implied trust relationship through their shared root domain. The shortcut trust shortens the path that authentication requests must travel to connect the peer domains.

Realm trusts exist between a forest root and an external Kerberos domain. Several operating systems rely on Kerberos-based authentication mechanisms, and the realm trust allows other Kerberos-enabled environments to be extended to include the Windows Server 2003 Active Directory. Trusts in Windows Server 2003 are not always external to the forest. In the next section, we will look at trust relationships that exist within the forest.

Trusts Within a Forest

Windows Server 2003 provides trust relationship control between forests, realms, and domains. Within a single Active Directory forest, as domains are created, two-way transitive trusts are automatically created. This is the built-in internal trust relationship provided by Windows Server 2003 by default between all domains in a forest.

Internal Transitive Trusts

When users authenticate in their own domain, they are provided with a Ticket-Granting Ticket (TGT). This TGT provides a mechanism for the user to access other resources throughout the local forest or any forest available via a trust. The user's TGT is used to negotiate with various servers throughout the forest until a KDC in the resource domain is reached. The KDC in the resource domain provides a service ticket to the user if the user is supposed to be given authorization to the requested resource. This entire process starts from the user's home domain and follows the trust path to the forest root. From the forest root, the request is passed up the resource domain tree until the request reaches a proper KDC in the resource domain. In a fairly complex forest design, this trust path may become quite lengthy, resulting in delayed access to resources, also known as *latency*. The trusts that create the trust path are all internal, transitive trusts that are automatically created as each domain is created within a single forest. Let's see how we can improve the performance of this trust path.

Two default trust types are automatically created in a Windows Server 2003 Active Directory forest when a new domain is created. Table 4.9 illustrates the trust types and their properties.

Table 4.9 Default Windows Server 2003 Trust Types

Trust Type	Transitivity	Direction	Description
Parent and child	Transitive	Two-way	This trust type connects child domains to parent domains within a domain tree
Tree-root	Transitive	Two-way	This trust type connects domains at the root of each domain tree with other (peer) tree root domains

There are times in a design that the default trust types within a forest do not provide sufficient results. When existing default trusts cannot provide sufficient performance, you can create other trusts to improve performance.

Shortcut Trusts

In an effort to reduce latency, if users frequently access resources in a separate domain tree, you can create a shortcut trust to shorten the trust path that authentication traffic must follow. This shortcut trust is a trust relationship between domains in the same forest. Domains within separate trees in the forest, where access to resources in the other domain is frequently required, use the shortcut trust as a means to provide direct authentication traffic between the two domains.

Now that we have our forests and domains accounted for and we have established the needed trust relationships between forests and domains, it is time to plan our OU design.

Designing the Organizational Unit Model

OUs are the smallest container objects in Active Directory. OUs provide organization, as the name implies, as well as administrative delegation capabilities. In the following sections, we will explore the various applications of OUs and discuss the best practice for their execution.

Just like the larger containers of forests and domains, best practice for OU design follows a few designated models. (The various OU design models were discussed in greater detail in Chapter 2, which presents a more concise look at the various OU designs available.) Now, let's begin by looking at the benefit of using OUs to delegate.

Delegation

EXAM
70-297
OBJECTIVE
2.1.2

One of the greatest benefits OUs provide is delegation. In this section we will analyze the three major OU models in practical use and discuss the best-practice design
of each. With OU delegation providing such a large benefit to Active Directory
administration, we will place most of the emphasis on that topic.

Microsoft recommends three scenarios in which OU creation is beneficial:

- For delegation of administrative tasks

- For division of users with unlike policy requirements

- For simplified resource administration

We will see one of the three standard models for OUs in Active Directory, which
organizes by function. The next section provides an analysis of OUs organized geographically. Finally, we will look at OUs organized by object type.

Delegating by Function

Delegating by function provides an Active Directory design that closely mimics the
organization's hierarchical structure. Each department in the organization becomes an
OU in this model. Delegating by function provides a familiar approach to organization
because the OU structure mimics the basic corporate structure. Also, administrative
overhead is reduced because basic administrative tasks will likely be the responsibility
of an individual from the department that the OU represents. Figure 4.7 illustrates an
OU hierarchy based on delegation by function.

Figure 4.7 Delegation of OUs by Function

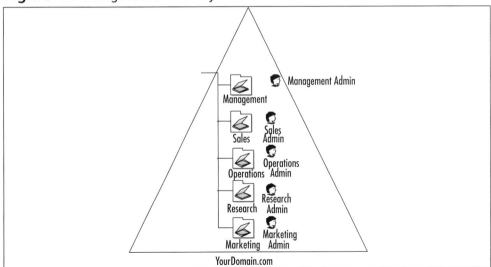

Delegating by Geography

Delegation by geography or location provides a hierarchical model that mimics the organization's geographic distribution. Each region or office has its own OU; subsequently an individual at that particular location may be tasked with basic administrative duties. This OU structure provides a reasonably stable network design, because office locations do not usually change very frequently. The disadvantage of this model is that certain locations may house several functions, resulting in an OU structure that requires a significant amount of administrative overhead. Figure 4.8 illustrates an OU hierarchy based on delegation by geography.

Figure 4.8 Delegation of OUs by Geography

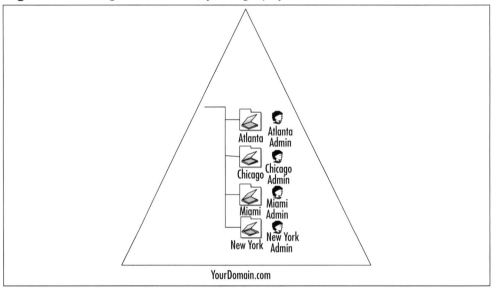

Delegating by Object Type

In an OU designed to delegate by object type, specific users within the Active Directory are tasked with administration of specific objects. For example, an organization may have a printer administrator, a Web server administrator, an e-mail administrator, or an administrator of any other type of object within Active Directory. This type of delegation is usually implemented in larger networks in which the personnel cost involved in maintaining a staff specialized for each type of object is less prohibitive. Figure 4.9 illustrates an OU hierarchy based on delegation by object type.

Figure 4.9 Delegation of OUs by Object Type

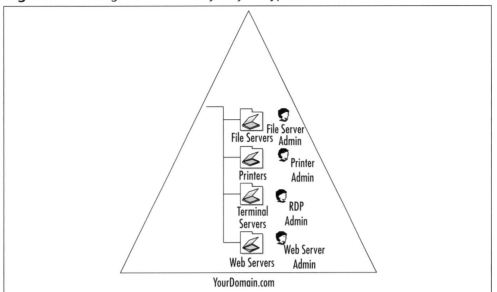

 TEST DAY TIP

Delegation is an important feature that has greatly expanded on the limitations of Windows NT 4.0. We discuss delegation in various places throughout the chapter as well as in the exercises. Make sure you know the various objects and capabilities available through Active Directory to accomplish various means of delegation.

Ownership

Ownership plays a significant part in Active Directory design. Every object within Active Directory has an owner. Object owners have the right to modify properties and contents of their objects within AD. Owners also have the right to delegate control of objects within AD. Forest owners may elect to delegate administration of the domains contained within them to other users within the AD infrastructure. Domain owners may delegate control of OUs within the domain to other users. Likewise, OU owners are responsible for the objects and data stored within OUs. This hierarchical environment based on ownership, delegation, and organizational structure is what provides such granular control within Active Directory.

Responsibility of Owners

OU owners are responsible for data management of data stored within the Active Directory. Because of their responsibilities, OU owners have to be very familiar with operational and security policies and procedures that are in place on the network. OU administrators have control over only the OUs that have been delegated to them by higher-level domain or forest administrators. OU owners may be responsible for the following:

- Account management tasks within their OU

- Workstation and member server management for systems that are members of their assigned OU

- Delegation of authority to local administrators within their assigned OU to further divide administrative responsibilities incurred

As we discussed earlier in this chapter, designing an AD infrastructure requires careful definitions of autonomy and isolation requirements. Once the autonomy and isolation requirements are understood, ownership roles and container boundaries and hierarchies may be more readily defined. Let's take a look at the process of assigning owners.

Assign Owners

We have been analyzing AD containers throughout this chapter. Each container provides an organizational structure and a means to delegate through a hierarchy. The top-level senior IT administrators own forest containers. From the forest container downward through the hierarchy, ownership is assigned or delegated to users. Users are generally given responsibility for object management through assignment of ownership. The forest owner is the owner for all objects within the AD infrastructure. Subcontainers such as domains and OUs are assigned in a hierarchical format. Forest owners assign ownership of domains to users, who will be domain administrators. Domain administrators will assign ownership of OUs to users, who will be OU administrators. It is possible that within an OU, child OUs may be created and delegated to other individuals. This delegation is assigned and controlled through the use of the forest, domain, and OU containers provided by AD.

In the next section, we will see how objects may have special policies applied to them to affect the users' environments and how the use of Group Policy can affect the overall OU design.

Group Policy

EXAM
70-297
OBJECTIVE
2.1.1

Group Policy was introduced with Windows 2000, when Microsoft first released Active Directory. Group Policy is a major extension to system policies as used in Windows 9x and Windows NT. System and Group Policies both provide a centralized method for modifying the users' desktop experience through remote registry adjustments. Group Policy is used to configure groups of users' and computers' environments to predefined settings. The settings are configured through the Microsoft Management Console (MMC) and stored in a Group Policy Object (GPO) that can be subsequently linked to containers within Active Directory to provide a consistent environment throughout the enterprise. The GPO consists of files that reside in the SYSVOL folder. Group Policy can provide some of the more simple centralized tasks, such roaming profile setup and folder redirection, to more complex tasks such as Internet Explorer configuration settings and software deployment. Let's look at a couple of examples of what Group Policy can do while we examine the recommended approach for accomplishing each task.

Group Policy implementation follows an inheritance structure whereby subcontainers (or child containers) inherit the policies of their parent containers (by default). Implementing a policy at the domain or high-level OU will result in the application of that policy throughout all objects in the container (and all child containers) unless specific measures have been taken. Now let's look at a few examples of Group Policy implementation.

In our first example, several users in your environment have to connect to a terminal server on your network to access a specialized application. The users will be working from any of the Windows 2000 Professional client systems on your network. You want to make sure that Microsoft Terminal Services client is installed on all workstations used by a specific group of users, no matter which workstation they use to access network resources. You also want to make sure that user data and items from the Start menu are consistently available, no matter which workstation a user uses to access the network. To provide the desired configurations for each client, you will have to implement roaming profiles, folder redirection, and Intellimirror software deployment features. This design will require two different GPOs to provide one set of configurations for all users while providing the Terminal Services Advanced Client to the group of users accessing the specialized application.

At the domain level, apply folder redirection through the Group Policy settings located at User Configuration | Windows Settings | Folder Redirection. Redirect the My Documents folder to a network share to ensure all user documents are available throughout the domain to each individual user. This Group Policy could be applied to the default domain policy or created as a separate policy and linked at the domain level to ensure its application to all users within the domain. The Start menu may be redirected the same way that the My Documents folder is redirected. Apply redirection to the Start menu from User Configuration | Windows

Settings | Folder Redirection and redirect the Start menu for each user to a network share.

At this point, we have accomplished two of our three stated goals for this example. Finally, we can distribute the Terminal Services Advanced Client (TSAC) to a specific group of users by placing the users in their own OU. We link a GPO to this OU to install the Terminal Services Microsoft Installer (MSI) package on the workstations used by our targeted group. Because we want to make sure the software is installed on all workstations used by our specialized group of clients, we have to assign the software to the users through our GPO. To configure this GPO, we go to User Configuration | Software Settings | Software Installation in the Group Policy MMC. From here, we can assign a network-shared package to our group of users. When our users log in to a new workstation, the software will be automatically installed for them.

In this example, we will configure an OU design based on the company outlined in Figure 4.9 and Table 4.10.

Table 4.10 YourCompany.com Corporate Structure

Location	Department	Resources
Miami	Sales	File servers
	Marketing	Printers
	Production	Workstations
		Domain controllers
		Special apps servers
Atlanta	Sales	File servers
	Marketing	Printers
	Product Support	Workstations
		Domain controllers
Houston	Sales	File servers
	Marketing	Printers
	Product Support	Workstations
		Domain controllers
New York	Executive Management	File servers
	Senior IT	Printers
	Product Support	Workstations
	R & D	Domain controllers
		Web servers

Continued

Table 4.10 YourCompany.com Corporate Structure (**Continued**)

Location	Department	Resources
Phoenix	Sales	File servers
	Marketing	Printers
	Product Support	Workstations
		Domain controllers
Los Angeles	Sales	File servers
	Marketing	Printers
	Production	Workstations
	Product Support	Domain controllers
		Special apps servers

1. The first part of our design encompassed forest and domain design decisions, as outlined earlier in this chapter. Now we have to decide on an OU structure. The options here include structures based solely on location, department (functional group), or object type. It is also possible to design a hybrid environment that encompasses aspects of each individual design.

2. Due to the volume of accounts in this organization and the centralized IT design, significant delegation will take place in this design to provide adequate support for each location.

3. This company would benefit from a hybrid design that first uses a geographic delegation model, nested with a function delegation model. Figure 4.10 illustrates the OU design.

Figure 4.10 Completed OU Design

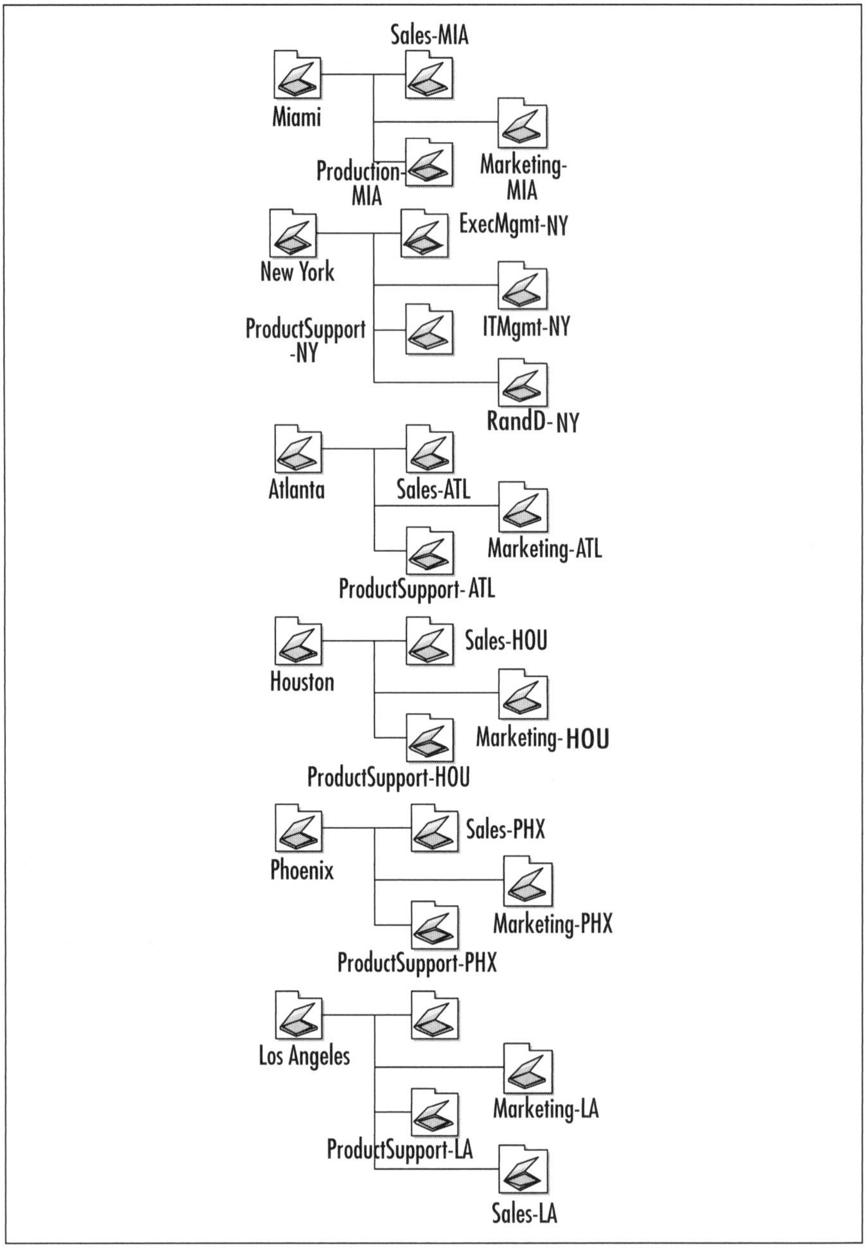

[figure showing a hierarchical OU design with folder icons:

Miami → Sales-MIA, Marketing-MIA, Production-MIA

New York → ExecMgmt-NY, ITMgmt-NY, RandD-NY, ProductSupport-NY

Atlanta → Sales-ATL, Marketing-ATL, ProductSupport-ATL

Houston → Sales-HOU, Marketing-HOU, ProductSupport-HOU

Phoenix → Sales-PHX, Marketing-PHX, ProductSupport-PHX

Los Angeles → Marketing-LA, ProductSupport-LA, Sales-LA]

EXAM
70-297
OBJECTIVE
2.1.1

Impact on OU Design

In our example, our user requirements dictated our OU design. GPO design requirements are often met by providing the right OU design. Because specific users within the organization required a certain software package, in this case the requirements worked well with an OU design based on function. Structuring the OUs around the functional groups within the organization provided a mechanism for segregating user desktop configurations, allowing us to provide specialized configurations for one particular group of users. Within this same design, we may elect to delegate administration for our specialized group to a manager within that functional group.

We can provide the necessary tools and necessary rights to delegate account maintenance and day-to-day account management to this individual. To simplify network management, we may grant the responsibility to change passwords and to create and disable accounts to this individual. In this way, a large organization with thousands of users may grant a certain level of autonomy to functional groups, geographically defined groups, or groups responsible for specific objects within the Active Directory.

Defining the Group Policy Object Approach

Since its introduction with Windows 2000, Group Policy has been a major focal point. Because Group Policy provides for more than 1000 different desktop and system alterations, each affecting the users' experience to simplify management and thereby reduce costs of ownership, expect this topic to continue to garner a large amount of attention when you're designing an AD infrastructure.

In this section, we will expand on our earlier example while also adding some new examples to illustrate the benefits and proper design of Group Policy and GPOs. We also analyze different default GPOs and see how each plays a role in our AD design. We will further expand the concept of delegation and see in greater detail how GPOs and a proper OU infrastructure can provide simplified administration through delegation of tasks. Let's begin by looking at the requirements for Group Policy implementation.

Requirements

Group policies affect Windows 2000-, Windows XP-, and Windows 2003-based machines. Implementation of policies for Windows 9x- and Windows NT-based machines is accomplished through the limited capabilities of the system policy editor for the respective operating systems. Windows 9x and Windows NT system policies provided limited lockdown and deployment capabilities in Windows NT-based domains and still provide only limited capabilities for Windows 9x and Windows NT clients within an Active Directory environment. Several features are available through Group Policy that were not available using the previous generation system policy editor.

System Policy settings that can be specified on Windows 9x- and Windows NT-based systems with System Policy Editor (Poledit.exe) can be characterized as having the following traits:

- They apply only to domains.

- Control over them may be extended by user membership in security groups.

- They lack security. A user is able to change them with the registry editor.

- They overwrite user preferences.

- They remain in users' profiles, occasionally beyond their intended life cycle. Once a registry setting is set using Windows NT 4.0 System Policy, the setting remains until the policy is reversed or the registry is edited directly.

- They are limited in function to specific desktop behavior based on registry settings.

Windows 2000 Group Policy provided more than 650 settings, exhibiting a broad range of options for user environment management. Windows 2000 Group Policy exhibits the following traits:

- Works within Active Directory or can be defined locally

- Extensible with MMC or .adm files

- Stores settings securely

- Maintains user preferences

- If the policy is changed or removed, settings are not left in the users' profiles

- Can be applied to users or computers in a specified Active Directory OU

- User or computer membership in security groups provides further control

- Can be used to configure security settings

- Provides logon, logoff, startup, and shutdown script capabilities

- Provides software installation and maintenance

- Can be used to redirect folders

- Provides maintenance capabilities for Internet Explorer

Windows Server 2003 provides more than 200 improvements and enhancements to Windows 2000 Active Directory Group Policy. The new enhancements include configuration capabilities for the Control Panel, error reporting, Terminal Services, remote assistance, networking and dialup connections, network logon, Group Policy, roaming profiles, client DNS settings, and others. Two new additions to Windows Server 2003 Group Policy are the new Group Policy Management Console (GPMC) and Windows Management Instrumentation (WMI) filtering facilities.

GPMC provides an interface for simulating Group Policy implementations as well as reporting functionality and other new ease-of-use features. WMI filtering provides

Group Policy deployment control based on available criteria provided by WMI, relying on information such as type of network card, disk space, and other environment information available through WMI.

In the next section, we will see how Group Policy fits into the various OU models discussed earlier in this chapter.

The OU Model

Earlier in this chapter, we reviewed three models for delegation using OUs. In this section, we analyze each of the three models, reviewing the benefits of each with regard to Group Policy implementation. The three models are:

- Functional
- Geographic
- Object type

Best practice dictates that OU implementations should not rely on significant depth through nesting. Also, it is considered best practice to use as few OUs as possible to achieve the desired results. As mentioned previously, grouping by function means placing objects and accounts by organizational function or department. This OU model works well with Group Policy because users and systems that are used to perform the same basic function will typically have the same software and configurations. A Group Policy may be applied to the functional OU to provide this consistent environment. This model may prove to be less beneficial in smaller organizations in which very few people make up each functional group. In this case, the number of OUs that have to be deployed to accomplish the desired results will prove counterproductive to administrative simplification due to the high ratio of OUs to users.

The geographic model works well in small to midsize organizations in which each satellite office may require specific configurations that are dependent on location. This model is often used in conjunction with the functional model to provide nested OUs that model geography and function. The geographic OUs will be used for delegation, while the functional OUs will typically be used for configuration control.

The object type model is typically used in very large organizations. This model provides consistent application of configuration settings to groups of systems. For example, an individual may be responsible for messaging server administration. If a specific set of new configurations should be applied, it may be applied to the OU containing the messaging servers through a linked GPO. Again, the object type model typically works best in very large organizations in which large groups of similar objects may be the responsibility of an individual or group within the overall organization.

EXAM WARNING

As we saw earlier in this chapter, forest and domain designs are based on high-level functionality and the existing network infrastructure. OUs are the real opportunity to mirror a company's actual organization structure. Be prepared to have your mettle tested on OU design and how it fits into an organization's departmental structure.

What Do We Hope to Achieve?

In designing an infrastructure for GPO deployment, the axiom "A picture is worth a thousand words" certainly applies. So far in this chapter, we have seen design constraints that apply to our AD design. Typically, the user base, the link speeds, and previous design constraints play a part in the overall AD design. This should be plotted in a logical diagram to reflect the hard limitations imposed by other factors in our design. From here, we should see how features that we expect to apply through linked GPOs fit into our existing infrastructure design.

By seeing the existing constraints and matching what we hope to achieve to those constraints, we can see what is missing from our AD design with regard to Group Policy. The remaining organization of our AD infrastructure will typically be left up to one of our OU delegation models. This is the time to evaluate or reevaluate the OU delegation models to see how our design can best benefit from one or a combination of the delegation models. Again, we want to achieve our desired results with as few OUs as possible and with as few GPOs as possible. A properly created GPO design provides an environment with a reduced total cost of ownership (TCO) by locking systems down and providing a consistent, standard configuration to groups of machines while providing an overall environment that is simple to implement and maintain.

Let's take a look at the GPOs and their specific applications now.

How Many and Where Applied?

We want to apply as few GPOs as possible, built around an OU design that includes enough OUs to accomplish simplified organization while still providing the necessary delegation requirements. GPOs do not have to be linked to OUs. It is possible to link GPOs to domain and site containers as well. You should evaluate your AD environment and determine where specific settings should be applied. Settings that will affect users throughout your environment should be applied to the domain. It is recommended that domain policies are created and linked to the domain independently of the default domain policy. Although it is possible to link GPOs to sites, a good AD design will typically provide an OU structure that mimics the site design so GPOs may be linked to those OUs instead. The best design will provide all of the required user and system configuration settings with the fewest GPOs possible.

Developing & Deploying…

The GPO Deployment Balancing Act

A famous Dr. Seuss book states, "Life is a balancing act." Similarly, the process of Group Policy design and deployment is also a balancing act. Designing a Group Policy deployment requires a thorough analysis of the desired results before the first GPO is ever created. Create too many GPOs, and you are defeating the purpose of GPOs. If your design has too many GPOs, you will have to invest a significant amount of overhead to maintain the environment. The purpose of GPOs is a consistent, low-overhead environment. With each GPO that is added to your design, you increase the amount of overhead.

GPOs provide a granular design, compared to their system policy predecessors. The fewer GPOs that are used in a design, however, the decreased degree of granularity provided. So, often you will find that a design involves a tradeoff between this granular design and the overhead required to implement and maintain the GPOs. One final tradeoff comes into play in designing a GPO deployment—security. Using GPOs, you can configure various security settings for machines throughout the AD infrastructure.

Often, simplified administration or a reduction in administrative overhead means a less diligent approach to security. The security balance lies somewhere between the most secure, non-networked, unplugged PC that provides no benefit to its user to the PC with the least secure, networked, administrative rights for everyone, which compromises the security of your entire network, including all your data and services. Because a one-size-fits-all approach to enterprise security does not exist, a single, simple GPO does not really provide the best fit for enterprise security. Again, to balance the needs of disparate systems and users, multiple GPOs typically have to be applied to meet the needs and design requirements for security. Once again, we attempt to balance between a granular approach that provides a best fit for everyone involved and a singular approach that requires the least amount of overhead to design and maintain. There is no perfect solution or a single correct answer involving GPO deployments. It is a balancing act between each of the factors discussed here.

EXAM
70-297

OBJECTIVE
2.7.1

Delegating the Group Policy

Earlier in this chapter, we discussed delegation and the reasons for using the delegation capabilities in Active Directory. We can delegate control of basically any object within Active Directory. Also earlier in this chapter, we analyzed the basics of Group Policy and looked at GPOs. So, it would seem only natural to delegate control and administration of the newest objects in our analysis—GPOs. In this section, we discuss delegation of GPOs, and we will see the two administrative models used in information technology enterprise design and how they affect Group Policy design and delegation.

IT management can be accomplished through two different administrative models:

- The centralized management model, whereby a single individual or group of individuals makes all decisions that affect the enterprise infrastructure, provides services, and administers the AD forest and all its contents

- The distributed management model, in which each business unit, department, or division is responsible for the information technology services, infrastructure, and administration for their respective portion of the Active Directory infrastructure

Let's begin with an analysis of the centralized management model.

Centralized Management

Centralized IT management does not mean that administrative tasks are handled only by an individual or a group. It means that an individual or a group is ultimately responsible for the necessary administrative tasks throughout the enterprise. A centralized management model may still utilize AD's delegation capabilities to delegate specific tasks for an Active Directory container. It is possible to delegate the following tasks through Active Directory:

- GPO creation

- GPO management

- Performing the following tasks on sites, domains, and OUs:

  - GPO link management for a given site, domain, or OU

  - Group Policy modeling analyses for objects in that container

  - Group Policy results analysis for objects in that container

- WMI filter creation

- Individual WMI filter editing and management

 TEST DAY TIP

The area of management structure is a hot topic in many organizations. Often, users complain that they do not have sufficient rights within the network to accomplish their job functions, while administrators usually complain that users have too much access throughout the network, which in turn causes high administrative overhead to undo what a few users have done. Make a note of the differences between centralized management and distributed management and how this affects the Active Directory design.

It should be noted that Group Policy modeling and results analysis tasks are not applicable to sites. The administrative model your organization uses will help you determine which tasks shall be delegated and to which AD containers you should delegate the tasks. Generally, in a centralized management model, simpler tasks such as changing passwords and possibly other accounting tasks will be delegated at the OU level. Again, specific configurations that should affect all users within your organization will typically be applied at the domain level. It is considered best practice to link GPOs to the highest container possible, using permissions and inheritance properties to filter the effects on child containers. Remember that Group Policy follows an inheritance structure in which child containers and objects generally inherit the settings applied to parent containers. Administrators may choose Block Policy inheritance on certain levels to alter the effects of a particular Group Policy from being inherited by a container. Likewise, an administrator may want to ensure that a policy is enforced. In this particular case, the administrator has the option to select Enforce (No Override) to prevent owners and administrators of child containers from blocking the policy application. Although a centralized management model may not be entirely centralized in administrative operation, a distributed model is completely decentralized.

Distributed Management

In distributed IT management, an individual or a group is not ultimately responsible for the necessary administrative tasks throughout the enterprise. In the distributed management model, different functional groups within an organization are ultimately responsible for the IT administration of their respective infrastructures.

Designing and implementing a distributed management model is highly dependent on the Active Directory container hierarchy. A distributed management model is basically a management model that provides service isolation or, at a minimum, data isolation, as discussed earlier in this chapter. Depending on the degree of trust that exists between the different managing entities, you may choose to create a multiple-forest design, a multiple-domain design, or a delegated OU design. In the event that a multiple-domain or delegated OU design is implemented, service isolation will not be provided. Also, in a multiple-domain or delegated OU environment, you are sharing the AD schema and portions of AD partitions between entities. This will reduce the administrative and implementation expenses associated with an AD deployment, but it will also compromise the administrative isolation.

A properly designed AD environment provides capabilities to delegate GPO creation, GPO links, and GPO reporting functions to qualified individuals who operate within the portions of the organization that their respective OU, site, or domain represents. This system ensures that administration is not completely the onus of the IT administrators, providing self-sufficiency for individual departments or offices where it may be reasonably delegated. In the next exercise, we see how to delegate GPO functionality to a group responsible for an OU within Active Directory.

EXERCISE 4.03

DELEGATING A GROUP POLICY OBJECT TO A SECURITY GROUP

In this exercise, we will create a special group (GPO-Admins-ATL) to administer Group Policies and GPOs for one of the geographic OUs (the Atlanta OU) created in our last exercise. We will grant permission to create, link, delete, and generate GPOs.

1. First, we need to download and install the Group Policy Management Console (gpmc.msi). Download the file from www.microsoft.com/downloads/details.aspx?FamilyId=C355B04F-50CE-42C7-A401-30BE1EF647EA&displaylang=en.

2. Once installation is complete, we work from Active Directory Users and Computers to create the necessary OU structure. Choose **Start | All Programs | Administrative Tools | Active Directory Users and Computers**.

3. Create an OU structure as shown in Figure 4.11.

Figure 4.11 The Atlanta OU Structure

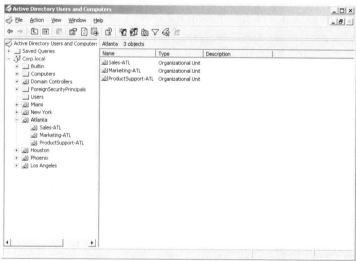

4. Now create a new domain global security group for the GPO-Admins-ATL group. Right-click **Atlanta OU**, then select **New | Group**. Create the **GPO-Admins-ATL** global group.

5. Click **OK** to finish creating the group to which the Atlanta GPOs will be delegated.

6. Right-click the newly created group, and select **Properties**.

7. From the **Member of** tab, select **Add**.

8. Type **g** and click **Check Names**. Highlight the **Group Policy Creator Owners** group as shown in Figure 4.12.

Figure 4.12 Adding the New Group to the Group Policy Creator Owners Group

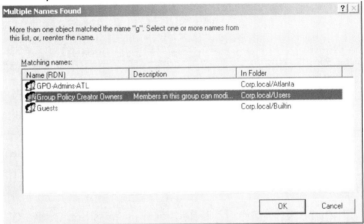

9. Click **OK** three times to complete the group membership portion of this exercise.

10. When the Group Policy Management Console is not installed, GPOs are created and administered by right-clicking the container where the policy would be applied in the Active Directory Users and Computers MMC snap-in. Right-click **Atlanta OU**, and select **Properties**.

11. From the **Atlanta Properties** dialog box, select the **Group Policy** tab, as shown in Figure 4.13.

Figure 4.13 The Group Policy Tab; Group Policy Management
Console Installed

12. Click **Open** to open the Group Policy Management Console.

13. Click the OU that you want to delegate Group Policy to, and
     select **Delegation** in the right pane.

14. Click **Add** in the right pane, and add the **GPO-Admins-ATL**
     global group that you created earlier in this exercise, as shown in
     Figure 4.14.

Figure 4.14 Adding Delegation Permissions to the GPO-Admins-ATL
Global Group

15. From the **Permission** drop-down box in the right pane, add the
     GPO-Admins-ATL global group to the other permissions, as
     shown in Figure 4.15.

Figure 4.15 Adding the Remaining Permissions for Complete Delegation

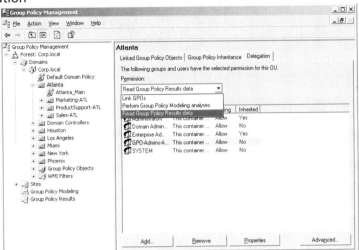

16. Close the **Group Policy Management** MMC to complete the delegation of control. Members of the GPO-Admins-ATL global group now have permissions to create GPOs, link them to the Atlanta OU or OUs contained within the Atlanta OU, perform Group Policy modeling analyses, and read Group Policy results data.

Mandatory Policy Settings

When Active Directory is installed and configured on a Windows Server 2003 server, default Group Policies are installed. The two Group Policies installed by default are the Default Domain Policy and the Default Domain Controllers Policy. The default policies should not be modified. If an existing policy requirement conflicts with the default policies, a separate policy should be configured instead of modifying the default policies.

The Default Domain Policy specifies settings that control the following security configurations:

- Password policy

- Account lockout policy

- Kerberos policy

The Default Domain Controllers Policy specifies settings that control the following:

- User rights assignment

In the following sections, we will look at the Default Domain Policy and Default Domain Controllers Policy in greater detail.

Default Domain Policy

Default Domain Policy controls security settings involving password and account policy settings, including Kerberos Policy. Figure 4.16 illustrates the password policy settings for the Windows Server 2003 Default Domain Policy. Table 4.11 lists each policy, with brief descriptions explaining the policy settings available.

Figure 4.16 Default Domain Policy: Password Policy Settings

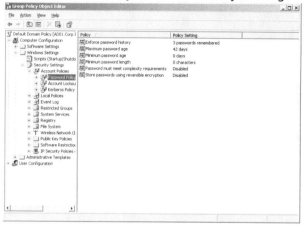

Table 4.11 Password Policies with Descriptions

Policy	Description
Enforce password history	Maintains a list of previously used passwords. Users must use a new password not currently residing on this list.
Maximum password age	Controls how long a user may use a given password before he or she is forced to change the password.
Minimum password age	Prevents users from circumventing the password history by repeatedly changing passwords during one session in an effort to use a preferred password.
Minimum password length	Forces users to use passwords of a specific minimum length to ensure greater security.

Continued

Table 4.11 Password Policies with Descriptions (**Continued**)

Policy	Description
Password must meet complexity requirements	Forces users to use a combination of capitals, lowercase letters, numbers, and special characters to ensure greater security.
Store passwords using reversible encryption	Stores a clear-text password (used by CHAP in RRAS and Digest Authentication in IIS).

Best practice specifies a password history with a small maximum password age. Password complexity requirements with a minimum of eight characters in password length are the preferred settings for password length and complexity settings. Increasing password length in conjunction with enabling password complexity will greatly increase the level of security provided by Windows Server 2003. As is the case with any security setting, however, the design will ultimately be a tradeoff between the cost incurred by the increased level of support required to administer the tighter security and the cost of a security breach.

The Default Domain Policy also provides predefined account lockout policy settings, as mentioned previously. The account lockout threshold is the only predefined item for account lockout policy, as shown in Figure 4.17.

Figure 4.17 Default Domain Policy: Account Lockout Policy Settings

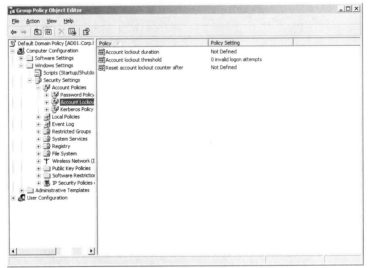

Also, as mentioned previously, the Default Domain Policy provides predefined Kerberos policy settings as well. The Kerberos policy settings define Kerberos ticket life settings and clock synchronization settings, as shown in Figure 4.18.

Figure 4.18 Default Domain Policy: Kerberos Policy Settings

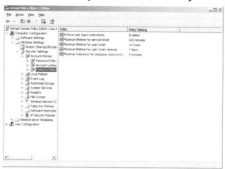

EXAM
70-297
OBJECTIVE
2.4
2.4.1
2.4.2

Developing & Deploying…

Designing Strategies for Account Policies

When designing user account policies, ensure that the settings described previously are carefully chosen, because they will affect each and every account in the domain. These settings should also be chosen so as to meet company and regulatory policies and standards that exist within your organization. Furthermore, consider closely options such as Password must meet complexity requirements and Account lockout threshold.

Password complexity, when enabled, will ensure that all users choose passwords with three different character types, from the groups a–z, A–Z, and 0–9, and special characters such as @, #, and &. However, if users are not educated and told how to choose complex passwords and are not used to doing so, most will struggle to choose a password that meets the complexity requirements. For this reason, complexity may need to be disabled within your environment, because its enablement might result in a huge increase in calls being logged with Help desks, thus outweighing the benefits of more secure passwords.

Similarly, if account lockout has never been used before, or if users are used to their accounts being locked only after a large number of bad logon attempts, any changes to the lockout threshold may result in an increased number of issues as a result of locked out accounts. Applications that use service accounts to logon, may attempt to logon many times in quick succession, if an initial logon fails, thus resulting in a locked account. As a result, the threshold should be carefully considered, and ideally not set too low such that accounts become locked after only a small number of bad logon attempts.

In addition to carefully considering these policies with respect to users in general, you should also consider how to handle special accounts such as administrative and service accounts. Consider segregating these accounts by placing them in separate organization units, so they may be easily identified and subject to tighter controls and policies. Furthermore, consider placing administrative workstations inside segregated OUs so that these machines

Continued

(Continued)

may also be further locked down. As an example, RDP sessions to Domain Controllers via a Terminal Services client may be restricted via Group Policy to only those machines located inside a specific OU. Those machines added to the special OU are then those used by the Domain Admins, which then adds another layer of security to Domain Controller access. In addition, because all administrative machines are located in the same OU, different audit policies may be applied to those machines so that activity on those machines may be closely monitored and controlled.

Now let's take a look at the Default Domain Controllers Policy.

The Default Domain Controllers Policy

Numerous user rights assignment settings are predefined in the Default Domain Controllers Policy. Figure 4.19 illustrates the predefined user rights assignment settings for the Windows Server 2003 Default Domain Controllers Policy.

Figure 4.19 Default Domain Controllers Policy: User Rights Assignment

As Figure 4.19 illustrates, several options are predefined in the Default Domain Controllers Policy. The main functions provided by this predefined policy control users' abilities to accomplish administrative and non-administrative tasks in an Active Directory environment. One of the more common settings provided by the User Rights Assignment portion of the Default Domain Controllers Policy is the capability to Add workstations to domain, granting the right to join systems to the current domain environment. Other policies control the capabilities to log on locally, log on through Terminal Services, and back up files and folders on the system, just to name a few. In the next section, we will discuss best practice and review some common settings used in Active Directory Group Policy.

Other Policy Settings

Best practice dictates that GPOs should be linked to the highest container possible. This ensures that policy settings are not unnecessarily repeated in an AD design. As discussed earlier in this chapter, best practice also dictates that the Default Domain Policy and Default Domain Controllers Policy should not be modified. Conflicting policy settings should be accomplished by creating a new GPO and linking it to the Domain or Domain Controllers OUs.

In a network environment, server data is generally routinely backed up for disaster protection. It is far less common for workstations to be backed up on a routine basis. For this reason, in the past administrators had to educate users as to the importance of using the network-mapped drives to store their files. In spite of this, users might end up saving documents locally—probably to the My Documents folder. Fortunately, Group Policy provides folder redirection capabilities to redirect the My Documents folder to a network share. This circumvents the possibility that a user's data may not be backed up because the user may store his or her data locally to the My Documents folder instead of the network share. Some other common settings include configuring the connection settings through the Internet Explorer Maintenance settings policy folder and software installation under the Software Settings folder. The connection settings configuration options provide a copy of the local Internet Explorer connection settings to all clients that the policy applies to. The software installation configuration option provides a method for deploying software to remote users from a network share.

All the policy settings defined by a GPO are divided into two sections: user policy settings and machine policy settings. This ensures that configuration options exist for user accounts as well as computer accounts. Certain scenarios dictate machine configuration requirements; other scenarios may dictate user configuration requirements. In the following sections, we will analyze the user and machine policy options in greater detail.

User Policy Settings

User policy settings provide configuration options to control users' desktop settings, software availability, and software settings. User policy settings are applied when a user logs on to the domain. Some common user policy settings are the logon and logoff script capabilities, which provide an avenue to apply various scripted settings, including printer mapping, drive mapping, and time synchronization functions. Another common policy is the folder redirection policy. This policy provides folder redirection for the My Documents folder (a recommended practice), application data, the Start menu, and desktop redirection. Software deployment can be controlled through the user policy settings to ensure that certain software packages are available to users. Also, common Internet Explorer settings may be centrally configured using the user policy settings.

As you can see, Group Policy provides a significant amount of control over many aspects of the users' experience. The user policy settings may be disabled if only machine policy settings are configured.

Machine Policy Settings

Machine policy settings provide configuration options to control machines' desktop settings, software availability, and software settings. Machine policy settings are applied when a machine starts. Like the user policy settings, machine policy settings provide control over various aspects of the system environment. Software may be deployed to machines, and startup and shutdown scripts may be applied in a similar fashion to users' logon and logoff scripts. Remote assistance settings and Group Policy control settings may be configured through the machine policy settings as well. In total, between the user policy settings and the machine policy settings, you can define more than 1,000 different configuration options through Group Policy. The machine policy settings may be disabled if only user policy settings are configured.

Exploring Groups and Roles

We have discussed the concept of delegation several times throughout this chapter, but up to this point we have not really discussed how delegation can be accomplished. In this section, we will see how you can use group membership to provide different types of delegation. Next, we will see how you can use roles to control administration and application access.

Delegation Using Groups

Delegation using groups is generally divided in to two classes: data access groups and administrative access groups. In the following sections, we will analyze and compare the use of groups for administrative and data purposes.

Data Access Groups

Data access groups are used in conjunction with DACLs to regulate users' access to resources in Active Directory. The DACL contains access control entries (ACEs) that determine the users' access to a given object.

Windows Server 2003 includes three types of security groups to provide data access control:

- Domain local groups
- Global groups
- Universal groups

Domain local groups are placed within the DACLs to provide permissions. Domain local groups can have the following members: accounts, global groups, and universal groups, all from any domain if the domain functional level is set to Windows 2000 Native Mode or higher. These groups can also have other domain local groups from within the same domain as members. Domain local groups, as their name implies, are local to the particular domain where they are created.

TEST DAY TIP

The most important aspect of networking to most users is that they can access the resources they need. Once that goal is accomplished, the next major concern for most users is the speed with which they can access resources. Providing the lowest latency, fastest service possible is reflective of proper design and tuning. Make sure you know a few methods for tuning the network performance (scheduling replication traffic, setting costs, or disabling unneeded settings such as user or machine configurations in GPOs).

Global groups provide a mechanism for access control beyond the local domain. Global groups can have the following members: accounts from the same domain and other global groups from the same domain if the domain functional level is set to Windows 2000 Native Mode or higher. Global groups are applicable forestwide.

Universal groups provide a mechanism to nest like groups throughout the forest. Universal groups can have the following members: accounts, computer accounts, other universal groups, and global groups from any domain if the domain functional level is set to Windows 2000 Native Mode or higher.

The domain functional level affects the types of groups available and their behavior. Table 4.12 illustrates the various group types and their required domain functional levels.

Table 4.12 Group Types and Their Required Domain Functional Levels

Domain Feature	Windows 2000 Mixed Windows	Windows 2000 Native	Windows Server 2003
Universal groups	Enabled for distribution groups Disabled for security groups	Enabled for both security and distribution groups	Enabled for both security and distribution groups
Group nesting	Enabled for distribution groups Disabled for security groups, except for domain local security groups that can have global groups as members	Enabled Allows full group nesting	Enabled Allows full group nesting
Converting groups	Disabled No group conversions allowed	Enabled Allows conversion between security groups and distribution groups	Enabled Allows conversion between security groups and distribution groups

Administrative Access Groups

Administrative access groups are used to control administrative rights in Active Directory. These groups are the delegated groups, like the ones we created and implemented in Exercise 4.03. Several built-in administrative access groups exist within Windows Server 2003 Active Directory. Table 4.13 illustrates many of the common administrative access groups.

Table 4.13 Common Administrative Access Groups

Group	Function
Backup Operators	Overrides security for the purpose of backing up data
Print Operators	Administers domain printers
DHCP Administrators	Gains administrative access to the DHCP service
HelpServicesGroup	Group for the Help and Support Center
Enterprise Admins	Administers domains and forest
Schema Admins	Allows modification rights to the schema
Group Policy Creator Owners	Group allowed to create group policies
DnsAdmins	Administers DNS servers

Each of the groups listed in Table 4.13 provides some type of special functions with Active Directory. Administrative delegation typically involves adding users to one of the groups listed in the table.

Understanding User Roles

User roles in Active Directory may be used in conjunction with the new Authorization Manager utility to configure role-based administration. Authorization roles are designed based on a user's job function. Authorization roles may be used to:

- Authorize access

- Delegate administrative privileges

- Manage interaction with computer-based resources

Roles should be identified within any organization, and thorough planning and documentation should follow role identification. Every role that will be created within an organization should have a specific management policy to ensure that roles are needed and not being misused. In the following sections, we will see how role requirements can be determined. Next, we will use the role requirements to create and manage roles.

Identifying Roles

When you use role-based administration in an Active Directory environment, you must define specific job functions and clearly specify their respective access and administrative requirements. Mapping this information out will provide a clear path for our role-based administrative design.

An example of a role-based administrative function might include a financial officer responsible for authorizing purchases and generating financial reports. Other common roles can include OU owners, user object manager, password administrator, and printer manager. Understanding the user's basic role and access requirements that this role will need to complete the job function allows us to define the necessary structure to provide the user with sufficient rights to complete his or her tasks as well as sufficient management to ensure that the role is being used properly. In the next exercise, we will extend delegation to further encompass role-based administration.

EXERCISE 4.04

DELEGATING BY GROUP

In this exercise, you will create a group structure to which you will delegate control over an OU. Then you'll customize a Microsoft Management Console for the delegated tasks. Begin by opening a blank MMC.

1. Choose **Start | Run**, type **MMC**, and click **OK**.

2. From the blank MMC, choose **File | Add/Remove Snap-in**. Your screen should resemble Figure 4.20.

Figure 4.20 Add a Snap-in: Listing the Snap-ins

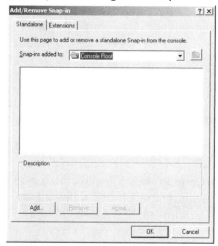

3. From the Add/Remove Snap-in dialog box, select **Add**.

4. From the Add Standalone Snap-in dialog box, select **Active Directory Users and Computers** from the **Available Standalone Snap-ins:** list and click **Add**, as shown in Figure 4.21.

Figure 4.21 Adding the Active Directory Users and Computers Snap-in

5. Click **Close** to close the Add Standalone Snap-in dialog box.
6. Click **OK** to begin using the new MMC, as shown in Figure 4.22.

Figure 4.22 Adding the Active Directory Users and Computers Snap-in

7. Now we have a standard Active Directory Users and Computers MMC, with a few extra options. Select **Active Directory Users and Computers** in the left pane, followed by the domain name. From the right pane, right-click **Atlanta OU**, and select **New | Group** to add a group.

8. Create an **Admins_ATL** global group, as outlined in Exercise 4.03.

9. Now right-click **Atlanta OU** again, and select **Delegate Control**.

10. Click **Next**. From the **Delegation of Control Wizard**, select **Add...** and add the **Admins_ATL** group to the delegation list.

11. Click **Next**.

12. Select **Create, delete, and manage user accounts**, as illustrated in Figure 4.23.

Figure 4.23 Delegating Account Creation Policy

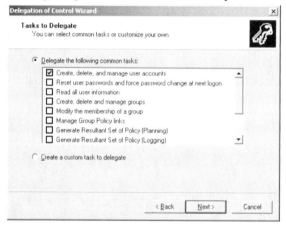

13. Click **Next** to continue the delegation process.

14. Select **Finish** to complete the delegation process.

Creating and Managing Roles

The Authorization Manager is a new utility available in Windows Server 2003 that provides role-based account creation and management capabilities. This utility will help us translate the information we compiled in the previous section to usable account settings for our role-based administration. Using the previous example, we could take the financial officer's job requirements to develop a role-based policy using the Authorization Manager.

Generally, an organization wants to monitor roles as part of standard management practice to ensure that only properly authorized users are members of groups with administrative capabilities. Most organizations will elect to audit the use of each of the high-level roles to ensure that users are accountable for their actions. Without a suitable auditing policy in place, a proper system of checks and balances does not exist to protect the directory from unauthorized access and modifications. Auditing and proper management ensure that delegated functions are handled properly while still reducing the need for completely centralized administration.

In the next section, we will see how Active Directory's logical structure is configured to utilize the underlying physical network infrastructure.

Defining Replication Topology

Active Directory has a lot more intelligence built into it compared to Windows NT 4.0 with regard to replication control and site awareness. Here we take a look at the physical network design and how Active Directory may be configured to accommodate the networking conditions available through our network infrastructure. First, we should ensure that when the term *replication* comes up, the concept is completely understood. For a complete understanding of the terms and concepts in replication, refer to Chapter 2, where the basic topologies and terminologies were spelled out in more detail.

Active Directory replication involves the process in which changes are distributed and tracked between domain controllers. The actual data that is replicated is broken into partitions. When all partitions are replicated to another domain controller, the process creates a full replica. Not only does the full replica contain all attributes of all directory partition objects, it is also both readable and writeable. Three full, writeable directory partition replicas exist on every domain controller as follows:

- **Schema partition** Contains all class and attribute definitions for the forest. There is one schema directory partition per forest.

- **Configuration partition** Contains replication configuration information and other information common across the forest. There is one configuration directory partition per forest.

- **Domain partition** Contains all objects that are stored within a given domain. There is one domain directory partition for each domain in the forest.

Now that we have a basic understanding of what is being replicated, let's take a look at how replication takes place in a Windows Server 2003 Active Directory environment.

New Features

Windows Server 2003 has improved on the replication capabilities of Active Directory by providing a new feature called *link replication*. Link replication provides a mechanism for incremental replication of multivalued attributes. An example of this feature: When a user's membership in a group is changed, only the changed information is replicated throughout Active Directory. In the past, a change in group membership would propagate replication of the entire group. Group membership is an example of a multivalued attribute that benefits from the new link replication system.

Active Directory provides a truly revolutionary improvement over the Windows NT 4.0 SAM-based single-master replication model. Multimaster replication provides administrators with the capability to make changes to information on any domain controller within the domain, with the guarantee that changes will be propagated to all the domain controllers within the domain. This two-way process provides capabilities to make modifications to information within the domain from multiple-domain controllers at any given moment. In the next section, we will see how Active Directory's logical infrastructure may be configured to provide awareness of the network's physical topology.

Collating Network Data

Let's look at how Active Directory provides configuration options to provide network infrastructure awareness. Active Directory sites, site links, scheduling, and bridgehead servers all work together to provide for controlled WAN traffic between LANs, ensuring controlled replication of Active Directory data between disparate locations.

Identifying Active Directory Sites and Subnets

In the early days of Windows NT 4.0, the Internet was barely a thought on most people's minds, and the notion of network connectivity typically extended only as far as the office LAN. As the Internet quickly grew in popularity and the need for interconnectivity between offices increased, Windows NT 4.0's original design concepts for domain functionality began to show its age. As the network began to extend its reach, network infrastructure designs became more important to a properly functioning domain.

With the introduction of Windows 2000, Microsoft introduced Active Directory and with it site containers. A *site container* is an AD object that may be configured to mimic the physical layout of LAN segments of the overall network design. In a TCP/IP network, providing WAN connectivity typically means providing a Layer 3 routed environment in which different IP subnets are used to segregate traffic. Each LAN (or VLAN) belongs to its own subnet to group its respective machines. This subnet grouping is how TCP/IP understands whether to use local discovery and communication techniques or whether remote discovery and communication techniques will be used. We can associate the subnet information to an Active Directory site to provide network infrastructure awareness to Active Directory. This awareness also extends to the actual links between subnets, the expensive WAN traffic.

Each AD site may be configured with a site link to mimic the WAN link connecting the sites. This site link may be configured to reflect the available bandwidth or preference that the link has in the network design using a cost metric. In other words, let's say that a slow link exists between two offices. Elsewhere, another link exists from one of the offices to a third office. Site links may be configured to utilize a preferred route for replication traffic. This is not an IP preferred route, as seen in IP routing protocol data, but a preferred route understood by Microsoft Active Directory. Table 4.14 illustrates the Microsoft-recommended cost values for common bandwidths.

Table 4.14 Recommended Costs for Common Links

Available Bandwidth (Kbps)	Cost
9.6	1024
19.2	798
38.4	644
56	586
64	567
128	486
256	425
512	378
1024	340
2048	309
4096	283

Figure 4.24 illustrates a multioffice design with link costs attached.

Figure 4.24 A Multioffice Network with Costs

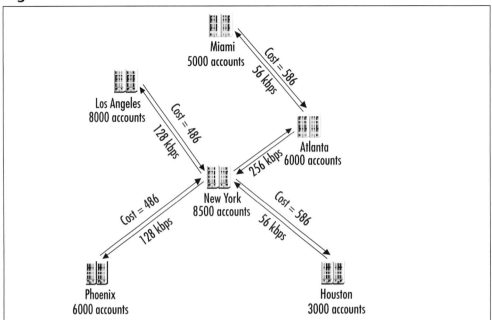

Active Directory uses its understanding of sites to adjust replication between domain controllers. This knowledge of sites provides for different replication intervals for intersite versus intrasite replication. *Intrasite replication* (replication within a site) takes place using a ring topology that Active Directory predefines as each domain controller is introduced to the site. The *Knowledge Consistency Checker (KCC)* is responsible for defining the replication topology for intrasite replication. This ring topology, in conjunction with a triggered update system, ensures fast replication and consequently fast convergence for changes to Active Directory and its objects.

Intrasite replication occurs over a logical bidirectional ring. This ring emerges with no more than three hops from the source domain controller to the last destination domain controller, with a replication interval of five minutes per replication cycle. If no changes are made to Active Directory, replication occurs every hour to ensure proper synchronization of the AD database between all domain controllers.

Intersite replication occurs, by default, every 180 minutes (or three hours) between sites. The default cost for a site link is 100, and scheduling capabilities as well as alternative transport methods are offered to accommodate most links. Reliably connected WANs should elect to use RPC connectivity (select IP from Active Directory Sites and Services). If a reliable link does not exist between sites, the SMTP replication transport is available to carry piecemeal replication data over the site link. SMTP should be used where a reliable WAN link cannot be provided.

NOTE

SMTP replication does not provide for replication of the Active Directory domain partition. This means that if SMTP replication is to be used as the replication transport, it is recommended that the sites be maintained in separate domains for this reason. Also, replication schedules do not pertain to SMTP replication. SMTP replication relies on the mail delivery scheduling to control SMTP replication.

As discussed earlier, intrasite replication occurs only between certain domain controllers on the predetermined replication ring. Intersite replication, on the other hand, occurs only between *bridgehead servers.* Bridgehead servers are the replication gateways between sites. You can configure a preferred bridgehead server or multiple preferred bridgehead servers to control replication partner selection between sites. Windows Server 2003 introduces some new features for bridgehead servers.

The Inter Site Topology Generator (ISTG) has been significantly modified from the ISTG of Windows 2000 Server. Default intrasite replication latency has been reduced from 15 minutes to one minute. Multiple bridgehead servers cannot be configured. A new compression algorithm reduces the CPU load on the bridgehead servers. The repadmin.exe tool has been enhanced to allow reading and management operations for multiple domain controllers. The site limit jumps from 200 sites to 5,000 sites along with a new complex algorithm that helps improve the scalability. A special improvement has been introduced for very large hub-and-spoke topologies. Increasing the forest functional level to Windows Server 2003 provides the majority of improvements for Windows Server 2003 replication. Finally, after increasing the forest functional level, the new Active Directory Load Balancing tool, adlb.exe, supplied in the resource kit, helps improve performance settings for replication traffic.

Now that we have defined mechanisms for controlling replication traffic, let's see how we can put together an environment that will accommodate our administrative requirements while also accommodating the replication requirements for our Active Directory.

Some of the features that make up Microsoft's flexible, loose consistency multimaster system are:

- **Multimaster capabilities** This means that a directory partition can have several writeable replicas that must be kept consistent between domain controllers in the same forest.

- **Loose consistency** The replicas may not be consistent with each other at any particular point in time. Changes can be applied at any time to any full replica.

- **Convergence** All replicas are guaranteed to converge on the same set of values if the system is allowed to reach a steady state where all updates have been completely replicated.

The Active Directory replication model provides several benefits over the previous replication design used by Windows NT 4.0. The major benefits to Active Directory's replication model are the following:

- Dependency on the time synchronization service (W32Time) is minimized, compared with other forms of synchronization.

- Active Directory replication is based on the globally unique identifiers (GUIDs) for directory objects, not on the distinguished names (DNs). This design feature ensures that changes are always replicated to the correct object. AD is therefore able to differentiate between a deleted object and a new object with the same DN.

- Updates contain only the changed attribute values, not the entire object. This minimizes conflicts between updates to an object where attribute-level conflict might occur in an object-based update system. Also, detection and resolution capabilities exist within this attribute-level replication system. This helps minimize the amount of data replicated.

- Site awareness provides a method to minimize WAN communication traffic through replication data compression between sites. Replication traffic moves through the organization based on site topology, which is designed around the underlying network topology. This provides administrators with a mechanism to control replication traffic more precisely.

  Site awareness and a choice of multiple transports provide replication flexibility between various topologies. Replication topologies are automatically generated within sites, and clients are able to intelligently select "nearby" domain controllers using the client's IP address to determine in which site the client is located.

- Sites are independent from the directory partition structure, so replication configuration remains flexible.

- Replication protocol traffic is minimized, so speed over high-latency communication links is improved.

EXAM WARNING

This is not necessarily a TCP/IP exam or a network infrastructure design exam, but both of these topics play a very important factor in network site design as well as domain design. Make sure you understand the basics of subnetting and its effect on traffic directing in a network. Know the difference between local TCP/IP traffic and remote traffic and how subnets play a part in local and remote traffic.

EXERCISE 4.05

CONFIGURING SITES

In this exercise, you will configure sites and a site link for the Atlanta and Miami sites, as shown in Figure 4.24.

1. Begin by opening Active Directory Sites and Services from **Start | All Programs | Administrative Tools | Active Directory Sites and Services**.

2. Our first site will be the Atlanta site. Create a new site named **Atlanta**. Right-click **Sites**, select **New | Site**, and enter the name **Atlanta**.

3. Next, we will create the **Miami** site. Right-click **Sites** and select **New | Site**. Enter the site name **Miami**.

4. We will create a new site link later in the exercise, but for now we'll leave the Miami (and Atlanta) sites within the default site link. Enter the name for the site and select **DefaultIPSiteLink**, as shown in Figure 4.25.

Figure 4.25 Linking the Site Link to the New Site

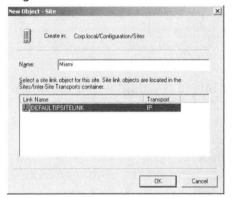

5. Click **OK**. A message box appears, outlining the remaining required steps, as shown in Figure 4.26.

Figure 4.26 New Site Message Box

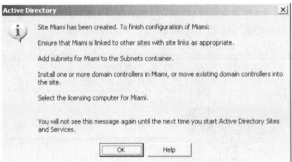

6. Click **OK**.

7. Now we will create a new site link. Click **Inter-Site Transports** in the left pane. Right-click **IP** in the left pane, and select **New Site Link** (see Figure 4.27).

Figure 4.27 Creating a New Site Link

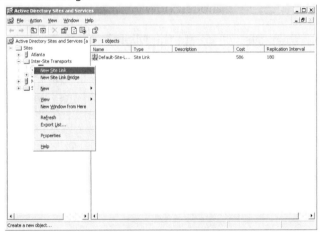

8. Enter **Miami-IP-Atlanta**, add the **Miami** and **Atlanta** sites, and press **Enter** to name the site link. Now double-click the **Miami-IP-Atlanta** site link to open the Properties box shown in Figure 4.28. Change the cost to **586** to reflect the recommended link cost for a 56kbps link. Change the value found in **Replicate every** as deemed appropriate for your environment.

Figure 4.28 Site Link Properties Box

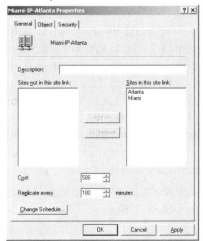

9. Click **OK** to complete the site link setup.

10. The Miami and Atlanta subnets are 10.10.0.0/16 and 10.8.0.0/16, respectively. Now we need to create a subnet object for each of these subnets and associate these subnets with the appropriate site. In the left pane, right-click **Subnets**, and select **New Subnet**.

11. Enter the subnet address of **10.10.0.0** and the subnet mask of **255.255.0.0** in the appropriate places. Select **Miami** as the site object, as shown in Figure 4.29. Click **OK**.

Figure 4.29 Associating the Site with a Subnet

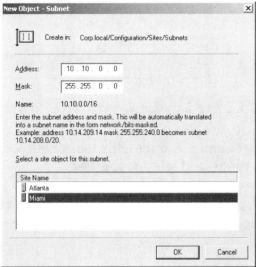

12. Repeat Steps 10 and 11 with the information for Atlanta's subnet and site.

13. Now a server must be associated with the Miami site. It is not uncommon to install Active Directory on servers in one site, only to physically move the server to its intended site upon completion. This process would warrant moving the server. In our example, we will create the server object in the Miami site. Double-click the **Miami** site in the left pane. *Note:* If a domain controller is installed in one site and then the subnet in which it exists is moved to a different site, the domain controller will need to be *manually* moved to the new site.

14. Right-click the **Servers** container within the Miami site container, and select **New | Server**.

15. Enter the name for the new server, as shown in Figure 4.30.

Figure 4.30 Adding a Server to a Site: Specifying the Server Name

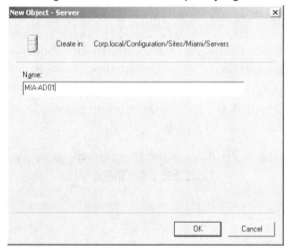

16. Click **OK** to finish adding the server to the Miami site.

17. Finally, we have to add a license server to the site. Double-click the **Miami** site in the left pane. Right-click **Licensing Site Settings**, and select **Properties**.

18. From the **Licensing Site Settings Properties** dialog box, select **Change**, and enter the server information for the server that will handle licensing duties for the Miami site.

19. Click **OK**. Verify that the Licensing Site Settings Properties dialog box information is correct, as shown in Figure 4.31, then click **OK**.

Figure 4.31 Confirming the Licensing Server Information

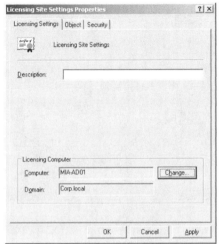

20. Now Active Directory understands the site connectivity between Miami and Atlanta and is able to replicate data between the sites based on the parameters supplied in the exercise.

Selecting a Replication Topology

The two most common replication topologies are the ring topology and the hub-and-spoke topology. As a general rule, a centrally managed design uses a hub-and-spoke topology, while a distributed management design uses a ring or possibly a modified mesh. Figure 4.32 illustrates a ring topology, typically used in a distributed management environment. Again, refer to Chapter 2, where replication topologies are described in more detail.

Figure 4.32 A Ring Replication Topology

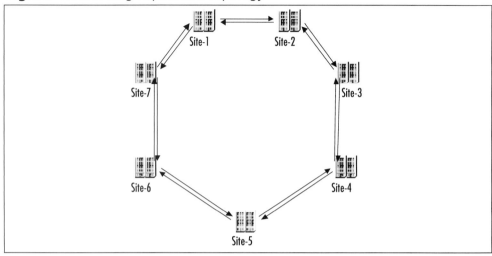

Figure 4.33 illustrates a hub–and–spoke topology, typically used in a centralized management environment.

Figure 4.33 A Hub-and-Spoke Replication Topology

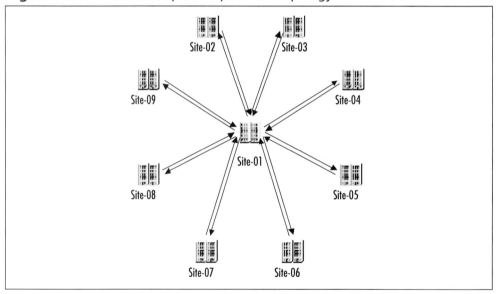

A good replication topology design provides the right balance among cost, redundancy, latency, and administrative overhead.

Creating a Replication Diagram

In an Active Directory design that encompasses a few sites, designing and configuring replication might not warrant a complex diagram illustrating every detail. However, as an organization grows, or if you are designing a large-scale implementation, a good diagram will simplify the design process. Figure 4.34 illustrates an example of a replication diagram.

A replication diagram should reflect site links and replication schedules to determine site link replication overlap availability.

Figure 4.34 Replication Diagram

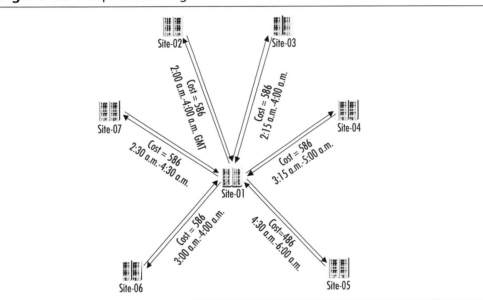

TEST DAY TIP

With the abundance of inexpensive broadband connectivity, WAN bandwidth is fast becoming a commodity in network design. Just because it is becoming more plentiful does not mean that it should be taken for granted in a design, however. Design your Active Directory sites to be frugal with bandwidth whenever possible. WAN connections, even if they were originally allocated for replication traffic, rarely provide connectivity for a single service or function. Expect the WAN bandwidth usage to be a hotly contested item within the network. Distributed computing capabilities are gradually moving a great deal of the original mainframe-type services off the desktop and back to a centralized server design. This has a huge effect on the amount of bandwidth that will be available on a network.

Summary of Exam Objectives

Standards simplify administration and provide consistency in design. Active Directory works well with standardization because of the container structure of its overall design. Enterprisewide standardization extends beyond the overall internal structure of Active Directory. Forestwide standardization affects the topmost container and all of its contents. Domainwide standardization affects a single domain within Active Directory and all of its contents including OUs and possibly sites. Every item within AD is considered a container or an object. Each item within the Active Directory provides for simplified administration by following naming standardization and also by following a standardized structure.

The forest is the topmost container within Active Directory and consequently the seat of administrative control. The degree of control needed within an AD design will determine whether a single forest should be implemented or whether a design will require multiple forests.

The number of domains required within an Active Directory design is affected by the available bandwidth between locations and the number of users in the overall environment, among other factors. Domain naming and the domain hierarchy is made available through a standardized naming system based on the naming system provided by the Domain Name Service (DNS). Not all designs are based entirely on a clean-slate approach. Three design approaches are available for the domain design and implementation strategy: in-place upgrade, restructuring, and a migration to a pristine environment.

Windows Server 2003 supports three different authentication mechanisms: LM (the weakest and supported by older Windows 9*x* clients), NTLM (version 1 supported by Windows NT4 pre-SP4 clients and version 2 supported by Windows NT4 SP4 and newer clients), and Kerberos (supported by Windows 2000, Windows XP, and Windows Server 2003 clients). The clients within your environment should be carefully identified so that the authentication approach may be designed to cater for a heterogeneous environment while maximizing security.

When authentication is required between domains or forests, trusts are required. Windows Server 2003 creates transitive, two-way trusts by default between all domains in an Active Directory forest. Different types of trusts are available to areas external to Windows Server 2003's Active Directory. The following trust types are available: External trusts (established between a domain in the forest and a domain in another forest), Realm trusts (established between Windows Server 2003 domains and non-Windows Kerberos realms), Forest trusts (established between two Windows Server 2003 forests), and Shortcut trusts (established between two domains in the same forest and used to optimize cross-domain authentication).

Organizational Units (OUs) are the smallest Active Directory containers. OUs may provide delegated administrative control without providing full-fledged administrative capabilities. OUs should be created for one of the following reasons: delegation of administrative tasks, simplified resource administration, and group policy deployment. The three OU designs generally used and advocated by Microsoft are designed by function, geography, and object type. A typical OU design will often utilize all three of these design options, so as to best reflect the nature of the organization.

Every object within Active Directory has an owner. Active Directory container owners are responsible for the container properties and for the subcontainers that are subordinate to the container in their possession. Owners may assign or delegate ownership of subcontainers to other users within the Active Directory. Container owners are responsible for account management of objects within their OU(s), management of machine acccounts in their OU(s), and delegation of authority to local administrators within their assigned OU(s) to further divide administrative responsibilities.

Group Policy Objects (GPOs) are objects within Active Directory that contain user and computer configuration settings. GPOs are linked to containers within Active Directory to provide consistent control over the user or computer configurations within that container. As a best practice, use as few GPOs as possible to accomplish the desired result. The right to create, edit, and manage GPOs may be delegated, like any other object within Active Directory, using the new Group Policy Management Console (GPMC). Group Policy management may be performed centrally, where one group are responsible for all GPOs, or in a distributed fashion, where OU owners (for example) are responsible for creating, editing, linking, and managing their own GPOs. Two default GPOs exist and are linked to the root of the domain and to the Domain Controllers OU. These two GPOs contain many security settings that should be carefully considered and configured, according to your environment.

Group membership provides a mechanism to control access to resources as well as a mechanism to control administrative rights in Active Directory. User roles are associated to job functions or tasks within an organization. Microsoft's new Authorization Manager provides role-based account creation and management capabilities.

Active Directory replicates the following information (partitions) among domain controllers:

- **Schema partition** Contains all class and attribute definitions for the forest. There is one schema directory partition per forest.

- **Configuration partition** Contains replication configuration information and other information for the forest. There is one configuration directory partition per forest.

- **Domain partition** Contains all objects that are stored within a particular domain. There is one domain directory partition for each domain in the forest.

Active Directory provides a replication mechanism that is multi-master, loosely consistent, and convergent. Active Directory replication occurs between (intersite) and within (intrasite) sites. Intersite replication occurs between the bridgehead servers of those sites involved. Intersite replication occurs on a three-hour interval by default and may be controlled through scheduling, modifying the replication interval, or modifying the transport method used (IP or SMTP). Active Directory intrasite as well as intersite replication is controlled by the Knowledge Consistency Checker (KCC). Intrasite replication occurs on a five-minute interval, extending to no more than three hops within a replication ring. When designing a replication topology, consider the following replication topologies:

- **Ring topology** Distributed network model
- **Hub-and-spoke topology** Centralized network model
- **Fully meshed** All sites are connected to all other sites via LAN and/or WAN links

Exam Objectives Fast Track

Defining Standards

- ☑ Standardization provides consistency and predictability in design.
- ☑ Standards may exist enterprisewide, forestwide, or domainwide.
- ☑ Object naming is the most commonly standardized item.

Defining the Forest Structure, Hierarchy, and Naming Strategy

- ☑ Forest designs must provide for service autonomy, service isolation, data autonomy, and/or data isolation.
- ☑ Organizational forest, resource forest, and restricted access forest models are used to accommodate autonomy and isolation requirements.
- ☑ Available bandwidth and the number of users in the organization will determine whether a single domain or multiple domains will be required.

Defining Authentication Mechanisms

- ☑ From weakest to strongest, LAN Manager, NTLM v1, NTLM v2, and Kerberos authentication are all authentication mechanisms supported by Windows Server 2003.

☑ Four trust types are available:

- External trusts—non-transitive trusts providing either one-way or two-way trust

- Realm trusts—transitive or non-transitive trusts providing either one-way or two-way trust

- Forest trusts—transitive trusts providing one-way or two-way trust

- Shortcut trusts—transitive trusts providing one-way or two-way trust

☑ Transitive, two-way trusts are created by default between all domains in the same forest.

Designing the Organizational Unit Model

☑ OUs are created to delegate administrative tasks, to create divisions of users with dissimilar policy requirements, and to simplify resource administration.

☑ OUs delegate by function, geography, or object type (or a hybrid thereof).

☑ OU owners are responsible for account management, workstation and member server management, and delegation of authority within their assigned OU(s).

Defining the Group Policy Object Approach

☑ Group Policy implementation follows an inheritance structure whereby subcontainers (or child containers) inherit the policies of their parent containers.

☑ Create as few GPOs as necessary and link to multiple containers as needed.

☑ GPO management may be delegated using the Group Policy Management Console (GPMC).

Exploring Groups and Roles

☑ Data access is controlled through discretionary access control lists (DACLs) placed on objects.

☑ Administrative access is controlled through administrative rights through Active Directory.

☑ The Microsoft Authentication Manager provides role-based account creation and management.

Defining Replication Topology

☑ Sites link physical network constraints and connection information to Active Directory's logical structure.

☑ Intrasite replication is notification based, uses RPC, uses a frequency of 15 seconds, is controlled by the KCC, and uses a ring topology.

☑ Intersite replication is schedule based, uses RPC, uses a frequency set by the Admin (default: three hours), is controlled by the KCC, and uses a topology built by the Admin using sites, links, and costs.

☑ ISTG has been significantly modified from the ISTG of Windows 2000 Server.

☑ Default intrasite replication latency has been reduced from 15 minutes to one minute.

☑ Multiple bridgehead servers cannot be configured.

☑ A new compression algorithm reduces the CPU load on the bridgehead servers.

☑ The repadmin.exe tool has been enhanced to allow reading and management operations for multiple domain controllers.

☑ The site limit jumps from 200 sites to 5,000 sites along with a new complex algorithm that helps improve the scalability.

☑ A special improvement has been introduced for very large hub-and-spoke topologies. Increasing the forest functional level to Windows Server 2003 provides the majority of improvements for Windows Server 2003 replication.

☑ After increasing the forest functional level, the new Active Directory Load Balancing tool, adlb.exe, helps improve performance settings for replication traffic.

Exam Objectives
Frequently Asked Questions

The following Frequently Asked Questions, answered by the authors of this book, are designed to both measure your understanding of the Exam Objectives presented in this chapter and to assist you with real-life implementation of these concepts. You will also gain access to thousands of other FAQs at *www.ITFAQnet.com*.

Q: As a username standard, why can't we use first names as usernames?

A: In smaller organizations that do not expect to grow, first names may suffice as usernames, but as any organization grows, the likelihood of having two individuals with the same first name increases. Consequently, the naming convention will have to be modified at that time.

Q: How does a lack of a standard naming system create more administrative overhead?

A: The lack of a standard naming system requires an administrator to search for the existence of a name before creating an object, and once an object is created, it might be difficult to find certain objects due to the lack of consistent naming.

Q: What is the difference between enterprisewide and forestwide standards?

A: Enterprisewide refers to the scope of the systems within an organization. The organization may include multiple forests, or it may use a single forest. Forestwide refers to the scope of a single forest.

Q: What is more expensive to achieve, autonomy or isolation?

A: A design that requires isolation is generally more expensive than a design that requires autonomy, because a separate domain or forest is required in the former.

Q: Is there a preferred number of forests or domains for a best-practice design?

A: Generally, to keep costs to a minimum, a design should use as few forests and domains as possible to achieve the desired design goals.

Q: Are there any tools available to aid in a Windows NT 4.0 enterprise migration to Windows Server 2003?

A: The Active Directory Migration Tool (ADMT) provides domain migration assistance for administrators and engineers tasked with migrating an NT 4.0 environment to Window Server 2003.

Q: What is the preferred authentication mechanism for a current Windows network?

A: Kerberos authentication is considered the preferred authentication mechanism for a modern Microsoft Windows network, because it is the most secure mechanism supported by Windows 2000, Windows XP, and Windows Server 2003.

Q: Does installation of Active Directory Client Extensions on a Windows 98 system provide Kerberos authentication for the Windows 98 client?

A: The Active Directory Client Extensions, when installed on Windows 98, update the supported authentication mechanism to NTLM v2. Kerberos authentication is not provided by installing the client extensions.

Q: Can an Active Directory design interact with other vendors' Kerberos implementations?

A: Yes. Creating a realm trust will allow an Active Directory implementation to interoperate with other Kerberos implementations (UNIX, Linux, etc.).

Q: Is there a preferred OU design model?

A: There is no preferred OU design model. You should utilize an OU design model that closely reflects your organization's business and/or physical structure.

Q: When delegating by geography, does Active Directory adjust replication to accommodate the geographical bounds represented by the OUs?

A: No. OUs representing geographical boundaries do not facilitate replication adjustments by Active Directory. Active Directory sites and site links are designed to accommodate the nuances of WAN connectivity, providing a mechanism for adjusting replication traffic.

Q: Is a model based on object type a best fit for an environment of 20 users and computers?

A: Typically, a model based on object type is used in a very large environment. It is generally considered cost prohibitive to implement a model based on object type in a small environment.

Q: Can we use Group Policy Objects (GPOs) to control desktop settings on our Windows 98 clients?

A: No. Windows 98 systems may be controlled through the Windows 98 System Policy Editor (poledit.exe) or through scripting; GPOs apply only to Windows 2000, Windows XP, and Windows Server 2003 systems.

Q: Is it possible to apply Group Policy settings to a specific group of machines based on a criteria like disk space or other system information?

A: Yes. Windows Server 2003 introduces Group Policy WMI filtering capabilities. Using WMI scripting, GPO application may be controlled by various system criteria.

Q: We want to implement a domainwide policy. Should I just modify the default domain policy to achieve our desired goal?

A: No. Best practice dictates that the default domain policy and the default domain controller policy should not be modified. Instead, create a new policy to accomplish the required result and give this policy a higher precedence than the default policy.

Q: Is there a benefit to a centralized management policy over a distributed management policy?

A: Centralized policy does not necessarily mean that all administration is accomplished from a centralized location or group. If a centralized approach will fit with your design, combining this approach with proper delegation should result in an efficient implementation that keeps costs to a minimum.

Q: How do data access groups provide for lower total cost of ownership?

A: A data access group is delegated control of an object or resource within Active Directory without actually providing administrative capabilities to any other resources within Active Directory. This offloads administrative responsibilities to a group that may be better positioned to control access permissions to the resource. This offload of administrative responsibilities should reduce the TCO.

Q: What utility do I use for role-based administration?

A: Download the Microsoft Authorization Manager from the Microsoft Web site. The Authorization Manager is used to manage role-based administrative controls.

Q: We have two replica domain controllers located at different sites and connected by a problematic link. How do we adjust the replication between these systems to accommodate the problematic link?

A: SMTP replication is designed specifically for unreliable or problematic links between domain controllers. You will have to place the domain controllers in separate domains, however, because the domain partition is not replicated over an SMTP site link.

Q: If a domain controller fails in an Active Directory environment, can account management be accomplished from another domain controller, or does it have to be promoted like an NT 4.0 BDC?

A: Active Directory provides for multimaster replication, which means that account management can be accomplished from any domain controller within the domain.

Q: Our satellite office has been using the WAN link to connect to a domain controller in the main office for authentication. Will clients authenticate against a server that is local to them if we place a domain controller at the satellite office?

A: If the satellite office is configured as a separate site from the main office, replication traffic may be controlled between the domain controllers. Clients, being site aware, will seek out servers that are on the same subnet as they are on.

Q: Our company hosts all the IT personnel at the corporate office, while several other employees are located at other small offices around the state. Which replication topology should we use for this environment?

A: Because this is a centrally administered infrastructure, the best design approach would likely be a hub-and-spoke design.

Self Test

A Quick Answer Key follows the Self Test questions. For complete questions, answers, and explanations to the Self Test questions in this chapter as well as the other chapters in this book, see the Self Test Appendix.

1. Your organization has five locations connected as shown in Figure 4.35. Analog dialup and ISDN connections are non-persistent connections. Specify transport for each link.

   Figure 4.35 Site Design

   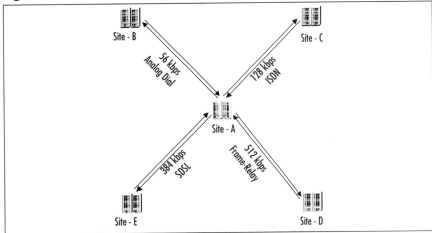

   A. A–B (Transport = IP), A–C (Transport = IP), A–D (Transport = IP), A–E (Transport = SMTP)

   B. A–B (Transport = SMTP), A–C (Transport = SMTP), A–D (Transport = IP), A–E (Transport = SMTP)

   C. A–B (Transport = SMTP), A–C (Transport = SMTP), A–D (Transport = IP), A–E (Transport = IP)

   D. A–B (Transport = IP), A–C (Transport = IP), A–D (Transport = IP), A–E (Transport = IP)

2. You have been given the task of designing an OU structure for a client. The client has a dedicated network administrator located at the corporate offices. Each of the remaining 11 offices has 20 users relying on Internet connectivity to interact with a specialized Web application at the corporate office. Users log on to a Windows Server 2003 Active Directory domain for workstation security. You want to delegate basic account administration to one user at each of the remote offices. How can this best be accomplished?

A. Create a geographical OU design. Use the Delegation of Control wizard to create a customized Microsoft Management Console and Taskpad. Create a special administrator group for each location, and delegate the appropriate tasks to this group. Place each OU administrator in their respective groups.

B. Create a functional OU design. Use the Delegation of Control wizard to create a customized Microsoft Management Console and Taskpad. Create a special administrator group for each location, and delegate the task to this group. Place each OU administrator in his or her respective group.

C. Create an object type OU design. Use the Delegation of Control wizard to create a customized Microsoft Management Console and Taskpad. Create a special administrator group for each location, and delegate the task to this group. Place each OU administrator in their respective groups.

D. Create a functional OU design. Use the Delegation of Control wizard to create a customized Microsoft Management Console and Taskpad. Place each OU administrator in the Domain Administrators group.

3. Your organization consists of a single forest with a root domain and three child domains: namaerica.yourcorp.com, samerica.yourcorp.com, and europe.yourcorp.com. The structure is illustrated in Figure 4.36. Users who belong to the management groups from each domain must have access to resources in each of the other domains. How can this be achieved, using best practice wherever possible?

Figure 4.36 Multidomain Access

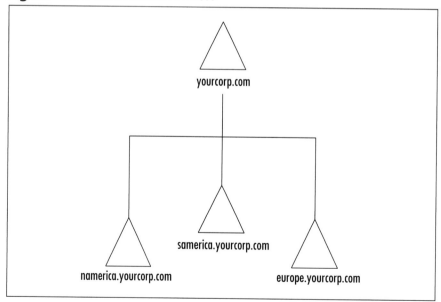

A. Create a global group for the management groups in each domain. Nest the global groups in a global group in the root domain. Create domain local groups in each domain and place the root global group in each domain local group. Use the domain local groups to control access to resources.

B. Create a domain local group for the management groups in each domain. Nest the domain local groups in a universal group in the root domain. Create domain local groups in each domain and place the universal group in each domain local group. Use the domain local groups to control access to resources.

C. Create a domain local group for the management groups in each domain. Nest the domain local groups in a global group in the root domain. Create domain local groups in each domain and place the root domain global group in each domain local group. Use the domain local groups to control access to resources.

D. Create a global group for the management groups in each domain. Nest the global groups in a universal group. Create domain local groups in each domain and place the universal group in each domain local group. Use the domain local groups to control access to resources.

4. Your company will be collaborating with another company in the design of a new cobranded product. Users from the partner company need access to project data. How can you guarantee that users from the partner organization cannot access resources beyond the shared project data?

A. Place the group for remote users on each resource where access should be granted and assign proper permissions. Remove the Everyone group from all sensitive resources. Place the remote users' group on all sensitive resources and select Deny for the Full Control option on sensitive resources.

B. Place the group for remote users on each resource where access should be granted and assign proper permissions. Select Deny for the Full Control option on sensitive resources for the Everyone group.

C. Place the group for remote users on each resource where access should be granted and assign proper permissions. Place the remote users' group on all sensitive resources and select Deny for the Full Control option on sensitive resources.

D. Place the group for remote users on each resource where access should not be granted and assign the proper permissions. Select Deny for the Full Control option on sensitive resources for the Everyone group.

5. Your organization contains more than 3000 users and utilizes a distributed administration model. Using the features available in Active Directory, decide who should be assigned the responsibility to control access to a file server in the marketing department in your Phoenix office.

    A. The domain administrators should control access to all resources.

    B. The enterprise administrators should control access to all resources.

    C. A domainwide File Server Administrators group should control access to all file servers.

    D. A manager or office administrator for the marketing department in Atlanta should control access to the file server.

6. Twelve users within your department require access to the latest reports generated by your sales department. What access level will the users require to accomplish the desired tasks?

    A. The users will require Read permission only.

    B. The users will require Read and Execute permission only.

    C. The users will require Modify permission only.

    D. The users will require Full control.

7. You have been assigned a new project to control users' access to specialized Web-based applications within your organization. Which Windows Server 2003 tool will you use to help you control role-based authorization?

    A. The IIS Permissions wizard

    B. Active Directory Users and Computers

    C. Authorization Manager

    D. Resultant Set of Policies (RSoP)

8. Your organization consists of 12 offices connected through fractional T-1 links. Each office houses between 300 and 500 users and computers. Each office except the main office has the same corporate organization structure. Within each office are sales, engineering, and operations departments. The main office also has a department that encompasses the executive managers. How many OUs will a best-practice design encompass?

    A. 37 OUs will provide the best design.

    B. 24 OUs will provide the best design.

    C. 12 OUs will provide the best design.

    D. 320 OUs will provide the best design.

9. Your Active Directory design is illustrated in Figure 4.37. Users in east.namerica.yourcorp.com frequently access resources in the east.samerica.yourcorp.com. Users have been complaining about the time it takes to access resources in the other domain. How can you improve the time required to access the resources?

Figure 4.37 Infrastructure for Question #9

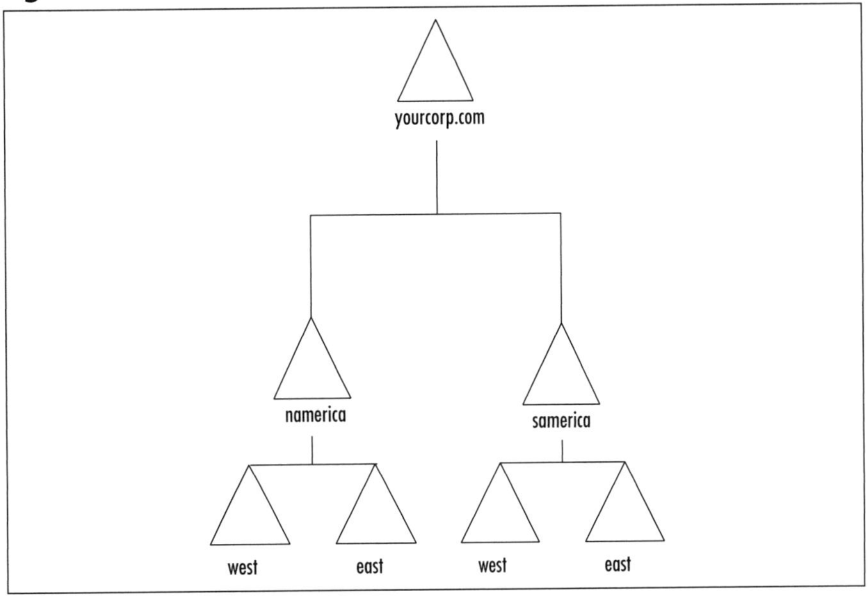

A. Create an external trust between east.namerica.yourcorp.com and east.samerica.yourcorp.com.

B. Create a realm trust between east.namerica.yourcorp.com and east.samerica.yourcorp.com.

C. Create a forest trust between east.namerica.yourcorp.com and east.samerica.yourcorp.com.

D. Create a shortcut trust between east.namerica.yourcorp.com and east.samerica.yourcorp.com.

10. Your organization's IT admin model is split geographically, and each region needs a separate domain. Your organization has four regions (NAmericas, SAmericas, EMEA, and APAC). What namespace is appropriate for your organization?

A. Create four regional domains. The first domain should be the root. The remaining three will be child domains to the root.

B. Create five regional domains. Each region will be a child domain.

    C. Create one domain. Each region will have its own domain controller in the domain.

    D. Create a root domain. The remaining four will be child domains to the root.

11. You are consolidating network resources for your organization. Which names are considered valid NetBIOS name? (Choose two answers.)

    A. RAPID|DESIGN

    B. RAPIDDESIGN

    C. RAPID~DESIGN

    D. RAPIDDESIGNDOMAIN

12. Your organization uses a Windows NT 4.0 domain design based on three resource domains and one master domain. The resource domains are NAMERICA, SAMERICA, and AUSTRALIA. The master domain is CORP. The overall design hosts 1500 users and computers. Consistent password policy, schema definitions, and account settings will apply throughout your organization, once upgraded to use Windows Server 2003 and Active Directory. All sites are connected via 256kbps fractional T1s. Design a migration strategy for this organization.

    A. Upgrade the master domain to Windows Server 2003. Create an OU design to mimic the resource domains. Next, upgrade the resource domains to Windows Server 2003. Move all accounts from the resource domains to their respective OUs in the master domain. Dissolve the resource domains.

    B. Upgrade each domain in place from Windows NT 4.0 to Windows Server 2003.

    C. Upgrade only the Windows NT 4.0 master domain to Windows Server 2003. Move the accounts from the resource domains to the Windows Server 2003 domain.

    D. Upgrade all the domains to Windows 2000 Server. Upgrade the master domain to Windows Server 2003.

13. Your current network design consists of a Windows 2000 Active Directory domain with four Windows NT 4.0 domains external to the forest. Users in one of your NT 4.0 domains will require more stringent password and account lockout policies than the rest of your organization. The total number of accounts within your organization currently does not exceed 2500 users. Your offices are all connected via 128kbps ISDN and 512kbps fractional T1s. How will you upgrade this design so that all domains exist within the same Active Directory forest?

A. Upgrade the Windows 2000 domain in place. Create OUs for three of the four Windows NT 4.0 domains. Upgrade the Windows NT 4.0 domains to Windows Server 2003 domains. Restructure your enterprise design by moving all objects from the three NT 4.0 domains that will share password and account policies with the root domain, to the newly created root domain OUs. Leave the fourth domain as a separate domain in the forest, with its own password and account lockout policies.

B. Upgrade the Windows 2000 Server domain to Windows Server 2003 and create OUs for each of the NT 4.0 domains. Upgrade the NT 4.0 domains to Windows Server 2003. Move all accounts to their respective OUs in the root domain.

C. Upgrade the Windows 2000 domain in place. Upgrade the Windows NT 4.0 domains to Windows Server 2003. Apply the password and account policies on the domain that requires more stringent settings.

D. Upgrade the Windows 2000 domain to Windows Server 2003 and create OUs for each of the NT 4.0 domains. Move the accounts from three of the NT 4.0 domains to their respective OUs. Upgrade the remaining NT 4.0 domain to Windows Server 2003. Configure the specialized security settings on the domain that was just upgraded.

14. Your Active Directory design includes a single forest, a single domain, and an OU infrastructure based on both geography and function. Your design requirements specify that users in one location must operate with a more stringent password policy than the other locations. Design a Group Policy deployment strategy for this scenario.

A. Create two separate GPOs—one providing standard password options and the other providing tighter security requirements. Link the tighter-security GPO to the location OU requiring more stringent password requirements, and link the other GPO to the domain. Set the high-security GPO to a higher precedence.

B. Create another domain and relocate the OU with the more stringent security requirements to the new domain. Create a GPO and configure its policy requirements to provide the more stringent password policy requirements.

C. Create another forest and relocate the OU with the more stringent security requirements to the new forest. Create two GPOs (one for each domain) and configure the policy requirements for each GPO accordingly.

D. Create another domain and relocate the OU with the more stringent security requirements to the new domain. Create a GPO and configure the policy requirements for the new GPO to provide the less stringent password policy requirements.

15. Your network design consists of two Active Directory forests, each with a single domain. You want to ensure that all workstations except the management workstations in the genericforest1.com forest run a shutdown script to clean up files left over from a specialized application. How do you configure Group Policy to accomplish this task, expending as little administrative overhead as possible?

    A. Place each of the management workstations in its own OU. Apply the GPO to the domain within each forest, and block inheritance for the Management Workstations OU.

    B. Place each of the management workstations in a security group. Apply the GPO to the domain within each forest, and change the GPO permissions so that the Management Workstations group is denied the apply Group Policy permission.

    C. Place each of the management workstations in its own OU. Apply the GPO to the domain within each forest, and create a conflicting GPO with higher precedence to block the domain GPO.

    D. Place each of the management workstations in its own group. Apply the GPO to the domain within each forest, and grant Read and Apply permission for the Management Workstations group.

Self Test Quick Answer Key

For complete questions, answers, and explanations to the Self Test questions in this chapter as well as the other chapters in this book, see the Self Test Appendix.

1. **C**
2. **A**
3. **D**
4. **A**
5. **D**
6. **A**
7. **C**
8. **A**
9. **D.**
10. **D**
11. **B, C**
12. **A**
13. **A**
14. **B**
15. **A**

Chapter 5

MCSE 70-297

Name Resolution

Exam Objectives in This Chapter:

Introduction

The next chapter deals with name resolution strategies. Specifically, we discuss DNS and WINS considerations in this chapter, and how best to implement these technologies so as to provide an efficient, robust, scalable, and available name resolution strategy.

Unlike prior versions of Windows, which relied heavily on WINS as their primary resolution mechanism, Windows 2000 and Windows Server 2003 primarily use DNS for name resolution. The first subjects discussed are the implementation of DNS, the namespace, and how Active Directory may be dovetailed into any existing Berkeley Internet Name Daemon (BIND) deployment.

Next, we discuss zones and their configuration and storage options, followed by the strategies for securing the namespace, servers, zones, and records through delegation. We then examine how DNS records need to be registered by various types for name resolution to function properly. A description of how to make full use of the interoperability of DNS, WINS, and DHCP follows, which will help you to ensure that all necessary DNS records are registered in a timely fashion.

We then move onto the design and implementation of a WINS infrastructure. This begins with a discussion of how best to design a WINS topology across a large enterprise and how to ensure the uniqueness of NetBIOS names in a large, disparate organization.

This is followed by a description of the various available approaches for deploying a WINS topology, and how WINS servers should be configured for optimal replication performance, especially in larger environments. Subjects such as burst mode and the use of static entries are discussed. The subject of WINS is rounded out with a description of different methods for distributing the responsibilities for managing WINS through delegation.

Understanding DNS Design

Design is all about optimization. A good design makes everything and everybody work better, but a bad design can result in disaster. In reality, you will know that you have a good design when all services are transparent to your clients and no one even thinks to talk about it. This is because a bad design brings all kinds of undesirable attention. With name resolution and DNS in particular, the goal is to provide your clients with the ability to quickly and easily locate the hosts they want with technology that is absolutely transparent to them. Fortunately, Windows Server 2003 DNS can take you very close to this goal. The remainder of the steps you need to take will be through a sound design that includes the following components:

- DNS namespace

- DNS zones

- DNS servers

This section of the chapter will start with the broadest topic, the DNS namespace, and then focus on the zones that constitute the namespace, and finally describe the servers that actually perform the duties of resolving host names and forwarding requests.

The Namespace

A namespace, strictly defined, is a set or group of names that are assigned according to some naming convention. DNS uses a hierarchical namespace that partitions names into top-level domains, which can be subdivided into subdomains, and then into zones. You or your organization would register a unique domain name and then use it along with a naming convention to aggregate and identify all of the hosts that are connected to your network.

This may sound patronizing and blatantly obvious, but it needs to be stated: the most important step in creating a DNS namespace is choosing a name. After all, name resolution would not be name resolution without a name to resolve. Settling on a name could prove to be the most difficult, politically charged step in the entire process of planning your deployment because everyone will have their own ideas that they believe are the best, or are at least better than yours. Rather than get into the dynamics of dispute resolution, we will present some conventions and guidelines that could make this process easier on everyone's nerves. The name should have the following characteristics:

- It should represent the organization.

- It should be long enough to be descriptive but short enough to be easily remembered.

- It must contain only legal characters (characters that are allowed by all the operating systems in use).

Additionally, you might want different internal and external domain names.

For the purposes of designing and managing name resolution in practical terms for this chapter, we will be using a fictitious organization, Name Resolution University, which is an IT training school devoted to teaching DNS. The school has chosen an external domain name of learnaboutdns.com, and an internal domain of nru.corp. Figure 5.1 depicts Name Resolution University's network.

Figure 5.1 Name Resolution University's Physical Locations and DNS Domains

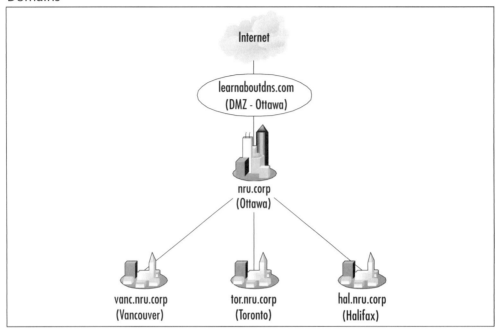

It is important at this point to make the distinction between internal and external namespaces. Both work in exactly the same way, however they are used for different purposes. They are both organized hierarchically, contain zones and resource records, and use the same types of servers. The key difference is that an external namespace is exposed to a public network (the Internet) and makes its resources publicly accessible to anyone searching for them, while the internal namespace is for managing resources on a private network. The private network may be connected to the public network, but users on the public network cannot search for resources on the private network. As an example, extranet.learnaboutdns.com signifies that the server called "extranet" exists in the learnaboutdns.com external namespace. With the appropriate configuration (such as routing and port forwarding, among others), the server can be physically connected to any network, even Name Resolution University's private network, but it is registered within the learnaboutdns.com namespace and accessible to any user with an Internet connection. On the other hand, intranet.nru.corp is accessible only to individuals who are granted direct access to Name Resolution University's private network. To further complicate things, intranet.nru.corp and extranet.learnaboutdns.com can be the same server registered using different *A* (Address) and *CNAME* (Canonical Name) resource records in the internal namespace. Resource record types and their uses are described later in the chapter.

The first guideline, "It should represent the organization," has two meanings. The name of your DNS namespace should represent the organization, and the structure of the namespace should reflect the structure of your organization. Because potential students and other organizations that need to contact the school will use an external domain name, a name was chosen that clearly identified the purpose of the organization. The internal namespace will use nru.corp as its root—hosted in the head office in Ottawa—and will use the name of its three campuses (Halifax, Toronto, and Vancouver) as the names of subdomains and zones. For example, the name of the internal DNS zone for the Vancouver campus will be vanc.nru.corp. The public will use learnaboutdns.com as part of the URL for its Web presence and as the domain for electronic messaging. There will be several hosts connected directly to the Internet in the school's external namespace: www.learnaboutdns.com (the main Web site), educ.learnaboutdns.com (the online training portal), and mail.learaboutdns.com (the external messaging gateway).

The second principle is one that is sometimes overlooked. Had the company chosen nameresolutionuniversity.com, frequent visitors to its Web site may end up getting carpal tunnel syndrome by typing in the URL over and over again. Learnaboutdns.com is half the length of the company's name, but equally as descriptive and probably more easily remembered. A shorter domain name is also less prone to being misspelled by external visitors. A domain that is too short could be nru.com. Yes, NRU is a valid abbreviation for Name Resolution University, but it is also valid for Neurobiology Research Unit, Niagara Rugby Union, and New River University. This, too, could be confusing. Just ask perplexed fans of professional golf who visited www.pga.com and found the Web site for the Potato Growers Association (this was amicably resolved between the two associations). For employees and students of Name Resolution University, NRU is significant to them as the name of the organization to which they are affiliated.

There is also a standard set of characters that are permitted for use in DNS host naming. This standard is set in RFC 1123 (www.ietf.org/rfc/rfc1123.txt). According to RFC 1123, all numerals *0* through *9*, lowercase letters *a* through *z*, all uppercase letters *A* through *Z*, and hyphens (-) can be used within a domain name. Therefore, any of the following could have been chosen as our domain name for Name Resolution University instead of nru.corp:

- NRU123.corp
- NruCorp.123
- N-R-U.corp
- NRU.CORP

There are vast numbers of combinations that you could use for your namespace. In fact, Windows Server 2003 DNS allows you even to use characters outside the recommended character set. In Windows Server 2003, Microsoft has expanded DNS character support to include enhanced default support for UTF-8, which is a

Unicode transformation format. The UTF-8 protocol allows for use of extended ASCII characters and translation of UCS-2, a 16-bit Unicode character set that encompasses most writing standards. By including UTF-8, Windows Server 2003 DNS enables a much wider range of names than you can get using ASCII or extended ASCII encoding alone. This being said, you may want to avoid using extended character sets if you have a requirement for interoperability with legacy operating systems, such as Windows NT 4.0.

When naming an internal domain, you have much more flexibility than you do with external namespaces. With an external namespace, you have to conform to one of the predefined top-level domains: .com, .net, .org, .edu, .mil, .int, .gov, .biz, .info, .name, .pro, .coop, .museum, .aero, and the two-letter country abbreviations, such as .us for the United States, .ca for Canada, and .uk for the United Kingdom. When creating an Internet namespace, you can use these predefined top-level domains to name your IP-based nodes only if you want them to be seen via the Internet through the use of fully qualified domain names (FQDNs), and even then, the general public is free to register names only with .com, .net, .org, .biz, .info, and the country abbreviations. All the rest of the top-level domains have restrictions for their use. On the other hand, if you are creating an internal DNS namespace that will be used only for your own internal network, you are not restricted as to how it is designed or implemented. In Exercise 5.01, you will learn more about namespaces.

EXERCISE 5.01

CREATING A WINDOWS SERVER 2003 DNS NAMESPACE

In this exercise, we walk through the steps for creating Name Resolution University's parent internal domain. To complete this exercise, you need a PC running Windows Server 2003 Server Edition. Insert the Windows 2003 Server CD-ROM into your CD-ROM drive, and let's begin our exercise:

1. If the CD-ROM starts automatically, cancel out of the autorun by clicking **Exit**.

2. Click **Start | Control Panel** and choose **Add or Remove Programs**.

3. Click the **Add/Remove Windows Components** icon.

4. Scroll down the list of components until you come to the **Network Services** component. Highlight it and then click **Details**.

5. In the list of Network Services Subcomponents, highlight **Domain Name System (DNS)** and then select the empty check box next to it. Next, click **OK** to continue. When the Network Subcomponents window closes, click **Next**. The DNS service will begin to install.

6. Click **Finish** once the installation has finished.

7. Next, click **Start**, and then click **Administrative Tools | DNS**.

8. When prompted to connect to a DNS server, click **This Computer** and then click **OK**. The DNS Management console will open.

9. Right-click the server name and select **Configure a DNS Server** from the shortcut menu.

10. When the Configure a DNS Server Wizard window appears, click **Next**.

11. When prompted to select a type of server to configure, choose **Create forward and reverse lookup zones** and click **Next**.

12. When asked if you want to create a forward lookup zone now, choose **Yes, create a forward lookup zone now (recommended)** and click **Next**.

13. You will be prompted to select a zone type. Choose **Primary Zone** and click **Next** (zone types are explained later in the chapter).

14. When prompted for the name of the zone, enter nru.corp, because this will be the first DNS server for the nru.corp domain. Click **Next** to continue.

15. When prompted for the zone filename, leave the default filename (nru.corp.dns) and click **Next**.

16. When prompted to allow dynamic updates, select **Do not allow dynamic updates** (if necessary) and click **Next**. Select **Yes, create a reverse lookup zone now** when asked if you want to create a reverse lookup zone now, and then click **Next**.

17. Again, this will be a primary zone, so click **Primary Zone** and then click **Next** when asked to select a zone type.

18. When prompted to enter a network ID, you will want to enter the first three IP octets of the subnet that this DNS zone will be used to resolve. For example, we use 192.168.0 for the first three octets. Notice that the reverse lookup zone name is entered for you. Click **Next**.

19. You will be prompted to create a reverse lookup zone file. Leave the default filename and click **Next**. The default filename should be 0.168.192.in-addr.arpa.dns if you followed our IP address schema.

20. Again, choose **Do not allow dynamic updates**, then click **Next** to continue.

21. Next you will be prompted about forwarders; we discuss for-
     warders later in this chapter. For now, when asked if this DNS
     server should forward queries, select **No, it should not forward
     queries**. Then click Next.

22. Click **Finish** to complete the DNS zone configuration process.
     Your parent domain namespace has been created.

Getting back to our example, Name Resolution University has already registered
learnaboutdns.com for its (external) Internet servers, and it is decided that a separate,
internal namespace is required. After tabling different namespace suggestions, you
decide on nru.corp as your parent domain name. At the time of this writing, .corp is
not a top-level domain currently in use (or planned) on the Internet. A list of top-
level domains is available at www.icann.org/tlds. Internet users, therefore, will not be
able to resolve IP-based nodes within your internal network without direct access to
your internal DNS server records. There may come a time when you need to provide
either full DNS resolution for the Internet or referral to an external namespace.
Integrating internal and external namespaces will be discussed later in this chapter. In
theory, there are three possible design options:

■ Active Directory hosting the only DNS namespace

■ Active Directory hosting its own DNS namespace

■ Active Directory within an existing DNS implementation

The desired option will depend on your organization's existing DNS infrastructure, the desire or requirement to preserve the existing infrastructure, and any business
or technical requirements to add functionality that the current infrastructure does not
offer.

Active Directory Hosting the Only DNS Namespace

This design is the most straightforward to design and implement. There are no concerns over interoperability because, quite simply, there is no other internal DNS that
requires integration. The only other service to which you may need to connect is an
external namespace, such as a Demilitarized Zone (DMZ) that hosts your Web presence, or the Internet. You have the greatest number of options for choosing zone
types and replication methods.

The one feature of Windows Server 2003 that will definitely present itself as an
attractive option is the use of *Active Directory-integrated (ADI) zones*. Figure 5.2
depicts a typical internal DNS domain where only Windows Server 2003 DNS is
used for the entire namespace and DNS infrastructure. The benefits of Active

Directory-integrated zones are discussed in detail later in the chapter. In brief, the following benefits can be realized:

- No zone files to manage

- Use of multi-master replication for DNS zone transfer

- Increased speed of Active Directory replication

- Integrated management of Active Directory domains and DNS namespaces from the same management console

- Automatic synchronization of zone data to domain controllers (DCs), regardless of whether the domain controller is also a DNS server

Figure 5.2 nru.corp Hosted in the Only Namespace

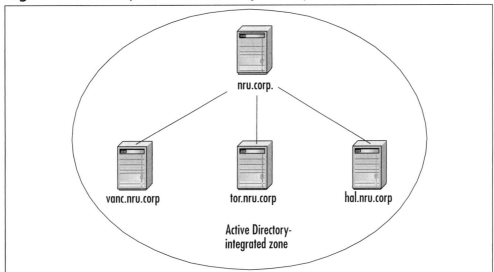

If Active Directory is hosting its own namespace, it can use a standalone internal domain. The internal and external domain names are unrelated, and that adds to the security of the DNS infrastructure and enables the organization to tailor the namespace to its own naming conventions. In our example, the organization can use the domain name learnaboutdns.com for its external namespace and nru.corp for the internal namespace.

The advantage to this model is that it provides the organization with a unique internal domain name. The disadvantage is that two separate namespaces, internal and external, must be managed. There is also the possibility that using an internal domain that is unrelated to your external domain might create confusion for users because the namespaces do not reflect a relationship between internal and external resources.

In the event that the internal domain must be publicly accessible, you might have to register both the internal and external domain names with a domain registrar.

Active Directory Hosting Its Own DNS Namespace

The next option is similar in design to the option just described, with the exception that the Active Directory namespace connects to another internal rather than an external namespace. Active Directory-integrated zones can be used for the Active Directory namespace, but in the event that the Active Directory-integrated namespace needs to replicate with a non-Active Directory namespace, standard zones must be used for replication between the Active Directory namespace and the third-party namespace. This makes integration somewhat more difficult and may limit the number of features available to those that are supported by the third-party DNS service. In our example, vanc.nru.corp is an Active Directory-integrated zone that is hosted by Windows Server 2003, but it is delegated to from an existing DNS hierarchy that is using BIND.

In our example, as shown in Figure 5.3, the organization has an internal namespace with the domain name nru.corp, and vanc.nru.corp is a subdomain, or child domain, of the nru.corp root. The internal subdomain will be the parent domain for additional child domains that will be created in the future. Because child domains are immediately subordinate to the domain name of the parent, the child domain for the finance department in Vancouver in our example, when added to the vanc.nru.corp namespace might have the domain name fin.vanc.nru.corp.

Figure 5.3 vanc.nru.corp in Its Own Namespace

There are several advantages to this option. First, only one name needs to be registered with a domain registrar if the internal namespace needs to be publicly accessible. Second, all internal domain names are globally unique because the namespace is contiguous. Finally, the delegation administration is more straightforward because the internal and external domains can be managed separately.

The main disadvantage is that there will be zone files to manage. However, zone files were probably being used already and this option would add one more for replication for the Active Directory-integrated zone. Furthermore, zone transfers between the child domain and the parent, or in our example, the domain root, are unsecured. Finally, although the Active Directory-integrated zone can enjoy the benefits of being integrated with Active Directory, these benefits cannot be extended to the rest of the DNS infrastructure.

Active Directory Within an Existing DNS Implementation

If you are migrating to Windows Server 2003 or integrating Windows Server 2003 DNS with a third-party DNS infrastructure such as BIND on UNIX or Linux, you do not need to change the namespace design used in your third-party DNS infrastructure. Although the design does not need to change, this option presents the fewest available features for use in the implementation. In essence, the number of available features is the "lowest common denominator" between Windows Server 2003 and the installed third-party DNS service. Notably, Active Directory-integrated zones, and all of the benefits that come with them, cannot be used. This design option (shown in Figure 5.4) presents the greatest integration challenge. More details on interoperability with these DNS services are explored in the next section.

Figure 5.4 vanc.nru.corp on Windows Server 2003 Within an Existing DNS Infrastructure

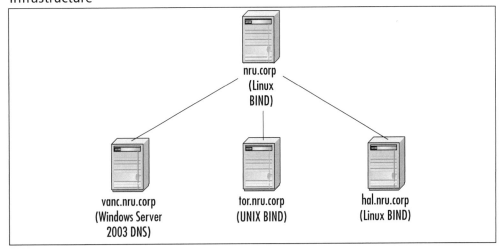

That being said, integration in this situation has many meanings and depends directly on which DNS features are required for your organization. If the existing DNS environment already supports the required features, then the integration with Windows Server 2003 DNS should prove to be very straightforward. If the current DNS environment is not addressing your organization's requirements, however, the degree of complexity increases by an order of magnitude. The integration may not be technically impossible, but the integration process could end up being more complex than the organization (or you and your colleagues) are willing to take on.

Interoperability

Windows Server 2003 DNS is standards-compliant and interoperates with other implementations of DNS, including Microsoft Windows NT version 4.0 and all versions of BIND. This can be very helpful if there is a requirement to preserve a third-party DNS infrastructure. That being said, in this situation, integration has many meanings and depends very directly on which DNS features are required for your organization. If the existing DNS environment already supports the required features, then the integration with Windows Server 2003 DNS should prove to be very straightforward. However, if the current DNS environment is not addressing your organization's requirements, the degree of complexity increases by an order of magnitude. The integration may not be technically impossible, but the integration process could end up being more complex than the organization (or you and your colleagues) are willing to take on.

EXAM WARNING

Make sure that you know all about the features of the various versions of BIND, especially those features that can be used for interoperability with Active Directory.

The degree to which third-party or legacy Windows DNS is interoperable with Windows Server 2003 DNS depends on the DNS version that is being used. Table 5.1 compares the features that are supported in Windows Server 2003 DNS and older versions of DNS in Windows and BIND:

Table 5.1 Feature Comparison

Feature	Windows Server 2003	Windows 2000	Windows NT 4.0	BIND 9	BIND 8.2	BIND 8.1.2	BIND 4.9.7
Supports RFC 2782: A DNS Resource Record (RR) for specifying the location of services (DNS SRV, defined later in this chapter)	X	X	X	X	X	X	X
Dynamic update	X	X		X	X	X	
Secure dynamic update based on the GSS-Transaction signature (TSIG) algorithm	X	X					
WINS and WINS-R records	X	X	X				
Incremental zone transfer	X	X		X	X		
UTF-8 character encoding	X	X					
DNS MMC snap-in	X	X					
Dnscmd.exe (defined later in this chapter)	X	X					
Active Directory-integrated zones	X	X					
Storage of zones in the DNS application directory partition	X						
Aging and scavenging of obsolete records	X	X					
Stub zones (defined later in this chapter)	X	X		X			
Conditional forwarding	X			X			
Per-record permissions or Access Control Lists	X	X					

As an example, if your current DNS environment is supported by servers running BIND 4.9.7, and Dynamic Updates are required, the version of BIND should be upgraded to at least 8.1.2 to offer this feature in conjunction with Windows Server 2003 DNS. BIND version 9 provides the greatest degree of interoperability with Windows 2003 in a heterogeneous DNS environment. Because non-Windows clients can use Windows Server 2003 DNS for resolution, it may make sense from a business and technical perspective to replace non-Windows DNS with Windows DNS in order to take advantage of the features that Windows Server 2003 DNS offers. Two possible examples of this would be if the nature of your organization's business requires that the DNS infrastructure be hardened by using the Secure Dynamic Updates feature of Active Directory-integrated zones, or where the effort that is currently invested in managing DNS must be reduced for financial reasons and the Aging and Scavenging of Obsolete Records feature has been demonstrated to accomplish this.

DNS Zones

Each "level" of the DNS hierarchy represents a particular zone within DNS. For the actual DNS database, a *zone* is a contiguous portion of the domain tree that is administered as a single separate entity by a DNS server. The zone contains resource records for all of the names within the zone. If Active Directory-integrated zones are not being used, there will be zone files that will contain the DNS database resource records that are required to define the zone. If DNS data is Active Directory-integrated, the data is stored in Active Directory and not stored in zone files. The following list identifies the types of zones used in Windows Server 2003 DNS:

- Primary
- Secondary
- Active Directory-integrated
- Reverse lookup
- Stub

Primary and secondary zones are standard (that is, non-Active Directory-integrated) forward lookup zones. The principal difference between the two is the ability to add records. A standard primary zone is hosted on the master servers in a zone replication scheme. Primary zones are the only zones that can be edited, whereas secondary zones are read-only and are updated only through zone transfer. DNS master servers replicate a copy of their zones to one or more servers that host secondary zones, thereby providing fault tolerance for your DNS servers. DNS standard zones are the types of zones you need to use if you do not plan on integrating Active Directory with your DNS servers.

An Active Directory-integrated zone is an authoritative primary (forward lookup) zone in which all of the zone data is stored in Active Directory. As mentioned previously, zone files are not used or necessary. Active Directory-integrated zones are the only type of zones that can use multi-master replication and Active Directory security features. Standard and Active Directory-integrated zones will be compared and contrasted later in the chapter.

A *reverse lookup* zone is an authoritative DNS zone that is used primarily to resolve IP addresses to network resource names. This zone type can be primary, secondary, or Active Directory-integrated. Reverse lookups traverse the DNS hierarchy in exactly the same way as the more common forward lookups.

Stub zones are a new feature introduced in Windows Server 2003. They contain a partial copy of a zone that can be hosted by a DNS server and used to resolve recursive or iterative queries. A *recursive* query is a request from a host to a resolver to find data on other name servers. An *s* query is a request, usually made by a resolver, for any information a server already has in memory for a certain domain name. Stub zones contain the Start of Authority (SOA) resource records of the zone, the DNS resource records that list the zone's authoritative servers, and the glue address (A) resource records that are required for contacting the zone's authoritative servers. Stub zones are useful for reducing the number of DNS queries on a network, and consequently the resource consumption on the primary DNS servers for that particular namespace. Basically, stub zones are used to find other zones. A stub zone can be created in the middle of a large DNS hierarchy to prevent a query for a distant zone within the same namespace from having to ascend, traverse, and return over a multitude of zones.

Zone Transfer

Zone transfer is the process of copying the contents of the zone file on a primary DNS server to a secondary DNS server. Using zone transfer provides fault tolerance by synchronizing the zone file in a primary DNS server with the zone file in a secondary DNS server. The secondary DNS server can continue performing name resolution if the primary DNS server fails. Furthermore, secondary DNS servers can transfer to other secondary DNS servers in the same hierarchical fashion, which renders the higher level secondary DNS server as a master to other secondary servers. Three transfer modes are used in a Windows Server 2003 DNS configuration:

- **Full Transfer** When you bring a new DNS server online and configure it to be a secondary server for an existing zone in your environment, it will perform a *full transfer* of all the zone information in order to replicate all the existing resource records for that zone. Older implementations of the DNS service also used full transfers whenever updates to a DNS database needed to be propagated. Full zone transfers can be very time-consuming and resource intensive, especially in situations in which there is not sufficient bandwidth between primary and secondary DNS servers. For this reason, incremental DNS transfers were developed.

■ **Incremental Transfer** When using *incremental zone transfers*, the secondary server retrieves only resource records that have changed within a zone so that it remains synchronized with the primary DNS server. When incremental transfers are used, the databases on the primary server and the secondary server are compared to see if any differences exist. If the zones are identified as the same (based on the serial number of the *start of authority* resource record), no zone transfer is performed. If, however, the serial number on the primary server database is higher than the serial number on the secondary server, a transfer of the delta resource records commences. Because of this configuration, incremental zone transfers require much less bandwidth and create less network traffic, allowing them to finish faster. Incremental zone transfers are often ideal for DNS servers that must communicate over low-bandwidth connections.

■ **DNS Notify** The third method for transferring DNS zone records is not actually a transfer method at all. To avoid the constant polling of primary DNS servers from secondary DNS servers, *DNS Notify* was developed as a networking standard (RFC 1996) and has since been implemented into the Windows operating system. DNS Notify allows a primary DNS server to utilize a "push" mechanism for notifying secondary servers that it has been updated with records that need to be replicated. Servers that are notified can then initiate a zone transfer (either full or incremental) to "pull" zone changes from their primary servers as they normally would. In a DNS Notify configuration, the IP addresses for all secondary DNS servers in a DNS configuration must be entered into the notify list of the primary DNS server to pull, or request, zone updates.

Each of the three methods has its own purpose and functionality. How you handle zone transfers between your DNS servers depends on your individual circumstances.

Test Day Tip

Remember that full and incremental transfers actually transfer the data between the DNS servers and that DNS Notify is not a mechanism for transferring zone data. It is used in conjunction with AXFR (full transfer) and IXFR (incremental transfer) to notify a secondary server that new records are available for transfer.

Identifying DNS Record Requirements

A Resource Record (RR) is to DNS what a record is to a database. A *Resource Record* is part of DNS' database structure that contains the name information for a particular host or zone. Table 5.2 contains an aggregation of the most popular RR types that have been collected from the various RFCs that define their usage:

Table 5.2 RR Types

Record Type	Common Name	Function	RFC
A	Address Record	Maps FQDN to 32-bit IPv4 address	RFC1035
AAAA	IPv6 address record	Maps FQDN to 128-bit IPv6 address	RFC1886
AFSDB	Andrews files system	Maps a DNS domain name to a server subtype that is either an AFS version 3 volume or an authenticated name server using DCE or NCA	RFC1183
ATMA	Asynchronous Transfer Mode address	Maps a DNS domain name in the owner field to an ATM address referenced in the atm_address field	
CNAME	Canonical name or alias name	Maps a virtual domain name (alias) to a real domain name	RFC1035
HINFO	Host info record	Specifies the CPU and operating system type for the host	RFC1700
ISDN	ISDN info record	Maps an FQDN to an ISDN telephone number	RFC1183

Continued

Table 5.2 RR Types (Continued)

Record Type	Common Name	Function	RFC
KEY	Public key resource record	Contains a public key that is associated with a zone. In full DNSSEC (defined later in this chapter) implementation, resolvers, and servers use KEY resource records to authenticate SIG resource records received from signed zones. KEY resource records are signed by the parent zone, allowing a server that knows a parent zone's public key to discover and verify the child zone's key. Name servers or resolvers receiving resource records from a signed zone obtain the corresponding SIG record, then retrieve the zone's KEY record.	
MB	Mailbox name record	Maps a domain mail server name to the host name of the mail server	RFC1035
MG	Mail group record	Maps a domain mailing group to the mailbox resource records	RFC1035
MINFO	Mailbox info record	Specifies a mailbox for the person who maintains the mailbox	RFC1035
MR	Mailbox renamed record	Maps an old mailbox name to a new mailbox name for forwarding purposes	RFC1035
MX	Mail exchange record	Provides routing info to reach a given mailbox	RFC974
NS	Name server record	Specifies that the listed name server has a zone starting with the owner name. Identify servers other than SOA servers that contain zone information files.	RFC1035

Continued

Table 5.2 RR Types (Continued)

Record Type	Common Name	Function	RFC
NXT	Next resource record	Indicates the nonexistence of a name in a zone by creating a chain of all of the literal owner names in that zone. It also indicates which resource record types are present for an existing name.	
OPT	Option resource record	One OPT resource record can be added to the additional data section of either a DNS request or response. An OPT resource record belongs to a particular transport level message, such as UDP, and not to actual DNS data. Only one OPT resource record is allowed, but not required, per message.	
PTR	Pointer resource record	Points to another DNS resource record. Used for reverse lookup to point to A records	RFC1035
RP	Responsible person info record	Provides info about the server admin	RFC1183
RT	Route-through record	Provides routing info for hosts lacking a direct WAN address	RFC1183
SIG	Signature resource record	Encrypts an RRset to a signer's (RRset's zone owner) domain name and a validity interval	

Continued

Table 5.2 RR Types **(Continued)**

Record Type	Common Name	Function	RFC
SOA	Start of Authority resource record	Indicates the name of origin for the zone and contains the name of the server that is the primary source for information about the zone. It also indicates other basic properties of the zone. The SOA resource record is always first in any standard zone. It indicates the DNS server that either originally created it or is now the primary server for the zone. It is also used to store other properties such as version information and timings that affect zone renewal or expiration. These properties affect how often transfers of the zone are performed between servers that are authoritative for the zone.	RFC1537
SRV	Service locator record	Provides a way of locating multiple servers that provide similar TCP/IP services	RFC2052
TXT	Text record	Maps a DNS name to a string of descriptive text	RFC1035
WKS	Well known services record	Describes the most popular TCP/IP services supported by a protocol on a specific IP address	RFC1035
X25	X.25 info record	Maps a DNS address to a public switched data network (PSDN) address number	RFC1183

The official IANA (Internet Assigned Numbers Authority) list of DNS parameters can be found at www.iana.org/assignments/dns-parameters, and a really good DNS glossary can be found at www.menandmice.com/online_docs_and_faq/glossary/glossarytoc.htm.

NOTE

Windows Server 2003 DNS allows you to restrict which servers and zones are allowed to register name server (NS) resource records. Using the dnscmd command-line tool, you can set your environment to allow NS resource records to be created only by specific domain controllers. You can also use the dnscmd command-line tool to specify servers that you do not want to be able to create NS resource records.

Domain Controller Service Records

In order for Active Directory to function properly, the DNS servers that host the Active Directory zones must provide support for Service Location (SRV) resource records described in RFC 2052, "A DNS RR for specifying the location of services (DNS SRV)." In the introduction to the RFC document, an SRV RR is defined as "a DNS RR that specifies the location of the server(s) for a specific protocol and domain (like a more general form of MX)." As described in Table 5.2, SRV resource records map the name of a service to the name of a server offering that service by providing a way of locating multiple servers offering similar TCP/IP services. In the context of Windows Server 2003 and Active Directory, clients and domain controllers query DNS for SRV records to determine the IP addresses of domain controllers. Although it is not a hard and fast technical requirement of Active Directory, it is highly recommended that DNS servers provide support for DNS dynamic updates described in RFC 2136, entitled "Dynamic Updates in the Domain Name System (DNS UPDATE)." This will reduce the amount of effort required to enter individual host names for potentially every host in your network. Active Directory depends on DNS as a locator service. Therefore, in a network in which DNS is based primarily on BIND, you might want to upgrade the version of BIND to version 8.1.2 or later so that dynamic updates are supported, and enable *Dynamic DNS* (*DDNS*, discussed later in this chapter) for certain Windows-based servers, such as domain controllers.

The Windows Server 2003 DNS service provides support for both SRV records and dynamic updates. If Windows NT 4.0 (pre-Service Pack 4) or versions of BIND prior to 8.1.2 are being used, you should verify that they support the SRV RR at a minimum; BIND 4.9.7 supports the SRV RR, but not Dynamic Update. A DNS server that supports SRV records but not dynamic update must be manually updated with the contents of the Netlogon.dns file created by the Active Directory Installation wizard during the promotion of a Windows Server 2003 to a domain controller.

If you enable dynamic update on the relevant DNS zones in Windows Server 2003, the following entries will be created automatically:

- **_ldap._tcp.\<DNSDomainName\>** Enables a client to locate a domain controller in the domain named by \<DNSDomainName\>. A client searching for a domain controller in the domain nru.corp would query the DNS server for _ldap._tcp.nru.corp.

- **_ldap._tcp.\<SiteName\>._sites.\<DNSDomainName\>** Enables a client to find a domain controller in the domain and site specified (such as _ldap._tcp.lab._sites.nru.corp for a domain controller in the Lab site of nru.corp).

- **_ldap._tcp.pdc._msdcs.<DNSDomainName>** Enables a client to find the PDC Emulator flexible single master operations (FSMO) role holder of a mixed- or native-mode domain. Only the PDC of the domain registers this record.

- **_ldap._tcp.gc._msdcs.<DNSForestName>** Found in the zone associated with the root domain of the forest, this enables a client to find a Global Catalog (GC) server. Only domain controllers serving as GC servers for the forest will register this name. If a server ceases to be a GC server, the server will deregister the record.

- **_ldap._tcp. ._sites.gc._msdcs.<DNSForestName>** Enables a client to find a GC server in the specified site (such as _ldap._tcp.lab. _sites.gc._msdcs.nru.corp).

- **_ldap._tcp.<DomainGuid>.domains._msdcs.<DNSForestName>** Enables a client to find a domain controller in a domain based on the domain controller's globally unique ID (GUID). A *GUID* is a 128-bit (8-byte) number that is generated automatically for the purpose of referencing Active Directory objects. This mechanism and these records are used by domain controllers to locate other domain controllers when they need to replicate, for example.

- **<DNSDomainName>** Enables a client to find a domain controller via a normal Host (A) record.

Host and Alias Records

This may sound like a gross oversimplification, but host and alias records are used to record the host names and hosts' aliased names. This is really the heart and soul of DNS. There are three essential (and most commonly used) resource records for identifying hosts on a DNS-supported network: *Start of Authority (SOA)*, *Address (A and AAAA)*, and *Canonical Name (CNAME)*, which is also known as an *Alias record*.

SOA resource records identify the name of the root of the zone and contain the name of the server that is the primary source for information about the zone. They also provide other basic information about the zone, such as version information, zone renewal or expiration time thresholds, and information on how zone transfers will transpire between other primary DNS servers that are the SOA for other zones. Because it indicates the DNS server that either originally created it or is now the primary server for the zone, the SOA resource record is always first in any standard zone. In an Active Directory-integrated zone, the domain controller used to view the SOA record is always listed as the SOA.

A (Address) resource records are used for setting the primary name for hosts, and each maps a DNS domain host name to an Internet Protocol (IP) version 4 32-bit address. The AAAA resource record performs the same function, except that it is used exclusively for mapping a DNS domain host name to an IPv6 host address. Address (A) resource records will constitute the vast majority of records in the DNS database because every TCP/IP host that needs to be identified by name will need one. They can be entered in the database manually, or automatically through Dynamic Update, if that feature is enabled.

TEST DAY TIP

IPv6 and 128-bit addressing will not be covered on the exam. The difference between A and AAAA resource records were included in case someone, or the exam, decides to throw you a curve ball when discussing resource record types, or if "the Internet" decides to adopt IPv6 in the near future, which looks unlikely unless a sudden shortage of addresses occurs.

CNAME (Canonical Name) records are used for creating aliases for hosts. According to Microsoft and RFC 1035, this resource record type "maps an aliased or alternate DNS domain name in the owner field to a canonical or primary DNS domain name specified in the canonical_name field." The canonical or primary DNS domain name used in the data is required and must resolve to a valid DNS domain name (A RR) in the DNS namespace. A common example would be when the host that is acting as the primary mail server for the company (such as exch2000.tor.nru.corp) would be given an alias of "mail" in the root of nru.corp and CNAME record in the database for mail.nru.corp. Therefore, a query for record "mail.nru.corp" would return "exch2000.tor.nru.corp" and this would then in turn, be resolved to an IP address.

Pointer Records

Strictly speaking, *pointer (PTR)* resource records are used to allow special names to point to some other location in a domain as specified in the targeted_domain_name field. In Windows Server 2003 DNS this record type is used primarily for reverse lookups. By definition, a PTR record provides information that points to another DNS domain name location, even corresponding hosts, which must have a valid address resource record, in a forward lookup zone. Simply put, PTR records translate IP addresses to DNS host names.

Identify Zone Requirements

The DNS system is a collection of zone files that are spread throughout the Internet as well as private networks. Internet zone files break up the DNS namespace into smaller pieces that can be easily managed. Zones allow for the distribution of data but also for the management of localized DNS databases. By managing local DNS databases, you can manage your own zone files by setting your own zone boundaries and selecting DNS settings that will affect only your own resource records. By dividing your parent domain into smaller zones, you improve the performance and manageability of your DNS structure.

Using Name Resolution University as an example, we can break up the nru.corp namespace into several zones. We could, in fact, create a separate zone for each office, making the local administrators responsible for the management of their own DNS names within their zones. Another option is to create separate zones based on the continent on which the offices reside; however, this might not be the best idea based on communication issues. The reason for this is that if you decided to make the Vancouver office the managing zone file for vanc.nru.corp and any other Canadian subzones that may be created in the future, and the quality and speed of communications were poor, the subzones in Toronto and Halifax would all feel the impact (Toronto is thousands of kilometers from Vancouver, and Halifax is actually at the opposite end of North America). If the Toronto and Halifax offices are relatively small and without the proper IT staff, however, you might indeed want to make the Vancouver office the managing DNS zone for tor.nru.corp and hal.nru.corp. You need to decide how best to break up your DNS zones within your environment. Some things you need to take into consideration when planning DNS zones are:

- **Traffic Patterns** You can use System Monitor to get DNS server statistics and review DNS performance counters. You will also want to review client-to-server traffic to see how much of the traffic is going between clients and servers and DNS queries, especially when the queries are running over WAN connections.

- **Link Speed** What types of network links exist between the DNS servers? Are these links active 24/7 or only at particular times of the day?

- **Caching-Only Versus Full DNS Server** If an office is a small, remote office, does it need its own server or can it use a caching-only server? A *caching-only server* is a DNS server that does not host any DNS zones but rather performs name resolution and stores the results in its own cache. This is discussed in greater detail in the Servers section later in this chapter.

Identify Zone Placement

DNS zones are used to divide the namespace and use servers to allocate resources and divide services. Namespaces and zones are two sides of the same coin; they both work hand in hand. As described earlier, the namespace must be designed to meet business requirements and make optimal use of technology resources such as available bandwidth within and between sites. Subdividing the namespace into zones will make it easier for DNS to manage the use of available bandwidth, which will increase performance. Furthermore, it will enable the delegation of administrative responsibility to other reliable network administrators, which will ease your workload. The key issues to consider when subdividing the DNS "real estate" are the use of forwarders and root hints, and the choice of what type of server to use. Servers will be described in greater detail in the next section.

DNS forwarding is simply the mechanism in which one DNS server passes on an unresolved query to another DNS server for resolution. A query will be forwarded until an affirmative or negative response is reached. Typically, zones are used to cordon off a particular location of the organization so that all of that location's networked resources are aggregated in one place in DNS. It is worth noting that, although this is true of DNS, Active Directory is a special case in that one zone is required per domain and the zone hierarchy must match the domain hierarchy in the forest. If a remote location frequently queries for a particular location's resources and there is an associated zone file, a copy of the zone file can be stored on the remote location's DNS server as a secondary zone. This will accelerate the speed at which DNS queries are resolved because individual queries will be resolved on the local DNS server and not sent across the WAN. Proper placement of zone files and configuration of forwarders will make optimal use of available bandwidth.

Developing & Deploying…

Root Hints and Forwarders

There are two ways to direct DNS queries out of your organization: root hints and DNS forwarders. *Root hints* are simply pointers to DNS servers that are higher in the DNS hierarchy, sometimes to the most authoritative DNS servers on the Internet. Root hints are used to configure servers that are authoritative for non-root zones such that they can discover authoritative servers that manage domains located at a higher level of the namespace or in other subtrees. The best use of root hints is on internal DNS servers at lower levels of the namespace. Root hints should not be used for querying DNS servers outside your organization; DNS forwarders are better equipped for performing this function.

DNS forwarders are DNS servers on your network that are used to forward DNS queries for a separate DNS namespace from internal DNS clients to DNS servers that can resolve the query. In a manner of speaking, the key difference between root hints and forwarders is that forwarders create a chain of DNS servers that ascend the DNS hierarchy, while root hints shoot right for the top. You designate a DNS server on a network as a forwarder by configuring the other DNS servers in your network to direct those queries that cannot be resolved to that particular server. A DNS forwarder is the sole means for enabling name resolution for host names in external namespaces, notably the Internet. It can also improve the efficiency of name resolution by

Continued

(Continued)

offloading the processing of queries to other DNS servers, rather than performing some very resource intensive, constant replication of external namespaces. A new DNS feature that was introduced with Windows Server 2003 is Conditional forwarding, which uses forwarders that can be configured to forward queries according to specific domain names to make name resolution more efficient.

In Windows Server 2003, there is a new method of forwarding queries to an external domain for resolution, Conditional forwarding. *Conditional forwarders* can be configured to forward DNS queries based on specific domain names. With conditional forwarders, a DNS server can forward queries to specific DNS servers based on the specific domain names that are being requested within the queries instead of having the DNS servers follow the typical resolution path all the way to the root domain. A conditional forwarder forwards only queries for a specific domain that is specified in the forwarder's list. If a conditional forwarder entry does not exist, the query will be sent to the default forwarder. Conditional forwarders improve upon regular forwarding by adding a name-based condition to the forwarding process. For example, Name Resolution University is partnering with Acme DNS Software. Name Resolution University and Acme DNS Software inform each other of the names of their respective DNS servers to include in each others' DNS. The result is that when users on Name Resolution University's network need to query for resources on Acme DNS Software's network, conditional forwarding routes these queries directly to Acme DNS Software's DNS server. All other queries will follow the conventional path for resolving names (that is, up to the authoritative DNS server for the root top-level domain, if necessary).

When a DNS client sends a query to a DNS server, the DNS server looks at its own database to see if the query can be resolved using its own zone data. The server will also examine its cache of resolved queries and send the data back to the client that sent the query. If the DNS server is configured to forward for the domain name designated in the query, the query is forwarded to the IP address of the DNS forwarder that is associated with that domain name. If the DNS server has no forwarder listed for the name designated in the query, it attempts to resolve the query using standard recursion. You can use conditional forwarders to enhance and improve upon both internal and external name resolution.

EXAM WARNING

Expect a trick question on the exam about stub zones. The exam might present a scenario in which both stub zones and Conditional forwarders are possible answers. Remember that with a stub zone, certain records exist on the DNS server hosting the stub zone, whereas a Conditional forwarder is used to forward DNS resolutions to specific DNS servers based on domain name.

In planning your DNS namespace, you will encounter situations in which you might need to use any of the types of forwarders that we discussed. The way you configure your forwarders within your environment will affect how well queries are answered. If your forwarding scheme is poorly designed, it will affect your ability to properly direct and resolve these queries. For this reason, you need to consider some issues prior to implementing forwarders into your environment:

- **Keep it simple** Implement only as many forwarders as necessary for optimum resolution performance. If possible, don't overload internal DNS servers with dozens of DNS forwarders. Keep in mind that every time a DNS server attempts to process a query, it first attempts to resolve it locally, and then forwards it sequentially through its list of known DNS forwarders. This creates additional overhead by using system resources to complete the query request.

- **Balance is key** One common mistake in using DNS forwarders is pointing multiple internal DNS servers to a single external DNS forwarder. This practice simply creates a bottleneck within your environment. To keep a DNS forwarder from becoming a bottleneck—and a single point of failure—consider creating more than one DNS forwarder and load-balance your forwarding traffic.

- **No "chains of love"** Unless it is completely unavoidable, do not chain your DNS servers together in a forwarding configuration. In other words, if you are configuring your internal DNS servers to forward requests for www.learnaboutdns.com to server X, do not configure server X to forward requests for www.learnaboutdns.com to server Y, and so on. Doing so will just create additional overhead and increase the amount of time it takes to resolve a query.

- **Know your forwarders** In our discussion of conditional forwarders, we mentioned how they could be used for Internet resolution outside your environment. If you plan to use conditional forwarders in this manner, make sure that you know where these forwarders are and who is managing them. For example, make sure that company XYZ is not using a third-party DNS hosting company (such as www.mydns.com) to host its DNS names. You must also be sure you trust your forwarders to be available and that their IP addresses do not change. These servers can potentially be anywhere in the world and run by any number of people.

■ **Remember the big picture** Keep your entire infrastructure in mind when you are configuring a forwarding scenario. In our Name Resolution University example, it wouldn't make sense to forward requests from the Vancouver office to the Halifax office, considering that the query would have to cross North America. Because there are other network "hops" between Vancouver and Halifax, this would be inefficient. Examine your network bandwidth prior to implementing DNS forwarders, and even when sufficient bandwidth exists, try to keep your DNS forwarders in the same physical location as your internal DNS servers.

By following these simple guidelines, you will make client query requests much more streamlined and avoid creating administration nightmares for yourself.

Active Directory Integrated versus Primary Zones

At the beginning of the chapter, several zone types were identified and described. Two principal zone types in Windows Server 2003 are primary and Active Directory-integrated. There are good reasons for using both types of zones. However, one type will be more appropriate than the other depending on how your DNS needs to function once the design has been implemented. This section will describe each zone type and where it would be most appropriately used.

Primary and secondary zones are standard (that is, non–Active Directory-integrated) zones. The principal difference between the two is the ability to add records. A standard primary zone is hosted on the master servers in a zone replication scheme. Primary zones are the only zones that can be edited, whereas secondary zones are read-only and are updated only through zone transfer. DNS master servers replicate a copy of their zones to one or more servers that host secondary zones, thereby providing fault tolerance for your DNS servers. DNS standard zones are the types of zones you need to use if you do not plan on integrating Active Directory with your DNS servers.

An Active Directory-integrated zone is basically an enhanced primary DNS zone. An Active Directory-integrated zone is a primary DNS zone that is stored in Active Directory and thus can, unlike all other zone types, use multi-master replication and Active Directory security features. It is an authoritative primary zone in which all of the zone data is stored in Active Directory. As mentioned previously, zone files are not used or necessary. Integrating DNS with Active Directory produces the following additional benefits:

- **Speed** Directory replication is much faster when DNS and Active Directory are integrated. This is because Active Directory replication is performed on a per-property basis, meaning that only changes that apply to particular zones are replicated. Because only the relevant information is to be replicated, the time required to transfer data between zones is greatly reduced. On top of this, a separate DNS replication topology is eliminated because Active Directory replication topology is used for both ADI zones and AD itself.

- **Reduced Administrative Overhead** Anytime you can reduce the number of management consoles that you have to work with, you can reduce the amount of time needed to manage information. Without the advantage of consolidating the management of DNS and Active Directory in the same console, you would have to manage your Active Directory domains and DNS namespaces separately. Moreover, your DNS domain structure mirrors your Active Directory domains. Any deviation between Active Directory and DNS makes management more time-consuming and creates more opportunity for mistakes. As your network continues to grow and become more complex, managing two separate entities becomes more involved. Integrating Active Directory and DNS provides you with the ability to view and manage them together as a single entity.

- **Automatic Synchronization** When a new domain controller is brought online, networks that have integrated DNS and Active Directory have the advantage of automatic synchronization. Even if a domain controller will not be used to host the DNS service, the ADI zones will still be replicated, synchronized, and stored on the new domain controllers.

- **Secure Dynamic DNS** Additional features have been added that enhance the security of secure dynamic updates. These features will be discussed in the "DNS Security Guidelines" section later in this chapter.

DNS Zone Storage Options

With Windows Server 2003, DNS zones can be stored in the domain or application directory partitions of Active Directory. As it relates to DNS, the official definition of a *partition* from Microsoft is that it is a data structure within Active Directory used to distinguish data for different replication purposes. The only way to take advantage of zone storage options is to install Windows Server 2003 and employ Active Directory-integrated zones for DNS.

The ability to choose the type of directory partition that serves as the repository for DNS zone data is new because application partitions themselves are a new feature of Windows Server 2003. A domain partition contains information about objects within a domain. An *application directory partition* contains specialized data that is intended for local access or limited replication. Two application partitions are created by default as soon as the domain-naming master is upgraded. Any other application directory partitions must be created manually.

The purpose of having a choice of zone storage options is to increase the scalability of Active Directory. Once DNS is integrated with Active Directory, all DNS data is replicated throughout the domain (or forest). Active Directory-integrated zone data is stored in domain partitions by default. There might be situations, however, in which an organization has grown to such a size that a particular location may rarely, if ever, need to access resources in another particular location. In this case, there is no need to have constantly replicated zone data flowing in and out of that location's domain controller, especially if it happens to be across a slow or saturated WAN link. This is where storing zone data in application partitions is especially beneficial. Zone data for particular zones can be stored in application partitions that are then replicated to domain controllers local to the people who need it. Furthermore, the scheduling of replication of this data can be optimized to suit the location's requirements for the currency of the data.

Storing Zones in Application Partitions

In Windows Server 2003, DNS zones can be stored within the domain or in Active Directory data structures used specifically for replication purposes, known as *application directory partitions*. In the most generic sense, application directory partitions are most often used to store dynamic data. Because data changes more often than the configuration information for a forest, the replication scope and frequency of an application directory partition can be set for each partition. The replication features of Active Directory are utilized, and the replication data can be fine-tuned to suit the type of data stored on the partition. In the context of DNS, DNS zones can be stored in Active Directory to take advantage of the ability to finely tune the parameters that govern the replication of zone data in Active Directory–integrated zones. This is especially beneficial in large, geographically dispersed networks, in which subtle changes in zone data can have far reaching effects if not properly replicated in a timely fashion.

In a standard zone configuration, DNS zones are stored in the %systemroot%\system32\dns folder inside a .dns file. Each .dns zone file corresponds to a zone that is stored on a particular DNS server. For example, the zone file for the Vancouver office of Name Resolution University would be vanc.nru.corp.dns.

Active Directory-integrated zones, on the other hand, store their zone data in the Active Directory tree under the domain or application directory partition. Each zone is stored in a container object known within the *dnsZone* class of objects; the actual container is identified by the name of the zone that has been created. In an integrated zone configuration, only primary zones can be stored within Active Directory. If your DNS server is going to host a secondary zone, it will continue to store the primary Active Directory-integrated zone in a dnsZone container within Active Directory, but any secondary zones will be stored in standard text files. This occurs due to the *multi-master replication model* of Active Directory, which removes the need for secondary zones when all zones are stored in Active Directory. In the multi-master replication model, any authoritative DNS server can be designated a primary source for a DNS zone. Because the zone file is stored in the Active Directory database, any DNS server that is also a domain controller can update it. Because any domain controller can update the master DNS database within Active Directory, there is no need to create a secondary DNS zone for Active Directory-integrated zones. This is also a good time to mention the fact that the DNS Notify feature in Windows Server 2003 does not apply to Active Directory-integrated DNS zones, simply because there will never be a secondary DNS server for a primary DNS server to notify.

TEST DAY TIP

Don't get confused about zone storage. If you get a question that relates to zone storage of Active Directory zones, remember that Active Directory-integrated zones are always stored in the dnsZone class of objects within Active Directory. A server that contains an Active Directory-integrated zone, however, can still host a standard primary or secondary zone. These zone files will be stored in %systemroot%\system32\dns, even though the Active Directory-integrated zones are stored in Active Directory.

In an earlier section, three of the major advantages of zone integration with Active Directory were identified as speed, integrated management, and automated synchronization. Each of these three advantages is realized due to the way DNS is stored within the Active Directory structure. A fourth advantage, which we discuss in the section "DNS Security Guidelines," is the capability of having secure dynamic updates in your environment. All these features exist simply due to the way DNS is stored in Active Directory in an integrated configuration.

Delegation and Security

Whenever you expose your system to the outside world, you are leaving your environment open to attacks by hackers. To an attacker, a DNS server is fair game just as as a Web server, a mail server, or any other server that is accessible to the outside world is. To take it a step further, we all know very well that attackers do not await us only on the Internet. Chances are that probably at least one employee in your organization is unhappy with his position, the company, or life in general. Because information is readily available on the Internet on how to perform all different types of network-based attacks, it does not take an elite computer guru to figure out how to attack your network.

Whether you are dealing with attackers on the Internet, attackers on your internal network, or most likely, both, Microsoft has made some great strides in incorporating security features into Windows Server 2003 DNS. Because DNS administration in a large organization can be very labor intensive, the responsibility for administering the namespace and the servers that support it can be delegated to trusted individuals and groups. Second, with Windows Server 2003, you can configure DNS to secure DNS clients, secure your DNS namespace, protect the services that run DNS on the Windows server, secure DNS zone transfers by implementing secure dynamic updates, and secure DNS resource records. Lastly, one of the better advancements in Windows Server 2003 is the implementation of DNSSEC (discussed later in this chapter).

Delegation

To further enhance security for a Windows Server 2003 DNS server with Active Directory-integrated zones, you can adjust the security settings in *discretionary access control lists* (*DACLs*). The DACL for a particular zone can be viewed and managed through the DNS Management console under the Security tab of the zone properties. DACL properties for a DNS zone are similar to NTFS and sharing security properties, with which you should already be familiar. You can use the DACL to specify full control, read, write, create all child objects, and delete child objects or special permissions for users and/or groups. The default setting for authenticated users is Create All Child Objects, which is the minimum required permission for a user to use secure dynamic updates. For example, domain controller records may be secured with DACLs so that only domain controllers can update those records. Similarly, a sensitive DNS record relating to a particular corporate application may be secured with DACLs.

For more information on adjusting DACL security settings, visit www. microsoft.com/technet/treeview/default.asp?url=/technet/prodtechnol/ windowsserver2003/proddocs/datacenter/sag_DNS_pro_ModifySecurityZone.asp.

DNS Security Guidelines

One of the easiest and most common things that you can do is split your DNS namespace into *internal* and *external* zones. In cases in which you want to keep the Internet-standard DNS top-level domain structure (.com, .net, .edu, and others), you can do this quite easily by creating a child domain off your parent domain and managing that zone on an internal DNS server.

For example, if the think tank at Name Resolution University decides that they want to keep the learnaboutdns.com domain name constant throughout their internal and external networks, they can create a zone called internal off their DNS server that hosts learnaboutdns.com and delegate authority to an internal DNS server that will manage internal.learnaboutdns.com. Of course, you could always take this a step further, as we did earlier in this chapter, and create an internal domain that does not directly comply with Internet standards, such as our nru.corp internal DNS namespace.

Once the internal DNS server has been configured inside your network and the DNS database has been populated, you will want to have the two DNS servers possess the ability to communicate with each other. However, because you are making the effort to separate your internal and external DNS namespaces, you definitely don't want outsiders to be able to get access to your internal DNS servers. The best (and easiest) way to keep outsiders from gaining access to your internal DNS server is to configure your firewall to *explicitly* allow only UDP and TCP port 53 communications between the servers. By doing so, the external DNS server accepts only TCP and UDP port 53 requests (from within the internal network) from the internal DNS server, and the internal DNS server accepts only TCP and UDP port 53 requests (from within the external network) from the external DNS server.

Next, configure your internal DNS server to forward all queries for external names to your external DNS server. In the previous section, you learned how to configure forwarders in Windows Server 2003 DNS, and this is a great place to apply those concepts. Lastly, once you have configured your internal DNS server to point to your external DNS server, you need to configure your clients to point to the internal DNS server for name resolution. By doing this, you are restricting all DNS queries to pass from the client to the internal DNS server and then to the external DNS server. Of course, you will want to keep your internal DNS server from being a single point of failure, so setting up a second internal (and external) DNS server is a good idea.

The previous scenario is a very general yet very easy way to secure your DNS servers. It's also a very good baseline for adding security to your name resolution strategy. In the sections to come, we discuss some of the concepts and features that Microsoft has put forth relating specifically to DNS and DNS security within Windows Server 2003. In the next section, we discuss the three levels of security that Microsoft has developed for DNS.

Levels of DNS Security

DNS security, like many other forms of security, is a relative term. For some, simply implementing a firewall and placing their DNS server behind it is sufficient security. For others, only the latest and greatest top level of security will satisfy their needs. To assist you with your DNS security configurations for Windows Server 2003, Microsoft has broken security into three separate levels for comparison purposes:

- Low level
- Medium level
- High level

As you apply different security features to your DNS namespace, you systematically move from a lower level of security to a higher level (Reference: www. microsoft.com/technet/prodtechnol/windowsserver2003/proddocs/deployguide/ dnsbd_dns_oxet.asp).

Low-level security, as defined by Microsoft, is basically using the default configuration settings when DNS for Windows Server 2003 is installed. Typically, you do not want to run a DNS server under this configuration due to the fact that it is so wide open. The characteristics of a DNS server set for low-level security are as follows:

- **Full Exposure to the Internet** Your DNS namespace is completely exposed to the Internet, meaning that Internet users can perform DNS lookups on any PC within your infrastructure. Typically, port 53 is open bi-directionally on your firewall.

- **Zone Transfer** Your DNS servers can transfer zone information to any server.

- **DNS Root Hints** Your DNS servers are configured with root hints that point to the root server on the Internet.

- **DNS Listener Configuration** Your DNS servers have been configured to listen to any and all IP addresses configured for the server. For example, if you have a server running on two subnets, it will listen for requests on both subnets.

- **Dynamic Update** Dynamic update is allowed on your DNS server. This means that users are allowed to update their resource records at will.

A medium-level configuration is what you will typically see and implement into an environment. The medium-level characteristics offer a higher level of protection than low-level security, while not becoming so restrictive that it makes it difficult to operate. The characteristics of a DNS server set for medium-level security are as follows:

- **Limited Exposure to the Internet** Only certain DNS traffic is allowed to and from your DNS server. Typically, port 53 traffic is allowed only to and from certain external DNS servers. The external DNS servers are typically on the outside of your firewall. DNS lookups for external IP addresses are first forwarded to these external DNS servers.

- **Zone Transfer** Your DNS servers can transfer zone information only to servers listed in NS records for the zone(s) being transferred.

- **DNS Root Hints** Internet DNS root hints are present only on the DNS servers outside of your firewall.

- **DNS Listener Configuration** Your DNS servers have been configured to listen only on specified IP addresses.

The high-level configuration characteristics are very similar to those of the medium-level configuration. However, one key difference between medium and high levels is that a high-level configuration contains a domain controller as well as a DNS server, and the DNS zone information is also stored within Active Directory. The other key characteristics of high-level configuration for DNS as compared to medium level are as follows:

- **No Exposure to the Internet** Your DNS server does not communicate with the outside world under any circumstances.

- **DNS Root Hints** DNS root hints for your internal servers point exclusively to internal DNS servers that host root information for your internal namespace.

- **Dynamic Update** Dynamic update is allowed, but only for secure dynamic updates, which requires that the zone be stored in Active Directory.

There is no management console setting in Windows Server 2003 that allows you to select whether your DNS server will function on a low, medium, or high level of security. These are simply guidelines that you can use in developing your DNS infrastructure. You should match your DNS configuration to the three levels to determine if the security of your DNS server meets the security needs of your organization.

One constant in computer networks is that no matter what type of security you implement in your environment, your environment will never be completely secure. There will always be someone out there who wants to see if he can penetrate the safeguards you have put into place in your network. Knowing what threats exist and being diligent in keeping your network secure from known and recently discovered threats are your best bet for maintaining a secure environment. The first precaution you can take for any resource connected to your network is to ensure that all of the latest patches and service packs have been applied. Taking action on the vulnerabilities that the software publishers have acknowledged and addressed will go a long way in protecting your network. The following sections discuss what action you can take that are specific to securing your DNS infrastructure.

Using Secure Updates

When it comes to Windows Server 2003 DNS, one of the first things you should do is to make yourself familiar with the concept of dynamic DNS updates. Dynamic DNS updates allow a computer on your network to register and update its DNS resource records whenever a change occurs, such as a change of computer name, or periodically, simply to refresh the record. Dynamic DNS updates were intended to reduce the amount of administrative work in terms of updating DNS databases each time a machine was brought online, moved, or renamed.

Configuring & Implementing…

Secure Dynamic DNS

By virtue of it being dynamic, Dynamic DNS (DDNS) is designed for ease of administration. Clients register themselves and update their records whenever they receive an IP address from Windows Server 2003 DHCP. If you are the administrator of a DNS zone, the last thing you want is to have a bunch of unauthorized clients polluting the zone with unwanted resource records. This situation will add to your frustration levels, not to mention your workload, for cleaning out these DNS infidels. Fortunately, Windows Server 2003 DNS and its Windows 2000 Server predecessor have the "Scavenge Old Records" utility so that resource records of a certain age can be eliminated with a single click. This is great for old records, but what can be done before these records have reached their expiration date? Windows Server 2003 DNS has the answer: Secure DDNS.

Secure Dynamic Update is available only for Active Directory-integrated zones. If the target DNS zone is not Active Directory integrated and you want to implement this feature, you must change the zone type to Active Directory-integrated before attempting to run any of the procedures described later. Secure Dynamic Update is not available for servers running Windows Server 2003, Web Edition.

The problem arises when unauthorized clients register with DDNS. If a large number of these clients are registered with a given zone, the zone database increases in size and the speed for DNS queries decreases. Secure DDNS avoids this by requiring an update of the DNS record by an authorized DHCP server. When the Windows Server 2003 DHCP Server service is authorized in an Active Directory-integrated zone, it has full control of all DNS zones and records. As a result, the DHCP Server service can update or delete any DNS record that is registered in a secure Active Directory-integrated zone. When an unauthorized client attempts to register itself through DDNS, the

Continued

(Continued)

DHCP Server can simply overwrite that record in DNS. Only clients joined to the domain and with a valid Kerberos ticket can perform Secure DDNS updates. If a DHCP server is to perform this task, it must be a member of the DNS Proxy group.

To configure Secure Dynamic Updates from the DNS Snap-in in MMC:

1. Open the **DNS** Snap-in in MMC.

2. In the console tree, right-click the target DNS zone and click **Properties**.

3. On the **General** tab, ensure that the zone type is Active Directory-Integrated.

4. In the Dynamic updates section, click **Secure only**, as shown in Figure 5.5.

Figure 5.5 Configuring Secure Dynamic Updates

To configure Secure Dynamic Updates from the command line:

1. Open a Command Prompt window.

2. Type **dnscmd [ServerName] /Config {[ZoneName]** or **[..AllZones]} /AllowUpdate 2**, for example "dnscmd nameserver1 /Config{vanc.nru.corp} /AllowUpdate 2".

All elements of this string are required. "dnscmd" is the name of the command-line program. This is followed by ServerName (the host name or the IP address of the target DNS server), or a dot (.) if you are running dnscmd locally on the target DNS server. The /Config switch specifies that the com-

Continued

(Continued)

mand will change the configuration of the server. At this point, you can enter the ZoneName that you want to secure or you can type **..AllZones** to secure all Active Directory-integrated zones hosted on the target DNS server. The fully qualified domain name (FQDN) of the target zone must be entered as the ZoneName. **/AllowUpdate 2** triggers the re-configuration of the target DNS server to allow Secure Dynamic Update. If the **2** is omitted, the target DNS zone will be set to perform standard dynamic updates only.

In Windows Server 2003, Microsoft has taken the concept of dynamic DNS updates a step further. When a DNS zone is integrated with Active Directory, it has the added advantage of potentially utilizing secure dynamic updates. When DNS is configured to use secure dynamic updates, only computers that have been authenticated to the Active Directory domain can perform dynamic updates. In Windows Server 2003, dynamic DNS updates are disabled by default when standard zones are used. However, when a zone becomes an Active Directory-integrated zone, secure dynamic DNS updates are turned on by default. If you want to allow clients to be able to use non-secure DNS updates on a Windows Server 2003 DNS server (using either standard or Active Directory-integrated zones), you need to enable this option manually using the Nonsecure and secure setting (see Figure 5.5).

EXAM WARNING

Remember that dynamic updates can be configured only as "secure only" for Active Directory-integrated zones.

The DNS Security Extensions Protocol

The last topic that we discuss in this section is Microsoft's support for the *DNS Security Extensions* (*DNSSEC*) protocol. DNSSEC is a set of extensions to DNS that adds the capability to authenticate resource records and was designed to protect the Internet from certain attacks. DNSSEC uses public key cryptography with digital signatures to provide a process for a requestor of resource information to authenticate the source of the data. DNSSEC offers reliability that a query response can be traced back to a trusted source, either directly or through a hierarchy that can extend all the way to the parent DNS server.

In DNSSEC, a DNS zone has its own public and private key pair that is used to encrypt and decrypt digital signatures. DNSSEC works by adding three additional record types into DNS—NXT, KEY, and SIG—that will be used for authentication:

- The NXT key is used for creating a chain of certificate owners and for listing the resource records that do not exist for a particular zone.

- The KEY record stores the public key information for a host or zone.

- The SIG record stores a digital signature associated with each set of records.

When a resource record in a zone is signed using a private key, DNSSEC-aware resolvers containing the secured zone's public key can determine whether resource information received from the zone is authentic. If a resolver receives an unsigned record set when it expects a signed one, it determines that there is a problem and therefore will not accept the information that has been retrieved. A typical DNSSEC-enabled query occurs as follows:

1. First, the resolver must query the root server using the root server's public key (which is well known) to find out the DNS server that is authoritative for a particular zone as well as the public key for that zone.

2. The resolver then sends a DNS query to the authoritative server for the zone for which it had requested the public key in Step 1.

3. The DNS server receives the query and responds to the resolver with the requested information as well as the SIG record that corresponds to the DNS zone.

4. The resolver receives the resource record as well as the SIG record and authenticates the resource record using the known public key (which was obtained in Step 1).

5. If the resolver can authenticate the resource record and SIG, it will accept the resource record information. If it cannot authenticate the information, it will discard it.

You might be asking yourself what happens if a DNS server does not have a resource record for a particular query in its database. For this purpose, a third type of record has been added to DNS as part of the DNSSEC implementation: the NXT (next) record. When a DNS server responds to a query that it does not have a matching record for, the DNS server sends an NXT record. The NXT record contains the name of the next DNS entity that exists in the zone as well as a list of the types of records (NS, SOA, MX, and others) present for the current name. The purpose of the NXT record is to not only inform the requestor that a particular resource record does not exist, but it also prevents the DNS server from becoming a victim of a replay attack. In a *replay attack*, a third party that is sitting between the two replays information to the second party that it has previously received from one of the parties.

NXT records thwart replay attacks by verifying the order in which certificates were signed. The NXT record contains the name of the next record that exists within a zone. From our example, the following records exist in the vanc.nru.corp domain:

- alpha.vanc.nru.corp

- beta.vanc.nru.corp

- delta.vanc.nru.corp

- omega.vanc.nru.corp

- zeta.vanc.nru.corp

Frank, who is a very unhappy instructor at Name Resolution University, is familiar with the concept of a DNS replay attack. Frank makes a request to a DNSSEC-enabled DNS server for the resource record of kappa.vanc.nru.corp. Because this host does not exist in our table, Frank is sent an NXT record for delta.vanc.nru.corp, which is the record just *prior* to where *kappa* would exist. This NXT record contains the name of the next existing server in the zone, which is omega.vanc.nru.corp.

Frank decides that he wants to cause a little havoc in the Phoenix office. He performs a replay attack on a fellow instructor, Karen. Karen sends a query to the same DNS server for the IP address of alpha.vanc.nru.corp. Before the DNS server can respond to Karen's query, Frank sends his stored NXT record to Karen. Because the NXT record was signed by the DNS server, Karen's computer verifies the record as authentic. However, when Karen's computer views the NXT record, it sees that the NXT record is that of delta.vanc.nru.corp, and because *alpha* does not fall between *delta* and *omega*, Karen's computer can assume that the record is invalid and discard it.

To learn more about DNSSEC, visit www.dns.net/dnsrd/rfc/rfc2535.html, which is the original RFC on DNSSEC. You might also want to check out www.dnssec.net, which is a great portal for Web sites related to DNSSEC.

Using DNSSEC

As far as Windows Server 2003 support for DNSSEC, we have some good news and some bad news. First, the bad news: it does not support all the features listed in RFC 2535. The good news is that it does cover "basic support" for DNSSEC as described in RFC 2535. The basic support functionality as described in the RFC states that a DNS server must possess the capability to store and retrieve SIG, KEY, and NXT resource records. Any secondary or caching server for a secure zone must have at least these basic compliance features.

EXAM WARNING

For questions relating to DNSSEC, remember the new keys (SIG, KEY, and NXT) and the functions they perform. Also remember that a Windows Server 2003 DNS server can function only as a secondary DNSSEC server.

Server Support

Because Windows Server 2003 meets only the basic support functionality for DNSSEC, it can be configured to operate only as a secondary DNSSEC-enabled DNS server. This means that a Windows Server 2003 DNS server cannot perform such functions as signing zones or resource records, or validating SIG resource records. When a Windows Server 2003 DNS server receives a zone transfer from a DNSSEC-enabled DNS server that has resource records, it writes these records to the zone storage as well as the standard DNS resource records. When the Windows Server 2003 DNS server receives a request for a DNSSEC resource record, it does not verify the digital signatures; rather, it caches the response from the primary server and uses it for future queries.

Client Support

In Windows Server 2003 (and Windows XP Professional), the DNS client cannot read or store a key for a trusted zone, nor can it perform authentication or verification. When a Windows 2003/XP client initiates a DNS query and the response contains DNSSEC resource records, the DNS client returns these records and caches them in the same manner as any other resource records. However, at the time of this writing, this is the maximum amount of support that Windows Server 2003 and Windows XP clients have for DNSSEC.

DNS Servers

Servers are used to "execute" the design; therefore, each server must be adequately sized and placed for the number of queries it will be resolving, and must be assigned the proper role. The roles assigned to the servers involved in the provision of name resolution create the physical infrastructure. When it comes to designing the network infrastructure that provides name resolution services, there are some general design principles that should be followed:

- Place resources closest to the clients that need them.

- Employ technology that increases the availability of the service.

- Make the design easy to manage once implemented.

DNS servers can be configured in three ways; each type corresponds with the zone that the server hosts or a function it performs:

- Primary

- Secondary

- Caching-only

A primary DNS server hosts read-write copies of zone data, has a DNS database of resource records, and resolves DNS queries. A secondary DNS server hosts a read-only copy of zone data. A secondary DNS server periodically checks for changes made to the zone on its configured primary DNS server and performs full or incremental zone transfers as needed.

A caching-only name server does not host any DNS zones, but performs name resolution using forwarders or root hints, and stores the results in its cache. All DNS servers cache queries that they have resolved; however, caching-only servers only perform queries, cache the responses, and return the results. They are not authoritative for any domains, and the information they contain is limited to what has been cached while resolving queries. When determining when to use this kind of server, note that when this server is initially started, it has no cached information. This information is obtained over time as client requests are serviced. They are ideal for conserving bandwidth on low-speed WAN links, because DNS-related traffic decreases as the cache is populated. In addition, caching-only servers do not perform bandwidth-intensive zone transfers. We will explore caching-only servers in Exercise 5.02.

EXERCISE 5.02

INSTALLING A CACHING-ONLY DNS SERVER

1. Install and configure the DNS service on your local domain controller.

2. Add the DNS Snap-in MMC:QUERY:

   a. Click **Start | Run**, type **mmc** in the Open box, and click **OK**.

   b. On the **File** menu, click **Add/Remove Snap-in**.

   c. In the Add/Remove Snap-in dialog box, click **Add**.

   d. In the Add Standalone Snap-in dialog box, click **DNS**, click **Add**, and then click **Close** to finish.

   e. Click **OK** in the Add/Remove Snap-in dialog box.

3. Expand the DNS Snap-in tree.

4. Do *not* add any zones (this will be a cache-only implementation).

5. Right-click the **Server** entry in DNS Manager and open the **Properties** dialog. Select the **Forwarders** tab and add the following to the IP address list **(10.63.32.200 and 10.63.32.161)**. Next, select the **Root Hints** tab, as shown in Figure 5.6. Ensure that only one entry is in the Root Servers list (192.168.1.5).

Figure 5.6 Configuring a DNS Server as Caching-Only

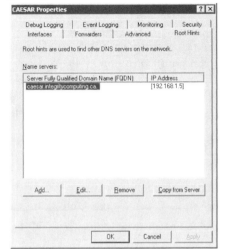

6.   Once you have completed modifying the settings on the DNS server, you will need to modify the settings for your local DHCP server. In the properties for the DHCP server, you will need to enter the IP address for the DNS server you just created. Then set the first DNS server entry to be the IP address for that DNS server.

Each zone must have at least one authoritative DNS server, which hosts a primary or secondary copy of zone data. Ideally, the main DNS servers for the entire organization should reside as close to the core of the network as possible. For performance reasons, there should be a DNS server in each location, even if it is simply a caching-only server. Larger locations may have their own secondary servers. In a homogeneous Microsoft environment, a domain controller in every location hosting Active Directory-integrated partitions would serve the entire organization very well indeed. Furthermore, Windows Server 2003 DNS is cluster-aware. Therefore, you can configure a cluster of DNS servers for high availability, using Microsoft Cluster Services for failover or network load balancing.

The number of servers required to adequately host your DNS infrastructure is directly proportional to the number of queries that need to be resolved. A large organization does not need a large number of DNS servers in every situation. Depending on the type of work being done and the applications being run, a small number of individuals can generate a substantial amount of DNS traffic. According to Microsoft, a server equipped with a 750MHz Intel Pentium III, or equivalent, can resolve up to 10,000 queries per second. DNS queries are the same in essence as queries to any database, and consequently, DNS servers should be configured accordingly. Database operations are processor and memory intensive, and depending on the amount of zone data being stored, they can be disk intensive as well. Increasing the speed of the processor will have a positive impact on the time to resolve DNS queries, but not as much as increasing the amount of memory. DNS data is cached in memory, which is accessed more quickly than disk by a vast order of magnitude, and it stands to reason that more memory means a larger amount of cached data. This is also discussed in the DNS Servers section of Chapter 7, "Server Sizing and Placement."

Interoperability with WINS and DHCP

DNS is a powerful, valuable service on its own. However, Microsoft has designed it so that it can be integrated with other network services to optimize the features of both DNS and these other services. WINS and DHCP are two very likely candidates for integration on any size network because the integration reduces the amount of administrative effort for system administrators.

Integrating DNS with WINS

Windows Server 2003 DNS enables you to support an existing WINS deployment by allowing you to configure a DNS server to query a WINS server. If NetBIOS is required and your servers are running Windows 2000 or Windows Server 2003 DNS, you can enable WINS lookup in DNS. When this is enabled, DNS servers forward requests to WINS, which will resolve any names that the DNS servers fail to resolve.

For a smooth integration with DNS, use only characters that are "legal" for DNS. (Refer to the section entitled The Namespace earlier in this chapter.) Specifically, do not use extended characters in NetBIOS names, notably underscores (_) and periods (.). For the sake of interoperability, your DNS naming standards should govern your NetBIOS naming standards because the DNS naming standards are more restrictive and you will avoid no end of headaches by working with the narrower choice of standards.

Integrating DNS with DHCP

The Windows Server 2003 DHCP server service can be integrated with Windows Server 2003 DNS to perform DNS dynamic updates and secure DNS dynamic updates for DHCP clients. This eliminates the need for administrators to update DNS records manually when a client workstation's IP address changes. This is available to clients running Windows 2000, Windows XP, or Windows Server 2003, but not to clients running any earlier versions of Windows. To enable DHCP to perform dynamic DNS updates on behalf of legacy Windows clients, the default client preference settings can be used. Furthermore, clients using WINS for name resolution cannot make an explicit request for dynamic DNS updates. However, the DHCP service can be configured to update both the PTR and the A resource records to accommodate WINS-only clients.

When using multiple DHCP servers and secure dynamic updates, add each of the DHCP servers as members of the DnsUpdateProxy global security group so that any DHCP server can perform a secure dynamic update for any record. Otherwise, when a DHCP server performs a secure dynamic update for a record, that DHCP server is the only computer that can update the record.

Follow this procedure to configure dynamic update for DHCP clients and servers:

1. In the DHCP snap-in, select and right-click the DHCP server you want to configure, and then click **Properties**.

2. In the server name Properties dialog box, click the **DNS** tab.

3. On the DNS tab, select the **Enable DNS dynamic updates according to the settings below** check box.

4. On the DNS tab, select the dynamic update method you want: either always updating DNS A and PTR or updating the records only when requested by the DHCP client.

If DHCP will perform DNS dynamic updates, install the DHCP service on a member server and not on a domain controller. In the event that DHCP must be installed on a domain controller and is configured to perform secure dynamic updates on behalf of clients, you should specify a user account that will be used to update the DNS records.

Understanding WINS Design

Windows Internet Name Server (WINS) is the Microsoft implementation of a NetBIOS name server as described in RFC 1001 and RFC 1002. Basically, WINS consists of a database that is populated with NetBIOS names and corresponding IP addresses that can be distributed throughout the enterprise. This database is populated by WINS clients registering their names and addresses with the WINS server whose address is configured on the WINS client. WINS servers then replicate the NetBIOS name and IP address pairs to other WINS servers that are set up as replication partners.

WINS design principles are the same as for DNS. The big difference between WINS and DNS with Windows Server 2003 is that WINS is becoming increasingly irrelevant with every new release of Windows, and starting with Windows 2000, DNS became the main name resolution and location service because of Active Directory. Microsoft continues to provide backward compatibility and integration with legacy products and applications. In fact, regardless of its increasing obsolescence, Microsoft continues to add new features to WINS to improve the service. One of the goals of an Active Directory implementation is the eventual elimination of NetBIOS and WINS. NetBIOS belongs to the category of proprietary advertising protocols, such as IPX/SPX, and as such, it is "chatty" and consumes more bandwidth than its more efficient cousins that use a location service for finding network resources.

As far as the exam is considered, the most critical thing to keep at the front of your mind is how the WINS database is replicated most efficiently across an enterprise that spans multiple locations. If there are applications in your organization that must use WINS, they are most likely important enough to keep operating efficiently, or else they would have been upgraded to use DNS. Therefore, it is critical to begin the design of WINS infrastructure with a serious investment in the creation of a strategy.

Strategy

Because WINS has been replaced by DNS as the essential name resolution service used within Windows networks, it is an optional component that should be added as is any other optional component, with forethought to design, integration, and impact on other essential services. When designing your WINS strategy the following issues must be taken into consideration:

- Number of locations

- Available WAN links and bandwidth

- Applications that require WINS

Once these items have been enumerated, evaluated, and documented, you can start creating the WINS topology. The essential function that will need to be addressed is the replication of the WINS database across those little lines that connect the locations on your organization's network diagram. A naming convention for NetBIOS hosts, a replication scheme for WINS servers in all locations, and methods for optimizing WINS performance will need to be explored and developed. These issues and others will be addressed in the sections that follow.

Ensuring Unique NetBIOS Names

The NetBIOS namespace is flat, meaning that there is no hierarchy to provide context for hosts in different locations. DNS is hierarchical; therefore, hosta.vanc.nru.corp is not the same as hosta.nru.corp. In WINS, each name must be unique, and there must be a mechanism to convert the NetBIOS name to an address. WINS is the mechanism; however, it is up to the network architect to devise a scheme to ensure that the names are unique across the whole enterprise and not just within each location or business. One possible approach is to create a naming scheme that incorporates NetBIOS naming restrictions yet is specific to some characteristic of the organization that would make the name unique.

According the RFC, NetBIOS names are 16 characters in length. Names can be registered as unique (one owner) or as group (multiple owner) names. For WINS, Microsoft permits the first 15 characters of a NetBIOS name to be specified by the user or administrator, and reserves the sixteenth character of the NetBIOS name to indicate a resource type (00-FF hex), such as Workstation, File Server, Messenger, or domain controller, as shown in the Type column of Figure 5.7. Many popular third-party software packages also use this character to identify and register their specific services.

Figure 5.7 Registering NetBIOS Names and Services with WINS

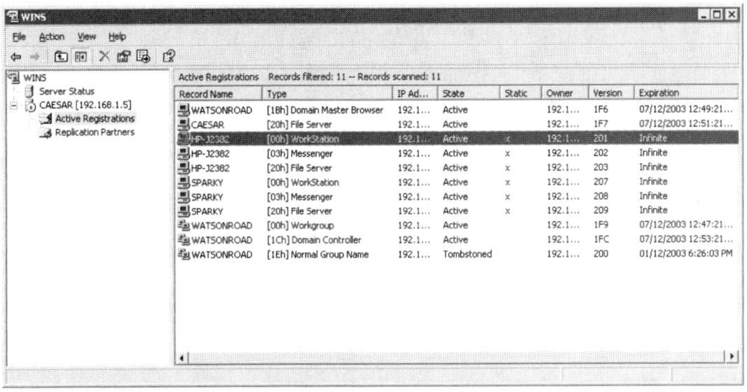

Given that names must be at most 15 characters in length (the sixteenth character is reserved), something must be used within these constraints to ensure a unique name. This "something" will be up to your imagination. Some suggestions might be to use something truly unique, such as an asset tag number or serial number, or some combination of host name and location, such as RECEPTION-VANC. To complicate things further, the NetBIOS name can contain any alphanumeric characters and the following additional characters: ! @ # $ % ^ & ( ) - _ { } ~. Bear in mind that many of these non–alphanumeric characters are not compatible with DNS; therefore, it is a good idea to avoid using these characters whenever possible, because many of your NetBIOS names will also need to be registered in a DNS zone. One solution is to replace NetBIOS-compliant names with DNS-compliant names to ensure that all names adhere to existing DNS naming standards, as we discussed earlier.

EXAM 70-297
OBJECTIVE 3.2.1

WINS Topologies and Replication across the Enterprise

WINS is one of those services that, if you must have it, everyone needs access to it. And much like DNS, an enterprise solution is required, because deploying WINS in an enterprise environment calls for multiple WINS servers to be completely inter-connected in some way. It must be carefully designed and managed to ensure there is minimal degradation of performance when providing the service to other locations within your organization, specifically across potentially slow WAN links.

Replication

According to Microsoft, *replication* is defined as "the process of copying updated data from a data store or file system on a source computer to a matching data store or file system on one or more destination computers to synchronize the data."

When configuring WINS replication across WANs, the two most important issues are:

- Whether your WINS replication occurs over slower WAN links
- The length of time required for all replicated changes in the WINS database to converge and achieve consistency on the network

The frequency of WINS database replication between WINS servers is a major design issue. The WINS server database must be replicated frequently enough to prevent the downtime of a single WINS server from affecting the reliability of the mapping information in other WINS servers. However, the time interval between replications cannot be so small that it interferes with network throughput.

Replication Frequency

Network topology can influence your decision on replication frequency. For example, if your network has multiple hubs connected by relatively slow WAN links, you can configure WINS database replication between WINS servers on the slow links to occur less frequently than replication on the LAN or on fast WAN links. This reduces traffic across the slow link and reduces contention between replication traffic and WINS client name queries.

Replication Designs

After determining the replication strategy that works best for your organization, map the strategy to your physical network. For example, if you have chosen a hub-and-spoke strategy, indicate on your network topology map which sites have the "hub" server and which have the "spoke" servers.

 EXAM WARNING

Most, if not all, WINS questions on the exam will focus on the appropriate replication scheme given available bandwidth. Focus on the size of WAN links in the exhibits and choose where the push/pull partners should be located.

The key to effective WINS design is managing the bandwidth that it uses, and there is no more important contribution toward the performance and availability of WINS than to create a proper replication design. The primary means of accomplishing this is by choosing the correct WINS topology and selecting the proper role for servers acting as replication partners given the available bandwidth. The two recognized choices for WINS topologies are the Hub-and-Spoke model and the Fully Meshed model. In addition, the WINS servers that participate in these topologies can be configured to be push partners, pull partners, or push/pull partners. These topologies and concepts are explored next.

Push versus Pull

In order to present consistent location information to clients, the WINS service has an integrated replication mechanism. There are two types of replication, push and pull, and replication is accomplished by configuring WINS servers as replication partners. Microsoft defines a *pull partner* as a WINS component that requests replication of updated WINS database entries from its push partner, while a *push partner* is a WINS component that notifies its pull partner when updated WINS database entries are available for replication. A push/pull partner combines both of these functions. Figure 5.8 is a diagram of these replication mechanisms.

When a WINS server is configured as a pull partner, it queries its replication partner to determine if any updates are available at a predefined interval. Pull partners should be used if the following conditions exist:

- You have slow WAN links or a congested LAN
- You need to consolidate WINS database updates that consume bandwidth
- You want to exercise control over when the WINS database is updated

When a WINS server is configured as a push partner, the WINS server notifies its replication partner, or partners, that WINS database updates are available. WINS servers that are configured as push partners should be used in the following conditions:

- In a LAN or over high-speed WAN links
- The bandwidth consumed by frequent WINS replication updates is not causing congestion
- WINS databases need to be constantly updated

WINS push-and-pull replication can address availability issues between the local network and remote locations. By adding a WINS server to a remote location, you can increase the availability of the WINS service in the event that a WAN link or router fails.

Hub and Spoke

The Hub-and-Spoke topology is best suited for large, distributed networks. WINS servers in each physical location connect to a central WINS server, or if business requirements dictate, a WINS server cluster. Clustering will increase performance and availability through Windows clustering technology's load-balancing and failover capabilities, respectively. This configuration ensures that the WINS database on each server in each location contains the addresses for every host on the network.

Figure 5.8 Hub-and-Spoke Replication Topology

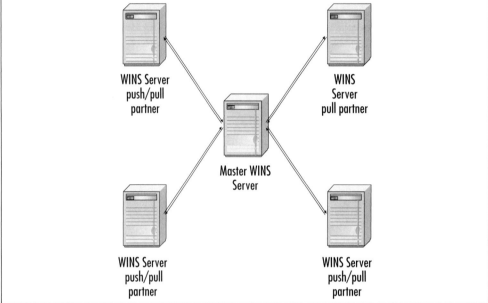

The type of replication partner you choose for each WINS servers depends on the available bandwidth between the central WINS server and the particular location. For locations that are connected by high-speed, high-capacity links, the "spoke" WINS servers can be configured as push/pull partners. For locations that are connected by slower links, a better choice would be to configure the replication partner as a pull partner.

There are several advantages to employing this topology. First and foremost is the topology's ability to scale as the organization grows. WINS servers can be added to any of the spokes with relative ease because there is only one replication partner to configure, the WINS master server. The second advantage is that, once implemented, this design is more easily managed than the Fully Meshed model. There is only one central database that requires care and feeding, and there are fewer replication links to manage.

The disadvantage to this model is that there may be some latency in updating all spokes in a large, distributed environment. If replication schedules for some of the spokes are out of synchronization with other spokes, especially spokes that are pull partners, there may be a delay for an update in one spoke to be replicated in the master database and then picked up by another spoke. A second and more troublesome disadvantage to using a WINS master server in the hub is that the hub is a single point of failure for the entire organization. If this topology is chosen, the reliability of the WINS should be fortified by ensuring that there is redundancy for the database. Furthermore, the WINS database at the hub of the organization should also be well maintained to prevent any corruption in WINS data. Corrupted data that is replicated to the spokes or that breaks replication altogether could cause costly interruptions in service.

Fully Meshed

The Fully Meshed topology is best suited for smaller networks that are limited to a single location, or multiple locations that are connected by high-speed, high-capacity links. In the Fully Meshed topology, every WINS server is configured as a replication partner to every other WINS server, as shown in Figure 5.9.

Figure 5.9 Fully Meshed Replication Topology

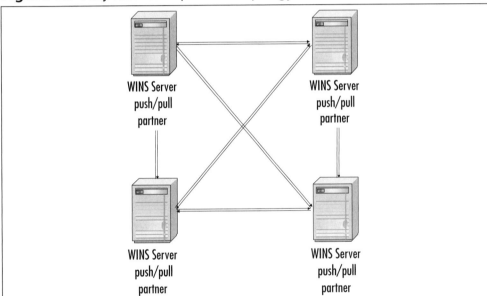

The type of replication partner you choose for each WINS server is less important for this topology than for the Hub-and-Spoke model. Because accommodating many locations and low bandwidth are not prominent factors, WINS servers can be comfortably configured as push/pull partners.

The advantage to employing this design is the speed of replication. Interconnected WINS servers in a high-speed network can be kept up to date in almost real time. Replication intervals can be shortened to ensure that all changes are replicated very soon after they have been committed to the database.

The disadvantage is that this topology can become unmanageable very quickly if the organization grows. Because every WINS server is configured as a replication partner to every other WINS server, the number of relationships will increase exponentially as more servers are added. WINS replication could potentially saturate the network, and any inconsistencies in replication would be difficult to troubleshoot due to the sheer volume of replication partnerships that would need to be investigated.

TEST DAY TIP

Use push replication only in areas of high bandwidth, such as on a contiguous LAN segment. Use pull replication across low-bandwidth connections, such as WAN links. Pull replication enables the conservation of bandwidth because it allows replications across slow links to be scheduled in times of off-peak use.

Advanced WINS Optimization

Although the greatest amount of optimization will be accomplished by choosing the most appropriate WINS topology and replication scheme for your organization, there are a few options for tweaking WINS for even better performance and improved availability. The two primary options for WINS optimization are:

- Making use of WINS Burst Handling Mode
- Using static entries in the WINS database

TEST DAY TIP

There are no significant user interface differences between Windows 2000 and Windows Server 2003 for WINS. You will be able to administer WINS in Windows Server 2003 in exactly the same way you would have (or are still doing) in Windows 2000.

Burst Handling Mode

Despite the shift away in reliance from WINS as the principal means of name resolution and toward DNS that began with Windows 2000, Microsoft is still adding features to WINS. Burst Handling is one those new WINS features. Burst Handling enables WINS to supports high volumes of simultaneous WINS client name registration. In previous versions of WINS, a WINS server would became saturated and performance would degrade when a large number of clients tried to register their

NetBIOS names at the same time. In Burst Handling mode, when the WINS server is under stress, and the number of outstanding registrations exceeds a predefined threshold, the WINS server responds positively to clients that submit a registration request before the WINS server has processed and entered these updates in the WINS server database. The WINS server immediately sends a relatively short, random Time to Live (TTL) lease length to all WINS clients. The short TTL lease length forces WINS clients to reregister after the excessive WINS registration traffic subsides, thus decreasing the load on the network by varying the delay interval to distribute the load on the WINS server at a manageable level. We will explore burst-handling levels in Exercise 5.03.

EXERCISE 5.03

CONFIGURING BURST HANDLING LEVELS IN WINS

Using the WINS MMC Snap-in, you can configure the level of burst handling for the server, which modifies the size of the burst queue.

To configure burst handling:

1. In the WINS MMC Snap-in, right-click the **appropriate WINS server**, and then click **Properties**.

2. Select the **Advanced** tab from the [server name] properties dialog box as shown in Figure 5.10.

Figure 5.10 Setting a Burst Handling Threshold in WINS

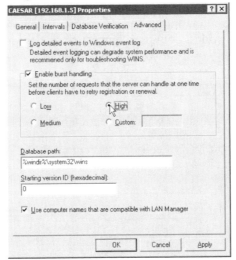

3. In the Enable burst handling section, select **Low (300)**, **Medium (500)**, **High (1000)**, or **Custom (between 50 and 5000)** as the burst queue size.

Static Entries

When most people think of WINS (if people actually stop and think about it), it is considered a dynamic service in which everything happens automatically. However, WINS has the capability to accept static entries for use with computers that do not directly use WINS. If a server cannot register a NetBIOS name directly with a WINS server, its name and IP address can be added to an Lmhosts file on systems that need to access that server, or else DNS can be used.

The use of a static WINS mapping can accelerate the speed of responding to queries when resolving the names of popular network resources. As a bit of background, there are two methods available for populating entries in the WINS database:

■ **Dynamically** WINS clients can directly contact a WINS server to register, release, or renew their NetBIOS names.

■ **Manually** An administrator can use either the WINS console or command-line tools to add or delete static entries.

 EXAM WARNING

Never add static mappings for computers that can directly use WINS. Doing so can cause undesirable problems, such as demanding additional work to migrate, delete, or tombstone these mappings in a replicated WINS environment.

Moreover, there are three ways that static entries can be manually added:

■ Through the WINS console (see Figure 5.11)

Figure 5.11 Adding a Static Entry in WINS Through MMC

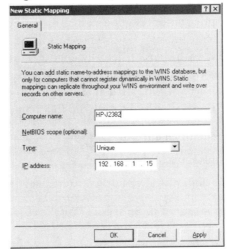

- At the command-line using netsh (netsh add name [Name=]*ComputerName* [IP=]{*IPAddress*}) (See Figure 5.12)

Figure 5.12 Adding a Static Entry from the Windows Command Prompt

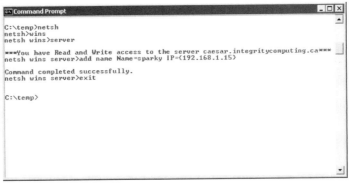

- By importing an Lmhosts file

Unlike dynamic mappings, which can age and be automatically removed from WINS over time, static mappings remain in WINS until they are removed. They must be removed manually just as they were added manually. By default, if during an update process WINS is presented with both a static and dynamic-type entry for the same name, the static entry will be preserved. You can, however, use the Overwrite unique static mappings at this server (migrate on) feature provided with WINS to change this behavior. This feature is useful in simplifying the update of legacy NetBIOS b-node (broadcast-only) clients that will be upgraded to support WINS.

Summary of Exam Objectives

Design is all about optimization. A good design makes everything work better because it creates synergy among the components that it integrates. The services that come out of a good network design actually appear transparent to clients. On the other hand, bad network design makes everything more noticeable, but not in a positive light. The goal of network infrastructure design is the transparent delivery of services to the client. To accomplish this goal, the following objectives must be achieved:

- Increase the performance of the service
- Increase availability of the service
- Reduce the administrative burden to manage the servers

Name resolution is one of those services that should be absolutely transparent to the client.

When it comes to designing the network infrastructure that will provide name resolution services, there are some general design principles that should be followed.

- Place resources closest to the clients that need them
- Employ technology that increases the availability of the service
- Make the design easy to manage once implemented

The namespace should reflect the organization, and consideration should be given as to whether separate internal and external namespaces should be created. The namespace should be divided into zones for ease of management and to improve the response time for queries. Windows Server 2003 DNS can integrate with legacy and third-party DNS, such as Windows NT 4.0 and BIND on UNIX or Linux, respectively. It can also be integrated with Active Directory to take advantage of the increased speed, integrated management, automated synchronization, and improved security that Active Directory-integrated zones offer. To assist in scaling Active Directory for large, geographically dispersed organizations, zones can be stored in application partitions so that the replication of zone data can be fine-tuned according to the requirements of the locations that need it.

WINS is not the essential name resolution service that it was with Windows NT 4.0. However, it has been not only preserved, but enhanced in Windows Server 2003. The same design goal for WINS is still relevant: provide the most up-to-date replication of the WINS database that will not adversely impact the performance of the Wide Area Network. A Fully Meshed topology can be used in a small environment, but it will quickly become unmanageable as more WINS servers are added. For larger, more distributed networks, the Hub-and-Spoke model is more appropriate. Push replication can be used over high-speed network connections, such as a LAN; however, only pull replication should be used over lower-speed WAN links. Static entries can be used for hosts that cannot dynamically update WINS, and a new feature in Windows Server 2003, Burst Handling, can improve the consistency of the WINS database by ensuring that all WINS clients can register their updates, even during peak registration periods.

Exam Objectives Fast Track

DNS Design

☑ A namespace is a grouping in which names are used to represent other types of information such as IP addresses and set rules to determine how names can be created and used.

☑ The first step to planning your DNS namespace is to get a snapshot of your entire organization and choose a parent domain name that represents your organization.

☑ Often it is advisable to create an internal DNS namespace with a non-standard name that is separate from the external or public DNS namespace.

☑ BIND can interoperate with Windows Server 2003 DNS, but using only features that are common to both products.

☑ There are four types of zones in Windows Server 2003: standard primary, standard secondary, stub zones, and Active Directory-integrated zones.

☑ A forwarder is a server configured with the DNS service that is used to forward DNS queries for external DNS names to DNS servers outside a private network. Conditional forwarders are DNS servers that can be used to forward queries based on specific domain names.

☑ Only Active Directory-integrated zones can realize the benefits of secure dynamic updates, Active Directory-integrated storage, and granular permissions on resource records.

WINS Design

☑ The Hub-and-Spoke topology is best suited for large distributed networks with a high number of replication partnerships.

☑ The Fully Meshed topology is more appropriate for networks with few, if any, remote locations in which all network resources are interconnected with high-speed links, such as a Local Area Network.

☑ Configure WINS servers as pull replication partners that are in remote offices at the end of slow WAN links.

☑ Burst Handling can enable a WINS server to respond to many more simultaneous registration requests without dropping requests than could previous versions of WINS.

☑ Static entries can be used to provide WINS clients with the capability to query network resources that do not use WINS. Static entries must be deleted manually.

Exam Objectives Frequently Asked Questions

The following Frequently Asked Questions, answered by the authors of this book, are designed to both measure your understanding of the Exam Objectives presented in this chapter, and to assist you with real-life implementation of these concepts. You will also gain access to thousands of other FAQs at *www.ITFAQnet.com*.

Q: What should be the first step in planning my DNS namespace?

A: First, take a look at your company as a whole. Do you have remote offices? Will they need to have DNS servers? Will these DNS servers need to have administrative control over their DNS zones? Once you have determined your corporate needs, you can take other issues into consideration, including the separation of internal and external namespaces, Active Directory integration, and third-party DNS server support.

Q: Is there any advantage to upgrading my Windows 2000 DNS servers to Windows Server 2003?

A: Absolutely. The addition of new features in Windows Server 2003, including conditional forwarders and stub zones alone makes the change to Windows Server 2003 DNS important. It also makes sense to upgrade your DNS servers to Windows Server 2003 if you plan to upgrade your Active Directory infrastructure to Windows Server 2003.

Q: We have a large investment in UNIX servers that host our DNS infrastructure, and we want to support as many new features of Windows Server 2003 as possible. Should we decommission our UNIX servers in favor of Windows Server 2003 DNS? If not, what should we do?

A: Windows Server 2003 has been designed to conform to Internet standards as spelled out in the IETF's RFCs. In addition, Microsoft has added many new features to Windows Server 2003 DNS. Many of these features are supported in the latest version of BIND, version 9. If your requirements for DNS are supported in BIND 9, then it can be configured to interoperate with Windows Server 2003 DNS.

Q: I am setting up a small project office that will be connected to our branch office by VPN over a 128-Kbps DSL connection. What can I do to ensure that the maximum amount of bandwidth is available for file transfers?

A: Concerning DNS, you should install a caching-only DNS server in the new project office. DNS queries will go through your main branch office until the local caching-only DNS server's database begins to populate. After a few days, the most popular queries will be resolved by the DNS server in the project office, and only the queries that cannot be resolved will pass over the WAN link.

Q: We need to preserve our WINS infrastructure because we have critical applications that still need it. Our problem is that the servers occasionally become overwhelmed with registration requests from WINS clients, and we do not want to add any more WINS servers. What can we do?

A: There is a WINS feature in Windows Server 2003 called Burst Handling. In Burst-Handling mode, the WINS server responds positively to clients that submit a registration request before the WINS server has processed and entered these updates in the WINS server database. The WINS server immediately sends a relatively short, random Time to Live (TTL) lease length to all WINS clients. The short TTL lease length forces WINS clients to reregister after the excessive WINS registration traffic subsides. You can enable Burst Handling on your WINS servers and set the threshold to "High" so that up to 1000 client requests can be handled simultaneously before the WINS server is overwhelmed.

Q: Because Microsoft has switched to DNS and I do not want to manage WINS anymore, can't I simply shut down WINS and force everyone to use DNS?

A: Although eliminating NetBIOS is a goal for most Active Directory migration projects, shutting down the WINS server is something that should be done carefully. There may be legacy clients and applications that rely on WINS and any interruption in business operations may prove to be especially unwelcome. Rather than shut down WINS all at once, after identifying an upgrade path for these legacy clients and applications, a better step would be to gradually tombstone records in the WINS database until all records have been affected. Once you are sure that no one or nothing is using WINS, then the records can be deleted and the WINS server can be decommissioned. You may find that eliminating WINS is impossible without a significant investment of time and money.

Self Test

A Quick Answer Key follows the Self Test questions. For complete questions, answers, and explanations to the Self Test questions in this chapter as well as the other chapters in this book, see the Self Test Appendix.

1. On occasion, clients need to resolve DNS records for external resources. When this occurs, the client sends its query to its appropriate internal DNS server. The DNS server sends additional queries to external DNS servers, acting on behalf of the client, and returns the query information to the client once the server obtains it. What type of query occurs when a DNS server is used as a proxy for DNS clients that have requested resource record information outside their domain?

   A. Recursive query

   B. Iterative query

   C. Reverse lookup query

   D. External query

2. You are creating a standard primary zone for your company on a Windows Server 2003 DNS server, and you want to enable secure-only dynamic DNS updates on your standard primary zone for clients within your office. You open the **DNS management** console, access the **Properties** window of the primary zone, and notice that the only options available for dynamic updates are

None and **Non-secure and Secure**. What is preventing you from enabling secure-only dynamic DNS updates on this zone?

A. You cannot use secure-only dynamic DNS updates unless your zone is an Active Directory-integrated zone.

B. The Secure Dynamic Updates feature is not available in Windows Server 2003.

C. After creating the zone, you must stop and restart the DNS server service.

D. You can just use the Non-secure and Secure option, because clients will attempt to use secure dynamic updates first.

3. One of your coworkers has been tasked with finding various ways to reduce the amount of network traffic that passes over the WAN. Your colleague approaches you with the idea of setting up DNS Notify for your Active Directory-integrated DNS zones. You inform him that although this is a good idea for reducing DNS traffic, it will not work in your organization's environment. Why might this be true?

A. DNS Notify is used to notify secondary servers of changes to the DNS database on the primary server. Because secondary servers do not exist in Active Directory-integrated zones, DNS Notify cannot be implemented.

B. DNS Notify is not available on the Windows Server 2003 operating system. However, an Active Directory-integrated zone can function as a secondary server using DNS Notify on a BIND server that functions as the primary server.

C. DNS Notify cannot run on your Windows Server 2003 server *unless* you place your zone files into an application directory partition.

D. This is not true. You can use DNS Notify in your environment as long as you add the list of secondary servers to notify in the properties of the primary server.

4. You are creating a new standard primary zone for the company you work for, Name Resolution University, using the domain nru.corp. You create the zone through the DNS management console, and now you want to view the corresponding DNS zone file, nru.corp.dns. Where do you need to look in order to find this file?

A. You cannot view the zone file because it is stored in Active Directory.

B. You can look in the %systemroot%\system32\dns folder.

C. You cannot view the DNS file except by using the DNS management console.

D. The DNS zone file is actually just a key in the Windows Registry. You need to use the Registry Editor if you want to view the file.

5. Your manager is concerned that the DNS servers in your network could be susceptible to name spoofing and wants to implement DNS security in your environment. He asks you to research the implementation of DNSSEC onto your existing Windows Server 2003 DNS servers. After researching DNSSEC, you explain to your boss that your Windows Server 2003 DNS servers can act only as secondary servers while running DNSSEC. Why is this so?

A. A Windows Server 2003 DNS server can run only as a secondary server when using DNSSEC because it meets only the basic requirements of DNSSEC.

B. A Windows Server 2003 DNS server can run only as a secondary server when using DNSSEC because a DNSSEC primary server can run only on BIND.

C. A Windows Server 2003 DNS server can run only as a secondary server when using DNSSEC because you must purchase the additional DNSSEC module for Windows Server 2003 in order for your server to function as a primary DNS server.

D. A Windows Server 2003 DNS server can indeed run as a primary or secondary server when using DNSSEC, as long as it is configured correctly.

6. Your company has an existing DNS infrastructure that uses BIND 8.2 on Linux at its head office to host the root domain for the entire company, and it needs to integrate a subdomain that contains a group of Windows Server 2000 servers in a homogeneous Windows environment. These servers are in a branch office in another city and your manager wants to conserve bandwidth consumed by DNS. You suggest that full transfers of zone data should be avoided. Is this possible? If so, how can this be accomplished?

A. Yes because, if the subdomain is configured as an Active Directory-integrated zone, DNS replication can occur at the same time as Active Directory replication.

B. Yes, because BIND 8.2 supports incremental zone transfer.

C. No, because BIND 8.2 does not support incremental zone transfer.

D. No, because this version of BIND and Windows Server 2003 DNS cannot interoperate.

7. Your organization is running a heterogeneous DNS infrastructure that consists of Intel servers running Windows Server 2003 and RISC-based UNIX machines running BIND 9. Your organization just merged with another of equal size, and the new DNS domains will become subdomains of your existing domains. What is the best way to bring the new DNS hierarchy in so that all resources can be located in the new amalgamated domain?

   A. Implement conditional forwarders.

   B. Implement Active Directory-integrated zones.

   C. Implement stub zones.

   D. Implement DNSSEC.

8. Active Directory-integrated zones store their zone data in the Active Directory within a domain or application directory partition. Each zone is stored in a container object, which is identified by the name of the zone that has been created. To which class does this type of container object belong?

   A. dnsZone

   B. dns-Zone

   C. .dnsZone

   D. Active Directory zone

9. You are the only network administrator in the head office of a chain of 20 local 24-hour video rental stores. All of the 20 local stores are connected to the head office by a 10Mbps LAN extension to facilitate the replication of large database updates on an hourly basis. Your video rental software uses NetBIOS and WINS to locate point-of-sale terminals, servers in the video store, and the various laptops and workstations used by the video store managers and head office personnel. What is the best choice for the WINS topology you should implement?

   A. Hub and spoke with all stores configured as pull partners

   B. Hub and spoke with all stores configured as push/pull partners

   C. Fully meshed with all stores configured as pull partners

   D. Fully meshed with all stores configured as push/pull partners

10. Your company just acquired another company, and it has been decided that the two former head offices will be connected with a full T-1 connection. The five branch offices in your organization are connected to your head office with fractional T-1 links, and the four newly acquired branch offices continue to use their 128Kbps-ISDN connections to their head office. You have been assigned the responsibility of creating a WINS infrastructure for the new enterprise. Which of the following recommendations will you make? Choose all that apply.

A. Make all offices from the newly acquired organization pull partners.

B. Make all offices from the newly acquired organization push/pull partners.

C. Make all offices from your organization pull partners.

D. Make all offices from your organization push/pull partners.

E. Deploy a Hub-and-Spoke topology with "hub" WINS servers in each of the head offices.

F. Deploy a Hub-and-Spoke topology with a "hub" WINS server in one of the head offices.

G. Deploy a Fully Meshed topology for all WINS servers in the new organization.

Self Test Quick Answer Key

For complete questions, answers, and explanations to the Self Test questions in this chapter as well as the other chapters in this book, see the Self Test Appendix.

1.	**A**	6.	**B**
2.	**A**	7.	**C**
3.	**A**	8.	**A**
4.	**B**	9.	**B**
5.	**A**	10.	**A, D, F**

Chapter 6

MCSE 70-297

Remote Access and Address Management

Exam Objectives in This Chapter:

3.3	Design security for remote access users.
3.5	Design a remote access strategy.
3.3.1	Identify security host requirements.
3.3.2	Identify the authentication and accounting provider.
3.5.1	Specify the remote access method.
3.3.3	Design remote access policies.
3.5.2	Specify the authentication method for remote access.
3.3.4	Specify logging and auditing settings.
3.6	Design an IP address assignment strategy.
3.6.1	Specify DHCP integration with DNS infrastructure.
3.6.2	Specify DHCP interoperability with client types.

Introduction

A further consideration when designing an Active Directory network infrastructure is that of remote access and the management of IP addresses. The methods used to gain remote access into the organization's network and the users and locations used for remote access can impact the implementation of Active Directory and must therefore be carefully considered. Additionally, because Dynamic Host Control Protocol (DHCP) is widely used as a way of managing IP addresses (through scopes), this topic must also be included in any design and implementation plans.

The chapter starts with a discussion of remote access, the available methods, and the locations from which remote access must be provided. Furthermore, the available authentication methods need to be assessed in light of the fact that multiple clients may need to gain remote access.

Moving on to the RAS implementation itself, we discuss the implications of an RAS deployment with respect to Active Directory, the policies that are available for users as well as machines, the chosen authentication strategy and how it is to be implemented, and accounting strategies. The final RAS topic discussed is auditing—an often overlooked but nevertheless important aspect of an RAS solution, because without auditing, we have no way to identify security breaches nor any way to assess who uses the RAS solution, how often, and for what purpose.

The second half of the chapter deals with IP address management and the use of DHCP. Most Active Directory network infrastructure deployments include a DHCP solution, used to assign IP addresses and IP configuration.

The topic begins with a discussion of how IP addresses and subnets should be mapped to DHCP scopes (and/or superscopes), which are then used to assign IP address and configuration data to clients on the associated subnet. Once the scopes have been identified, identify settings that are common to all scopes as well as those that may vary from place to place or from scope to scope.

This discussion is followed by a review of best practices for DHCP server placement and how best to provide failover and redundancy in the event that a DHCP server fails. Lastly, the integration of DHCP with DNS is discussed, as are the considerations of the various clients and the many different DHCP options they support.

Remote Access Service Servers

Almost anyone performing business over the Internet today requires some sort of remote access solution. For example, information technology staff might need to connect from locations outside the office to correct problem situations. Traveling executives often need to dial in from a hotel to check for important information. Sales personnel might need to connect to verify price and inventory status. Telecommuters working from home and managers working from small branch offices might need to access centralized information and data. Health professionals may need to connect from remote locations to access centralized medical data. Benefit specialists with retirement funds might need to connect from client homes or workplaces to determine projected benefits or update client information. Remote access has become more and more a critical business function. In fact, remote access has become a standard IT service requirement in most businesses, large or small. It has become a central part of the business IT strategy, and users expect it to be there when they need it—secure, reliable, and available.

Windows 2000 and Active Directory brought distinct advantages to IT groups in regard to remote access implementation. Windows Server 2003 builds on those advantages and adds new improvements and capabilities. Using the available built-in tools, IT managers and architects can design and implement solutions that meet and exceed the requirements of their specific industries.

Developing & Deploying…

Network Access Quarantine

Windows Server 2003 provides several improvements to Windows remote access. One of the most useful features, the Network Access Quarantine Control feature, allows you to quarantine specific users. How does it work? If a client system attempting to connect to your network via remote access isn't running the software you have specified, such as a specific service pack or a virus scanner, those client systems can be quarantined and won't be allowed to access your network.

This feature can be somewhat difficult to work with. Network Access Quarantine Control delays normal remote access to your network while your script examines and validates the configuration of the client computer. This delay could cause problems with applications that are intended to run immediately after the connection is complete. You can't use this feature if you have wireless or authenticated switch clients, either, because the service requires the use of the Routing and Remote Access service and the ability to run a post-connect script on the client. Specific details for working with this feature can be downloaded from the following URL: www.microsoft.com/windowsserver2003/techinfo/overview/quarantine.mspx.

One of the biggest choices you need to make is whether to choose Windows authentication over RADIUS and why. RADIUS stands for Remote Authentication Dial-in User Service and is defined in RFC 2865 and RFC 2866. The first thing you need to remember is that there are two types of authentication providers: Windows authentication and RADIUS authentication. Windows authentication uses a Windows 2000 or Windows Server 2003 computer to authenticate remote access requests. RADIUS authentication uses a RADIUS server to authenticate remote access requests.

In Windows Server 2003, the Internet Authentication Service (IAS) implements an RFC-compliant RADIUS server and proxy. This means that a Windows Server 2003 machine running the Routing and Remote Access service can also be configured as a RADIUS client. With this feature, you can accept dial-in or virtual private network (VPN) clients to be authenticated using the RADIUS server.

Many factors will come into play as you decide how you're going to deliver remote access services to your users. The design and deployment of RAS with Active Directory is much easier if you use a structured approach in dealing with the difficulties you encounter during your implementation. A good strategy to help you meet your objectives, especially in large projects, would include the following steps:

- Define your requirements.

- Analyze your alternatives.

- Create a conceptual design.

- Create a detailed design.

- Perform a pilot implementation.

- Deploy the design into production.

Over the next few pages, we'll look at the components of this strategy broken down into the requirements and the implementation. Defining these requirements consists of three steps: identifying remote access users, machines, and locations; assessing and defining authentication requirements. You then can perform the actual implementation. The first step in meeting these requirements, however, is to determine the organization's RAS needs.

The Requirements

You could make or break your RAS project based on the clarity of your requirements. Your requirements must be clearly defined and well documented. If they're not, you might partially meet your needs but fail to take into account other required aspects of your remote access needs. The first step in making sure that you're getting the information you need is to identify who and what needs remote access.

Identifying Remote Access Users, Machines, and Locations

One of the first questions you need to ask yourself is, how big is the group that needs remote access? Another question you need to ask concerns where, geographically, the majority of this group (or population) is located. You'll also need to know during what times and from what time zones this group or groups will be accessing your network via remote access. The level of security, or how restrictive you need the network to be, is also an important factor you'll need to address. Finally, you also need to examine your business and security policies regarding remote access.

The answers to these types of questions will most often be determined by first identifying the key stakeholders, such as the IT director or the CIO, and the business sponsors who need and use the remote access service. Once identified, you need to interview these individuals and develop the list of requirements. Once you have this list identified, the players on the list need to be grouped and prioritized and a consensus built around these requirements as those from which you will build your remote access strategy and from which your solution will be developed.

You'll also want to develop an understanding of the habits and needs of the staff who will be using remote access. This will help you define the remote access system requirements and how the Active Directory needs to be configured and deployed to support your mobile users. First, however, you need to look at the various remote access technologies and determine which will meet your requirements.

Assessing and Defining a Remote Access Method

Determining the remote access technology you will use to meet the remote access requirements of your organization is a critical and, by definition, necessary first step in designing a functional solution to your remote access needs. In developing a solid remote access strategy, your job is to fully understand the features and capabilities of the various remote access technologies, how those technologies are deployed and managed, and what additional technologies might be needed to provide a complete remote access solution. RAS is not like installing a new server. Don't hesitate to seek assistance from outside your IT organization. The money you save in the long run will be well worth the short-term added expense.

One of the first steps in the discovery and analysis phase is to consider the various components and protocols of the International Standards Organization's (ISO) Open Systems Interconnection (OSI) model (commonly referred to as ISO/OSI) and the relationships and capabilities that are inherent in them.

Head of the Class...

ISO/OSI Review

As mentioned previously, ISO/OSI is short for the International Standards Organization Open System Interconnection model. This ISO/OSI model defines a network framework for implementing an agreed-on format by which various vendors' equipment can communicate. Basically, the model identifies and defines all the functionality required to establish, use, define, and dismantle a communication session between two network devices, no matter what the device and no matter who the manufacturer. This is a good thing.

Keep in mind that under this model, all communication processes are defined in seven distinct layers, with specific functionality assigned to each layer. Some companies, such as Microsoft and other proprietary systems, combine multiple-layer functionality into one in their particular version, but most, if not all, of the functionality of the original OSI model layers is incorporated by the various vendors. For this reason, most discussions of computer-to-computer communication begin with a discussion of the OSI/ISO model. Table 6.1 illustrates the OSI reference model.

Table 6.1 The OSI Reference Model

Layer	Description
7	Application
6	Presentation
5	Session
4	Transport
3	Network
2	Data link
1	Physical

Layer 1 of the OSI reference model is often referred to as the *bottom layer*. This may be partly because the usual representation of the model places Layer 1 at the bottom. Layer 1 is the physical layer, and it is here that responsibility for the transmission of the data actually exists. This means that the physical layer operates with only 1s and 0s and is responsible for receiving incoming streams of data, one bit at a time, and then passing them up to the next layer, the data link layer. Examples of Layer 1 transmission media include coaxial cabling, twisted-pair wiring, and fiber optic cabling.

The next step up the ISO/OSI ladder is Layer 2, called the *data link layer*. Layer 2 is responsible for providing end-to-end validity of the data being transmitted and therefore deals with frames. A frame contains the data and local destination instructions for the data. That means nothing else is

Continued

(Continued)

required for communication on the local LAN. The physical and data link layers provide all the necessary information required for communication at the local LAN level. Figure 6.1 demonstrates a data link layer domain.

Figure 6.1 The Physical and Data Link Layers

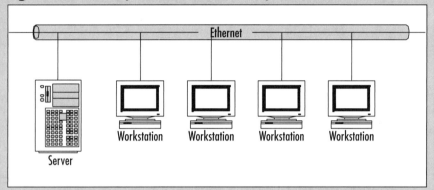

At Layer 3, the *network layer,* internetworking is enabled. At this layer, communication between networks occurs. It is here that the route to be used between the source and the destination is determined. No native transmission error detection/correction method occurs here, however. Some manufacturers' data link layer technologies do support reliable delivery, but the OSI/ISO model doesn't make this assumption. As a result, Layer 3 protocols such as IP generally assume that Level 4 protocols such as TCP will provide the error detection/correction functionality.

Figure 6.2 illustrates a similar network to that shown in Figure 6.1. The difference here is that a second, identical network has been connected via a router. A router isolates data link layer domains so that the only way the two domains can communicate is by using network layer addressing.

Figure 6.2 This Network Requires Network Layer Addressing

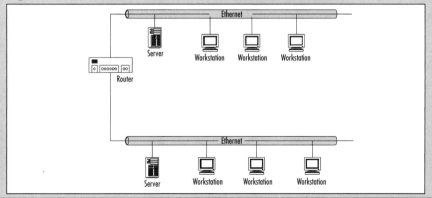

Continued

(Continued)

> At the network layer, protocols can transport data across the LAN segments or even across the Internet. These are called *routable protocols* because their data can be forwarded by routers beyond the local network. IP, IPX (Novel's Internetwork Packet Exchange), and AppleTalk are examples of these routable protocols. Each has its own Layer 3 addressing architecture. The dominant routable protocol is IP, and most discussions deal only with IP fundamentals.
>
> As we prepare to leave the network layer, keep in mind that its use is optional. The use of the first two layers is required, but no application is required to use the network layer. The network layer is required only if two communicating systems reside on different networks or if the two communicating applications require its service.
>
> Just like the data link layer, the fourth layer, the *transport layer*, is responsible for the end-to-end integrity of data transmissions. The main difference between the two is that the transport layer can provide this function beyond the local LAN. If a packet is either damaged or lost in transmission, this layer automatically requests the data be retransmitted. It is also responsible for resequencing the data packets that may have arrived out of order.
>
> Layer 5 is the *session layer*. This layer's functionality is sometimes handled by many protocols in the same layer that protocol handles the functionality of the transport layer. Remote procedure calls (RPCs) and quality-of-service protocols such as RSVP, the bandwidth reservation protocol, are both examples of session layer protocols.
>
> Layer 6 is known as the *presentation layer* and is responsible for how the data is encoded. There are many different data encoding schemes. Layer 6 is responsible for translating data between otherwise incompatible encoding schemes; it can also be used to provide encryption and decryption services.
>
> Finally, the seventh layer is the *application layer*. It is here that the interface between user applications and network services exists.

As mentioned previously, during the discovery and analysis phase, you need to consider the various components you will use to build your RAS. Table 6.2 describes many of the common remote access components and protocols as they relate to the ISO/OSI model. Once you know your organization's requirements for remote access, it's easy to identify the components you already have and the ones you need.

Table 6.2 Common RAS Components and the ISO/OSI Model

OSI Model	Common RAS Components	Microsoft Windows Server 2003 RAS Features
Layer 7	FTP, SMTP, HTTP, RLOGIN, DHCP, BOOTP	Active Directory, FTP Server, DHCP Server, Quality of Service
Layer 6	Lightweight Presentation Protocol	
Layer 5	LDAP, DNS, NetBIOS	DNS Server, Active Directory, WINS
Layer 4	TCP, NetBIOS, UDP	
Layer 3	IP	Routing and Remote Access Services
Layer 2	CHAP, PPP, PPTP	Routing and Remote Access Services
Layer 1	Analog, ISDN, ADSL, Frame Relay	

The standards organizations have adopted several technologies for remote access, and these are supported by the leading equipment manufacturers and telecommunication vendors. On the lower end of the scale you will find analog dial-up with speeds up to 56Kbps using V.90 modems over the public switched telephone network (PSTN). Basic Rate ISDN was a consideration in the past, although less expensive and more attractive alternatives are available today.

Broadband and ADSL technologies offered over cable TV and standard telephone lines, respectively, quickly became viable transmission mechanisms for both business and home users in the search for remote access capabilities. Other viable alternatives on the horizon include satellite and wireless solutions such as digital cellular, 900MHz, and other radio-wave technologies. In some cases today these technologies might not offer the speed, performance, and reliability of more traditional broadband carrier technologies, but as they improve, you should take them into account in your survey of available technologies.

Assessing and Defining the Authentication Requirements

Before we discuss assessing and defining the authentication requirements, it's important that we understand the underlying concepts of the authentication process. Why, you might ask? If you understand how authentication works in concept, it will be a lot easier to troubleshoot logon and authentication problems.

Head of the Class…

How Does the System Authenticate a User?

Users are authenticated in Windows Server 2003 environments by first locating a domain controller and then using the proper authentication protocol. The process is completely transparent to the user. The only thing the user has to do is provide a username and password. Basically, what's happening here is that the users are proving to the system that they are who they say they are and that they should be allowed access to the system. The computer authenticates the user, or verifies his identity, and then builds an access token on the system that contains all the security identifiers (SIDs) that are associated with this user's account.

There are two ways that the computer can use to locate the domain controller: using the Windows 2003 Resolver and DNS or using the NetBIOS Resolver and NetBIOS name resolution. Windows 2000 systems and later will try the DNS Resolver first and will use the NetBIOS Resolver only if no domain controller can be located via DNS.

The Windows 2003 Resolver will query DNS for specific SRV resource records to locate the domain controller. The procedure is as follows:

1. The client computer queries the DNS for a list of domain controllers located within the DNS site. Domain controllers are identified in DNS as LDAP SVR records in:

   `_ldap.<sitename>._sites.dc_msdcs.<domain>`

2. The client computer then sends an LDAP UDP query to Port 389 on the domain controllers to identify which domain controllers are available.

3. The client computer uses the response it receives to the previous query to decide which domain controller is located closest. If no domain controllers respond, the client computer queries DNS for LDAP SRV records in:

   `_ldap._tcp.dc_msdcs.<domain>`

4. The client computer attempts to locate one of the domain controllers listed in the response to the previous query.

5. On locating a domain controller, the client computer sends it a logon request.

Should the Windows 2003 Resolver be unable to locate a domain controller using DNS, the NetBIOS Resolver will attempt to locate one. The 1B record only contains the primary domain controller (PDC) for the domain. The 1C record contains a list of the first 25 registered DCs in the domain. This procedure is as follows:

Continued

(Continued)

1. The NetBIOS Resolver queries the NetBIOS interface for entries for the *Domainname <1B>* NetBIOS name that identifies the domain.

2. If the system is a WINS client, the WINS server is queried for *Domainname <1C>*, which provides a list of DCs in the domain.

3. The client computer then connects with one of the DCs in the list.

4. If the WINS server is not available or if there are no name registration records for *Domainname <1C>*, the client computer then broadcasts in an attempt to locate a DC.

Windows Server 2003 supports several network authentication protocols. The key protocols include Kerberos Version 5, NT LAN Manager (NTLM), Secure Socket Layer/Transport Layer Security (SSL/TLS), and .NET Passport Authentication. Table 6.3 provides a quick checklist of the protocols used in authentication and their purposes. The authentication protocol used will depend on the application requesting access to the resource.

Table 6.3 Authentication Protocols

Protocol	Description	Purpose
Kerberos Version 5	A standard Internet protocol for authenticating users and systems. This is the primary authentication protocol used by Windows Server 2003.	Network authentication. Allows for the mutual authentication of both users and resources.
NT LAN Manager (NTLM)	NTLM is the primary NT authentication protocol.	Network authentication. Used to authenticate computers in Windows NT domains.
Secure Socket Layer/ Transport Layer Security (SSL/TLS)	This is the primary authentication protocol used when accessing secure Web servers.	Network authentication. Based on X.509 public key certificates.
.NET Passport Authentication	This protocol allows the .NET Passport authentication to be used for IIS 6.	Network authentication. Enables the use of Active Directory information in the authentication of Internet, intranet, and extranet users.
Microsoft Challenge Handshake Authentication Protocol Version 2 (MS-CHAP v2)	A Challenge Handshake-Authentication Protocol (CHAP) based authentication protocol providing mutual authentication.	Network and dial-up authentication. Uses separate encryption keys for sending and receiving.

Continued

(Continued)

Table 6.3 Authentication Protocols

Protocol	Description	Purpose
Extensible Authentication Protocol (EAP)	Designed as an extension to Point-to-Point Protocol (PPP), EAP provides greater extensibility and flexibility in the implementation of authentication methods for the PPP connection.	Network and dial-up authentication. Provides support for additional authentication methods such as smart cards.
Password Authentication Protocol (PAP)	A very simple, plain-text authentication protocol.	Network and dial-up authentication. Sends passwords in open text.
Extensible Authentication Protocol—Transport Level Security (EAP-TLS)	This protocol uses Transport Level Security (TLS) to provide authentication in establishing a PPP connection.	Network authentication. Provides for the authentication over wireless connections.

As mentioned earlier, Kerberos Version 5 is the default authentication protocol for Windows Server 2003. This industry-standard protocol provides for mutual authentication of both clients and servers and is based on shared-secrets cryptography.

Whenever Windows Server 2003 is installed as a DC, it automatically becomes a Kerberos Key Distribution Center (KDC) service. The KDC's job is to authenticate Kerberos clients; it is responsible for holding all client passwords and account information. The KDC provides both the Authentication Service (AS) and a Ticket Granting Service (TGS) that's required in Kerberos authentication.

The KDC service:

- Is part of the Local Security Authority Process (lsass.exe)
- Uses Active Directory as its account database
- Starts automatically on all DCs
- Cannot be stopped

Actually, that last statement is not entirely true. The KDC service actually can be stopped. But because turning off the service would prevent the domain controller from allowing users to log onto the network, for all practical aspects, the service cannot be stopped if the server is to continue to function properly. However, technically, the service can be stopped.

Let's walk through a brief example of how Kerberos authentication works. You can follow along in Figure 6.3:

Continued

(Continued)

1. When the client computer logs on, it submits a request for authentication to the KDC.

2. If the request is successful, the KDC sends the client a Ticket Granting Ticket (TGT). The TGT is used as a session ticket for all further communications with the KDC.

3. When the client computer needs to connect to a server, it uses the TGT to request a session ticket for the server from the TGS running on the DC.

4. If the client computer is allowed to access the server, the TGS sends a ticket to the client.

5. The client computer then presents the session ticket to the server that it is trying to communicate with. The server accepts the identity of the client computer because the ticket indicates that the user has been authenticated by a trusted authority (in other words, the DC).

6. The server can also identify itself back to the client at this point.

Figure 6.3 Kerberos Authentication

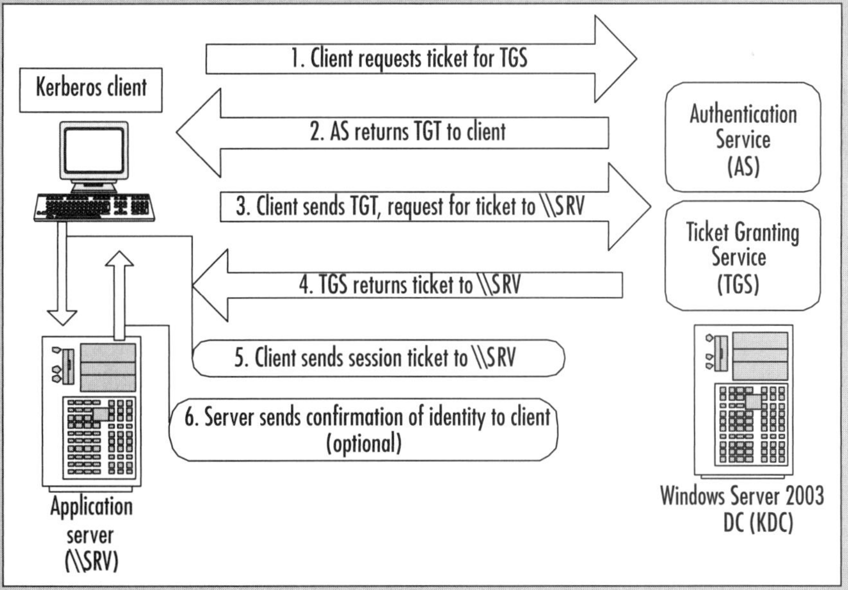

- Kerberos client
- 1. Client requests ticket for TGS
- 2. AS returns TGT to client
- 3. Client sends TGT, request for ticket to \\SRV
- 4. TGS returns ticket to \\SRV
- 5. Client sends session ticket to \\SRV
- 6. Server sends confirmation of identity to client (optional)
- Application server (\\SRV)
- Authentication Service (AS)
- Ticket Granting Service (TGS)
- Windows Server 2003 DC (KDC)

The Kerberos tickets are maintained in a local cache and are aged. They're of no value after they have expired. That means that the client computer must get a new ticket from the KDC when it is ready to reconnect to the remote server.

Continued

(Continued)

> The default length of time Kerberos tickets are valid is eight hours. This interval can be modified using the Group Policy for the site, domain, or organizational unit. The system will flush the cache and destroy all tickets when the user logs off. Because these tickets are time sensitive, it is extremely important that the system time for all client computers be synchronized with the domain controller. Keep in mind that domain controllers in a forest are automatically synchronized using the Windows Time service.
>
> Although, as we stated, the default length of time Kerberos tickets are valid is eight hours, the ticket can be refreshed over and over for a period of seven days. It's only when the current ticket can no longer be refreshed and has expired that a new ticket must be obtained from the KDC.
>
> Windows Server 2003 and Windows 2000 domains together act as Kerberos realms. Trust relationships allow for cross-realm authentication. The Key Distribution Center Service account *krbtgt* is used to authenticate a DC when it is authenticating users or client computers in other domains.

 EXAM WARNING

Remember that existing connections aren't affected by expired tickets. Any attempt at a new connection with a server will require a new ticket from a KDC. So, if you have a user connected to a resource and that user's ticket expires, the user will experience no problem continuing to work with the resource to which he or she is currently connected. It is only after the ticket expires or the user disconnects and attempts to connect to the resource again that the user will require a new ticket.

Now that we've examined the authentication protocols and discussed the default Kerberos protocol, let's return to the problem of defining and accessing the authentication requirements. Choosing remote access components to implement, deciding how to implement those components, and designing your Active Directory tree to support and manage those components to the advantage of your organization depend on several factors.

Designing an Active Directory tree and namespace for remote users has a negative impact on performance. To compensate for this issue, a well-designed Active Directory tree and namespace needs to consider the quantity and location of your Global Catalog (GC) servers. Remember that the GC provides an indexed catalog that speeds searches for network resources. That's important for remote users.

Other issues that you need to consider include:

1. Who needs remote access in your organization?

2. Where do those users expect to connect from? Is there just one remote location, or are there multiple locations?

3. What kind of security does each user or group of users require when accessing the network from the remote location?

4. What applications and/or services will each user or group of users need to access?

5. Do any of the applications or services require or benefit from Terminal Services?

6. Does your organization use dial-up or VPN servers?

7. Do you need to connect remote locations, such as small branch offices?

8. What dial-up or bandwidth options are available at each site?

9. Are you using Windows RAS, IAS, or a separate routing device such as a Cisco VPN router?

10. What's the best configuration for your Active Directory site topology that will optimize access for remote offices with small bandwidth?

11. How will you authenticate your remote users? What level of authentication and data encryption will you require?

As you plan your strategy, whether to implement a complete Windows Server 2003 RAS or to implement specific components, keep in mind that your remote users, telecommuting home users, and branch offices have different requirements. These requirements will evolve and expand over time. Let's turn our attention now to the implementation of an RAS.

The Implementation

One of the first aspects of RAS implementation is the actual setup of the RAS. Let's look at that process before we go any further. We should first create a checklist that we can follow when setting up Windows Server 2003 as a remote access server. To set up Windows Server 2003 as a remote access server, follow these steps:

1. Any necessary network adapters should be installed and configured.

2. The Routing and Remote Access Service should be installed.

3. Because this is going to be a remote access server and will therefore provide the Routing and Remote Access Service, although RIP or OSPF are optional components, you must choose one to be configured.

4. The remote access devices must be configured.

5. The DHCP Relay Agent must be installed and configured.

6. A WINS or DNS name server must be installed.

Because this Windows Server 2003 machine will be used as a remote access server, you'll need to install at least two network adapters on it. The necessary drivers need to be installed, the TCP/IP protocol must be installed, and IP addresses need to be configured on all the network adapters. Table 6.4 shows how the IP addresses for the remote access server might be set up.

Before we go any further, we need to discuss the design considerations—why you would choose RIP or OSPF over the other. Let's start with RIP. Keep in mind that the maximum number of hops for RIP networks is 15 routers. The server will consider any and all non-RIP learned routes to be two hops. Static routes are all considered to be non-RIP learned routes. This means that any RIP-based network that uses servers running Routing and Remote Access will have a maximum hop count of only 14 routers. You really should consider using only RIP Version 2, but then again your network could contain routers that won't support RIP Version 2. In this case, you need to consider the fact that RIP Version 1 does not support classless interdomain routing (CIDR) or variable-length subnet mask (VLSM) implementations. If your network is using either or both of these, you'll need to reexamine your desire to use RIP. Other items you'll want to look at include RIP Version 2 simple password authentication and how RIP performs autostatic updates across demand-dial interfaces. Considering these issues up front may help prevent problems with your implementation. For a more detailed look at these considerations, see *www.microsoft.com/technet/prodtechnol/windowsserver2003 /proddocs/standard/sag_rras-ch3_03b.asp*.

With Open Shortest Path First (OSPF), you have similar issues you must consider. There are three levels of OSPF design. Those three levels are autonomous system design, area design, and network design. When you use the autonomous system design, one thing to consider is subdividing the OSPF autonomous system into areas that can be summarized. You might also want to subdivide your IP address space into a network/area/subnet/host hierarchy. If you're considering the area design, you should consider ensuring that all your areas are assigned network IDs that can be expressed as a small number of summary routes. You'll also want to have your areas stay under 100 networks. For network design, consider assigning router priorities, and make your least busy routers the designated router and the backup designated router. For a more detailed look at these considerations, see *www.microsoft.com/ technet/prodtechnol/windowsserver2003/proddocs/standard/sag_rras-ch3_04b.asp*.

Table 6.4 Typical Network Adapter Setup

Network Card	Connected To	IP Address
1	External Internet backbone	192.168.0.1
2	Internal Intranet subnet	192.168.1.1

Your next step is to enable RRAS on your Windows Server 2003 machine. Exercise 6.01 will walk you through this process.

EXERCISE 6.01

CONFIGURING WINDOWS SERVER 2003 AS A STATIC ROUTER

In the following exercise, we'll configure a Windows Server 2003 server as a static router. This procedure is relatively simple. You need to be logged in with Administrator privileges to perform the following setup procedures. From a security best-practice perspective, you should consider using the *Run As* command rather than logging in with Administrator credentials. If you are logged in using an account other than the Administrator account, just right-click the application you want to run and choose the **Run As** option. The Run As dialog window will appear, similar to what is shown in Figure 6.4. Simply choose the administrator account you want to use and type in the password for this account. Then click the **OK** button. The application will now run using the Administrator's permissions.

One point to remember is that normally a straight user account will not be able to access your Windows Server 2003 system. In Figure 6.4, the *psummitt* account is a Backup Operator on Aries or it would not be able to access the machine. By using the *texascyclone* account, all we've done is allow the application to run under the Administrator permissions.

Figure 6.4 Choose an Administrator Account in Run As

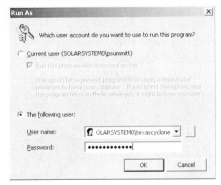

In this exercise, you will configure your Windows Server 2003 server as a static router. The steps you need to follow are:

1. If the server you're setting up as an RAS is a member of an Active Directory domain and you're not a domain administrator, you'll need to have your domain administrator add the computer account of this server to the **RAS and IAS Servers** security group in the domain that this server is a member of. Alternatively, if you have a domain administrator's account but are logged on using your user account, you could use Run As, as described previously. You can do this in one of two ways:

   ■ Add the computer account to the RAS and IAS Servers Security group using Active Directory Users and Computers.

   ■ Use the *netsh ras add registeredserver* command.

2. Click **Start | Administrative Tools | Routing and Remote Access**. You should now see something similar to Figure 6.5.

Figure 6.5 Routing and Remote Access Service

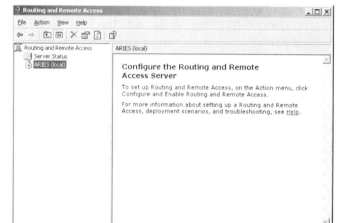

3. The default is that the local computer will be listed as a server. You can add other servers by right-clicking **Server Status** in the console tree on the left and then clicking **Add Server**.

4. As shown in Figure 6.6, click the appropriate option in the **Add Server** dialog box, and then click **OK**.

Figure 6.6 The Add Server Dialog Box

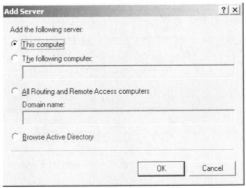

5. As shown in Figure 6.7, right-click the server you want to enable in the console tree on the left of the Routing and Remote Access window, and then click **Configure and Enable Routing and Remote Access**.

Figure 6.7 Click Configure and Enable Routing and Remote Access

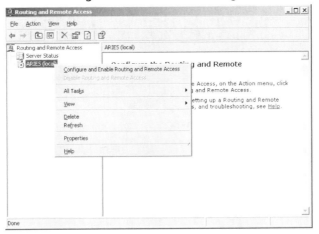

6. The Routing and Remote Access Server Setup Wizard starts. Click the **Next** button.

7. Choose **Custom configuration**, as shown in Figure 6.8, and then click the **Next** button.

Figure 6.8 Choose Custom Configuration

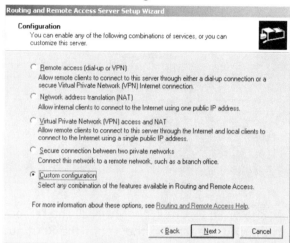

8. Choose the **LAN routing** option, as shown in Figure 6.9, and click the **Next** button.

Figure 6.9 Choose the LAN Routing Option

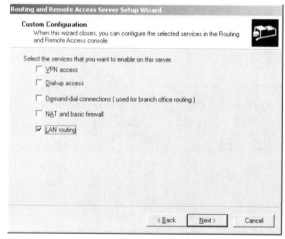

9. You'll see a summary of the options you've chosen (as shown in Figure 6.10), and you're now ready to complete the setup wizard. Verify the selections you have made, and then click the **Finish** button.

Figure 6.10 Finishing the Setup Wizard

10. A window now appears, telling you the Routing and Remote Access Service has been installed (see Figure 6.11) and asking if you want to start the service. Click **Yes**, and the setup wizard will complete.

Figure 6.11 Start the Routing and Remote Access Service

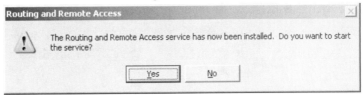

11. Now we add a static default route to the server. We still have the Routing and Remote Access window open, and it should look something like Figure 6.12. Right-click **Static Routes** in the left pane, and then click **New Static Route**.

Figure 6.12 The Routing and Remote Access Window

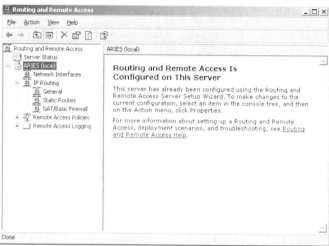

12. Choose the interface you want to use for the default route (see Figure 6.13). In the Destination box, type **0.0.0.0**. Do the same in the Network mask box. Setting both to 0.0.0.0 specifies the default route.

Figure 6.13 Choose Your Interface

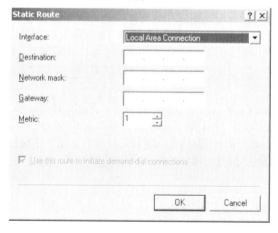

13. In the Gateway box, you'll need to do one of the following:

   ■ If this is a demand-dial interface, select the **Use this route to initiate demand-dial connections** check box. This will initiate a demand-dial connection when any traffic matching this route occurs. The Gateway option will be unavailable.

- ■ If the interface is either an Ethernet or Token Ring LAN connection, type the IP address of the interface that is on the same network segment as the LAN interface.

14. In the Metric box, type the number **1** and click **OK**. That's it. You've completed adding a default static IP route to your router.

In the previous exercise, you configured your Windows Server 2003 server as a static router. Along the way you installed the Routing and Remote Access Service, set up LAN routing, and assigned static routes. You accomplished all this using the graphical interface that Windows Server 2003 provides. You'd follow the same process for any other route that you would want to add. You could also do this from the command prompt. What you would need to do is:

1. Open the command prompt.

2. Type the following: **Route add destination mask subnet mask gateway metric costmetric if interface.**

    Where:

- ■ *destination* specifies either an IP address or hostname for the network or the host.

- ■ *subnet mask* specifies the subnet mask that is to be associated with this route entry. This entry defaults to 255.255.255.255.

- ■ *gateway* specifies either an IP address or a hostname for the gateway or router to use when forwarding.

- ■ *costmetric* assigns a metric cost ranging from 1 to 9,999 to use in calculating the fastest, most reliable route. This defaults to 1.

- ■ *interface* specifies the interface you want used for the route. If you don't specify the interface, it will be determined from the gateway IP address.

So, to add a static route to the 192.168.1.0 network that uses a subnet mask of 255.255.255.0, a gateway of 192.168.0.1, and a cost metric of 2, you would type: **Route add 192.168.1.0 mask 255.255.255.0 192.168.0.1 metric 2.**

The exercise you just finished simply showed you how to set up an RAS with a static route. Exercise 6.02 demonstrates how to set up the RAS with a VPN.

 EXAM WARNING

Don't forget that you need to set up the incoming connections. An incoming connections dial-up network connection must exist in your network and in your Dial-up Connections folder before the service can be enabled. If you don't have one already configured, the wizard will give you the opportunity to configure one.

EXERCISE 6.02

INSTALLING AND ENABLING YOUR WINDOWS SERVER 2003 VPN SERVER

You saw in the previous exercise how simple it is to install and set up a Windows Server 2003 RAS server; setting up and enabling a VPN server is just as simple. Follow these steps:

1. Click **Start | Administrative Tools | Routing and Remote Access**. You'll see a screen similar to Figure 6.14. If you didn't perform the previous exercise and have never set up the Routing and Remote Access Service, you'll see a red circle in the Server icon. If, however, you did perform the previous exercise or if you set up your server to be an RAS server when you were installing the Windows Server 2003 software, you'll see a green arrow.

Figure 6.14 The Service Has Previously Been Enabled

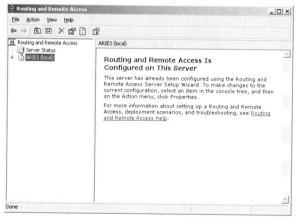

2. The icon representing your server will either have a red circle or a green arrow pointing up in the lower right-hand corner of the icon. You might need to reconfigure your server if the service has already been turned on. You can do this by right-clicking the server icon and choosing **Disable Routing and Remote Access** from the drop-down menu. When prompted, click **Yes** to continue. Your server icon should now have the red circle rather than the green arrow.

3. Now you're going to configure the server. Right-click the server's icon and choose **Configure and Enable Routing and Remote Access** to start the setup wizard. Click **Next** to continue.

4. Select the **Remote access (dial-up or VPN)** option, as shown in Figure 6.15, and then click the **Next** button.

Figure 6.15 Choose Remote Access

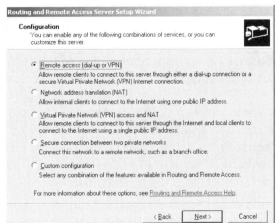

5. Check the **VPN** check box, and then click the **Next** button again.

6. You'll now see the VPN Connection screen shown in Figure 6.16. Select the network interface that's connected to the Internet, and then click the **Next** button again.

Figure 6.16 Choose the Interface Connected to the Internet

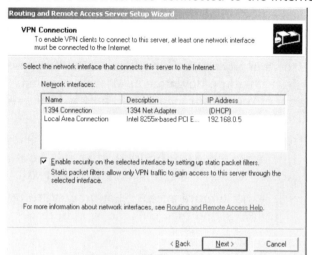

7. Next up will be the IP Address Assignment window. Here you have two choices: automatically assign IP addresses or assign addresses from a specified range of addresses. Of the two, the **Automatically** option is the easier to administer unless there is no DHCP server present, in which case you must specify a range of static addresses. Choose **Automatically** if you have a DHCP server you can use to assign IP addresses to the remote clients. Choose **From a specified range of addresses** if the remote clients can be given an address from only a manually specified pool of addresses. Click **Next** to continue.

8A. If you chose **From a specified range of addresses** in Step 7, you'll see the Address Range Assignment window next. Click the **New** button, and in the Start IP address box, type the first IP address in the range of addresses you want to use. You next need to type the last IP address in the range you've chosen. Windows Server 2003 will automatically calculate the number of addresses for you. Click the **OK** button to return to the Address Range Assignment window, and then click the **Next** button to continue to Step 9.

8B. If you chose **Automatically** in Step 7, when you clicked the **Next** button you automatically came to this step. If not, you'll choose **From a specified range of addresses** and then, when you click the **Next** button at the end of that step, you arrive here. In any event, at this point you need to simply accept the default value of

No, use Routing and Remote Access to authenticate connection requests, and click the **Next** button to continue.

9. Finally, click **Finish** to turn on the Routing and Remote Access Service and to configure the server as a remote access server.

EXAM WARNING

If you configure a pool of IP addresses on the RAS server, this eliminates the dependency of the RAS server contacting the DHCP and simplifies the process a bit. You need to make sure, however, that your address pool does not overlap configured address ranges that are available on your network DHCP servers or any previously defined address on the network. This is a common error that you can prevent by keeping the pool of addresses available to your RAS separate and unique from any other on the network. You should also ensure that the pool of addresses is large enough to cater to your remote access community.

Now that you have the Routing and Remote Access Service up and running and are accepting VPN connections, you might want to think about security for a moment. The Windows Server 2003 IPSec security protocol provides end-to-end security of your datastream using encryption, digital signatures, and hashing algorithms. IPSec protects the actual packets of data, not the link itself. As a result, IPSec provides security even on insecure networks, and only the computers actually involved in the communication are even aware of it. IPSec provides a number of security features:

- Authentication using digital signatures to identify the sender

- Integrity through the use of hash algorithms, ensuring that the data has not been altered

- Privacy through encryption that protects the data from being read

- Anti-replay, which prevents unauthorized access by an attacker who resends packets

- Nonrepudiation through the use of public-key digital signatures that prove the message's origin

- Dynamic rekeying that allows keys to be generated during communication so that the different transmissions are protected with different keys

- Key generation using the Diffie-Hellman key agreement algorithm, which allows computers to agree on a key without having to expose it

- Key lengths that are configurable to allow for export restrictions or highly sensitive transmissions

IPSec works in a relatively simple way. For data to be transmitted and protected between two IPSec-enabled computers, the two computers need to agree on which keys, mechanisms, and security policies they will use to protect the data. This agreement, or negotiation, produces an SA, or a security association. The first SA established between the two computers, called Internet Security Association and Key Management Protocol (ISAKMP), provides the method of key exchange. Using ISAKMP to provide protection, the two computers then negotiate the production of a pair of IPSec SAs and keys. These two keys include one for inbound and one for outbound transmissions. The SAs include the agreed-on algorithm for encryption and integrity and the agreed-on IPSec protocol to use. The two IPSec protocols that could be used are:

- Authentication Header (AH), which provides data authentication, integrity, and anti-replay to IP packets

- Encapsulating Security Payload (ESP), which provides confidentiality along with data authentication, integrity, and anti-replay to IP packets

The next step is to consider the impact that the Windows Server 2003 Active Directory will have on your installation. An Active Directory implementation consists of several phases, and each phase will affect the way the AD implementation performs. The problem we face is that there is no default implementation plan and no set of standard rules to apply. In fact, each implementation will be different. This is primarily due to the fact that each organization's needs differ from those of other organizations.

 EXAM WARNING

Keep in mind that remote access policies are stored on the server that hosts the RRAS. This fact is so important that it bears repeating. Even when part of an Active Directory network, the remote access policies are stored on the server that hosts the RRAS.

Active Directory Implications

All user, group, and computer account information is stored in the Windows Server 2003 Active Directory. These user, group, and machine accounts are organized into containers called *organizational units (OUs)*. There's no limit to the number of OUs that can exist within an individual domain. And when it comes to user, group, and machine accounts, the Windows Server 2003 Active Directory can hold more than a million objects.

For this reason, the Windows Server 2003 domain isn't tied to any specific number of accounts, and domains can be created and joined together in any organizational structure you like. The Active Directory can contain one domain or many. Remote locations can now participate in the enterprise domain structure.

In addition to account-related information, domain security policy information is also stored in the Active Directory. The information that is maintained includes properties that allow users to use the system. Passwords are examples of the information stored here. These security objects need to be protected from unauthorized access. As a result, security and directory services are tightly integrated with one another.

If permissions for a specific object are configured, its security descriptor will contain a discretionary access control list (DACL) with SIDs for the users and groups who are allowed or denied access. If auditing is configured for the object, the security descriptor also contains a system access control list (SACL) that controls how the security subsystem audits attempts to access the object.

Defining Security Policies

Security policies in Windows Server 2003 and Windows 2000 are more complicated than they were in previous versions of the operating system. A user's access ability is determined by a combination of the dial-in properties for the user's network account and the remote access policies. With remote access policies, a user can be allowed or denied access based on factors such as time of day, the group to which the user belongs, and the type of connection being requested, among other things.

EXAM WARNING

There is a difference between authentication and authorization. Know this difference! *Authentication* is the process of identifying a user. *Authorization*, on the other hand, is the process of allowing or denying a user access to a system and the objects on that system based on the user's identity. Authorization is performed when the client sends the user's username and password to the server using an authentication protocol. The authentication process then makes sure that the individual is who he or she claims to be but says nothing about the user's access rights.

Understanding the Default Policy

Let's take a few minutes to look over the default policy that is set in Routing and Remote Access when you install. By default, both Windows Server 2003 and Windows 2000 RAS ship with a default RAS policy. You find this policy in the RRAS snap-in under the remote access server by selecting the Remote Access Policies object and looking in the details pane on the right, as shown in Figure 6.17.

Figure 6.17 Default RAS Policy Properties

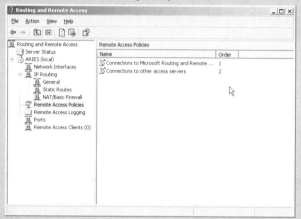

As you can see, two policies are listed. Double-click the first policy, **Connections to Microsoft Routing and Remote Access Server**, and open the Settings dialog box, shown in Figure 6.18.

Figure 6.18 Default Remote Access Policy Properties

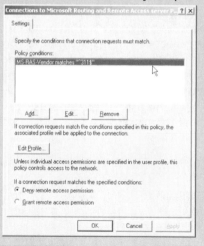

Continued

(Continued)

> As you can see in Figure 6.18, one condition is shown in the policy conditions window. The policy shown says MS-RAS-Vendor matches ^311$. Lower in the figure you can see that it says that if a connection request matches the specified conditions, the RAS is to deny the remote access permission. What this all means is that if the version of the RADIUS client is ^311$, the connection will be denied. Any other RADIUS client not meeting that version number will not be subject to this policy and will therefore move on to the next policy shown in Figure 6.17.
>
> The second policy shown in Figure 6.17 is Connections to other Access Servers. It is the first policy, however, that is the default RRAS policy for the server and therefore the one that you need to modify to match your organization's needs.

EXAM WARNING

Keep in mind that many people confuse the terms "permission" and "policy" and use them as if they were interchangeable. Permissions are set on a user account and are denied by default. The dial-in permission set on the user account overrides the permission option in the Properties dialog box except in the case of the native-mode administration model, where all user accounts are set to Control Access Through Remote Access Policy.

An essential part of planning for remote access involves making a decision as to the model for administering remote access permissions and connection settings that you will use. There are three basic models:

- Access by user

- Access by policy in a Windows 2000 mixed or Windows Server 2003 interim domain

- Access by policy in a Windows 2000 native or Windows Server 2003 domain

There's enough variation in these models that, should you attempt to mix them, you can pretty much count on confusing everyone, including yourself. No matter what, plan to fully test your access policies so that you know that you're getting the results you planned to get.

In the next two sections, we look at setting up policies on two levels: user and machine. Keep in mind that this discussion is superficial and seeks only to demonstrate some of the best practices involved in choosing your administration model.

User Policies

As we discussed earlier, there are three models for remote access policies: access by user, access by policy in a Windows 2000 mixed or Windows Server 2003 interim domain, and access by policy in a Windows 2000 native or Windows Server 2003 domain. Let's examine each of these briefly.

Looking first at the access by user administrative model, we notice that remote access permissions are determined by the remote access permissions in the Dial-in tab of the Properties dialog box for the user account, as shown in Figure 6.19.

EXAM WARNING

Notice that the third option in Figure 6.19, Control Access through Remote Access Policy, is grayed out and not available to choose. You will see this condition when you deal with user accounts in Windows Server 2003 and Windows 2000 mixed domains. Watch for this indicator in questions on the exam.

Figure 6.19 User Account Remote Access Permissions

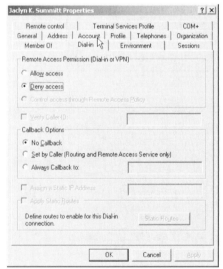

To enable or disable an individual user's remote access permissions, all you need to do is set the Remote Access Permission to either Allow Access or Deny Access. This is probably the simplest of all three of the administration models. It works fine when the number of users is small and the time of access is uncomplicated.

The setting here of either allow or deny effectively overrides any remote access permission setting on the remote access policy. As we said earlier, you could use multiple administration methods, but you're asking for trouble if you do. Connections must match the conditions of the policy, but if multiple policies or profile settings don't match, connection attempts could be rejected, as shown in Figure 6.20.

Figure 6.20 Administering Access by User

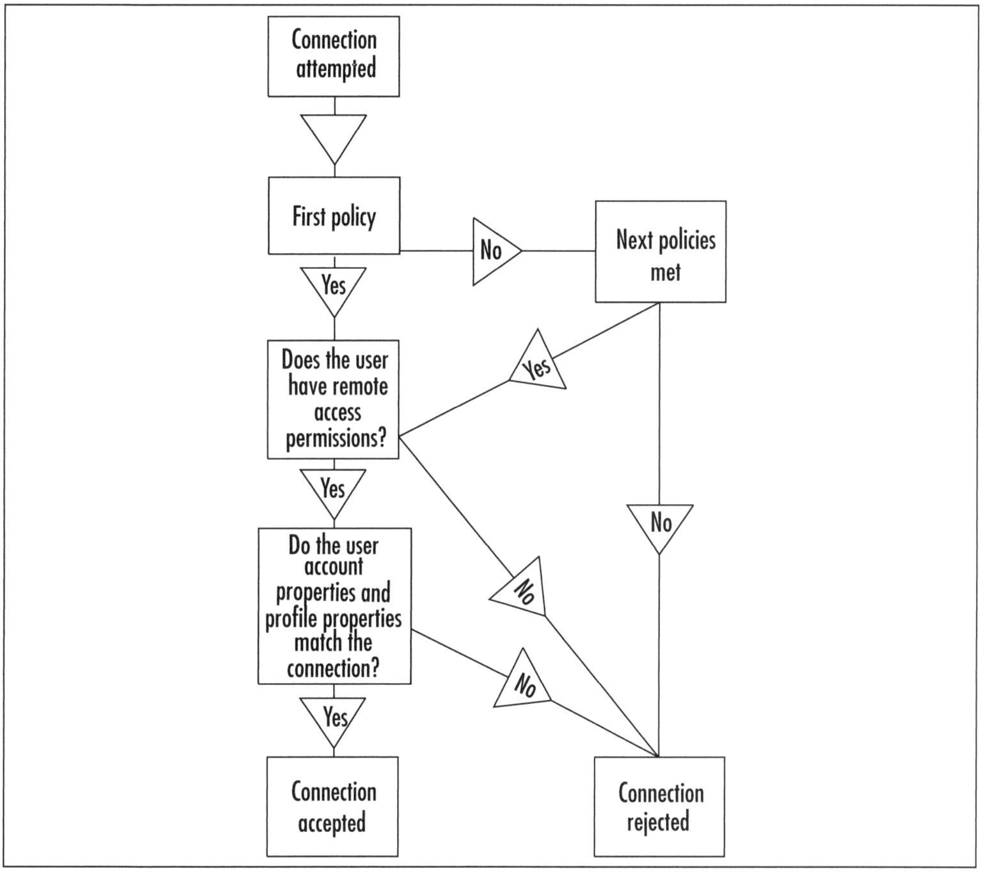

In the access-by-user model, access is controlled in one of the following three ways:

- **Explicit Allow** Here, the remote access permission for the user is set to Allow Access. No conflicts exist among a policy, the settings for the profile, or the dial-in properties for the user account.

- **Explicit Deny** The remote access permission for the user is set to Deny Access. End of story.

- **Implicit Deny** In this case, the connection attempt doesn't match the conditions set in any remote access policy.

Keep in mind that, in the access-by-user model, access is determined solely by the settings in the Properties dialog box for the individual user account. Take a look again at Figure 6.18 and notice that it is set to deny access. If the Allow Access is set in Figure 6.19, that deny setting doesn't mean anything. Again, in the access-by-user model, access is determined solely by the settings in the Properties dialog box for the individual user account.

In the administer-access-by-policy model in a Windows 2000 mixed or Windows Server 2003 interim domain, the remote access permissions on every user account are set to allow access. Here, the default remote access policies are deleted or demoted, and separate remote access policies are created for the various types of connections that will be allowed. In this model, access is controlled in one of the following three ways:

- **Explicit Allow** In this case, the attempted connection matches all the conditions of the policy, subject to the profile settings and the user account dial-in properties.

- **Explicit Deny** Here, the attempted connection matches the conditions of a policy but not the profile settings.

- **Implicit Deny** The attempted connection doesn't match the conditions of any remote access policy.

Finally, in the administer-access-by-policy model in a Windows 2000 native or Windows Server 2003 domain, you have two alternatives for controlling access:

- Set the remote access permissions on every user account to Control Access through Remote Access Policy.

- Determine your remote access permissions by the Remote Access Permission setting on the remote access policy.

In using either of these methods, you control access through:

- **Explicit Allow** On the remote access policy, the remote access permission is set to Grant Remote Access Permission. The attempted connection matches the conditions of the policy, subject to the profile settings and the user account dial-in properties.

- **Explicit Deny** On the remote access policy, the remote access permission is set to Deny Remote Access Permission. The attempted connection matches the conditions of the policy.

- **Implicit Deny** The attempted connection doesn't match the conditions of any remote access policy.

TEST DAY TIP

Looking at questions that deal with these permission setups, don't forget that if the access-by-policy administrative model for Windows Server 2003 or Windows 2000 native domain is being used and you're not using groups to specify which users get access, you need to make sure that the Guest account is disabled and the remote access permission for this account is set to deny access. Otherwise, the default permissions for the Guest account will allow access when it shouldn't be allowed.

Machine Policies

One of the first policies you will probably want to set up regards what servers in your network can actually run RAS. You can create a security policy that designates the servers that can actually run the Remote Access Service by first creating two new GPOs, as follows:

- The first GPO you'll create should be named **Disable RAS**. This GPO will disable the RAS service. The policy will be assigned at the domain node so that it affects every computer in the domain.

- The second GPO you'll create should be named **Enable RAS**. This GPO autostarts RAS and sets security on the service so that only the Administrators group (and local system) will have access to the service. This policy is assigned to the RAS server's OU, allowing it to override the **Disable RAS** GPO defined at the domain level. This means that only those computers in the RAS server's OU will be able to, and actually must, run RAS.

To create the RAS server OU, first load the Active Directory Users and Computers Snap-in.

1. Click **Start | All Programs | Administrative Tools | Active Directory Users and Computers**.

2. Right-click the domain name, choose **New**, and click **Organizational Unit**, as shown in Figure 6.21.

Figure 6.21 Choose Organizational Units

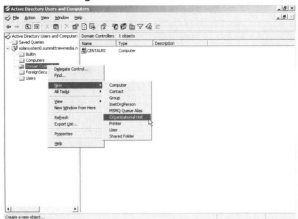

3. In the Name text box, type **RAS Servers** and then click the **OK** button, as shown in Figure 6.22.

Figure 6.22 Enter the Name of Your Organizational Unit

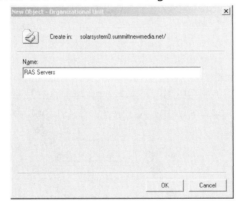

4. Close the Active Directory Users and Computers Snap-in.

Next you need to create a new domain-level GPO to disable the RAS. To do this, you must first load the Group Policy Snap-in. There are two ways you can accomplish this. The simplest method is to use the Active Directory User and Computer Snap-in that you just closed, right-click the domain name, choose **Properties**, and then choose the **Group Policy** tab. Another way is to follow the these steps:

1. Click **Start | Run**. In the **Open** text box, type **mmc /s**.

2. On the File menu, choose **Add/Remove Snap-in**, as shown in Figure 6.23.

Figure 6.23 Click Add/Remove Snap-in

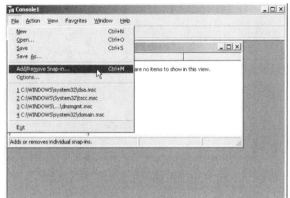

3.   Click **Add**, as shown in Figure 6.24.

Figure 6.24 Click Add

4.   Choose **Group Policy Object Editor** from the list, and click **Add**, as shown in Figure 6.25. The Select Group Policy Object dialog box is displayed, as shown in Figure 6.26.

Figure 6.25 Add Group Policy Object Editor

Figure 6.26 The Select Group Policy Object Window

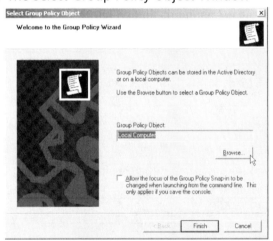

5. Click the **Browse** button, as shown in Figure 6.26. The Browse for a
    Group Policy Object dialog box shown in Figure 6.27 will open. Note that
    the RAS Servers OU is listed as a possible location where you can link the
    GPO. The Disable RAS GPO, however, belongs with the domain.

Figure 6.27 The Browse for a Group Policy Object Window

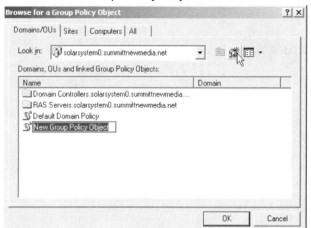

6. Click the **Create New Group Policy Object** icon, as shown in Figure 6.27. Modify the default name of the new GPO. Name it **Disable RAS**, and click **OK**. Click **Finish**.

7. Click the **Close** button in the Add Standalone Snap-in dialog box.

8. Click **OK** to close the Add/Remove Snap-in dialog box.

9. In the scope pane of the console, expand **Disable RAS**, and navigate to **Computer Configuration**, to **Windows Settings**, and then to **Security Settings**.

10. Select **System Services**.

11. In the list of service names, double-click **Routing and Remote Access**, as shown in Figure 6.28.

Figure 6.28 Double-Click Routing and Remote Access

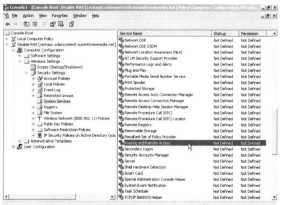

12. Select the **Define this policy setting** check box, as shown in Figure 6.29.

Figure 6.29 Select Define This Policy Setting

13. Select the **Disabled** option, as shown in Figure 6.29, and click **OK**.

14. Close the Group Policy Snap-in.

15. When prompted to save the console settings, click **No**.

The Disable RAS policy has now been established for the domain. You now need to create the Enable RAS policy, as discussed earlier. You can follow the same process we've discussed so far.

Identifying an Authentication and Accounting Strategy

The Internet Authentication Service (IAS) is the central component in Windows Server 2003 for authenticating, authorizing, and auditing users who connect to a network through a VPN or dial-up access. The IAS server is an implementation of a RADIUS server and proxy. RADIUS is the authentication protocol most commonly used by Internet service providers (ISPs). Another common usage is in the authentication of clients for network area storage (NAS) devices.

IAS uses the data stored on the domain controller, which relates to users and groups, to verify the authentication requests received through the RADIUS protocol. When the RADIUS server is part of an Active Directory domain, the server uses the directory services as its user account database. Keep in mind that both the RAS service and the IAS service can be hosted on the same machine.

When you configure the RAS properties, you'll need to select RADIUS as the authentication provider. If you need to change a server to RADIUS authentication, follow these steps:

1. Right-click the name of the server you want to change in the Routing and Remote Access Snap-in. Choose **Properties** from the shortcut menu.

2. Choose the **Security** tab and, under Authentication provider, select **RADIUS Authentication**. Now click **Configure**.

3. Click the **Add** button. Provide the server name. This can be either the hostname or the IP address for the IAS server. If the IAS server is already installed, you won't need to change the shared secret. If the IAS server is not installed, you'll need to change it. The two servers, the RAS and the IAS servers, share a secret that is used to encrypt messages sent between them. The two services must share the same secret.

4. Click **OK** when you're finished.

Let's look a little deeper into the subject of RADIUS for a moment. RADIUS operates using a simple client/server protocol. It uses this protocol for both authorization and accounting. The client machine will send encapsulated UDP information to the server, which will then respond in the appropriate manner.

As stated, all RADIUS messages use UDP for transmission. Each UDP diagram contains one, and only one, RADIUS message. A RADIUS access message is sent by default from the client or proxy to the server using the UDP destination port of 1812 and an ephemeral source port. RADIUS accounting messages, in contrast, are sent using a UDP destination port of 1813 and an ephemeral source port. When a response to either type of message is sent, the source and destination ports are reversed.

Early implementations of RADIUS used UDP port 1645 for access and UDP port 1656 for accounting messages, but this conflicted with two other protocols: Diametrics and Sa-msg-port. To avoid those conflicts, RADIUS now uses UDP ports 1812 and 1813. The IAS included with Windows Server 2003, as with most modern RADIUS servers, allows the administrator to choose the port the RADIUS server will use for authentication and accounting messages.

Authentication messages are defined in RFC 2865. These messages basically enable the RADIUS client to authenticate and authorize connection attempts. There are four RADIUS authentication messages sent between the RADIUS client and server. These messages are Access-Request, Access-Challenge, Access-Accept, and Access-Reject. There are two primary methods for these message exchanges to transpire. The first is Access-Request followed by Access-Accept. Here, the RADIUS server authenticates and authorizes a connection on the client's behalf. The second method is Access-Request followed by Access-Reject. The process here is that the RADIUS server is unable to successfully authenticate and authorize a connection on behalf of the RADIUS client. The RADIUS client can attempt to get new credentials at this point and then submit a new Access-Request.

There is also a third, less seen type of exchange, known as Access-Challenge. Here, the client sends an Access-Request to the server. The server responds with an Access-Challenge. The RADIUS client then obtains additional information from the access client and submits another Access-Request. The RADIUS server can send multiple Access-Challenge messages.

You'll also need to configure the RAS for RADIUS accounting. This can be done when you are first setting up the RAS server, or you can change a server to RADIUS accounting by following these steps:

1. Open the **Routing and Remote Access Snap-in** and right-click the name of the server you want to change. Choose **Properties** from the shortcut menu.

2. Choose the **Security** tab and, under **Accounting provider**, select **RADIUS Accounting**. Click **Configure**. Click **Add**.

3. Provide the server name. This can be either the hostname or the IP address of the IAS server.

4. If IAS is already installed, you don't need to change the shared secret. If IAS is not installed, you do need to change the shared secret. Again, the RAS and the IAS servers share a secret that is used to encrypt messages sent between them. The two services must share the same secret.

5. Click **OK** when you're finished.

Defining the Audit Strategy

One of the first components of an audit strategy is setting a logging level. A good audit and logging strategy is important to the proper maintenance of your network and the systems that are used on it. Before we get more deeply into defining your audit strategy, we need to deal with the logging question.

Just what you want to log will be one of the most important questions you'll ask yourself. Defining an extensive logging and auditing strategy will lower the performance of your server and of your network. Doing too little logging and auditing will leave you without the information you need to determine the source and cause of problems that arise. Your best option regarding logging is to log only those options you really need. Then, when you don't need a particular type of log data anymore, stop recording it.

Setting the logging levels for RAS is simple. First open the RAS module and then right-click the server you want to administer. Choose **Properties**, and then click the **Logging** tab (see Figure 6.30). You're now confronted with several radio button options showing the various types of events for which you can set up logging.

The default is to log all errors and warnings. You can also check the check box that will cause logging of additional Routing and Remote Access information that will assist in debugging.

Figure 6.30 Setting the Logging Level

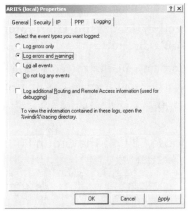

Auditing both events and objects can help you manage the security of your Active Directory domain, thereby ensuring the effectiveness of your security strategy. Remember that the more you audit, the bigger the logs. Reviewing huge logs can be an extremely painful process. It's therefore very important that you decide on an auditing policy that protects your network without creating a huge administrative task at the same time. Keep in mind that the very act of auditing will decrease your network's performance.

To enable auditing on any of the options listed in Table 6.5, either open the **Default Domain Policy MMC** (if you have one) or perform the following steps:

Table 6.5 Auditing Options

Events	Activation
Account logon	Domain controller receives a logon request
Account management	User account or group is created or changed
Directory service access	Active Directory object is accessed
Logon	User logs on or off
Object access	Object is accessed
Policy change	Policy affecting security, user rights, or auditing is modified
Privilege use	User right is used to perform an action
Process tracking	Application executes action to be tracked

Continued

Table 6.5 Auditing Options (Continued)

Events	Activation
System events	Computer is rebooted or shut down or other event occurs that affects security

1. Open **Active Directory Users and Computers** from the **Administrative Tools** directory.

2. Right-click your domain name in the console tree on the left, and choose **Properties** from the shortcut menu that's offered.

3. Click the **Group Policy** tab and then click **Edit**, as shown in Figure 6.31.

Figure 6.31 Choose Edit on the Group Policy Tab

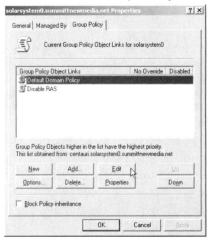

4. In the console tree on the left side of the window, click your way through **Computer Configuration | Windows Settings | Security Settings | Local Policies** to reach **Audit Policy**, as shown in Figure 6.32.

Figure 6.32 Navigate Your Way to Audit Policy

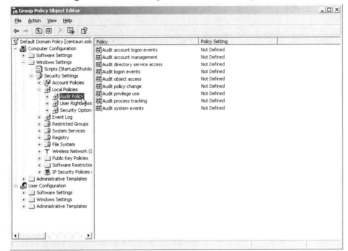

5. Right-click the event category you want to audit, and choose **Properties** from the shortcut window.

6. As shown in Figure 6.33, check the box to define the policy setting, and then check the options to audit either successful or failed attempts, or both.

Figure 6.33 Define Your Event Policy

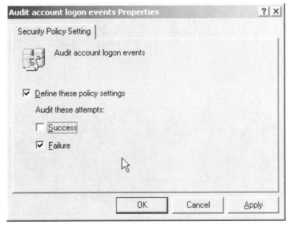

Now that you've defined the policy setting to audit Active Directory objects, create audit settings for an object by following these steps:

1. Right-click the object (user, group, file, printer, and so on) that you want to audit, and choose **Properties** from the shortcut menu.

2. Choose the **Security** tab, as shown in Figure 6.34, and then click the **Advanced** button as shown.

    Figure 6.34 Click the Advanced Button on the Security Tab

3. Click the **Auditing** tab, and then click **Add**, as shown in Figure 6.35, to set up auditing for a group or user.

    Figure 6.35 Click Add to Set Up Auditing

    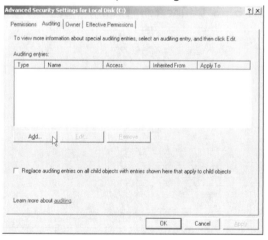

4. Select the security principals whose actions you want to audit, as shown in Figure 6.36.

Figure 6.36 Choose the Object to Audit

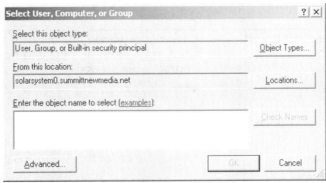

5. Choose the events you want to audit, as shown in Figure 6.37. Table 6.6 lists the various options and defines them. Click **OK** when you're finished.

Figure 6.37 Choose the Events to Audit

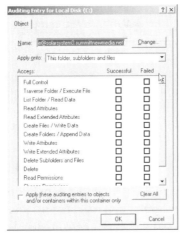

Table 6.6 File System Events That Can Be Audited

Event	Activation
Traverse Folder/Execute File	When a person passes through a folder on the way to a parent or child folder or when an application is run
List Folder/Read Data	When a folder is opened or data is viewed in files
Read Attributes	When the attributes on a file or a folder are viewed

Continued

Table 6.6 File System Events That Can Be Audited (Continued)

Event	Activation
Read Extended Attributes	When the extended attributes of a file or folder, which are defined and created by applications and programs, are viewed
Create Files/Write Data	When files are created inside a folder or a file is changed, overwriting existing information in the file
Create Folders/Append Data	When folders are created inside a folder being audited or information is added to an existing file
Write Attributes	When a file or folder attribute is changed
Write Extended Attributes	When extended attributes of files or folders, which are defined and created by applications and pro-grams, are changed
Delete Subfolders and Files	When a file or subfolder is deleted
Delete	When a specific file is deleted
Read Permissions	When permissions for a file or folder are viewed
Change Permissions	When permissions for a file or folder are modified
Take Ownership	When ownership of the file or folder changes

Remember that every event tells you something. Sometimes it might not be something you need to know. Know what and why you are auditing. You'll probably want to keep your auditing to a minimum unless there's a problem. In that case, extend the level of auditing on those objects for which you suspect a problem. When you have the problem solved, bring the auditing levels back to a minimum.

IP Address Management and DHCP

The simple truth is that any TCP/IP-based network of any size needs to use DHCP. The DHCP server dynamically supplies client machines with IP addresses and network configuration information. DHCP can be considered an essential service on most TCP/IP networks. Small networks need at least one DHCP server. Larger networks can use multiple DHCP servers to split the address space and provide fault tolerance.

When designing your DHCP networks, you'll want to take many factors into account, including:

- Draw yourself a map of your network. Make sure you show each physical and logical subnet and the routers between the various subnets.

- If the network uses routers to subnet the network, do the routers support forwarding DHCP broadcasts? Most new routers do, but that option must be turned on.

■ Sectioning the IP address range between two servers will provide fault tolerance. Keep in mind that DHCP servers can't communicate with one another, so they can't share addresses. Therefore, give 80 percent of the addresses to one server and 20 percent to a second server. (This is sometimes called the 80/20 rule.) If one of the two servers goes down, clients can still receive IP addresses from the other server. Another option is to set up a DHCP server cluster. The cluster could handle all the addresses.

■ Depending on the speed and reliability of your network and the links between your subnets, the routers between can be configured to forward DHCP broadcasts (or you could add a DMCP relay agent). Another option is to place a second DHCP server on a different physical subnet. You could also deploy a pair of DHCP servers to each physical subnet.

■ If you're planning to use the DHCP server to update DNS records for legacy clients, don't run the DHCP service on a domain controller. Doing so would create a security risk. The use of secure dynamic updates can be compromised by running the DHCP server on a domain controller. This problem occurs when the DHCP server is configured to perform registration of DNS records on behalf of its clients. If you place your DHCP servers and domain controllers on separate computers, you'll be able to avoid this problem. You can find more help on this specific topic in the DNS Help topic of the Windows Server 2003 Help system. Check under the Dynamic Updates topic.

■ Remember that the recommendation is that a single DHCP server can provide services for 10,000 or fewer clients and 1000 or fewer scopes; therefore, make sure you size your servers appropriately.

■ DHCP servers access their disk drives very frequently. Make sure you use either a disk drive with a fast access time or a hardware RAID disk controller. Faster storage means better DHCP performance.

■ If you are still using any Windows NT 4 domain controllers, make sure you have them upgraded to Windows Server 2003.

Let's take a quick look at the ways we can set up a DHCP server.

Developing & Deploying...

Installing DHCP for Windows Server 2003

Probably the simplest way to set up the DHCP service is to use the Configure Your Server Wizard to install it. The wizard will also walk you through creating a new scope. A second option is to manually install it through the Add/Remove Programs tool. In this section we'll take a look at both options.

You'll need to know first if you have a working DNS server in your network environment. Validating your DNS server is quick and easy. Click **Start | Run**, and type **cmd** in the text box. Press **Enter**, and then type the following into the command window: **Ping DNS Server Name**.

Press **Enter**, and if you see the following message in the command window, you don't have a working DNS server: **Unknown Host: DNS Server Name**.

Keep in mind that for both installation methods you will probably need to have your Windows Server 2003 installation CD available. Let's first take a look at installing using the wizard:

1. Click **Manage Your Server** from the Administration menu to start the wizard.

2. In the Manage Your Server window, choose the **Add or Remove a role** option.

3. You should now be looking at the Preliminary Steps window. This is a reminder that there are certain things you should do at this point before you go on. After you've made sure that you've accomplished all of those tasks, click the **Next** button.

4. The next window will be the Choosing the Server Role window. Here you need to choose the role you want to add to this server. As you can see in Figure 6.38, we've chosen the DHCP role to add. Now click the **Next** button.

Figure 6.38 Choosing the Server Role

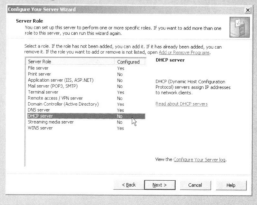

Continued

(Continued)

5. The Summary of Selections window will now be displayed. Make sure all the options you've chosen are displayed, and click the **Next** button again. The wizard will now enter the Scope Configuration Wizard. Click the **Next** button as shown.

6. The New Scope Wizard will now ask you to name and describe the new scope, as shown in Figure 6.39. This information helps to quickly identify the scope when you have multiple scopes running on the server. Type in a name and description, and click the **Next** button as shown.

Figure 6.39 Naming the Scope

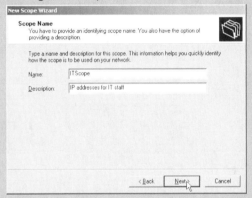

7. The wizard will now walk you through assigning the IP address range, as shown in Figure 6.40. Type in the starting IP address and then the ending IP address. The length and subnet mask will be automatically entered. If you prefer, you can modify either of these if you want to use a different subnet mask. After you have entered this information, click the Next button.

Figure 6.40 Assigning the IP Address Range

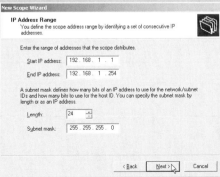

Continued

(Continued)

8. The New Scope Wizard, as shown in Figure 6.41, will now offer you the ability to add an exclusion range. Exclusion ranges can be used for servers and other objects that are assigned a permanent IP address. For instance, as you'll see in the next few pages, the router (the default gateway) for this subnet is assigned the IP address 192.168.1.1. We don't want the DHCP to assign this address to another client machine, so we exclude that address here. Once you've entered your starting and ending IP addresses for the exclusion, click the **Add** button, and the range will be moved down to the excluded address range list box. You can now either add another exclusion range or click the **Next** button to move on.

Figure 6.41 Adding Exclusion Ranges

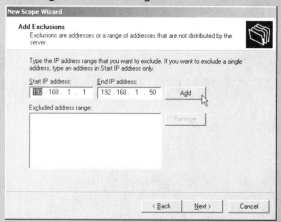

9. As shown in Figure 6.42, the wizard will now give you the ability to change the lease duration. The lease duration defaults to eight days. We more fully discuss how the lease duration works in the Setting the DHCP Lease Duration sidebar. For now, unless you have reason to change it, simply accept the default and click the **Next** button.

Continued

(Continued)

Figure 6.42 Setting the Lease Duration

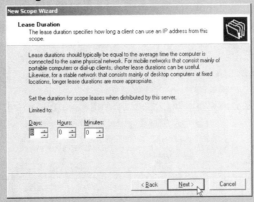

10. The wizard next gives you the opportunity to set the DHCP options. You can choose to configure them at a later time or now. In this example, we are going to configure these options now. Click the **Next** button.

11. As discussed earlier, one of the first options you can set, as is shown in Figure 6.43, is the IP address for the router, or the default gateway. Type in the IP address and click the **Add** button. If there are more addresses, add them one at a time. When you're finished, click the **Next** button.

Figure 6.43 Set the IP Address for the Default Gateway

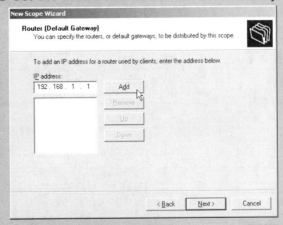

12. The wizard now gives you the opportunity to set the domain name and DNS address, as shown in Figure 6.44. When you've

(Continued)

finished entering the domain name and added and resolved any DNS servers you want to add, click the **Next** button as shown. Speaking of resolved, you'll notice the Resolve button on the window. You can enter the name of your server and then click the **Resolve** button and it will resolve the IP address of that server on the network.

Figure 6.44 Setting the Domain Name and DNS

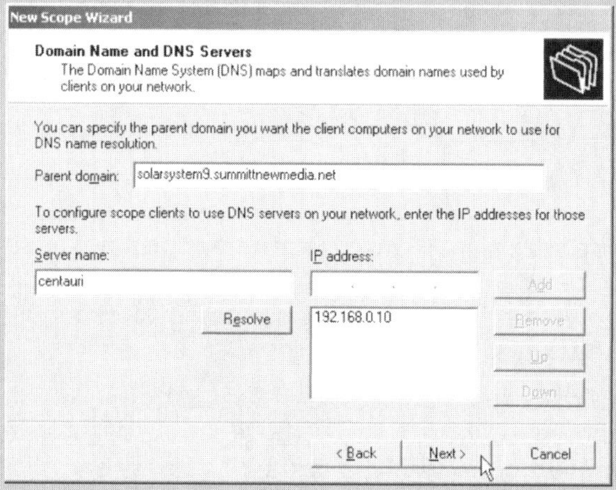

13. The next step provides you the opportunity to designate the IP address and name of your WINS server, as shown in Figure 6.45. Again, you can use the Resolve button as discussed previously. After you have entered and added your WINS server, you can click the **Next** button.

Figure 6.45 Adding the WINS Server

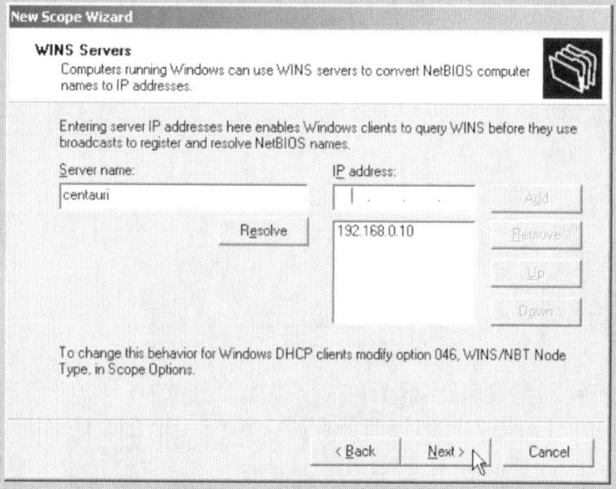

Continued

(Continued)

14. The wizard will now give you the opportunity to activate the scope. Unless you have a specific reason not to, go ahead and activate the scope. Click the **Next** button, and then click the **Finish** button twice. Your DHCP server is installed and a scope has been activated.

At this point, however, the DHCP server is not authorized by the Active Directory. We'll look at how to authorize the server in just a moment. First, let's look at manually installing the service.

You can manually install the DHCP service by following these instructions:

1. Click **Start | Settings**, and then choose the **Control Panel**.

2. Double-click **Add or Remove Programs**, and then click the **Add/Remove Windows Components** option.

3. In the Windows Component Wizard, shown in Figure 6.46, click **Network Services** in the Components box, and then click the **Details** button.

Figure 6.46 Choose Network Services Details

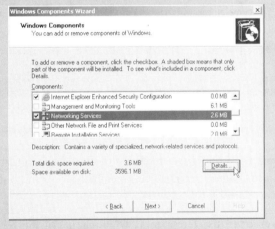

4. As shown in Figure 6.47, choose the **Dynamic Host Configuration Protocol (DHCP)** check box if it's not already selected. Click **OK**.

Continued

(Continued)

Figure 6.47 Choose Dynamic Host Configuration Protocol

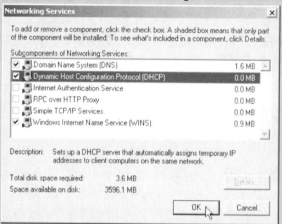

5. In the Windows Components Wizard, click **Next** to start the Windows Server 2003 setup. Insert the Windows Server 2003 installation CD, if prompted, and the necessary files will be copied and installed on your computer.

6. When setup is complete, click the **Finish** button.

7. To configure your DHCP server, select **Start | Administrative Tools | DHCP**. Right-click the server and choose **New Scope**. Then follow the previous steps.

Authorizing the DHCP server is the last phase of this process, and we will cover it next.

Before going on, a few pages back we discussed configuring the DHCP options during installation. There are four levels at which you can configure those options in Windows Server 2003 DHCP servers. Those options are:

- **Server options** These apply to all clients of the DHCP server. You should probably use these options sparingly. The main use would be for parameters common across all scopes installed on the server.

- **Scope options** These are the most used type of options. They apply to all clients within a specific scope. Also, they override any server options set on the DHCP server.

- **Client options** These are options that can be specified for a specific individual client. These options are especially useful when specific computers need special options. Remember that client options override all other options, including class options.

- **Class options** These are options that are specific to types of clients. These types, or classes, of clients could be vendor-class clients such as Windows 98 clients or user-class clients such as RAS clients. Class options aren't used very often. For more information concerning creating and using class options, consult the Help system and the Resource Kit.

Now that you've installed the DHCP server and configured your scopes, you first need to find out if your DHCP server is authorized and, if it's not, to authorize the DHCP server on your Active Directory network. If you don't, it won't be allowed to hand out addresses. You may even get the message:

`The DHCP Server servername is not authorized in the directory...`

You can determine whether your DHCP server has been authorized in Active Directory using the Active Directory Sites and Services console. Look in the configuration container in the \Configuration\Services\NetServices folder. All authorized DHCP servers will show up here. The container can also be viewed in the DHCP Snap-in. You'll probably work in this snap-in, as shown in Figure 6.48, more often than in the Active Directory Sites and Services console.

Any DHCP server running on a Windows Server 2003 or Windows 2000 Server system must register and be authorized by the Active Directory. This is not true of DHCP servers running on Windows NT 4.0 or other operating systems such as Linux. To authorize a DHCP server in Active Directory, perform the following steps:

1. Log on to the server as a user who has membership in the Enterprise Administrators group or who has been granted the right to authorize new DHCP servers.

2. Open the DHCP **mmc** Snap-in and select **DHCP** at the root of the console window.

3. Click **Manage authorized servers** from the Action menu.

4. Click the **Authorize button** in the dialog box that appears.

5. Enter the name or IP address of the DHCP server you want to authorize, and then click **OK**.

Another option is to right-click the DHCP server you want to authorize in the DHCP Snap-in, as shown in Figure 6.48, and then choose **Authorize** from the displayed options.

Figure 6.48 Authorizing the DHCP Server in Active Directory

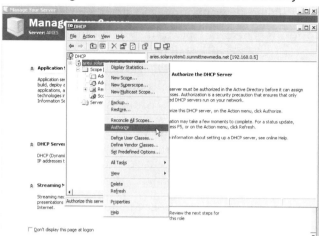

Finally, before we continue, we need to make sure that we understand the DHCP request/offer/lease process and, as suggested earlier, how to go about setting the DHCP lease duration.

Setting the DHCP Lease Duration

The DHCP service is a process that responds to client requests. When a computer that is a DHCP client boots up on the network for the first time, a four-step process is initiated.

1. The client machine broadcasts a request for an IP address. The request is broadcast on Port 67 and is known as a *DHCP Discovery Broadcast*.

2. Any and all DHCP servers that exist on the local network subnet will respond to the client with a direct *DHCP Offer*. If there are no local DHCP servers but there is a relay agent and it has forwarded the client's broadcast to a remote DCHP server, that server responds with the DHCP Offer.

3. It's first come, first served as the client takes the first offer it gets and responds with another broadcast, which is known as a *DHCP Request*. This request confirms the IP address it received from the DHCP server. A relay agent will forward the request when needed. A server whose offer was not accepted puts the offered IP address back into its address pool.

Continued

(Continued)

4. The DHCP server whose offer was accepted then responds with a *DHCP Acknowledgment* message that includes the lease duration and any other configuration information that the server has been set up to provide. At the point at which the client receives the acknowledgment, it then binds the new address to its IP stack and starts using it.

The DHCP server gives out addresses according to a specific selection algorithm. Basically, the server starts handing out addresses from the bottom of its scope range and works its way toward the top. It won't give out a previously used, expired address to a new client until all unused addresses are exhausted. After all addresses are used at some point, the server then assigns addresses that were released or expired, based on the amount of time the address has been available. Addresses that haven't been used for the longest amount of time are the server's first choice for reuse. Keep in mind, though, that as with all other lease assignments, the server will use conflict-detection techniques to make sure the IP is, in reality, unused.

Both the server and the client have ways to check for IP duplication. The server can be configured to ping an IP address before it assigns that address to a client. This option is turned off by default as the functionality is largely duplicated as we will see in a moment by the client. This method requires that the ping request fail before the DHCP server will go ahead and issue an IP address to the client. This means that the more pings, the longer the process will take. Each ping takes about a second. If successful, the DHCP server selects another address and pings it before issuing it to the client. To set up the conflict-detection method on the server, follow these directions:

1. Right-click the server in the DHCP console and choose **Properties**.

2. Click the **Advanced** tab.

3. Set **Conflict detection attempts** to a number greater than zero. A word to the wise: A number greater than 2 is not a good idea. This number determines how many times your DHCP server will test an IP address before leasing it to a client. The DHCP server uses the Packet Internet Groper (ping) process to test available scope IP addresses before including these addresses in DHCP lease offers to clients. If the ping is successful, the IP address is in use on the network. As a result, the DHCP server won't offer to lease that specific address to a client. If, however, the ping request fails and times out, the IP address is considered not to be in use on the network. The DHCP server then offers the address to a client. Keep in mind that each additional conflict-detection attempt delays the DHCP server response by a second while

Continued

(Continued)

waiting for the ping request to time out. This increases the load on the server.

4. Click **OK**.

The client sends out an ARP broadcast on the local subnet before it replies to a DHCP offer with a DHCP Request. This broadcast is aimed at determining if a local host is already using the IP address that the DHCP server offered. If it determines that the address is already in use, it will send a DHCP Decline broadcast back to the DHCP server and make another DHCP Discovery broadcast. The server that offered the declined IP marks as bad that specific IP address in its pool and keeps from reissuing it again by adding it to its list of active leases with the name BAD_ADDRESS. When you see this entry in the Active Leases list and you are able to determine that the system that caused the error is no longer on the network, you can release that address back into the pool by deleting it from the Active Leases list.

The IP address that's provided to the client is good as long as the lease duration lasts. The default lease time for a Windows 2000 DHCP server is three days, while that for the Windows Server 2003 DHCP server is eight days. Either can be modified by the administrator. Renewals take place in the following manner:

- Halfway through the lease period, the client will attempt to contact the DHCP server and renew the lease by sending a directed DHCP Request. If the request is successful and is able to renew, the client machine gets a full new lease on the same IP address it was using. If, on the other hand, it fails to contact the server at the 50 percent point of the lease, it continues to use the leased IP address.

- When 85.5 percent, or seven-eighths, of the lease time has expired, the client again tries to contact the DHCP server to renew the lease. If it fails this time, it will continue to attempt renewal at regular intervals until the lease expires. At that point, the client will drop the address it has been using and will initiate a DHCP Discovery broadcast. This will continue every five minutes until a server responds to the broadcast.

- As well as the renewal requests described, the client will attempt to renew its lease every time it restarts. This attempt occurs even if the lease has expired while the server was offline.

Any time any of the configuration options that the DHCP server provides are changed since the client's last renewal, they'll be updated on the client as needed.

Continued

(Continued)

> If the client's lease expired while the client was offline and the IP address it was given has been reissued to another client, the DHCP server will respond to the client's renewal request with a Negative Acknowledgment (NACK). A NACK can also occur when the scope that the client had received its lease from has been deactivated by an administrator. At any point that a client receives a NACK in response to a renewal request, the client immediately ceases to use the IP address it was previously assigned and starts sending out DHCP Discovery broadcasts to obtain a new IP address lease.
>
> The duration of the scope's lease helps determine the amount of network traffic that DHCP clients will generate, especially when the DHCP is configured to send updates to the DNS. Compared to other network services, the DHCP service doesn't produce an undue amount of traffic, but traffic should be monitored so that an accurate picture of the actual bandwidth being used can be determined.
>
> Lease duration also affects the amount of time that the DHCP server can be offline before problems might arise. With the default lease of eight days provided by the Windows Server 2003 DHCP server, most clients will have a remaining lease of between four and eight days because of the continuous nature of the lease process. If the DHCP server were taken offline for two or three days but the network environment was otherwise stable, the only clients that would encounter trouble would be new clients that have never received the initial IP lease. All other clients would be good for at least four days.
>
> The bad side of long durations is that changes to the scope IP options take longer to propagate to the clients. In our example, if a new DNS server was added to the network, it would take at least four days before most of the clients would receive the updated DNS entry from the DHCP server.

Although it may appear that there is some work involved in setting up and maintaining DHCP servers on your network, the alternative—static address configuration—is labor intensive and not practical for large networks. Our next goal is to understand scopes and superscopes and how subnets might be mapped to either.

Address Assignments

A *scope* is simply a range of possible IP addresses on a network. It's used to set aside a range or a pool of consecutive IP addresses that can then be distributed to clients. The scope provides information to the clients about the lease time for the addresses given out and other configuration options given to the client, such as those we discussed earlier. A scope can span up to a single subnet. When the addresses in a scope have been exhausted, you might want to add another scope, as long as the new scope doesn't belong to the same subnet as any existing scope. Of course, the more logical course of action would be to redesign the underlying network topology.

When you create multiple scopes, it's important to understand that clients from one logical subnet won't be able to obtain IP addresses from a scope that relates to a different subnet than the one to which they currently belong. The reason for this is that the other scope relates to a different logical subnet. If you want your clients to be able to use addresses from other scopes, you'll need to combine your scopes into a larger administrative entity known as a *superscope*.

A superscope is a collection of scopes gathered together into a single administrative grouping. There are three main reasons that you might want to use superscopes:

- A scope is running out of IP addresses.

- You need to renumber the IP network and therefore move the clients from one set of addresses to another.

- You want to use two DHCP servers on the same subnet for redundancy.

When you create a superscope, you enable clients to obtain or renew leases from any scope within the superscope. This is true even if they contain addresses from a different logical subnet.

We've already walked through the physical process of creating a scope. The decisions that you need to make when creating a scope include:

- The starting and ending addresses of the range you want to use

- The subnet mask of the subnet in question

- Whether there are clients using static IP addresses within this range that will need to be excluded from the pool

- The amount of time the lease duration should be for the IP addresses leased from this scope

- The IP configuration information you want to pass to clients, in addition to the IP address and the subnet mask

- Whether you need to reserve specific IP addresses for specific clients

DHCP Security Considerations

Although DHCP servers don't rank high on the hacker target list, there are several vulnerabilities that you need to address:

- The number of IP addresses within each scope is limited. This means that an unauthorized user might launch a denial-of-service (DoS) attack on your network by requesting and acquiring a large number of IP addresses from the DHCP server.

- A DoS attack on your DNS can also be initiated by a hacker performing a large number of DNS dynamic updates through the DHCP.

- An unauthorized user might also set up a rogue DHCP server that would provide improper addresses to your network clients.

- Keep in mind that any user who gets an IP address from the DHCP is also getting the addresses of the DNS and the WINS. That user can then either obtain more information from those servers or attack them straight out.

Your best defense against these problems is to limit the physical access potential hackers might have to your network. Actually being able to plug into the network makes the hacker's job that much easier. Here are some basic security concepts you need to remember:

- Implement and maintain firewalls. Close all ports you don't absolutely need open.

- If you're running any wireless networks, don't broadcast the service set identifier (SSID). Use 128-bit wired equivalent privacy (WEP) encryption. This will keep users from obtaining a lease unless and until they provide the appropriate WEP key.

- Use MAC address filters.

- Consider the use of VPN tunnels.

Finally, make sure that you maintain and review your DHCP audit logs. By default, they're located in the %windir%\System32\Dhcp folder.

Configuring & Implementing…

Fault-Tolerant DHCP

Without an IP address, a computer can't communicate with other computers on your network or even connect to the Internet. As discussed previously, most computers will have a period of time without having to worry about network connectivity problems should your network lose the DHCP server. However, new computers on the network, returning laptops, or little used systems that haven't recently logged on won't be able to get access to the network should the DHCP fail.

In this section, we look at a couple of different options that will make the DHCP more fault tolerant. These options include the use of split scopes and clustering.

Using split scopes requires the use of two DHCP servers for load balancing and redundancy. To set up split scopes, perform the following steps:

Continued

(Continued)

1. Create scopes for all the valid IP addresses that the DHCP servers you're setting up are going to manage.

2. Set up exclusions so that your primary DHCP server will handle 80 percent of the address pool and the secondary server will handle the other 20 percent.

3. Create a superscope on both servers that contains all valid scopes for the physical subnet. You can do this by selecting the appropriate DHCP server from the console tree, and then choosing the **New Superscope** command from the **Action** menu. Now name the superscope, and then select the member scopes to be included in it.

It is not the purpose of this chapter to describe how to set up and maintain server clusters. The basic steps to get a DHCP server up and running in a cluster are:

1. Install the DHCP server and set it up on the cluster. Recommended practices suggest that scopes not be configured until the DHCP service is completely set up on the cluster, as described here.

2. Launch the **Cluster Administrator** from the Administrative Tools folder on the All Programs menu.

3. Select the cluster you want to use to host the DHCP service.

4. Choose the **Configure Application** command from the File menu to open the Configure Application Wizard.

5. Click the **Next** button in the first page, and then choose the **Use an Existing Virtual Server** option. Next select the appropriate group. If you haven't already done so, choose the **Create A New Virtual Server** option, and use the wizard to create a new virtual server.

6. In the Create Application Cluster Reference page, choose **Yes, Create A Cluster Resource For My Application Now** option. Next choose the DHCP resource type, and then click **Next**.

7. Enter a name and a description for the DHCP resource, and then click **Next** again.

8. Now, click **Advanced Properties**, click the **Dependencies** tab, and then click **Modify**.

9. Double-click the IP address, physical disk, and the network name you want to use for the DHCP server cluster. Those dependencies will now appear as dependencies. When you're finished, click **OK**,

Continued

(Continued)

> modify the properties of the resource if you want, and then click **OK** again.
>
> 10. Click the **Next** button in the Application Resource Name and Description page. Now specify where the DHCP database should be stored. Next, click the **Next** button.
>
> 11. Review your settings, and then click **Finish** to complete the wizard.
>
> 12. Make sure that your resource is displayed in the correct group, and then right-click the resource and choose **Bring Online** from the shortcut menu. This will enable the DHCP server to begin servicing clients.
>
> 13. Authorize the DHCP server in the Active Directory.

DNS Integration and Client Interoperability

Windows Server 2003, Windows XP, and Windows 2000 clients have the ability to automatically update their forward lookup records with the DNS server if they receive a new IP address from the DHCP server. No extra action needs to be taken by the DHCP or DNS in these cases. The reverse lookup or PTR records on the DNS server do require updating, and the Windows Server 2003, Windows XP, and Windows 2000 clients explicitly request that the DHCP server update those records on their behalf. This action does require communication between the DHCP and the DNS.

Windows 9*x* (which includes Windows 95, 98, 98SE, and ME) and Windows NT clients can't update their resource records themselves. The DHCP server has to do it for them. However, you need to enable this feature first. When enabled, the DHCP server updates an earlier client's forward and reverse lookup records when the client obtains a new IP address.

To enable these earlier clients to function with DHCP and dynamic DNS, follow these steps:

1. Choose the DHCP server or the scope on which you want to permit dynamic DNS updates.

2. Right-click and choose **Properties**, and then click the **DNS** tab.

3. Make sure the **Enable DNS dynamic updates according to the settings below** check box is selected.

One last point before we finish: Your DHCP database relies on a database engine much like that used by Exchange. There's practically no limit to the number of lease records that the database can hold. This database is largely self-maintaining and will compact itself occasionally during idle time. This compaction is necessary to resolve corruption errors that might arise.

Generally, when the database is corrupted, you'll see errors popping up in the System Event log. These common errors are errors 510, 1022, and 1850. Sometimes, taking the database offline and compacting it will correct your errors. When this fails, you probably will need to restore from a tape backup. These error events are discussed in the following Microsoft articles.

- **Error 510** *http://support.microsoft.com/default.aspx?scid=kb; en-us;216793*

- **Errors 1022, 1850** *http://support.microsoft.com/default.aspx?scid=kb; en-us;173396*

Summary of Exam Objectives

In this chapter, we discussed two main topics as they apply to the Active Directory and security. Those two topics are the Routing and Remote Access Service (RRAS) and the Dynamic Host Control Protocol (DHCP). One of the first RRAS topics we examined was how to design security for remote access users.

This design process involves assessing the requirements, defining appropriate remote access methods, and determining which authentications methods are available and which are appropriate for the environment. In particular, we discussed the subject of RADIUS, which focuses on the authentication of remote users. We also looked at accounting as well as policies and how these may be utilized. Next up was the subject of auditing, where we examined available settings and some suggested best practices.

We also discussed the implementation of RRAS and included several exercises that help illustrate both the different roles an RRAS server may assume as well as the ease with which the administrator can install and configure these roles. We covered the roles of a static router and VPN server, and we discussed the use of IPSec in conjunction with VPNs.

Then we turned our attention to DHCP. We began with a discussion of how the first step in any DHCP design should involve an assessment of both the network environment and the requirements of the DHCP implementation. These two aspects should help you design the optimum DHCP system. Along the way, we explained how to install, configure, and authorize a DHCP server and offered some best practices for parameters such as lease duration and conflict detection.

We then moved on to discuss scopes and superscopes and how you can decide on the best approach for your organization. Naturally, any organization needs to consider the availability and security of a DHCP implementation, so we also covered how DHCP may be configured to be fault redundant in a number of different ways, ranging from the use of split scopes to the use of clustered servers. From a security point of view, we discussed ways in which the DHCP servers may be protected, such as by blocking ports on firewalls and restricting the authorization of new DHCP servers in Active Directory. To conclude, we discussed the integration of DHCP with DNS and how different client types and their support for DNS can be catered to by Windows Server 2003 DHCP.

Exam Objectives Fast Track

Remote Access Service Servers

☑ Know the roles of the Remote Access Service (RAS) and the Routing and Remote Access Service (RRAS). The purpose and role of the RRAS is to authorize and service requests from remote users. The purpose and role of the RAS is to allow mobile or off-site users to connect to the network through the RRAS.

☑ Know the authentication providers. Authentication is provided by either Windows authentication or by RADIUS authentication.

☑ Know the various authentication methods used for RAS. These methods are Extensible Authentication Protocol (EAP), Microsoft Encrypted Authentication Version 2, Microsoft Encrypted Authentication, Encrypted Authentication, Shiva Password Authentication Protocol, unencrypted password, and unauthorized access.

☑ Know where you need to set dial-in permissions.

☑ Know what options can be set with remote access policies.

IP Address Management and DHCP

☑ Know how DHCP services work in a Windows Server 2003/Windows 2000 network. Make sure you understand how IP leases are requested and granted by DHCP. Be sure to understand the lease renewal and release process. Know what happens when a client fails to renew a lease.

☑ Know the difference between scope properties and options and how and why they are assigned.

☑ Know the time frames involved with DHCP leases. Understand that the client always requests an extension or a new lease when half the lease time is up. If it fails to connect to the DHCP server, it will try again when 87.5 percent of the lease time is up.

☑ Know how to install and configure DHCP. Understand the address pool, the address lease, reservations, and the various forms of scope options.

☑ Know how to integrate DNS with DHCP. Understand the steps for this integration and how it keeps the network records correct and current.

☑ Know how to authorize DHCP servers in Active Directory. Use Active Directory to your advantage. Make sure you know the steps needed to incorporate the DHCP process.

Exam Objectives
Frequently Asked Questions

The following Frequently Asked Questions, answered by the authors of this book, are designed to both measure your understanding of the Exam Objectives presented in this chapter and to assist you with real-life implementation of these concepts. You will also gain access to thousands of other FAQs at *www.ITFAQnet.com*.

Q: I need to devise implement a remote access solution using Windows Server 2003. What are the processes I should follow to deploy an RAS solution?

A: The suggested approach is to define requirements, then create a conceptual design, followed by a detailed design; deploy a pilot implementation; and finally deploy into production, to all necessary users.

Q: What are the available authentication mechanisms for an RAS solution?

A: RAS may utilize Kerberos, NTLM, LM, SSL, and TLS as well as MS-CHAP, EAP, and PAP.

Q: What are some of the typical ways in which a Windows Server 2003 RAS server may be utilized?

A: A Windows Server 2003 RAS server may be configured to act as a router, between external and internal networks; or as a VPN server, allowing secure VPN connections into the internal network from external clients.

Q: How can I restrict access to my Windows Server 2003 RAS server?

A: Access to a Windows Server 2003 RAS server can be restricted with the use of policies. Policies may be used to allow certain users access while blocking others.

Q: I want to implement a centralized authentication, accounting, and auditing strategy for my Windows Server 2003 RAS solution. How can I achieve that?

A: This can be achieved with a RADIUS solution. RADIUS provides authentication, accounting, and auditing methods and support for RAS solutions. Windows Server 2003 includes its own implementation of RADIUS, known as Internet Authentication Service, or IAS.

Q: I need to deploy DHCP within my environment. How should I plan the deployment?

A: A DHCP deployment should begin with an assessment of the network topology, followed by an assessment of the placement, hardware specification, and fault-tolerance requirements of the DHCP servers. Finally, determine if BOOTP relays are required and whether DHCP is to be used to register DNS records.

Q: I need to restrict the installation of new DHCP servers within my Active Directory environment. How can this be achieved?

A: DHCP servers cannot provide IP address data to clients until they have been authorized in Active Directory. This authorization can be performed only by an Enterprise Admin.

Q: I need to provide a fault-tolerant DHCP solution but cannot afford extra servers or hardware. What are my options?

A: Instead of deploying additional servers and using split scopes, for example, longer lease periods can offer a degree of fault tolerance. If a DHCP server is unavailable, clients can remain unaffected until their lease expires. If a lease period of 10 days is used, then on average, a client will remain unaffected by a DHCP outage for five days. This should be ample time to resolve the issue and bring the DHCP server online again.

Self Test

A Quick Answer Key follows the Self Test questions. For complete questions, answers, and explanations to the Self Test questions in this chapter as well as the other chapters in this book, see the Self Test Appendix.

1. You are the network administrator for your organization. Your Windows Server 2003 domain consists of two sites, six domain controllers, and 500 Windows XP Professional and Windows 2000 Professional workstations. Most of your domain members are in St. Louis, but about 50 are in Jefferson City. You need to connect these two locations in a secure but more cost-effective manner than your current configuration. Currently, your organization is using leased lines between the two sites. What Windows Server 2003 solution would be your best choice?

    A. Add IPSec and create a dial-on-demand router.

    B. Create a VPN using the Internet as a backbone.

C. Create a VPN and implement Layer 2 Tunneling Protocol using the Internet as a backbone.

D. Create a VPN and implement IP filtering on the routers.

2. After spending hours setting up and configuring your remote access solution, you discover that users are still being denied access to your network. You've even carefully created a remote access policy and associated profile for the inbound connections. What could be the cause of your problem?

A. You have forgotten to associate the policy with the appropriate group or OU.

B. You haven't activated the policy and associated profile.

C. The user's permissions are set for Control Access through Remote Access Policy, and the policy is set for Deny Access.

D. The policy is set for Control Access through Users Permissions, and the users' permissions are set to Deny Access.

3. Your executive director has asked you to create and design a secure remote access solution for your organization. What two tunneling protocols are available using Windows Server 2003 Remote Access Services?

A. Point-to-Point Tunneling Protocol (PPTP)

B. Layer 2 Tunneling Protocol (L2TP)

C. Layer 4 Tunneling Protocol (L4TP)

D. Internet Protocol Security (IPSec)

4. Assume that the network configuration depicted in Figure 6.49 is purely a Windows Server 2003 network. How must the RAS server be configured to facilitate DHCP assignment of IP addresses to dial-up network client computers?

Figure 6.49 Image for Question #4

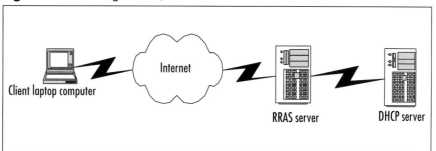

A. The dial-up network client computers must get an IP address from the RAS server. A block of IP addresses must be excluded on the DHCP servers, and the RAS server must be configured to assign addresses to the client computers.

B. The RAS server must be configured as a DHCP client computer.

C. The RAS server must be configured to allow dial-up network client computers to use DHCP to obtain an IP address.

D. The RAS server must be configured to use DHCP to obtain IP addresses on behalf of dial-up network client computers.

5. You're the administrator of a Windows Server 2003 computer named MySystem. MySystem is a standalone server outside any Windows Server 2003 or Windows 2000 domain. You want to use MySystem as am RAS server. You need to configure the dial-in properties of a user to allow that user to connect to the RAS. Which of the following is the correct procedure for doing so?

A. Open the Local Users and Groups Snap-in. Set the dial-in properties on the Dial-in tab of the user account properties of that user.

B. Open the Active Directory Users and Computers Snap-in. Set the dial-in properties on the Dial-in tab of the user account properties of that user.

C. Open the Active Directory Users and Computers Snap-in. Set the modem dial-in properties on the Dial-in tab of the user account properties of that user.

D. Open the Local Users and Groups Snap-in. Set the modem dial-in properties of the Advanced tab of the user account properties for that user.

6. You've just taken on the responsibility of serving as administrator for a Windows Server 2003 domain controller named OrgDC1. OrgDC1 exists within a Windows 2003 Server domain that is running in native mode. Your IT director wants OrgDC1 to act as the RAS server. You need to configure the user dial-in properties to allow connection attempts. You open the Active Directory Users and Computers Snap-in and try to set the dial-in properties on the Dial-in tab of the user account properties. Which of the following options should be available for you to choose? (Choose all that apply.)

A. Apply 128-bit Encryption

B. Remote Access Permission

C. Apply SSL

D. Verify Caller ID

E. Apply Static Routes

    F.   Callback Options

    G. Assign a Static IP Address

7. You're the administrator of a Windows Server 2003 computer named FileServer4. FileServer4 resides on a subnet within your network. All Windows Server 2003 computers except the DHCP server itself use DHCP to configure IP addressing. You've just discovered that FileServer4 is intermittently failing to connect to the other Windows 2003 Server computers on the network. It doesn't happen all the time, but it is happening. You're not sure if other clients are having the same problem. Which two of the following solutions would help to solve this problem?

    A. Decrease the duration of the DHCP leases for all servers.

    B. Increase the duration of the DHCP leases for all servers.

    C. Provide static IP addressing for all clients.

    D. Provide static IP addressing for all servers.

    E. Make sure that DHCP reservations are configured for all clients.

    F.   Make sure that DHCP reservations are configured for all servers.

8. You are the network administrator for your organization. Your network consists of a single Windows Server 2003 domain. Your domain consists of Windows Server 2003 computers, Windows 2000 Server computers, Windows XP Professional computers, Windows 2000 Professional computers, and Windows NT 4.0 Workstation computers. You administer two Windows Server 2003 DNS servers, two Windows 2000 WINS servers, and two Windows Server 2003 DHCP servers. All servers in your network have been assigned static IP addresses. All client computers are DHCP clients. Both the servers and the clients are configured as WINS clients. You want all clients in the domain to be dynamically registered in DNS. What should you do?

    A. Configure the DNS zone for the domain to use WINS forward lookup, and make sure that the Do not replicate this record check box is cleared.

    B. Configure the DHCP servers to register your DHCP clients in DNS.

    C. Configure an Active Directory integrated zone for the domain.

    D. For all your client computers in your domain, manually configure DNS parameters, and then run the *ipconfig/registerdns* command from the command prompt in a DOS window.

9. You are the administrator for your organization's network. This network consists of a single Windows Server 2003 domain. One of the Windows Server 2003 computers in your domain, ProximaCentauri, provides RRAS. ProximaCentauri is set up to use the default remote access policy. You are setting up new user accounts on the domain. What remote access permissions will be set for the new user accounts?

   A. Control Access through Remote Access Policy

   B. Deny Remote Access Permission Policy

   C. Allow Access

   D. Deny Access

10. You are one of the network administrators for your organization's network. The network consists of a single network subnet and contains a Windows 2000 server computer named Sneezy that runs the DNS server service. All your client computers are running either Windows XP Professional or Windows 2000 Professional, and they are all configured with static IP addresses. The clients are also configured to use Sneezy for DNS name resolution. Johann, another administrator, has installed Windows Server 2003 on another computer named Bashful. Johann has also installed the DNS server service and the DHCP server service on Bashful. He has configured the DHCP server to issue dynamic IP addresses to client computers and has configured the DHCP server to configure client computers to use Bashful for DNS name resolution. You have reconfigured all client computers to use DHCP to obtain IP addressing information, and you have uninstalled the DNS server service from Sneezy. Suddenly, all your users are calling and letting you know that they can no longer access any network resources by name. You need to ensure that they can access those network resources by name. What should you do?

   A. Delete the Hosts file on each of the client computers.

   B. Run the *ipconfig/registerdns* command on each of the client computers.

   C. Configure the DNS server on Bashful to include a static A (host) record that contains the name and IP address of Sneezy.

   D. Reconfigure each client computer to remove Sneezy's IP address from the list of DNS servers and to obtain a list of DNS servers automatically via DHCP.

11. You're the network administrator for your organization's Windows Server 2003 domain. The domain consists of a single Windows Server 2003 domain controller named Lion and 25 desktop client computers running Windows XP Professional and Windows 2000 Professional. Your network connects to the

Internet via a T1 line. All IP addresses in your network are static. You've set up an RRAS on a Windows Server 2003 computer named Tiger to provide VPN access, as shown in Figure 6.50. Tiger is a member of the domain. At one of the Windows 2000 Professional client machines on the domain, you use the *Ping* command to search for Tiger, and you receive a reply. At Tiger, you run *ipconfig* and notice that the subnet mask is 0.0.0.0. What could be the problem?

Figure 6.50 Your Organization's Windows Server 2003 Domain for Question #11

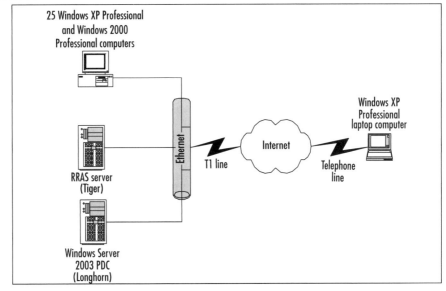

A. There is another computer with the same NetBIOS name.

B. There is another computer with the same IP address.

C. The Routing and Remote Access Service has assigned an Automatic Private IP Addressing (APIPA) address to the Windows XP Professional laptop computer.

D. The DHCP server has assigned an APIPA address to the Windows XP Professional laptop computer.

12. You are the network administrator for your organization, and your network consists of one DHCP server running on a Windows Server 2003 computer named Bradbury; three Windows Server 2003 computers named Heinlein, Clark, and deCamp serving as domain controllers; two DNS servers named Stephenson and Gibson running on Windows Server 2003 computers; one WINS server named Brunner running on Windows Server 2003; five file servers named Burke, Hillerman, Koontz, Brin, and Fitzhugh running on

Windows 2000 Server computers; 275 Windows XP Professional and Windows 2000 Professional client computers; and two UNIX servers named Clancy and Chrichton. All your file servers except Brin rely on DHCP for IP addressing. You relocate Brin to another subnet, and none of your clients can access it any longer. You take the following actions:

- Reconfigure Brin to provide DNS service.

- Reconfigure Brin to provide DHCP service.

- Delete Brin's static entry from the DNS database.

What has been accomplished by your efforts? (Choose all that apply.)

A. Brin's security has been optimized.

B. Brin's performance has been optimized.

C. Brin will be accessible even if relocated again across subnets.

D. Brin will be accessible even if relocated again within the same subnet.

E. Brin is now accessible.

13. You're the network administrator for your organization's Windows Server 2003 network. Your network contains a remote access–enabled server. You set the dial-in permissions for the user accounts to control access through remote access policy. When users attempt to connect to the RAS, what happens?

A. All connection attempts must meet the profile requirements of all policies.

B. All connection attempts must meet conditions of all policies.

C. All connection attempts are accepted.

D. All connection attempts are rejected.

14. You are the administrator for your organization. Your organization maintains a small (25-user) Ethernet network. The network is a single-segment network with a standard IP addressing scheme. Host IP addresses are limited, so when your executive director asks you to set up dialup network access for your traveling benefits staff of three, you decide to use a different network ID for dial-up client computers. You set up a domain controller Windows Server 2003 computer with a modem and then configure RAS to assign IP addresses for dial-up client computers using a different network ID. When you test the dial-up procedure, you find that you can log on to the network; however, you do not have access to the rest of the network. What did you forget to do?

A. You must enable routing in the RAS computer's TCP/IP configuration.

B. You cannot use a different network ID for RAS client computers than you use on the network to which the RAS computer belongs. You must configure dial-up client computers to use the network's DHCP services.

C. You must assign static IP addresses to the dial-up client computers.

D. You must add the new network ID to the RAS computer's routing table.

15. You are the administrator for your multihomed network (which has multiple connections to the Internet, for purposes of availability and redundancy). Until recently you managed your IP addressing manually. With the addition of several hundred new users, you have decided to reassess the situation and configure your workstations to use DHCP. You have started the service and configured your DHCP scopes. Because you have several segments, you have several scopes to configure. Hosts are getting IP addresses, so it seems that you have configured your DHCP service correctly, but you find out rather quickly that workstations can't communicate with other systems on different segments. Computers are able to connect to other computers on their own segment. You have verified that DHCP is working correctly. Assuming that your hosts connect using an IP address, what could be the problem?

A. The lease time is too short.

B. DNS is not configured in his DHCP scope.

C. The default gateway hasn't been set.

D. The subnet mask on the DHCP scope is set incorrectly.

Self Test Quick Answer Key

For complete questions, answers, and explanations to the Self Test questions in this chapter as well as the other chapters in this book, see the Self Test Appendix.

1.	**D**	9.	**D**
2.	**C**	10.	**D**
3.	**A, B**	11.	**B**
4.	**D**	12.	**C, D, E**
5.	**A**	13.	**D**
6.	**B, D, E, F, G**	14.	**A**
7.	**D, F**	15.	**C**
8.	**B**		

Chapter 7

MCSE 70-297

Service Sizing and Placement

Exam Objectives in This Chapter:

4.2   Design an Active Directory implementation plan.

4.3   Specify the server specifications to meet system requirements.

4.2.1   Design the placement of domain controllers and global catalog servers.

4.1   Design a DNS service placement.

4.2.3   Select the domain controller creation process.

4.2.2   Plan the placement of flexible operations master roles.

Introduction

Now that we've decided what type of infrastructure is required, we need to decide where to place the associated services so we can provide the optimum service to the end users and applications. In conjunction with this task, we also need to decide how to size the servers that provide these services, so that they can cope with both the demands of today and the increased demands of tomorrow. The first phase when planning the placement of services is to assess the service levels that need to be adhered to. These might already be available from existing infrastructure deployments, but it is likely that they will need to be amended or tailored to meet the new demands of an Active Directory Services and Network infrastructure. For example, the organization might stipulate that a user must be authenticated within a set time period after supplying credentials. We also discuss how service placement should be determined by various factors such as user populations, nearest hub site, available bandwidth, and so on. Based on these factors, locations can be banded and assigned the appropriate types and quantities of services as deemed necessary.

Any large project that involves the deployment of infrastructure to many disparate locations needs a well thought-out and tested plan. The next phase is, therefore, to create such a plan for the deployment of services throughout the organization. This plan should ensure that minimal disruption occurs, and that the deployment is completed within the required time frame. Finally, we move on to the creation, sizing, and placement of the services themselves. We discuss how to size a domain controller (DC), Global Catalog (GC) server, and DNS server, and how to best place such services based on the factors previously discussed. We also discuss how best to safely and securely promote a server to become a DC. The chapter also includes a review of Flexible Single Operations Master (FSMO) roles, what they are, where they should be placed, and how they can be recovered in the event of a failure.

The Planning Phase

The key to designing service placement is understanding the environment, what the expectations of Active Directory performance are, and what service levels exist within the organization. These factors, when assessed and understood, will help you to place the needed services in appropriate quantity at the proper locations. Understanding the environment means that we determine who the users of Active Directory are, where they are, and how they intend to use the infrastructure. Naturally, if a location houses many users, but only a small fraction of those users need access to Active Directory infrastructure components, then there might be little need to deploy infrastructure to that location. We also examine how network topologies and WAN links can influence service placement—these factors must also be assessed and properly understood before decisions can be made.

The topic of expectation will also influence placement designs. Although it might appear prudent to place services only in locations with large user communities, locations might exist with fewer users who have a requirement that all logons are performed within a very short time period. Alternatively, a location might house an application that needs fast GC lookup capabilities. Finally, any existing service level agreements (SLAs) in place between the IT department and the rest of the organization should be closely scrutinized so that they are still adhered to once the Active Directory infrastructure components have been deployed throughout the organization. For example, if a location has an SLA that mandates that a Windows NT DC be housed there, then it is unlikely that this SLA can be achieved without the placement of a DC/GC, when designing infrastructure placement for Active Directory.

Requirements

In an ideal world, where all locations have large, highly resilient and redundant links to hub locations, available bandwidth is plentiful, all locations and links are highly secure, and budgetary constraints are nonexistent, the subject of service placement would be moot.

All locations, regardless of size and geography, would receive as much infrastructure as they have physical space for (in such an ideal world), or, alternatively, if management and administrative costs are to be minimized, then all infrastructures would be placed in central locations with little or no infrastructure in the smaller locations.

Both of the preceding scenarios are extreme examples of how an enterprise, distributed system might be designed in an ideal world. Unfortunately, we do not live in this ideal world. Instead, we have the following issues with which to contend:

- Unreliable WAN links

- Nonredundant WAN links

- Expensive, overused WAN links

- Physically insecure locations

- IT hardware budgets

Each of the preceding factors contributes to the need for a service placement strategy, such that services are kept secure, are justified, and are shown not to have any detrimental effect on the existing environment. Because we rarely have carte blanche control over service placement, we often find ourselves in the situation where two or more requirements are weighed against each other. This type of "conflict" can occur between, for example, logon time and replication overhead. This section examines these types of factors and requirements, and discusses how each might influence the service placement design.

Logon Time

Everyone wants to be able to switch a Windows desktop machine on and be working in a productive manner as soon as possible. Ideally, in the extreme case, we would all like to be working instantly, within moments of powering our machines on.

The reality is that, even with the fastest hardware, it takes time to boot into Windows and log on with your user account. There are many factors involved in this boot process, such as operating system initialization, startup scripts, group policy, logon scripts, and authentication to a domain.

Startup and logon scripts are located in the SYSVOL share, which is replicated using the File Replication System (FRS) between each DC in the same domain. Naturally, if a user attempts to log on to a DC across a slow WAN link, the time taken to execute scripts and any spawned processes is bound to far exceed the time taken for a similar user to start up and log on when communicating with a DC in his or her location.

In addition to startup and logon scripts, another factor that can affect boot time is the application of Group Policies. In basic terms, the more Group Policy Objects (GPOs) a computer and user need to process at boot and logon, the longer the process will take. For example, if a GPO is linked to the domain and a second GPO is linked to the organizational unit (OU) where the user's computer account exists, and a third GPO is linked to where the user account exists, then the boot and logon process will include the processing of three GPOs, including any startup and logon scripts they might contain.

When designing service placement, therefore, we must take into consideration the actual time to start up. This time will be affected by three factors:

- Complexity of startup and logon scripts

- Number of group policies processed for the computer and user

- Network speed from client to DC, DNS server, and GC

Complexity of Scripts

All too often, administrators will exclude remote locations from receiving infrastructure on the basis that the connecting WAN link is perceived to have sufficient speed and capacity to cope with traffic demands. Unfortunately, without proper testing and simulation of the new environment, the issue of increased logon time due to complex startup and logon scripts can be easily overlooked. It is highly recommended that all scripts be thoroughly tested in an environment that simulates the actual production environment. In conjunction with this testing, efforts should be made to remove as much complexity from startup and logon scripts as is feasible.

Developing & Deploying...

Simplify Startup and Logon Scripts

Often, an organization will develop logon scripts that perform user drive mappings by enumerating the groups a user is a member of and then performing mappings accordingly. This process, if not optimized, can prove to be expensive and time consuming at logon. If logon scripts simply perform many "if member" style operations to determine which mappings a user should receive, then many lookups per user logon are required. These must be performed by a DC. Regardless of whether a DC is located near the user or not, this approach can potentially slow the logon process.

An alternative approach uses a group naming convention that contains all the logic required to perform the mapping without performing multiple lookups on a DC. For example, if user jbloggs is a member of group map_t_server01_share1 and map_s_server02_share2, then his T: drive is mapped to \\server01\share1 and his S: drive is mapped to \\server02\share2. There is no longer a need to perform "if member" queries as the user logs on, which can greatly optimize the logon process.

Number of Group Policies

We have already mentioned how startup and logon scripts might affect the time taken to boot a Windows machine. A closely related factor is that of group policies. Each policy defined applying to client computer and/or user must be processed before the startup and logon process can complete.

This can be best explained through an example. Let us assume that user jbloggs located in OU=Admin, OU=London, OU=UserAccounts, DC=mydomain, and DC=com uses a Windows XP machine that is a member of domain mydomain.com and is located in OU=London, OU=Workstations, DC=mydomain, and DC=com. By default, every domain has a default domain Group Policy defined at the root of the domain. Let's also assume that Group Policies are defined at the Workstations OU (named WorkstationsGPO) as well as the UserAccounts OU (named UserAccountsGPO).

This implies that before jbloggs is able to work productively on his Windows XP machine, three group policies must be processed—the machine and user parts of the default domain policy, the machine-only part of WorkstationsGPO, and the user-only part of UserAccountsGPO. Naturally, the more processing required within each Group Policy, the longer boot and logon will take. In addition, having more Group Policies to process means that more time is required to boot and log on.

When designing an OU structure and a Group Policy model, it is important to be aware that although group policies can be advantageous (because they can be used to control and lock down the environment), they can also have adverse effects on the Active Directory environment. If too many policies are defined or each requires a large amount of time to complete, the boot and logon process will be adversely affected. A balance must be sought between security and control, and operational functionality.

TEST DAY TIP

The subject of Group Policy processing over slow WAN links will most likely appear on the exam. You should be aware of the Group Policy settings available to change the behavior of Group Policy if a slow link is detected, and the ramifications of changing these settings. These settings and their descriptions can be found by following the links as such: Computer Configuration\Administrative Templates\System\Group Policy and Computer Configuration\Administrative Templates\System\User Profiles

Client to Infrastructure Connectivity

Having simplified the logon and startup scripts to optimize the logon process, we also need to ensure that the user has a DC "close by" that can satisfy the logon and startup scripts and any processes spawned by these scripts. We discuss the placement of DCs, DNS servers, and GC servers later in this chapter, but it is important to appreciate the ramifications of DC, DNS server, and GC server placement with respect to user startup and logon.

It is easy to overlook, but if the client performing the startup and logon process does not have a DC in the same site, or if the nearest DC is located across a slow WAN link, then the startup/logon process can be greatly impacted.

The Domain Controller Location Process

When a Windows client starts up, it attempts to locate a DC so that the user can be permitted to log on and access resources within the enterprise. It is important that the associated processes are understood so that you can more easily resolve startup and logon issues. This location process is as follows:

1. The client contacts a DNS server, as configured in its IP settings.

2. If the client has yet to determine in what site it resides, the client requests a complete list of DCs registered in DNS for the client's domain. If the client has previously determined the site in which it resides (by requesting that information from a DC in a previous logon attempt), then it simply requests a list of all DCs in that site, in the same domain as the client.

Head of the Class...

Continued

(Continued)

3. The client contacts each DC in turn (at random) and waits 0.1 seconds for a reply. The client stops contacting DCs when all have been contacted successfully or the client has at least attempted to contact the DCs.

4. When a DC responds to the request sent in Step 3, the client tries to match the DC's domain and site to that of its own. If the client had previously determined its site membership, then it will simply request a list of DCs from that site. The client then ensures that it has not changed site membership since last boot, by requesting that a DC in the list has the same site membership as the client. However, if the client does not know which site it resides in, or it has changed site membership since last boot, then a request is sent to the selected DC asking that it determine the site in which the client resides.

   ■ If a match is found, the DC is used for the logon process and cached for all subsequent authentication requests.

   ■ If a match is not found, then another DC is selected that responded in Step 3.

5. If no DCs match the criteria, then the process returns to Step 1, but this time, the client requests a list of DCs in its own site only, which was determined in Step 4.

Self-Sufficient Locations

Many organizations have smaller locations around the world that have slow, high-latency, unreliable, and nonredundant WAN links to their nearest hub location. Even though these locations have poor network links, they can require high availability for the Active Directory infrastructure so that their business is not interrupted. The nature of the business conducted at the smaller locations might dictate that they require continuous access to the Active Directory infrastructure, even in the event that connectivity to all other locations is lost (the WAN link(s) fail(s)). This requirement can be achieved only by deploying all of the necessary infrastructure locally so that the location becomes "self-sufficient."

This might sound straightforward on the surface, but just what infrastructure is actually required so that the location is deemed self-sufficient? You can see that the Active Directory infrastructure required to provide a self-sufficient startup and logon are as per Table 7.1.

Table 7.1 Active Directory Infrastructure Required for Self-Sufficiency

Required Infrastructure Component	Reason for Requirement
DC from the user's domain	Authenticates user to the domain and provides Kerberos tickets for authorization.
GC from the user's forest	Needed at logon so user's Universal Group memberships can be enumerated. Required if users log on using a user principal Name (UPN). Will also be required if Active Directory Integrated applications are installed that require that the user be able to search for application data; for example, Exchange 2003.
DNS server hosting forest root domain zone	Required to locate the local GC server for the user's forest.
DNS server hosting user's domain zone	Required to locate the local DC for the user's domain.

It can clearly be seen that although other factors such as increased cost might dictate that such a location not receive all the infrastructure components listed in Table 7.1, for reasons of self-sufficiency they are required. Such a requirement must be factored into any service placement designs.

Security

DCs house the Active Directory database, which is used to store sensitive information relating to the business and the people working within the organization. The security of the database is of paramount importance, along with the physical security of the DCs housing it. With these requirements in mind, it is important to assess all locations to ascertain if they are capable of securely housing a DC and other Active Directory infrastructure components. For example, a scoring system could be implemented that assigns a number of points to each security aspect that the location adheres to or meets. An example of such a system is shown in Table 7.2.

Table 7.2 shows how points are assigned based on the level of security offered by the individual aspects. For example, placing a DC in a rack rather than leaving it on a desk or floor is awarded only one point. However, if the DC is located in a segregated locked rack within a managed, audited, and locked communication room, then this is awarded five points.

Table 7.2 Location Security Points System

Security Aspect	Points	Explanation
DC in rack	1	It is a basic requirement that the DC (and ideally other Active Directory infrastructure servers) be located in a communications room rack, as opposed to a desk or on the floor of an office.
DC in locked rack	2	The next layer of security is to ensure that the rack referred to above is locked.
DC in locked rack located in locked communication room	3	The room containing the rack should also be locked.
As above plus access to locked room managed and audited	4	Access to infrastructure such as DCs should be carefully controlled. Because of this, access to the communication room should be managed and audited.
As above plus DC and Active Directory infrastructure in dedicated rack	5	The ultimate security configuration would be to place DCs in separate racks, so that access to them can be controlled on a more granular level.

Many organizations will have large, central communications rooms and suites that house the entire infrastructure used throughout the enterprise. However, other organizations with remote locations often need to place infrastructure in smaller, less well-managed environments. It is therefore recommended that all locations are carefully assessed, and only those locations that meet the minimum criteria have infrastructure deployed. The minimum criteria will vary from one organization to another and should be developed based on your own company's requirements. A system such as that found in Table 7.2 would help to arrive at a minimum set of criteria, however.

 EXAM WARNING

The exam will most likely ask questions that relate to infrastructure placement, based on factors such as physical security. Be aware that DCs should always be located in secure sites.

Service Levels

It might be tempting to treat the placement of infrastructure components as a precise science by assigning a points, or similar, system. However, as discussed in Chapter 1, "The Assessment Stage," existing SLAs agreements might override any decisions made thus far. Although all other requirements discussed thus far might dictate that a particular location should not receive any Active Directory infrastructure components, SLAs in place between the business and the IT department might dictate that logon times and access to resources should occur within a prescribed time. These SLAs can be achieved only if the necessary infrastructure components are located at the locations covered by the SLAs. It is imperative that all such agreements be carefully assessed and understood, their ramifications appreciated, and their requirements factored into any service placement designs.

Replication Overhead

Thus far, we have considered various factors that tend to denote where infrastructure should be deployed. However, for every DC deployed, there is associated replication traffic overhead. Although the deployment of a DC to each location is an ideal situation from the end-user's perspective, administrators (who have extra infrastructure to manage, maintain, and monitor) have to weigh this ideal against the increased overhead incurred and the increased demand placed on the WAN links between each location.

It is important that testing and measurement of additional network services be carried out, so that the extra demand placed on the network links can be assessed. A decision must be made regarding whether those network links are able to cope with such a demand, or whether extra bandwidth and/or lower latency should be considered. This factor clearly conflicts with other factors already described, such as faster logon times. The decision therefore needs to be made as to whether logon times should be optimized or replication traffic minimized. It might also be necessary to compromise between the two. Only careful testing and in-depth discussions with all involved parties can help decide where the right balance lies.

TEST DAY TIP

The exam will expect WAN links and available bandwidth to be considered when placing infrastructure components. Look out for questions that ask you to place infrastructure within an enterprise that has locations connected to hub sites by low bandwidth WAN links. Be careful to assess whether additional replication traffic can be supported if placing infrastructure in such locations.

NOTE

The book *Active Directory: Notes from the Field* released by Microsoft Press has lots of very detailed information regarding the effects of Active Directory on network traffic. It extensively covers the effects on Active Directory as objects are added and/or changed within the database. Although the facts and figures within that publication are relevant to one particular implementation, it is a useful book to have close at hand when assessing the impact that Active Directory replication traffic might have on your network WAN links.

Active Directory-Aware Applications

Active Directory is a database that is used to store objects that exist within the organization. In addition to storing objects such as users and groups, Active Directory can also be used to store data relating to applications. Access to this Active Directory-stored data can dictate where DCs are located. For example, if an application stores configuration data in Active Directory that needs to be available to users in a particular location, then a DC should be placed at that location. If a DC is not placed at the location, then the application that stores its data in Active Directory might not perform at an optimum level.

This requirement, as with any other factor, must be weighed carefully. For example, it should be assessed to ascertain which locations have this specific requirement and whether these locations could suffice with obtaining that data from a remote DC, across a WAN link. The effect on logon and application responsiveness and performance should be measured carefully to determine whether Active Directory infrastructure is required.

TEST DAY TIP

Questions that include Exchange 2000 or Exchange 2003 as a factor should be examined carefully. Locations that have these messaging systems deployed will most likely require a GC to be deployed in their site so that Exchange has a consistent, fast connection to it.

User Populations

The final factor that influences the placement of Active Directory infrastructure is user populations. We now focus on the distribution of users in the organization and how infrastructure will need to be dispersed throughout it. Of all the factors considered thus far, it is likely that user populations will have the greatest bearing on Active Directory infrastructure component placement.

An organization will want to place infrastructure close to its users. However, organizations, especially larger organizations, will most likely have a small number of locations with many users, and a larger number of locations with small user populations. The role of the designer or architect of an Active Directory infrastructure deployment is to perform the following functions:

- Document each location and the number of users at that location.

- Assess the type of users at each location and determine if they require Active Directory authentication 24 hours per day, 7 days per week.

- Determine if the users require Active Directory authentication even in the event of a WAN failure.

- Create user population bandings (for example, band A has 1–10 users, band B has 11–100, etc.).

- Deploy the appropriate Active Directory infrastructure components to each location based on the user population banding assigned to that location and the other factors mentioned previously.

Much of this assessment will have been performed in the "Assessment Phase" that was described in Chapter 1. All that remains now is for the factors described thus far to be used together within an algorithm to produce a definitive statement as to whether each location within the organization should have Active Directory infrastructure components deployed. This algorithm and how it can be constructed and used during the deployment phase is described next.

The Implementation Plan

Having examined all the factors that influence service placement, we now need to start to put all these factors together and create an implementation project plan. This plan will include the development of an algorithm that will take all the information relating to the factors described previously and assign appropriate Active Directory infrastructure components to the relevant locations. Having decided where infrastructure components need to be placed, a deployment plan is then required that describes when locations receive these components in a phased approach.

Developing a Service Placement Algorithm

As previously stated, in an ideal world, we would place Active Directory infrastructure at every location within the organization. However, especially in larger, global companies, this is often not feasible due to various political, budgetary, or security-related issues. Consequently, we need a way to assign infrastructure components in a subjective manner, such that decisions can be explained and justified to management. All too often, infrastructure components are deployed for no tangible reasons.

For example, the environment might have grown organically or via mergers and acquisitions. Designing service placement should introduce a degree of subjectivity and remove ambiguity where possible. This can be done only by developing an algorithm that both decides which locations should receive infrastructure components and justifies the need for that infrastructure from budgetary, operational, and political points of view.

One such algorithm used by the author placed the factors into bands and then assigned weighted scores to each band. Therefore, locations with 1 to 10 users receive a score of 1; locations with 11 to 50 users receive a score of 2; and so on. Tables 7.3 through 7.8 further illustrate this algorithm.

Number of Users

Table 7.3 illustrates a suggested weighted points assignment for user population numbers.

Table 7.3 Weighted Points Assignment for User Populations

Location User Population	Points Assigned
1–10	1
11–50	2
51–100	5
101–250	10
251–500	20
501–1000	30
1001–5000	50
5001–10,000	100
10,001+	200

Bandwidth

Table 7.4 illustrates a suggested weighted points assignment for location bandwidth values.

Table 7.4 Weighted Points Assignment for Location Bandwidth

Bandwidth to Nearest Hub Location	Points Assigned
0–63Kb	100
64–127Kb	50
128–511Kb	30
512–1023Kb	20
1–2MB	10
2–5MB	5
5–10MB	2
>10MB	1

WAN Redundancy

Table 7.5 illustrates a suggested weighted points assignment WAN redundancy.

Table 7.5 Weighted Points Assignment for WAN Redundancy

WAN Redundancy	Points Assigned
Yes	0
No	50

WAN Latency

Table 7.6 illustrates a suggested weighted points assignment for WAN latency.

Table 7.6 Weighted Points Assignment for WAN Latency

WAN Latency	Points Assigned
1–10ms	1
11–20ms	2
21–30ms	5
31–40ms	10
42–50ms	20
51–100ms	50
>100ms	100

Service Levels

Table 7.7 illustrates a suggested weighted points assignment for user population numbers.

Table 7.7 Weighted Points Assignment for Service Levels

Service Levels	Points Assigned
No service level in place (1)	1
Service level in place, but contingency for WAN failure not required (2)	10
Contingency for WAN failure required (3)	100

Spoke Sites Supported

Table 7.8 illustrates a suggested weighted points assignment for spoke sites supported.

Table 7.8 Weighted Points Assignment for Spoke Sites Supported

Spoke Sites Supported	Points Assigned
0	0
1	5
2	10
3	20
4	30
5	50
>5	100

The Algorithm

Now that we have assigned scores to each factor and to each band within these factors, all that remains is for each location's data to be collated and assigned scores as per the previous tables. We then need to define a score that must be reached in order for a location to receive Active Directory infrastructure components. An example algorithm is given in Table 7.9 where 10 locations, each with different characteristics, are compared. For each location, every characteristic is assigned a score and then the scores are totaled. In the next example, the following logic is used to determine if the location should receive infrastructure components:

- If a location scores less than 100 points total, then it does not receive any infrastructure components.

- If a location receives more than 100 points total, then it receives infrastructure components; specifically, a DC, GC server, and a DNS server.

- If a location receives more than 200 points total, then it receives infrastructure components—specifically, a DC, GC server, and a DNS server—and should be considered for multiple instances of each component.

Table 7.9 contains two values within each table cell—one depicts the value relating to the factor shown in the column header, and the other depicts the score assigned from Tables 7.3 through 7.8. The Total column contains the sum of all scores for each location. Finally, the Infra Required? column contains the word *No* and the value 0 if the location does not qualify for infrastructure components, or *Yes* and either the value 1 (the location qualifies for infrastructure components) or the expression >1 (if the location qualifies for multiple instances of infrastructure components).

The factor of security is not included in the algorithm. If a location cannot satisfy the criteria defined for the deployment of a DC, then it should not receive such infrastructure under any circumstances. This factor can, therefore, override all the factors included in the preceding table. For this reason, security is not included in the table. The factor of Active Directory-aware applications is also not included in Table 7.9. This is because if a location hosts such an application, and it requires Active Directory infrastructure components in order to function, then the requisite components should be deployed to the location, regardless of all other factors.

Table 7.9 Combining the Scores to Determine Infrastructure Requirements

Location	Users	Bandwidth	Redundancy	Latency	Service Level	Spoke Sites	Total	Infra Required?
A	12 (2)	128Kb (30)	No (50)	50ms (20)	2 (10)	0 (0)	112	Yes (1)
B	46 (2)	256Kb (30)	Yes (0)	30ms (5)	2 (10)	0 (0)	47	No (0)
C	152 (5)	1Mb (10)	Yes (0)	10ms (1)	3 (100)	1 (5)	121	Yes (1)
D	232 (10)	512Kb (20)	No (50)	50ms (20)	2 (10)	0 (0)	110	Yes (1)
E	469 (20)	1Mb (10)	Yes (0)	20ms (2)	2 (10)	2 (10)	52	No (0)
F	754 (30)	768Kb (20)	No (50)	20ms (2)	2 (10)	1 (5)	117	Yes (1)
G	1241 (50)	2Mb (10)	No (50)	10ms (1)	3 (100)	3 (20)	231	Yes (>1)
H	2467 (50)	5Mb (5)	Yes (0)	10ms (1)	2 (10)	5 (50)	116	Yes (1)
I	5612 (100)	10Mb (2)	Yes (0)	10ms (1)	3 (100)	10 (100)	303	Yes (>1)
J	13,483 (200)	40Mb (1)	Yes (0)	10ms (1)	3 (100)	20 (100)	402	Yes (>1)

Interesting points to mention about the results of Table 7.9 include:

- Although Location B has more users than Location A, it does not qualify for infrastructure while location A does qualify. This is largely because location B has a redundant link to another location, while location A does not.

- Location E, although it does have a high user population, it also has a redundant, high-speed WAN link to another location that has a low latency value. The WAN characteristics in this model outweigh the high user population.

Naturally, the previous algorithm is merely an example, and different values can be assigned to each band within each factor. Indeed, different bands can also be created. The purpose of the algorithm depicted earlier is not to show the only way in which infrastructure placement can be determined, but is simply a tool that should be used as a way to remove the ambiguity normally involved when assigning infrastructure components to locations.

It should also be noted that although the previous model offers a more precise way of assigning infrastructure components, a mechanism should be available to override the results for any location. Additional factors can exist (not discussed in this chapter) that dictate that infrastructure components must or must not be deployed to a particular location. The results of the model should be discussed with all interested parties such that overriding factors can be allowed to surface and therefore be discussed.

Table 7.9 can be presented to management and the sponsors of any Active Directory design in such a way that the infrastructure required might be justified and quantified in a more scientific manner. When presented without objectivity and ambiguity, such proposals will have a much better chance of being approved and for budgets to made available for the project.

Create a Project Plan

We have now reached the point where we know which locations require Active Directory infrastructure components and which do not. Now it is time to formalize a plan that dictates how those components are deployed in a structure manner. When creating such a plan, various factors will dictate how infrastructure components are deployed and which locations receive such components first. It is likely that the largest hub locations will receive infrastructure first, followed by smaller hub locations, and then finally the smaller, satellite sites.

However, this deployment according to location size must be reconciled with any other deployment plans. For example, if a deployment of Windows XP is planned, then the order in which locations are to receive the new desktop operating system should be factored into the deployment plans of Active Directory infrastructure. Whatever the most important factors are within your particular organization, it is vitally important that a structure plan is devised that dictates how and when infrastructure is to be deployed, such that minimal disruption occurs and other related plans are taken into account when possible.

Sizing and Availability

To better understand where Active Directory infrastructure needs to be placed and how the hosting servers should be specified, we need to examine the requirements of components that comprise Active Directory. Each domain within Active Directory will require a certain amount of disk space and thus contribute to the overall size of the Active Directory database. Likewise, each Application Directory partition and DNS zone stored in Active Directory has its own requirements that must be considered when designing the DC, GC, and DNS servers. The following sections discuss each of these components, how they should be sized based on your organization, and therefore how the servers hosting these components need to be specified.

We start by examining Active Directory and which factors affect the size of the database. We then move on to DCs, the promotion of a member server into a DC and how that can be managed in an automated fashion, what specification a DC should have, and where DCs should be placed, depending on various factors within the environment. We then focus on GC servers and the additional factors and requirements that affect their sizing and placement along with a similar discussion relating to DNS servers.

Finally, we examine FSMO roles. These roles are housed on DCs within the forest and must be located according to various rules and best practices. Each role is discussed in detail, including the rules, best practices, and failover procedures.

Active Directory

The Active Directory database is comprised of discrete partitions, or naming contexts. Each of these partitions will consume space within the database, and the amount of space consumed by each partition will be influenced by various factors. Windows Server 2003 Active Directory supports four different partitions:

- Schema
- Configuration
- Domain
- Application Directory partitions

Each of these partition types serves its own purpose and contributes to the overall database size in different ways. Generally, the Schema and Configuration partitions do not contribute a significant amount to the database size. Therefore, the following section examines the contributions from the Domain and Application Directory partitions only.

Sizing Domain Partitions

Calculating the precise size of each Domain partition within an Active Directory forest is not a trivial task. The Domain partition size is dependent on a huge number of object types, each of which consumes a different amount of space in the database. Therefore, traditionally, there has not been a simple way to calculate the space requirements of an Active Directory database.

Each object type has a number of mandatory attributes that must be assigned data; and a number of additional, optional attributes that might be assigned data. Therefore, each object within the domain might consume different amounts of space within the database, depending on the number of attributes that are assigned data. For example, a group object, in general, will consume more space than a user object will, and a group with 1000 members will consume more space in the database than will a group with only 100 members. Such complexity often implies that a calculation is possible only once all objects have been created and configured appropriately, which can be accomplished only once the entire environment has been built and all objects have been created. A calculation of the database size before the environment has been built is, therefore, practically impossible.

However, Active Directory is now a mature product, with many organizations—large and small—using the technology for many different purposes. This maturity has brought with it experience and a better understanding of how the Active Directory database size grows depending on the nature of the environment itself. Microsoft and existing users of Active Directory now understand how the database size relates to the number of users, for example, via a rule of thumb:

Size of domain partition in GB = (number of users in domain / 1000) * 0.4

Stated in words, the preceding expression states that for every 1000 users in the domain, 0.4GB of space inside the Active Directory database is required. It is immediately obvious that this expression is an approximation at best, because it does not include factors such as group types, number of group members, number of user attributes populated with data, and so on. However, experience has shown that this expression allows administrators and architects to estimate the size of the database before deployment, and thus size and specify DCs and GC servers accordingly. For organizations with fewer than 10,000 users, this model might prove less useful. Instead, the Active Directory Sizer tool, available from Microsoft's Web site, might prove more useful and provide a more accurate estimate of the Active Directory database size. This is discussed further in the sidebar *Active Directory Sizer Tool*. We discuss how best to size and specify DCs in the section *Domain Controller Sizing and Specification*, and GC servers are discussed in the section *Global Catalog Sizing and Specification*.

Configuring & Implementing…

Active Directory Sizer Tool

Thus far, we have focused on Active Directory implementations with 1000 users or more. However, many implementations involve smaller numbers than this, and for these installations, a useful sizing tool is Microsoft's Active Directory Sizer, which can be downloaded from Microsoft's Web site at *www.microsoft.com/windows2000/downloads/tools/sizer/default.asp*. Once downloaded, simply install the software, using the file setup.exe.

The Active Directory Sizer tool can be invoked via **Start | All Programs | Active Directory Sizer | Active Directory Sizer**. Within the Active Directory Sizer interface, you can specify your domain topology and your site and site link topology. The tool will use these to suggest how many DCs should be deployed and where.

For example, in Figure 7.1, two domains (mydomain.com and child1.mydomain.com) have been configured, along with five sites. The first domain houses 20 users and is a placeholder domain, while the second domain has 500 users, spread across sites: London, Singapore, Sydney, New York, and HQ. Site links have also been defined between various sites.

Figure 7.1 The Active Directory Sizer Interface

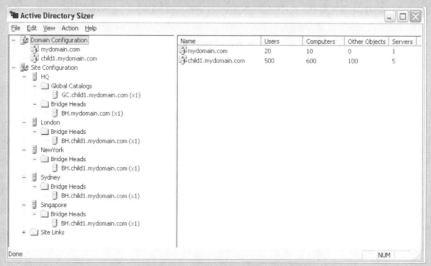

Although the Active Directory Sizer tool is a useful utility for smaller installations, it does not scale well for larger implementations, where many sites, site links, and other administrative, political, and technical factors all affect the overall Active Directory design as well as the design of Service Placement. It is suggested that the Active Directory Sizer tool be used only in smaller organiza-

Continued

(Continued)

> tions where there are less than 1000 users, and even then, the suggestions it produces should be ratified by an experienced consultant or by Microsoft.
>
> As can be clearly seen, the Active Directory Sizer tool has made several suggestions, including the number and location of DCs, and whether these DCs will also act as bridgehead servers (BSs). In the previous example, we can see that the tool suggests that we place a DC for mydomain.com along with a DC for child1.mydomain.com in the site HQ. It then further suggests that each of the other four sites has a DC for child1.mydomain.com deployed, each of which will act as BSs in its respective sites.

Table 7.10 shows how the number of users in a domain affects the approximate size of the corresponding domain partition.

Table 7.10 Domain Partition Size versus Number of Users in the Domain

Number of Users in Domain Partition (GB)	Approximate Size of Domain
1000	0.4
2000	0.8
5000	2.0
10,000	4.0
25,000	10.0
50,000	20.0
100,000	40.0
500,000	200.0
1,000,000	400.0

Active Directory Database Fragmentation

Although the previous section described how to approximate the size of the domain partition, over time the database size will slowly but surely increase, even if the number of objects remains constant. The reason for this increase is fragmentation. In the same way that a hard disk becomes fragmented, so does the Active Directory database. As objects are removed, space is marked as available in the database. However, when new objects are added, they might require more space than has been freed up by the deletions. The new objects take up additional space inside the database, and the overall database size increases over time.

The result is that the database becomes pitted with empty spaces (that objects consumed before their deletion), and newer records that could not be accommodated within the empty spaces often occupy the end of the database. Consequently, the database size increases even though the number of objects within the database might have remained constant throughout. If we take the analogy of a file system, then defragmentation can occur at any time. However, it is recommended that all files be closed before the defragmentation begins, so that all files can be manipulated during the defragmentation process. However, Active Directory databases can be defragmented in one of two ways—the first occurs automatically and periodically at each DC, with no need for human intervention, while the second method requires the DC to be taken offline. The first method simply rearranges the database in a more efficient manner. The second method both rearranges the database and reclaims unused disk space.

DCs automatically defragment their local copy of the Active Directory database every 24 hours using the first method mentioned in the previous paragraph. However, the overall database size remains unchanged by this process, because the process never releases disk space back to the system. Over an extended period of time, an Active Directory database can grow considerably, despite the fact that it contains considerable free space.

So that the database can be both defragmented and reduced in size, it must be defragmented (or compacted) "off line." This is the second type of defragmentation process mentioned previously, and can be performed only by an administrator when the DC is booted in Directory Services Restore mode. The command-line utility ntdsutil is then used to compact the database, after which the DC can be booted back into normal mode. The steps required to defragment the database offline are described in Exercise 7.01.

EXERCISE 7.01

PERFORMING AN OFFLINE DEFRAGMENTATION OF THE ACTIVE DIRECTORY DATABASE

1. Back up the system state data for fault tolerance purposes.

2. Boot or reboot the computer.

3. When prompted, press **F8** during Windows Server 2003 startup.

4. Select **Directory Services Restore Mode (Windows domain controllers only)** in the Windows Advanced Options menu that appears, and press the **Enter** key.

5. Select your operating system (for example, **Windows Server 2003, Enterprise**) and press the **Enter** key.

6. You will see a number of checks performed while the system is booting and eventually will receive the Safe Mode logon prompt.

7. Log on by providing the password for the local administrator account (as provided during the dcpromo process, when the server was promoted to the role of DC) and clicking the **OK** button.

8. Click the **OK** button in the dialog box that notifies you that Windows is running in safe mode.

9. Open a command prompt.

10. Type **ntdsutil** to enter the Ntdsutil utility. Note that this is a command-line utility, so the command prompt will change to ntdsutil:.

11. Type **files**. The command prompt should change to display file maintenance:.

12. Type **compact to <drive>:\<directory>** to create a defragmented and compacted copy of the Active Directory database in the specified new location. For example, **compact to C:\ADTemp** creates a defragmented, re-indexed, and resized database file in the C:\ADTemp directory, as shown in Figure 7.2. The location specified can be on a local disk or a mapped network drive. If there are spaces in the path to where the file needs to be placed, it must be surrounded in quotes; for example, **"compact to c:\ad\july defrag"**.

Figure 7.2 The Ntdsutil compact to Command

13. Type **quit** to return to the ntdsutil: prompt.

14. Type **quit** again to exit the utility.

15. Open Windows Explorer and rename the previously used ntds.dit file to ntds.old.dit. This step is not specified by Microsoft and is for fault tolerance purposes. As mentioned, an offline defragmentation is very invasive. It is possible that the compacted file will be corrupt and that Active Directory will not start. If you don't take this step, you will be forced to do a system state restore to recover the previous database file. By simply renaming it, you can boot back into Directory Services Restore mode, delete the corrupt file, and rename ntds.old.dit back to ntds.dit to recover the system.

16. In Windows Explorer, copy the new ntds.dit file from the location you specified using the **compact to** command to the location of the primary ntds.dit file location.

17. In Windows Explorer, delete all files that end with the LOG extension in your Active Directory log files folder.

Application Directory Partitions

A new feature of Active Directory in Windows Server 2003 is the Application Directory Partition (ADP). An ADP can be used to store data pertinent to a particular application, for example, and the data in the ADP can be replicated to any subset of DCs in the forest deemed appropriate. These ADPs are discrete partitions within the database, and as such, each ADP consumes an amount of space within the database. Sizing each individual ADP cannot be done precisely. However, one should be aware that additional ADPs can be created as the Active Directory installation matures, and therefore it is the responsibility of the design team and administrators to ensure that DCs have sufficient free disk space such that they can house any needed ADPs in the future.

NOTE

In order that ADPs can be created and configured, the DC hosting the Domain Naming Master (DNM) FSMO role must first be upgraded to Windows Server 2003.

Domain Controller Sizing and Specification

We have examined how the Domain and Application Directory partitions influence the size of the Active Directory database and how to estimate the size of domain partitions based on number of users within each domain. In this section, we focus on the DCs housing this database and how they should be best configured, promoted, and placed for optimum performance and service.

We begin by looking at best practices for DC hardware configuration, focusing on components such as disk, memory, and CPU. Next, we examine any specific placement considerations, and then we discuss the promotion phase, the options available, and how the process can be automated and controlled.

Choosing a Specification

Estimating the requirements of a DC's hardware configuration is as difficult as estimating the size of the Active Directory database before deployment. The demands of one environment will be different from any other. It is difficult to predict the load and therefore the ideal hardware configuration of a DC.

Microsoft has set out some basic recommendations for DC CPU and memory requirements, and some suggested best practices for disk configurations. These recommendations can be found in the *Windows Server 2003 Resource Kit Deployment Guide*, available at *www.microsoft.com/windowsserver2003/techinfo/reskit/deploykit.mspx*. These recommendations and best practices are explored further in this section, beginning with disk configurations and disk space requirements. We then move on to CPU and memory recommendations.

Minimum Requirements

In addition to DC specific requirements, the minimum system requirements for Windows Server 2003 as set out by Microsoft must be adhered to. These requirements are detailed in Table 7.11.

Table 7.11 Windows Server 2003 Minimum System Requirements

Requirement	Standard Edition	Enterprise Edition	Datacenter Edition
Minimum CPU speed	133MHz	133MHz for *x86*-based computers; 733MHz for Itanium-based computers	400MHz for *x86*-based computers; 733MHz for Itanium-based computers
Recommended CPU speed	550MHz	733MHz	733MHz
Minimum RAM	128MB	128MB	512MB
Recommended minimum RAM	256MB	256MB	1GB
Disk space for setup	1.5GB	1.5GB for *x86*-based computers; 2.0GB for Itanium-based computers	1.5GB for *x86*-based computers; 2.0GB for Itanium-based computers

Disk Configuration

Each DC houses a local copy of the Active Directory database. The DCs can, therefore, be thought of as "database servers" and thus configured and optimized in much the same way as a database server. In addition to the Active Directory database, each DC stores transaction log files relating to the database and a local operating system. These different components each have their own requirements from a disk configuration standpoint, because some are read intensive while others are write intensive. The trick to configuring disks in a DC is to meet the needs of all (or as many as possible) of these components.

Microsoft makes several recommendations concerning both disk configuration and disk space requirements. These are summarized in Table 7.12 and extracted from the *Windows Server 2003 Deployment Guide* available at *www.microsoft.com/windowsserver2003/techinfo/reskit/deploykit.mspx*.

Table 7.12 Recommended Domain Controller Disk Configurations

Component	Operations Performed	Disk Configuration
Operating system	Read and write operations	RAID 1
Active Directory log files	Mostly write operations	RAID 1
Active Directory database and SYSVOL files	Mostly read operations	RAID 5 or RAID 0+1

Other relevant statements made in the same Microsoft paper include the following:

- For DCs accessed by fewer than 1000 users, all four (database, logs, operating system, SYSVOL) can be collocated on the same RAID 1 array.

- For DCs accessed by more than 1000 users, do the following:

  1. Place logs and database on separate RAID arrays.

  2. Place SYSVOL and the database on the same RAID array.

Disk Space Requirements

Microsoft suggests the following minimum requirements for the four DC components:

- **General** Assume a GC server stores 100 percent of all object data for its local domain partition and 50 percent for all other domain partitions. This is covered in further detail in the section *Global Catalog Server Sizing and Specification*.

- **Database** Allow for 0.4Gb per 1000 users. This was already discussed in the previous section *Disk Configuration*.

- **Logs** Allow at least 500MB free space.

- **SYSVOL** Allow at least 500MB free space.

- **Operating System** Allow at least 1.5GB free space.

Memory and CPU

Microsoft has published some best practices for DC memory and CPU requirements that depend on the number of users being supported in the site where the DC is located. Table 7.13 summarizes the suggested minimum specifications, as found in the *Windows Server 2003 Deployment Guide* available at *www.microsoft.com/windowsserver2003/techinfo/reskit/deploykit.mspx*.

Table 7.13 Recommended Domain Controller CPU and Memory Requirements

User Per Domain in Site	Number of Domain Controllers Required	CPUs Required Per Domain Controller	Memory Required Per Domain Controller
1–499	One	1 x 850MHz+	512MB
500–999	One	2 x 850MHz+	1GB
1000–2999	Two	2 x 850MHz+	2GB
3000–10,000	Two	4 x 850MHz+	2GB
> 10,000	One per 5000 users	4 x 850MHz+	2GB

Experience shows that whereas fast processors are important when configuring DCs, the more essential component is physical memory. DCs host several critical processes and services, including the Kerberos Key Distribution Center, the Active Directory database, and (optionally) DNS, each of which has its own memory demands on the DC.

The process LSASS.EXE, for example, uses more memory as the Active Directory database grows. It is highly recommended, therefore, that DCs deployed into forests where a large number of objects and hence a large Active Directory database exist have 2GB or more of RAM installed, because excessive paging might be experienced if less RAM is installed. Monitor the memory used by the LSASS.EXE process as well as paging activity on DCs and add more RAM to DCs if deemed necessary.

Naturally, it is difficult to predict the precise requirements for CPU and memory. It is therefore of paramount importance that these components be monitored over a period of time such that bottlenecks and potentials issues can be predicted and addressed before any detrimental effects are seen in the Active Directory environment. Solutions such as the Microsoft Operations Manager (MOM) or NetIQ's Application Manager can be used to monitor DC components and perform trend analyses. This can help predict whether changes are required to DC components.

Placement Considerations

Traditionally, Microsoft has not published hard rules for deciding where to locate Active Directory infrastructure components. Recently, however, they have provided some detail and recommendations via the Windows Server 2003 Deployment Resource Kit. This covers DC, GC, FSMO, and DNS service placement and suggested algorithms for each. DC and GC placement discussions follow.

Microsoft has never published a definitive algorithm for deciding which locations should have DCs installed and which should be able to cope without local DCs. The flow diagram in Figure 7.3 offers a basic algorithm, found in the Windows Server 2003

Deployment Resource Kit. It focuses on remote administration, physical security, and WAN availability and performance. Although it asks only the most basic questions about the location and WAN links, it can be seen that if a location has poor WAN availability and requires 24x7 authentication, then a DC will always be required, according to the algorithm. The stated example is often the case in a large, distributed financial organization's network; thus, most or all locations will qualify for a DC.

Figure 7.3 A Suggested Algorithm for Determining Domain Controller Placement

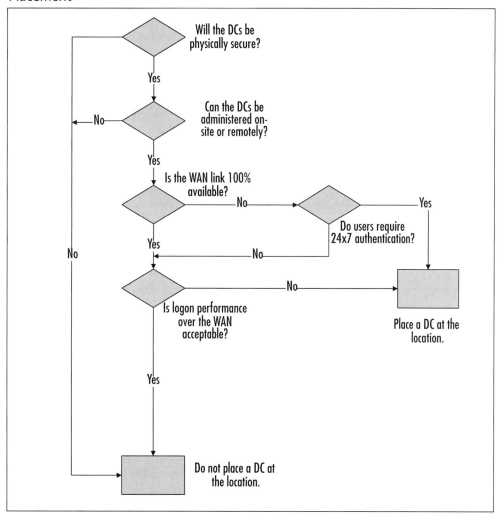

An algorithm has already been described in the section *The Implementation Plan* that helps identify locations that should receive Active Directory infrastructure components, in the form of a DC and/or GC server. Microsoft also has documented its

own suggestions regarding DC placement. Table 7.14 shows Microsoft's suggestions regarding the number of DCs that should be deployed to a location, based on user population at that location. Up to a population of 1000 users, one DC is believed to suffice, while populations between 1000 and 10,000 should receive two DCs. Beyond 10,000, one DC should be deployed for each 50,000 users in the location.

Table 7.14 Microsoft Recommended Number of Domain Controllers Per Site

User Per Domain in Site	Number of Domain Controllers Required
1–499	One
500–999	One
1000–2999	Two
3000–10,000	Two
> 10,000	One per 5000 users

The Promotion Strategy

Now that we have decided where DCs are to be placed and their specifications, we need to agree on the methodology that will be used for the promotion of a Windows Server 2003 member server into a DC. The promotion phase is split into two stages—the first deals with a review of the server's configuration, ensuring that it is ready to be promoted to a DC. The second stage, started once stage one has been completed successfully, is the actual promotion. This stage can be performed manually, automatically after stage one checks complete, or even automatically as a separate process, after the completion of the operating system installation onto the member server, without having performed any checks. In this section, we examine all of these options in turn, as well as post-promotion checks.

Pre-Promotion Checks

Before commencing with the promotion of a member server into a DC, several checks and best practices should be performed to ascertain whether the server is ready and able to be promoted. These checks are described in the Table 7.15.

Table 7.15 Pre-Promotion Check List

Pre-Promotion Check	Explanation and Benefit
Check event logs for boot-related issues	Before promoting a member server, it is of paramount importance that the server boots without errors or issues. Check the event logs for any installation- or boot-related issues and resolve them before continuing.

Continued

Table 7.15 Pre-Promotion Check List (**Continued**)

Pre-Promotion Check	Explanation and Benefit
Configure event logs	The number of events logged by a DC is likely to be greater than the number logged on a member server. Consequently, the event log sizes and wrapping properties should be altered appropriately. A Group Policy should implemented at the DC's OU to facilitate these settings.
Configure services	Certain services configured to start automatically might not be required within your organization, or might be viewed as potential areas of vulnerability. Review all services and disable those that are not required or deemed vulnerable to attack. Consider using a Group Policy at the DC's OU level to implement such changes so they are standardized and enforced across all DCs.
Check IP configuration	Ensure that IP configuration is correct. Execute **ipconfig /all** from a command prompt and check that DNS and WINS settings are correct as well as subnet mask and default gateway(s). Correct any misconfigurations found.
Check network connectivity	Once IP configurations are checked, network connectivity should be checked. Execute **netdiag /v** from a command prompt and ensure that connectivity to DNS and WINS occurs without issue. Correct any issues found.
Configure the page file	If the prospective DC has multiple physical disks, or multiple disk arrays, consider placing page files on all of these disks so the paging load is spread across multiple disks.
Check FSMO availability	In order for a member server to be promoted, connectivity to one or more FSMO roles is required. If you are creating a new domain in an existing forest, for example, the DNM must be available. If a new DC is being created in an existing domain, then the RID Master must be available. Ensure that these roles are available, and that the prospective DC can resolve their names and connect to the DCs hosting these roles.

Continued

Table 7.15 Pre-Promotion Check List (Continued)

Pre-Promotion Check	Explanation and Benefit
Back up the server	Before promoting a member server to a DC, it is a best practice to back up the server including the system state and any other services and applications it hosts. The backup may then be used to restore the server to its original state if the promotion phase fails.
Check DNS connectivity	Use **nslookup** and/or **ping** to ensure that a DNS server hosting the appropriate Windows Server 2003 DNS zone(s) can be located. If a new domain is being created via the promotion phase, then ensure that the corresponding DNS zone is available and that DDNS updates are permitted in that zone.

Manual Promotion

The most popular approach to promoting servers to become DCs is the manual approach. This approach offers the administrator complete control over the promotion phase and is the suggested approach of the author that should be adopted, at least until the promotion of servers is fully understood by the administrators of Active Directory. Once this process is fully understood and administrators are comfortable with automating the process, then this can be done using an answer file. This automated approach is covered in the section *Automated Promotion*.

The manual approach involves the installation of a Windows Server 2003 member server followed by promotion using the utility dcpromo, which can be launched via **Start | Run dcpromo <Enter>**. The various options available during the promotion phase are described in Table 7.16.

Table 7.16 Manual Promotion Options

Option	Action	Examples
Additional DC or Member Server	Select whether the server is to become a new member server or a new DC	If creating a new DC in an existing domain, choose **Additional Domain Controller**. If demoting a DC to a member server, choose **Additional Member Server**.

Continued

Table 7.16 Manual Promotion Options (**Continued**)

Option	Action	Examples
DC Type	Select **Additional domain controller for an existing domain** or **Domain controller for a new domain**	If adding a DC to an existing domain, choose **Additional domain controller for an existing domain** and go to option **Domain Name**. Otherwise, choose **Domain controller for a new domain** and go to option **Create New Domain**.
Create New Domain	Select **Domain in a new forest** or **Child domain in an existing domain tree** or **Domain tree in an existing forest**	If establishing a new domain and a new forest, choose **Domain in a new forest**. If creating a new domain in an existing domain tree, choose **Child domain in an existing domain tree**. If creating a new domain and new tree in an existing forest, choose **Domain tree in an existing forest**.
New Domain Name	Type the DNS name of the new domain	Type **mycompany.com**, for example.
NetBIOS Domain Name	Type the NetBIOS name of the domain	Type **mycompany**, for example
Domain Name	Type the existing DNS domain name	Type **oldcompany.com**, for example
Database and Log Folders	Specify the locations for the database and log files	Place database folders in d:\database and log files in e:\logs, for example.
Shared System Volume	Specify the location for the SYSVOL folder	Place SYSVOL folder in c:\ windows\sysvol, for example.
Permissions	Select **Permissions compatible with pre-Windows 2000 server operating systems** or **Permissions compatible only with Windows 2000 or Windows Server 2003 operating systems**	If users from older, legacy clients need to query Active Directory, choose **Permissions compatible with pre-Windows 2000 server operating systems**. Otherwise, select **Permissions compatible only with Windows 2000 or Windows Server 2003 operating systems**.

Continued

Table 7.16 Manual Promotion Options **(Continued)**

Option	Action	Examples
Directory Services Restore Mode Administrator Password	Type the password to be used when booting the DC into Directory Services Restore mode (DSRM).	When booting into DSRM, a local logon must be performed because Active Directory is not available. Type the password to be assigned to the local administrator account.

Once all the information required has been given, a summary window appears that details all the information provided. This summary should be reviewed, and if found to be correct, then the promotion can be started.

Automated Promotion

Rather than directly provide answers to various questions and thus promote a member server to a DC manually, the process can be automated using a dcpromo answer file, which contains all required answers to questions posed by the promotion phase. Dcpromo can be executed in the following way: dcpromo /answer:*answerfile.txt* where *answerfile.txt* is the name of a text file that contains all the required responses to all dcpromo questions. Naturally, the answers provided in the text file will vary depending on whether the DC is establishing a new domain, new domain tree, or new forest, or simply being added to an existing domain. The various options available and their applications are listed in Table 7.17. This is followed by several example answer files, covering some of the promotion options available.

Table 7.17 Automated Promotion Options

Option	Possible Values (Defaults in Bold)	How and When Used
AllowAnonymousAccess	Yes/No. No default.	Used to determine whether anonymous access is permitted to user and group information.
AdministratorPassword	No default.	Specifies the local admin password assigned to a server after demotion.
AutoConfigDNS	**Yes**/No.	Determines whether DNS should be automatically installed and configured on the DC.

Continued

Table 7.17 Automated Promotion Options (Continued)

Option	Possible Values (Defaults in Bold)	How and When Used
ChildName	No default.	Name of the new child domain being created (for example, new.child.com).
CreateOrJoin	Create/**Join**.	Create = create new forest. Join = create a new domain tree and join to existing forest.
CriticalReplicationOnly	No values. No default.	Specifies that only critical replication should occur during dcpromo, and that the remaining replication should occur after the new DC is rebooted.
DatabasePath	**%systemroot%\NTDS**	The path to the Active Directory database file (NTDS.DIT).
DomainNetBIOSName	No default.	The NetBIOS name of the domain.
DNSOnNetwork	**Yes**/No.	Yes = DNS client is left configured "as is." No = DNS client is auto-configured to use the new DC as its preferred DNS server.
IsLastDCInDomain	Yes/**No**.	Indicates that this is the last DC in the domain (used during a demotion).
LogPath	**%systemroot%\NTDS**	The path to the Active Directory log files.
NewDomainDNSName	No default.	The fully qualified DNS name of the new domain.
Password	No default.	The password to be used (along with "username") during the promotion phase.
ParentDomainDNSName	No default.	The DNS name of the parent domain.
RebootOnSuccess	Yes/**No**.	Yes = reboot when dcpromo completes. No = do not reboot when dcpromo completes.

Continued

Table 7.17 Automated Promotion Options (**Continued**)

Option	Possible Values (Defaults in Bold)	How and When Used
ReplicaDomain DNSName	No default.	The existing DNS name into which the DC is to be pro moted.
ReplicaOrMember	Replica/**Member**.	Replica = promote the server to a DC in an existing domain. Member = demote a DC to a member server in the domain.
ReplicaOrNewDomain	Domain/**Replica**.	Domain = promote the server as the first DC in a new domain. Replica = promote the server to a DC in an existing domain.
ReplicationSourceDC=	No default.	The name of the DC from which Active Directory objects are to be replicated, during the promotion.
SafeMode AdminPassword	No default.	The DC local admin password used in Restore mode.
SiteName	**Default-First-Site**.	The site into which the DC is to be placed.
SYSVOLPath	**%systemroot%\SYSVOL**.	The path to the SYSVOL share.
TreeOrChild	Tree/**Child**.	Tree = establish a new domain tree in an existing forest. Child = create a new child domain in an existing domain tree.
UserDomain	No default.	The domain in which the "user-name" exists, used during the promotion phase.
UserName	No default.	The username used during the promotion.

Example Answer File

A new domain tree in a new forest can be established as follows:

```
[DCINSTALL]

ReplicaOrNewDomain=Domain

TreeOrChild=Tree

CreateOrJoin=Create

NewDomainDNSName=<fully qualified DNS domain name >
```

DNSOnNetwork=yes

DomainNetbiosName=<Netbios domain name>

AutoConfigDNS=yes

SiteName=[active directory site name (optional)]

AllowAnonymousAccess=no

DatabasePath=%systemroot%\ntds

LogPath=%systemroot%\ntds

SYSVOLPath=%systemroot%\sysvol

SafeModeAdminPassword=<admin defined offline admin account password>

CriticalReplicationOnly=No

RebootOnSuccess=yes

Post-Promotion Checks

Once a DC has been deployed, several checks and amendments should be performed before the DC is "production-ready." These are described in Table 7.18.

Table 7.18 Post-Promotion Checks

Task	Explanation
Default Containers	When creating a new domain, ensure that after the first DC has been promoted, the default containers (such as Users, Computers, and ForeignSecurityPrincipals) exist.
Domain Controllers OU	When creating a new domain, ensure that the Domain Controllers OU exists.
Site Membership	When a DC has been promoted, ensure that it exists in the correct Active Directory site.
Active Directory Database	Ensure that the database file NTDS.DIT exists in the correct location.
GC	If the DC is to act as a GC server, enable that role using the Active Directory Sites and Services MMC snap-in as follows: 1. Navigate to **Sites | <SiteName> | Servers | <DCname> | NTDS Settings**. 2. Right-click **Properties**. 3. Select **Global Catalog**.

Continued

Table 7.18 Post-Promotion Checks **(Continued)**

Task	Explanation
	If the DC is the first one in a new forest, it should be assigned the GC role automatically, as part of the promotion phase. Use the preceding steps to verify that this is the case.
SYSVOL	Use the command **net share** to verify that SYSVOL has been shared and is available.
DNS Records	Ensure that all DC (and GC) DNS resource records are registered correctly. Look for resource records of type –kerberos and _ldap in locations: _msdcs.dc._sites.siteName._tcp _msdcs.dc._tcp.
Remote Desktop	The remote desktop feature is installed but not enabled by default. It is suggested (although not a requirement) that this option be enabled so that the DC can be managed remotely. This can be done via: **Start	Control Panel	System	Remote tab	Allow users to remotely connect to this computer**.
Event Logs	Check all event logs, in particular System and Directory Services, and ensure that the DC is functioning correctly. Search for errors occurring at boot (in the System log) or that relate to replication issues (found in the Directory Services log).

Global Catalog Server Sizing and Specification

We previously discussed how a DC should be sized and configured in some detail. However, some or all of the DCs in the Active Directory forest(s) will also act as GC servers. The following section discusses the additional requirements of the GC role beyond that found for the DC role. We start with a discussion of the additional requirements regarding disk space, CPU, and memory, and then proceed to evaluate the additional placement factors and requirements.

Additional Requirements

The space requirements for GC servers is equivalent to the space requirements of a DC in the same domain, plus half the sum of all other DC space requirements in other domains.

Written as a formula, this is:

$$\text{Space}_{GC} = \text{SpaceLocal}_{DC} + 1/2\ \Sigma(\text{SpaceOther}_{DC})$$

Table 7.19 illustrates the estimated space requirements in a forest with five domains and compares the requirements of DCs versus GCs.

Table 7.19 Global Catalog versus Domain Controller Disk Space Requirements

Users Per Domain	Domain Controller Requirement	Global Catalog Requirement
2000	2 * 0.4 = **0.8GB**	0.8 + ? (1.6 + 2.4 + 3.2 + 4.0) = **6.4GB**
4000	4 * 0.4 = **1.6GB**	1.6 = ? (0.8 + 2.4 + 3.2 + 4.0) = **6.8GB**
6000	6 * 0.4 = **2.4GB**	2.4 = ? (0.8 + 1.6 + 3.2 + 4.0) = **7.2GB**
8000	8 * 0.4 = **3.2GB**	3.2 = ? (0.8 + 1.6 + 2.4 + 4.0) = **7.6GB**
10,000	10 * 0.4 = **4.0GB**	4.0 = ? (0.8 + 1.6 + 2.4 + 3.2) = **8.0GB**

Placement

Microsoft has never published a definitive algorithm for deciding which locations should have a GC installed and which should be able to cope without one. The flow diagram in Figure 7.4 offers a basic algorithm, found in the Windows Server 2003 Deployment Resource Kit. It focuses on application requirements, user populations, WAN availability, and roaming users.

It can be seen that if a local application requires a GC (or the location has more than 1000 users or has roaming users), then a GC is required. If the specified criteria are not met, but WAN availability is 100 percent, then a GC is not required. Otherwise, Universal Group membership caching might be sufficient. (We discuss this subject further in the sidebar *Universal Group Membership Caching*.)

Perhaps the most important factor when choosing GC placement is the subject of Active Directory-aware applications. These include Exchange 2000 and 2003, and other applications that store data in Active Directory and require a GC search to retrieve that data. If such a requirement exists, then a GC server should be deployed to each location that hosts that application.

Figure 7.4 Flow Diagram Indicating when a Global Catalog Server Is Required

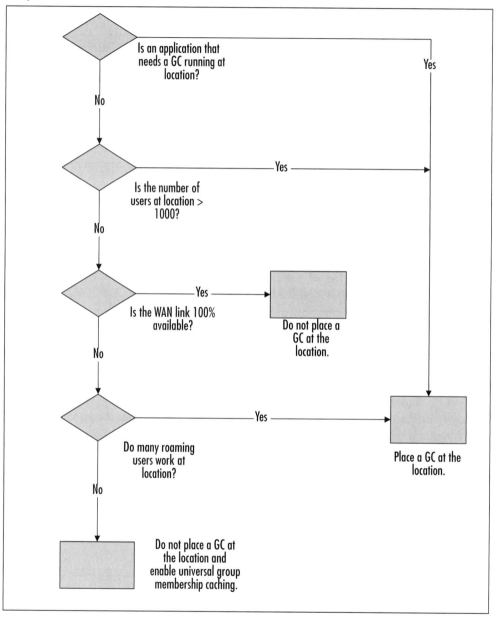

Configuring & Implementing...

Universal Group Membership Caching

By default, each user must be authenticated by a GC server at logon, so that the user's Universal Group membership can be enumerated. Universal Groups can exist in any domain and the user can be a member of any of these Universal Groups, some of which might deny the user access to one or more resources.

It is therefore necessary to contact a GC server at logon to enumerate the user's Universal Group memberships and thus ascertain which resources he or she has been denied access to. By default, if a GC server cannot be found during the logon process (and cached credentials are not found on the client), then a logon cannot succeed. This requirement for a GC has often been the overriding factor when deploying GC servers to small branch offices. These offices might be connected to hub sites where other GC servers exist, but the users at the branch office require constant logon capabilities, even in the event that the WAN link to the hub site fails. This requirement can be met only by deploying a GC server to each location that requires logon capabilities in the event of a WAN failure.

Windows Server 2003 introduces a new feature that helps to address this limitation and potentially aid in the removal of GC servers that were deployed purely to aid the logon process. This new feature is known as "Universal Group membership caching" and is enabled on a per-site basis. This feature is available as long as all DCs in the remote office have Windows Server 2003 installed, and the Active Directory site (corresponding to the location) is configured to cache Universal Group memberships from a specific site that itself has one or more GC servers.

When a user logs on at the remote location, the DC contacts a GC server and retrieves and stores that user's Universal Group memberships. This information is stored indefinitely for each user and is refreshed every eight hours, by default.

Note: this new feature does not remove the need for a GC server to be deployed to a location if an application at that remote location requires access to a GC server, such as Exchange 2000 or 2003. The remote DC(s) cache Universal Group memberships, but in all other respects behave as DCs and not GC servers.

This new feature is enabled per site and is implemented using the Active Directory Sites and Services MMC snap-in. Figure 7.5 illustrates how this feature is enabled for a particular Active Directory site. In the figure, site "London" caches Universal Group memberships from site "NewYork."

Continued

(Continued)

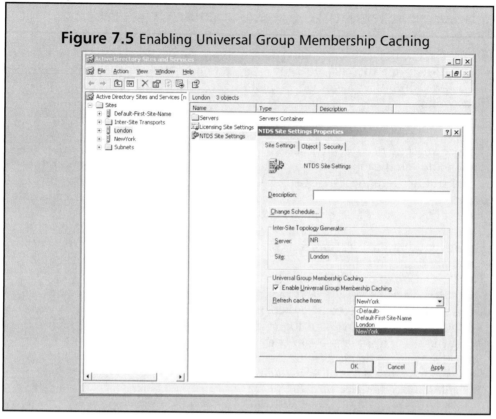

Figure 7.5 Enabling Universal Group Membership Caching

DNS Servers

We have discussed how a DC and a GC server should be sized and configured in some detail. However, some or all of the DC/GC servers in the Active Directory forest(s) will also act as DNS servers, hosting zones for the domains in the forest. The following section discusses the additional requirements of the DNS server service role beyond that found for the DC and GC Server roles. Additional information relating to the DNS Server service, server placement, and zone placement can be found in Chapter 5, "Name Resolution."

Specification

The roles of DC and GC server are generally very demanding and require suitably specified and configured servers, as seen in previous sections. The DNS role, by comparison, places much smaller demands on the hosting server.

The DNS service itself has a very small demand and resource requirement from a server when compared to the demands of the DC and GC roles. The additional demands placed on a DNS server are likely to be memory sufficient to manage the number of DNS records housed by the server and disk space to house the zones. When configuring servers to house DNS zones, it is worth considering whether the zones will be stored in Active Directory (Active Directory integrated) or in BIND text files. If the former, then the disk space requirements calculated for Active Directory itself should suffice, but if the latter, then additional disk space should be factored into server designs for these (relatively small) text files.

Each resource record housed by a Windows Server 2003 DNS server consumes approximately 100 bytes of memory. Table 7.20 depicts RAM requirements versus number of resource records housed by the server.

Table 7.20 RAM Requirements versus Resource Records Housed

Number of Resource Records	RAM Requirements
100	10Kb
1000	100Kb
2000	200Kb
5000	500Kb
10,000	1MB
50,000	5MB
100,000	10MB
250,000	25MB

Flexible Single Master Operations Roles

The final subject covered in this chapter, is that of Flexible Single Master Operations (FSMO) roles. The acronym FSMO is frequently pronounced as "fuzmo" or "fizmo." FSMO roles, their purpose, governing rules, and best practices are all discussed in this section.

We start by explaining in some detail what FSMO roles are and why they are needed. Each role has a specific purpose and several have rules that govern where they can be placed within the enterprise. We then examine best practices for FSMO role placement, based on both the rules mentioned previously as well as other factors. The final topic covered relating to FSMO roles is the subject of failover and recovery.

Background

Before embarking upon a discussion relating to FSMO role placement and recovery, we first need to describe each FSMO role, what it is, and how it relates to the Active Directory. Certain roles, for example, are more critical to the day-to-day operation of Active Directory than others. In addition, certain FSMO roles must be housed and placed according to rules that must be adhered to regardless of the environment.

There are five FSMO roles in all—two per forest and three per domain. In a forest with five domains, there will be 2 (forest) and 5 * 3 (domain) FSMO roles for a grand total of 17. Let us discuss and describe each FSMO role is turn.

Domain Naming Master

An Active Directory forest may contain many domains. Each domain in the forest must have a unique fully qualified domain name (FQDN), which is the DNS representation of the domain name. With a pure multimaster implementation, it would be theoretically possible to create two additional domains in the forest at the same time with the same FQDN if the domain creation was performed on different DCs in the forest.

It is the job of the DNM to ensure that each domain created has a unique name within the forest. The DNM role must therefore be assigned to precisely one DC in the forest. The DNM role is therefore said to be a forestwide FSMO role, because only one DNM role exists in any one Active Directory forest.

As well as ensuring that all domains in the forest have unique names, the DNM is also responsible for maintaining the authoritative list of domains in the forest. This list is stored in the Partitions container, within the Configuration partition.

LDAP://CN=Partitions,CN=Configuration,DC=<domain>

Although all DCs have a read-write copy of the Configuration partition, only the DNM role holder is able to make changes to the list of domain partitions listed in the Partitions container. If a domain is renamed or removed, the DNM must be contacted so that the list of domains can be updated accordingly. It is also the responsibility of the DNM role to add and remove cross-references to domains in external Active Directory forests.

Figure 7.6 shows how ADSI Edit can be used to view the current holder of that role within a forest.

Figure 7.6 The Domain Naming Master FSMO Role Holder

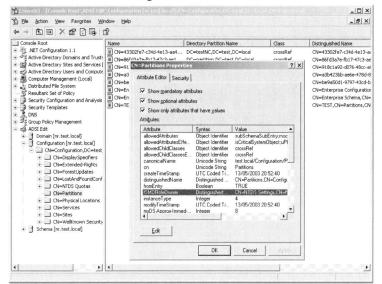

Schema Master

Every object within Active Directory must obey certain rules concerning the attributes and data stored as part of the object. These rules, along with the list of permitted object types and attributes, are all stored in the schema. The schema exists as a partition within Active Directory and is replicated as a read-only partition to every DC in the forest. However, if changes need to be made, such as the addition of a new object or attribute, then one DC needs a copy of the Schema partition that can be written to and thus altered.

The DC that houses the Schema Master (SM) FSMO role is the only DC in the forest that can have schema amendments made to its copy of the Schema partition. The SM role is therefore the second of the two forestwide FSMO roles.

LDAP://CN=Schema, CN=Configuration, DC=<domain>

Figure 7.7 shows how ADSI Edit can be used to view the current holder of that role within a forest.

Figure 7.7 The Schema Master FSMO Role Holder

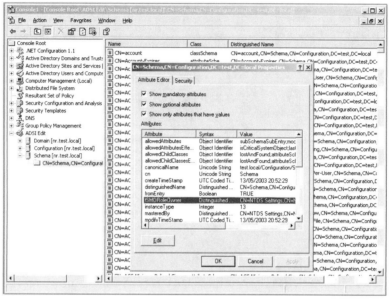

Primary Domain Controller Emulator

A Windows NT DC was either built as a Primary Domain controller (PDC) or as a backup domain controller (BDC). Each Windows NT domain has precisely one PDC and one or more BDCs. All changes to the domain occur on the PDC, which are then replicated to all BDCs in the same domain. This model is referred to as "single master," because all changes, including password changes, occur on one DC (the PDC), and changes cannot be made on any other DCs in the domain.

Although Active Directory DCs perform changes to the database in a multi-master fashion (changes can be made on any DC), the concept of a PDC is still required for compatibility with older systems and for several other tasks, which we describe later. The Active Directory "equivalent" of the Windows NT PDC is the PDCe. The reason for the addition of the word *emulator* will become apparent as we further describe the role of the PDCe.

If Windows NT BDCs exist in an Active Directory forest, where the PDC has been upgraded to Windows Server 2003, then these BDCs still behave as though they were within a Windows NT domain—they are unable to make changes to objects in the domain and receive all replication from the PDCe. This single master topology ceases to exist once all BDCs have been upgraded to Windows 2000 or Windows Server 2003, however. Furthermore, if Windows NT, 95, 98, or Me clients exist in the domain (which do not have the Active Directory client installed), they will perform, for example, all password changes on the PDCe for the domain. In the same way that the Windows NT PDC acted as the Domain Master browser, the Windows Server 2003 PDCe also acts as the Domain Master browser, for any clients requiring network browse capabilities. In these respects, the PDCe emulates the functions provided in a legacy PDC found in a Windows NT domain. This is the reason why the Windows Server 2003 PDC is known as a PDCe.

In addition to providing PDC emulation functions, a Windows Server 2003 PDCe also provides other single master operations. For example, when a user changes his or her password on a Windows Server 2003 DC, other than the PDCe, that password change is urgently replicated to the PDCe for the domain. Urgent replication does not adhere to the normal replication rules used by Active Directory, but instead the change is replicated "as soon as possible." The same logic is applied to changes of a user's account lockout status. If a user's account is unlocked by an administrator on a DC other than the PDCe, this change is urgently replicated to the PDCe for the domain.

The behavior just described is required, because Active Directory uses a multi-master model for updates to objects. For example, if a user has his or her password changed by an administrator on DC A, but the user is authenticated by DC B, the logon attempt with the new password will fail, because the new password would likely not have replicated from DC A to DC B. The urgent replication of the new password from DC A to the PDCe mitigates this issue because when DC B receives a logon attempt with an invalid password, before declining the logon attempt it first checks with the PDCe as to whether a newer password exists for the user that might have been changed on another DC. If a newer password is found on the PDCe and it matches the password supplied by the user at DC A, then the logon attempt is permitted. Refer to Figure 7.8 for a graphical representation of this process.

Figure 7.8 The Password Replication Algorithm

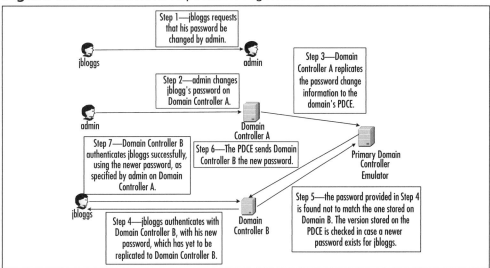

The PDCe in each domain acts as the authoritative time source for that domain. Each DC in the domain synchronizes its time from the PDCe in the same domain, and each nonroot domain PDCe then synchronizes its time from the PDCe in the forest root domain. This PDCe in the forest root domain is therefore the authoritative time source for the entire forest and should itself synchronize with an external time source.

The final role of the PDCe is that it is used to implement all changes to GPOs by default. This single master approach ensures that the same GPO cannot be amended by two different personnel at the same time on different DCs. This behavior is implemented by the Group Policy Editor MMC snap-in, although it is not enforced. It is highly recommended, however, that GPO changes be performed on the PDCe so that conflicting changes to GPOs do not occur.

Figure 7.9 shows how ADSI Edit can be used to view the current holder of that role within a forest.

Figure 7.9 The Primary Domain Controller Emulator FSMO Role Holder

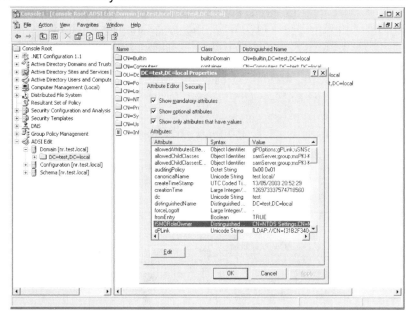

Protection of Privileged Groups

Head of the Class…

An often-undocumented role performed by the PDCe in each domain is that the PDCe reapplies permissions applied to the AdminSDHolder object to all privileged groups in the domain (and all direct and indirect group members). The ACL entries applied to the AdminSDHolder object (located in the System container of each domain in the forest) are applied to each privileged group (and members) in the domain on a periodic basis. This is done so as to ensure that privileged groups (and their members) such as the Domain Admins group cannot be assigned different ACLs that might allow a nonprivileged user to add himself or herself to the Domain Admins group.

This feature is implemented via a process called SDPROP that runs within the lsass.exe process. SDPROP executes every 60 minutes on the PDCe, applies the same ACLs found applied to the AdminSDHolder object to all privileged groups, and removes any inherited permissions that might have been inadvertently applied from the parent container or OU. Although this feature was designed to protect the privileged groups (such as Domain Admins, Schema Admins, Enterprise Admins, and all members), it can also be used to further lock down these groups. For example, the ability of the Authenticated Users group to read the memberships of these privileged groups can be removed by simply removing Authenticated Users from the ACL applied to the AdminSDHolder object.

RID Master

When a new security principal is created (user, group, or computer object), it is assigned a unique Security ID (SID). This SID is comprised of two parts—a domain SID (which is the same for all objects in the same domain) and a relative ID, or RID (which is unique within the domain). Because security principals can be created on any DC in the domain, and RIDs must be unique across the domain, a mechanism is required for ensuring that different DCs never allocate the same RID to different objects. This is achieved via the RID Master FSMO role via the following logic. The process starts when the first DC is built in an Active Directory domain. This DC assumes the role of RID Master for that domain. It also generates a unique domain SID and creates a pool of RIDs, which is used to generate SIDs for new security principals created on the new DC. Thus far, we have no possibility of creating objects with conflicting SIDs because we have only one DC in the new domain, but when additional DCs are built, we need a way of ensuring that each DC assigns a unique SID to each new security principal.

This uniqueness is achieved by assigning precisely one DC in each domain as being responsible for distribution of pools of RIDs to each of the DCs in the domain. For example, if a new DC is built in a domain, during the promotion phase it contacts the RID Master for the domain and requests a pool of RIDs. The RID Master will assign a pool of unique RIDs to the new DC and not assign any RIDs from that pool to any other DC. Because no two DCs have been assigned the same RIDs from the RID Master, all security principals will be created with a unique RID and thus a unique SID.

In time, DCs will exhaust their pool of RIDs, and if the pool is not replenished in a timely fashion, the DC will be unable to create any more security principals. To avoid this issue, DCs contact the RID Master when they still have a small proportion of their RID pool left. This allows the DC to continue assigning RIDs to new security principals for a short time even if the RID Master role is unavailable. Further information can be found in the *Failover and Recovery* section.

Infrastructure Master

Within an Active Directory forest, there can exist several domains. Frequently, users in one domain will be added as members of groups in other domains. When changes to the underlying user account properties (such as the name of the account) that relate to group membership occur (in say, domain A), there needs to be a way for the referenced object to be updated (in say, domain B).

The Infrastructure Master role is responsible for updating the referenced objects whenever changes are made in the source domain. The first DC built in each domain will assume, by default, the Infrastructure Master role, and this role is thus said to be domainwide.

Placement

Having examined the functions and roles placed by each FSMO, it becomes apparent that certain FSMOs need to be placed in appropriate places throughout the enterprise, so that Active Directory can operate in an optimized fashion. The default holder of all domain FSMO roles is the first DC built into the domain, and the default holder of the forest FSMO roles is the first DC built into the forest. These defaults might not be appropriate in your organization. The following section examines these placement requirements and best practices and makes suggestions that should be kept in mind when DC and FSMO placement strategies are being designed.

Domain Naming Master

The Domain Naming Master role will be housed on the first DC built in the forest, by default. Rules and best practices are described in Table 7.21.

Table 7.21 Domain Naming Master Placement Guidelines

Recommendation	Explanation
It is highly recommended that this FSMO role be housed on a DC in the forest root domain.	This approach makes for an environment that is easier to administer and manage.
The role *must* be housed on a DC that is also a GC server, unless the Active Directory forest functionality level has been raised to Windows Server 2003 level.	This ensures that the Domain Naming Master has a partial copy of all nonlocal domains in the forest.
The Domain Naming Master role should be located on the same DC that houses the Schema Master role.	Both forestwide FSMO roles are rarely used and need to be tightly controlled and managed. This can be done by placing both forestwide roles on the same DC.
The Domain Naming Master should be located physically near to where domain creations and removals are to occur.	If the role is located on a DC with poor connectivity, issues or delays might occur during the creation or removal of domains in the forest.

Schema Master

The Schema Master role will be housed on the first DC built in the forest by default Rules and best practices are described in Table 7.22.

Table 7.22 Schema Master Placement Guidelines

Recommendation	Explanation
It is highly recommended that this FSMO role be housed on a DC in the forest root domain.	This approach makes for an environment that is easier to administer and manage.
The Schema Master role should be located on the same DC that houses the Domain Naming Master role.	Both forestwide FSMO roles are rarely used and need to be tightly controlled and managed. This can be done by placing both forestwide roles on the same DC.
The Schema Master role should be located physically near to the user or application that will be responsible for making schema changes.	If the role is located on a DC with poor connectivity, issues or delays might occur when schema modifications are being made.

Primary Domain Controller Emulator

The PDCe role will be housed on the first DC built in each domain in the forest by default. Rules and best practices are described in Table 7.23.

Table 7.23 Primary Domain Controller Emulator Placement Guidelines

Recommendation	Explanation
If the PDCe and RID Master roles can safely be housed on the same DC, then place the PDCe and RID Master roles on the same DC.	Legacy clients such as Windows 9x and Windows NT will target the PDCe for the creation of new security principals. As a result, the PDCe might be a large consumer of RIDs, thus requiring good connectivity to the RID Master.
If the load on the PDCe role dictates that it be separated from the RID Master role, then ensure that the PDCe and RID Master roles are located in the same site, with direct replication links.	If the PDCe and RID Master need to be split over separate DCs, they should be well connected so that the PDCe can replenish its RID pool in a timely fashion, given that the PDCe might prove to be a large consumer of RIDs in the domain.
Place the PDCe role at or near the largest site according to user population.	Because the PDCe receives password and account lockout changes from all other DCs, this role should be located near to the largest user community so that any latency-related issues are minimized. It is likely that this location also houses the administrators of the domain and those responsible for Group Policy. It is also recommended that the PDCe role be located near to these administrators so that changes to GPOs occur in a timely fashion.

RID Master

The RID Master role will be housed on the first DC built in each domain in the forest by default. Rules and best practices are described in Table 7.24.

Table 7.24 RID Master Placement Guidelines

Recommendation	Explanation
If the PDCe and RID Master roles can safely be housed on the same DC, then place the PDCe and RID Master roles on the same DC.	Legacy clients such as Windows 9x and Windows NT will target the PDCe for the creation of new security principals. As a result, the PDCe might be a large consumer of RIDs, thus requiring good connectivity to the RID Master.
If the load on the PDCe role dictates that it be separated from the RID Master role, then ensure that the PDCe and RID Master roles are located in the same site with direct replication links.	If the PDCe and RID Master need to be split over separate DCs, they should be well connected so that the PDCe can replenish its RID pool in a timely fashion, given that the PDCe might prove to be a large consumer of RIDs in the domain.

Infrastructure Master

The Infrastructure Master role will be housed on the first DC built in each domain in the forest by default. Rules and best practices are described in Table 7.25.

Table 7.25 Infrastructure Master Placement Guidelines

Recommendation	Explanation
If the domain has at least one DC that is not also a GC server, then place the Infrastructure Master role on a DC that is not also a GC server.	In order that the Infrastructure Master can update references made to objects in other domains, it must be located on a DC that is not also a GC server. Because GC servers have partial copies of all nonlocal domains, they are always up to date. The Infrastructure Master role, if housed on a GC, will therefore never become aware of changes made in nonlocal domains and thus never update the objects in its own local domain.
If the forest has only one domain, then the Infrastructure Master role can be placed on any DC in the domain.	In a single domain forest, no references exist between one domain and another, so the Infrastructure Master role is not relevant.
If all DCs in the domain are also GC servers, then the Infrastructure Master role can be placed on any of these DCs.	If all DCs in a domain are also GC servers, then the Infrastructure Master role has no work to do and, again, is irrelevant.

Failover and Recovery

From time to time, FSMO roles will need to be relocated from one DC to another. This might be due to planned maintenance and therefore a reboot of a DC, or an unplanned software or hardware failure, which requires changes to be made to the DC such that it is unavailable for a period of time. In either case, the availability of the FSMO role affected by the downtime of the DC in question must be minimized to reduce impact on the Active Directory environment. This can be done only if the processes governing FSMO role transfer are understood.

If it is known in advance that a DC will be unavailable for a period of time, then the roles it hosts can be transferred in a graceful and controlled manner. If, however, a DC fails without prior warning, then the roles it holds cannot be moved gracefully and instead are seized using "brute force." Both methods of moving FSMO roles—transferring and seizing—are described further in the *Role Transfer* and *Role Seizure* sections, respectively. This is then followed by a description of standby servers, which are designated as available to receive FSMO roles in the event of a failure. Finally, the repercussions of moving each of the five roles are examined in more detail in the *Best Practices* section.

Role Transfer

The preferred method of moving FSMO roles from one DC to another is to transfer the role. When a role is transferred, the current role holder and the proposed role holder are able to replicate any pending Active Directory changes, before finally transferring the role itself. This ensures that any outstanding changes not yet replicated to other DCs are passed on to the DC receiving the FSMO role. A FSMO role should be transferred if the hosting DC is to be made unavailable for an extended period of time; for example, during a hardware upgrade.

Roles can be transferred using either the appropriate Microsoft Management Console (MMC) snap-in or using the command-line utility ntdsutil. More details regarding the methods available for transferring and seizing each FSMO role can be found in Table 7.26. Alternatively, when a DC is demoted, it will transfer all its FSMO roles to another suitable DC. Domainwide roles will be transferred to another DC in the same domain, while forestwide roles will be transferred to a DC in the same domain, or any DC in the forest if necessary.

Role Seizure

The alternative to transferring FSMO roles is role seizure. A role should be seized only if the current role holder cannot be contacted to transfer the role in a graceful manner. For example, if a DC experiences a serious hardware failure and is expected to be unavailable, then any roles it hosts that need to be moved will need to be seized, because they cannot be transferred online.

A role must be seized only as a last resort. Depending on the role in question, the effects of being without a role for a period of time can be negligible, but the ramifications of seizing a role and then bringing the original role holder back online can be catastrophic. The seizure of each role is discussed in more detail in the *Best Practices* section.

Standby Servers

FSMO roles are housed on precisely one DC at any one point in time. If the DC housing one or more FSMO roles fails, there is no way to automate the failover of the roles to another DC. Instead, if the role needs to be moved to another DC, for whatever reason, it must be done manually.

This failover can be facilitated with the use of standby servers. These servers do not have any special properties within Active Directory. The FSMO roles are not automatically failed over to these standby servers. Instead, in the event of a failure, FSMO roles are manually moved to one or more standby servers, which are "waiting in the wings" ready to assume ownership of FSMO roles.

It is suggested, therefore, that DCs be identified in each domain that are to assume FSMO roles in the event of a failure of a FSMO role holder in that same domain. To further enhance disaster recovery, consider placing the standby DC in an alternative location so that FSMO roles can be seized even in the event of a location-specific disaster.

It is further suggested that the standby servers have manual connection objects established with the FSMO role holders. This ensures that the standby servers and the FSMO role holders replicate in a timely fashion, and that, in the event of a seizure, one can be confident that the standby servers and FSMO role holders are synchronized with respect to FSMO data.

Best Practices

FSMO roles exist because certain operations must occur only on one DC, as opposed to any DC, so that conflicts are avoided. However, if a role is seized, one faces the dilemma of whether the original role holder can be brought online again in such a way in which the environment is not adversely affected. Table 7.26 addresses the issue of how best to handle a role seizure for each of the five FSMO roles. For each FSMO role, the following aspects of role transfer and seizure are discussed:

- **Repercussions of role not being available** Naturally, because certain operations can occur only on one DC in the forest or domain, if a role is unavailable, then the corresponding operations might not be performed. This aspect of Table 7.26 describes the functions that will not be available and the potential repercussions that might be experienced.

- **Ramifications of incorrect transfer or seizure** Incorrect transfer or seizure of a role can result in two DCs both assuming the same FSMO role and both allowing FSMO-related functions to occur on their local copies of the Active Directory database. The ramifications of such a scenario are described.

- **Recommended seizure procedures** In the event that a role must be seized as a last resort, it is important that the original role be brought back online only if the impact on the environment is minimal. Best practice recommendations are described for bringing an original role holder back online.

- **Impact** Where applicable, the potential impact for a given scenario is provided. High implies that the environment might be so adversely affected that large sections of the forest might need to be rebuilt. Medium implies that adverse conditions might exist but they can be resolved either in time or through remedial steps. Low implies that little or no impact will be realized, and that the changes or loss of service will not been noticed within the environment, unless under specific circumstances (detailed in Table 7.26).

- **Risk** Where applicable, the potential risk associated with a given scenario is stated. This is based on the probability of a particular scenario actually occurring. For example, the probability that two DCs both assume a particular FSMO role and that the same operation is performed on both DCs, thus resulting in a conflict, is generally very small and thus the resulting risk is also small.

Table 7.26 FSMO Role Transfer and Seizure Best Practices

Flexible Single Master Operation Role	Repercussions of Role Not Being Available	Ramifications of Incorrect Transfer or Seizure	Recommended Seizure Procedures	Available Transfer and Seizure Options
Schema Master	Changes cannot be made to the schema. Minimal impact and low risk (because schema changes occur rarely).	Two Schema Masters might exist at the same time, resulting in potentially conflicting schema changes being made. The schema might thus be corrupted. Huge impact but low risk (because schema changes occur rarely).	Never bring the original role holder back online. A corrupt schema might result that requires a rebuild of the entire forest. Instead, rebuild the old FSMO role holder and bring it back online as a new DC.	Seizure—via ntdsutil. Transfer—via ntdsutil or the Active Directory Schema MMC snap-in. Membership of the Schema Admins group is required.
Domain Naming Master	Domains cannot be added or removed from the forest. Minimal impact and low risk (because domain changes occur rarely).	Two Domain Naming Masters might exist and thus two domains might be created with the same name, or a domain might be removed on one role holder but not on the other FSMO holder. Huge impact but low risk (because domain changes occur rarely).	Never bring the original FSMO role holder back online. Domains might need to be rebuilt. Instead, rebuild the old FSMO role holder and bring it back online as a new DC.	Seizure—via ntdsutil. Transfer—via ntdsutil or the Active Directory Domains and Trusts MMC snap-in. Membership of the Enterprise Admins group or the root domain Domain Admins group is required.

Continued

Table 7.26 FSMO Role Transfer and Seizure Best Practices (Continued)

Flexible Single Master Operation Role	Repercussions of Role Not Being Available	Ramifications of Incorrect Transfer or Seizure	Recommended Seizure Procedures	Available Transfer and Seizure Options
PDC Emulator	Pre-Windows 2000 clients (without the DNS client installed) cannot log on or change passwords, and Windows NT BDCs are unable to replicate. Impact and risk depend on the number of legacy clients and BDCs. Group Policy changes might fail unless focus is changed to another DC, in which case, conflicting changes can be made to the same Group Policy.	Password validation might succeed or fail at random, and password changes can take longer to replicate. Medium impact but low risk.	Bring the original role holder back online, but expect a period of erratic password validation behavior. Normal behavior will resume, however, with no damage to the environment.	Seizure—via ntdsutil. Transfer—via ntdsutil or the Active Directory Users and Computers MMC snap-in. Membership of the Domain Admins group is required.
Infrastructure Master	Group memberships will not be updated when users are added to groups in other domains. Impact is likely to be minimal and risk is minimal.	Group memberships might be displayed incorrectly after changes are made in another domain. Impact is likely to be minimal and risk is minimal.	Bring the original role holder back online. Group membership changes will be updated and no damage will occur to the environment.	Seizure—via ntdsutil. Transfer—via ntdsutil or the Active Directory Users and Computers MMC snap-in. Membership of the Domain Admins group is required.

Continued

Table 7.26 FSMO Role Transfer and Seizure Best Practices (Continued)

Flexible Single Master Operation Role	Repercussions of Role Not Being Available	Ramifications of Incorrect Transfer or Seizure	Recommended Seizure Procedures	Available Transfer and Seizure Options
RID Master	DC's pool of 500 RIDs will be exhausted and no new security principals can be created. Large impact but low risk.	Two RID Masters might allocate the same RID pool to different DCs, resulting in corruption within the domain. Huge impact but low risk.	Never bring the original role holder back online. The domain might need to be rebuilt. Instead, rebuild the old FSMO role holder and bring it back online as a new DC.	Seizure—via ntdsutil. Transfer—via ntdsutil or the Active Directory Users and Computers MMC snap-in. Membership of the Domain Admins group is required.

TEST DAY TIP

If all DCs in the domain are also GC servers, then the impact and risk of being without an Infrastructure Master role for even an extended period are nil.

EXAM WARNING

Naturally, in the event of a disaster, all FSMO roles in the forest might need to be seized regardless of the impact, risk, or best practices just described. If such a disaster occurs, you should refer to the Microsoft white paper "Active Directory Disaster Recovery," which describes how to safely seize roles in such a scenario. This paper can be found at *www.microsoft.com/windows2000/techinfo/administration/activedirectory/addrstep.asp*.

Summary of Exam Objectives

Windows Server 2003 and Active Directory represent a distributed system, which uses multimaster replication of Active Directory data. For this complex system to perform in an optimum manner within your organization, it is essential that the components offering Active Directory services are configured and placed in appropriate locations throughout your organization.

The location, number, and configuration of DCs can greatly affect startup and logon times, because clients often need to process multiple scripts and/or Group Policies during the boot phase.

Although it is important to consider the users and their requirements, we also need to be aware that certain political, technical, and administrative issues (or even regulations) might be present within our organization. If this is the case, then these issues must also be factored in to our placement of service designs so that we adhere to any laws or regulations (appropriate to the type of business conducted) and meet the internal rules in place within the company.

Once we understand our requirements and the rules that must be adhered to, we need an implementation plan that describes and governs the implementation of Active Directory. This is important for a number of reasons. It helps manage the rollout and ensure that it occurs in a timely but controlled fashion that minimizes disruption to the organization during the implementation phase. Naturally, as part of this process, a method for installing and promoting servers to DC status should be defined so that the process can be repeated a number of times in a similar fashion.

In conjunction with placing services (such as DC and GC servers) throughout the organization, we saw how best to size these components to meet both current and future needs. DCs, GC servers, and DNS servers are often housed on the same physical server, yet each has different sizing and configuration needs. It is therefore important to understand the needs of the different roles and to configure server hardware and operating systems appropriately.

No design would be complete without discussing FSMO roles, their relevance, and how they should best be placed and managed. Although Active Directory uses a multimaster replication topology, certain events are managed in a single master fashion. These events are often critical to the organization, such as password changes, and so the availability of the FSMO roles and their hosting DCs is of paramount importance.

Exam Objectives Fast Track

The Planning Phase

- ☑ Identify locations that require self-sufficiency.

- ☑ Identify Active Directory-aware applications and their requirements.

- ☑ Understand the effects on logon time that service placement can have.

- ☑ Assess your organization's user populations.

- ☑ Understand what other factors affect service placement and how they might alter the placement design.

- ☑ Create an algorithm to be used to assign service components, which includes all factors understood to exist in your organization.

- ☑ Assess which other factors exist that might influence the schedule for deployment of infrastructure, such as any desktop deployments.

- ☑ Create an implementation plan.

Sizing and Availability

- ☑ Carefully forecast the size of the Active Directory database.

- ☑ Choose an appropriate hardware specification for DCs, GC servers, and DNS servers.

- ☑ Select an appropriate DC promotion process.

- ☑ Understand the rules that govern FSMO role placement.

- ☑ Choose appropriate locations for FSMO roles and plan for FSMO role holder failures.

- ☑ Understand the rules and ramifications of seizing and transferring FSMO roles.

Exam Objectives
Frequently Asked Questions

The following Frequently Asked Questions, answered by the authors of this book, are designed to both measure your understanding of the Exam Objectives presented in this chapter, and to assist you with real-life implementation of these concepts. You will also gain access to thousands of other FAQs at *www.ITFAQnet.com*.

Q: Why do Active Directory-aware applications affect service placement designs?

A: Active Directory-aware applications often require frequent and efficient access to a DC and/or GC server.

Q: Why do self-sufficient locations require infrastructure components?

A: Self-sufficient locations need access to Active Directory 24x7, regardless of WAN link failures. This can be achieved only if infrastructure is deployed locally.

Q: Why is it important to understand user population distribution?

A: Locations that house fewer users generally have less of a need for infrastructure than do locations with larger user populations. It is therefore important to understand where users are located and in what numbers.

Q: Why must I understand service levels when designing service placement?

A: Having assessed locations and user populations, it might be found that service levels dictate that a certain location must have 24x7 access to infrastructure components. This requirement will, therefore, influence service placement.

Q: Why is a project plan required when deploying infrastructure?

A: It is common for Active Directory infrastructure to be deployed to coincide with and support another deployment, such as a desktop or messaging implementation. A plan must be constructed that ensures that components are deployed as appropriate.

Q: Why should I consider automating the DC promotion process?

A: If automated, the DC promotion process does not require that an administrator perform the promotion and also removes any issues due to human error.

Q: What additional disk space requirements does the GC server have?

A: A GC stores a complete copy of its local domain and a copy of all objects from the other domains in the forest. It does not store all attributes and properties for the objects from these other domains, only the ones most likely to be used in a search.

Q: What additional RAM requirements does the DNS server service have?

A: The DNS server service requires 100 bytes of RAM per DNS resource record.

Q: When choosing a location for the Domain Naming Master FSMO role, what rules must I adhere to?

A: The Domain Naming Master FSMO must reside on a DC that is also a GC server.

Q: What other FSMO rules must be adhered to when placing FSMO roles?

A: The Infrastructure Master must not reside on a GC server, unless all DCs in the domain are GC servers.

Q: What are the ramifications of the RID Master FSMO role being unavailable?

A: DCs that exhaust their RID pool will not be able to request further RIDs and therefore will not be able to create additional security principals (for example, users and groups).

Q: Which FSMO roles can I safely bring back online, having previously seized the role?

A: The PDCe and Infrastructure Master FSMO roles can both be safely brought back online after a role seizure.

Self Test

A Quick Answer Key follows the Self Test questions. For complete questions, answers, and explanations to the Self Test questions in this chapter as well as the other chapters in this book, see the Self Test Appendix.

1. Your organization has many disparate locations. You have been tasked with designing Active Directory infrastructure placement. Which of the following might influence your design? (Choose all that apply.)

    A. User populations

    B. Available bandwidth

    C. Physical security

    D. Existing service levels

2. While assessing locations within your organization, you note that different locations can provide different levels of physical security for your DCs. Which of the following conditions should be met by a location being considered to receive a DC? (Choose all that apply.)

    A. A locked server cabinet

    B. A separate cabinet in which only the DC(s) are housed

    C. A lockable communications room

    D. A server located at the administrator's desk, for ease of administration

3. You have been tasked with estimating the size of the Active Directory database within each domain in your Active Directory forest. Which of the following algorithms or tools should be adopted when calculating this estimate? (Choose two.)

    A. Add 400MB for every 1000 users in the domain

    B. Assume an upper limit of 1GB

    C. Monitor the database size during deployment and use trend analysis

    D. Use the Microsoft Active Directory Sizer utility

4. You are a systems architect and have been tasked with designing the optimum configuration for the DCs within your organization. Which of the following disk configurations offers the optimum performance for a Windows Server 2003 DC, while offering high availability?

A. Database and SYSVOL using RAID 1, log files using RAID 1

B. Database and SYSVOL using RAID 0, log files using RAID 1

C. Database and SYSVOL using RAID 5, log files using RAID 1

D. Database and SYSVOL using RAID 5, log files using RAID 5

5. You are the Domain Administrator in an Active Directory domain. You have been tasked with promoting a member server to a DC in an existing domain. Which of the following checks and changes should be performed at the member server before the promotion begins? (Choose all that apply.)

A. Check event logs for errors

B. Check DNS connectivity

C. Disable the DHCP client service

D. Check connectivity to the RID Master FSMO role

6. A new DC needs to be created. Which command can be executed to initiate a manual server promotion at the appropriate member server?

A. promote.exe

B. dcpromo.exe

C. server2dc.exe

D. upgrade.exe

7. A new DC needs to be created in a remote office that does not have any onsite administrators. You want to build and promote a new server without granting a local user additional rights, and without traveling to the remote office. Instead, you create an answer file and plan to promote the server automatically once the operating system has been installed. Which command needs to be executed to initiate an automated server promotion?

A. dcpromo /answer:*answerfile.txt*

B. dcpromo /file:*answerfile.txt*

C. dcpromo /answerfile:*answerfile.txt*

D. dcpromo /auto:*answerfile.txt*

8. A server has been promoted to DC status and now needs to be configured as a GC server. Which application is used to configure the DC to act as a GC server?

A. Active Directory Users and Computers

B. Active Directory Domains and Trusts

C. Active Directory Sites and Services

D. Computer Management

9. You have been asked to assess an existing DC as to whether it has enough free disk space to cope with the GC role. What algorithm should you deploy when estimating the disk space requirements for a GC server?

A. Space required = size of local domain partition + ? sum total of all other domain partitions

B. Space required = size of local domain partition + ? sum total of all other domain partitions

C. Space required = size of local domain partition

D. Space required = size of local domain partition + sum total of all other domain partitions

10. You have been tasked with the design and placement of the Active Directory FSMO roles. Which of the following roles are forestwide and thus exist once only within any forest? (Choose all that apply.)

A. RID Master

B. PDC Emulator

C. Domain Naming Master

D. Schema Master

11. You have been asked to promote a new DC and establish a new domain and new domain tree within an existing forest. Which of the existing FSMO roles must be available in order for the promotion to succeed? (Choose all that apply.)

A. RID Master

B. PDC Emulator

C. Domain Naming Master

D. Schema Master

12. The DC housing the PDC Emulator role fails due to a hardware-related issue. It is likely that the hardware fault will take one to two days to fix. How could you, the domain administrator, address the fact that the PDCe role has been lost and ensure that the environment continues to function correctly? (Choose all that apply.)

A. Seize the PDCe role using ntdsutil

B. Seize the PDCe role using the Active Directory Sites and Services interface

C. Seize the PDCe role using the Active Directory Users and Computers interface

D. Promote an existing DC to the role of PDCe

13. The DC hosting the RID Master FSMO role in an Active Directory domain has failed due to a hard disk failure. You have been tasked with ensuring that the hardware fault is fixed and that the RID Master role continues to be available to the remaining DCs in the domain. What steps should you take?

A. Transfer the RID Master role to another DC.

B. Seize the RID Master role to another DC, fix the hardware issue on the original RID Master role holder, and reinstall Windows Server 2003 on that server before introducing it back into the domain.

C. Seize the RID Master role to another DC, fix the hardware issue on the original RID Master role holder, introduce the original role holder to the domain, and transfer the RID Master role back to its original owner.

D. Do not seize or transfer the RID Master role. Fix the hardware issue and boot the DC hosting the RID Master role.

Self Test Quick Answer Key

For complete questions, answers, and explanations to the Self Test questions in this chapter as well as the other chapters in this book, see the Self Test Appendix.

1.	**A, B, C, D**	8.	**C**
2.	**A, B, C**	9.	**B**
3.	**A, D**	10.	**C, D**
4.	**C**	11.	**C**
5.	**A, B, D**	12.	**A, C**
6.	**B**	13.	**B.**
7.	**A**		

Chapter 8

MCSE 70-297

The Physical Design

Exam Objectives in This Chapter:

Introduction

Continuing the theme of physical design, this chapter focuses on the aspect of Active Directory Network Services infrastructure and the considerations relating to physical components. As the previous chapter discussed topics relating to the physical design and placement of the Active Directory Services infrastructure, this chapter focuses more on the practical aspects of networking in support of Active Directory services.

The foundation of networking in any organization is the network topology, which includes routers, switches, network protocols, intranets, extranets, and connectivity to the Internet. If the underlying network is poorly designed or not able to scale to meet business demands, then any infrastructure layered on top will more quickly highlight these limitations and shortcomings.

This chapter begins with a discussion of some of the best practices for designing a network topology, including routing, router placement, Internet connectivity, addressing and subnetting, and firewall considerations. These components all have a bearing on the infrastructure used "on top" of them and therefore require careful consideration when deploying an infrastructure.

Throughout the book we discussed the topology and behavior of a network within the perimeter of the network; however, access to the network from outside that perimeter requires specific attention. This involves the design and implementation of a remote access solution, which when scaled appropriately is robust, secure, flexible, and highly available, yet offers the external users access to all resources they need. We, therefore, discuss the considerations that need to be kept in mind when designing a network topology, such that a remote access solution can easily be integrated into whatever designs are chosen.

Networking and Routing

The first principle of building any reliable and scalable network is assessing and designing a network that can support your current requirements and scale to any future requirements. You need to ensure that you have a supported private internal IP addressing scheme and a properly registered external IP addressing scheme for your network.

Another factor that needs to be considered is how to properly segment the internal and external network. Careful consideration will need to be taken for router placement and security. This topic is discussed in the section *The Network Perimeter*.

Internet Connectivity

Let's first take a look at the external design of your network. In today's networks, Internet connectivity is essential. It provides a means of communication that is both cost effective and expedient. This Internet connectivity is used to support the business in many different ways. An internal network needs to connect to the Internet for such applications as research, e-mail, and e-commerce. It is very important when designing a network that steps are taken to ensure that your organization can connect to the outside and do business, and other organizations and customers can connect to your organization to conduct business. You learn about connecting your business to the Internet in Exercise 8.01.

EXERCISE 8.01

CONNECTING YOUR BUSINESS TO THE INTERNET

This is not a practical exercise where you will be able to walk through the steps in a hands-on fashion at the PC that hosts your newly installed version of Windows Server 2003. Nevertheless, it is an important exercise from the perspective that the knowledge of the steps is important for application in the real world. Certain things must be in place for an organization to be properly connected to the outside world and to be recognized and securely accessible by the public.

1. Assess your organization's business requirements for Internet connectivity. For example, investigate your organization's ability to or desire for hosting its own Web site or e-mail. Perhaps third-party hosting providers will take care of all hosting, and basic connectivity is all that is required.

2. Procure a link to the Internet from your selected telecommunications carrier and apply for a static IP address (or range of addresses), if required. This will most likely require a visit from an installer who will leave you with some networking equipment, such as a router, firewall, remote access device, or some combination of the three, and an active link to the Internet.

3. Ensure that the IP address for the public network is properly configured on the router's public network interface. Make sure that the router's private interface is configured with an IP address on one of your subnets that the entire organization can access. This will be the gateway address for the clients on your internal network.

4. Choose an available domain name that represents your organization and register it with a domain registrar. When choosing a top-level domain (TLD), you should aim to use .com or .biz if your organization is a company, or .org if your organization is a nonprofit group. TLDs are explained in Chapter 5, "Name Resolution."

5. Arrange for DNS hosting so that your newly registered domain name resolves to the IP address that will be used for your e-mail

and Web site hosts (either on your site or with a hosting provider). Your domain registrar usually takes care if this for you.

6.   With a way out for your organization, and perhaps a way in for the public if you went that route, you will need a way to secure the gateway between the private and public networks. Entire shelves of books have been written about firewalls and network security—read a few of them. The importance of securing this connection should never be underestimated. If you are using third-party hosting providers, then the concern over what traffic should be allowed disappears because only outgoing traffic is required and no public incoming traffic is permitted.

7.   Configure the clients on your private network to use the new gateway to the Internet. This can be done by configuring the IP address of the router's private interface as the default gateway in DHCP, or if you have only a handful of clients, it can be manually entered on every workstation.

Additional activities, such as firewall configuration, setting up a demilitarized zone (DMZ), port forwarding, installing a proxy server, traffic logging and auditing, and Web caching have not been covered in these seven basic steps, and would be better covered elsewhere. These steps will get you to the point where your organization can make full use of the Internet, and, if applicable, where the general public can make full use of the services you provide.

Designing the topology requires both a physical and logical approach. The "physical" approach to designing a network topology involves network design that matches the physical, or geographic locations, of your organization. You would use routers to segment the network according to where the clients on your network sit. The alternative to that would be to take a "logical" approach, where your topology would match an organization chart. Using technology embedded in networking hardware, such as virtual LANs (VLANs), you can aggregate individual client connections from many LANs who work together into VLANs. This provides the performance on the same physical LAN to individuals who could be scattered over many. Consequently, you will need to consider best practices in hardware *and* software to ensure that your organization can communicate efficiently and securely with the Internet. Connecting private networks to the Internet creates a whole new set of variables that will need to be considered.

EXAM WARNING

Be sure you have an understanding of the types of equipment and services that you can use to connect an organization to the Internet. The exam might ask you about the best solution for Internet connectivity based on the size of your organization.

For a small organization that does not host its own Web services and e-mail, the solution might be to use cable or digital subscriber line (DSL) to implement Internet connectivity, and use the Web hosting and messaging services offered by its Internet service provider (ISP). A larger organization might have to use a telecommunications carrier to provision it with a higher bandwidth solution, so that it can reliably host its own Internet- and Web-based services at a satisfactory performance level for its employees and for customers. This solution will require higher-end routers and firewalls to support and secure the traffic.

Domain Name Registration

Any organization that wants to conduct business over the Internet needs a domain name. To acquire an appropriate domain name, you need to deal with companies that specialize in registering these for you.

The first thing you need to do is choose a domain name. This will not be easy, because most organizations want a ".com" and most of these are taken. You will also need to research the chosen domain name to ensure that there are not any trademark conflicts. Once you have chosen the name, it is time to register it. There are many different registries available to help you with this. Please check *www.internic.net/alpha.html* for a list of approved registries.

Obtaining a registered domain name is useful for your organization to conduct business on the Internet. It is also useful to have a registered domain name for internal use with Active Directory. Maintaining a registered name internally helps to resolve any conflicts in the future. For example, you create your Active Directory domain with the name company.com, but company.com is already a registered domain name for a business on the Internet. Users on your internal network will probably not be able to access that site because their Web browsers will think it is internal. A good solution is to select an internal domain name with a suffix that is not a TLD (.com, .org, .net, .edu, .mil, and .gov) or any of the country-specific domains, such as .ca for Canada. An appropriate alternative might be a domain that ends in .dpt (for department) or .internal, or any other name that seems appropriate, but differs from a TLD.

Segmenting the Intranet from the Internet

Most organizations use two different yet similar methods of separating the internal network (intranet) from the Internet. Routers are used as both a standalone method and in conjunction with a firewall. Some routers have built-in firewall features to help alleviate having multiple pieces of equipment. Depending on how much work will be required of the router, it might make sense to have a separate firewall to offload the work from the router.

An *intranet* is an internal Web environment that serves an organization's personnel and is generally not accessible to the public. An *extranet* is a means of selectively extending an organization's intranet to individuals and organizations through the Internet who are not physically connected to the organization's network.

Routers will help to route IP traffic in and out of the intranet and Internet. Firewalls are mostly used to filter what IP traffic can pass from the Internet to the intranet. Proxy servers and authentication servers are used for filtering and monitoring what IP traffic flows from the intranet to the Internet. See Figure 8.1 for an example of how this segmentation is achieved with the use of routers with a firewall.

Figure 8.1 Private and Public Segmentation

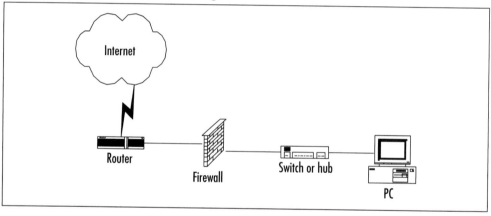

Proxy servers are very beneficial in separating the intranet from the Internet. Proxy servers provide for a means for your organization's users to access the Internet quickly and securely. Proxy servers can use caching to speed Internet access. For example, if User1 accesses *www.microsoft.com*, much of the content from that Web page is cached on the proxy server. When User2 accesses *www.microsoft.com*, User2 will pull some of the content from the local proxy server. This will allow User2 to receive the data at LAN speed. Because proxy servers are an intermediate step in the Internet process, the user's identity is masked behind the proxy server to allow for a more secure experience. Proxy servers also allow you to control what Web sites you don't want your users to access.

To allow internal and external clients to securely access the same resources from the LAN and across the Internet, respectively, place the desired Web infrastructure in a DMZ. A DMZ—also called a perimeter network—is a network segment between an organization's trusted internal network and an untrusted external network such as the Internet. This segment is protected on both sides by firewalls. The term *firewall* comes from the field of automotive manufacturing. In a car or truck, a firewall is the barrier that separates and protects the passenger compartment from the heat and noxious gases of the engine compartment. In networking, a firewall is a barrier between one network and another, typically an internal network and all manners of destruction that lurk on the Internet.

An organization would be wise to locate its Web, mail, and proxy servers that will be accessed by the public in a DMZ. Microsoft Internet Security and Acceleration (ISA) Server is an extensible enterprise firewall and Web cache server that would be suitable for use as both a firewall and a proxy server. A proxy server, like the name suggests, is a server that acts on behalf of other servers. Specifically, a proxy server operates as a relay between the client and server. For example, a proxy server conceals an organization's internal addressing scheme through Network Address Translation (NAT), and accelerates the retrieval of frequently accessed Web pages that are cached in memory on the proxy server. NAT converts the private IP addresses of an internal addressing scheme to one or more public IP addresses for the Internet by altering the packet headers to the new address and keeps track of each session. When packets return to the organization's network, NAT performs the reverse conversion to the IP address.

Exam Warning

Know the types of devices and services that can segment the Internet from an organization's intranet. It is important to know these devices and how they work. Firewalls, routers, proxy servers, RRAS, and NAT are all examples of these devices and services.

Network Topology Definitions

Physical topology is comprised of geometric components that make up the local area network (LAN) or wide area network (WAN). There are three basic physical topologies: bus, ring, and star. Whatever physical topology is used in the environment, the components of that topology are the same:

- **Subnets** A "division of a network into an interconnected, but independent, segment, or domain, in order to improve performance and security. Because traffic is often the heaviest within a department, and Ethernet is the common network technology, the subnet limits the number of nodes (clients, servers) that have to compete for available bandwidth to a confined geographic area" (*www.techweb.com/encyclopedia*).

- **Routers** Devices that interconnect different physical networks to connect these subnets into one or several contiguous networks, depending on how your organization's network architecture is designed.

- **Switches and hubs** Devices used to aggregate network connections from workstations and to connect different network segments within the same physical network. Switches create dedicated connections between network nodes to take advantage of all available bandwidth. Hubs merely connect all nodes together and the available bandwidth is shared.

- **Perimeter defenses** Consist of devices and software that sit at the edge of your network, most commonly between your internal network and the Internet, and protect the integrity of your network by controlling what traffic is allowed to enter and leave. These devices include firewalls, anti-virus scanners and gateways, and virtual private networking (VPN) devices, among others.

Bus Topology

Bus topology uses an open-ended cable in which all network devices are connected. Both ends of this cable must be terminated. Generally, this topology is not used much anymore and is best suited for small networks because it does not require the use of a switch or hub. Support for this topology has become limited in recent times. See Figure 8.2 for an example of bus topology.

Figure 8.2 Bus Topology

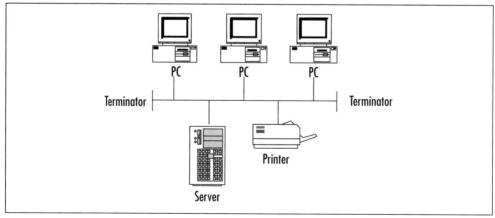

Ring Topology

Ring topology uses a cable that is connected to all network devices, but in a ring formation. In this topology, there is no termination because there are no open ends. In the early days, there was a physical ring (see Figure 8.3). This became a problem because if the ring was broken in any place, your network communication failed. Once IBM introduced Token Ring, a concentrator was used to create a logical ring (see Figure 8.4). In this case, if one of the connections was broken, the ring continued around without losing network communication. There are still networks in existence that use this topology; however, generally, new networks are not designed in this fashion.

Figure 8.3 Physical Ring Topology

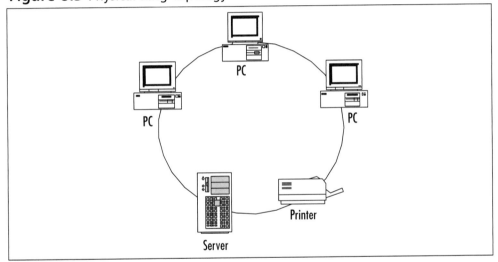

Figure 8.4 Token Ring

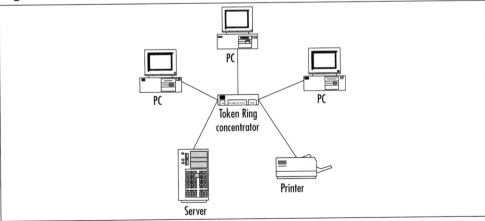

Star Topology

Star topology is the most common physical topology used today. In a star topology, each device is connected centrally to a concentrator (switch or hub). The star topology looks similar to how Token Ring is physically set up. However, the star topology is physically and logically the same. Each device is independently connected to the media and does not have to concern itself with how the other devices are connected. See Figure 8.5 for an example of the star topology.

Figure 8.5 Star Topology

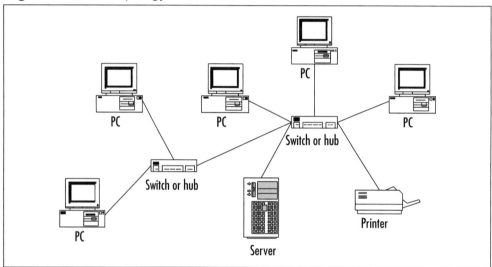

TEST DAY TIP

Do not torture yourself with deliberating about the subject of which topology to use in a new design. The majority of newer networks consist of star topologies. Just know what they are and what they look like.

EXAM
70-297

OBJECTIVE
4.5.1

Segmenting the Organization into Subnets

A subnet is just a way of taking a complete network and reducing it to manageable and optimized chunks. When designing a network, you want to create a network that will be both fast and secure. Creating subnets will help you to achieve this goal by reducing the size of the network and thus help to control network traffic.

In some instances, you will create subnets to separate groups of devices from one another. For example, you might want to have all of your servers on the same subnet.

You might also want to have each floor of your building on a different subnet. Both of these are good practices for creating subnets.

You will also create subnets out of necessity; for example, if your network consists of a WAN. You might have an office in New York City and an office in Philadelphia. These offices will be separated by expensive slow links. This will require the use of separate subnets. In addition, consider the amount of devices you have at each location. For example, if you have 2000 Windows XP Professional desktops at the Philadelphia office, you might have to segment these users into multiple subnets to better manage them.

When segmenting an organization into subnets, you will use routers or devices that can provide routing. You will also require an IP addressing scheme that will make managing the subnets easy. In the section *Addressing and DHCP* we discuss the addressing of the subnets further. In the section *Router Placement*, we discuss the placement of routers and routing devices in more detail.

EXAM WARNING

Segmenting a network will play heavily on this exam. You should know why and how you would segment a network. The "why" can be reasons such as isolating for security to physical separations, such as different buildings or floors.

EXAM
70-297

OBJECTIVE
4.5.3

Addressing and DHCP

The Dynamic Host Configuration Protocol (DHCP) service in Windows Server 2003 is used to provide automatic TCP/IP addressing and management of these addresses. In this section, we discuss what information a designer needs to gather to create a strong DHCP design.

These designs will consist of the three management features supported by DHCP:

- Scopes
- Superscopes
- TCP/IP options

These terms and the concepts behind them are described in depth in Chapter 3, "Developing the Network Services Design."

We will also look at the DHCP server and the DHCP client. It is important to understand the differences and uses of both. DHCP can distribute IP addresses from a pool (scope) of addresses, or it can always give a device the same IP address.

Why Use DHCP?

As networks increase in size and complexity, the need to ease the management of IP addressing becomes increasingly important. DHCP is a service to assign and manage the IP addresses. DHCP is a client/server process. For DHCP to be successful, there needs to be a DHCP server and a DHCP client. Windows Server 2003 can host the DHCP Server service to facilitate the assigning and managing of IP addresses. For each device that you want to automatically manage, there needs to be either a DHCP client or Bootstrap Protocol (BOOTP) Client.

DHCP is a message-based service. The client sends out a request for an address and the server responds to the request with an address. The DHCP server keeps track of what address it gives out. This is done to ensure that duplicate IP addresses are not distributed to the clients.

DHCP Design Requirements

One of the very first things you must consider with designing DHCP is how many hosts are in the environment and how many of them will be using DHCP. Keep in mind that not only your users will be using DHCP. Servers, printers, network devices, and other devices can benefit from the use of DHCP—or should we say that administration would benefit if all devices could use DHCP.

In addition to determining how many hosts are in your environment, you also need to determine how many subnets are required in your network design. These factors will help in determining how many scopes or superscopes you will need to include. Collecting this type of information will help you in the design of your Windows Server 2003 network and with the design of your Active Directory environment.

The first management feature to discuss further is *scopes*. A scope is a range of IP addresses that will be used by a subnet to assign needed IP addresses. These addresses are the first things that are set up and should be the first thing you consider when designing for DHCP.

The second management feature is *superscopes*. Superscopes are a grouping of scopes to support a particular subnet. Superscopes allow for allocating more IP addresses for a subnet without actually extending the scope. An important advantage of superscopes is their ability to use noncontiguous IP address ranges.

Scope options or *TCP/IP options* make up the third management feature of DHCP. These options allow you to create default TCP/IP settings to be delivered to the DHCP client when they receive the IP address assignment. Some of these options include domain name, gateway (router), and DNS servers.

There are four levels for defining these options on a DHCP server.

- **Default global options** These options are applied to all scopes on that DHCP server. By default, there are no global options—the admin must configure them manually.

- **Scope options** These options are applied to a particular defined scope.

- **Class options** If a client has a particular DHCP Class ID, it will receive the specified options. A DHCP Class ID can be set on a client, and then options can be issued from the DHCP server. This becomes useful if, for example, you wanted a particular option for the HR department.

- **Reserved client options** If you create a reservation for an IP address to go to a particular MAC address of a network adapter, then you can also define a particular option to associate with that reservation.

 EXAM WARNING

DHCP design might make up a large part of the exam. You might be asked questions that will require you to design scopes for DHCP. You might even have to provide redundancy for these DHCP servers. Always keep redundancy in your plan.

Head of the Class...

DHCP Superscopes

Let's discuss DHCP superscopes in more detail. Most importantly, why would you design superscopes into your network? Superscopes are used in environments with more than one DHCP server. When designed properly, they will eliminate DHCPNak (negative acknowledgment) that can occur when a scope for a subnet is split between two DHCP servers.

Here is the scenario: A DHCP client will renegotiate its IP address at 50 percent of the lease time with the server it originally received the IP address from. If it cannot renew the IP address at that time because the DHCP server is down or unavailable for some other reason, it will try again at 87.5 percent. This second attempt is called the *Rebuilding* state. This time, it sends a broadcast for the IP address instead of going straight to the DHCP server it originally received it from. If the other DCHP server receives the request, it will check its scope configurations and see that it does not service that IP address in any of its scopes. At that point, it will send the DHCPNak.

To avoid this problem, you can design your DHCP environment to use superscopes. Superscopes allow DHCP servers to have an understanding of the entire DHCP environment—both the scopes they manage and the scopes that other DHCP servers manage. The superscope will contain member

Continued

(Continued)

scopes. These member scopes will be scopes on that DHCP server that have addresses it can give out. Additionally, the superscope will contain scopes with exclusions, which are basically scopes that are live on other DHCP servers and are not controlled by that server.

Going back to our earlier example, when the nonmanaging DHCP server receives the request that was broadcast at the 87.5 percent time frame, the DHCP server will check the superscope for the IP address. When it sees that it is excluded, it will simply ignore the request. This will allow the IP address to finish out its lease and request a new IP address instead of trying to renew the current IP address.

Microsoft DNS Integration

An important feature of Windows Server 2003 DHCP services is that it can integrate with Microsoft DNS. Windows 2000 and later clients can register their IP addresses in DNS for name resolution. However, previous versions of these clients do not have this capability. Microsoft DHCP Server can register their IP addresses for them in Microsoft DNS. Furthermore, Dynamic Update is enabled on the DHCP server so that it will register IP addresses that it gives to the DHCP client with a Microsoft DNS server. By default, this option is not enabled and would need to be considered in your design if you are still supporting down-level clients.

TEST DAY TIP

Due to the features that are available in Active Directory-integrated zones, employing Windows Server 2003 DNS is always the best solution when designing DNS for a homogeneous Microsoft infrastructure. If a question does not specify the use of legacy Windows DNS or a DNS solution from a third party, it is a good bet that this is the solution that an exam will be looking for. Refer to Chapter 5 for a more detailed description of DNS zones and zone transfer.

DHCP Design Best Practices

As with anything, some general best practices and guidelines should be considered when designing a DHCP environment. These are not rules that must be followed, but are some methods of designing and deploying a strong DHCP environment. DHCP server requirements and placement are discussed in depth in Chapter 6, "Remote Access and Address Management."

To provide fault tolerance with DHCP servers, use at least two DHCP servers. You should use the 80/20 rule when creating your scopes. That means that on one

DHCP server, one scope should contain 80 percent of the address in the scope, and the other should contain 20 percent of the address. You will need to ensure that all TCP/IP options are the same on both servers. In addition, if you are using reservations for any of your clients, be sure to create that reservation on both DHCP servers to ensure that it can obtain its address from either DHCP server.

If you are deploying DHCP in a routed environment and there will not be a DHCP server in each of the physical subnets, use routers that support DHCP relaying or BOOTP relaying. If your routers do not support either, you can design a DHCP relay in that subnet. This relay will forward DHCP requests to a DHCP server for assignments.

When deploying DHCP servers, you should use Windows Server 2003. DHCP services under Windows Server 2003 allow for secure updates, authorization of DHCP servers, and Dynamic DNS (DDNS) services. With secure updates, the computer needs to be authenticated in Active Directory before an IP address is issued. With DHCP authorization, someone cannot bring up another Windows 2000 or 2003 DHCP server without authorizing it in Active Directory—to do so requires Domain Admin rights. With DDNS integration, the DHCP server can be set up to update DNS with the current IP address for a workstation that does not have the capability to perform the update.

Addressing

DHCP is useful in managing an IP network, but what addressing do you use? This brings us to the topic of using private and public IP addresses in your network. You need to make sure an appropriate addressing model is used, so as to ensure your network is designed properly.

Should you use a public IP address with your network? Well, this determination comes from examining the needs of your clients. If there is a need for your clients to have public IP addresses, then you will have to ensure that you have enough to satisfy them. In most cases, this is not necessary. It is very difficult to get a large amount of public IP addresses because of the limitation of how many are available. It is better to approach your internal address with the use of private addresses.

RFC 1918 contains ranges of IP addresses that can be used on an internal network. These IP addresses will not be routed on the public Internet, thus eliminating potential conflicts with private IP addresses getting on the public Internet. To use private IP addresses to access resources on the public Internet, you will need to include in your design a means to translate the private IP addresses to public IP addresses. This is done by using Network Address Translation (NAT). Many routers and firewalls support NAT. It is your job to ensure that you choose a router or firewall that supports NAT if you will be using private IP addresses.

Figure 8.6 shows how NAT works. First, PC-1 has an internal IP address of 192.168.1.101. The Internet router has an internal IP address of 192.168.1.1. Both of these IP addresses will not route on the public Internet because they are defined in RFC 1918. The router's public IP address of 222.222.25.1 is a routable IP address. What NAT will do is use the public address for PC-1. It will track on an internal table on the router the translation to ensure that communication between PC-1 and the Internet will occur. It does this by assigning a TCP/IP port number to the 192.168.1.101 address. For example, 192.168.1.101 equals 222.222.25.1 port 11001. Clients outside the router reply to the internal client using 222.222.25.1 port 11001, and the router then translates this to 192.168.1.101 and forwards packets to the internal client.

Figure 8.6 Network Address Translation (NAT)

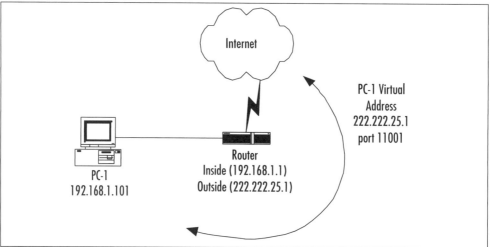

IP Subnetting

In the real world, not every organization is given a public IP address range that will accommodate all devices that require an IP address—there simply are not enough IP addresses to go around. To address this shortage, an organization can do one of two things: use internal addresses from special ranges of IP addresses that are designated for internal, or private use only, or use subnetting of a public IP address to add further scalability within the internal subnets. Let's look at a simple IP subnetting scheme that follows the first approach, which is used in many organizations. For our example, we are talking about Net10.

Net10 comes directly from RFC 1918 (*Address Allocation for Private Internets*). This RFC references current best practice in addressing an organization's intranet without affecting the public Internet. There are three blocks of addresses from which you can choose:

Developing & Deploying...

Continued

(Continued)

- Class A (10.0.0.0–10.255.255.255)
- Class B (172.16.0.0–172.31.255.255)
- Class C (192.168.0.0–192.168.255.255)

We will now discuss how you can use the Class A range (Net10) in defining your organization's subnets. First, the default mask for Net10 is an 8-bit mask (255.0.0.0). Using the default mask would give us one subnet that could support 16,581,375 hosts. This would not meet the needs of most, if any, organizations. What we would require is subnetting, for the purpose of creating more subnets that can contain a small amount of hosts.

The first thing you would need to do is find out how many subnets your organization has or will have. Do not forget to plan for scalability in gathering the amount of subnets needed. Another consideration you will need to gather is the amount of hosts in a subnet. Once we have this information, we can plan our subnet addressing accordingly.

To keep this example simple, we will assume that there are no more than 254 users in a subnet. If this is the case, we can use a 24-bit mask (255.255.255.0). A 24-bit mask will allow for 254 users per subnet and allow for 16,581,375 subnets. This will give you plenty of room for scalability. The following list will give you an idea of the ranges you will use for deployment:

- 10.0.0.1–10.0.0.254 (mask 255.255.255.0)
- 10.0.1.1–10.0.1.254 (mask 255.255.255.0)
- 10.10.0.1–10.0.0.254 (mask 255.255.255.0)
- 10.10.1.1–10.0.1.254 (mask 255.255.255.0)

Router Placement

Router placement in your network is important in controlling access and bandwidth. Let's do a quick review of the need for routers in a network. Routers are used as a border for broadcast domains (subnets). Every device on each side of a router can broadcast information to other devices on the same subnet. These broadcasts can be requests for IP addresses (DHCP requests) so that clients can communicate on the network. They can also be requests for IP addresses for another client via the NetBIOS protocol. By default, routers do not let this traffic pass between the subnets; hence the need for devices such as DHCP relays.

Routers also serve as devices that can route data from one host to another. They use different routing protocols to learn the easiest path from one subnet to another, even across multiple routers. Figure 8.7 is an example of how routers segment a network into different subnets. The router in Figure 8.7 is dividing four subnets. The first subnet is a client subnet in which PC-1 is located—192.168.1.x /24. The /24 represents a 24-bit subnet mask, which is 255.255.255.0. The second subnet is a client subnet in which PC-2 is located—192.168.2.x /24. The third subnet is a server or data center subnet in which the Windows 2003 Server is located—192.168.100.x /24. The last subnet is the Internet—222.222.25.x /24. As you can see in Figure 8.7, the router serves to route traffic between the subnets and to contain broadcasts from traveling across to the subnets.

TEST DAY TIP

Any exam questions on routing will primarily focus on how to use routers to connect disparate subnets; therefore, knowledge of IP addressing and calculating subnets is essential. These subnets could be within the same building or on different continents, but the principles are the same. Know where to place the routers (for example, with the router's interfaces pointing to different subnets) and how to calculate a subnet with enough available hosts to accommodate the number of nodes in a particular location.

Figure 8.7 Router Placement

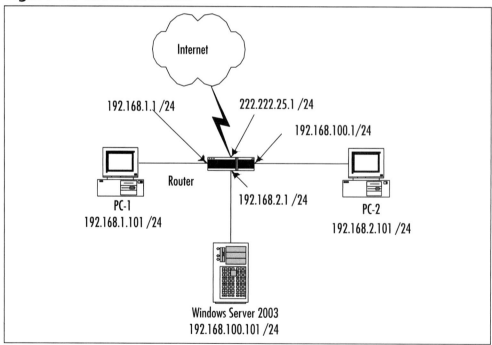

It is important when designing a network that you assess the current router placement or design a new router placement that will provide a fast and stable network. The following are considerations when designing router placement.

- **Performance** You want your clients to communicate with your servers with minimal impact. If you place too much complexity in your design, you can impact the performance of the network. Start simple and grow the design from that point.

- **Redundancy** Examine how downtime can affect the business. If the business cannot tolerate any downtime, you will need to design redundancy into your router placement. This means that you will need to provide multiple paths to the business-critical servers and services. Redundancy can also help with performance.

- **Scalability** It is important that the router placement accommodate growth in the network. You want to install routers that can handle more users and subnets than are currently in the environment.

- **Manageability** Any router you place in the environment must be easy to manage and monitor. It is important that you can proactively gauge performance and potential issues before they happen.

- **Security** One of the main advantages to a router is its ability to provide a security boundary. With a router, you can control what type of traffic can flow through it. When designing the placement of the routers, take into consideration what traffic must flow through the router and what traffic should be blocked. Certain subnets might have special requirements in controlling what flows through. For example, a Human Resources department might require that only the IP address assigned to their workstations be allowed through a router to their servers.

- **Cost** Cost should always be a consideration. Because of budgetary constraints, you need to be realistic in placement of your routers. One router with multiple ports might cost less than multiple routers.

The Network Perimeter

Security is one of the most important aspects of a network design. Protecting your network from the outside is difficult. You need to ensure that you design your network with this protection in mind. We are not just talking about the Internet. There are other ways in which threats can get into your network that need to be considered. Your network perimeter will consist of a combination of firewalls, routers, and, perhaps, remote access equipment.

Your router is your first line of defense against the Internet. You can use IP filtering to control what data gets through to your network. You should also consider a firewall in your design. The firewall will serve as an important device in controlling access to your network. A firewall is designed to better handle network perimeter security than a router can and should always be used in a network design. By design, a firewall inspects incoming and outgoing packets and compares them to a configured set of rules to determine if they should be denied access, dropped, or permitted to pass through to the connected network. A router merely reassigns packets based on the address and port without inspecting the type of packet. Routers can filter by address, but firewalls are much more granular and can filter by MAC address, IP address, TCP and UDP port, and protocol, among others. Therefore, the ability to configure rules for controlling the type of traffic that is permitted to pass through a firewall provides the organization with a much greater degree of control over the integrity of the network and the activity of the clients that connect to it.

Another access into your network can come from dial-up remote access. If there is a need to have dial-in access to your network, you will need to secure this access. You will need to ensure that you allow only dial-in to your network to occur through a device that provides authentication and auditing.

As mentioned earlier, Microsoft ISA Server is a product to consider in this design for securing the network perimeter. This product can provide firewall and dial-up protection for your network. There are also solutions available from other vendors you can consider if ISA does not fit your needs.

TEST DAY TIP

These days, security is job one. That goes for Microsoft solutions as well. Always steer toward answers on the exam that provide a security advantage.

Protecting Active Directory

Network perimeter security planning plays a key role when it comes to Active Directory. Active Directory is the database of many objects in your environment. It houses usernames, computer names, and passwords. It is vital that you create perimeter security to protect this investment. Dangerous elements on the Internet and telephone lines pose a real threat.

If you allow these elements to compromise an Active Directory domain controller (DC), you are giving them the keys to your organization. They can access any information that used Active Directory as its authentication mechanism. Another thing to keep in mind is that if they cannot access the Active Directory DC to gain administrative power, they might be able to crash the DC with denial-of-service (DoS) attacks, resulting in downtime and financial consequences.

A best practice to protecting your Active Directory is not to have it exposed to the Internet. Keep it behind a firewall and safe from those dangerous elements. Use a tier approach if you need to authenticate to Active Directory from the Internet. One example of this would be the RADIUS server discussed in the section *Designing Requirements for Remote Access Infrastructures*.

EXAM 70-297

OBJECTIVE 4.6 4.6.2

Designing Requirements for Remote Access Infrastructures

Let's face it, today, almost every organization needs a way for its clients to connect to the internal, private network when they are not in the office. These connections are necessary for accessing files and checking e-mail, among other things. When you design these solutions, you need to determine what type of access will be required. The following are questions you will need to ask when beginning to design your remote access infrastructure:

- Will the clients require VPN or will they dial in directly?

- Will partners need to access your network?

- Will the WAN design require the use of the Internet to piece it together using VPNs?

- Will there be a need for demand dialing to connect to remote offices?

Remote access solutions have broad requirements for design and implementation. We will dive in a little deeper to determine the requirements for a remote access design. We will discuss why you need a remote access solution and what information you need to collect to design the solution. We will discuss the perimeter requirements to ensure that the designs can securely accommodate connections from outside the network. We will discuss what is required to allow partners to connect from an extranet perspective.

Finally, we will discuss what is required to establish the remote access solution within the company. This will incorporate how the design interfaces with the current or proposed environment.

Design Requirements

Before designing what hardware and/or software you would need for the remote access solution, you need to determine how your remote access solution will be used. There is certain data you need to collect to ensure you are designing a remote access solution that will fit the needs of the environment and meet the needs of the future.

The first question you need to answer is, how many clients will need to access the network remotely? A good rule of thumb is determining how many clients have notebook computers. These users are mobile for a reason. It will also help to find out if there are any work-at-home users. The organization might have supplied these users with home workstations that will connect back to the environment. You will need this information so you can scale the server(s) to meet the demand.

The next question you need to answer is, are there any partners who will require access to your network environment? If so, what do they need access to? With this information, you can determine how to properly design the VPN and/or dial-up access to allow partners to get to the necessary information. This can also work in reverse. You might have to design the solution to allow a connection to come from your network and access information on the partner's network. In that case, you will need to ensure that the partners can't come back into your network from theirs while the connection is established.

Next, will there be any sites that will require a VPN or dial-in solution to connect them to the network? This is very important because you might have business needs that require these remote sites to deliver or obtain data from the main network. This data might be e-mail or even Active Directory authentication. The solution you might have to establish could be dial-on-demand using VPN, ISDN, or analog telephone lines.

As you can see, there are many pieces of information you need to collect in determining the design requirements for the remote access solution. Next, we will discuss what hardware and software requirements will be needed to make the design work.

Perimeter Requirements

The perimeter is the point at which all remote access will flow into your network environment. Whether access is coming in from your clients or partners for dial-in or VPN, they will access your network through the perimeter. Let's look at what is needed at the perimeter to establish a remote access solution.

Windows Server 2003 is a good solution for implementing on the perimeter to support the remote access solution and provide security for this solution. Windows Server 2003 right out of the box can support dial-in access and VPN access by using Routing and Remote Access Server (RRAS). It can also provide TCP/IP filtering to help protect it from intruders. This is important because it will be located at the perimeter of the network.

Figure 8.8 shows how Windows Server 2003 can be used at the perimeter of the network. Each step in the following list follows the numbering in Figure 8.8:

1. The laptop user connects to the Internet.

2. The user initiates a VPN connection that is routed to your network via the Internet.

3. The perimeter router allows the VPN session through to terminate on the Windows Server 2003 RRAS server.

4. The user is a virtual node on the same local network as the Microsoft Exchange 2000 Server and can retrieve his or her e-mail.

Figure 8.8 Windows 2003 Server RRAS

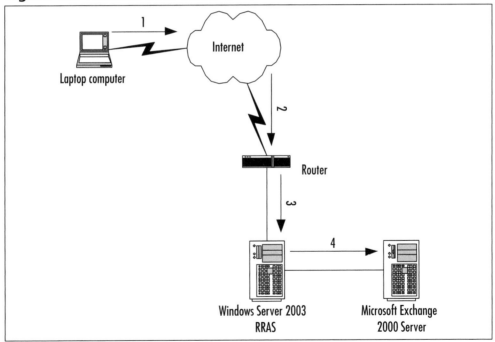

Extranet Requirements

To support an extranet, you and your selected partners need to ensure that you are using a secure remote access solution and that they are using methods for connecting to your network that are compatible with your remote access solution. This could be a Web browser, but you might find that the best solution is typically a site-to-site VPN. Windows Server 2003 can provide this solution with the use of RRAS and dial-on-demand.

Figure 8.9 shows how the site-to-site VPN works. In Step 1, when traffic that is destined for your network from your partner's network occurs, using the existing Internet connection, a VPN connection is initiated from your partner's Windows Server 2003 RRAS. In Step 2, the VPN connection is established with your Windows Server 2003 RRAS. This is done with the assistance of dial-on-demand and can occur in either direction.

Figure 8.9 Site-to-Site VPN

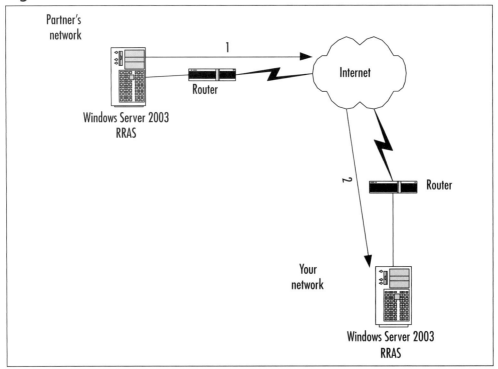

Intranet Authentication Requirements

To support a secure remote access solution, you need to establish authentication. To support authentication, you will have requirements on your intranet that will be accessed from the perimeter remote access solutions.

You have two choices for authentication:

- Windows Authentication
- Remote Authentication Dial-In User Service (RADIUS)

Windows Authentication

If you are planning on only one RRAS server, then using Windows Authentication will suffice. Your Windows Server 2003 with RRAS will use Active Directory for authentication if it is a member server. If it is a standalone server, it will use its internal user database.

Figure 8.10 shows an example of Windows Server 2003 RRAS as a member server and the steps a user would take to make a secure connection from outside the network.

1. The laptop user connects to the Internet.
2. The user initiates a VPN connection that is routed to your network via the Internet.
3. The perimeter router allows the VPN session through to terminate on the Windows Server 2003 RRAS server.
4. The Windows Server 2003 RRAS server used Windows Authentication to authenticate the user with the Active Directory DC.
5. Authentication is approved and the user's VPN is established.
6. The user is virtually a node on the network and can connect to the Microsoft Exchange 2000 Server to retrieve e-mail.

Figure 8.10 Windows Authentication

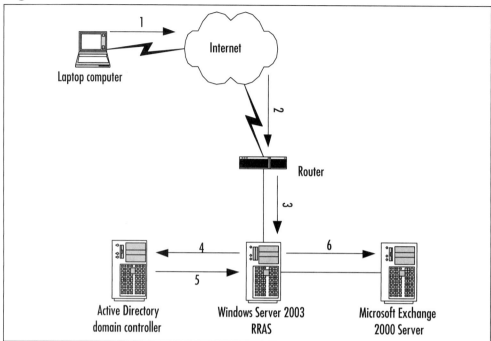

RADIUS

If you are planning to incorporate more than one RRAS server, then Windows Server 2003 should be configured to use RADIUS for authentication purposes. RADIUS is an access control protocol that uses a challenge/response method for authentication. Each Windows Server 2003 RRAS server acts as a RADIUS client. Each of these RADIUS clients authenticates via a top-level RADIUS server, which itself can then authenticate to Active Directory.

Figure 8.11 shows an example of Windows Server 2003 in a RADIUS setup.

1. The laptop user connects to the Internet.

2. The user initiates a VPN connection that is routed to your network via the Internet.

3. The perimeter router allows the VPN session through to terminate on the Windows Server 2003 RRAS server.

4. The Windows Server 2003 RRAS server uses the RADIUS client to authenticate the user with the RADIUS server.

5. The RADIUS server authenticates the user with the Active Directory DC.

6. The authentication approval is sent back to the RADIUS server.

7. Authentication is approved at the RADIUS client and the user's VPN is established.

8. The user is a virtual node on the network and can connect to the Microsoft Exchange 2000 Server to retrieve e-mail.

Figure 8.11 RADIUS Authentication

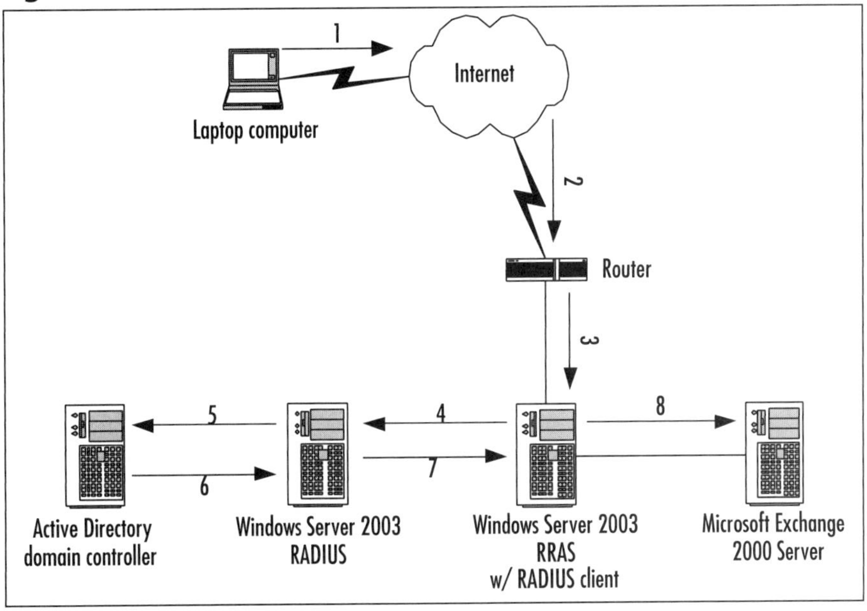

RADIUS Policies

Another intranet requirement is policies. RRAS policies allow you to control connection times, user and group access, connection security, and others. Using these policies is beneficial for creating a secure RRAS environment. There might be a time of day in which you do not want users to connect because of maintenance. You might also want to force users to use L2TP instead of PPTP for security reasons. Policies allow you to control how you want clients to connect to your organization's network. This is discussed in greater detail in Chapter 6.

⚠ EXAM WARNING

Know when to use RADIUS servers. Keep in mind that it depends on the complexity of the RAS solution and the size of the organization.

Determining Sizing and Availability of Remote Access Infrastructure

Now that we know what we need to design a remote access solution, we have to determine how much of it we require. As with designing any network, you need to know how it is going to be used. You also need to know how many hosts will be using the network. The same goes for remote access.

Let's now look at some of the best practices and principles for sizing the remote access solution. We are going to determine what and where we should place these solutions. We are also going to examine the level of scalability and availability we need to design into the solution.

Sizing Remote Access Components

How many and how powerful should your remote access components be to support your environment? Well, the first thing you need to determine is how many users will need to connect remotely via VPN and/or dial-in. You will also need to determine any other remote access clients, such as site-to-site. This is the starting point for sizing.

Many network designs today tend not to use dial-in because of cost and speed. A better choice is VPN because it does not require the provisioning of additional analog or ISDN lines within the company. With the advent of cable modems and DSL, many companies and users prefer VPN for accessing the organization's network.

Sizing for remote access is a difficult task. A general rule-of-thumb is the 8:1 rule; that is, for every eight users, you should provide one port (dial-in or VPN). Given that rule, you must after implementation monitor these ports to determine that they require being increased. Windows Server 2003 can support 1000 concurrent VPN connections, which equates to 8000 users per server. Keep in mind that this would require robust server hardware in a configuration that is carefully managed and monitored.

Placing Remote Access Components

We covered the requirements for placing remote access components earlier in Sections 4.6 and 4.62.

Now let's look at where we should place these devices and why. It is important that we place these devices where they can function efficiently and securely. Functionality and security is always a constant trade-off. For example, a network can be locked down to the point where it is barely usable. Alternatively, security measures can be ignored to give clients the greatest degree of latitude in using the network; however, the network could be easily crippled by an attack, rendering it nonoperational. The art of designing any system that has a security aspect associated with it is to get the right balance between security and operation.

If we are dealing with a Windows Server 2003 server that is providing only dial-in access to the network, then it makes sense to place this server inside the network perimeter. Because users are only dialing into the server, we do not have to worry about many of the attacks that could be waged from the Internet. For someone to penetrate the network via this type of server they would need to first be authenticated.

If we are deploying a Windows Server 2003 server that is providing VPN access to the network, it should be placed in a DMZ behind a firewall. This will help to protect the server from most attacks, and the DMZ will isolate the inside network

Figure 8.12 Securing a VPN Server

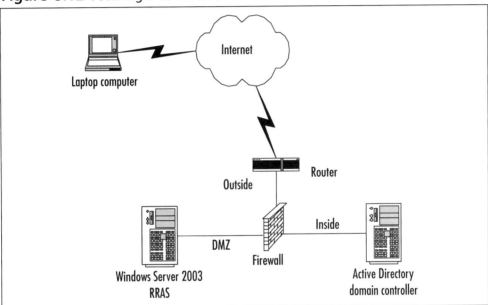

from that server in the event it is compromised. See Figure 8.12 for an example.

To reduce cost for connecting remote offices, you can design dial-on-demand routing into your infrastructure. Windows 2003 RRAS server can support dial-on-demand routing. To use dial-on-demand, you need to install RRAS and set it to detect requests beyond the local subnets. This is done by using the RRAS server as a gateway. A gateway is merely a point of access from one network to another. In this context, the RRAS server will initiate and receive outgoing and incoming dial-up connections to another similarly configured server on the perimeter of another network. When a connection needs to be established, it will connect to the destination according to the routing table. Encryption can be used with dial-on-demand. You have a choice for the connection: "no encryption," "optional encryption," or "require encryption." The encryption will work only if it is connecting to another Windows 2000 or Windows Server 2003 RRAS server.

Providing Scalability, Availability, and Failover

It is important that you provide a remote access solution that can scale for the future. A good start is the use of Windows Server 2003. Because each server is capable of providing up to 1000 concurrent VPN connections, you have a solution that is scalable. What will become important is that you provide the scalability in the hardware to ensure that the server can maintain more connections than are required. Monitoring the server's system resources is the key to maintaining this availability.

When installing RRAS on a server, you will be given the choice of creating a pool of IP addresses to give to clients or to use DHCP for IP addressing. A safe bet is to use DHCP for IP addressing. Using DHCP will allow you to better manage your organization's IP addressing. The RRAS server will reserve 10 IP addresses from the DHCP server when the service starts. Once these are used up, it will reserve another 10 IP addresses. If your RRAS server is located where it does not have access to the DHCP server, then you might want to provide a pool of addresses for the RRAS server to use for clients.

Availability and failover go hand-in-hand. To ensure availability, you need to provide the means for failover. The easiest way to do so is to provide multiple remote access servers. You can then either provide users with multiple remote access entries or with a dial-in solution and a VPN solution. Giving them both choices will help to lessen the impact of a failure.

Another consideration for remote access availability and failover is providing dial-on-demand for backing up routers. For example, you can use RRAS to provide a backup if your Internet connection goes down. With dial-on-demand, you can use asynchronous telephone lines, cable, DSL, X.25, or ISDN to provide the dialing access. These connections will need to be set up, and in the case of cable or DSL, you might need to establish a VPN if the connection will be to another site via a site-to-site VPN.

Summary of Exam Objectives

This chapter covered one of the most important parts of designing a network and Active Directory. Without a good physical assessment and design, you cannot be successful in designing the logical network and Active Directory. These things need to be in place before moving forward.

One of the first sections we discussed was *Networking and Routing*. This section encompassed the physical aspect of how we are going to communicate within our network and beyond. This included Internet connectivity, where we talked about the importance of connecting to the Internet; for example, e-mail and e-commerce. We also discussed how we segment the Internet and the intranet. We covered the importance of using routers and firewalls. This included why it is important to protect your network and, most importantly, Active Directory. We covered the need to register a legal domain name for your organization and how to get started. We then took a look at the different types of topologies that you might find when assessing an organization's existing network. This included the bus and ring topologies, which are not in much use today. We looked at the star topology, which is the most popular and the one you will most likely run into or design.

Next, we jumped into segmenting this physical network into subnets. Subnets let you take a large network and break it into more manageable pieces. We covered how to properly address these subnets using TCP/IP subnetting. We looked at proper router placement and why this is necessary. We also covered how DHCP can be used to help with the assignment and management of TCP/IP addresses.

Digging deeper into DHCP we looked at how Microsoft's DHCP can be integrated with DNS. We looked at some best practices to support redundancy and availability. This included using multiple DHCP servers and superscopes. It also included the use of DHCP relays where the protocol could not pass a router to have communication between the server and the client.

Finally, we covered remote access and the importance of it. We looked at the design of it, which included assessing how much is needed to accommodate your organization. We covered the requirements for designing and implementing such a solution. This included RRAS solutions on the perimeter, and protecting and segmenting them from the intranet and Internet. We looked at what is required for the clients and partners who might connect to your organization. We also looked at solutions like RADIUS to provide support for larger deployments of remote access.

All of the preceding pieces go into the physical design of your organization's network. It is important that you provide a strong assessment of any current environment so you can provide a strong foundation for a new network environment.

Exam Objectives Fast Track

Networking and Routing

☑ An organization needs to connect to the Internet to support research, e-mail, and e-commerce.

☑ You need to have a valid registered domain name if your organization wants to perform business on the Internet.

☑ You should have a valid registered domain name to be used for Active Directory.

☑ Routers route traffic between the intranet and the Internet. They also route traffic between segments or subnets in your intranet.

☑ Firewalls should be used to help protect your intranet from elements on the Internet.

☑ The main components of a physical topology are subnets, routers, switches and/or hubs, and perimeter defenses (firewalls).

☑ Networks should be segmented into subnets to reduce the management size of the network.

☑ The three management features of DHCP are scopes, superscopes, and TCP/IP options.

☑ A DHCP scope is a range of sequential IP addresses to be assigned from a DHCP server to a DHCP client.

☑ DHCP superscopes provide a mechanism for managing more than one DHCP server in an organization.

☑ DHCP TCP/IP options are additional information assigned to the DHCP client. These are set at the server.

☑ Using DHCP reduces the size and management of assigning IP addresses to hosts.

☑ To use DHCP, you must have a DHCP server and DHCP clients.

☑ DHCP relay can be used if there is not a local DHCP server and the router(s) will not allow DHCP requests to cross them.

☑ Microsoft DHCP can integrate with Microsoft DNS to provide proper name resolution in a dynamic environment.

☑ Private IP addresses should be used in an organization as referenced in RFC 1918.

☑ NAT can be used to provide private-to-public address translation so that intranet users can communicate on the Internet.

Designing Requirements for a Remote Access Infrastructure

☑ Remote access is driven by the demand of the organization and partners.

☑ Microsoft RRAS can provide VPN and dial-in solutions for an organization.

☑ The RRAS server should be placed on the perimeter network to allow access and to block bad elements from the Internet.

☑ RADIUS can be used as a solution for integrating multiple RRAS servers with one authentication point.

Determining Sizing and Availability of Remote Access Infrastructure

☑ Windows Server 2003 can support 1000 concurrent VPN connections.

☑ Windows Server 2003 RRAS server can be configured to support dial-on-demand routing. To deploy dial-on-demand, you need to install RRAS on a perimeter server and configure it to listen for requests that originate beyond local subnets.

☑ Deploying redundant hardware and software in support of RRAS and VPN will dramatically increase the reliability and availability of the secure remote access solution.

Exam Objectives
Frequently Asked Questions

The following Frequently Asked Questions, answered by the authors of this book, are designed to both measure your understanding of the Exam Objectives presented in this chapter and to assist you with real-life implementation of these concepts. You will also gain access to thousands of other FAQs at *www.ITFAQnet.com*.

Q: Why do I need to register a domain name to perform business on the Internet?

A: To properly account for all businesses on the Internet, there needs to be a legal registration of the domain name. To enable a customer to find your organization, business legal registration is required.

Q: Why are firewalls important to an organization using the Internet?

A: Firewalls provide a means of filtering incoming traffic to your organization's intranet. Some of the incoming traffic might be of a malicious intent. Routers can provide some of this filtering also, but is it best to offload this work to the firewall.

Q: How and why would a partner to my organization connect using remote access?

A: If a partner needs to access an application or transfer data that business has deemed necessary, then a secure connection might be necessary. This can be done simply by allowing the partner to VPN from one client or as complex as creating a site-to-site VPN to virtually connect the organizations. It will all depend on the necessity.

Q: How do I know how many VPN connections to create to support my organization?

A: A good rule-of-thumb is the 8:1 rule. Create one connection for every eight users who will require VPN access.

Q: I have three RRAS servers in my design; what is the best way to implement this solution?

A: You can include RADIUS in your design. This will create a tiered support for the RRAS solution by allowing all of the RRAS servers to use RADIUS for authentication. RADIUS will handle communication back to Active Directory. This will allow you to centralize the solution.

Self Test

A Quick Answer Key follows the Self Test questions. For complete questions, answers, and explanations to the Self Test questions in this chapter as well as the other chapters in this book, see the Self Test Appendix.

1. In designing the network for Chapter Five Industries, you have been given the requirement that the company will be hosting its own Web site. What is the first thing you should do to ensure that the company will be able to achieve e-commerce on the Internet?

   A. Design the router placement

   B. Design the firewall filters

   C. Obtain a domain name

   D. Design the capacity

2. Chapter Five Industries has only one connection to the Internet—a 512K Frame Relay. There are 500 users in this network. These users are complaining that the Internet is slow. The Internet connectivity is set up as shown in the following diagram. What could be done to enhance the users' Internet experience without incurring too much cost?

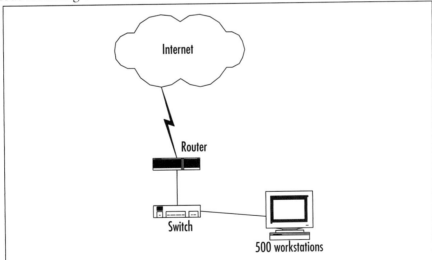

   A. Increase the bandwidth of the Internet connection

   B. Install a proxy server

   C. Install another router for the users

   D. Install a firewall

3. You have just finished creating the new physical network design for Chapter Five Industries. You now need to create IP subnets to coincide with the new design. What is the minimum amount of IP subnets you will need to design?

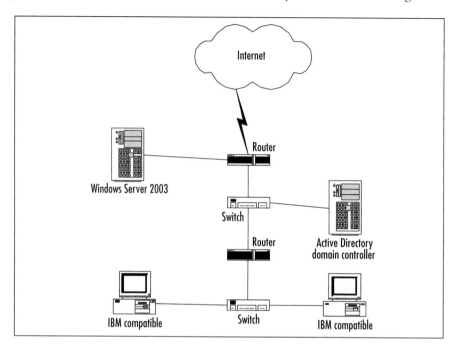

A. Two

B. Three

C. Four

D. Six

4. You have been given the following network WAN design. Philadelphia has 200 users, New York has 100 users, Atlanta has 200 users, and Los Angeles has 50 users. You need to create a private address scheme that will satisfy the design. The Frame Relay cloud and router interfaces already are using a 203.45.9.x IP addressing assigned by the ISP. What would be the best IP addressing to use in this design?

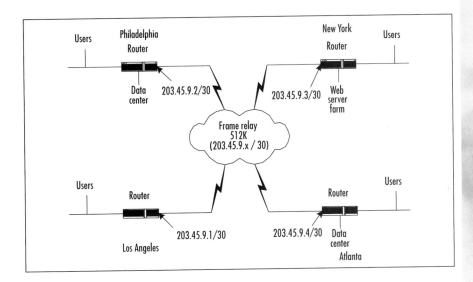

A. Philadelphia Users (192.168.1.x /24), Philadelphia Data Center (192.168.2.x /24); New York Users (192.168.3.x /24), New York Web Server Farm (192.168.4.x /24); Los Angeles Users (10.0.3.x /24); Atlanta Users (10.0.1.x /24), Atlanta Data Center (10.0.2.x /24)

B. Philadelphia Users (100.0.1.x /24), Philadelphia Data Center (100.0.2.x /24); New York Users (100.0.3.x /24), New York Web Server Farm (100.0.4.x /24); Los Angeles Users (100.0.5.x /24); Atlanta Users (100.0.6.0 /24), Atlanta Data Center (100.0.7.0 /24)

C. Philadelphia Users (192.168.1.x /24), Philadelphia Data Center (192.168.2.x /24); New York Users (192.168.3.x /24), New York Web Server Farm (192.168.4.x /24); Los Angeles Users (192.168.5.x /24); Atlanta Users (192.168.6.x /24), Atlanta Data Center (192.168.7.x /24)

D. Philadelphia Users (10.1.0.x /8), Philadelphia Data Center (10.1.0.x /8); New York Users (10.1.0.x /8), New York Web Server Farm (10.1.0.x /8); Los Angeles Users (10.1.0.x /8); Atlanta Users (10.1.0.x /8), Atlanta Data Center (10.1.0.x /8)

5. You have just finished designing and installing a Window Server 2003 DHCP server. You have three subnets in your network. Subnet A contains the Windows Server 2003 DHCP server. Subnets B and C contain user workstations. You receive a call that users in subnet B cannot get on the Internet. You perform an IPCONFIG on one of the workstations and get an IP address of 169.224.221.5. What could be the problem? (Choose two.)

A. You excluded the 169.224.221.x range on the DHCP server.

B. There is no scope created for this subnet.

C. The router is set to filter the 169.224.221.x range from accessing the Internet.

D. The router is not forwarding BOOTP requests.

6. The HR Department has become concerned about security lately and would like to ensure even internally that its users and servers are safe from unfriendly elements. They are not as concerned about speed as they are about security and logging. What device could be used to securely segment the HR Department users and servers from the rest of the organization?

A. Router

B. Switch

C. Firewall

D. Proxy server

7. Your current network design has three sites with 470 users. Over the next three years, there are 10 more sites planned. There will also be about 2000 users added to the environment. Because of performance issues with having too many computers on a single subnet, there is a limit of 200 computers per subnet. Using the private Class C IP addressing, what subnet mask would allow for the future expansion?

A. 255.255.240.0

B. 255.255.254.0

C. 255.255.255.0

D. 255.255.252.0

8. You need to design failover into your Internet connectivity solution. You are going to be using your RRAS server to accomplish this failover. What types of telephony connection can you use to provide dial-on-demand? (Choose all that apply.)

A. X.25

B. TCP/IP

C. DSL

D. Asynchronous telephone line

9. You have remote offices in San Diego and Seattle. To save money, you have designed dial-on-demand into your solution. These sites occasionally need to attach to the Internet. They also need to occasionally attach to the main office in Philadelphia. You want to make these connections as secure as possible. All of the offices are using Windows Server 2003 servers for RRAS. How would you

set up the encryption options on the RRAS servers in the branch office for dial-on-demand routing?

A. For the Internet connection, set "require encryption." For the main office connection, set "optional encryption."

B. For the Internet connection, set "no encryption." For the main office connection, set "no encryption."

C. For the Internet connection, set "optional encryption." For the main office connection, set "optional encryption."

D. For the Internet connection, set "optional encryption." For the main office connection, set "require encryption."

10. You are designing a dial-on-demand solution for a small organization of 50 users. They need only the RRAS for connecting to the Internet. There will be an IDSL (128K/128K) line used for this connection. What will be your biggest concern with this solution?

A. Encrypting access to the Internet

B. Bandwidth utilization

C. Setup and maintenance of the solution

D. Cost of the solution

11. You are designing a VPN solution for an organization. There will be 100 users who will need to connect to the organization using VPN. How may VPN ports should you establish in your design to meet the requirements?

A. 100

B. 50

C. 13

D. 10

12. You are designing a VPN solution for a large organization. Users will be connecting from the Internet to three RRAS servers in the Philadelphia office. What is the best solution for authenticating these users?

A. Use a RADIUS server with Active Directory authentication

B. Use the RRAS servers with standalone authentication

C. Use the RRAS servers with Active Directory authentication

D. Use a RADIUS server with standalone authentication

Self Test Quick Answer Key

For complete questions, answers, and explanations to the Self Test questions in this chapter as well as the other chapters in this book, see the Self Test Appendix.

1. **C**	7. **C**
2. **B**	8. **A, C, D**
3. **C**	9. **D**
4. **C**	10. **B**
5. **B, D**	11. **C**
6. **C**	12. **A**

Appendix A

MCSE 70-297

Self Test Answers and Explanations

This Appendix provides complete Self Test Answers and Explanations for each Chapter.

Chapter 1 The Assessment Stage

1. You are part of a team of consultants that will be designing the network infrastructure and Active Directory for a multinational company. Your team is approached by the head of one of the organization's business units, who is proposing his own design for Active Directory that has been modeled after the organization chart, with each business unit having an OU that is named after its director. How would you rate this design?

   A. It is a good design because it follows the organization chart.

   B. It is a good design because it follows the flow of information from management to employees.

   C. It is a bad design because it does not account for changes in the organization.

   D. It is a bad design because it does not account for available bandwidth.

   ☑ Answer **C** is correct. Corporate reorganization can render this design irrelevant in one fell swoop. The information flow that needs to be accommodated is between or among critical systems and the units who make the greatest use of them, not from manager to employee.

   ☒ Answer **A** is incorrect because the organization chart is a good reflection of the structure of the organization, but it is only one factor among several that should be considered. Answer **B** is incorrect because the flow of information that needs to be accommodated is between or among critical systems and the units who make the greatest use of them, not from manager to employee. Answer **D** is incorrect because the reason for it being a bad design is not that it does not account for available bandwidth, but that it is based on a faulty premise.

2. You have been asked to assess your current domain structure as part of the planning to migrate to the version of Active Directory on Windows Server 2003. You have been asked to keep the company's business objectives at the front of your mind when conducting your assessment. What documents will be especially useful to you?

   A. Organization charts

   B. Documented business processes

   C. The annual report to shareholders

   D. Financial statements

   E. The geographic locations of offices

☑ Answers **A**, **B**, and **E** are correct. Organization charts will list the organization's business units and depict their interrelationships. Documented business processes will explain how information is used and passed within and among systems and business units. The geographic layout of the organization is important for determining the physical path that information must take from one office to another. All of these documents will factor into Active Directory design.

☒ Answers **C** and **D** are incorrect. Annual reports are full of information about the company's past performance and projected performance for the future, as well as information on personnel and the company's direction. However, it might contain little if any information that will contribute to the overall quality of the design. The financial statements will not provide any useful information.

3. Your design team is handed documents that describe the company's organization and is assured that they are current, although no one can tell you when the documents were last updated. How should you proceed with this new found information?

A. Trust the documents and proceed.

B. Verify when they were last updated and make changes if necessary.

C. Ignore the documents and create new ones by conducting your own investigation.

D. Create a design based on industry best practices and recommend making organizational changes to accommodate the design.

☑ Answer **B** is correct. In all likelihood, these documents represent a good starting point; however, the information should be validated and amended appropriately.

☒ Answer **A** is incorrect because proceeding with information that is potentially out of date could result in a design that is not suited to the current organization. Answer **C** is incorrect because even if the documents are slightly out of date, updating information and amending the information is less time consuming than starting from scratch. This being said, if the information is grossly out of date and bears absolutely no resemblance to the current organization, you might need to investigate and re-create the documentation. However, the most prudent first step is to attempt to validate the information rather than immediately dismiss it out of hand. Answer **D** is incorrect because the purpose of the exercise is to arrive at a design that supports the business objectives of the organization. Best practices are useful as guidelines but they are not necessarily appropriate for every organization.

In addition, corporate reorganization to support an IT infrastructure design would be appropriate only in the most dysfunctional organizations, but then again if the organization is dysfunctional, a new infrastructure design would not be its primary concern.

4. When they find out about the impending upgrade of the network infrastructure, representatives from your company's business units approach you demanding assurances that existing service levels will apply after the migration is complete. How should you respond?

    A. Inform them that you cannot make any promises at this point in the migration.

    B. Inform them that you will assess past performance against the existing service levels to see if the existing service levels are still valid.

    C. Inform them that Windows Server 2003 is definitely more reliable than what is currently running and they should expect an improvement in service.

    D. Inform them that the new network infrastructure design is being constructed with the existing service levels as a primary consideration and they will be kept informed as the design evolves.

    ☑ Answer **D** is correct. Service levels for systems that will be affected by the implementation of the new network infrastructure design must be considered an important factor when developing the design. By keeping the channels of communication open between your design team and the affected business units, you will be able to better manage everyone's expectations during and after the implementation.

    ☒ Answer **A** is incorrect because the importance of service levels, especially to those business units, cannot be de-emphasized or dismissed. Answer **B** is incorrect because, although the validity of existing service levels is important when renegotiating service level agreements, managing the expectations of business units and gathering their input is more valuable for the quality of the design and the success of the project. Answer **C** is incorrect because it cannot be assumed that a new product will improve the reliability of an existing system simply because it is new. The way in which the product is implemented, used, and managed determines its reliability.

5. You have been asked to conduct a hardware inventory of all of the servers running in your company to determine their state of readiness for the impending upgrade to Windows Server 2003. What hardware information should you capture? (Select all that apply.)

A. Hard disk size

B. Serial number

C. Date of manufacture

D. CPU

E. Amount of RAM

F. Warranty status

☑ Answers **A**, **D**, and **E** correct. Disk capacity, CPU type and speed, and the amount of memory are three of the key indicators to determine whether a server can handle the new version of Windows or not.

☒ Answers **B**, **C**, and **F** are incorrect. The serial number is useful for asset management and potentially as a unique identifier for the computer, but does not determine the computer's compatibility with Windows Server 2003. The date of manufacture provides the age of the computer, but it is also not a factor. An older computer might be able to be upgraded to meet current hardware standards. Warranty status is another red herring. It has no bearing on a machine's usefulness.

6. You are migrating your company's Web servers from Windows NT 4.0 to Windows Server 2003, Standard Edition. What are the most important components to examine to see if your existing hardware can support the new version? (Select all that apply.)

A. SSL accelerator

B. Amount of RAM

C. NIC type and speed

D. Hard disk capacity

E. Number of processors

☑ Answers **B** and **D** are correct. The amount of memory and the hard disk capacity are the two major components in this list that have noticeably different requirements between Windows NT 4.0 and Windows Server 2003, Standard Edition.

☒ Answers **A**, **C**, and **E** are incorrect. Apart from the fact that they might not be supported by Windows Server 2003 if they are obsolete, the components in A and C are not factors in determining whether the server is ready to receive the upgrade. Windows NT 4.0 and Windows Server 2003, Standard Edition support the same number of processors.

7. You have been asked to conduct an inventory of all software that is running on your company's servers. What are the primary benefits for creating a design that can be derived from the data collected during a software inventory? (Select all that apply.)

   A. Determining if your company has an adequate number of licenses for the number of users

   B. The portability of applications from Windows to Unix

   C. The degree of compatibility of the software that will be installed with existing software that will not be upgraded

   D. Finding software that is no longer in use

   ☑ Answers **A** and **C** correct. It is critical that your company be in a legal licensing position to avoid the potential for public embarrassment by failing a software audit. By determining the number of required licenses, you will be able to provide a more accurate estimate of the cost for implementing the design. In addition, any design that is created must not jeopardize the stability of business operations by introducing incompatible software. The inventory will assist in identifying pitfalls so that any potential software conflicts can be resolved in advance of the implementation.

   ☒ Answer **B** is incorrect because a software inventory will not determine the portability of an application. That is best left up to vendor research or with a separate development project at another time. Answer **D** is incorrect because software that is not in use will not need to be accommodated in the design or during the implementation. It might prove valuable if you discover that you are needlessly paying for licenses or support and you can save your company some money that would be wasted, but it is not a design benefit.

8. You are assessing your current version of the DNS design for your company, specifically the placement of DNS zones. The company is based in North America and has many branch offices throughout the continent. What are the key issues you need to consider when making your assessment? (Select all that apply.)

   A. Use of caching-only servers

   B. The version of Windows DNS that is being used in the branch offices

   C. Link speed

   D. Traffic patterns

   E. Use of conditional forwarders

   F. Client configuration

☑ Answers **A**, **C**, and **D** are correct. When planning DNS for a widely dispersed network, the optimal use of available bandwidth is the primary concern. Link speed and traffic patterns should govern how the namespace will be subdivided into zones, what type of servers will be used, and where they will be placed. Caching-only servers should be used to conserve the amount of bandwidth used over slow WAN links.

☒ Answers **B**, **E**, and **F** are incorrect because they are all secondary or even tertiary concerns in relation to making optimal use of available bandwidth.

Chapter 2 Developing the Active Directory Infrastructure Design

1. Your organization is comprised of six different business units. Each requires a certain level of independence from each of the other businesses within the Active Directory environment. Which of the following terms are relevant when considering the level of independence required? (Choose all that apply.)

   A. Isolation

   B. Autonomy

   C. Independence

   D. Restriction

   ☑ Answers **A** and **B** are correct. As discussed in the section Assessing and Designing the Administrative Model, the terms that Microsoft has introduced so that different levels of independence can be assessed are *isolation* and *autonomy*. *Isolation* implies that exclusive access is required, whereas *autonomy* simply means that independence is needed, but without exclusive rights.

   ☒ Answers **C** and **D** are incorrect. Although terms such as *independence* and *restriction* can be used in a general sense to describe the segregation of one business from another, they are not specific terms used within Microsoft guidelines, nor within this book.

2. You are the project manager for a large Active Directory design and deployment project within an organization. Several disparate businesses want to co-exist in the same Active Directory environment. Which administrative roles need to be defined within each business, such that the level of isolation and autonomy can be designed appropriately to meet the needs of these administrative groups? (Choose all that apply.)

   A. Service administrators

   B. Domain administrators

    C. Server administrators

    D. Data administrators

    ☑ Answers **A** and **D** are correct. Service Admins and Data Admins were defined in the section Assessing and Designing the Administrative Model as the two types of administrators that must be defined and evaluated. Service Admins are responsible for the configuration and maintenance of the Active Directory infrastructure, while Data Admins are responsible for the data contained therein. The level of isolation or autonomy required by both these groups will largely affect forest, domain, and OU designs.

    ☒ Answers **B** and **C** are incorrect. Domain Admins is a specific Service/Data Admin group, but is not the only such admin group. It is not sufficient to evaluate this role alone. Similarly, Server Admins are one Service/Data Admin group, but on their own do not represent all the Service or Data Admins.

3. During the assessment of administrative requirements, one group expresses the need to have complete, exclusive access to and control over the schema within Active Directory. Which of the following terms describes their requirement, in terms of independence?

    A. Autonomy

    B. Isolation

    C. Exclusive access

    D. Restricted access

    ☑ Answer **B** is correct. When exclusive access is required, then this is termed isolation. Because the schema is shared across the entire Active Directory forest, if any one group requires exclusive control over it, then that group must deploy a separate forest.

    ☒ The term *autonomy* implies independence, but without exclusive control. This is, therefore, not the appropriate level of independence and renders Answer **A** incorrect, although it is a term that is used with respect to Active Directory design and independence. Answers **C** and **D** are not terms used to describe independence with respect to Active Directory design.

4. An organization has several, disparate businesses, which for legal reasons cannot share data with any other part of the organization. These businesses must ensure that their data cannot be accessed from any other business. Which of the following models meets these requirements?

A. Separate OU per business

B. Separate domain per business

C. Separate forest per business

D. Separate, segmented network per business

☑ Answer **C** is correct. Each business clearly requires data isolation, which can be achieved only with a separate forest.

☒ Answers **A**, **B**, and **D** are incorrect. Separate OUs and separate domains, although offering autonomy, do not offer isolation. A segmented network, although offering isolation at the physical level, precludes any type of data access from the business to nonisolated businesses, within the organization. This is therefore too restrictive, and instead, a firewall approach in conjunction with a separate forest is the ideal solution.

5. An application requires that extensions to the schema be made. However, the existing Active Directory design houses several disparate businesses, some of which do not require these schema changes. How might the application be deployed, while leaving the schema in the "shared" forest unchanged, so that users can access the application with existing credentials?

A. Deploy a separate domain within the existing forest. Deploy the application in the new domain.

B. Deploy a separate forest. Deploy the application in the new forest with no trust to the other forest.

C. Deploy a separate forest. Deploy the application in the new forest and establish a trust to the other forest.

D. Deploy the application in the existing forest.

☑ Answer **C** is correct. Schema changes are forestwide, because the schema is shared across all domains in the forest. If changes to the schema are not acceptable, then a separate forest must be established. Furthermore, if access to the application is required from the forest using existing credentials, then a trust must also be created.

☒ Answers **A** and **D** imply that the application is deployed into the existing forest, along with the associated schema changes. This is not acceptable. Answer **B** meets all the requirements except the ability to access the application with existing credentials. Without a trust in place, a separate set of credentials would be required for each user of the application.

6. Two Active Directory sites each have a DC that hosts a replica of an application partition. No site link exists between these two sites. What can be done to initiate replication of the application partition data between these two sites?

   A. Create manual connection objects.

   B. Create a site link bridge.

   C. Create a site link.

   D. Merge the sites into one, new site encompassing both DCs.

   ☑ **All Answers are correct**. Manual connection objects can be created between the two DCs. Two unidirectional connection objects are required. A site link bridge will also enable the two sites to replicate, if there is a common site with which both share a link. These two links can then be "combined" to form a site link bridge, bridging the gap between the two sites. Another solution is to simply create a site link. However, if the underlying network has no direct connection between the sites, then a site link bridge should be favored. Finally, the two sites could be merged—meaning that all subnets within both sites are to be removed from their current sites and added to a new "supersite." The two DCs would then replicate using intra-site replication rules, thus not requiring a site link. Again, this might not be reflective of the underlying network topology, and a bridge might be favorable.

   ☒ None

7. You are designing Active Directory for an organization comprised of several functional groups. Each group needs autonomous control over its objects, but not isolation at the service or data level. How should each group be segregated from each other group to meet these requirements in the simplest way possible?

   A. Create a separate domain.

   B. Create a separate forest.

   C. Create a separate OU.

   D. Create a separate site.

   ☑ Answer **C** is correct. A separate OU for each group gives those groups autonomy over their own objects and the ability to delegate rights over those objects. It also enables the groups to link group policy to their own OU. This meets their requirements as set out.

☒ Answers **A**, **B**, and **D** are incorrect. A domain or forest does meet the requirements, but also offers several features that are not required, and more importantly, adds complexity to the design, which can be avoided by using separate OUs instead. A separate site is appropriate for replication design, but not for segregation of Active Directory objects such as users, groups, and computers.

8. Your organization has three regional Windows NT 4.0 user domains. This split was designed due to the limitations of the Windows NT Secure Accounts Manager (SAM) database. Each user domain is managed autonomously by its own region. When designing Active Directory for the organization, how should these regions be segregated so that no change to the Administrative model is required?

A. In separate domains.

B. In separate forests.

C. In separate sites.

D. In separate OUs.

☑ Answer **D** is correct. Because the only reason for splitting the environment into regional domains was due to SAM limitations, there is no technical reason to keep the regions separate when designing Active Directory. However, each region manages its objects and requires autonomy over those objects—this can be achieved with a separate OU per region.

☒ Answers **A**, **B**, and **C** are incorrect. A domain or forest does meet the requirements, but also offers several features that are not required, and more importantly, adds complexity to the design, which can be avoided by using separate OUs instead. A separate site is appropriate for replication design, but not for segregation of Active Directory objects such as users, groups, and computers.

9. When designing a group policy strategy for your Active Directory implementation, the following requirements are identified: all member servers must receive a core set of policies; all servers must receive a role-specific set of policies; all servers must receive a regional-specific set of policies. How can this be achieved?

A. Create an OU structure that splits servers by role, and then by region.

B. Create an OU structure that splits servers by region, and then by role.

C. Create an OU structure that splits servers by role. Apply local policies on each server as appropriate.

D. Create an OU structure that splits servers by region. Apply local policies on each server as appropriate.

☑ Answer **B** is correct. It is more likely that servers are managed on a regional basis than by role. The first level of segregation, therefore, should be regional. Each region can then manage their own servers and further segregate their servers by role. Finally, Group Policy can be set at the server OU, the regional OU, and the role OU levels.

☒ It is unlikely that servers would be managed by role and not by region, so Answer **A** is incorrect. Answer **B** is also incorrect for the same reason. Answer **D** is incorrect because local policies will be overwritten by OU-based policies, which can result in undesired policy settings on the regional servers.

Chapter 3 Developing the Network Services Design

1. You have been hired to design the network services for Blue Bell Corp. Blue Bell is planning on implementing Windows Server 2003 network services with Active Directory that will be migrated from their existing Novell NetWare and Unix systems. Which of the following services must you design before implementing these network services?

   A. DHCP

   B. DNS

   C. WINS

   D. RRAS

   ☑ Answer **B** is correct. Only DNS is an absolute requirement of Active Directory.

   ☒ Answer **A** is incorrect because although you must use TCP/IP, you can manually apply static IP addresses to all the network hosts. Answer **C** is incorrect because you do not require NetBIOS naming for Active Directory. Answer **D** is incorrect because you do not need to have routing and remote access services implemented on Windows Server 2003 in order for Active Directory to be installed and configured.

2. You are the network administrator for Jim's Garages. The Jim's Garages network is distributed throughout the United States and Canada. The main location has several hundred users, whereas there are 75 satellite locations directly connected to the main location with fewer than 10 users at each site. You want to deploy DHCP. You have configured all satellite offices to use APIPA in the event of a WAN link failure. How many DHCP servers will you require if you want to make sure the DHCP service has high availability to the network?

A. 1

B. 2

C. 75

D. 76

☑ Answer **B** is correct. You should be able to have two DHCP servers to ensure availability.

☒ Answer **A** is incorrect because a single server will not provide the business requirement of the DHCP server always being available. Answer **C** is incorrect because this is the number of satellite locations and you do not need a DHCP server for each location. Answer **D** is incorrect because this is the number of satellite locations plus the main location. You can configure routers between the satellite offices and the main site to forward the DHCP messages.

3. You have configured a DHCP server on segment A. Your client is connected to segment B. You cannot obtain an IP address lease. Which of the following can be configured to resolve the problem?

A. DHCP Relay Agent

B. DHCP Discover

C. DHCP Offer

D. DHCP Request

☑ Answer **A** is correct. DHCP Relay Agent is correct because this is a special forwarder that can be configured on a router to ensure that DHCP messages are sent to the DHCP server from a DHCP client on a different segment.

☒ Answers **B**, **C**, and **D** are all incorrect because these are three of the four phases of the DHCP leasing process.

4. You have been monitoring the network traffic on a segment of your network. This segment is one where no client has been able to lease an IP address from the DHCP server that has been configured on a different segment. You find that there is a DHCP message type that is being transmitted on the network. Which of the following messages are you most likely seeing?

A. DHCPDISCOVER

B. DHCPOFFER

C. DHCPREQUEST

D. DHCPACK

☑ Answer **A** is correct. DHCPDISCOVER is correct because this is the DHCP message that is transmitted from the client to the DHCP server.

Because this is a broadcast message, any client that is configured to attempt to lease an IP address will send out a DHCPDISCOVER message in order to locate a DHCP server.

☒ Answers **B**, **C**, and **D** are all incorrect because the DHCPOFFER and DHCPACK messages are transmitted from a DHCP server to the client, and the DHCPREQUEST message is directed to the DHCP server from the client once the client knows the DHCP server's IP address. Because the server does not exist on the subnet that is being monitored and because no client is obtaining IP address leases, the only message that should appear in the network monitor is DHCPDISCOVER.

5. You are upgrading a Windows NT network to Windows Server 2003. The current network has three domains, which you intend to keep. You want to make certain that each domain has its own DNS zone, and that the solution is redundant. Take into consideration that each zone consists of 5000 or fewer hosts. What is the minimum number of DNS servers that will you need to plan for?

A. 2

B. 3

C. 4

D. 6

☑ Answer **A** is correct. You can host multiple zones on a single DNS server. Because you need two servers for each zone, you can create one server with three zones and a second server with three copies of the zones. A DNS server can host far more than 15,000 records.

☒ None

6. You are the network administrator for Blue Bell Corp. Blue Bell uses the Web site *www.bluebell.com*. Users are comfortable with the bluebell.com name and are expecting to use that for the Active Directory that you are implementing. You are concerned about the security of internal hosts if you use the same domain name for the Web site as well as the Active Directory. Which of the following can you implement to provide security?

A. Dynamic DNS

B. Round Robin DNS

C. Clustered DNS servers

D. Split Brain DNS

☑ Answer **D** is correct. Split Brain DNS is correct because the use of both an internal and an external DNS zone can provide a way to prevent public queries from infiltrating the private network while using the same domain name both externally and internally.

☒ Answer **A** is incorrect because this is a method for clients to be able to register their own Address and Pointer records in the DNS database. Answer **B** is incorrect because Round Robin DNS is a method for multiple DNS records to take turns sending clients to different servers that provide identical services, thus increasing availability of the servers. Answer **C** is incorrect because configuring a cluster of DNS servers does not add any security to the network.

7. You have been recently hired by Jim's Garages to design their DNS network. Jim's Garages has had a heavy load on their existing DNS server and performance has been slow. Which of the following methods can increase performance?

A. Dynamic DNS

B. DHCP

C. Cluster services

D. Split Brain DNS

☑ Answer **C** is correct. Clustering can increase the performance of a DNS server by combining the capabilities of two (or more) servers. Clustering improves performance and provides a failover system in the event of a single server outage.

☒ Answer **A** is incorrect because this is a method for clients to be able to register their own Address and Pointer records in the DNS database. Answer **B** is incorrect because DHCP is a service designed to provide IP address leases to client computers. Answer **D** is incorrect because Split Brain DNS is a system that provides for both an internal and external zone for the same namespace in order to protect internal systems from infiltration by the public network.

8. You are the network administrator for Blue Bell Corp. You have 1200 servers that provide network services, such as file sharing and printer sharing, on the network. These servers are frequently installed, moved, added, changed, or retired from the network. You want to implement an automatic method for managing the DNS record registration for the servers. Which of the following should you implement?

A. Dynamic DNS

B. DHCP

C. Round Robin DNS

D. Split Brain DNS

☑ Answer **A** is correct. Dynamic DNS, or DDNS, is a system in which each
server can automatically register its own Address and Pointer records in the
DNS database.

☒ Answer **B** is incorrect because this is a method of automatically leasing IP
addresses to clients. Answer **C** is incorrect because it is a method of using
multiple DNS records to increase performance of the servers they point to.
Answer **D** is incorrect because it provides for the use of internal and
external DNS zones in order to preserve security of private systems.

9. You are the network designer for Jim's Garages. You have been asked by management to use the existing DNS servers for the migration to Windows Server
2003 with Active Directory. Which of the following should you do first?

A. Upgrade the servers to Windows NT 4.0.

B. Contact the manufacturer to find out if the existing DNS system is compatible.

C. Review the network topology to see if there will be sufficient availability.

D. Determine the number and size of each DNS server.

☑ Answer **B** is correct. The first thing you should do is contact the manufacturer of the existing DNS system to find out if there are any compatibility
issues with Windows Server 2003 Active Directory. This includes determining whether the DNS system supports SRV RRs (a requirement), and
whether features such as Dynamic DNS are supported.

☒ Answer **A** is incorrect because there is no need to upgrade servers to
Windows NT 4.0. Answer **C** is incorrect because you would review the
network topology after you determine whether there are compatibility
issues. Answer **D** is incorrect because you would determine the number and
size of the DNS servers after you determine compatibility.

10. Your Unix network uses a version of BIND that is incompatible with Windows
Server 2003 Active Directory. You want to maintain the existing BIND implementation for the namespace example.com. Your only Active Directory domain
will be named example.local. Which of the following must you do to make this
system function?

A. Nothing, it should work fine using just the existing BIND implementation.

B. Install another BIND server to manage example.local.

C. Install a Windows Server 2003 DNS server to manage example.local.

D. Create two primary zones for example.local.

☑ Answer **C** is correct. You can use a version of DNS that is not compatible
with Active Directory as long as you are not using that version to manage

the zones for the Active Directory domains. As long as the Active Directory domain example.local is using the Windows Server 2003 DNS version, it should function correctly.

☒ Answer **A** is incorrect because the question states that the version of BIND was not compatible, so it cannot be used. Answer **B** is incorrect because the version of BIND was considered incompatible. Answer **D** is incorrect because the number and type of zones will not drive the compatibility of the DNS server.

11. You are the network administrator for Old School. Old School has a Windows NT 4.0 network with a couple of Windows NT 3.51 servers providing DNS and WINS services for name resolution. There is also a Windows NT 4.0 server providing RRAS and DHCP services. You have been given the go-ahead to install a new Windows Server 2003 DC. Your plans are to install the new server hardware with Windows NT 4.0 as a backup domain controller (BDC). Then, you intend to promote it to a primary domain controller (PDC), and finally you want to upgrade it to Windows Server 2003. Before you perform the upgrade to Windows Server 2003, which of the following must you install first to avoid any compatibility problems?

A. DHCP

B. WINS

C. DNS

D. RRAS

☑ Answer **C** is correct. DNS is correct because the version of DNS used in Windows NT 3.51 is incompatible with Windows Server 2003 Active Directory. Because you are installing a DC, you will need to have Active Directory.

☒ Answers **A**, **B**, and **D** are all incorrect because DHCP, WINS, and RRAS are not necessary for a DC to be installed or to function.

12. As the Webmaster for an intranet, you manage all servers and server design for any application that is shared on the intranet. Management has asked you to share a new application. You find out that the application requires NetBIOS names on the network. Which two of the following methods can you use to resolve NetBIOS names to IP addresses?

A. WINS

B. DNS

C. HOSTS

D. LMHOSTS

☑ Answers **A** and **D** are correct. WINS is the centralized NetBIOS name resolution service offered in Microsoft networks, whereas LMHOSTS is the
manually configured file on a computer that contains NetBIOS name to IP
address mapping records. Either or both can be used on a network to provide NetBIOS name resolution.

☒ Answers **B** and **C** are incorrect because DNS is the centralized service providing name to IP address resolution, and HOSTS is the manually configured file containing the name to IP address mapping records.

13. You are the network administrator for Fast Trax research department. Your business unit consists of 5000 users. The rest of the company is about 30,000 users.
You install a DHCP server to provide IP addresses to your clients who dial in to
your own business unit's remote access server. You find that the server is not
providing IP addresses. Which of the following could be the problem?

A. You did not authorize the DHCP server in Active Directory.

B. You did not activate the DHCP scope.

C. You did not configure the routers to forward the DHCP broadcasts.

D. Any or all of the above.

E. None of the above.

☑ Answer **D** is correct. Any of the first three answers could be the reason why
your clients are not receiving IP address leases from your DHCP server.

☒ Answer **E** is incorrect because the first three answers are all correct.

14. Your network has a RADIUS server that provides remote access client authentication and accounting services. The network also uses a third-party remote
access solution. One of the company's business units wants to have a private
remote access server with its own dial-up numbers. They already have a server
running Windows Server 2003 that is not being used for any other purpose
than DHCP services to 75 client computers. Which of the following is the
most cost-effective method to comply with their request yet maintain RADIUS
authentication?

A. Install an additional third-party remote access server for the business unit.

B. Add another third-party remote access server to the main pool.

C. Enable and configure RRAS on the existing W2K3 server as a RADIUS
client with RADIUS authentication back to the RADIUS server.

D. Enable and configure DHCP on the existing W2K3 server.

☑ Answer **C** is correct. There is little cost involved with enabling and configuring RRAS on the existing server and making it function with the
existing RADIUS implementation.

☒   Answers **A**, **B**, and **D** are incorrect because the first two involve excess cost in new hardware and software while the last does not provide the remote access or RADIUS services that were requested.

15. You have been tasked with designing a new Windows Server 2003 Active Directory forest. The network is currently a combination of Novell NetWare, Unix, and Windows NT 4.0. All client computers use HOSTS files and statically applied IP addresses. Your network is expecting to quadruple in the next year due to a merger that is being finalized. You want to reduce administration of IP addresses. Which of the following services must you implement before installing the first Active Directory DC?

A. DHCP

B. DNS

C. WINS

D. DDNS

☑   Answer **B** is correct. DNS is required to be installed and configured prior to installing an Active Directory DC. Although it is possible to install and configure DNS during the first DC's DCPROMO process, you should have the DNS plans completed to ensure that the configuration is accurate. If you do not have DNS installed before or during the DCPROMO process, then the server will fail to install the Active Directory.

☒   Answer **A** is incorrect because DHCP is recommended for IP address management reduction, but is not required for installing a DC. Answer **C** is incorrect because WINS is not required for DC installation. Answer **D** is incorrect because DDNS is recommended for reducing administration of IP addresses, but it is not required by DC installation

16. You are the network administrator for Black Jack Groceries. You have an existing Windows NT 4.0 domain infrastructure of three domains named HQ, Produce, and Wholesale. The network relies solely on WINS for name resolution. You are planning to install a new Active Directory domain named blackjack.com. You will then restructure the HQ and Produce domains into blackjack.com. You do not plan to upgrade or restructure the Wholesale domain. All blackjack.com users will require access to the Wholesale domain, and all Wholesale users will require access to blackjack.com. Your company's written security policy prevents the use of LMHOSTS and HOSTS files. Which of the following is required?

A. DHCP must be configured on all servers in the Wholesale domain.

B. DNS must be configured on all servers in the Wholesale domain.

C. WINS must be configured on all DCs in the Wholesale and blackjack.com domains.

D. DNS must be configured on all DCs in the Wholesale and blackjack.com domains.

☑ Answer **C** is correct. You must have WINS configured on the DCs of the Wholesale domain and the blackjack.com domain. WINS is required for domains to perform NetBIOS name resolution over TCP/IP when establishing and maintaining the external trust relationship between the two domains.

☒ Answer **A** is incorrect because DHCP does not need to be configured, although it is a recommended service. Answers **B** and **D** are incorrect because DNS does not need to be configured on the Wholesale DCs or servers. They can use WINS, which is required for Windows NT 4.0 to resolve NetBIOS names over TCP/IP because LMHOSTS cannot be used.

17. You have a network with two subnets. All the DCs for your Windows NT 4.0 domain named JHN are on Subnet A. WINS and DHCP run on a member server of the JHN domain. You have installed a new Active Directory domain named resources.ababab.com on Subnet B. DNS (which is configured to accept dynamic registrations from clients) runs on the DC dc1.resources.ababab.com. You have attempted to create a trust relationship between JHN and resources.ababab.com and it has failed. Which protocol is most likely at fault?

A. WINS

B. DNS

C. DHCP

D. DDNS

☑ Answer **A** is correct. Because the Windows NT 4.0 domain is dependent on WINS, you will need it to be configured on both domains in order for an external trust relationship to be created across the subnet. If the two domains existed on the same subnet, then the NetBIOS name resolution mechanism would default to broadcasts for dc1.resources.ababab.com and the JHN domain would then be found.

☒ Answer **B** is incorrect because DNS is required only for external trust relationships between Windows 2000 or later domains. Answers **C** and **D** are incorrect because DHCP and DDNS are not required to facilitate trust relationships.

18. You have been hired to plan the WINS configuration for a large intranetwork consisting of 50,000 client computers, 558 servers, and 40 DCs. These computers are distributed throughout 78 physical sites, 7 of which are considered "large" because each has more than 4000 users. The majority of sites are connected directly to the headquarters site. Your goal is to reduce the WINS convergence

time, yet maintain availability of WINS services. Which of the following can help meet that goal?

A. Add WINS to each of the 40 DCs. Have each DC contact its nearest neighbor for WINS replication.

B. Add WINS to a single server located at the headquarters site.

C. Install WINS servers at each large site. Configure all WINS servers to block all other replication partners except for the WINS server at the headquarters site.

D. Install WINS on servers at each large site. Configure all WINS servers to accept all other WINS servers as replication partners.

☑ Answer **C** is correct. Because the large sites contain more than 50 percent of the network's users, you should ensure that WINS is immediately available to them. In addition, you should configure all servers to replicate with a single central server, which reduces convergence of any changes on the network to a two-step replication.

☒ Answer **A** is incorrect because installing WINS on 40 DCs and allowing them to replicate in domino fashion will increase convergence time above what's necessary. Answer **B** is incorrect because using a single WINS server does not provide the availability requested in the solution. Answer **D** is incorrect because configuring all WINS servers as replication partners will increase convergence time.

Chapter 4 Designing the Logical Components

1. Your organization has five locations connected as shown in Figure 4.35 on page 590. Analog dial-up and ISDN connections are non–persistent connections. Specify transport for each link.

A. A-B (Transport = IP), A-C (Transport = IP), A-D (Transport = IP), A-E (Transport = SMTP)

B. A-B (Transport = SMTP), A-C (Transport = SMTP), A-D (Transport = IP), A-E (Transport = SMTP)

C. A-B (Transport = SMTP), A-C (Transport = SMTP), A-D (Transport = IP), A-E (Transport = IP)

D. A-B (Transport = IP), A-C (Transport = IP), A-D (Transport = IP), A-E (Transport = IP)

☑ Answer **C** is the correct answer because the nonpersistent connections should rely on SMTP transport.

Figure 4.35 Site Design

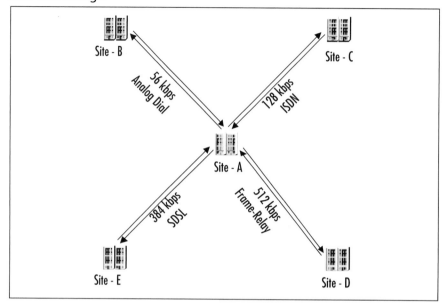

☒   Answer **A** is incorrect because the site transports are not the recommended types for the available connections. The dialup link should use SMTP, and the SDSL should use IP. Answers **B** and **D** are incorrect because the site link transports are incorrect.

2. You have been given the task of designing an OU structure for a client. The client has a dedicated network administrator located at the corporate offices. Each of the remaining 11 offices has 20 users relying on Internet connectivity to interact with a specialized Web application at the corporate office. Users log on to a Windows Server 2003 Active Directory domain for workstation security. You want to delegate basic account administration to one user at each of the remote offices. How can this best be accomplished?

A. Create a geographical OU design. Use the Delegation of Control wizard to create a customized Microsoft Management Console and Taskpad. Create a special administrator group for each location, and delegate the appropriate tasks to this group. Place each OU administrator in their respective groups.

B. Create a functional OU design. Use the Delegation of Control wizard to create a customized Microsoft Management Console and Taskpad. Create a special administrator group for each location, and delegate the task to this group. Place each OU administrator in his or her respective group.

C. Create an object type OU design. Use the Delegation of Control wizard to create a customized Microsoft Management Console and Taskpad. Create a special administrator group for each location, and delegate the task to this group. Place each OU administrator in their respective groups.

D. Create a functional OU design. Use the Delegation of Control wizard to create a customized Microsoft Management Console and Taskpad. Place each OU administrator in the Domain Administrators group.

☑ Answer **A** is correct because it delegates control without overextending the user's capabilities. Also, the OU structure closely mimics the organizational structure of the company without creating too many OUs.

☒ Answer **B** and **C** is incorrect because its OU design does not mimic the organizational structure to a great enough extent to provide the needed control over delegation. Answer **D** is incorrect because the design provides weak security by providing too much administrative power for the delegated users.

3. Your organization consists of a single forest with a root domain and three child domains: namaerica.yourcorp.com, samerica.yourcorp.com, and europe.yourcorp.com. The structure is illustrated in Figure 4.36. Users who belong to the management groups from each domain must have access to resources in each of the other domains. How can this be achieved, using best practice wherever possible?

Figure 4.36 Multidomain Access

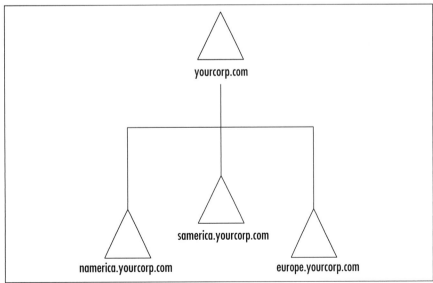

A. Create a global group for the management groups in each domain. Nest the global groups in a global group in the root domain. Create domain local groups in each domain and place the root global group in each domain local group. Use the domain local groups to control access to resources.

B. Create a domain local group for the management groups in each domain. Nest the domain local groups in a universal group in the root domain. Create domain local groups in each domain and place the universal group in each domain local group. Use the domain local groups to control access to resources.

C. Create a domain local group for the management groups in each domain. Nest the domain local groups in a global group in the root domain. Create domain local groups in each domain and place the root domain global group in each domain local group. Use the domain local groups to control access to resources.

D. Create a global group for the management groups in each domain. Nest the global groups in a universal group. Create domain local groups in each domain and place the universal group in each domain local group. Use the domain local groups to control access to resources.

☑ Answer **D** is the correct answer because it follows the best practice of placing AGULP (Accounts, Global Groups, Universal Groups, Domain Local Groups, Permissions).

☒ Answers **A, C,** and **D** are incorrect because the group nesting described does not follow best practice.

4. Your company will be collaborating with another company in the design of a new cobranded product. Users from the partner company need access to project data. How can you guarantee that users from the partner organization cannot access resources beyond the shared project data?

A. Place the group for remote users on each resource where access should be granted, and assign proper permissions. Remove the Everyone group from all sensitive resources. Place the remote users' group on all sensitive resources, and select Deny for the Full Control option on sensitive resources.

B. Place the group for remote users on each resource where access should be granted, and assign proper permissions. Select Deny for the Full Control option on sensitive resources for the Everyone group.

C. Place the group for remote users on each resource where access should be granted, and assign proper permissions. Place the remote users' group on all sensitive resources, and select Deny for the Full Control option on sensitive resources.

D. Place the group for remote users on each resource where access should not be granted, and assign the proper permissions. Select Deny for the Full Control option on sensitive resources for the Everyone group.

☑ Answer **A** is correct because it follows the best practice of removing the Everyone group from access to resources while also explicitly denying access to the users who should never have access to the resources.

☒ Answer **B** is incorrect because the options selected will remove access for everyone, including internal company users who should have access to the resources, not just the users that should be blocked. Answer **C** is incorrect because the Everyone group should be removed from the access control list. Answer **D** is incorrect because the remote users will be denied access by both methods but not granted access to any resources.

5. Your organization contains more than 3000 users and utilizes a distributed administration model. Using the features available in Active Directory, decide who should be assigned the responsibility to control access to a file server in the marketing department in your Phoenix office.

A. The domain administrators should control access to all resources.

B. The enterprise administrators should control access to all resources.

C. A domainwide File Server Administrators group should control access to all file servers.

D. A manager or office administrator for the marketing department in Atlanta should control access to the file server.

☑ Answer **D** is correct because this design places an individual that is close to the resource in charge of access. This person will likely have the best understanding of personnel and access requirements for resources within is or her own department, compared to an administrator who is located in another department or possibly even in another geographic location.

☒ Answers **A** and **B** are incorrect because in a large environment with thousands of users, enterprise or domain administrators will quickly become overburdened if tasked with the responsibility to control access to all resources within the Active Directory design. Answer **C** is incorrect because a dedicated file server administrator will not have the personnel understanding and access requirements for every department within the enterprise.

6. Twelve users within your department require access to the latest reports gener-
    ated by your sales department. What access level will the users require to
    accomplish the desired tasks?

    A. The users will require Read permission only.

    B. The users will require Read and Execute permission only.

    C. The users will require Modify permission only.

    D. The users will require Full control.

    ☑ Answer **A** is correct because it provides sufficient privilege for the users to
        complete the required task.

    ☒ Answers **B, C**, and **D** are incorrect because they provide greater privileges
        than necessary for the users to complete the required tasks.

7. You have been assigned a new project to control users' access to specialized
    Web-based applications within your organization. Which Windows Server 2003
    tool will you use to help you control role-based authorization?

    A. The IIS Permissions wizard

    B. Active Directory Users and Computers

    C. Authorization Manager

    D. Resultant Set of Policies (RSoP)

    ☑ Answer **C** is the correct answer. The Authorization Manager provides a
        mechanism for role-based authorization control.

    ☒ Answer **A** is incorrect because the IIS Permission wizard is a utility within
        Microsoft Internet Information Service (IIS) used to set proper permissions
        for Web resources. Answer **B** is incorrect because Active Directory Users
        and Computers does not control authorization. Answer **D** is incorrect
        because the RSoP utility is used to monitor the effect of GPOs.

8. Your organization consists of 12 offices connected through fractional T-1 links.
    Each office houses between 300 and 500 users and computers. Each office
    except the main office has the same corporate organization structure. Within
    each office are sales, engineering, and operations departments. The main office
    also has a department that encompasses the executive managers. How many
    OUs will a best-practice design encompass?

    A. Thirty-seven OUs will provide the best design.

    B. Twenty-four OUs will provide the best design.

    C. Twelve OUs will provide the best design.

    D. Three hundred twenty OUs will provide the best design.

☑ Answer **A** is the best answer. This design (12 Sales OUs, 12 Engineering OUs, 12 Operations OUs, and 1 Executive Managers OU) uses a hybrid design utilizing a geographic model at the top level and a functional model within each geographic OU.

☒ Answers **B** and **C** are incorrect because 24 OUs do not provide enough structure to mimic the corporate organizational structure. Answer **D** is incorrect because 320 OUs would provide nearly an OU for each account. This defeats one of the major reasons for using OUs: simplification of the environment.

9. Your Active Directory design is illustrated in Figure 4.37. Users in east.namerica.yourcorp.com frequently access resources in the east.samerica.yourcorp.com. Users have been complaining about the time it takes to access resources in the other domain. How can you improve the time required to access the resources?

Figure 4.37 Infrastructure for Question #9

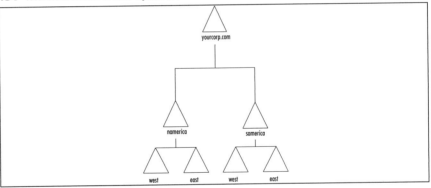

A. Create an external trust between east.namerica.yourcorp.com and east.samerica.yourcorp.com.

B. Create a realm trust between east.namerica.yourcorp.com and east.samerica.yourcorp.com.

C. Create a forest trust between east.namerica.yourcorp.com and east.samerica.yourcorp.com.

D. Create a shortcut trust between east.namerica.yourcorp.com and east.samerica.yourcorp.com.

☑ Answer **D** is the correct answer. Shortcut trusts shorten the authentication path required to access resources that exist in other trees in an Active Directory forest.

☒ Answer **A** is incorrect because external trusts are used to connect AD forests to Windows NT 4.0 domains. Answer **B** is incorrect because realm trusts are used to connect Active Directory forests to other Kerberos realms. Answer **C** is incorrect because a forest trust is used to connect multiple forests.

10. Your organization's IT admin model is split geographically, and each region needs a separate domain. Your organization has four regions (NAmericas, SAmericas, EMEA, and APAC). What namespace is appropriate for your organization?

   A. Create four regional domains. The first domain should be the root. The remaining three will be child domains to the root.

   B. Create five regional domains. Each region will be a child domain.

   C. Create one domain. Each region will have its own domain controller in the domain.

   D. Create a root domain. The remaining four will be child domains to the root.

   ☑ Answer **D** is correct. The best approach for a regional model uses an empty root domain with each region represented by a child domain.

   ☒ Answers **A**, **B**, **C** are incorrect. Answers **A**, **B**, and **C** do not produce the desired results.

11. You are consolidating network resources for your organization. Which names are considered valid NetBIOS name? (Choose two answers.)

   A. RAPID|DESIGN

   B. RAPIDDESIGN

   C. RAPID~DESIGN

   D. RAPIDDESIGNDOMAIN

   ☑ Answers **B** and **C** are considered valid NetBIOS names. A NetBIOS name may consist of the following characters: ! @ # $ % ^ & ( ) - _ ' { } . ~ Spaces and the following characters are considered invalid: \ * + = | : ; " ? < > , Also, a 15-character limitation exists within NetBIOS naming.

   ☒ Answer **A** is incorrect because | is not a valid symbol. Answer **D** is incorrect because it is longer than 15 characters.

12. Your organization uses a Windows NT 4.0 domain design based on three resource domains and one master domain. The resource domains are NAMERICA, SAMERICA, and AUSTRALIA. The master domain is CORP. The overall design hosts 1500 users and computers. Consistent password policy, schema definitions, and account settings will apply throughout your organization, once upgraded to use Windows Server 2003 and Active Directory. All sites

are connected via 256kbps fractional T1s. Design a migration strategy for this organization.

A. Upgrade the master domain to Windows Server 2003. Create an OU design to mimic the resource domains. Next, upgrade the resource domains to Windows Server 2003. Move all accounts from the resource domains to their respective OUs in the master domain. Dissolve the resource domains.

B. Upgrade each domain in place from Windows NT 4.0 to Windows Server 2003.

C. Upgrade only the Windows NT 4.0 master domain to Windows Server 2003. Move the accounts from the resource domains to the Windows Server 2003 domain.

D. Upgrade all the domains to Windows 2000 Server. Upgrade the master domain to Windows Server 2003.

☑ Answer **A** is correct. The design requirements reflect a single-forest, single-domain model. OUs often can replace Windows NT 4.0 domains for delegation of control, as long as password and user rights will be consistent throughout the organization.

☒ Answer **B** is incorrect because upgrading in place will not provide the best design possible based on the criteria. Answer **C** is incorrect because Windows NT 4.0 does not provide provisions for moving domain accounts to other domains. Answer **D** is incorrect because there is no need to upgrade to Windows 2000 Server as an intermediate step to a Windows Server 2003 upgrade. Also, the design specified does not provide a single-forest, single-domain design, which seems the best fit for the requirements.

13. Your current network design consists of a Windows 2000 Active Directory domain with four Windows NT 4.0 domains external to the forest. Users in one of your NT 4.0 domains will require more stringent password and account lockout policies than the rest of your organization. The total number of accounts within your organization currently does not exceed 2500 users. Your offices are all connected via 128kbps ISDN and 512kbps fractional T1s. How will you upgrade this design so that all domains exist within the same Active Directory forest?

A. Upgrade the Windows 2000 domain in place. Create OUs for three of the four Windows NT 4.0 domains. Upgrade the Windows NT 4.0 domains to Windows Server 2003 domains. Restructure your enterprise design by moving all objects from the three NT 4.0 domains that will share password and account policies with the root domain, to the newly created root domain OUs. Leave the fourth domain as a separate domain in the forest, with its own password and account lockout policies.

B. Upgrade the Windows 2000 Server domain to Windows Server 2003 and create OUs for each of the NT 4.0 domains. Upgrade the NT 4.0 domains to Windows Server 2003. Move all accounts to their respective OUs in the root domain.

C. Upgrade the Windows 2000 domain in place. Upgrade the Windows NT 4.0 domains to Windows Server 2003. Apply the password and account policies on the domain that requires more stringent settings.

D. Upgrade the Windows 2000 domain to Windows Server 2003 and create OUs for each of the NT 4.0 domains. Move the accounts from three of the NT 4.0 domains to their respective OUs. Upgrade the remaining NT 4.0 domain to Windows Server 2003. Configure the specialized security settings on the domain that was just upgraded.

☑ Answer **A** is correct. Because one of the domains has different password and security requirements compared with the other domains, it will have to remain a separate domain. The remaining domains may be consolidated to the root domain.

☒ Answer **B** is incorrect because one domain will have to remain separate for password policy settings. Answer **C** is incorrect because most of the domains can (and should) be consolidated. This design keeps them all separate. Answer **D** is incorrect because accounts in an NT 4.0 domain may not be moved to another domain.

14. Your Active Directory design includes a single forest, a single domain, and an OU infrastructure based on both geography and function. Your design requirements specify that users in one location must operate with a more stringent password policy than the other locations. Design a Group Policy deployment strategy for this scenario.

A. Create two separate GPOs—one providing standard password options and the other providing tighter security requirements. Link the tighter-security GPO to the location OU requiring more stringent password requirements, and link the other GPO to the domain. Set the high-security GPO to a higher precedence.

B. Create another domain and relocate the OU with the more stringent security requirements to the new domain. Create a GPO and configure its policy requirements to provide the more stringent password policy requirements.

C. Create another forest and relocate the OU with the more stringent security requirements to the new forest. Create two GPOs (one for each domain) and configure the policy requirements for each GPO accordingly.

D. Create another domain and relocate the OU with the more stringent security requirements to the new domain. Create a GPO and configure the policy requirements for the new GPO to provide the less stringent password policy requirements.

☑ Answer **B** is the correct answer because separate password policy requirements require separate domains. Creating a domain for the more stringent policy requirements will provide the best solution.

☒ Answer **A** is incorrect because separate GPOs will not accommodate separate password policy requirements within the same domain. Answer **C** is incorrect because there is no need to create a separate forest for this scenario. Answer **D** is incorrect because the more stringent policy needs to be created. The existing policy for the original domain should suffice.

15. Your network design consists of two Active Directory forests, each with a single domain. You want to ensure that all workstations except the management workstations in the genericforest1.com forest run a shutdown script to clean up files left over from a specialized application. How do you configure Group Policy to accomplish this task, expending as little administrative overhead as possible?

A. Place each of the management workstations in its own OU. Apply the GPO to the domain within each forest, and block inheritance for the Management Workstations OU.

B. Place each of the management workstations in a security group. Apply the GPO to the domain within each forest, and change the GPO permissions so that the Management Workstations group is denied the apply Group Policy permission.

C. Place each of the management workstations in its own OU. Apply the GPO to the domain within each forest, and create a conflicting GPO with higher precedence to block the domain GPO.

D. Place each of the management workstations in its own group. Apply the GPO to the domain within each forest, and grant Read and Apply permission for the Management Workstations group.

☑ Answer **A** is correct because it applies the desired functionality while following best practice.

☒ Answer **B** is incorrect because you cannot directly assign permissions to workstations. Answer **C** is incorrect because writing two GPOs to accomplish this task does not follow best practice, because the desired result may be accomplished without modifying the default GPOs and without creating two GPOs. Answer **D** is incorrect because the Read and Apply permissions will cause a GPO to affect objects associated to that GPO.

Chapter 5 Name Resolution

1. On occasion, clients need to resolve DNS records for external resources. When this occurs, the client sends its query to its appropriate internal DNS server. The DNS server sends additional queries to external DNS servers, acting on behalf of the client, and returns the query information to the client once the server obtains it. What type of query occurs when a DNS server is used as a proxy for DNS clients that have requested resource record information outside their domain?

   A. Recursive query

   B. Iterative query

   C. Reverse lookup query

   D. External query

   ☑ Answer **A** is correct. A recursive query is a request from a host to a resolver to find data on other name servers.

   ☒ Answer **B** is incorrect because an iterative query is a request, usually made by a resolver, for any information a server already has in memory for a certain domain name. Answer **C** is incorrect because the client was querying with a host name, not an IP address. Answer **D** is incorrect because the question specified that a query was made to a proxy DNS server, not necessarily a DNS server in a higher-level external domain.

2. You are creating a standard primary zone for your company on a Windows Server 2003 DNS server, and you want to enable secure-only dynamic DNS updates on your standard primary zone for clients within your office. You open the DNS management console, access the Properties window of the primary zone, and notice that the only options available for dynamic updates are None and Non-secure and Secure. What is preventing you from enabling secure-only dynamic DNS updates on this zone?

   A. You cannot use secure-only dynamic DNS updates unless your zone is an Active Directory-integrated zone.

   B. The Secure Dynamic Updates feature is not available in Windows Server 2003.

   C. After creating the zone, you must stop and restart the DNS server service.

D. You can just use the Non-secure and Secure option, because clients will attempt to use secure dynamic updates first.

☑ Answer **A** is correct. Secure dynamic updates are available only in Active Directory-integrated zones.

☒ Answers **B**, **C**, and **D** are incorrect. Secure Dynamic Updates are definitely available in Windows Server 2003. Generally speaking, the DNS service does not need to be restarted after a configuration change. Finally, if secure dynamic updates are disabled or not available, clients will not have access to this feature.

3. One of your coworkers has been tasked with finding various ways to reduce the amount of network traffic that passes over the WAN. Your colleague approaches you with the idea of setting up DNS Notify for your Active Directory-integrated DNS zones. You inform him that although this is a good idea for reducing DNS traffic, it will not work in your organization's environment. Why might this be true?

A. DNS Notify is used to notify secondary servers of changes to the DNS database on the primary server. Because secondary servers do not exist in Active Directory-integrated zones, DNS Notify cannot be implemented.

B. DNS Notify is not available on the Windows Server 2003 operating system. However, an Active Directory-integrated zone can function as a secondary server using DNS Notify on a BIND server that functions as the primary server.

C. DNS Notify cannot run on your Windows Server 2003 server unless you place your zone files into an application directory partition.

D. This is not true. You can use DNS Notify in your environment as long as you add the list of secondary servers to notify in the properties of the primary server.

☑ Answer **A** is correct. DNS Notify works only with secondary servers, which Active Directory-integrated zones do not have.

☒ Answer **B** is incorrect because DNS Notify is available with Windows Server 2003, but is not required for Active Directory-integrated zones, for which there are no secondary servers. Answer **C** is incorrect because in this instance, the use of application directory partitions is not required to run DNS notify. However, if used effectively, they can be used to reduce the amount of DNS-related WAN traffic. Answer **D** is incorrect because your statement to your colleague is absolutely true.

4. You are creating a new standard primary zone for the company you work for, Name Resolution University, using the domain nru.corp. You create the zone through the DNS management console, and now you want to view the corresponding DNS zone file, nru.corp.dns. Where do you need to look in order to find this file?

   A. You cannot view the zone file because it is stored in Active Directory.

   B. You can look in the %systemroot%\system32\dns folder.

   C. You cannot view the DNS file except by using the DNS management console.

   D. The DNS zone file is actually just a key in the Windows Registry. You need to use the Registry Editor if you want to view the file.

   ☑ Answer **B** is correct. The default location of zone files for primary and secondary zones is %systemroot%\system32\dns.

   ☒ Answer **A** is incorrect because primary zones are not stored in Active Directory; only Active Directory-integrated zones are stored in Active Directory. Answer **C** is incorrect because the contents of the zone file can be viewed with a text editor. Answer **D** is incorrect because zone file data is not stored in the registry.

5. Your manager is concerned that the DNS servers in your network could be susceptible to name spoofing and wants to implement DNS security in your environment. He asks you to research the implementation of DNSSEC onto your existing Windows Server 2003 DNS servers. After researching DNSSEC, you explain to your boss that your Windows Server 2003 DNS servers can act only as secondary servers while running DNSSEC. Why is this so?

   A. A Windows Server 2003 DNS server can run only as a secondary server when using DNSSEC because it meets only the basic requirements of DNSSEC.

   B. A Windows Server 2003 DNS server can run only as a secondary server when using DNSSEC because a DNSSEC primary server can run only on BIND.

   C. A Windows Server 2003 DNS server can run only as a secondary server when using DNSSEC because you must purchase the additional DNSSEC module for Windows Server 2003 in order for your server to function as a primary DNS server.

   D. A Windows Server 2003 DNS server can indeed run as a primary or secondary server when using DNSSEC, as long as it is configured correctly.

☑ Answer **A** is correct. According to RFC 2535, there is only basic support for the DNSSEC that is implemented in Windows Server 2003. The RFC lists six requirements for full support of DNSSEC, all of which Windows Server 2003 doesn't meet. It does, however, meet, the requirements for basic support.

☒ Answer **B** is incorrect because although DNSSEC is implemented in the latest release of BIND 9, DNSSEC can run on systems other than BIND. Answer **C** is incorrect because DNSSEC is not a separate module; it is a feature of Windows Server 2003 that ships with the operating system. Answer **D** is incorrect because at this point in time a Windows Server 2003 DNS server can run only as a secondary server when using DNSSEC.

6. Your company has an existing DNS infrastructure that uses BIND 8.2 on Linux at its head office to host the root domain for the entire company, and it needs to integrate a subdomain that contains a group of Windows Server 2000 servers in a homogeneous Windows environment. These servers are in a branch office in another city and your manager wants to conserve bandwidth consumed by DNS. You suggest that full transfers of zone data should be avoided. Is this possible? If so, how can this be accomplished?

A. Yes because, if the subdomain is configured as an Active Directory-integrated zone, DNS replication can occur at the same time as Active Directory replication.

B. Yes, because BIND 8.2 supports incremental zone transfer.

C. No, because BIND 8.2 does not support incremental zone transfer.

D. No, because this version of BIND and Windows Server 2003 DNS cannot interoperate.

☑ Answer **B** is correct. BIND 8.2 is the earliest version that supports incremental zone transfer and can interoperate with Windows Server 2003 DNS.

☒ Answer **A** is incorrect because Active Directory-integrated zones cannot be used where BIND and Windows Server 2003 DNS are fully integrated. Answer **C** is incorrect because BIND 8.2 does support incremental zone transfer. Answer **D** is incorrect because BIND and Windows Server 2003 can interoperate, with the caveat that only the features that are supported in both versions can be integrated.

7. Your organization is running a heterogeneous DNS infrastructure that consists of Intel servers running Windows Server 2003 and RISC-based UNIX machines running BIND 9. Your organization just merged with another of equal size, and the new DNS domains will become subdomains of your existing

domains. What is the best way to bring the new DNS hierarchy in so that all resources can be located in the new amalgamated domain?

A. Implement conditional forwarders.

B. Implement Active Directory-integrated zones.

C. Implement stub zones.

D. Implement DNSSEC.

☑   Answer **C** is correct. Stub zones contain the SOA and A records for all of the authoritative DNS servers in the DNS hierarchy, and they could greatly facilitate the location of network services for both former companies. Both BIND 9 and Windows Server 2003 support stub zones.

☒   Answer **A** is incorrect because conditional forwarders assist in streamlining the forwarding of DNS queries, while stub zones will identify the newly added subdomains. BIND 9 supports conditional forwarders, but Answer **C** provides for the better solution. Answer **B** is incorrect because BIND 9 does not support Active Directory-integrated zones. Answer **D** is incorrect because DNSSEC guards the integrity of DNS data and is not used for identifying the location of domains.

8. Active Directory-integrated zones store their zone data in the Active Directory within a domain or application directory partition. Each zone is stored in a container object, which is identified by the name of the zone that has been created. To which class does this type of container object belong?

A. *dnsZone*

B. *dns-Zone*

C. *.dnsZone*

D. Active Directory zone

☑   Answer **A** is correct. dnsZone is the name of the container object used to store zone data in Active Directory.

☒   Answers **B**, **C**, and **D** are incorrect because they are not identified correctly.

9. You are the only network administrator in the head office of a chain of 20 local 24-hour video rental stores. All of the 20 local stores are connected to the head office by a 10Mbps LAN extension to facilitate the replication of large database updates on an hourly basis. Your video rental software uses NetBIOS and WINS to locate point-of-sale terminals, servers in the video store, and the various laptops and workstations used by the video store managers and head office personnel. What is the best choice for the WINS topology you should implement?

A. Hub and spoke with all stores configured as pull partners

B. Hub and spoke with all stores configured as push/pull partners

C. Fully meshed with all stores configured as pull partners

D. Fully meshed with all stores configured as push/pull partners

☑ Answer **B** is correct. The burden of managing the replication partnerships of the fully meshed model would be onerous for a team of people, let alone a single network administrator. The 10Mbps LAN extension provides enough bandwidth that WINS replication does not need to be carefully managed, and push/pull replication partnerships can be used.

☒ Answer **A** is incorrect because although the hub-and-spoke model is the right choice, pull replication partnerships are not necessary due to the ample amount of available bandwidth. Answers **C** and **D** are incorrect because the fully meshed model would be onerous for a team of people to manage, let alone a single network administrator. If each server were connected to every other server, there would be 380 total relationships (20 servers × 19 replication relationships) to troubleshoot when problems arise.

10. Your company just acquired another company, and it has been decided that the two former head offices will be connected with a full T-1 connection. The five branch offices in your organization are connected to your head office with fractional T-1 links, and the four newly acquired branch offices continue to use their 128Kbps-ISDN connections to their head office. You have been assigned the responsibility of creating a WINS infrastructure for the new enterprise. Which of the following recommendations will you make? Choose all that apply.

A. Make all offices from the newly acquired organization pull partners.

B. Make all offices from the newly acquired organization push/pull partners.

C. Make all offices from your organization pull partners.

D. Make all offices from your organization push/pull partners.

E. Deploy a hub-and-spoke topology with "hub" WINS servers in each of the head offices.

F. Deploy a hub-and-spoke topology with a "hub" WINS server in one of the head offices.

G. Deploy a Fully Meshed topology for all WINS servers in the new organization.

☑ Answer **A**, **D**, and **F** are correct. The offices at the end of the slow links should be made pull partners so that they can control the schedule for replication. The offices at the end of the fractional T-1 links should have sufficient available bandwidth to be push/pull partners. The hub-and-spoke model is the most manageable topology. However, it is best to have the master WINS database in one location so that the spoke will not be out of synchronization in case the schedules do not mesh.

☒ Answers **B**, **C**, **E**, and **G** are incorrect. The available bandwidth is too low to make the newly acquired offices push/pull partners, and likewise there is enough bandwidth for the original branch offices so that they do not need to be pull partners. The master copy of the WINS database should be in one location, and a fully meshed topology is not well suited to a distributed environment.

Chapter 6 Remote Access and Address Management

1. You are the network administrator for your organization. Your Windows Server 2003 domain consists of two sites, six domain controllers, and 500 Windows XP Professional and Windows 2000 Professional workstations. Most of your domain members are in St. Louis, but about 50 are in Jefferson City. You need to connect these two locations in a secure but more cost-effective manner than your current configuration. Currently, your organization is using leased lines between the two sites. What Windows Server 2003 solution would be your best choice?

    A. Add IPSec and create a dial-on-demand router.

    B. Create a VPN using the Internet as a backbone.

    C. Create a VPN and implement Layer 2 Tunneling Protocol using the Internet as a backbone.

    D. Create a VPN and implement IP filtering on the routers.

    ☑ Answer **D** is correct. You should create a VPN between the two sites. By implementing IPSec and L2TP and the IP filters they imply, you will be able to count on the data transport being safe between the two sites and that only authorized packets will be allowed to enter either site.

    ☒ The two requirements are that the solution be secure and more cost-effective. Although adding IPSec does make Answer **A** more secure, the use of a dial-on-demand router does not make the solution more cost-effective. Answer **B** offers more cost-effectiveness but does not provide the necessary security. Answer **C** offers cost-effectiveness, but L2TP does not in and of itself offer secure connections. To make this solution fulfill the requirements, IPSec needs to be added to the mix.

2. After spending hours setting up and configuring your remote access solution, you discover that users are still being denied access to your network. You've

even carefully created a remote access policy and associated profile for the inbound connections. What could be the cause of your problem?

A. You have forgotten to associate the policy with the appropriate group or OU.

B. You haven't activated the policy and associated profile.

C. The user's permissions are set for Control Access through Remote Access Policy, and the policy is set for Deny Access.

D. The policy is set for Control Access through Users Permissions, and the users' permissions are set to Deny Access.

☑ Answer **C** is correct. After the connections are configured, the administrator can use RRAS policies to control connections to the client. Remember that policies comprise conditions that are examined first. These conditions consist of settings such as time of day, group membership, IP address, service type requested, protocol, and so forth. Permissions (user properties) are then examined. These permissions consist of Allow Access, Deny Access, or Control Access through Remote Access Policy. Finally, the profiles, which define the kind of access the user will receive, are examined. Again, remember that RRAS policies are stored on the server, not in Active Directory. The default RRAS policy setting is called Allow Access if Dial-in Permission Is Enabled and is set for Deny Access. This means that all users in your native-mode network will be denied access until the administrator explicitly grants them dial-up access in their Dial-up Networking proper- ties. Mixed-mode networks do not offer the Control Access through Remote Access Policy permission. Here, Allow and Deny are the only per- missions available. In this situation, the user setting would be to Control Access through Remote Access Policy, and the policy must have been set to Deny Access.

☒ User access is determined through the permissions and profiles. In this sce- nario, all users are being denied access, so there is no appropriate group or OU to which the policy should have been associated. Therefore, Answer **A** is incorrect. Answer **B** is incorrect because, again, access is determined through permissions and profiles. Policies and profiles are not activated. Answer **D** stipulates that the access is controlled through user permissions and that the policy has set them. Just the reverse is true. User settings deter- mine how access is controlled, so Answer **D** is incorrect.

3. Your executive director has asked you to create and design a secure remote access solution for your organization. What two tunneling protocols are avail- able using Windows Server 2003 Remote Access Services?

A. Point-to-Point Tunneling Protocol (PPTP)

B. Layer 2 Tunneling Protocol (L2TP)

C. Layer 4 Tunneling Protocol (L4TP)

D. Internet Protocol Security (IPSec)

☑ Answers **A** and **B** are correct. Two tunneling protocols are available under Windows Server 2003 Remote Access Services: Point-to-Point Tunneling Protocol (PPTP) and Layer 2 Tunneling Protocol (L2TP).

☒ There is no such protocol as Layer 4 Tunneling Protocol, so Answer **C** is incorrect. IPSec provides for secure networking over TCP/IP by providing end-to-end security for all communication on the network and is therefore not a tunneling protocol. Answer **D** is therefore incorrect.

4. Assume that the network configuration depicted in Figure 6.49 is purely a Windows Server 2003 network. How must the RAS server be configured to facilitate DHCP assignment of IP addresses to dial-up network client computers?

Figure 6.49 Image for Question #4

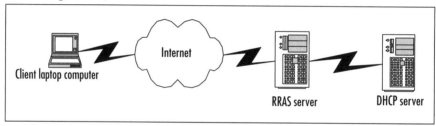

A. The dial-up network client computers must get an IP address from the RAS server. A block of IP addresses must be excluded on the DHCP servers, and the RAS server must be configured to assign addresses to the client computers.

B. The RAS server must be configured as a DHCP client computer.

C. The RAS server must be configured to allow dial-up network client computers to use DHCP to obtain an IP address.

D. The RAS server must be configured to use DHCP to obtain IP addresses on behalf of dial-up network client computers.

☑ Answer **D** is correct. A RAS server can be configured to obtain IP addresses from DHCP on behalf of its client computers.

☒ Answer **A** is incorrect because the dial-up network client computers can use the same scope as local DHCP client computers. Answer **B** is incorrect because whether the RAS server is a DHCP client computer has no bearing on the question. Answer **C** is incorrect because the dial-up client computer does not contact DHCP directly.

5. You're the administrator of a Windows Server 2003 computer named MySystem. MySystem is a standalone server outside any Windows Server 2003 or Windows 2000 domain. You want to use MySystem as an RAS server. You need to configure the dial-in properties of a user to allow that user to connect to the RAS. Which of the following is the correct procedure for doing so?

   A. Open the Local Users and Groups snap-in. Set the dial-in properties on the Dial-in tab of the user account properties of that user.

   B. Open the Active Directory Users and Computers snap-in. Set the dial-in properties on the Dial-in tab of the user account properties of that user.

   C. Open the Active Directory Users and Computers snap-in. Set the modem dial-in properties on the Dial-in tab of the user account properties of that user.

   D. Open the Local Users and Groups snap-in. Set the modem dial-in properties of the Advanced tab of the user account properties for that user.

   ☑ Answer **A** is correct. For a standalone server, a user's dial-in properties are set on the Dial-in tab of the user account properties in the Local Users and Groups snap-in.

   ☒ Because MySystem is a standalone server, it will not have an Active Directory Users and Groups snap-in, so Answers **B** and **C** are incorrect. In both standalone and Active Directory-based servers, the dial-in properties, not the modem dial-in properties, are set in the user account. This makes both Answers **C** and **D** incorrect.

6. You've just taken on the responsibility of serving as administrator for a Windows Server 2003 domain controller named OrgDC1. OrgDC1 exists within a Windows 2003 Server domain that is running in native mode. Your IT director wants OrgDC1 to act as the RAS server. You need to configure the user dial-in properties to allow connection attempts. You open the Active Directory Users and Computers snap-in and try to set the dial-in properties on the Dial-in tab of the user account properties. Which of the following options should be available for you to choose? (Choose all that apply.)

   A. Apply 128-bit Encryption

   B. Remote Access Permission

   C. Apply SSL

   D. Verify Caller ID

   E. Apply Static Routes

   F. Callback Options

   G. Assign a Static IP Address

☑ In an Active Directory-based server, you can set the dial-in properties on the Dial-in tab of the user account properties in the Active Directory Users and Computers snap-in. The Dial-in tab includes several options: Answer **B**, Remote Access Permission (Dial-in or VPN); Answer **D**, Verify Caller ID; Answer **F**, Callback Options; Answer **G**, Assign a Static IP Address; and Answer **E**, Apply Static Routes.

☒ Neither Answer **A** nor Answer **C** are included options on the Dial-in tab of the user account properties in the Active Directory Users and Computers snap-in.

7. You're the administrator of a Windows Server 2003 computer named FileServer4. FileServer4 resides on a subnet within your network. All Windows Server 2003 computers except the DHCP server itself use DHCP to configure IP addressing. You've just discovered that FileServer4 is intermittently failing to connect to the other Windows 2003 Server computers on the network. It doesn't happen all the time, but it is happening. You're not sure if other clients are having the same problem. Which two of the following solutions would help to solve this problem?

A. Decrease the duration of the DHCP leases for all servers.

B. Increase the duration of the DHCP leases for all servers.

C. Provide static IP addressing for all clients.

D. Provide static IP addressing for all servers.

E. Make sure that DHCP reservations are configured for all clients.

F. Make sure that DHCP reservations are configured for all servers.

☑ Answer **D**, **F** are correct. For servers, it is recommended that static addressing be used, so Answer **D** is correct. If static IP addressing is not going to be used for servers, then, at the very least, configure DHCP reservations for those servers, which would make Answer **F** correct as well. Clients using static host name resolution may require that critical servers, such as a file server, maintain their IP address configurations so that the client can find them.

☒ Decreasing the duration of the DHCP lease for the server will do nothing to solve the problem and probably would make it worse, so Answer **A** is incorrect. Increasing the duration of the lease, although possibly extending the time between problems, will still not solve the problem; therefore, Answer **B** is incorrect. The status of the address schema used for the clients is not the problem, so both Answers **C** and **E** are incorrect.

8. You are the network administrator for your organization. Your network consists of a single Windows Server 2003 domain. Your domain consists of Windows Server 2003 computers, Windows 2000 Server computers, Windows XP Professional computers, Windows 2000 Professional computers, and Windows NT 4.0 Workstation computers. You administer two Windows Server 2003 DNS servers, two Windows 2000 WINS servers, and two Windows Server 2003 DHCP servers. All servers in your network have been assigned static IP addresses. All client computers are DHCP clients. Both the servers and the clients are configured as WINS clients. You want all clients in the domain to be dynamically registered in DNS. What should you do?

A. Configure the DNS zone for the domain to use WINS forward lookup, and make sure that the Do not replicate this record check box is cleared.

B. Configure the DHCP servers to register your DHCP clients in DNS.

C. Configure an Active Directory integrated zone for the domain.

D. For all your client computers in your domain, manually configure DNS parameters, and then run the *ipconfig/registerdns* command from the command prompt in a DOS window.

☑ Answer **B** is correct. Remember, you want to enable dynamic registrations for all client computers in the domain. This is accomplished by configuring the DHCP servers to automatically update client information in the DNS for all Windows clients. This is accomplished by first opening the DHCP console and then right-clicking the DHCP server you want to configure and choosing Properties. Your next step is to select the DNS tab and then select Automatically update DHCP client information in DNS. This will allow your DHCP server to register the Windows XP Professional and Windows 2000 Professional clients in the DNS zone. In order to get the Windows NT 4.0 Workstation clients registered, you need to select Enable updates for DNS clients that do not support dynamic updates. Finally, click OK.

☒ Configuring the DNS zone to use WINS forward lookup, the DNS service would be able to use WINS servers to look up names not found in the DNS domain namespace by checking the NETBIOS namespace managed by the WINS. By clearing the Do not Replicate this record check box, the only thing you accomplish is that this would prevent records retrieved from WINS from being replicated to other servers during zone transfers. Neither of these two settings give you the ability to dynamically register your clients in the DNS, so Answer **A** is incorrect. Answer **C** is incorrect because an Active Directory-integrated zone is not required for dynamic registration of your clients in the DNS. Finally, the *ipconfig/registerdns* command is used to manually force a refresh of the clients in your DNS. This does not accomplish the requirement of dynamically registering all clients in the DNS, so Answer **D** is incorrect.

9. You are the administrator for your organization's network. This network consists of a single Windows Server 2003 domain. One of the Windows Server 2003 computers in your domain, ProximaCentauri, provides RRAS. ProximaCentauri is set up to use the default remote access policy. You are setting up new user accounts on the domain. What remote access permissions will be set for the new user accounts?

A. Control Access through Remote Access Policy

B. Deny Remote Access Permission Policy

C. Allow Access

D. Deny Access

☑ Answer **D** is correct. By default, new user accounts in a Windows Server 2003 domain are not granted dial-up access to a remote access server.

☒ By default, the Administrator and Guest accounts on a standalone remote access server are set to Control Access through Remote Access Policy. ProximaCentauri, however, is part of the domain, and the default here is to deny access, so Answer **A** is incorrect. Answer **B**, as with a Grant Remote Access Permission, is available in individual policies, not individual users, and is therefore incorrect. Remember that individual users' remote access permissions override policy settings. Finally, users are not granted dial-up access by default, so Answer **C** is incorrect.

10. You are one of the network administrators for your organization's network. The network consists of a single network subnet and contains a Windows 2000 server computer named Sneezy that runs the DNS server service. All your client computers are running either Windows XP Professional or Windows 2000 Professional, and they are all configured with static IP addresses. The clients are also configured to use Sneezy for DNS name resolution. Johann, another administrator, has installed Windows Server 2003 on another computer named Bashful. Johann has also installed the DNS server service and the DHCP server service on Bashful. He has configured the DHCP server to issue dynamic IP addresses to client computers and has configured the DHCP server to configure client computers to use Bashful for DNS name resolution. You have reconfigured all client computers to use DHCP to obtain IP addressing information, and you have uninstalled the DNS server service from Sneezy. Suddenly, all your users are calling and letting you know that they can no longer access any network resources by name. You need to ensure that they can access those network resources by name. What should you do?

A. Delete the Hosts file on each of the client computers.

B. Run the *ipconfig/registerdns* command on each of the client computers.

C. Configure the DNS server on Bashful to include a static A (host) record that contains the name and IP address of Sneezy.

D. Reconfigure each client computer to remove Sneezy's IP address from the list of DNS servers and to obtain a list of DNS servers automatically via DHCP.

☑ Answer **D** is correct. You changed the TCP/IP configuration on the clients, and they're now receiving their address and network mask dynamically instead of by static assignment. You must also change the configuration so that the clients will obtain DNS server addresses automatically also. Currently, the clients are still configured to get DNS information from Sneezy.

☒ Answer **A**, deleting the Hosts file, won't change the basic problem. It doesn't appear that the Hosts file is being used anyway. Answer **B** is also incorrect because the clients are still configured to use the now–nonexistent DNS Sneezy. Running this command would simply force the clients to attempt to register at Sneezy. Finally, Answer **C** would be an exercise in futility. You already uninstalled the DNS server from Sneezy, so it would do no good whatsoever to add a host record for Sneezy at the DNS Bashful.

11. You're the network administrator for your organization's Windows Server 2003 domain. The domain consists of a single Windows Server 2003 domain controller named Lion and 25 desktop client computers running Windows XP Professional and Windows 2000 Professional. Your network connects to the Internet via a T1 line. All IP addresses in your network are static. You've set up an RRAS on a Windows Server 2003 computer named Tiger to provide VPN access, as shown in Figure 6.50. Tiger is a member of the domain. At one of the Windows 2000 Professional client machines on the domain, you use the *Ping* command to search for Tiger and you receive a reply. At Tiger, you run *ipconfig* and notice that the subnet mask is 0.0.0.0. What could be the problem?

Figure 6.50 Your Organization's Windows Server 2003 Domain for Question #11

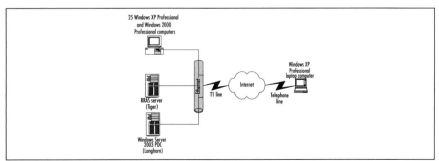

A. There is another computer with the same NetBIOS name.

B. There is another computer with the same IP address.

C. The Routing and Remote Access Service has assigned an Automatic Private IP Addressing (APIPA) address to the Windows XP Professional laptop computer.

D. The DHCP server has assigned an APIPA address to the Windows XP Professional laptop computer.

☑ Answer **B** is correct. Using the *ipconfig /all* command on Tiger checks the computer's current TCP/IP settings. When 0.0.0.0 is returned as the subnet, there's another computer on the network with the same IP address.

☒ Answer **A** is incorrect because the existence of 0.0.0.0 as the subnet is an indication of a duplicate IP address, not a duplicate NetBIOS name. Answer **C** is incorrect because it is the lack of a DHCP server, not an RRAS server, that causes an APIPA address to be assigned. Because the client is able to connect successfully to the Internet, the problem has to do with connecting to the VPN and nothing else. Answer **D** is incorrect because APIPA addresses are assigned when a DHCP server cannot be located when a computer is first started.

12. You are the network administrator for your organization, and your network consists of one DHCP server running on a Windows Server 2003 computer named Bradbury; three Windows Server 2003 computers named Heinlein, Clark, and deCamp serving as domain controllers; two DNS servers named Stephenson and Gibson running on Windows Server 2003 computers; one WINS server named Brunner running on Windows Server 2003; five file servers named Burke, Hillerman, Koontz, Brin, and Fitzhugh running on Windows 2000 Server computers; 275 Windows XP Professional and Windows 2000 Professional client computers; and two UNIX servers named Clancy and Chrichton. All your file servers except Brin rely on DHCP for IP addressing. You relocate Brin to another subnet, and none of your clients can access it any longer. You take the following actions:

- Reconfigure Brin to provide DNS service.

- Reconfigure Brin to provide DHCP service.

- Delete Brin's static entry from the DNS database.

What has been accomplished by your efforts? (Choose all that apply.)

A. Brin's security has been optimized.

B. Brin's performance has been optimized.

C. Brin will be accessible even if relocated again across subnets.

D. Brin will be accessible even if relocated again within the same subnet.

E. Brin is now accessible.

☑ Answers **C**, **D**, and **E** are correct. The DHCP service centralizes and manages the allocation of TCP/IP configuration information by assigning IP addresses automatically to computers configured as DHCP clients. By configuring Brin for DNS and DHCP and then deleting the previous static entry from the DNS database, you have made Brin accessible again to the clients on the network. Because you have configured Brin for both DHCP and DNS, you have also made sure that Brin will be accessible even if it is relocated on the subnet or moved to another subnet.

☒ Answses **A** and **B** are incorrect. Configuring Brin for DNS and DHCP will do nothing toward optimizing either Brin's security or performance.

13. You're the network administrator for your organization's Windows Server 2003 network. Your network contains a remote access-enabled server. You set the dial-in permissions for the user accounts to control access through remote access policy. When users attempt to connect to the RAS, what happens?

A. All connection attempts must meet the profile requirements of all policies.

B. All connection attempts must meet conditions of all policies.

C. All connection attempts are accepted.

D. All connection attempts are rejected.

☑ Answer **D** is correct. By default, users are not granted dial-in permissions. You must therefore change the dial-in setting to Grant Remote Access Permission to allow your users to dial in.

☒ Connection attempts need to meet the profile requirements of the policy applied for the user or group of users. By default, connections are denied, so Answers **A**, **B**, and **C** are incorrect. You must change this setting to Grant Remote Access Permission.

14. You are the administrator for your organization. Your organization maintains a small (25-user) Ethernet network. The network is a single-segment network with a standard IP addressing scheme. Host IP addresses are limited, so when your executive director asks you to set up dialup network access for your traveling benefits staff of three, you decide to use a different network ID for dial-up client computers. You set up a domain controller Windows Server 2003 computer with a modem and then configure RAS to assign IP addresses for dial-up client computers using a different network ID. When you test the dial-up procedure, you find that you can log on to the network; however, you do not have access to the rest of the network. What did you forget to do?

A. You must enable routing in the RAS computer's TCP/IP configuration.

B. You cannot use a different network ID for RAS client computers than you use on the network to which the RAS computer belongs. You must configure dial-up client computers to use the network's DHCP services.

C. You must assign static IP addresses to the dial-up client computers.

D. You must add the new network ID to the RAS computer's routing table.

☑ Answer **A** is correct. You must enable routing in the RAS computer's TCP/IP configuration. The modem connected to the RAS server is no different than a network interface card as far as TCP/IP is concerned. You can log on to the RAS computer because it is a domain controller; however, because routing is not enabled, you are not logically connected to the rest of the network.

☒ Answers **B**, **C**, and **D** are incorrect. Routing has not been configured in any of these options.

15. You are the administrator for your multihomed network (which has multiple connections to the Internet, for purposes of availability and redundancy). Until recently you managed your IP addressing manually. With the addition of several hundred new users, you have decided to reassess the situation and configure your workstations to use DHCP. You have started the service and configured your DHCP scopes. Because you have several segments, you have several scopes to configure. Hosts are getting IP addresses, so it seems that you have configured your DHCP service correctly, but you find out rather quickly that workstations can't communicate with other systems on different segments. Computers are able to connect to other computers on their own segment. You have verified that DHCP is working correctly. Assuming that your hosts connect using an IP address, what could be the problem?

A. The lease time is too short.

B. DNS is not configured in his DHCP scope.

C. The default gateway hasn't been set.

D. The subnet mask on the DHCP scope is set incorrectly.

☑ Answer **C** is correct. DNS hasn't been configured in your DHCP scope. If the destination computer isn't on the local segment, TCP/IP needs to know where to send the request. The default gateway is that place the request needs to be sent.

☒ The default lease time is three days; therefore, the lease time is not the cause, and Answer **A** is incorrect. If your hosts are connecting using an IP address, DNS is not needed, so Answer **B** is incorrect. If the subnet mask were configured incorrectly, chances are that the host could not communicate with other hosts on the same subnet at all, so Answer **D** is incorrect.

Chapter 7 Service Sizing and Placement

1. Your organization has many disparate locations. You have been tasked with designing Active Directory infrastructure placement. Which of the following might influence your design? (Choose all that apply.)

   A. User populations

   B. Available bandwidth

   C. Physical security

   D. Existing service levels

   ☑ Answer **A** is correct. As discussed in the section The Planning Phase, user populations can influence the design, because it might be deemed appropriate to place infrastructure only in locations with large user populations. Answer **B** is also correct. Bandwidth must be factored into the design so that replication traffic does not saturate smaller WAN links. Physical security must be assessed so that DCs are not deployed into locations that cannot guarantee their safety, making Answer **C** correct. Finally, Answer **D** is correct because service levels must be examined, because any agreements in place must be honored within the Active Directory design.

   ☒ None.

2. While assessing locations within your organization, you note that different locations can provide different levels of physical security for your DCs. Which of the following conditions should be met by a location being considered to receive a DC? (Choose all that apply.)

   A. A locked server cabinet

   B. A separate cabinet in which only the DC(s) are housed

   C. A lockable communications room

   D. A server located at the administrator's desk, for ease of administration

   ☑ The Active Directory database should be secured in much the same way as any other company data would be. If the data stored within Active Directory was to become available to a competitor, the ramifications could be dire. The DC(s) should therefore be secured in a locked cabinet, or room, which offers an extra level of protection to the server and the database itself. It should therefore be locked in a server cabinet (Answer **A** is thus correct) that is ideally dedicated to the DC so only the administrators of that server have physical access to it (Answer **B** is thus correct). The cabinet itself should be located inside a lockable communications room (Answer **C** is thus correct).

☒   Answer **D** is incorrect. A DC should not be located at an administrator's desk where it can be physically accessed by any member of staff or visitors to the office premises.

3. You have been tasked with estimating the size of the Active Directory database within each domain in your Active Directory forest. Which of the following algorithms or tools should be adopted when calculating this estimate? (Choose two.)

A. Add 400MB for every 1000 users in the domain

B. Assume an upper limit of 1GB

C. Monitor the database size during deployment and use trend analysis

D. Use the Microsoft Active Directory Sizer utility

☑   The rule of thumb offered by Microsoft is to assign 400MB of disk space for each 1000 users. Answer **A** is therefore correct. However, Microsoft's own Active Directory Sizer can also be used to estimate the size of the Active Directory database and will offer basic suggestions for DC sizing and configuration. Answer **D** is therefore also correct.

☒   Answer **B** is incorrect because it states that an upper limit exists, which is not the case. Large organizations will notice that their database grows beyond 1GB. Answer **C** is incorrect because it suggests that trend analysis be used, but this assumes that the database will grow in a linear fashion, which is unlikely because the deployment is unlikely to occur in such a way.

4. You are a systems architect and have been tasked with designing the optimum configuration for the DCs within your organization. Which of the following disk configurations offers the optimum performance for a Windows Server 2003 DC, while offering high availability?

A. Database and SYSVOL using RAID 1, log files using RAID 1

B. Database and SYSVOL using RAID 0, log files using RAID 1

C. Database and SYSVOL using RAID 5, log files using RAID 1

D. Database and SYSVOL using RAID 5, log files using RAID 5

☑   Answer **C** is correct. The Active Directory database is mostly read from, whereas the log files are mostly written to. RAID 5 offers optimized read performance, and RAID 1 offers optimized write performance.

☒ Answers **A** and **B** are incorrect because they do not optimize the database for reads. Answer **D** is incorrect because it does not optimize the log files for writes.

5. You are the Domain Administrator in an Active Directory domain. You have been tasked with promoting a member server to a DC in an existing domain. Which of the following checks and changes should be performed at the member server before the promotion begins? (Choose all that apply.)

A. Check event logs for errors

B. Check DNS connectivity

C. Disable the DHCP client service

D. Check connectivity to the RID Master FSMO role

☑ Before promoting a member server, the event logs should be checked for errors; otherwise, the promotion might fail due to an existing issue. Answer **A** is therefore correct. Without correct DNS connectivity, the promotion is sure to fail, because the server will need to perform DNS lookups to locate other DCs in the domain from which it can replicate Active Directory data. Answer **B** is therefore correct. Answer **D** is correct because during the promotion phase, the new DC will attempt to acquire a pool of RIDs to be assigned to new security principals created within its local Active Directory database. The server must be able to contact the domain's RID Master.

☒ Answer **C** is incorrect. Although a DC should be configured with a static IP address, the DHCP client service is required, because this service is responsible for registering the DC's Host and Reverse DNS records.

6. A new DC needs to be created. Which command can be executed to initiate a manual server promotion at the appropriate member server?

A. promote.exe

B. dcpromo.exe

C. server2dc.exe

D. upgrade.exe

☑ Answer **B** is correct. When promoting a server into a DC, dcpromo.exe can be run to initiate the promotion phase.

☒ Answers **A**, **C**, and **D** are incorrect. The commands promote.exe, server2dc.exe, and upgrade.exe do not exist.

7. A new DC needs to be created in a remote office that does not have any onsite administrators. You want to build and promote a new server without granting a

local user additional rights, and without traveling to the remote office. Instead, you create an answer file and plan to promote the server automatically once the operating system has been installed. Which command needs to be executed to initiate an automated server promotion?

A. dcpromo /answer:*answerfile.txt*

B. dcpromo /file:*answerfile.txt*

C. dcpromo /answerfile:*answerfile.txt*

D. dcpromo /auto:*answerfile.txt*

☑ When using dcpromo in an automated fashion, the correct syntax to use when specifying an answer file is given in Answer **A**.

☒ Answers **A**, **B**, and **C** are incorrect All three are incorrect syntax for use by dcpromo when automating a promotion of a server to DC status.

8. A server has been promoted to DC status and now needs to be configured as a GC server. Which application is used to configure the DC to act as a GC server?

A. Active Directory Users and Computers

B. Active Directory Domains and Trusts

C. Active Directory Sites and Services

D. Computer Management

☑ Answer **C** is correct. A DC is configured to provide GC services using the Active Directory Sites and Services MMC snap-in.

☒ Answers **A**, **B**, and **D** are incorrect. The Active Directory Users and Computers snap-in is used to manage users, groups, and computer objects in Active Directory. Answer **A** is therefore incorrect. The Active Directory Domains and Trusts snap-in is used to view and manage trusts in Active Directory, and thus Answer **B** is incorrect. The Computer Management snap-in is used to manage the local and/or remote computers in Active Directory, thus Answer **D** is also incorrect.

9. You have been asked to assess an existing DC as to whether it has enough free disk space to cope with the GC role. What algorithm should you deploy when estimating the disk space requirements for a GC server?

A. Space required = size of local domain partition + ? sum total of all other domain partitions

B. Space required = size of local domain partition + ? sum total of all other domain partitions

C. Space required = size of local domain partition

D. Space required = size of local domain partition + sum total of all other domain partitions

☑ The algorithm in Answer **B** is used to estimate the size of the database housed by a GC server.

☒ Answers **A**, **C**, and **D** are incorrect Answer **A** adds the wrong proportion of data from nonlocal domains, and Answer **C** does not add any additional data for nonlocal domains. Answer **D** is incorrect because it assumes that a GC stores all data from all domain partitions, which is not the case.

10. You have been tasked with the design and placement of the Active Directory FSMO roles. Which of the following roles are forestwide and thus exist once only within any forest? (Choose all that apply.)

A. RID Master

B. PDC Emulator

C. Domain Naming Master

D. Schema Master

☑ Answers **C** and **D** are correct. Both the Domain Naming Master and the Schema Master FSMO roles are forestwide roles and thus exist only once in any given Active Directory forest.

☒ Answers **A** and **B** are incorrect. The FSMO roles PDC Emulator and RID Master are domainwide and exist once per domain in a forest.

11. You have been asked to promote a new DC and establish a new domain and new domain tree within an existing forest. Which of the existing FSMO roles must be available in order for the promotion to succeed? (Choose all that apply.)

A. RID Master

B. PDC Emulator

C. Domain Naming Master

D. Schema Master

☑ Answer **C** is correct. When a new domain is created, the Domain Naming Master FSMO roleholder must be contacted so as to ensure that the new domain name is unique within the forest.

☒ Answers **A**, **B**, and **D** are incorrect. The RID Master is contacted only when a new DC is created in an existing domain and when a DC needs to replenish its pool of RIDs. Answer **A** is therefore incorrect. The PDC Emulator does not need to be contacted during the promotion of a DC;

therefore, Answer **B** is incorrect. The Schema Master need only be contacted when schema changes are made; therefore, Answer **D** is incorrect.

12. The DC housing the PDC Emulator role fails due to a hardware-related issue. It is likely that the hardware fault will take one to two days to fix. How could you, the domain administrator, address the fact that the PDCe role has been lost and ensure that the environment continues to function correctly? (Choose all that apply.)

    A. Seize the PDCe role using ntdsutil

    B. Seize the PDCe role using the Active Directory Sites and Services interface

    C. Seize the PDCe role using the Active Directory Users and Computers interface

    D. Promote an existing DC to the role of PDCe

    ☑ Answers **A** and **C** are correct. The PDCe role has been lost unexpectedly and thus must be seized. This can be done using either the command-line utility ntdsutil or the Active Directory Users and Computers MMC snap-in.

    ☒ Answers **B** and **D** are incorrect. There are no FSMO roles that can be managed using the Active Directory Sites and Services snap-in, so Answer B is incorrect. The concept of promoting a DC to status of PDCe exists in Windows NT4, but is not valid when discussing Windows Server 2003 and FSMO roles. Answer D is thus incorrect.

13. The DC hosting the RID Master FSMO role in an Active Directory domain has failed due to a hard disk failure. You have been tasked with ensuring that the hardware fault is fixed and that the RID Master role continues to be available to the remaining DCs in the domain. What steps should you take?

    A. Transfer the RID Master role to another DC.

    B. Seize the RID Master role to another DC, fix the hardware issue on the original RID Master role holder, and reinstall Windows Server 2003 on that server before introducing it back into the domain.

    C. Seize the RID Master role to another DC, fix the hardware issue on the original RID Master role holder, introduce the original role holder to the domain, and transfer the RID Master role back to its original owner.

    D. Do not seize or transfer the RID Master role. Fix the hardware issue and boot the DC hosting the RID Master role.

    ☑ Answer **B** is correct. For the RID Master FSMO role to remain available, it must be seized to another DC in the same domain. Once the hardware issue has been fixed, Windows Server 2003 must be reinstalled on the orig-inal FSMO roleholder before it can be introduced back into the domain. If not rebuilt beforehand, your domain will have two RID Masters for a period of time, each of which might attempt to assign the same pool of RIDs to different DCs.

☒ Answers **A**, **C**, and **D** are incorrect. The RID Master role cannot be trans-ferred because the original roleholder is not available. Answer A is therefore incorrect. As stated, the original roleholder must be rebuilt before being introduced back into the domain, so Answer **C** is also incorrect. Answer **D** is incorrect because this approach implies that the RID Master role will be unavailable while the DC's hardware issue is being addressed. This does not meet the requirements laid out in the question.

Chapter 8 The Physical Design

1. In designing the network for Chapter Five Industries, you have been given the requirement that the company will be hosting its own Web site. What is the first thing you should do to ensure that the company will be able to achieve e-commerce on the Internet?

   A. Design the router placement

   B. Design the firewall filters

   C. Obtain a domain name

   D. Design the capacity

   ☑ Answer **C** is correct. The first thing you should do is research and obtain a domain name. You want to ensure this is taken care of before someone else obtains the same name.

   ☒ Answer **A** is incorrect, because you can design the placement of the routers after you obtain the domain name. This is an important step but not the first step. Answer **B** is incorrect, because you need to have a domain name first and determine what information will need to be filtered. Answer **D** is incorrect, because you will build the determination of the capacity of the information when designing the router placement.

2. Chapter Five Industries has only one connection to the Internet—a 512K Frame Relay. There are 500 users in this network. These users are complaining that the Internet is slow. The Internet connectivity is set up as shown ion the following the diagram. What could be done to enhance the users' Internet experience without incurring too much cost?

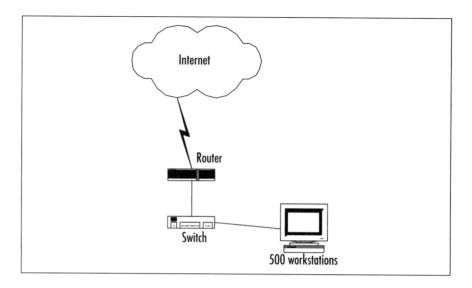

A. Increase the bandwidth of the Internet connection

B. Install a proxy server

C. Install another router for the users

D. Install a firewall

☑ Answer **B** is correct. Installing a proxy server will allow for caching to help speed the download of Web site content for frequently used Web sites.

☒ Answer **A** is incorrect, because this would increase the cost too much. The proxy server is a more cost-effective solution. Answer **C** is incorrect, because installation of another router would not eliminate the bottleneck that the users are experiencing. Both routers would still need to communicate through the same Internet pipe. Answer **D** is incorrect, because a normal firewall will not perform the caching function needed to increase performance.

3. You have just finished creating the new physical network design for Chapter Five Industries. You now need to create IP subnets to coincide with the new design. What is the minimum amount of IP subnets you will need to design?

A. Two

B. Three

C. Four

D. Six

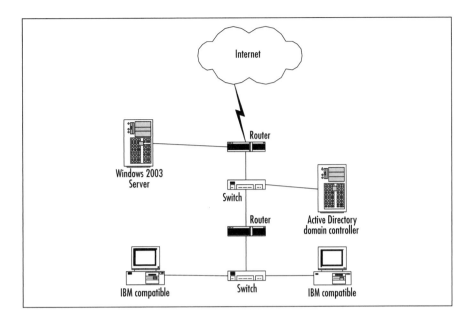

☑ Answer **C** is correct. Minimally, you will require a subnet on the outside, a subnet for the Windows Server 2003 server, a subnet between the two routers to support the Active Directory DC, and a subnet to support the IBM-compatible user systems.

☒ Answer **A** is incorrect, because it does not accommodate all of the necessary segments of the physical design. Every side of a router needs at least one IP subnet. Answer **B** is incorrect, because it does not accommodate all of the necessary segments of the physical design. The Windows Server 2003 server might be the common mistake here because it does sit by itself on a separate IP subnet. Answer **D** is incorrect, because it does not meet the minimum IP subnets. You need at least four IP subnets. If the bottom switch that is connected to the IBM-compatibles were a router, then it would require two more subnets to satisfy the design.

4. You have been given the following network WAN design. Philadelphia has 200 users, New York has 100 users, Atlanta has 200 users, and Los Angeles has 50 users. You need to create a private address scheme that will satisfy the design. The Frame Relay cloud and router interfaces already are using a 203.45.9.x IP addressing assigned by the ISP. What would be the best IP addressing to use in this design?

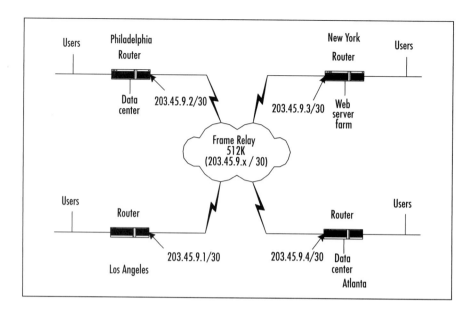

A. Philadelphia Users (192.168.1.x /24), Philadelphia Data Center
    (192.168.2.x /24); New York Users (192.168.3.x /24), New York Web
    Server Farm (192.168.4.x /24); Los Angeles Users (10.0.3.x /24); Atlanta
    Users (10.0.1.x /24), Atlanta Data Center (10.0.2.x /24)

B. Philadelphia Users (100.0.1.x /24), Philadelphia Data Center (100.0.2.x
    /24); New York Users (100.0.3.x /24), New York Web Server Farm
    (100.0.4.x /24); Los Angeles Users (100.0.5.x /24); Atlanta Users (100.0.6.0
    /24), Atlanta Data Center (100.0.7.0 /24)

C. Philadelphia Users (192.168.1.x /24), Philadelphia Data Center
    (192.168.2.x /24); New York Users (192.168.3.x /24), New York Web
    Server Farm (192.168.4.x /24); Los Angeles Users (192.168.5.x /24);
    Atlanta Users (192.168.6.x /24), Atlanta Data Center (192.168.7.x /24)

D. Philadelphia Users (10.1.0.x /8), Philadelphia Data Center (10.1.0.x /8);
    New York Users (10.1.0.x /8), New York Web Server Farm (10.1.0.x /8);
    Los Angeles Users (10.1.0.x /8); Atlanta Users (10.1.0.x /8), Atlanta Data
    Center (10.1.0.x /8)

☑ Answer **C** is correct. With the low number of users at each site, a Class C
    private address can be used. It will allow for 254 hosts per subnet.

☒ Answer **A** is incorrect, because even though the IP addressing would work,
    it is not the best answer because of the inconsistent use of both a Class A
    and a Class C private addressing. Answer **B** is incorrect, because 100.x.x.x
    is not a private address assigned through RFC 1918. These are Internet

routable addresses and might cause conflicts in the future. Answer **D** is incorrect, because it is not the most effective use of NET10 private addressing. It will work in this scheme but would allow for an overabundance of IP address per subnet.

5. You have just finished designing and installing a Window Server 2003 DHCP server. You have three subnets in your network. Subnet A contains the Windows Server 2003 DHCP server. Subnets B and C contain user workstations. You receive a call that users in subnet B cannot get on the Internet. You perform an IPCONFIG on one of the workstations and get an IP address of 169.224.221.5. What could be the problem? (Choose two.)

A. You excluded the 169.224.221.x range on the DHCP server.

B. There is no scope created for this subnet.

C. The router is set to filter the 169.224.221.x range from accessing the Internet.

D. The router is not forwarding BOOTP requests.

☑ Answer **B** is correct, because if a scope was not created for subnet B, then the workstation will receive the automatic IP address. This is the address that was given during the IPCONFIG. Answer **D** is correct, because if the router does not forward the DHCP Request, then the client will not receive an address and get the same results as not having a scope. You will need to enable BOOTP on the router or implement a DHCP Relay to fix this problem.

☒ Answer **A** is incorrect, because 169.224.221.x is an automatic IP address that the client negotiates if it cannot find a DHCP server. Answer **C** is incorrect, because if the client received the automatically negotiated IP address, it would not receive a gateway (default router). Therefore, it would not even reach the router.

6. The HR Department has become concerned about security lately and would like to ensure even internally that its users and servers are safe from unfriendly elements. They are not as concerned about speed as they are about security and logging. What device could be used to securely segment the HR Department users and servers from the rest of the organization?

A. Router

B. Switch

C. Firewall

D. Proxy server

☑ Answer **C** is correct. A firewall will help to isolate and protect the HR users and provide stronger logging options for evaluating attempted intrusion.

☒ Answer **A** is incorrect, because a router might not be able to provide the level of logging dictated by the HR department. Answer **B** is incorrect, because switches do not provide that level of security and isolation. Answer **D** is incorrect, because proxy servers are not an optimal solution for segmenting a subnet.

7. Your current network design has three sites with 470 users. Over the next three years, there are 10 more sites planned. There will also be about 2000 users added to the environment. Because of performance issues with having too many computers on a single subnet, there is a limit of 200 computers per subnet. Using the private Class C IP addressing, what subnet mask would allow for the future expansion?

   A. 255.255.240.0

   B. 255.255.254.0

   C. 255.255.255.0

   D. 255.255.252.0

☑ Answer **C** is correct. Because we want to limit the computer to 200 per subnet for performance, we need to design around that number. A subnet mask of 255.255.255.0 would allow for 254 users per subnet.

☒ Answer **A** is incorrect, because a subnet mask of 255.255.240.0 would provide for 4096 hosts. This is way above the limit. Answer **B** is incorrect, because a subnet mask of 255.255.254.0 would provide for 512 hosts. Answer **D** is incorrect, because a subnet mask of 255.255.252.0 would provide for 1024 hosts.

8. You need to design failover into your Internet connectivity solution. You are going to be using your RRAS server to accomplish this failover. What types of telephony connection can you use to provide dial-on-demand? (Choose all that apply.)

   A. X.25

   B. TCP/IP

   C. DSL

   D. Asynchronous telephone line

☑ Answers **A**, **C**, and **D** are correct. X.25, DSL, and asynchronous telephone line are all acceptable means of using dial-on-demand routing. You can also use cable and ISDN.

☒ Answer **B** is incorrect, because TCP/IP is the protocol that will be used in the communication, not the medium of the communication.

9. You have remote offices in San Diego and Seattle. To save money, you have designed dial-on-demand into your solution. These sites occasionally need to attach to the Internet. They also need to occasionally attach to the main office in Philadelphia. You want to make these connections as secure as possible. All of the offices are using Windows Server 2003 servers for RRAS. How would you set up the encryption options on the RRAS servers in the branch office for dial-on-demand routing?

   A. For the Internet connection, set "require encryption." For the main office connection, set "optional encryption."

   B. For the Internet connection, set "no encryption." For the main office connection, set "no encryption."

   C. For the Internet connection, set "optional encryption." For the main office connection, set "optional encryption."

   D. For the Internet connection, set "optional encryption." For the main office connection, set "require encryption."

   ☑ Answer **D** is correct. If you set the Internet connection to "optional encryption," if the ISP is using a Windows 2000 or Windows Server 2003 RRAS server, then encryption will be used. If they are not, then encryption will not be used, but you will still be able to connect to the Internet. If you set the main office connection to "require encryption," encryption will always be used. Because the entire organization is using Windows Server 2003, they will be compatible.

   ☒ Answer **A** is incorrect, because if you "require encryption" for the Internet, you might not be able to establish a connection if they are not using Windows 2000 or 2003 servers. Answer **B** is incorrect, because if you set the main office connection to "no encryption," you are not making the connection as secure as possible. Answer **C** is incorrect, because you should force the main office connection to "require encryption" to ensure you have a secure connection.

10. You are designing a dial-on-demand solution for a small organization of 50 users. They only need the RRAS for connecting to the Internet. There will be an IDSL (128K/128K) line used for this connection. What will be your biggest concern with this solution?

   A. Encrypting access to the Internet

   B. Bandwidth utilization

   C. Setup and maintenance of the solution

   D. Cost of the solution

☑   Answer **B** is correct. Because of the 128K link to the Internet and 50 users who might try to connect, bandwidth will be limited.

☒   Answer **A** is incorrect, because there should not be a need to encrypt your connection to the Internet. Encryption will occur from the users to the Internet resources to which they attach. Answer **C** is incorrect, because setup and maintenance will be easy with Windows Server 2003. Answer **D** is incorrect; because you are using IDSL, the cost will be low compared to a leased-line solution.

11. You are designing a VPN solution for an organization. There will be 100 users who will need to connect to the organization using VPN. How may VPN ports should you establish in your design to meet the requirements?

A. 100

B. 50

C. 13

D. 10

☑   Answer **C** is correct. Using the 8:1 rule-of-thumb, you would need to have at least 13 VPN connections. 100 / 8 = 12.5 (rounded up to 13)

☒   Answer **A** is incorrect, because 100 would be overkill; this works under the assumption that all users will connect all the time. Answers **B** and **D** are incorrect, because they do not fit the 8:1 rule-of-thumb; 50 would be too many, and 10 would be too few.

12. You are designing a VPN solution for a large organization. Users will be connecting from the Internet to three RRAS servers in the Philadelphia office. What is the best solution for authenticating these users?

A. Use a RADIUS server with Active Directory authentication

B. Use the RRAS servers with standalone authentication

C. Use the RRAS servers with Active Directory authentication

D. Use a RADIUS server with standalone authentication

☑   Answer **A** is correct. The RADIUS server will serve to centralize the authentication process in a tier capacity. Using Active Directory will maintain a centralized repository for authentication whether the user is remote or local.

☒   Answer **B** is incorrect, because it is best to centralize the authentication process. Answer **C** is incorrect, because it is best to use the tiered process for enhanced security. Answer **D** is incorrect, because it is best to use Active Directory to maintain a centralized repository for authentication whether the user is remote or local.

Index

A

A records, 162
A resource records, 338
AAAA resource records, 338
access control lists (ACLs), managed by data
    administrators, 83
accountability, 98
accounting strategy, for remote access, 422–424, 451
Acknowledge message (DHCP), 191
ACLs (access control lists), managed by data
    administrators, 83
Active Directory (AD)
    ADPs and, 485
    deployed organization-wide by service
        administrators, 82
    DNS and, 156, 318–361
    environment for, assessing, 1–77
    infrastructure designs for, 79–153
        accessing impact of proposed designs, 65–69
    interoperability issues and, 33
    network perimeter security planning and, 549
    partitions in, 478
    physical design for, 529–567
    supportability for, identifying, 56–58
    WINS and, 186, 361–371
Active Directory database
    defragmenting, 482–484
    size of, 478–485
Active Directory Integrated zones (ADI zones), 55,
    160, 177, 331, 373, 379
    benefits of, 324
    vs. primary zones, 344
Active Directory Migration Tool (ADMT), 303
Active Directory namespace, 231–233
Active Directory Service Interfaces (ADSIs), 244
Active Directory Sizer Tool, 479–481
AD. See Active Directory
address records, 338
ADI zones. See Active Directory Integrated zones
administrative access groups, 281
administrative models
    assessing/defining, 3–16, 80–86, 147
    formulating changes in, 15
    limitations found in, 12–14
AdminSDHolder object, 509
ADMT (Active Directory Migration Tool), 303
ADPs. See Application Directory Partitions
ADSIs (Active Directory Service Interfaces), 244
aging, configuring DNS for (exercise), 178
AH (Authentication Header), 410

algorithms
    for DC placement, 488–490
    for GC server placement, 499
    for placement of services, 472–477
alias records, 338
APIPA (Automatic Private IP Addressing), 193
Application Directory Partitions (ADPs), 110, 346,
    478, 485
application layer (OSI reference model), 390
applications
    assessing impact of proposed designs and, 66
    data related to stored in Active Directory, 471, 522
audit strategy, for remote access, 424–430, 451
authentication
    vs. authorization, 411
    intranets and, 553–555
    mechanisms for, defining, 243–254, 298, 300
    remote access and, 385, 391–397, 422–424, 450
Authentication Header (AH), 410
authentication protocols, 393, 451
Authorization Manager, 284
authorization, vs. authentication, 411
automatic connection objects, 135
Automatic Private IP Addressing (APIPA), 193
autonomy, 81, 83–86, 147
    cost and, 303
    domain design and, 103
    forest design and, 86–96
    functional domains and, 112–114
    vs. isolation, 85, 103
        illustrated by OUs, 130
    using without isolation, 149
availability, remote access and, 558

B

b-nodes, 186
backup domain controllers (BDCs), 46, 506
backup user accounts, 94
bandwidth
    collating data about, 60
    mapping, 62
    service placement algorithm and, 473
    SLAs and, 18
BDCs (backup domain controllers), 46, 506
Berkeley Internet Name Domain (BIND), 57,
    328–330
Bootstrap Protocol (BOOTP), 189
bottlenecks, identifying, 48
bottom layer (OSI reference model), 388
bridgehead servers (BSs), 138–140, 289

631

S

Microsoft® Windows® Server 2003
Enterprise Edition 180-Day Evaluation

The software included in this kit is intended for evaluation and deployment planning purposes only. If you plan to install the software on your primary machine, it is recommended that you back up your existing data prior to installation.

System requirements

To use Microsoft Windows Server 2003 Enterprise Edition, you need:

- Computer with 550 MHz or higher processor clock speed recommended; 133 MHz minimum required; Intel Pentium/Celeron family, or AMD K6/Athlon/Duron family, or compatible processor (Windows Server 2003 Enterprise Edition supports up to eight CPUs on one server)
- 256 MB of RAM or higher recommended; 128 MB minimum required (maximum 32 GB of RAM)
- 1.25 to 2 GB of available hard-disk space*
- CD-ROM or DVD-ROM drive
- Super VGA (800 × 600) or higher-resolution monitor recommended; VGA or hardware that supports console redirection required
- Keyboard and Microsoft Mouse or compatible pointing device, or hardware that supports console redirection

Additional items or services required to use certain Windows Server 2003 Enterprise Edition features:

- For Internet access:
  - Some Internet functionality may require Internet access, a Microsoft Passport account, and payment of a separate fee to a service provider; local and/or long-distance telephone toll charges may apply
  - High-speed modem or broadband Internet connection
- For networking:
  - Network adapter appropriate for the type of local-area, wide-area, wireless, or home network to which you wish to connect, and access to an appropriate network infrastructure; access to third-party networks may require additional charges

Note: To ensure that your applications and hardware are Windows Server 2003–ready, be sure to visit **www.microsoft.com/windowsserver2003**.

* Actual requirements will vary based on your system configuration and the applications and features you choose to install. Additional available hard-disk space may be required if you are installing over a network. For more information, please see **www.microsoft.com/windowsserver2003**.

Uninstall instructions

This time-limited release of Microsoft Windows Server 2003 Enterprise Edition will expire 180 days after installation. If you decide to discontinue the use of this software, you will need to reinstall your original operating system. You may need to reformat your drive.

This book is intended to be sold with two CD-ROMs. If this book does not contain two CD-ROMs, you are not getting the full value of your purchase.